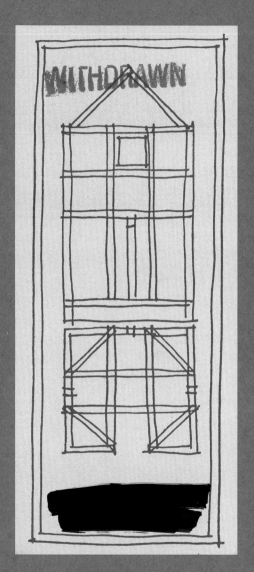

WITHDRAWN

MASTERPLOTS II

NONFICTION
SERIES

MASTERPLOTS II

NONFICTION SERIES

3

Mar-Sev

Edited by

FRANK N. MAGILL

SALEM PRESS

Pasadena, California   Englewood Cliffs, New Jersey

∞ The paper used in these volumes conforms to the
American National Standard for Permanence of Paper
for Printed Library Materials, Z39.48-1984.

Library of Congress Cataloging-in-Publication Data
Masterplots II: Nonfiction series/edited by Frank N.
Magill
   p. cm.
   Bibliography: p.
   Includes indexes
   1. Literature—Stories, plots. etc. 2. Literature—
History and criticism. I. Magill, Frank Northen, 1907-
  . II. Title: Masterplots 2. III. Title: Masterplots
two.
PN44.M345 1989   89-5877
080'.2'02—dc19   CIP
ISBN 0-89356-478-8 (set)
ISBN 0-89356-481-8 (volume 3)

LIST OF TITLES IN VOLUME 3

LIST OF TITLES OF VOLUME 3

A MARGIN OF HOPE
An Intellectual Autobiography

Author: Irving Howe (1920-   )
Type of work: Autobiography
Time of work: The 1930's to the early 1940's
Locale: Primarily New York City
First published: 1982

> *Principal personage:*
> IRVING HOWE, a prominent member of New York's intellectual
> circles

Form and Content

Irving Howe has been since the 1940's a prominent figure in American intellectual life as a literary critic, editor and anthologist, historian, and spokesman for Democratic Socialism. The subtitle of his book, *An Intellectual Autobiography*, alerts the reader to the work's focus. Indeed, *A Margin of Hope* is scanty on the personal side of Howe's life. His mother is briefly described as the stereotypical Jewish mother: "Strong, humorless, enclosing." His father receives more attention but mostly as the symbol of Howe's own ambivalent feelings toward the Eastern European immigrant world of his childhood. Not even their names are given. Howe alludes several times to his wife, but he fails to explain that he was married more than once. There is nothing about his two children. Perhaps most surprising is his failure to deal at length with his own writings. Some of his more important works are noted but without much in the way of explication. The work is primarily an account of the evolution of Howe's attitudes and beliefs.

The first four chapters—making up approximately 30 percent of the text—deal with Howe's formative years. Although he never says so, he was born in New York City on June 11, 1920, the son of David and Nettie (née Goldman) Howe. What appears to have been the most important influence on his childhood was the family's Depression-era fall from lower-middle to working class with the bankruptcy of his father's grocery store and the accompanying move from the West to the East Bronx. His father became a presser in the garment industry, his mother an operator. Although the family had its financial problems, there was still sufficient money to allow Howe to attend De Witt Clinton High School and then City College of New York. Howe was a precociously bookish youngster who cultivated "both a heightened social awareness and an adolescent cultural snobbism."

Although a loyal union member, his father was dismayed by Howe's left-wing political activism, first as a member of the Socialist Party's youth wing, the Young People's Socialist League, then as an adherent of the Trotskyist Socialist Workers Party, and finally, as a member of the splinter Trotskyist group headed by Max Shachtman. As Howe himself admits, he has difficulty in explaining why he became a Socialist. The conscious motive appears to have been the belief that "things had gone profoundly wrong." Even more important, however, was the way a political sect, such as the Trotskyists, with a comprehensive worldview offered the security of a defined sense of place, order, and coherence. "The movement," he recalls, "gave me something I would never find again and have since come to regard with deep suspicion, almost as a sign of moral derangement: it gave my life a 'complete meaning,' a 'whole purpose.'"

Howe found the classroom side of City College disappointing. More educationally valuable to him was his involvement in the debates that raged within the student body between the independent anti-Stalinist radicals and the Communist Party loyalists. After his graduation in 1940, he was editor of the Shachtman group's weekly, *Labor Action*, until he was drafted a few months after the bombing of Pearl Harbor. He spent most of the war shuffling papers at a remote base in Alaska, where he had ample leisure time for extensive reading. As he relates, "Enforced isolation and steady reading, together brought about a slow intellectual change. I remained passionately caught up with politics, but increasingly it became an abstract passion."

The next four chapters—making up approximately 40 percent of the text—deal with the narrow span of the decade following the end of the war. Those were the critical years of transition in Howe's life. In chapter 5 (appropriately titled "Into the World"), he tells of his gradual withdrawal from active involvement in the Shachtman group to try his hand as a free-lance intellectual; his work as Dwight Macdonald's assistant on *Politics* until that magazine's end in 1947; his four years as a part-time book reviewer for *Time*; and his entry into the circle of largely Jewish New York intellectuals centered on the *Partisan Review*. A separate chapter ("Literary Life: New York") details his experiences as a junior member of that formidably influential coterie before its fragmentation. Chapter 7 ("Loose-Fish, Still Flapping") recalls his association while living in Princeton, New Jersey, with the avantgarde writers around critic R. P. Blackmur (the poets John Berryman and Delmore Schwartz and novelist Saul Bellow), followed by his own appointment in 1953 to the English department of the newly founded Brandeis University.

Although Howe largely slides over the details in *A Margin of Hope*, those were probably his most productive years as a literary critic. His more important book-length works were *Sherwood Anderson* (1951), *William Faulkner: A Critical Study* (1952), and *Politics and the Novel* (1957). Politics, however, continued to engage his emotions most forcefully; at fifty pages, chapter 8, "Ideas in Conflict," is the book's longest. *The American Communist Party: A Critical History, 1919-1957* (1957)—coauthored with sociologist Lewis Coser—was a pioneering study that has remained an important source for later students. Howe's own intellectual trajectory was from Marxism to a vaguely defined Democratic Socialism. Nevertheless, there was simultaneously a strong feeling of hostility toward those intellectuals whom he believed had sold out by becoming apologists for American capitalism. Looking for a middle way between an outmoded and discredited Marxism and establishmentarian conformism, he was the moving force behind the founding in 1953 of *Dissent* as a journal of independent radical opinion to wage "polemical battle against our rightward-moving friends, especially those who had been less than lionhearted in standing up to McCarthyism."

In the early 1950's, Howe began to pursue what would remain one of his major interests in the years that followed: the preservation of at least the memory of the once-vibrant but dying Yiddish culture of Eastern Europe and New York City's Lower East Side. That effort—recounted in chapter 9 ("Jewish Quandaries")— resulted in a series of translations that Howe edited in collaboration with the Yiddish poet Elizier Greenberg and culminated in his authorship of the best-selling *World of Our Fathers* (1976). In 1961, Howe left Brandeis, during an apparent mid-life crisis, for what proved to be an unhappy two years at Stanford University before he returned to New York to teach at the Hunter College branch of the City University of New York. Yet the dominating preoccupation of his life in the 1960's—the subject of chapter 10 ("The Best and the Worst")—was how the bright promise of a revitalized reform impulse turned sour as the New Left succumbed to a mindless fanaticism.

The 1970's appear to him almost a void. "It's as if," he writes, "the years had simply dropped out of one's life and all that remains are bits and pieces of recollection." The "Fragments of a Decade" that stick in his mind are the rise of the feminist movement (with which he is warily sympathetic), his newfound enthusiasm for the ballet, and his father's death. He feels only revulsion for the "sordidness" of the era of Ronald Reagan: "It's as if the spirit of the old robber barons had been triumphantly resurrected, as if the most calloused notions of Social Darwinism were back with us, as if the celebrations of greed we associate with the late nineteenth century were reenacted a century later."

Analysis

A Margin of Hope has three major themes. The one that paradoxically receives the least attention in terms of space is his role as a literary critic. Howe—at least after his break with Marxism—eschewed any formal methodological framework. Although expressing a personal fondness for such individual New Critics as Allen Tate and John Crowe Ransom, he faults the New Criticism's narrow focus upon the text for its ignoring the social and historical context out of which a literary work emerged. In the final analysis, he remained a moralist "for whom criticism mattered because it could serve as open-ended humanist discourse."

Howe's moralism underlay what became his ambivalence toward literary modernism. In the 1930's, he had postulated an affinity between radical politics and avant-garde culture because of their shared hostility to bourgeois values. The award in 1949 of the Bollingen Prize for poetry to Ezra Pound, however, led him to have second thoughts. The controversy not only underlined how many of the giants of literary modernism had taken the reactionary side politically but also forced Howe to question what had been modernism's most cherished tenet, the principle of art for art's sake. In his later years, the primary focus of Howe's own literary interest shifted from the modernist authors to the Emersonian tradition in nineteenth century American literature.

The second theme is Howe's struggle to come to terms with his father, or, to be more accurate, with his father as symbol of his own Jewishness. Like many of his generation, Howe had subordinated ethnic and religious loyalties to socialist universalism. His latent sense of Jewish identity was reawakened by the Holocaust. Nevertheless, defining what his Jewishness meant proved to be a difficult problem. He remained nonreligious, even antireligious. He did become—belatedly, as a result of the 1967 war—an admirer of the state of Israel, though far from an unconditional enthusiast. His personal solution to coming to terms with his past lay in his efforts to preserve the legacy of secular Yiddish culture. The climax of that effort was the romanticized account of the lives of the Eastern European Jewish immigrants in *World of Our Fathers*—a world that as portrayed by Howe appeared peopled almost entirely by sensitive radicals or at least nascent New Dealers.

The third, and most important, theme in *A Margin of Hope* is the shattering of the millennialist hopes of socialism. "If these pages yield a common thread," he writes, "it can only be the idea that we have been witnesses to an age unique in its terribleness. . . . God died in the nineteenth century, utopia in the twentieth." Nowhere were radical dreams more thoroughly frustrated than in the United States: "There is a gathering of energies, a fusing of discontent. A movement springs up, buoyed by evangelical expectations. An encounter follows with American politics—its corruptions, its recalcitrance, its opportunism—and then a profound lapse into despair." In the wake of the debacle of the New Left, he was so disillusioned that he came to question whether there was any possibility of building in the United States "a radical movement both politically realistic and morally firm, devoted to the needs of the moment yet bringing to bear a larger vision of the good society."

Howe himself left the movement, even abandoned Marxism. Yet he remained loyal to what he had seen as the broader Socialist aspiration. His goal was "to keep a socialist kernel while dropping the Marxist shell." As he explains in his concluding reflections, "I am now inclined to think the case for socialism must be made increasingly on moral grounds: democracy in the work place as fulfillment of political freedom; an end to extreme inequalities of socio-economic condition; the vision of a humane society as one that requires a setting of cooperativeness and fraternity." At one crucial point, he underlines, his brand of Socialism "overlaps with liberalism. . . . With liberty you can struggle for greater equality; equality without liberty is a new mode of enslavement." He sees Socialism's future role in the United States as primarily acting as a goad to peoples' consciences by "offering an alternative vision of human possibility."

As a Trotskyist, Howe was inoculated against the Stalinism that infected so many self-styled progressive intellectuals in the 1930's. "The struggle to loosen the grip of Stalinism on the international Left," he remains convinced, "has been a crucial political experience of our century—even now by no means finished or completely successful." He strongly supported the American policies to contain Soviet expansionism in the aftermath of World War II. He similarly was one of the most outspoken antagonists of the New Left in the 1960's. The direction that the New Left took offended his deepest instincts: his anti-Stalinism, his devotion to democratic principles, his commitment to rationality.

Paradoxically, however, Howe directs his bitterest attacks against those of his former comrades on the left—such as the philosopher Sidney Hook and the group associated with *Commentary*—who moved too far to the right for his tastes. He became the exemplar of that phenomenon known as anti-anticommunism. His blind spot on this issue is the more surprising because Howe is fully aware of the extent to which the Stalinists had succeeded in infiltrating and controlling key social and cultural institutions during the 1930's. The difficulties in his position were most strikingly exemplified in his attitude toward the Vietnam War. He felt nothing but scorn for those in the antiwar movement who welcomed a North Vietnamese victory, but he could not bring himself to accept that support for the South Vietnamese regime was the lesser evil in a situation where there was no third alternative. The trouble was a legacy of his Trotskyist past: his almost visceral dislike of the one-time radical who "makes a safe politics out of anticommunism, correct as that anticommunism may be. He has lost that larger sympathy for the oppressed, that responsiveness to new modes of rebellion that a Socialist ought to have."

Critical Context

Given Howe's involvement in the controversies that had so bitterly divided American intellectuals over the preceding half century, the immediate critical reception to *A Margin of Hope* was strongly influenced by reviewers' political attitudes. There were those who thought him too rigidly anti-Soviet, others who found him the opposite. There were those who regarded his Socialism as too moderate, too gradualist, too reasonable to effect fundamental changes in American society; others who denied that one could be simultaneously a socialist and a democrat. The consensus was that here was a decent and well-meaning man who had struggled bravely to make sense of the world.

A Margin of Hope will probably not be ranked among the great autobiographies. Howe was not one of the movers and shakers of his time. As he freely admits, his influence upon the course of history was nil. While the *Partisan Review* group did have a significant impact upon American cultural life, Howe was no more than a secondary figure even within that circle. He founded no school of literary criticism. He was not responsible for discovering any neglected genius. He belonged to the tradition of the independent man of letters that could be traced back to Samuel Johnson. Nevertheless, he was not the equal of such contemporary examples as George Orwell or Edmund Wilson in terms of insight or importance. Although his interests were more political than aesthetic, Howe was neither profound nor novel in his thinking about man and society. Indeed, there was a strongly bookish quality to the evolution of his ideas. He appeared to respond not so much directly to events as to others' interpretations of those events. At most, his intellectual autobiography illuminates the thought processes of a narrow type: his generation of the intellectually inclined offspring of Eastern European Jewish immigrants.

Sources for Further Study

Atlas, James. "An Insurgent of the Mind," in *The New York Times Book Review*. LXXXVII (October 31, 1982), p. 1.

Decter, Midge. "Socialism and Its Irresponsibilities: The Case of Irving Howe," in *Commentary*. LXXIV (December, 1982), pp. 25-32.

Gornick, Vivian. "A Life of the Mind," in *The Nation*. CCXXXVI (January 1, 1983), pp. 20-22.

Lewis, R. W. B. "A Liberal Spirit," in *The New Republic*. XXXII (November 1, 1982), pp. 32-34, 36.

John Braeman

MARILYN

Author: Norman Mailer (1923-   )
With Lawrence Schiller
Type of work: New Journalism
Time of work: 1926-1962
Locale: Primarily Los Angeles
First published: 1973

Form and Content

    Marilyn owes its genesis to photographer Lawrence Schiller, who assembled some sixteen thousand photographs from the files of twenty-four photographers to create a special exhibition titled "Marilyn Monroe: The Legend and the Truth." It was Schiller who contacted Norman Mailer after this exhibition with the proposal that Mailer write the text for a book featuring the best of these photographs. Mailer originally planned to compose 25,000 words but ended with a text of 90,000 words. Schiller printed 118 photographs, including work by such notables as Richard Avedon, Milton H. Greene, Sam Shaw, and Eve Arnold. The arrangement of the photographs in relation to Mailer's text is rarely governed by principles of chronology or simple illustration. Mailer and Schiller deliberately place some photographs out of sequence in order to provide a sharp tonal contrast with the printed text or to create some kind of visual essay (sequences of photographs showing Marilyn on various beaches, for example). *Marilyn*, then, is a rich and complex work that can be appreciated on many levels, as a collection of stunningly effective photographs, as a boldly original text, or as a powerful combination of the two, constantly beckoning to the literal eye and to the eye of the imagination.

    Drawing extensively on two previously published books for his primary facts (*Norma Jean: The Life of Marilyn Monroe*, 1969, and *Marilyn Monroe*, 1960), Mailer quotes frequently from these secondary sources, using them more than twenty times. In addition, Mailer makes use of other background data gathered from another dozen primary sources he personally interviewed (all these primary and secondary sources, and all the photographers, are acknowledged in the last chapter of *Marilyn*). Describing himself as a kind of psychohistorian, Mailer tends to summarize the well-documented facts of Monroe's life and career, preferring to dwell on the psychic impact of key moments in her emotional life.

    Mailer moves in a chronological fashion, spending a considerable amount of time on Marilyn's unhappy childhood in Los Angeles and on the psychological consequences of her illegitimacy and inherited propensity for irrational behavior. Grandfather Monroe and Grandmother Della both went insane, and Marilyn's mother (Gladys Monroe Baker), a film cutter by trade, named her baby girl Norma Jean Baker (for her idols Norma Talmadge and Jean Harlow). Born in 1926, the child lived in a series of foster homes, a pattern that would continue until her first marriage, and she was shaped by such events as a near suffocation inflicted by her grandmother and the brutal shooting of her pet dog Tippy by an enraged neighbor. A shy, tongue-tied child emerges in this portrait, a child who quickly learns to pretend and to invent different versions of herself. In Mailer's view, Norma Jean grew up without any sustaining sense of self, and this crippling void at the center of her psyche would define her progressively tragic existence in the adult world.

After a brief marriage to young Jim Dougherty (she was sixteen, he twenty-five), her career was launched when a photographer from *Yank* magazine shot pictures of her at a defense plant where she worked spray-painting airplanes. Soon she attended charm school, dyed her hair blonde and was rechristened Marilyn Monroe by the public relations crew at Twentieth Century-Fox Studios. She became the girlfriend (and probable mistress) of veteran producer Joe Schenck. Her nose and jaw were surgically altered. She became the mistress of agent Joe Hyde, who interceded until finally Darryl Zanuck gave her a bit part in *As Young As You Feel* (1951).

She then entered her DiMaggio period, during which she was wooed by, married to, and finally divorced from Joe DiMaggio, whose rugged, masculine style did not mesh well with Marilyn's burgeoning interest in the art and craft of acting; soon she would become deeply involved with the famous director Lee Strasberg and his celebrated method acting. Nevertheless, the early days with DiMaggio were among her happiest, and their time together was marked by two of her most successful films, *Gentlemen Prefer Blondes* (1953) at the beginning of their relationship and *The Seven Year Itch* (1955) at its close.

Marilyn seemingly bounced from her relationship with the famous baseball star to a new attraction, Arthur Miller, a gentleman and an intellectual, who fulfilled the need for a close contact with drama. Miller was a celebrated writer of plays and scripts, a man who ultimately wrote a film (*The Misfits*, 1961) just for her, although her irrational behavior and obvious drug addiction during the shooting of the film finally destroyed this marriage, also.

Shortly after her celebrated singing for President John F. Kennedy's birthday, Marilyn was fired from the production of *Something's Got to Give*. In the last few weeks of her life, Marilyn continued her long-standing friendships with Peter Lawford, Robert F. Kennedy, and Frank Sinatra. Although her dependence on her psychologist and her shrinking financial resources were well-known to all of her friends at this time, no one seems to agree on the actual events of the night of her death, which was apparently the result of a massive overdose of barbiturates. She was only thirty-six, and her untimely death prompted Arthur Miller to write *After the Fall* (1964), an extended epitaph to his former wife, "a lovely if seldom simple woman."

Analysis

To read *Marilyn* is to experience one of the primary documents of New Journalism, the literary technique that dominated the 1960's and 1970's, especially in the work of Truman Capote, Tom Wolfe, Joan Didion, and Hunter S. Thompson. In New Journalism, the writer drops all pretenses of objectivity and distancing; the author, in fact, becomes part of the story, as Mailer himself demonstrated with great success in *The Armies of the Night: History as a Novel, the Novel as History* (1968). In *Marilyn*, he does not pretend to have known his subject personally (or to have participated in her life in the way in which he participated in the march on the Pentagon), but he does inject his candid opinions of those personages he does know, such as Arthur Miller.

One of the issues, then, in any critical analysis of *Marilyn* is Mailer's authority and the validity of his voice. Kate Millet and Germaine Greer have attacked Mailer as a sexist writer, and Mailer defends himself in such works as *The Prisoner of Sex* (1971) and *Pieces and Pontifications* (1982). Yet a close reading of Mailer reveals a rather complex and deeply sympathetic treatment of the character and personality of Marilyn Monroe, in spite of the considerable controversy created by the book (eight lengthy articles on aspects of this controversy appeared in *The New York Times* alone in 1973). In addition to being charged with sexism, Mailer was roundly criticized for purported plagiarism, and a libel suit was eventually filed against him. Thus, Mailer's attitude and methodology must figure into any critical appraisal of the book.

There is a considerable amount of Mailer's trademark prose style, a kind of high-energy assemblage of adjectives and nouns that yields such characterizations of Marilyn as "a sexual oven" with "a sweet little rinky-dink of a voice" for whom sex becomes "ice cream," a woman who "emanated sex" and whose womb was "fairly salivating in seed." Mailer also tallies Marilyn's well-documented clumsiness on the set and her tendency to make unforgettable bloopers. Mailer sees her as another Eliza Doolittle, and he quips, "If her blunders had hooks, they would be big enough to gaff marlin." At the same time that he recognizes her awkwardness and her sexual self (symbolized by her nude calendar poses), however, Mailer reveals a great sensitivity for Marilyn's soul. The body, he makes clear, was her tool, and she used it ruthlessly in the savage world of Hollywood. Yet within that body lay a vulnerable, perhaps schizophrenic woman whom Mailer can also praise. She could be a harridan or shrew on the set, always late, but these delaying tactics were her only defenses in a male-dominated industry that refused to let her break out of the "dumb-blonde" mold. Thus, Mailer argues, she played sick, and at times she became sick (she was plagued by menstrual cramps and mysterious, low-grade fevers), but in the end she won her way with nearly all of her directors, except John Huston (director of *The Misfits*). Mailer remarks that "fragility is her cruelest weapon" and that when she played the wounded doe it was the hunters around her who fell, not she. This axiom held true especially on the set of *Some Like It Hot* (1959), where she utterly exhausted Jack Lemmon and Tony Curtis, requiring them to do as many as forty takes of some scenes; and she improved as they began to wither. Nevertheless, these maneuvers exacted their toll; Marilyn became an addict and an insomniac. In Mailer's phrase, she popped sleeping pills like "cocktail party peanuts." This portrait of Marilyn is hardly the product of a woman hater or libertine; Mailer even discovers the letters of his name in an anagram of Marilyn

Monroe, surely a sign that he has fallen under her spell. (At the end of the book he breaks down in a most tender manner and wishes her "au revoir.") Perhaps he cannot gloss over her excesses, yet he redeems her by showing how her outbursts and vanities were the visible symptoms of a tormented and fragmented soul.

The controversy concerning plagiarism on Mailer's part is harder to analyze because Mailer, like all the New Journalists, insists that he is playing by a different set of rules and that, in order to present the psychological drama he must compose "a *species* of novel ready to play by the rules of biography." This is his defense for the numerous quotations from other writers and his defense against the charge of plagiarism because these quotations constitute part of the accepted tradition about Marilyn; thus, he must include them, and he does so openly, acknowledging all of his sources. In the end, because of out-of-court settlements, no suits were filed against Mailer. Even his thorniest allegation, namely that Marilyn's death was the result of a conspiracy, is based on unexplained discrepancies in the various affidavits connected with her death.

Critical Context

Marilyn can easily be understood as the product of perilous times, a book produced during the height of the Watergate affair, when public distrust of the federal government was at an all-time high. Conspiracy theories of one sort or another had been in the air since the assassination of John F. Kennedy, and such theories only multiplied after the subsequent assassinations of Martin Luther King and Robert F. Kennedy. Besides, as Mailer shows, undeniable links existed between the two Kennedy brothers and Marilyn Monroe. This book, then, must be reckoned as one of the representative documents of the decade in which it appeared. In its New Journalism style, in its heavy reliance on psychohistory, and in its conspiratorial outlook, it typifies the culture that produced it.

Marilyn also marks an important turning point in Norman Mailer's career: Having fought the big battles over the book and triumphed (a fact which he celebrated in an advertisement in *The New York Times Book Review* on December 9, 1973), Mailer had reached a new literary plateau. He was now free to become the celebrity and public figure, and he could devote himself to a new kind of project, a book with no immediate connection to American culture, a book that freed him from the bondage of the present, *Ancient Evenings* (1983).

Perhaps the most enduring contribution that *Marilyn* offers the reader is Mailer's concept of "factoids," "facts which have no existence before appearing in a magazine or newspaper." Marilyn herself was to drop many factoids on the plates of unsuspecting reporters. In the end, she had tragically lost the ability to distinguish between the facts and certain factoids she delivered (especially about her childhood) with all the earnestness of method acting. In Marilyn's tragedy, with all of its chilling consequences, Norman Mailer has left the reader with an idea that contains truly frightening implications, since factoids may be at the base of everything the reader so confidently assumes is real.

Sources for Further Study
Bloom, Harold, ed. *Norman Mailer*, 1986.
Clemons, Walter. Review in *Newsweek*. LXXXII (July 30, 1973), p. 71.
Kael, Pauline. Review in *The New York Times Book Review*. LXXVIII (July 22, 1973), p. 1.
Mills, Hilary. *Mailer: A Biography*, 1982.
The New Yorker. Review. XLIX (August 6, 1973), p. 87.

Daniel Guillory

MEMOIRS

Author: Pablo Neruda (Neftalí Ricardo Reyes Basoalto, 1904-1973)
Type of work: Memoir
Time of work: 1904-1973
Locale: Chile
First published: Confieso que he vivido: Memorias, 1974 (English translation, 1977)

> *Principal personages:*
> PABLO NERUDA, the author
> SALVADOR ALLENDE, the President of Chile from 1970 to 1973
> FEDERICO GARCÍA LORCA, a Spanish poet and Neruda's friend

Form and Content

Pablo Neruda died on September 23, 1973, in Santiago, Chile. Only twelve days earlier, the government of Salvador Allende, which Neruda strongly supported, had been overthrown in a bloody military coup. He was engaged in the final editing of his memoirs when death interrupted, so it is impossible to know what, if any, changes he would have made. The manuscript was prepared for publication by his wife, Matilde Neruda, and Miguel Otero Silva; the Spanish language edition first appeared in print the following year.

Memoirs is an appropriate title, for the book is far more a series of anecdotes linked by lyrical passages of poetic prose than it is an exhaustive, or even extensive, life history. For the most part, Neruda commits himself to the past tense, but he occasionally slips into the present tense, presumably to heighten the sense of imme-diacy in his account. The book is composed of twelve chapters, the contents of which are arranged chronologically. On occasion, however, Neruda will temporarily abandon chronology so that he can combine several incidents or impressions for thematic purposes. Neruda was an intensely political personality, and the narration of many of the incidents is charged with political implications. Still, it would not be fair to characterize *Memoirs* as an essentially political book or even one whose structure has been largely determined by political considerations.

The bulk of the book, as might be expected, is devoted to Neruda's adult life. Only the first chapter, "The Country Boy," deals with his childhood and adoles-cence. His school days, his first sexual encounters, even the loss of his virginity— all are treated rather cursorily. Neruda characterizes himself as a poet from his earliest boyhood, and it is clearly of his life as a poet that he wishes to speak. By chapter 2, "Lost in the City," he is boarding a third-class railway carriage for the trip to Santiago and the university. There he will quickly become involved with organizations of activist left-wing students, a colony of bohemian poets (most of whom are also students), and a gallery of eccentric characters from all walks of life. The tone of the book is set.

Analysis

Pablo Neruda's *Memoirs* have, if not a clear-cut theme, at least an unmistakable guiding principle: The book is an account of a poet's life. When Neruda falls in love, he is a poet in love. When he becomes politically engaged, he is a politically engaged poet. He believes in the fraternity of poets; throughout the book, he recounts with relish the endless hours of talking, drinking, and carousing with his fellow poets. Toward the end of chapter 4, "Luminous Solitude," Neruda devotes precisely one paragraph to his first marriage. It is 1930, and Neruda is Chilean consul in Batavia (now Djakarta, Indonesia). He weds María Antonieta Hagenaar, a tall, gentle young woman of a mixed Dutch and Malay background. He reports, significantly, that she knew nothing of the world of arts and letters. Chapter 5, "Spain in My Heart," is filled with anecdotes of Neruda's association with Federico García Lorca and other Spanish poets. The wife is a phantom presence, or no presence at all. Even Neruda's long diplomatic career was basically an adjunct to his poetry. In his youth, a minor diplomatic post was considered a suitable sinecure for a rising young Latin-American poet. Neruda states that the poet's appearance should match his singular calling: He should always dress in black.

The origins of Neruda's two great passions, poetry and the struggle of the proletariat, are not directly addressed in *Memoirs*. Probably it is unrealistic and unfair to expect him to reveal the precise moment when he knew he was a poet or the particular circumstance that caused him to identify with the oppressed of the world. At any rate, he does not.

Chapter 1 implies strongly that Neruda was born a poet—more particularly, a poet of nature. He was born at Parral, in central Chile, but spent his childhood at Temuco, the farthest outpost of civilization in the southern territories. He characterizes Temuco as Chile's frontier, its Wild West. It is a land of numbing cold, torrential rain, earthquakes, and a stirring volcano. It is also a land of tangled forests, rich in plant, insect, and animal life. Neruda describes his response to this landscape as euphoria, the poet's response. The book is peppered with italicized prose poems, the usual purpose of which is to establish a mood for the narrative passages that follow. These prose poems consistently employ the rich imagery of the natural world. Neruda recalls his first poem, written when he had barely learned to read, and how he tremblingly took it to his father and stepmother. His father absentmindedly dismissed the poem, asking the boy where he had copied it. The first instance of irresponsible literary criticism did, however, inadvertently acknowledge the poem's merit. Neruda refers to himself even at this tender age as a small boy poet, dressed in black.

The reader may also draw inferences about the development of Neruda's political attitudes. In chapter 1, he expresses sympathy for the Araucanian Indians, the original inhabitants of the land that would become Chile. Initially, the Spanish conquistadors drove them into the cold regions of southernmost Chile; later, the Chilean government instituted a pacification program for Araucania which was, in fact, an annihilation program.

Neruda's father was a conductor on a ballast train, so the boy was exposed early to the workingmen of the railroad. One in particular, a scar-faced laborer named Monge, would bring Neruda the exotic spiders and beetles he knew the boy prized. Monge would subsequently be killed as the result of falling from a train and tumbling down a precipice.

Neruda recalls how, as a poverty-stricken university student in Santiago, he observed the abuses of the oligarchy that dominated Chile and of the police who did the oligarchy's bidding. During his twenties, he served in consular posts at Rangoon, Burma; Colombo, Ceylon; Batavia, Java; and Singapore. He developed a hatred for colonialism and, judging from the tone of his reminiscences, a special antipathy toward the British. He decries their clannishness, insularity, and smugness. At one point, he states that when the British finally abandoned their empire, they left only poverty and starvation behind. Most objective observers would judge this something of an overstatement. It has often been noted that, of all the former colonial powers, Great Britain probably left the most behind in terms of government systems and infrastructure.

Neruda is a highly partisan writer, and his partisanship leads him not infrequently into hyperbole. For example, he refers to Adolf Hitler as "the Nixon of his era." Few of Richard M. Nixon's most virulent enemies would equate him with Hitler. At the time Neruda drew that comparison, however, Nixon was president of the northern Goliath that was actively subverting the socialist government that he, Neruda, had labored so long and hard to establish. In a reference to the notorious Scottsboro case, Neruda speaks of racist justice in the United States as if the adjective and the noun are permanent and inseparable companions.

Although Neruda's ideology had been solidly leftist from the beginning, the Spanish Civil War proved to be for him, as for so many of his generation, the galvanizing political experience. His dear friend Federico García Lorca, whom he considered Spain's greatest poet, was taken to be shot on a night when the two of them were to have attended a wrestling match together. Miguel Hernández, the peasant of the Spanish Levant, died of tuberculosis after three years of imprisonment. Neruda threw himself into the war effort by publishing *España en el corazón* (*Spain in the Heart*, 1946) in 1937. Republican soldiers at the front made the paper and operated the printing press for this remarkable book. Neruda states that, although he did not receive his party membership card until much later in Chile, he had considered himself a Communist ever since the war in Spain. No more could he indulge himself in the melancholy of *Residencia en la tierra* (1933, 1935, 1947; *Residence on Earth and Other Poems*, 1946, 1973), which was written during frequent periods of isolation and loneliness in the Orient. Henceforward, he must be one with the people, and his poetry must express the aspirations of mankind.

Still, it is poetry's aesthetic value rather than its ultimate utilitarianism which is always uppermost in Neruda's mind. Of all the horrors of the Spanish Civil War, it is García Lorca's murder which brands the Franco forces as monsters. That Spaniards from García Lorca's own Granada could kill their greatest poet is inconceivable. Neruda even characterizes the war as a Fascist attempt to deal poetry its death blow. He observes, however, that poetry, like a cat, has nine lives.

The last half of Neruda's *Memoirs* is largely an account of his political activities: his return to Chile and election to the senate, his persecution and flight from the reactionary government of González Videla, his years of exile in Europe. Toward the end of his life, he would be the Communist Party's candidate for the presidency of Chile, although he eventually withdrew in favor of Salvador Allende. While this account has some intrinsic interest, it does not yield many insights into Neruda's art.

Critical Context

Events conspired to make *Memoirs* an eagerly awaited book. Neruda, the recipient of the Nobel Prize in Literature in 1971, had also been a member of the Communist Party of Chile since July 8, 1945. He had been active in Allende's presidential campaign in 1970 and was named ambassador to France when the Popular Unity Party won the election. In the last years of his life, he labored both as a poet and as a practical politician to keep the Marxist government in power and to prevent civil war. The very dramatic situation—Neruda's completion of his autobiography, the overthrow of the Popular Unity government, Allende's violent death, and the poet's own death, all virtually coinciding—assured a sizable and expectant audience for the posthumously published *Memoirs*.

While indispensable to a study of Neruda's life and work, *Memoirs* is not a major contribution to the genre of autobiography. Critics have noted that Neruda's expansive tone is belied by his reticence concerning many subjects—a reticence that leaves gaping ellipses in his narrative. On page 130, for example, Neruda reveals that in 1937 he was living in Paris with Delia del Carril. She is next mentioned on page 216; it is 1952, and Neruda is leaving her for Matilde Urrutia. His only child, Malva Marina—who was born in Madrid on October 4, 1934, and died eight years later in Europe—is never mentioned at all. *Memoirs* cannot, therefore, be considered a work of self-revelation in the tradition of the confessions of Saint Augustine or Jean-Jacques Rousseau.

Neruda's anecdotes are entertaining, often fascinating, but they sometimes seem disingenuous as well. He states in his preface that many of his memories are blurred. In his reconstruction of them, the stories make the appropriate point almost too perfectly. Their climaxes, like those of artistic creations, are completely satisfying. Neruda's memories are the stuff of poetry to him, as all his perceptions have been since childhood. Consequently, Neruda the poet frequently takes the narrative out of the hands of Neruda the chronicler.

Neruda first states that he is a Communist on page 135 and mentions the fact several more times thereafter, but he states that he is a poet on the second page of his text and repeats that assertion several hundred times more, on virtually every page of the book. The pseudonym Pablo Neruda, assumed because his father objected to a son who wrote poetry, emphasizes this second identity. His subjective and uneven autobiography is a poetic response in prose to the facts of his life, and therein lies its value. It is not as a husband, father, or political activist that history will judge Pablo Neruda, but as a poet.

Sources for Further Study

Agosin, Marjorie. *Pablo Neruda*, 1986. Translated by Lorraine Roses.

Bizzarro, Salvatore. *Pablo Neruda: All Poets the Poet*, 1979.

Howes, Victor. Review in *The Christian Science Monitor*. March 8, 1977, p. 18.

Maurer, Robert. "A Confession of Life," in *Saturday Review*. IV (February 10, 1977), pp. 18-20.

Neruda, Pablo. *Pablo Neruda: Addresses, Essays, Lectures*, 1980. Edited by Emir Rodriguez Monegal and Enrico Mario Santi.

Rodman, Selden. Review in *National Review*. XXIX (March 18, 1977), p. 340.

Yglesias, José. Review in *The New York Times Book Review*. LXXXII (March 13, 1977), p. 3.

Patrick Adcock

MEMOIRS OF A DUTIFUL DAUGHTER

Author: Simone de Beauvoir (1908-1986)
Type of work: Autobiography
Time of work: 1908-1929
Locale: Paris
First published: Mémoirs d'une jeune fille rangée, 1958 (English translation, 1959)

> *Principal personages:*
> SIMONE DE BEAUVOIR, the author
> GEORGES DE BEAUVOIR, her father
> FRANÇOISE DE BEAUVOIR, her mother
> ELIZABETH MABILLE (ZAZA), her friend
> JACQUES LAIGUILLON, her cousin
> JEAN-PAUL SARTRE, a philosopher, her lifelong friend

Form and Content

From 1956 to 1958, Simone de Beauvoir composed the first of a series of autobiographical volumes that covered the course of her life. *Memoirs of a Dutiful Daughter* dealt with her childhood and youth to the age of twenty-one; it was followed by *La Force de l'âge* in 1960 (*The Prime of Life*, 1962), which dealt with her life from 1929 to 1944, *La Force des choses* in 1963 (*Force of Circumstance*, 1964), which brought her life up to the date of publication, and a final volume, a summary, *Tout compte fait* (1972; *All Said and Done*, 1974), which differed from the previous three in that it was organized thematically rather than chronologically. These autobiographical writings are among de Beauvoir's finest achievements. Her reconstructions of her life, even after consultations with cautious friends, retain a "disarming candor" that has led some critics to describe her as a modern Montaigne. Like the sixteenth century philosopher, she is a writer whose ability to combine introspective analysis with philosophical consideration has enabled her to produce "a truthful account of a life that could, and should, help others" (as Konrad Bieber claims) to understand themselves as well as some of the dominant social and political movements of the twentieth century.

Memoirs of a Dutiful Daughter reaches as much as fifty years back in time from the moment of its production. To compose the work, de Beauvoir was directed by a diary which she had begun as a young girl, fortified by a prodigious memory for detail which she combined with careful historical research, and guided by one of her most basic principles, the idea that one must be ruthlessly accurate, keenly analytic, and as dispassionate as possible about the self. In the first volume of her memoirs, she relates how her most esteemed faculty, her mind, was formed, and how her distinct sensibility developed. The course she charts is from a comfortable, sheltered Catholic childhood in the early days of the twentieth century, *la belle époque* of peace and serenity (which was actually a continuation of nineteenth century norms and assumptions), toward the emergence of a young woman who was intellectually self-confident, ready for pioneer political activity, committed to a life of writing, and disdainful of most social institutions and conventions.

The volume is divided into four books, the first an attempt to recapture the instinctive and impulsive young child's responses and reactions to the world, the second devoted to an understanding of the psychology of her parents and their world, the third tracing the uncertainty and doubt she felt as she began to reject the protective, pampered life for which her family had prepared her, and the fourth, in which she reaches adulthood and begins to share the intellectual and artistic life of some of the most influential people of the twentieth century. The structure of the book is like an ever-widening spiral from the compact realm of the self-centered child to the amorphous universe of the questioning adult. Through this pattern, an event is often analyzed and considered for all of its ramifications, then temporarily put aside, and later recollected in a larger, still-relevant context. The central themes of the work—individual growth and personal freedom, the responsibility of the artist to her work and of a person to her society, the flow of historical change, the nature of love and its relationship to a productive life—are all developed from an intensely personal perspective. The severe tone of de Beauvoir's voice is never modified in order to charm the reader. The intensity of the writing matches the intensity of the mind of the author, and the evocative power of de Beauvoir's prose has an appeal that derives from directness, honesty, and an uncompromising confidence in the reader's ability to match the writer's seriousness. This voice risked the condemnation of antagonist commentators, but succeeded in drawing responses such as Judith Okely's avowal, "She was our mother, our sister and something of ourselves."

Analysis

The first book of de Beauvoir's *Memoirs of a Dutiful Daughter* is the most creative and expressionistic of the four. Her approach to the earliest part of her life is in the spirit of William Wordsworth's epigram to his "Ode: Intimations of Immortality," here expressed as "The Child is the mother of the Woman." Since the realm of childhood is often almost an infinite distance from an adult's consciousness, and since de Beauvoir always speaks in the voice of a mature adult, the child who preceded the woman might be especially elusive and difficult to recapture. To close the distance, de Beauvoir projects her adult voice from the start—serious and erudite, with no concessions to the limits of a child's thought patterns or linguistic limitations—but uses it to convey emotional urgency, a total preoccupation with the self, and a wild willfulness which suggests the operations of the child's mind. The motto for this book might be Paul Gaugin's comment, "There is salvation only in extremes," for the young de Beauvoir is characterized by "impetuous vitality and a lack of all moderation." In the opening pages, she is presented in terms of her responses to phenomena that initially developed her senses, all of her reactions framed as versions of an absolute, permitting no alternative visions or possibilities.

If she does not like a certain food, she vomits. If she is forbidden to peel a plum, she runs howling down the boulevard. If she is denied the gratification of an impulse, she rages and sulks. As disturbing as they appear, these visceral outbursts are actually the basis for the beginning of the most important aspect of de Beauvoir's sense of her self, her discovery of the mind. She locates her earliest sense of her mental development in the wave of energy produced by frustrations and disappointments. To cope with these explosive outbursts, she begins to think about them—first in terms of the action itself, then in a primitive analysis of the nature of the action—and while there is no way for the young child to curb her instincts, she begins to acquire the means for a transformation that will reduce her discomfort.

This transformation is accomplished through an expansion of awareness. "Suddenly the future existed," she says, establishing time as a concept, removing the child from the trap of a perpetual present. She begins to discriminate among various foods, so that the senses serve rather than rule, an anticipation of the adult's prerogative of selection. While enjoying the sensual nature of the countryside, she becomes aware of the sources of her enjoyment in the landscape, thus adding the analytic to the instinctive. When stories are read to her, she imagines herself as one of the characters, assuming semilegendary proportions as a result of her connection with the significance of the printed word. Gradually, while retaining the physical immediacy of the child's world, she alters her points of reference so that the mind moves into prominence as a measure of reality, and events become occasions for thought as well as feeling. The connection between words and things follows directly, as de Beauvoir learns to read rapidly, driven by a curiosity about the "riches found in books" as well as an incipient interest in language itself.

In this book, de Beauvoir also begins to consider her parents' lives and character, but at first they are seen without fault, wrapped in an unquestioning love. Their dominance is accepted, and de Beauvoir traces the beginning of her intellectual life to her admiration of her father, the beginning of her spiritual life to her adoration of her mother, accepting the complete separation of those spheres without question. This is the only area, however, in which she accepts the conventional nature of things without considering alternatives. Even in her preteen years, she has a tremendous consciousness of shaping her own destiny so that reading leads to writing, which permits a shaping rather than an accepting of reality; dolls become not merely toys but "doubles," which open alternative visions of existence; goals begin to edge into her immediate plans, with teaching a possible vocation so that she can "form minds and mould character," a reflection of her desires for herself at this time.

Book 2 confronts the contradictions that have been gradually developing in her life. To this point, approximately age ten, she has been the "dutiful daughter" of the title, and while her sense of duty remains, the focus is shifted from a blind duty to her parents and the life they have prepared for her to a sense of duty to her self and her own fate. The original French word in the title, *rangée*, also means "patterned" or "arranged." As the innocence of childhood gives way before the intrusion of all the questions a brilliant, precocious, and highly inquisitive young girl might pose, the entire fabric of the society that her parents uphold begins to unravel. Although the events of World War I had already begun to change the world irrevocably, the de Beauvoirs were still living in the smug, self-assured contentment of the last decades of the nineteenth century, falsely secure in the illusion that their way of life was permanent. Their eldest daughter, however, had already begun to question some of the sacred assumptions of her parents' generation. For her, Catholicism provided no real explanation of the nature of the universe, and most rules of social conduct seemed designed to ratify hypocrisy—a major sin for one who believed in seeking the absolute truth.

The narrative progression of book 2 is from certainty to doubt as de Beauvoir adds personal experience to the continual development of her powers of analytic ability. The consequence is a feeling of displacement at childhood's end as adults still rule but with their authority no longer quite legitimate. Her questions extended directly into the world of adult decisions and when she did not receive satisfactory answers, the anxiety of uncertainty clouded her vision. As a compensation, she had begun to develop an intense friendship with Elizabeth Mabille (known as "Zaza") and an increasing dependence on the inspiration of literature. Her plan to study literature and then teach at the lycée was a disturbing and unconventional choice for a proper girl, and her confidence in the correctness of her decision was instinctive, not rational.

As subsequent events demonstrated, her decision was correct, but her confidence was immediately shaken by the circumstances that she faced. Still essentially under the control of her parents, she describes her situation at the beginning of book 3 as a kind of prison, and through the course of the book, she relates her attempts to escape into the freedom of her own life. The narrative pattern here is a systematic examination of possibility, beginning with an inclination toward public service, an idea that develops from an inspiring lecture delivered by a socialist speaker. Another possibility involves her first feelings of love as she begins to talk earnestly with her older cousin Jacques Laiguillon, a suave, sensitive young man she recalls as "the hero of my youth." Her discussions with Jacques lead her to her first acquaintance with modern art and literature, renewing her interest in being a writer by underscoring the relevance of literature to modern life. To activate this interest, she begins the diary which forms the basis for her autobiographical writing—a reflective, analytic, almost fiercely observant record of her life which enhances the mental skills she has been developing by concentrating impulsive thought into language. The diary also gives her the opportunity to begin to formulate the feminist philosophy which she presented in *Le Deuxième Sexe* in 1949 (*The Second Sex*, 1953). "What went on in one's body should be one's own concern" is typical of the entries on this subject. The diary solidifies her strong sense of individualism by acting as a kind of supportive "friend" prior to her actual contact with people who would share her ideas and outlook.

Another possibility for escape was the Sorbonne, where she began to assemble a cultural context within which to locate her own ideas. In examining the stance of the artist as outsider, particularly the poems of men such as Charles Baudelaire, Paul Verlaine, and Arthur Rimbaud, her own attempts to break away from the conventions of her parents' world gained validity.

None of these possibilities enabled her to move beyond the prison which held her between the "paradise of childhood" and "the world of men," however, and she continued to see her life primarily in terms of potentiality, with no immediate means for activating that energy. Her frustration drove her toward the nihilism of intellectual despair, but she was always carried back from this state by exultations of pure being in response to the variety of the world. Her consciousness of existence was shifting from the inner life of the extraordinary child to the outward inclination of a young woman reaching for direction. Her sense of enclosure is reflected in a narrative pattern of repetition with small variations within a circumscribed perimeter. In attempting to break out, she spends nights in bars and saloons, but in a curiously innocent way, still far too much her parents' "dutiful daughter" to abandon her ingrained precepts. Finally, near the end of the book, she mentions some of her fellow students, people destined for international celebrity, such as Simone Weil, Jean-Paul Sartre, the anthropologist Claude Lévi-Strauss, and the philosopher Maurice Merleau-Ponty. This is a foreshadowing of her imminent escape from "the labyrinth of the last three years" into the future.

Book 4 marks the emergence of Simone de Beauvoir, the young woman who is on the threshold of a life of engagement, emerging from a prison of uncertainty and parental suppression. Her preparation for her exams provides a focus for the energy that she has been scattering in many directions, and she passes them easily. Her continuing success in her studies helps her to formulate a self-image of an independent woman who has rejected the constraints of bourgeois norms. The excitement of living in the fabled Paris of the 1920's, with all the arts exploding in new directions, draws her into full participation in the world.

The final pages of the memoir follow de Beauvoir through the conclusion of two old friendships and the inception of a grand new one, signifying the end of her youth and the beginning of her adult years. Her break with her cousin Jacques and the tragic story of his decline, and the sudden death of her best friend, Zaza, which she attributes to a mental collapse brought on by parental demands, are symbolic of the ending of an era. The promise of a new age is heralded by Sartre's invitation, "I'm going to take you under my wing," and although his attitude seems paternalistic, she never presents herself in a subordinate role in their relationship, even while expressing her admiration for Sartre's intellect and character. Instead, she relates her feelings as she is captured by an absolute sense of love akin to other absolute states of being which she had known at the beginning of the memoir. As before, her individuality is not diminished by her commitment. The love she feels for Sartre is a justification for all of her struggles with modes of existence promoted by lesser people. In the lyric language she reserves for moments of special truth, de Beauvoir calls Sartre:

the double in whom I found all my burning aspiration raised to the pitch of incandescence. I should always be able to share everything with him. When I left him at the beginning of August, I knew that he would never go out of my life again.

Critical Context

Memoirs of a Dutiful Daughter is not only a vivid self-portrait but also a critical evaluation of French society during a period of transition. In the process of becoming the woman who could work for artistic and social freedom, de Beauvoir emphasizes her mental maturation, offering not only a very detailed and systematic description of the development of her mind but also an analytic explanation of her relationship to the basic propositions of the most brilliant French theoretical *savants*. Her friends were the precursors of Roland Barthes, Jacques Lacan, and the like, and her autobiographical writing is crucial to an understanding of the mind-forged power of the Left Bank activists who set the agenda for philosophical discourse until at least the 1960's.

In addition, Simone de Beauvoir's memoir places the foundations for the visionary feminist thinking of her middle years. *The Second Sex* was not only revolutionary in its examination of women in Western society but also a book which, as Carole Ascher points out, "made it all right" for a woman "to be an intellectual." Judith Okely describes it as a rare example of a female chronicle of apprenticeship that shares common themes of choice and struggle with such familiar male autobiographical novels as D. H. Lawrence's *Sons and Lovers* (1913), James Joyce's *A Portrait of the Artist as a Young Man* (1916), and Henry Miller's *Tropic of Cancer* (1934). "If the autobiography is sufficiently probing," Okely maintains, "it demands that the reader probe her own past." For readers of both sexes, the universality of individual experience expressed with singular eloquence remains as de Beauvoir's essential literary legacy.

Sources for Further Study

Ascher, Carole. *Simone de Beauvoir: A Life of Freedom*, 1982.
Bieber, Konrad. *Simone de Beauvoir*, 1979.
Cottrell, Robert D. *Simone de Beauvoir*, 1975.
Ellman, Mary. *Thinking About Women*, 1968.
Evans, Mary. *Simone de Beauvoir: A Feminist Mandarin*, 1985.
Leighton, Jean. *Simone de Beauvoir on Women*, 1975.
Marks, Elaine. *Simone de Beauvoir: Encounters with Death*, 1973.
Okely, Judith. *Simone de Beauvoir*, 1986.
Whitmarsh, Anne. *Simone de Beauvoir and the Limits of Commitment*, 1981.

Leon Lewis

MEMOIRS OF THE FORTIES

Author: Julian Maclaren-Ross (1912-1964)
Type of work: Memoir
Time of work: The 1940's
Locale: London
First published: 1965

> *Principal personages:*
> JULIAN MACLAREN-ROSS, a short-story writer, novelist, and
>   raconteur
> GRAHAM GREENE, a novelist
> CYRIL CONNOLLY, a journalist and literary critic
> DYLAN THOMAS, a Welsh poet
> J. MEARY TAMBIMUTTU, a Ceylonese impresario, editor of *Poetry
>   London*
> ALUN LEWIS, a Welsh poet and short-story writer, killed in World
>   War II before he turned thirty

Form and Content

Reminiscent of such colorful personalities as Marcel Proust and Oscar Wilde, Julian Maclaren-Ross, with his teddy-bear fur coat, malacca cane, white corduroy jacket, dark glasses, and lapel carnation, fit well into the bohemian atmosphere of the London literary scene of the 1940's. More important than the image he may have cut, however, is the fact that he was both a participant in and an observer of that scene, and, although he never fancied himself an official historian, his *Memoirs of the Forties* may be read as a kind of chronicle of Grub Street during that decade.

In the note at the beginning of *Memoirs of the Forties* Maclaren-Ross admits that he is not a professional literary man but rather a professional writer, and that anyone seeking scandal or inside accounts of literary politics would do well to seek them elsewhere. His stated goal is to portray as accurately as he can the various writers, publishers, editors, artists, and other personages with whom he came into contact during the 1940's. More than that, however, he emphasizes that he has tried to elude the trap open to writers of memoirs of falsifying incidents in order to make them more interesting to the reader. To achieve his goal, he presents what first strikes the reader as a random collection of conversations, incidents, and stories. Indeed, Maclaren-Ross readily confesses that he has a weakness regarding dates. Thus, in an exact chronological sense, neither he nor the reader can be sure when a particular conversation or incident took place. Emphasizing his photographic memory for details of such conversations and incidents, however, he assures the reader that they surely did occur as he narrates them and that they are, moreover, accurate. The reader, then, must not be overly concerned by the absence of an orderly chronology of events, situations, or conversations, but rather must take them all as they come and let the overall impressions develop as they may.

The book is divided into four sections—"Prologue," "The Forties," "Second Lieutenant Lewis," and "Some Stories." The prologue consists of three chapters that focus on Maclaren-Ross' struggles as a young writer seeking a publisher for his stories—a writer with, as he puts it, no useful connections to smooth the way. Sometimes selling vacuum cleaners, sometimes going on the dole, he makes his rounds among publishers on Grub Street until the British Broadcasting Corporation gives him the assignment of adapting Graham Greene's *A Gun for Sale* (1936) for radio. Although he does receive fifteen pounds for his efforts, the impending war and general bureaucratic delays bring the project to naught.

The second section of the book, "The Forties," consists of eight chapters, the first of which concerns Maclaren-Ross' meeting with Cyril Connolly, the editor of *Horizon*, and the latter's acceptance of the young writer's story "A Bit of a Smash in Madras" for publication. The second deals with some of Maclaren-Ross' army experiences and his meeting with Woodrow Wyatt, a young socialist barrister, who with his wife edited *English Story* and who agreed to publish some of his stories. The remaining chapters of this section are a series of portraits of notable people of the decade, including William Cooper Makins, Arthur Calder-Marshall, Dylan Thomas, J. Meary Tambimuttu, Peter Brooke, John Minton, Gerald Wilde, Robert Colquhoun, Robert Macbryde, Feliks Topolski, and Pablo Picasso.

The section titled "Second Lieutenant Lewis" is a chapter in itself—"A Memoir." It describes the meeting in the army in 1942 between the author and Alun Lewis. The last section, "Some Stories," consists of six stories: "Y List," the story of a soldier who suffers pneumonia and pleurisy; "I Had to Go Sick," the story of another soldier who becomes enmeshed in army red tape as he tries to get treatment for a bad leg; "A Bit of a Smash in Madras," the story of an Englishman in India, who hits a native while driving intoxicated and pulls what strings he can to extricate himself from the charges; "Five-Finger Exercise," the story of a thirty-six-year-old man seducing a sixteen-year-old girl; "Happy As the Day Is Long," the story of a happy-go-lucky Irishman who tries to bolster the spirits of a down-and-almost-out artist; and "The Swag, the Spy, and the Soldier," the story of a group of people living a bohemian existence and an unemployed former amusement-park worker who involves them in a case of theft.

Originally, Maclaren-Ross intended two more sections for his book—one titled "Ham" and the second "The Epilogue." Because of his untimely death in 1964, these were never completed.

Analysis

"I have an impression of unventilated corridors staled by cigarette smoke, of muzzy eyes; but a sort of Bohemia, dead for a decade, got staggering to its legs in the pubs between north and south Soho, the BBC and the MOI." So says V. S. Pritchett, speaking of the 1940's London literary scene in *New Statesman* (September 24, 1965). Such is the setting for Maclaren-Ross' *Memoirs of the Forties*. Or perhaps one should say the set, for the book is structured very much like a drama, or a series of scenarios in which the author brings to the stage a cast of characters who, each in his turn, play their roles. The author himself is the foil for most of them. As noted earlier, chronology is not significant. Characters appear in their own right and in their own time—and Maclaren-Ross, while a part of it, stands above it all. Thus, at the same time that he presents his characters, he can observe and comment on them. It is this strategy that enables him to give the reader insights into the realities of Grub Street and Soho and into the people who struggled there to build their careers and to find meaning in their lives as they circulated among such pubs as the Wheatsheaf, the Highlander, or the Horseshoe.

Not all of these characters lived their days waiting for the pubs to open or to close. Some, such as Connolly, editor of *Horizon*, made it possible for the fledgling writer to get his work into print. Connolly's round face, sloping shoulders, and shaggy brow belied his intellectual and artistic attributes. In his midthirties when Maclaren-Ross met him, he had published *Enemies of Promise*, a book of landmark importance to the generation of the 1940's. More important, he was an editor who understood the plight of such neophyte writers as Maclaren-Ross. Without editors such as Connolly, many self-styled, or real, creative geniuses would have languished in the endless acres of Soho pubs telling their stories to one another.

Juxtaposed to Connolly are such characters as Calder-Marshall, who always seemed to be "squinting against strong sunlight" and who tried to look the part of a workingman "without the features themselves being all that rough-hewn." He was, however, a person who knew the lay of the land well enough and who could put Maclaren-Ross in touch with prospective employers. Indeed, through Calder-Marshall, Maclaren-Ross obtained a position at Strand Films, a producer of documentary films. At Strand he met Dylan Thomas. With a bulbous nose that shone like a highly polished doorknob, Thomas was reluctantly writing documentary scripts. Put off at first by Maclaren-Ross' white corduroy jacket and fancy cane, Thomas urged him to try to look more sordid: "Sordidness, boy, that's the thing." The two, however, got along well and spent as much time in pubs as at Strand Films.

If Thomas had his eccentricities, so too did Tambimuttu, poet and founder-editor of *Poetry London*. "Tambi," a Ceylonese Christian, was, according to himself, a prince in his own country. Whether he meant Ceylon is not clear, for he once commented that a poet is a citizen of the world and that his principality is everywhere, "the Principality of the Mind." Soho, too, might have been called his principality—a Fitzrovia, as he called it. A literary entrepreneur, he was always full of plans, not only for himself but also for those who kept him company in the pubs. Most of these plans, however, never materialized, and Tambi eventually gave up his reign as Prince of Poetry Pundits in Soho and migrated to New York's Greenwich Village, where he found "fresh patrons, poetesses, and a new poetry review at his disposal."

Another player is Peter Brooke. With his high cheekbones and yellow eyes,

Brooke was one who seldom did anything by halves. A prodigious drinker, smoker, and womanizer, he tried his hand at songwriting, storywriting, and acting. Singing the Stein Song and drinking until all hours of the night, Brooke would spend the night at Maclaren-Ross' apartment and awake the next day shouting, "Wakey, wakey, rise and shine. It's past four in the afternoon and I could eat a horse. I could eat a fried cat." And so would begin another evening in the pubs, where, according to Maclaren-Ross, "gallons of beer, large measures of spirit, were poured upon mountains of whatever food was available." In the middle of it all was Brooke, bouncing around like a man trying to put out a fire.

Such a frenetic pace as that kept by Brooke was the norm, not the exception. Maclaren-Ross shifts, for example, to a number of painters whom he knew: John Minton, long and loose-jointed, who created exotic canvases and who once threw Maclaren-Ross bodily out of his apartment for allegedly interfering in his sex life; Gerald Wilde, known as the Mad Artist, whom Tambi supported and often kept locked up in a room so that he would work instead of drink; Robert Colquhoun and Robert Macbryde, fervent Scottish nationalists who moved through Soho followed by bevies of admiring young women.

With a cool detachment and a keen power of observation, Maclaren-Ross thus takes the reader on a fascinating journey through the pubs of Soho and introduces him to a gallery of bohemian characters of the 1940's who were real enough in life but who in print seem more to be products of a highly stimulated imagination.

Almost refreshing in its departure in tone from the rest of the book is the portrait of Alun Lewis, who seems indeed out of place among the characters who have gone before. A humble and modest Welsh army officer with a "deep tenderness toward life," he disdained the boozing and carousing that marked Soho and its inhabitants and would surely have been out of place there. The contrast that Maclaren-Ross draws between himself and Lewis is one of the more touching parts of *Memoirs of the Forties*. Where Lewis was humble and honest, Maclaren-Ross sees himself as arrogant and didactic; where Lewis felt sympathy and love, Maclaren-Ross sees himself feeling anger and contempt. Perhaps the latter is right when he says that in civilian life they would probably not have been friends. Yet that does not matter. Lewis was killed in action.

As for the six stories appended to the book, the first, "A Bit of a Smash in Madras," is probably the best. The setting is India (where, interestingly enough, Maclaren-Ross never traveled), but it really is Soho transferred to another continent. Of the other stories, "Five-Finger Exercise" stands out as a short piece that touches on human emotion in an unemotional way. These stories serve as a coda to the rest of the book. The characters are fictional, but one is hard pressed to distinguish them from the real ones whom Maclaren-Ross presents in the book. Indeed, they could exchange places, and the reader might be none the wiser.

Critical Context

The 1940's marked the high point of Julian Maclaren-Ross' literary career. During this decade he published in rapid succession three collections of short stories, *The Stuff to Give the Troops: Twenty-five Tales of Army Life* (1944), *Better Than a Kick in the Pants* (1945), and *The Nine Men of Soho* (1946), and two novels, *Bitten by the Tarantula: A Story of the South of France* (1945) and *Of Love and Hunger* (1947). The promise of these works, which are marked by a fresh, idiosyncratic style, was not fulfilled; in subsequent years, Maclaren-Ross' only significant publications were a reminiscence of his childhood, *The Weeping and the Laughter: A Chapter of Autobiography* (1953), intended to serve as the first installment of a multivolume autobiography (never completed), and the unfinished, posthumously issued *Memoirs of the Forties*.

The period covered by *Memoirs of the Forties* is treated in many other literary memoirs as well; the reader sees the same people and events from diverse and sometimes contradictory perspectives. Two fellow memoirists who must be read with Maclaren-Ross are Alan Ross, editor, poet, and cricket writer, and Anthony Powell, author of the twelve-novel sequence *A Dance to the Music of Time* (1951-1975). Ross, who was largely responsible for the publication of *Memoirs of the Forties*, includes a portrait of Maclaren-Ross in his memoir *Blindfold Games* (1986); in addition, his introduction to the 1984 Penguin edition of *Memoirs of the Forties* provides an excellent overview of Maclaren-Ross' life and work. Powell, whose fictional character X. Trapnel, featured in several novels in *A Dance to the Music of Time*, was based on Maclaren-Ross, recalls that colorful figure and his milieu in *The Strangers All Are Gone* (1982), the concluding volume of his memoirs, *To Keep the Ball Rolling* (1976-1982).

Sources for Further Study

Davenport, John. "Ghosts and Gargoyles," in *The Spectator*. October 1, 1965, p. 414.

Pritchett, V. S. "Those Were the Days," in *New Statesman*. LXX (September 24, 1965), pp. 446-448.

The Times Literary Supplement. Review. October 21, 1965, p. 937.

Toynbee, Phillip. Review in *The Observer*. September 12, 1965, p. 26.

Wilton Eckley

MEMORIES, DREAMS, REFLECTIONS

Author: Carl Gustav Jung (1875-1961)
Edited by Aniela Jaffé
Type of work: Autobiography
Time of work: 1875-1961
Locale: Switzerland, Austria, India, Italy, northern and eastern Africa, and the
United States
First published: Erinnerungen, Träume, Gedanken von C. G. Jung, 1962 (English
translation, 1963)

> *Principal personages:*
> CARL GUSTAV JUNG, a Swiss psychologist
> SIGMUND FREUD, the founder of psychoanalysis
> RICHARD WILHELM, a sinologist

Form and Content

In 1955, the Swiss psychologist Carl Gustav Jung celebrated his eightieth birthday
and published what he said would be his last book. The following year, his American publisher asked for an authorized biography or, better yet, an autobiography.
After some discussion and much resistance on Jung's part, it was decided that
Aniela Jaffé, his student and secretary of many years, would spend one afternoon a
week talking with him, would record his memories, and would edit them in the
form of an autobiography, with Jung as the narrator. The weekly conversations
began in the spring of 1957 and continued for another two years. By 1958, however,
Jung decided that he had not spoken adequately of his earliest years and wrote his
own account of his childhood and student years. In 1959, when Jung and Jaffé had
completed a first draft of the autobiography, he added a chapter, "Late Thoughts,"
and an account of his visit to East Africa. He thus gave to her a variety of material
from which to work: his own writing, which makes up 40 percent of the completed
book; transcripts of lectures to medical students, which form the basis of another
25 percent; and answers to her questions. He edited her writing, and she edited his.
Nevertheless, he thought of *Memories, Dreams, Reflections* as her project and asked
that it be left out of his collected works.

In the introduction, Jaffé explains her difficulty in getting Jung to talk about his
life. As a physician, he felt honor bound to keep the confidences of all who had
sought his help. As a public figure who had met many famous people, he chose to
remember only those whose destinies seemed somehow tied to his. As an old man
who had nearly died already and had recently lost his wife, he was preparing for
death, detaching himself from the outward details of his life and reflecting on the
inward meaning, most of all on the dreams and visions that had shaped his career
from within. His inner life had always been so intense that it threatened to eclipse
the outer. He had kept the innermost details secret from almost everyone. Now that
he wrote about them, however, it was only natural that they would dominate the

book. As Jung explains in the first sentences of his prologue, he had previously written in the language of science but he could not use it to describe himself because he could not observe himself scientifically. Therefore, he used the language of myth. What he wrote could not be judged true or false by any objective standard; he could only try to be true to his own myth.

Memories, Dreams, Reflections contains twelve chapters, of which the first half provide a chronological account of Jung's development up to mid-life. The first three chapters, based on Jung's written account, take him from his childhood in various vicarages through his years of secondary school and medical study at the University of Basel. The next three chapters, based on lectures, move from Jung's residency at the Burghölzli Mental Hospital in Zurich, through his relationship with Sigmund Freud, to his encounter with the unconscious and the development of what he came to call analytical psychology. The second half of the autobiography gives a more episodic account of Jung's later life. There are chapters on his esoteric studies of Gnosticism and alchemy, his creation of a private retreat on Lake Zurich, and his travels in Africa, the United States, and India. The last three chapters concern Jung's near-death experience after a heart attack in 1944, his views on life after death, and his thoughts on subjects such as good and evil. In a brief afterword, Jung writes in an age-old voice of wisdom and practically takes leave of himself as well as of his readers.

There are footnotes throughout the text—some by Jung as shorthand references to his many works, others by his English translators, but most of them by Jaffé to identify now-obscure people or to set remarks in context. There are also several appendices, which together account for about 10 percent of the book's 430 pages. Three appendices contain letters which had not yet been published when the book first appeared: letters from Freud to Jung and from Jung to his wife when he was on his travels. One appendix records Jung's memories of his closest male associate after Freud, the sinologist Richard Wilhelm, who is best known as the translator of the *I Ching* (sixth to third centuries B.C.; *Book of Changes*) and who introduced Jung to many aspects of Eastern thought. The last appendix reprints an odd tract titled *Septem Sermones ad Mortuos: Die sieben Belehrungen der Toten* (1916; *The Sermons of the Dead Written by Busilides in Alexandria, the City Where the East Toucheth the West*, 1925), which Jung recorded during his confrontation with the unconscious—it is not the work of his conscious intellect. Jung restricted this tract to his friends, fearing that it would seem too eccentric or artistic; nevertheless, its teachings became widely known through the novel *Demian* (1919; English translation, 1923), which was written by Hermann Hesse after he had undergone Jungian analysis. The German editions have further appendices: letters to a student and to a colleague; biographical sketches of two other men who influenced Jung, Théodore Flournoy and Heinrich Zimmer; a postscript to Jung's "Red Book," where he recorded further messages from the unconscious; and Jaffé's headnote to the "sermons" and her history of the Jung family, containing Jung's anecdotes of his first meeting with his future wife and his thought, "This is my wife." The appendices are followed by a glossary of Jungian terms, including now-familiar coinages such as "introvert" and "extrovert" and a list of his major works. The German editions offer a bibliography of works about Jung, and the English editions have a detailed index. Illustrations vary among the German, British, and American editions and are omitted from most paperback editions.

Analysis

The most haunting images in Jung's autobiography are from dreams and visions which came to him from his earliest years and which he kept secret for most of his life. When he was only three, he dreamed of an underground shrine that was consecrated to a phallic god. At twelve, he had a vivid mental image of God defecating on the great cathedral at Basel. At twenty, he dreamed that he was carrying a tiny candle in a dark wood, with unknown shadows in pursuit. As he tried to understand what was happening to him, he read voraciously and discovered that he really had two personalities: one growing and full of imperfections, the other ageless, wise, confident, still as a stone. After reading the work of Johann Wolfgang von Goethe, he decided that this must be a normal enough phenomenon though ignored by most people. After reading some of Friedrich Nietzsche's writings and seeing what the "No. 2" personality could do even to a man of culture, Jung determined to communicate exclusively through his "No. 1" personality and to explain the nighttime world in a daytime voice.

In *Memories, Dreams, Reflections*, Jung seems to speak in the accustomed voice of No. 1 but to speak quite openly about the experiences of No. 2. To some extent, the two personalities merge as the aging man becomes the archetype of the wise old man. No longer constrained to write in a scientific style, Jung abandons the long, numbered paragraphs and extensive bibliographies of his other books for a much more personal style. Without trying to summarize his work, much less to popularize it, he shows a continuity that would otherwise be difficult to see. His early psychiatric work taught him the importance of dream analysis; the study of dreams made him an early champion of Freud, who was then an outcast from the academic world; and his inability to discover why Freud insisted on sexuality as the sole basis of mental illness made him search for the symbolic power behind the biological function. His differences with Freud led inevitably to a severance of personal relations, and the break prompted Jung to study the way that one's personality type influences one's thought and action. The break also threw him headlong into the occult world that Freud had shunned, and his efforts to understand the primal elements of his own unconscious provided the impetus for his extensive research in the history of alchemic symbolism. Jung remarks:

> My life is what I have done, my scientific work; the one is inseparable from the other. The work is the expression of my inner development; for commitment to the contents of the unconscious forms the man and produces his transformations. My works can be regarded as stations along my life's way.

All my writings may be considered tasks imposed from within; their source was a fateful compulsion.

Jung's handiwork in stone at his lakeside retreat is described as a similar expression of an inner vision: Here he could live as a medieval man, as he did in his dreams and studies. Similarly, his travels took him to places where he could observe the primitive in himself; he learned more from conversations with Pueblo Indians in New Mexico and Elgonyis in Uganda than from many "civilized" Europeans, for native people speak the language of myth. The autobiography itself is an exercise in personal mythmaking, in which the hero confronts the monster of the unconscious and through his quest discovers his true identity. It provides a myth for modern man, who has largely ignored the stuff of which dreams are made.

Critical Context

Not without reason had Jung guarded his dreams and visions. He knew that they would serve only as ammunition for people who wanted to discredit psychology or his approach to it. And so they did. In an early review, the British analyst D. W. Winnicott described the autobiography as an account of a creatively managed case of schizophrenia. Later, in *C. G. Jung: The Haunted Prophet* (1976), the American analyst Paul Stern cited the daydreams of Jung's schooldays as evidence that he suffered from delusions of grandeur and was generally unstable; the autobiography seemed to Stern a Jungian bible in the form of parable. More sympathetic biographers such as Jung's friend Laurens van der Post have conceded that Jung suffered greatly, especially at mid-life, but regard his encounter with the unconscious as an essential act; if he was psychotic for a time, they point out, so is anyone in a thoroughgoing analysis. All biographers thus far have taken the shape of their stories (the *mythos* in the word's original sense) from Jung's myth.

Another ground for objection is what Jung has not said. Other than to Freud and his own parents, he gives no more than passing notice to any personal relationship. Critics are quick to cite his silence about Toni Wolff, his confidante and lover of nearly four decades, and there is only passing reference even to his wife in the English editions. "Reading the *Memories*," writes Gerhard Adler, "one is struck by the absolute uniqueness of Jung's personality, a uniqueness which also conveys the feeling of the great loneliness in which his genius had to exist." The book is so personal that it needs to be complemented by Jung's letters, where one finds what Adler calls "the personal flavor of involvement in the problem of his correspondents." Many biographies are now available as well, some with lavish illustrations, and there are such documentary films as *Matter of Heart* (1986). One case mentioned in the autobiography has been novelized in Morris L. West's *The World Is Made of Glass* (1983), and the more important case of Sabina Spielrein is the subject of an illuminating book by Aldo Carotenuto.

More recently, Jung has been assailed for his views of women. In large measure, the criticism is based on the common misconception that he considered men and women totally different and attributed specific historical contents to the archetypal form of the anima (female soul). In fact, Jung takes care to show how he himself attached specific personal content to a form that he believes to be found in everyone because it belongs to the collective experience of mankind. He notes that most of his patients were women, and most of his closest associates as well. His autobiography owes much to Jaffé's abilities as a listener. According to van der Post, she was so unsure of herself when she first came to Jung for analysis that she could not talk to him, but simply listened. In letters to her, Jung confided fantasies of which her dreams reminded him, and he thanked her once for responding to his work with "a creative resonance which is at the same time like a revelation of the feminine being." Although many autobiographies have grown out of collaborations, often bearing the phrase "as told to" on the title page, this one represents a "fusion" of efforts, as Jaffé called it, which is virtually unique.

Sources for Further Study
Carotenuto, Aldo. *A Secret Symmetry: Sabina Spielrein Between Jung and Freud*, 1982.
Franz, Marie-Louise von. *C. G. Jung: His Myth in Our Time*, 1975.
Freud, Sigmund, and C. G. Jung. *The Freud/Jung Letters*, 1974. Edited by William McGuire.
Jaffé, Aniela. *C. G. Jung: Word and Image*, 1979.
Jung, C. G. *Selected Letters of C. G. Jung, 1909-1961*, 1983. Edited by Gerhard Adler.
Jung, C. G., et al. *Man and His Symbols*, 1964.
Post, Laurens van der. *Jung and the Story of Our Time*, 1975.
Stern, Paul. *C. G. Jung: The Haunted Prophet*, 1976.
Wehr, Gerhard. *Jung: A Biography*, 1987.

Thomas Willard

MEMORIES OF A CATHOLIC GIRLHOOD

Author: Mary McCarthy (1912-   )
Type of work: Autobiography
Time of work: The early twentieth century
Locale: Minneapolis and Seattle
First published: 1957

> *Principal personages:*
> MARY MCCARTHY, the author, a young orphan
> KEVIN, one of her three brothers
> MRS. MCCARTHY, their paternal grandmother
> MARGARET SHRIVER, their grandaunt
> MYERS SHRIVER, their granduncle
> HARDY PRESTON, their maternal grandfather
> AUGUSTA PRESTON, their maternal grandmother
> MISS GOWRIE, Mary's Latin teacher

Form and Content

The sixth book of a prolific and prominent American writer, this collection includes eight essays interspersed with shorter pieces of commentary and preceded by an introduction. All but two of the eight chapters and the preface were first published, from 1946 to 1957, in *The New Yorker*, some in slightly altered form. The chapter title "Names" did not have prior publication, nor did the introduction, titled "To the Reader."

The book, like Mary McCarthy's childhood, is divided between two locales. The first two chapters center on Minneapolis, where Mary and her three brothers lived for five years with their paternal grandparents after the four young children were orphaned during the influenza epidemic of 1918. Mary, the oldest, was six when her parents died.

In the preface, the author describes her parents and their backgrounds, family life in Seattle, and the nature and importance of her religious faith as she was maturing. Briefly, she discusses her readers' various and conflicting responses to the essays as they were published separately, and she discourses on the difficulties of writing about her life when her principal resource was her own memory, a lively imagination, and a vague, sometimes faulty knowledge of certain facts. For example, she never knew her brothers as children after they were separated, and all the principal adult figures in her early life were dead or unavailable by the time she was writing these memoirs.

The remainder of the book is composed of recollections of her years in Seattle, where she lived with her mother's parents, the Prestons, the three boys having remained in Minneapolis. The period of time covered by this chronicle is approximately twelve years. Each chapter has a focus—each title suggesting an aspect of

McCarthy's life at a particular time—and each (except for the last one) is followed by a brief essay in which the writer meditates on some of the events and persons presented in the chapter and on the difficulty of distinguishing among truth, unreliable memory, and fantasy; this problem constitutes a principal theme of the book. Another concerns her Catholic upbringing; the third is the universal theme of growing from childhood to the verge of young womanhood.

Analysis

In the preface, McCarthy mentions that some of her readers have read the memoirs as fictions, questioning the Jewishness of her grandmother and the cruelty of her uncle, for example, while being fascinated by the odd behavior of people who were not in themselves unusual. The opposition by both sides of the family to the marriage of her father and mother; the weak health, high spirits, and extravagant, romantic nature of her father; the beauty and religious fervor of her mother, a convert; and, finally, the tragic deaths of her young parents (at twenty-nine and thirty-nine) are not extraordinary circumstances in themselves, but when combined in the life of one precocious and strong-willed child, they do acquire a fascinating strangeness, especially when narrated in a notably detached and objective manner. Thus, McCarthy describes herself as a passionate, intense, competitive girl while maintaining a dispassionate, almost aloof tone, often humorous and self-deprecating, never self-pitying or sentimental. The two strains of her Catholicism are important to an understanding of this book: One was of goodness and beauty, as exemplified by her mother and the Minneapolis priests and nuns, the other of dour narrow-mindedness, as personified by her grandmother McCarthy. For both aesthetic and intellectual reasons, the author does not regret having been a Catholic, though at the end of the preface she states that she is one no longer.

The inexplicably abusive treatment of the orphaned children is described in the first essay, "Yonder Peasant, Who Is He?" Victims of influenza themselves, the children were sequestered in their grandmother's sewing room until they recovered, after which they were moved to a nearby house under the guardianship of two middle-aged people, Grandaunt Margaret and her husband, Myers. Never directly informed of their parents' deaths, the children slowly came to the awful realization. Because of the deprivations and cruelty practiced on them, Mary and her brother Kevin regularly ran away and tried to enter an orphanage. In this chapter, only their pious and autocratic grandmother is described in detail; in the short commentary that follows, McCarthy expresses her purpose as having been to indict the privileged for indifferent treatment of the underprivileged. Viewing as an adult the peculiar circumstances of their deprived and penurious years in Minneapolis, McCarthy shows an understanding that was not available to her as a child, when she suffered without question or hope.

In the next essay, "A Tin Butterfly," McCarthy does pay more attention to individuals, particularly to Myers Shriver, her uncle by marriage. Childish crimes, such as defacing wallpaper, were disproportionately punished; the children were frequently beaten, often on the slightest pretext. What emerges is a portrait of an ignorant, brutal man who shamelessly ate special delicacies prepared by his wife while the children subsisted on such coarse fare as one might find in poorhouses described by Charles Dickens. A year after Mary was mercilessly beaten after having been unjustly accused of having taken a tin butterfly, the children were rescued by their Protestant grandfather. The commentary that follows confesses to some doubt and confusion about various elements in the story, but the desired effect has been created; the reader has already experienced the anger and pity that McCarthy must have known her account would elicit, and no amount of cool, objective analysis and correction can eradicate the feelings aroused by her vivid narration.

"The Blackguard" described Mary's return to Seattle, where she became Grandfather Preston's ward and entered the Sacred Heart Convent school as a five-day boarder. The blackguard of the title is thee poet George Gordon, Lord Byron, to whom one of Mary's teachers compared her, incurring Grandfather Preston's wrath until the teacher apologized. A number of details, McCarthy admits, are fictional, but the essay is an amusing one for its portrayal of her grandfather, the mother superior, the teacher, and Mary herself at the age of eleven, concerned for the salvation of the soul of her Protestant guardian.

The next essay, "C'est Le Premier Pas Qui Coûte," relates further events in Mary's convent schooling. Trying desperately to be noticed, Mary hit upon the idea of announcing that she had lost her faith. After undergoing some solemn sessions with the priests, Mary resolved to pretend to regain her faith out of a sense of obligation to others. The following commentary, as usual, points out some discrepancies in the story, but the central fact remains clear: Mary was a remarkable child with a strong sense of drama.

"Names" discusses the significance of family, baptismal, and confirmation names and concludes with a transition to the next stage in Mary's life: After a disastrous year in public school, Mary was sent to the Annie Wright Seminary, an Episcopal boarding school in Tacoma, Washington. "The Figures in the Clock" describes some of Mary's experiences there: learning Latin; acting in the play *Marcus Tullius*; being devoted to her Latin teacher, Miss Gowrie, one of the most memorable characters in the book; and getting caught in an escapade just before graduation.

Chronologically, the events described in "Yellowstone Park" occurred before those in the preceding essay, but McCarthy places the essay here because this episode involved a trip to Medicine Springs, Montana, to visit two schoolmates, a trip she was allowed to take only because she had told her grandfather that the trip would include a visit to Yellowstone Park—which never took place. Instead, she was introduced to adult pleasures for which she was not ready; her attempts to drink bootleg whiskey and gin, for example, are both pitiable and hilarious. The commentary that follows this essay claims that the story is true except for the name of the town and the names of the people involved. McCarthy then draws attention to her grandmother Preston, who has hardly been mentioned until this point, partly because she was still living when most of these memoirs were being written.

"Ask Me No Questions," the final and much longer essay, is devoted to a description and discussion of the appearance, personality, and mysterious behavior of Grandmother Preston and her two sisters. The writer describes the luxurious but curiously inhospitable home of her grandparents, their self-centered, ritualized lives, and finally, the death of her grandfather and then, after a period of senility, the death of her grandmother.

Critical Context

A central figure in the intellectual life of twentieth century America, Mary McCarthy has published more than twenty books as well as innumerable essays and reviews. Perhaps her best-known work is *The Group* (1963), a novel which traces the fates of nine Vassar College women in the 1930's. Appearing at a time when the revitalized feminist movement was beginning to gain attention, *The Group* became a best-seller and was widely discussed.

Memories of a Catholic Girlhood is considered by many critics to be a classic of autobiography; others have questioned the sincerity of McCarthy's attempt to distinguish fact from fantasy. One reviewer said, "Miss McCarthy, who writes better than most people, here writes better than herself." In 1987, McCarthy published *How I Grew*, a sequel of sorts to *Memories of a Catholic Girlhood*. While the latter centers on McCarthy's early years, *How I Grew* is primarily concerned with her experiences from the age of thirteen to twenty-one; nevertheless, there is some overlap between the two volumes. The consensus of reviewers was that *How I Grew* failed to match the quality of its predecessor as a self-portrait of a forthright, brilliant, and original writer.

Sources for Further Study

Gelderman, Carol. *Mary McCarthy*, 1988.
Grumbach, Doris. *The Company She Kept*, 1967.
Hardy, Willene Schaefer. *Mary McCarthy*, 1981.
McKenzie, Barbara. *Mary McCarthy*, 1966.
Stock, Irvin. *Mary McCarthy*, 1968.

Natalie Harper

MEMORY OF FIRE

Author: Eduardo Galeano (1940-   )
Type of work: History
Time of work: Genesis, the pre-Columbian period to 1700; *Faces and Masks,*
    1700-1900; *Century of the Wind,* 1900-1984
Locale: Principally Latin America, but also North America and Europe
First published: Memoria del fuego I: Los nacimientos, 1982 (*Memory of Fire I:*
    Genesis, 1985); *Memoria del fuego II: Las caras y las máscaras,* 1984 (*Memory*
    of Fire II: Faces and Masks, 1987); *Memoria del fuego III: El siglo del viento,*
    1986 (*Memory of Fire III: Century of the Wind,* 1988)

Form and Content

Although the trilogy *Memory of Fire* has been classified as a work of history, it is
a supremely personal and subjective history. The author, Eduardo Galeano, makes
no claim to being a historian; in fact, he specifically states the contrary. In school,
he found history courses to be like visits to a "waxworks" or "the Region of the
Dead," with the past "lifeless, hollow, dumb." His literary efforts have been a
reaction to such a view of history and the desire to make it vital again. The title
Memory of Fire reflects the author's purpose: "to contribute to the rescue of the
kidnapped memory of all America, but above all of Latin America, that despised
and beloved land." To preserve this important memory, Galeano wrote a unique
series of three books containing short episodes forming a mosaic of the many
elements contributing to America's past.

The format of the trilogy underlines the subjective nature of the work. Although
many voices are taken into account, the work reveals one vision, that of the author.
It is not an anthology, Galeano maintains, but to classify it as a novel, essay, epic
poem, testament, or chronicle is equally difficult—probably because it contains
elements of all of these. Every fragment is based on documentary information from
a series of sources listed in the back of each volume and referred to by number at
the end of the episode involved. The information upon which each fragment is
based comes from many types of sources, but the choices of what to include and
how to tell what happened reveal Galeano's own bias. The author recognizes that he
is not "neutral" in his reporting; he "takes sides" and the side he takes is clearly
that of the oppressed groups, whether Indian, black, poor, or female. Finding
traditional textbook history filled with lies and made to serve the function of
teaching people to "resign [themselves] with drained consciences to the present,"
Galeano presents his history as a vital part of stimulating change, using the repetition of ideas, episodes, and motifs so that the three volumes form one vision of the
rich Latin American tradition as well as the history of exploitation of people and
natural resources.

Genesis, the first volume of the trilogy, is divided into two parts: "First Voices"
and "Old New World." The "First Voices" are Indian myths of pre-Columbian

America, starting appropriately with a creation myth and ending with a prophesy of the "rule of greed." In between, the harmonious relationship of the Indian with nature is given a full range of expression through stories of many different tribes. As the section closes, a tale called "Authority" introduces a recurring theme, that the power of one group over another (in this case, men over women) is often based on a lie, which is passed from one generation to the next. In this way, he suggests, the rule of master over servant is maintained, once violence and murder have established it. Galeano then introduces three sections titled "Dangers," "The Spider Web," and "The Prophet" in which the arrival of the Europeans is foretold: "Men wearing clothes shall come, dominate, and kill." In contrast to the domination to come, the pre-Columbian Indians' life resembles Paradise.

The remainder of *Genesis* is a series of historical moments starting in 1492 on board Christopher Columbus' ship and ending in 1700 at the deathbed of Charles II. Each episode, whether focusing on a specific incident or an individual, has a heading with the year and location in addition to a title. Galeano consults various sources for his information and occasionally interpolates literal transcriptions which appear in italics.

Faces and Masks continues the same format as the second part of *Genesis*. This volume begins with an entry titled "Promise of America"—the search for paradise which the land of America stimulated in Indians as well as in the conquistadores— and ends with a second prophecy, speaking of the end of greed through struggle and the establishment of freedom. Historically, however, this book covers 1701 through 1900, the period of the wars of independence, and contains an almost overwhelming amount of violence and betrayal, which the positive tone of the final section cannot counterbalance.

Century of the Wind picks up at the beginning of the twentieth century. "The World Goes On," as the title notes, in spite of the belief of many that the world would end at midnight on the last day of 1899. Galeano traces modern developments in Latin America and its relations with the United States. Freedom is crushed repeatedly, but each time there is new rebellion. Galeano traces the present-day cycle through many turns and ends on the positive note of the irresistible life force, symbolized here by the "Maypole fiesta" and the "tree of life." As with the second volume, Galeano reaffirms the positive despite the horrors presented in the historical chronicle of this period.

The sum of the books of this trilogy is a mixed composition drawn from mythology, literature, historical accounts, newspapers, and other varied sources. The sheer number of sources—227 for *Genesis*, 361 for *Faces and Masks*, and 475 for *Century of the Wind*—shows the volume of material which went into creating this mosaic, intended to represent the whole of Latin American history and experience.

Analysis

That *Memory of Fire* is a personal statement on the part of the author quickly becomes clear. Galeano is not aloof from politics and the struggles of the poor and powerless; although the tone is controlled and the prose often stripped down to an essential statement of facts, the choice of episodes and persons as well as the vocabulary quickly reveals his sympathy with socialist aims. As such, some critics have reacted to the political overtones, while others have focused on the enormity of the task of writing a complete Latin American epic of this type, considering it impossible. Yet the majority seem to believe that, viewed as a subjective, personal collection of moments in this history, *Memory of Fire* is extremely successful in making history live, in capturing its electricity.

Because of the length of time involved, from pre-Columbian times through 1984, a format of connected fragments was used. These are joined together in a type of symphonic structure with themes or motifs that appear and reappear. In fact, the language of the individual entries, which often read like stories told in front of a campfire as part of the oral tradition, is often poetic and musical, though never florid. It has been suggested that a series of fragments is the most appropriate form for a history of Latin America: The land itself is splintered into individual countries, themselves splintered into factions and classes, with the result that there is no one Latin American identity, only a multitude of voices and faces. Galeano visualizes this history as one of conflict, a record of resistance to injustice and oppression.

Since *Memory of Fire* is clearly a personal chronicle, it is inevitable that the choice of documentary sources reflect a personal bias as well. Yet because the work is also a presentation of history, that choice is significant. The several hundred sources involved in the three volumes are a heterogeneous collection involving everything from myths and stories to newspaper reports and data gleaned from standard texts on the conquest and colonization. Galeano does not distinguish among the kinds of documents but rather borrows from them as they fit his total vision. The result underlines the fact that this is not a historian's history, certainly not an objective analysis or an attempt to weigh the validity of documents. In his sources are tales of magic along with reports and opinions based originally on insufficient evidence or even possible misinterpretation. The questions of what really happened and how to interpret it are important, particularly as Galeano attempts to unmask how the lies of history become the official version: for example, "The Government Decides That Peronism Doesn't Exist" and "The Government Decides That Truth Doesn't Exist." Another humorous illustration is the episode in which the President of Guatemala proclaims the Santa María volcano dormant despite the lava destroying Quetzaltenango. The ironic title reads, "The Government Decides That Reality Doesn't Exist."

The cyclical format of *Memory of Fire* is introduced in *Genesis*, in Spanish *los nacimientos* ("beginnings" or "births"). Appropriately, the first fragments deal with the "birth" of creation in a dream by God. The myth introduces the idea of cyclical time because woman and man will be born and die again and again: "They will never stop being born, because death is a lie." Much of the first section of *Genesis* then focuses on indigenous myths of nature. Only toward the end of the section is the prophecy of the "rule of greed" introduced: "Men will turn into slaves," and "the world will be depopulated, it will become small and humiliated."

Genesis then presents historical moments to illustrate the fulfillment of this prophecy. From the beginning, the Indians lose in the clash of cultures which Columbus' discovery causes. In a report ironically titled "Day of Glory," the few surviving Indians brought to Europe as trophies are paraded before a hostile audience which would have preferred gold or spices.

Religion and greed as causes of tremendous suffering in the Americas becomes the theme of *Genesis*. In separate fragments, six Indians are burned alive for the sacrilege of burying images of Christ and the Virgin (to fertilize their crops), and Aztec human sacrifices are juxtaposed to the burning of heretics by the Spanish Inquisition. In reaction to mistreatment of the Indians, protests begin to arise—first from Antonio de Montesinos and then from Bartolomé de las Casas.

European diseases and overwork wipe out whole populations of Indians, and the slave trade brings blacks from Africa to do the manual labor. The desire for freedom arises repeatedly, and the oppressed revolt: Lautaro and the Araucanians, the Tepehuanes from the Zacatecas mines, the escaped black slaves of the free city of Palmares, to name only a few in a long history. The revolt is followed by repression, which in turn will be followed by another revolt.

The irony of the Spanish exploitation of America's resources is a theme which is introduced early and followed through the wars of independence in *Faces and Masks*. Although the conquest was accomplished by Spaniards and many Indians and blacks paid with their lives for the gold which was sent to Europe, "the metals arriving from Mexico and Peru do not even leave a smell in Spain." European merchants and bankers outside Spain profited instead.

Although Galeano does not paint pre-Columbian America as a Garden of Eden, there is something like a Paradise Lost motif hooked into a hope for the future which he adds to *Faces and Masks* and *Century of the Wind*. Already in *Genesis*, there is an episode in which Mancio Serra de Leguízamo, one of the conquistadores of the Incas, is dying and confesses the inherent goodness he sees in the Indian way of life, with its community property and no greed. *Faces and Masks* starts with the idea that people have sought paradise in America and continues with a series of episodes illustrating that this hope for paradise remains unfulfilled. Galeano argues the case of the oppressed, demonstrating the crushing weight of history against the powerless while admiring the spirit of those who resist. The motif of the runaway slaves and the city of Palmares recurs, as does the question of the oppression of women, in *Genesis* with the case of Sor Juana Inés de la Cruz and then in *Faces and Masks* with Benjamin Franklin's sister Jane, whose "case will awaken no interest in historians."

As the wars of independence rage, the oppressed groups show their courage in the resistance against Spain, but the wealthy Creoles fear a real revolution of the underclasses. "Agrarian reform" alternately inspires hope in the poor and is suppressed by the wealthy, who fear the loss of their economic advantages. This reform is connected clearly with the Indians' idea of common property: "All belongs to all."

A main figure of *Faces and Masks* is José Martí, whose ideas are important to Galeano. Martí sees Latin America fighting to revive its "hidden and betrayed identity" rather than accept the one imposed by Europe or the United States. Here the theme of the mask from the title is most clearly emphasized. Galeano quotes Martí as writing: "We were a mask, with trousers from England, Parisian vest, jacket from North America, and cap from Spain." Latin America does not recognize the value of its own customs and language; starting with *Genesis*, Galeano interpolates episodes showing the devaluing of anything Indian or mestizo and continues in this volume to show that the attitude continues even after independence to apply to art, clothing, dance, customs, and literally anything that is an American product. The image left at the end of *Faces and Masks* is of an America plundering its raw materials to send overseas and working Indians, blacks, and the poor to do it. Nevertheless, freedom and the end of the rule of greed strike the last chords of the volume.

Century of the Wind reintroduces many of these themes as they apply to the twentieth century. Here the United States becomes the outside power with the strength to crush rebellions. At the same time, the question of the appeal of Marxism is introduced. The Peruvian poet José Carlos Mariátegui sees the depths of his country in the Indian communities, which are "unconquered in their socialist traditions of work and life." The events of Cuba and Nicaragua continue that thread.

Many grotesque dictators are introduced in short vignettes, and the suffering of the individual who resists is shown in the person of Miguel Mármol, who escapes death many times during the years of his long life. Events of modern Latin American history show a fragmented continent with individual countries waging war against their neighbors and thus squandering their resources, with the result that debts to foreign powers control their economies. Violent repression occurs whenever the questions of agrarian reform, divorce laws, higher wages, or nationalization are raised, since any of these challenge one or more powerful groups. A president who "dares to commit" reform, for example, Salvador Allende (Chile) or João Goulart (Brazil), is eliminated.

The many atrocities are recounted in tones of sadness and irony. The humor inherent in the human condition, specifically in the Latin American condition, is used to relieve the stark portrait the author paints. Even here, however, irony is Galeano's strongest weapon. "The Soccer War," for example, between El Salvador and Honduras seems impossibly absurd at one level yet horribly ironic at the same time, as two fragments of what was once a single republic define each other as the enemy and leave thousands dead in battle. In another example, the words "bad luck, human error, bad weather" from the official reports become an ironic litany in the account of the deaths of President Roldós of Ecuador, Omar Torrijos of Panama, and General Rafael Hoyos Rubio of Peru, all of whom had opposed powerful economic groups and died in suspicious plane crashes for it. To round out the irony,

Galeano uses an ironic juxtaposition of words ("benevolent multinational corporations"), a stylistic device which is almost a trademark of this trilogy.

Against the chronicle of torture, repression, and wars, Galeano repeatedly infuses an element of hope: Things could change. He writes of the Indians who are "guided by the ancient certainty that someday greed and arrogance will be punished," and he includes many episodes of brave individuals and groups who stand up for their beliefs in spite of almost certain death. At the end of *Century of the Wind*, Galeano closes with nine fragments, starting with "Against Forgetting," which express his purpose in compiling this personal epic. Believing with Carlos Quijano (publisher of the *Marcha* magazine) that forgetting is "the only death that really kills," Galeano makes *Memory of Fire* his pledge that this massive history and tradition will not be forgotten.

Critical Context

Modern Latin American history has often seemed to the outside world like an unending series of dictatorships, atrocities, and economic problems. Galeano's work attempts to balance that view with a vision of the dormant potential inherent in the people. For the Latin American, he gives expression to the turbulent history of the region, while at the same time he allows the outsider an insight into the many fragments which make up the Latin American experience. He reminds the reader of a rich culture outside that of Europe, which, although so greatly influenced by European civilization, has its own unique characteristics.

Eduardo Galeano's work stresses political and social questions which result from economic problems and the brutality of dictatorships. Politically engaged, he admires the heroic individuals who fight against oppression and uses his work to plead for solidarity against those who abuse power. His sympathies lie with the poor, and he sees in socialism a continuation of the Indian custom of common property, which he finds so admirable compared to the greed of big business and wealthy landowners. For expressing such opinions, he spent many years in exile. He finally returned to his homeland of Uruguay in 1984.

As a journalist, he contributed to *El Sol*, a socialist weekly, and was editor of *Marcha* and *Época*. His first international recognition came from his book *Las venas abiertas de América Latina* (1971; *Open Veins of Latin America: Five Centuries of the Pillage of the Continent*, 1973), which discusses the problem of underdevelopment in Latin America. From his collection of stories to his important novels, *La canción de nosotros* (1975; our song) and *Días y noches de amor y de guerra* (1978; *Days and Nights of Love and War*, 1983), Galeano writes in the tradition of recent Uruguayan fiction, which attempts to deal with the harsh realities of dictatorship and economic crisis along with the political movements demanding change. With *Memory of Fire*, he writes an epic view of the history of Latin America, showing the destructive forces in the clash of traditions which produced it and in the division between rich and poor which still dominates it. Bringing together history, literature, mythology—in fact, fragments of everything he finds significant—he produces a kaleidoscope of impressions, joined together through repeated themes and by the author's own desire to keep alive the memory of the past whose influence continues to be felt as Latin America forges its future.

Sources for Further Study

Broderick, Thomas. "Eduardo Galeano: *Memory of Fire: Genesis*," in *The Review of Contemporary Fiction*. VI (Fall, 1986), p. 144.

Christ, Ronald. "Dramas That Scorch: *Memory of Fire: I. Genesis*," in *The New York Times Book Review*. XC (October 27, 1985), p. 22.

Conant, Oliver. Review of *Memory of Fire: Faces and Masks* in *The New York Times Book Review*. XCII (March 1, 1987), p. 20.

Franco, Jean. "The Raw and the Cooked," in *The Nation*. CCXLIV (February 14, 1987), pp. 183-184.

McMurray, George R. *Spanish American Writing Since 1941: A Critical Survey*, 1986.

The New Yorker. "Eduardo Galeano." LXII (July 28, 1986), pp. 18-20.

Staggs, Sam. "Eduardo Galeano: In His Trilogy *Memory of Fire*, the Uruguayan Writer Attempts to Portray 'The Masked History' of America," in *Publishers Weekly*. CCXXXIII (June 3, 1988), pp. 64-65.

Susan L. Piepke

THE MESSAGE IN THE BOTTLE

Author: Walker Percy (1916-   )
Type of work: Cultural anthropology
First published: 1975

Form and Content

Although Walker Percy was trained as a physician, he never became active in his profession. During his internship at Bellevue Hospital, in New York City, he contracted tuberculosis. As a result, he was forced to spend nearly three years in convalescence, first at Lake Saranac, New York, and then at a sanatorium in Connecticut, in which he found himself in the bed once occupied by Eugene O'Neill. Percy's illness caused him to evaluate the sufficiency of the scientific, empirical education which he had received. He decided that it was excellent—so far as it went—but that it simply did not address the subjective experience of the individual. Thus, he began to read those authors—Søren Kierkegaard, Edmund Husserl, Martin Heidegger, Gabriel Marcel, Martin Buber, Jean-Paul Sartre, and Albert Camus—whose ideas constituted the foundations of existentialism and phenomenology. Convinced that research in those fields could best be conducted in fiction, Percy read widely in the nineteenth century Russian and the twentieth century European novel. He also began an extensive study of the philosophy of language, for language, he realized, was the only means by which individuals could communicate their experience of reality. This later study was made poignant by the discovery that his younger daughter had been born profoundly deaf and thus would never have the easiest access to symbolic meaning, sound.

From 1954 to 1975, Percy published essays in a wide variety of American journals. Several special concerns were represented by these journals: literature (*The Southern Review*, *The Sewanee Review*, and *Partisan Review*), Christianity, especially Catholicism (*Katallagete*, *Thought*, *The New Scholasticism*, and *The Modern Schoolman*), and psychology (*Psychiatry*, *The Journal of Philosophy*, and *Philosophy and Phenomenological Research*). Despite the diversity of the contexts in which they appeared, all the essays had a common concern: the significance of the symbol as the primary means by which humans communicate. It should be noted that none of the essays appeared in a publication devoted to the study of linguistics.

In 1975 these fourteen pieces and another, previously unpublished one, were published as *The Message in the Bottle*, a book of 335 pages. The title was taken from an essay which appears as the sixth chapter. The previously unpublished essay, "A Theory of Language," appears as the fifteenth and final chapter. The essays are not arranged in order of their original publication. The first essay, "The Delta Factor," appeared only in 1975, for example. All the essays retain their original title, except for "The Act of Naming," which is retitled "The Mystery of Language." As the seventh chapter, it is approximately at the center of the book.

Despite the book's origin as separate essays written over a longer period (resulting in a certain amount of repetition), *The Message in the Bottle* is intended as a coherent whole. The first and last essays, the last written, are designed to serve as the introduction and conclusion. With its scholarly, though unconventional, footnotes and its five-page bibliography, the book announces that it seeks as its primary audience specialists in the various fields of language studies. Periodically, Percy provides a model of his theory. At first, the figure is that of a triangle; it identifies the observer, the object seen and its name, as well as the mysterious gulf which exists between the latter two. Then the figure is expanded to a rectangle with the addition of a second person, who names the object and thus bridges the gulf, but in so doing he addresses an even more perplexing mystery: language. In the last essay a reversion to the triangular model makes the second person all the more conspicuous by his absence. The book stresses the fundamental significance, both for the race and for the individual, of intersubjectivity, in which one person names for another person some hitherto unknown aspect of their world. Thus, the book presents a radical anthropology: Before man, language was.

Analysis

The Message in the Bottle may be intended for those who specialize in the study of language, but it is not intended to be easily accessible to them. The book does not conform to the received ideas and techniques of the language establishment. Rather, Percy uses a very personal voice, personal references as evidence, a noncumulative argument, and various types of stylistic indirection—such as allusion, analogy, and repetition, especially of references to Helen Keller's breakthrough to language—all to frustrate his target audience. He knows that he must shake the specialists loose from a quick, preconceived reading of his text if he is to get them to see man-the-user-of-language in an entirely different light.

The book opens with a six-page bombardment of rhetorical questions, all of which are variations on the first one: "Why does man feel so sad in the twentieth century?" Such a prophetic evocation of biblical "latter days" is hardly the confident, assertive strategy usually used in a book that informs. Percy's answer is all the more unsettling, for it is merely another question:

> Is it possible that the questions about man's peculiar upside-down and perverse behavior, which he doesn't understand, have something to do with his strange gift of speech, which he also doesn't understand?

Percy contends that there is no adequate theory of language, the most distinctive human activity, because there is no adequate theory of man. The widely accepted scientific view, deriving from the ideas of Plato and the techniques of René Descartes, treats man as both a bodiless intelligence outside the world and an animal among other animals inside the world. The individual result is that all too often a human suffers from angelism-bestialism, vaunting his transcendent subjectivity and consigning all others to objectivity. The global result is that the twentieth century has witnessed both an explosion of knowledge and an explosion of violence.

The prevailing theory of language mirrors the split in the theory of man. The idealists, represented by Ernst Cassirer, emphasize the primacy of the isolated mind, as against the inclusive world, but cannot account for the transmission of thought from one mind to another. The behaviorists, led by B. F. Skinner, insist that the langauge act is no different from any other response that an inclusive world requires of its captive creatures. Thus, in behavior theory, thought never passes from one mind to another. Both views founder, according to Percy, because they ignore the role of the symbol, that mysterious construct between the observer and the observed, whose significance was first emphasized in the theory of language by the Scholastics in the Middle Ages.

In the world of *The Message in the Bottle*, then, language—mystery—precedes Percy, who does not enter until section 14 of chapter 1. Even then he enters not as an omniscient specialist but as a befuddled layman. He locates himself in history, twenty years earlier, as he was reading a book, Helen Keller's *The Story of My Life* (1903). He returned to that book often, because it contains a classic description of language acquisition cited by philosophers whose works he had been reading, among them Ernst Cassirer, Jacques Maritain, and Susanne Langer. Perhaps he also returned to it because his daughter, like Helen, was barred from language. On this occasion he saw something new: Others had understood that somehow, when Anne Sullivan had "spelled" "w-a-t-e-r" in one of Helen's hands, Helen suddenly understood that the stuff touching her other hand had been named. Thus, Helen reached symbolization and thereby created a world from chaos. Percy's advancement of the general understanding was the realization that the symbolic accomplishment occurs only when there is a Namer for the Hearer. Later, Percy acknowledges, he learned that Charles Sanders Peirce, an American psychologist of the late nineteenth century, had arrived at the same conclusion.

That human world-formation must begin with the act of hearing another person is significant not merely to the study of language acquisition but to any consideration of epistemology. From Plato on, with the ever-increasing importance of the scientific view seeing has increased its dominance over the other senses (the importance of the invention of the lens cannot be overemphasized here). In consequence, knowledge has become more and more a solitary experience, more and more primarily a matter of the quantification of externality by visualization, and therefore more and more mechanical in operation and abstract in content. At the same time, time has become visualized as uniform segments of length and thus has become space. Thus, the individual has become more and more alienated, deprived of a present because all space is standardized and deprived of a past and a future because time no longer provides him with a sense of continuity from a beginning to an ending. What is more, he has been taught to distrust and disavow any thoughts that are merely personal, for they are not pragmatic, measurable, or able to be duplicated; in short, they are not scientific.

It should be clear that Percy writes as one who has suffered from the malaise of the twentieth century. He underwent three years of unsuccessful analysis when he was barely into his twenties. It is little wonder that he is jubilant over his discovery that hearing is the foundation of knowledge, for that fact explodes all philosophies built on any form of dualism. From the beginning, the human is both incarnated and intersubjective, dependent upon the symbol, which is an analogy, not a quantification. Thinking about consciousness must be entirely reconstructed: Detached observation is not the original and purest consciousness but is rather a deprived deterioration. Percy reminds his readers that the etymology of "consciousness" is "knowing with." Solitary response to facts is not the only legitimate intellectual act as the positivists would have it; rather, the shared response to a symbol (joining different forms of being) is the supreme act of knowing. Percy's discovery was not only an intellectual breakthrough but also a religious conversion. Although he had become a Catholic a few years before, he must have gained from the Keller episode a radically deeper appreciation for the body of teaching, both biblical and institutional, that constitutes Christianity.

Percy wishes his readers to see that the naming act, "this is——," has its divine origin in the naming act which took place at the Last Supper, an act which symbolized a condition that had already existed throughout history and which instituted the means by which humans may celebrate that condition and its Incarnation. Human words are possible because of the Word; when John begins his book by writing, "In the beginning was the Word, and the Word was with God, and the Word was God," he is stating once and for all the Christian knowledge that language is sacred, that language is the medium through which a human can commune with God and his fellow humans. When Percy speaks of "the mystery of language," then, he is using "mystery" in both an open and a mysterious sense. To a scientist a mystery is merely a problem to be solved; in the New Testament mystery refers to both the revelation of God's design and the sacraments. Percy hopes that at some point in the book each of the members of his target audience will experience the same kind of breakthrough about the nature of language that he experienced in reading *The Story of My Life*. Yet he cannot openly state his intention. He hopes to write so seductively that at a certain point a transvaluation will occur so that his reader will return to the first words of the book—with its echoes of Genesis, the Gospel of John, and of Revelation, and really understand why they belong in a book about language and the only creature who possesses it:

> In the beginning was Alpha and the end is Omega, but somewhere between occurred Delta, which was nothing less than the arrival of man himself and his breakthrough into the daylight of language and consciousness and knowing, of happiness and sadness, of being with and being alone, of being right and being wrong, of being himself and being not himself, and of being at home and being a stranger.

Those words are *The Message in the Bottle*. They constitute what Percy calls a "piece of news from across the seas" (a statement appealing to faith) rather than a "piece of knowledge" (a statement subject to proof or disproof). It is noteworthy that "The Message in the Bottle," the title of the chapter preceding "The Mystery of Language," is chosen for the title of the entire book and thus to imply its intention. Percy concludes "The Message in the Bottle" by saying:

> In such times, when everyone is saying "Come!" when radio and television say nothing else but "Come!" it may be that the best way to say "Come!" is to remain silent. Sometimes silence itself is a "Come!"

In *The Message in the Bottle* Percy practices such silence. Unless the first sentence is fully appreciated, all 335 pages that follow are merely words.

Critical Context

Most frequently Walker Percy is viewed as a Southern writer, less often as an American writer. Certainly his placement in either of these categories is helpful, for he is thoroughly enveloped by his history and the contemporary context of both his region and his country. Then, too, his work is richly allusive to the literary tradition of his region and country. Nevertheless, both definitions, resting ultimately on secular values, fail to distinguish his work. He is fundamentally alienated from the world by his Christian faith. More must quickly be said to preclude misunderstanding: It is a faith enhanced by the thinking of such men as Saint Augustine, Saint Thomas Aquinas, Søren Kierkegaard, and Gabriel Marcel, and by all philosophical and scientific theory that is not distorted by secular dogmatism. What distinguishes his writing, then, is not his response to place but to time; facing an open, mysterious universe, he writes as a wayfarer to any other person who comes to believe that he too is a wayfarer.

The Message in the Bottle articulates from a different angle the worldwiew of Percy's fiction, which is "incarnational, historical, and predicamental." From such a perspective, the world is ordinarily a place of "everydayness," but there are those gracious moments when a sacramental symbol offers the individual the opportunity to experience holy excitement. In such a world (in which instruments of visuality are almost always prominent) one basic narrative occurs: A miserable, vision-dominated, solitary consciousness (prototypically the moviegoer) grasps or fails to grasp the opportunity to talk with another, to be Namer and Hearer and thus achieve intersubjectivity, full consciousness. *The Message in the Bottle* makes precisely the same set of statements about reality: In Percy's view a fiction of ultimate concerns has much more verisimilitude than the fiction concocted by secular science.

Sources for Further Study

Bigger, Charles. "Walker Percy and the Resonance of the Word," in *Walker Percy: Art and Ethics*, 1980. Edited by Jac L. Tharpe.

Poteat, Patricia Lewis. *Walker Percy and the Old Modern Age: Reflections on Language, Argument, and the Telling of Stories*, 1985.

Poteat, William. "Reflections on Walker Percy's Theory of Language," in *The Art of Walker Percy: Stratagems for Being*, 1979. Edited by Panthea Broughton.

Telotte, J. P. "Charles Peirce and Walker Percy: From Semiotic to Narrative," in

Walker Percy: Art and Ethics, 1980. Edited by Jac L. Tharpe.

Thornton, Weldon. "Homo Loquens, Homo Symbolificus, Homo Sapiens: Walker Percy on Language," in *The Art of Walker Percy: Stratagems for Being*, 1979. Edited by Panthea Broughton.

Lewis A. Lawson

THE MIDDLE PASSAGE
Impressions of Five Societies—British, French, and Dutch— in the West Indies and South America

Author: V. S. Naipaul (1932-   )
Type of work: Travel writing
Time of work: 1960-1961
Locale: England, Trinidad, British Guiana, Brazil, Surinam, Martinique, Antigua, and Jamaica
First published: 1962

Form and Content

In September, 1960, V. S. Naipaul returned to his native Trinidad after a decade's absence. In England he had studied at the University of Oxford and then embarked on a literary career, publishing three books set in Trinidad: the novels *The Mystic Masseur* (1957) and *The Suffrage of Elvira* (1958) and the collection of linked short stories *Miguel Street* (1959). Naipaul's return had been prompted by a grant from the government of Trinidad and Tobago, led by the historian Eric Williams, enabling him to revisit the country about which he had written in his fiction. Williams later expanded the terms and scope of Naipaul's scholarship, urging him to write, with government support, a book of nonfiction about the West Indies as a region. Naipaul was given a free hand to write whatever he pleased; Williams and his government later had cause to regret their generosity, for Naipaul produced an unflattering and highly critical account of life in the region.

Naipaul's purpose in writing *The Middle Passage* was to examine the nature of the colonial societies existing in the West Indies and on the northern coast of South America. The book is also a journey of self-exploration for the author. Throughout the book, Naipaul quotes from various sources; especially important are those quotations taken from the writings of earlier British travelers to the region, such as Anthony Trollope and the historian James Anthony Froude. The epigraph with which Naipaul begins his book and which establishes the direction of his argument is taken from the work of Froude, who wrote of the West Indies, "There are no people there in the true sense of the word, with a character and purpose of their own."

The first of the book's six sections is entitled "Middle Passage" and actually begins in England with observations on the crowds of lower-class West Indian immigrants arriving in search of a better life. Naipaul's book does much to explain why so many West Indians abandoned the islands for the hardships and uncertainties of life in the "Mother Country." On board a ship which is sailing almost empty on its return trip to the West Indies to pick up another load of emigrants, Naipaul finds that even his small group of fellow passengers becomes a Caribbean society in microcosm with its divisions based on color, race, financial standing, and territory of origin. Even before his arrival back in the West Indies, he has provided the reader with an introduction to many of the themes which he will explore.

Naipaul's tour of the West Indies lasted seven months and the book's organization follows the sequence of his travels. Fittingly, the first territory considered is Trinidad, the island of Naipaul's birth and presumably the only territory of which he already had firsthand knowledge; it is also Naipaul's principal point of reference for much of his analysis of the areas later visited. As a result, this second section, although making up only forty-five of the book's 222 pages, is the most ambitious, concentrated, and important. Naipaul shifts from a detached, ironic, and at times amused observer to a despairing, frustrated, and even hysterical participant.

As always, Naipaul is writing principally for a cosmopolitan and not a local audience; he touches on a wide range of topics in painting his highly critical portrait of a fragmented immigrant society composed of "various races, religions, sets and cliques" with no uniting nationalist feeling and no bond other than their shared island residence. Race and color are seen as the dominant factors of island life. Naipaul explores the genesis and development of racial attitudes as well as the crucial relationship between the main and often-antagonistic groups, the blacks and the East Indians (descendants of the indentured laborers brought from Asia to work on the sugar plantations after the emancipation of the slaves). Despite the appearances of "accord," Naipaul believes that "Trinidad in fact teeters on the brink of racial war."

The design of Naipaul's book leads him from Trinidad to the gradually more foreign and exotic and then back toward the more geographically and culturally familiar. The third and longest section of the book deals with British Guiana, which, although located on the mainland of South America, is a predominantly English-speaking and West Indian society, a colony where problems similar to those of Trinidad have been exacerbated by a long and brutal history of slavery and the particularly harsh system of indenture which followed.

In the fourth section of the book, Naipaul visits Surinam, formerly Dutch Guiana, and finds "the only truly cosmopolitan territory in the West Indian region" with even more racial and cultural diversity than Trinidad or British Guiana. There is an absence of racial or economic resentment directed toward the mother country and a genuine affection for the Netherlands; nevertheless, the hunger for an independent cultural identity, especially on the part of black intellectuals, has given rise to a Surinam nationalism which is "the profoundest anti-colonial movement in the West Indies."

The last two sections of the book are the shortest; they deal with Martinique and Jamaica. In Martinique, legally not a colony but an actual department of France, Naipaul feels stifled by the hypocrisy of a social system which proudly grants French citizenship to all while imposing rigid social stratification based on race. Assimilation with metropolitan France has not been economically liberating either, since the island is poor, underdeveloped, and as dependent as the meanest colony. Poverty and racial problems dominate Naipaul's perceptions of Jamaica; the Rastafarian movement is seen as a symptom of the island's desperate illness. The

Jamaican middle class seems to live in a world unrelated to that of the masses of urban and rural poor, and the world of the tourist is equally deceptive and unreal.

Analysis

The Middle Passage is a highly personal book in which West Indian society is observed and assessed by a native who candidly announces his biases. Naipaul's return to Trinidad is characterized as a confrontation with his youthful fears and wish to escape, feelings which were expressed but not examined in his earlier books. Not surprisingly, his reactions to Trinidad have not changed, but now, for the first time, he brings his considerable writing talents to a deliberate and factual analysis of the society which so perturbs him. Some critics have seen in Naipaul's book a distorted picture of the West Indies based on a careful selection of details designed to justify the author's own neurosis. Perhaps Naipaul anticipated this reaction and sought to obviate it by using quotations from a variety of writers, especially from earlier periods, to corroborate his observations.

Naipaul takes the title of his book from the name for the route traveled by the slaves as they were transported from Africa to the colonies of the New World. He also applies the term to the voyage taken by the present-day West Indians flooding into England, testimony to the failure and "futility of the West Indian adventure." Naipaul begins his section on Trinidad with quotations from Thomas Mann and Tacitus which reveal universal aspects of the profound psychological and cultural dislocation wrought by slavery and colonialism; there is also the implication that Naipaul sees West Indians as being in a confused state of transition, cut off from their ancestral roots yet without the confidence or resources to forge an identity independent of their former colonial masters. With the collapse of the plantation economy, the imperial powers have abandoned the region to its poverty and petty provincial concerns. The development of tourism, the result of economic necessity, has been accompanied by increasing foreign ownership and the raising of land prices beyond local means; the social and racial relationships between white visitors and black servants perpetuate old and unhealthy patterns. In Naipaul's opinion, tourism in the West Indies has led to dispossession and a new, self-imposed, slavery.

Naipaul, like Froude, does not see West Indians as possessing a culture of their own; instead they are living in what another writer, approvingly quoted by Naipaul, has called "a client culture and a client economy." During slavery, the culturally bereft Africans could only imitate what they understood of the ways and values of their masters, whites who were usually remote in every way from the best that Europe had to offer. Naipaul believes that with the retreat of the old colonialism, this mimicry of imperfect models has persisted and resulted in a society which values only the foreign and frequently second rate, a society whose ideals are the creation of advertising agencies and Hollywood "B" movies. For Naipaul, the West Indies remain uncreative. Widely recognized manifestations of a vigorous and original popular culture, such as the Trinidadian steel band, calypso, and Carnival, Naipaul finds only loathsome and depressing; the seeming happiness and gaiety of

Trinidadians in the face of all of their problems he finds "inexplicable."

In the West Indies, the problems of colonialism and race are inextricable. Because of his early experience, Naipaul is often startled when he meets New World blacks who speak Dutch, French, or Portuguese rather than English. It serves to remind him of "the condition of the Negro, who in the New World has been made in so many images." Robbed of his own language and culture, the New World black has adopted the values of his former white masters even to the point of scorning all things African, a rejection which Naipaul sees as "the greatest damage done to the Negro by slavery." Naipaul is disdainful of black intellectuals who see West Indian culture as part of the "Christian-Hellenic tradition," for inherent in this tradition is the assumption of black inferiority. Naipaul believes that for a black to identify himself with the Christian-Hellenic tradition is to indulge in "the West Indian fantasy" that "black will be made white." The more the black adopts the values of white civilization, the more he tries to make the European ideal his reality, the more he must become estranged from himself. Again and again Naipaul points to the fine shadings of color which West Indians recognize in categorizing one another; among the African-descended, embarked on "the weary road to whiteness," class and color are clearly linked.

The paradox, in which blacks aspire to a culture which demeans them, is compounded by the nature of the racial problem in Trinidad and British Guiana, where black hostility is not directed toward whites or coloreds (as is common in Jamaica, Martinique, and most of the other territories), but toward East Indians. According to Naipaul, there is racialism in both groups; the blacks' prejudice against the Indians is based on the bigotry toward all nonwhites which they have acquired from the European imperialists. The Indians' contempt for blacks arises from a combination of their own ethnocentrism and the racial attitudes they also have adopted from the whites.

Naipaul's analysis of the racial problems in the West Indies has met with considerable negative criticism, especially on the part of black intellectuals. While the East Indians of his own community are described as materialistic and philistine, practicing a debased religion cut off from its philosophical source, and while the local whites are also dismissed as superficial, placing value only in money and secure in their feelings of racial superiority, the burden of Naipaul's scathing critique falls upon the New World black. Those most provoked by Naipaul's views often seize upon the following statement, which is perhaps more offensive than originally intended: "Like monkeys pleading for evolution, each claiming to be whiter than the other, Indians and Negroes appeal to the unacknowledged white audience to see how much they despise one another." Naipaul is accused of having appropriated for himself the values and judgments of white imperialist society.

Naipaul believes that West Indian writers have failed to help the West Indian establish a true sense of self and situation because the writers too are partisans in the race war; he states that it would take "the most exquisite gifts of irony and perhaps malice, . . . of subtlety and brutality" to explore honestly the West Indian middle class. In *The Middle Passage*, Naipaul has used these very gifts to portray the whole of West Indian society.

Critical Context

At the time of Naipaul's return to Trinidad and the experiences described in *The Middle Passage*, he had already established himself as a young writer of considerable promise. He was seen to be a part of the West Indian literary renaissance which had begun in the late 1940's; in the view of some critics, however, his talent was devoted rather narrowly to writing unkind comedies of manners about a minority group on a remote and insignificant island. Among his West Indian audience, there were questions as to where Naipaul saw himself in relation to his subject matter; his sometimes derisive laughter was clearly not as warm and sympathetic as that of his fellow Trinidadian novelist Samuel Selvon.

Naipaul's trip came at a crucial time. Shortly before returning to Trinidad, he had completed but not yet published *A House for Mr. Biswas* (1961), a novel which some still regard as his first and preeminent masterpiece. This novel ended his period of apprenticeship and revealed an artistic range and a darkness of vision only hinted at in his earlier books. In writing *A House for Mr. Biswas* Naipaul was able to come to terms with his own early life, the life of his father, and the hermetic Trinidadian Hindu community, turning what might have been only personal or parochial concerns into a story with tragic and universal dimensions. In a sense, writing this novel liberated him to write *The Middle Passage*, an exploration of the wider social context in which he was reared. In *The Middle Passage* Naipaul eschewed the personal evasions possible to the writer of fiction and boldly spoke in his own voice about his vision of the colonial society. Soon after completing this first book of nonfiction, Naipaul took the next step on his journey of self-discovery, a voyage to India, the land of his ancestors, recounted in *An Area of Darkness: An Experience of India* (1964). Since then Naipaul has traveled widely and written about the spiritually unaccommodated and culturally rootless, especially in those places which receive little attention from the rest of the world. Beginning with *The Middle Passage*, Naipaul's nonfiction has also employed a quality of observation and a sheer technical brilliance which elevates most of it far beyond the level of superior journalism; it must be seen as an integral part of the artistic oeuvre of one of the late twentieth century's most important writers.

Sources for Further Study
Hammer, Robert D. *V. S. Naipaul*, 1973.
_____, ed. *Critical Perspectives on V. S. Naipaul*, 1977.
Thorpe, Michael. *V. S. Naipaul*, 1976.
Walsh, William. *V. S. Naipaul*, 1973.
White, Landeg. *V. S. Naipaul: A Critical Introduction*, 1975.

Douglas Rollins

MIDNIGHT OIL

Author: V. S. Pritchett (1900-   )
Type of work: Autobiography
Time of work: 1921 to the late 1940's
Locale: London, Paris, Ireland, Spain, and southern England
First published: 1971

> *Principal personages:*
> V. S. PRITCHETT, a young writer learning his craft
> WALTER PRITCHETT, his father
> BEATRICE MARTIN PRITCHETT, his mother
> DOROTHY RUDGE ROBERTS PRITCHETT, his second wife

Form and Content

V. S. Pritchett wrote *Midnight Oil* in his seventieth year. It is the second volume of his autobiography, a sequel to *A Cab at the Door,* which was published in both England and the United States in 1968 while he was a visiting professor at Brandeis University. This earlier volume deals with the period between the author's birth and his twentieth year; *Midnight Oil* takes up the story in 1921 with Pritchett's arrival in Paris, armed with twenty pounds sterling and the determination to become a writer. It recounts episodes in his life until after World War II.

The young Pritchett found life in Paris intoxicating; he vowed never to leave. Language and the sound of words had been his obsessions since childhood, and his stilted school French was soon enriched by young acquaintances and fellow workers, for, after fruitless efforts to find a job, he became a photographer's assistant. For the next two years he read voraciously and talked with people in cafés and in the streets. Then he would sit up late in his inexpensive room in Auteuil and try to write. He concluded eventually that he had nothing to say.

His first published piece was a joke, based on a remark heard in the street, which he had sent to one of the Paris papers. This success taught him that if he had nothing to say, he could at least write about what other people said. The discovery was enormously important: His best short stories are composed largely of conversation.

Looking back fifty years to the youth he was, Pritchett describes with gentle amusement his absurdities, his naïveté, his burning ambition. He appears to have total recall and reproduces lengthy conversations with his various acquaintances. Now, years later, he realizes that his isolation kept him from knowing anything about Sylvia Beach, James Joyce, Ernest Hemingway, and F. Scott Fitzgerald: He had not been aware that he was living at the center of a literary revolution. When he finally heard of Tristan Tzara he was angry because Tzara was smashing up a culture just as he was becoming acquainted with it.

After two years of struggle, Pritchett decided to return to London, where he was finally offered a position by *The Christian Science Monitor*'s London editor: He was told to describe the daily lives of ordinary people in Ireland as they coped with the civil war. Pritchett knew nothing about politics or journalism. His passion was for the scenery, the theater, and the Irish poets. He was able to talk with William Butler Yeats, Sean O'Casey, and Æ (George William Russell). It was in Ireland that he began to write stories.

Recalled by his paper, he returned to London with an Irish bride and in January, 1924, was sent to Spain as a correspondent. He was captivated by the Castilian landscape but found life in a small dark flat in Madrid cold and cheerless and the city dull. Nevertheless, he says that meeting with agnostics for the first time and with the students and professors of the University of Madrid proved to be some of the most valuable experiences of his youth. He quickly learned the language, made friends, and was introduced to José Ortega y Gasset, Miguel de Unamuno y Jugo, Federico García Lorca, and Pío Baroja y Nessi. Proud of being an amateur journalist, of not visiting the embassies or making friends with the English or Americans, he missed the big political news and wrote background pieces for his paper. He made many train trips in second- or third-class carriages, talking with the passengers, and he took long walks. His descriptions of the trains, the roads, the inns as they were in the 1920's present a strong and interesting contrast with modern Spain.

Back in London after further assignments in North Africa and the United States, Pritchett eked out a precarious living at various boring jobs until he decided to walk across Spain. The resulting book, *Marching Spain* (1928), embarrasses him now, although he still finds that it has originality and vigor. After its publication he received two contracts for books, sold some short stories, and was indeed an author. He moved to a country cottage in the south of England, wrote novels, and suffered from severe health problems until, he says, love and success cured him.

Throughout the book there are references to Pritchett's unhappy childhood, to family quarrels, to his long-suffering mother, a former Cockney shop girl who could still laugh after decades of subjugation, to his tyrannical, egotistical father, and especially to his father's belief in Christian Science. The last two chapters give a sympathetic account of the pitiful old age of his parents. His father, after the failure of his business, tried without success to become a Christian Science practitioner while his mother, who had never believed in Mary Baker Eddy's theories, spent hours a day lying on a couch and announcing that she was dying of cancer. Grieving over his mother's death—not from cancer—Pritchett for once allows the reader to share his deep feelings.

Analysis

The book bears this explanatory epigraph taken from the work of John Gay: "Whence is thy learning? Hath thy toil/ O'er books consum'd the midnight oil?" Indeed, Pritchett's toil has consumed the daylight as well as the midnight oil all of his life. Here is a record of the struggle of an essentially uneducated boy to become a writer. Along with this principal concern there are marvelous descriptions of scenery in Ireland and Spain; anecdotes with sprightly dialogue about scores of people from landladies to great statesmen; glimpses of the life of the lower classes in Paris in the 1920's, in Ireland during the early days of the civil war, in Spain under Miguel Primo de Rivera y Orbaneja and later during the Spanish Civil War, in England during World War II; and a few brief recollections of meetings with famous authors. Of all these aspects the first is by far the most important.

Describing the book Pritchett writes:

> There is a period when a writer has not yet become one, or just having become one, is struggling to form his talent, and it is from this period that I have selected most of the scenes and people in this book. It *is* a selection, and it is neither a confession nor a volume of literary reminiscences, but as far as I am able I have put in my "truth."

In setting down his truth Pritchett does not spare himself. He describes his lower-middle-class origins, his lack of university training, his occasional periods of laziness, his dislike of a regular desk job, his ignorance of current literary trends. He does not conceal, in fact he rather revels in, his sexual feelings both as a proud virgin and later. He does not hide his hatred of his father. Having lost his early belief in Christian Science, he ridicules ferociously his father's use of the "Divine Mind" to excuse all the inexcusable actions of his selfish life.

On the plus side, Pritchett relates his laudable efforts at self-education: He read exhaustively in English, French, and Spanish, sometimes using his lunch money to buy a book. There is a tinge of pride when he tells of how he lived on one-half of a small roll per day for six days rather than ask a friend for a second small loan. When his landlady realizes that he is literally starving, brings him a bowl of soup, and lends him five francs, he is truly grateful. He tells of long hikes over rough terrain and his acceptance without complaint of nights spent in filthy rooms which he shared with as many as seven other people. All of this he recounts without boasting of his endurance, just as he tells of his later life in the English countryside during the war, when he split wood, hauled water, took his turn at watching for fires on the roof of the *New Statesman*'s building, and tried to find time to continue writing. He simply states facts while minimizing the description of his emotional reactions.

Pritchett's first biographer, Dean R. Baldwin, in *V. S. Pritchett* (1987) claims that the two volumes of autobiography leave the reader with only a very sketchy idea of the real character of their author. It is certainly true that the reader wishes to know more about this fascinating man and more about his relations with the great literary figures of the era, yet a careful perusal of *Midnight Oil* reveals, as promised, the author's truth.

Approximately the first half of *Midnight Oil* is devoted to an account of Pritchett's efforts to learn to write, his lighthearted disregard of editors' assignments in favor of topics that interested him, in particular scenery and the drama in the lives of common people. He tells their stories instead of his own. When he does reveal personal details, he weaves them into an anecdote or dismisses his feelings in a few words. For example, when *The Christian Science Monitor* finally fired him, he comments, "I took this as a liberation." His autobiography is a series of anecdotes, many of which provided material for his short stories once he had discovered where his talent really lay.

The style of Pritchett's short stories, which has been compared with that of Guy de Maupassant and Ivan Turgenev, is present in *Midnight Oil*: His prose is simple, straightforward, unadorned. His ear for dialogue is extremely acute and his psychological understanding of the people he introduces is of the same depth as that found in his tales. He displays the same flashes of insight and understanding that make the characters in his short stories so recognizably human. His settings for these characters are established by the perceptive use of a few significant details. His fascination with the quirks and psychological hang-ups of ordinary middle-class people is abundantly evident. The unexpected turn of phrase so prevalent in his stories is also to be found in *Midnight Oil*.

Occasionally, the autobiographical origin of a later story is told at length; a case in point is "The Diver" in *The Camberwell Beauty and Other Stories* (1974). This is the tale of Pritchett's lost virginity and concomitant increase in literary creativity. In another instance, he quotes a remark made to him that became the focus of "Sense of Humour," thought by some critics to be Pritchett's best: A chance acquaintance in Ireland mentioned that he sometimes used his father's hearse to give his girl a ride. Pritchett's bitter contempt for his father, so evident in *Midnight Oil*, is softened to a pathetic, almost comic, portrait of an old man in "The Spree." *Midnight Oil* is autobiography as art rather than as history: Thirty years of Pritchett's adult life are completely omitted and most of the information he offers on his later years is superficial. Yet as art, the work is of a very high order.

Critical Context

The importance of *Midnight Oil* lies in its being a record of the making of a writer, one whose accomplishments have earned for him a knighthood, the presidency of the English PEN organization and later of the international PEN Club, an honorary membership in the American Academy of Arts and Letters, and honorary doctorates of literature from the University of Leeds and from Columbia University. V. S. Pritchett is an example of a vanishing species, the man of letters. He has written innumerable essays for, among other papers, *New Statesman* and *The Christian Science Monitor*, and a dozen books of literary criticism including *Balzac: A Biography* (1973), *The Gentle Barbarian: The Life and Work of Turgenev* (1977), and *The Myth Makers: Literary Essays* (1979). In 1969 he delivered the Clark lectures, titled "George Meredith and English Comedy," and earlier still had collaborated on *Why Do I Write? An Exchange of Views Between Elizabeth Bowen, Graham Greene, and V. S. Pritchett* (1948).

Pritchett's five novels, although published in both England and the United States, have been less successful than his other work. His numerous travel books, on the other hand, beginning with *Marching Spain* in 1928, have received wide acclaim. Yet it is his short stories that are his masterpieces, his enduring claim to fame. There are more than a dozen volumes of these gems and many more that have not been collected. These books paint striking vignettes of ordinary people in London, Paris, Dublin, and Madrid, haunting cameos of individuals or groups caught in a moment of crisis. These characters are in sharper focus than their author. Despite his two autobiographies and an article titled "Looking Back at Eighty" in *The New York Times* magazine, it is not possible to believe that one really knows this very private, very great man of letters.

Sources for Further Study

Allon, Dafna. "Reflections on the Art of Lying," in *Commentary*. LXXXI (June, 1986), p. 47.

Baldwin, Dean R. *V. S. Pritchett*, 1987.

Maxwell, William. Review in *The New Yorker*. XLVIII (June 17, 1972), p. 94.

Nichols, Lewis. "Talk with V. S. Pritchett," in *The New York Times Book Review*. LIX (April 25, 1954), p. 16.

Reid, B. L. "Putting in the Self: V. S. Pritchett," in *The Sewanee Review*. LXXXV (Spring, 1977), pp. 262-285.

Sheed, Wilfrid. Review in *The New York Times Book Review*. LXXVII (April 30, 1972), p. 3.

Dorothy B. Aspinwall

MIMESIS
The Representation of Reality in Western Literature

Author: Erich Auerbach (1892-1957)
Type of work: Literary criticism
First published: Mimesis: Dargestellte Wirklichkeit in der abendländischen Literatur, 1946 (English translation, 1953)

Form and Content

Erich Auerbach tackles a formidable topic in his scholarly investigation of the concept of mimesis. The Greek word, translated literally as "imitation," means for the literary scholar the method by which a writer imitates the real world around him and conveys a sense of that world to the reader. Central to any analysis of the concept is the identification of those elements of the narrative that transmit the sensory environment in which the action takes place. Auerbach offers the following description of the technical function of mimesis in a writer's work:

> Imitation of reality is imitation of the sensory experience of life on earth—among the most essential characteristics of which would seem to be its possessing a history, its changing and developing. Whatever degree of freedom the imitating artist may be granted in his work, he cannot be allowed to deprive reality of this characteristic.

His study of the concept leads him to explore a wide range of literary works, from the writings of the ancient Greeks through almost all Western literature to examples from twentieth century stream-of-consciousness novelists. Wherever he looks, he searches for "representations of everyday life," to discover ways "in which that life is treated seriously, in terms of human and social problems" or in terms of "its tragic complications."

Auerbach seeks to answer four key questions: What style best represents reality? What is the opposite of mimesis—fantasy, farce, rhetoric? What elements of realism influence the artist who writes intentionally nonrealistic literature? What cultural, historical, or literary phenomena affect the writer's attitudes toward contemporary reality and determine his obligation to represent it faithfully?

To formulate a comprehensive response, Auerbach scours the great works of Western literature—and many not-so-famous ones as well. Individual chapters highlight key passages from Homer's *Odyssey* (c. 800 B.C.); works by Roman writers Petronius, Ammianus Marcellinus, and historian Gregory of Tours; the *Chanson de Roland*; Chrétien de Troyes's *Yvain* (c. 1177-1181); Dante's *Inferno* (c. 1320); and Giovanni Boccaccio's *Decameron* (1349-1351). His examination of the Renaissance and the Enlightenment takes him to scenes from works by Antoine de Sales, François Rabelais, William Shakespeare, Miguel de Cervantes, Molière, and the Abbé Prévost. The writings of Friedrich Schiller, Stendhal, and the Goncourt brothers (Edmond and Jules de Goncourt), as well as passages from Honoré de Balzac and Émile Zola, serve him as examples of the way the concept of reality is dealt with by artists of the nineteenth century, the era in which the modern concept of realism emerges. A lengthy examination of a scene from Virginia Woolf's *To the Lighthouse* (1927) offers him a text to demonstrate what happens to the concept of reality in the hands of men and women who are his contemporaries.

In his exploration of Homer in the first chapter, Auerbach sets forth the problem he sees in representing reality. Homer's *Odyssey* presents an immediate, sensory experience, but it does not deal with the commonplace in a serious way. In contrast, Auerbach notes how the Bible treats common subjects seriously; however, the authors of the Books of the Bible show no interest in details of sensory experience, concentrating instead on the ability of their stories to illustrate some larger theme or serve some moral purpose. These are only some of the limitations he finds in classical texts. His examination of Roman writers shows how the lower classes are treated only in comic fashion, never as the subjects of serious or possibly tragic literature.

Compounding the problem is the insistence of classical authors on isolating particular styles as appropriate for discussing certain subjects. Hence, the high style is reserved for discussing the nobility—and for writing tragedy. Conversely, the low, colloquial style is the appropriate vehicle for comedy—and for dealing with the lower classes. The history of antiquity is essentially rhetorical, a mode of presentation antithetical to mimesis, since it ignores sensory experience in favor of stylistic flourish and finesse in argumentation. What he calls the biblical tradition exists side by side with this classical outlook, working at cross purposes with it, stressing the importance of the commonplace. In fact, Auerbach attributes the gradual dissolution of the separation of styles to the emergence and final triumph of Christianity, which conferred dignity on the common man.

Nevertheless, the rise of the courtly tradition in the Middle Ages, with its emphasis on idealism and its conscious rejection of the everyday in favor of the faraway, was a powerful force for restraining writers' tendencies to treat everyday reality seriously. The rise of the Renaissance gave impetus to artists' inclinations to present the world around them fully and without moral judgment, but the emergence of neoclassicism in Europe, especially in France, returned the idea of the ideal to prominence in society and hence in literature as well; the plays of Jean Racine and Molière stress the universal elements of mankind at the expense of representing real-life Frenchmen.

Not until the hegemony of style is broken—which happens infrequently for over two millennia—does Auerbach discover that serious attempts at realism come to dominate the literary scene. He identifies the emergence of modern realism with a single figure: Marie-Henri Beyle, who under the pen name Stendhal wrote the first truly realistic works in Western literature. His followers—Balzac, Gustave Flaubert, the Goncourts, Zola—brought the art of mimesis to its zenith. At least, that is what these artists thought; the writers of the twentieth century, armed with the tools of psychoanalysis, began to portray a reality that earlier writers could only imply, the reality of personality, which emerges as a result of many unconscious desires and fears. For the moderns, the apprehension of reality becomes a more complex activity; at the same time, the "moment" becomes more important, as these writers perceive that any man or woman, at any instant in life, can be the subject of interest and an example of the way the real world works upon the human consciousness.

What may seem astonishing to readers is that Auerbach deals with all the texts he selects for examination in the original language in which they were written— Homeric Greek, classical or medieval Latin, old French, Italian, Spanish, German, contemporary French, and English. The technique is important because Auerbach's starting point for his study is with language; he must deal with the original medium of the artist if he is to make a point about the way style and word choice convey or mask reality, and to do so by resorting to translation would vitiate the force of his argument. Ironically, he finds that he must forgo "discussing the rise of modern Russian realism" because such analysis "is impossible when one cannot read the works in their original language." Those readers who rely on a translation of Auerbach must pause momentarily to reflect on their limitations to appreciate the significance of his undertaking.

The English-language translation of *Mimesis* by Willard Trask runs to 576 pages; two paperback editions have made the text available to readers who still find this criticism as lively and intriguing as Rosemond Tuve, who wrote of *Mimesis* in an article in *The Yale Review* published a decade after the work appeared in German that the book remains "extraordinarily valuable"—not only because it is full of scholarly observations that expand the reader's understanding of literature but also because it is "interesting," an "old-fashioned" virtue that makes the book a pleasure to read.

Analysis

Because *Mimesis* is organized as a series of disparate examinations of specific texts, arranged so as to present a chronological sweep through Western literature, it may not be readily apparent to all readers what Auerbach's critical principles are. Nevertheless, the careful student of the work will discern Auerbach's method of scholarly analysis long before the author makes it clear in his own words. Late in his study, he notes that he has found success in "a method which consists in letting myself by guided by a few motifs which I have worked out gradually." He goes on to say that he tries these motifs out on a series of texts which have become familiar to him in the course of his philological activity.

Auerbach is principally a philologist, interested in the way language works. Every investigation of a text begins with an examination of its language: the words, the syntax, the construction of paragraphs, the juxtaposition of words and phrases, the use of dialogue and narration. Throughout, he engages in a process of induction: Specific texts are analyzed so that general principles may arise. Auerbach undertakes frequent comparison and contrast to show the inevitable similarities of technique that join realists of different centuries in their attempts to portray the world around them, or he exposes the limitations which their environments placed on their attempts to reduce the experiences of everyday life into writing. His underlying assumption is that the analysis of a key scene will give insight into the work as a whole; he assumes that the text is all of a piece, and that attitudes toward the subject and techniques of presentation remain constant throughout the work. That is certainly a large set of assumptions; yet as one reads this detailed study, one senses that Auerbach knows of what he speaks.

Though he may be hesitant to offer clean-cut definitions, it becomes clear that Auerbach equates "realism" with a vernacular presentation of sensory experiences, distinguished from the stylized presentation of many classical authors (even Homer is guilty of limited vision in this respect). Representing reality demands that the artist be open to all subjects and to all forms of treatment; his interest in life must be wide-ranging. He faults the writers of the classical tradition (and those of the Enlightenment as well) for stressing the importance of eternal truths and moral dicta at the expense of exploring the commonplace. Such writers deal almost exclusively with the upper classes, ignoring the multitudes whose lives form the milieu in which the actions of great men and women take place.

Auerbach insists that an accurate representation of reality must involve the artist in dealing with the social, economic, and political issues of his day. Hence, he can fault even Cervantes because "Don Quijote's adventures never reveal any of the basic problems of the society of the time." He gives high marks to the modern realists because in their works "real everyday occurrences in a low social stratum . . . are taken very seriously" and because these events "are accurately and profoundly set in a definite period of contemporary history." Absent from any direct commentary, however, is his view of the degree of mimesis present in the best historical novels.

Much of the analysis goes beyond literary or philological criticism, however, to examine the cultural and historical forces that shaped a writer's view of the world and his understanding of his role as a literary artist. Auerbach demonstrates his commonsense understanding of such forces in his discussions of medieval man's concept of time and of the importance of the otherworld, and in his analysis of the French Revolution as a catalyst for spurring mankind to rethink the role of the individual in society. Auerbach uses his investigations of literature to explore the way in which a people thought, to display their understanding of and attitudes toward human nature, and to reveal their metaphysics. Few scholars have attempted such a broad study; fewer still have succeeded in the way Auerbach has in making readers understand the power of literature.

Critical Context

While the notion of the mimetic as a principle of literature goes back to classical sources, specifically Aristotle, Auerbach is seen more properly to stand in a line of German philologists that reaches back to the nineteenth century, when modern philological scholarship began to rise in prominence in the European university community. The tradition actually has its roots in biblical exegesis, especially that form of study practiced by students of the Talmud, whose detailed analyses of specific texts of the Bible and associated commentaries survived for centuries and became the foundation for literary scholarship in a variety of forms. One reviewer has called Auerbach's work one of those "in the finest European tradition," that of the early twentieth century linguistic critics Karl Vossler, Leo Spitzer, and Benedetto Croce; for such men, "Europe is a constant interrogation whose literature is ever to be questioned anew, insistently."

In some ways, Auerbach's *Mimesis* shares the techniques of the New Critics, whose method of close textual analysis held the field in literary studies for almost half a century beginning in the 1920's, especially in the United States. Where Auerbach differs from such critics is in his willingness to see an interaction between the text and the world which it represents, a real world that exists outside it but impinges—through the consciousness of the artist—to give the work, for better or worse, its particular shape and sense of immediacy. Going far beyond the practice of textual analysis for its own sake, Auerbach's work is, in the opinion of another reviewer, the product of "a mind capable of making great and penetrating analyses of the nature of the human spirit as revealed in language and literature."

Sources for Further Study
Barrett, William. Review in *Saturday Review*. XXXVII (March 20, 1954), p. 21.
Boyd, John D. *The Function of Mimesis and Its Decline*, 1968.
Holdheim, Wolfgang. "Auerbach's *Mimesis* as Historical Understanding," in *Clio*. X (Winter, 1981), pp. 143-154.
Hughes, Serge. Review in *Commonweal*. LIX (February 5, 1954), p. 454.
Landauer, Carl. "*Mimesis* and Eric Auerbach's Self-Mythologizing," in *German Studies Review*. XI (February, 1988), pp. 83-96.
Lyons, John D., and Stephen G. Nichols, Jr. *Mimesis: From Mirror to Method, Augustine to Descartes*, 1982.
Morrison, Karl F. *The Mimetic Tradition of Reform in the West*, 1982.
Schwartz, Delmore. Review in *The New York Times Book Review*. LVIII (November 29, 1953), p. 40.
Tuve, Rosemond. Review in *The Yale Review*. XLIII (Summer, 1954), pp. 619-622.

Laurence W. Mazzeno

MINDS, BRAINS, AND SCIENCE

Author: John Searle (1932-   )
Type of work: Philosophy
First published: 1984

Form and Content

Minds, Brains, and Science is a slightly revised version of John Searle's 1984 Reith lectures, a series of six half-hour lectures broadcast by the British Broadcasting Corporation. These lectures were established by Bertrand Russell in 1948. Because the Reith lectures are popular and discuss issues of wide appeal, the essays are aimed at an audience without a scholarly background in the discipline of philosophy. The popular level is typified by Searle's avoidance of specialized terms such as "epiphenomenalism" in favor of Standard English.

The form of the book reflects the original lectures and consists of six brief but related essays which occupy eighty-seven pages. The book is 107 pages long and includes a five-page introduction, a fourteen-item bibliography, and a five-page index. Searle comments that he had originally intended to publish the lectures as a conventional book with a complete scholarly apparatus but decided that doing so would vitiate the purpose of the series: "Complete accessibility to anybody who is interested enough to try to follow the arguments."

The contents of the book are devoted to an exploration of the place of human beings, whom Searle defines as "intentionalistic," in a universe which science describes as consisting of "unconscious physical particles." The first three chapters, devoted to discussing aspects of the human mind, form a unit. The first explores the nature of the human mind as opposed to the brain and the body, which are demonstrably physical entities. Searle argues that problems arise when modern philosophers and psychologists use language derived from the work of René Descartes which suggests that there is an underlying distinction between the mind on one hand and the brain and body on the other. Searle states that modern philosophers must develop new terminology based on modern scientific knowledge, suggesting that the mind and all the functions associated with it (consciousness, intentionality, subjectivity, and mental causation) are related to the brain (and therefore to the body) just as a solid is to the properties of the molecules of which it is constituted. He argues that desires, beliefs, and emotions are caused by the neurophysiological functioning of the brain.

In chapter 2, Searle investigates the popular modern subject of artificial intelligence, especially that form which views the relationship of the mind to the brain in terms of the relationship of computer software to computer hardware. Searle argues that computers cannot think because they are limited to purely formal processes, which he compares to the syntactical aspects of language, rather than being able to deal with the meaningful processes that characterize human thought patterns, which he compares to the semantic properties of language. He points out that the operations of the human mind involve more than syntax and that it is specifically those functions which a computer cannot duplicate. Thus, the computer analogy is inaccurate.

Searle uses the background presented in the second chapter to launch a formal attack in the third, which is on cognitive science. He notes that the efforts of scientists to explain the functions of the mind by analogy to the latest technological device (in this case, computers) is simply the most recent in a series of analogies, including those made by Gottfried Wilhelm Leibniz to a mill and by Sigmund Freud to hydraulic and electromagnetic systems. Searle argues that although human beings, like computers, follow rules, there is an important difference: When human beings follow rules, "meanings cause behaviour," because the rules have a semantic component.

Chapters 4 and 5 turn away from the subject of the first three to discuss the nature of human action and the nature of the social sciences. In chapter 4, Searle suggests that since the most important function of the human mind is intentionality, intentionality also characterizes human actions, which are affected by beliefs and desires as well. Even an action that appears simple to an observer—leaving the room, for example—may have different mental causes. He points out that when psychologists discuss repression, they mean that one intentional state has been transformed into another but they do not deny that the actions are at some level intentional. The argument in chapter 4 leads directly into that of chapter 5, in which Searle suggests that methods used effectively in the natural sciences are not appropriate for human behavior, because human behavior differs from natural events. Natural phenomena follow scientific laws, "universal generalisations about how things happen." In contrast, the social sciences are actually "theories of pure and applied intentionality." Searle supports his argument by considering economics, which is not based on universal generalizations. Instead, it presupposes certain understandings about the intentions of people which influence their behavior, such as the desire of entrepreneurs in a capitalistic system to make money. As a result, Searle argues, when human intentions and practices change, the science of economics must change also.

The first five chapters lay the groundwork for the sixth, in which Searle discusses free will. He points out that human beings seem to be characterized by a desire to define themselves as free, an idea seemingly at odds either with the determinism of Newtonian physics or the indeterminacy of quantum mechanics. Searle rejects the doctrine known as "compatibilism," which states that free will and determinism are compatible with each other in some unspecified way. He argues, however, that the existence of intentionality suggests that human actions include the experience of freedom; for example, even a person who is forced to do something at gunpoint can consider the possibility of acting differently. His conclusion is that human beings are in some evolutionary way predisposed to believe in free will and cannot "give up the conviction of freedom because that conviction is built into every normal, conscious intentional action."

Analysis

Minds, Brains, and Science is intended to explain the functioning of the human mind and argue for the existence of free will using modern materialistic arguments and making no appeal to religious concepts. Despite its use of accessible terminology and its straightforward argument, the book is clearly controversial, because Searle attacks dualism, Chomskyan linguistics, behavioralism, cognitive psychology, and the belief in artificial intelligence, all of which have many supporters, both scientists and lay people. At the same time, Searle asserts that human beings have free will, an idea that seems at odds with his materialism, and he does so from a point of view that rejects the dualistic tradition deriving from René Descartes, which suggests that the mind is more than the molecular structure of the brain and that free will and determinism therefore coexist. Searle grounds his arguments in appeals to common sense, and readers' acceptance of them therefore depends on their acceptance of Searle's examples and analogies.

The first three chapters, which outline Searle's ideas about the mind-brain/body question and his critique of artificial intelligence and cognitive psychology, depend on a series of analogies. He argues that the relationship of the mind to the brain is like that of a macrocosmic object such as a solid to the microcosmic molecules of which it is constituted; from this analogy, he concludes that the functions of consciousness, intentionality, subjectivity, and mental causation are simply part of the neurophysiology of the brain. He asserts that consciousness exists and that one should accept the fact, rejecting the dualistic idea that the existence of consciousness proves that the mind is more than its material components. He does not, however, provide an analysis of the errors of the Cartesian dualists but simply asserts that their views are incorrect. Furthermore, he does so not from the point of view of philosophers who argue for panpsychism, such as Charles Hartshorne in *The Logic of Perfection and Other Essays in Neoclassical Metaphysics* (1962), who avoids dualism by attributing intentionality to all physical levels of being, including atoms. Nor does he argue from the point of view of philosophers who avoid both dualism and panpsychism by hypothesizing a hierarchical organization of the universe in which human beings differ from organisms on the other levels. Similarly, Searle begins from a non-transcendentalist position rather than by refuting the position taken by the transcendentalists that mental states are not caused by neurological functions alone.

Searle's argument that computers cannot think is based on an analogy different from that in chapter 1. In chapter 2, he compares the formal manipulation of symbols by a computer to a man—ignorant of Chinese and left alone in a room—who would be able to produce sentences intelligible to a Chinese speaker by manipulating Chinese characters with the aid of a book of rules. He argues that a computer program merely simulates rather than replicates the functions of the mind and that the program never has semanticity. In addition to showing the limits that he perceives among those who study artificial intelligence, Searle shows the limitations of grammarians, such as Noam Chomsky, who have suggested that the rules of language are merely syntactic.

Searle's analogy, however, deals only with those mental functions which are involved with the use of language; a reader must extrapolate from linguistics to other mental functions he discusses. Furthermore, a reader must accept Searle's assumption that the "Chinese room" provides a good analogy for artificial intelligence, a fact which has been questioned by philosophers such as Georges Rey. Finally, although Searle implies that a computer could not be designed with semanticity and that its hardware could not be designed to replicate the biological functions of the brain and therefore produce mental functions, he does not develop his reasons in detail. It is possible to argue that if human beings could produce a perfect duplication of understanding, the replicant would be able to understand.

Acceptance of the second chapter is necessary for acceptance of the third, in which Searle argues that it is a mistake to use the computer analogy to explain the workings of the mind because computers cannot think. He suggests that the computer is neither more nor less exact as a metaphor for the brain than were earlier technological metaphors. His disbelief in the accuracy of the metaphor leads him to question the research carried on by students of cognitivism. Although he demonstrates that the earlier technological metaphors have proved inaccurate, he asserts rather than proves that the computer metaphor is also incorrect, asking his readers to agree that he has discredited an entire field of research.

Chapters 4 and 5, which deal with intentional human actions and the nature of the social sciences, are based on a kind of materialistic but nondualistic reasoning similar to that of the first three chapters. The chapter on intentionality argues that all human actions are intentional and that they can be explained only by reference to mental contexts, conscious or unconscious, a fact which means that "actions differ from other natural events in the world." Just as his view of the human mind is nontranscendentalist, however, his view of intentionality is that it is not transcendental but separate from causality. He does not clearly state the difference between intentional and psychological states, and his theory of intentionality makes the mind basically self-referential: It is aware of itself and its functions, but since it is a biological phenomenon mental states and the actions dependent on them are subjective. Similarly, in chapter 5 he suggests that the difference between the natural and social sciences is that the former are capable of being explained in terms of generalizations, whereas the latter are capable of being understood only in terms of intentionality. All the social sciences are basically self-referential, because their categories cannot be defined in physical terms and they must be studied in terms of "the intrinsically mental character of social and psychological phenomena."

The self-referentiality of the human mind, of human action, and of the study of the social sciences leads Searle finally to argue for the existence of free will in self-referential terms. Searle suggests that modern science is incompatible with the traditional doctrine of free will, because true freedom would mean that every person would be capable of changing "the causal order of nature." Because sciences such as physics have shown that the world is determined by the structure of its molecules and there is no reason to disbelieve the sciences, Searle suggests that it seems improbable that human beings have free will but that it nevertheless exists. Just as a reader who accepts Searle's premises is likely to agree that the mind exists because of a consciousness of his own mental states, so he is likely to agree that free will exists because a belief in free will is a part of intentionality.

The matter-of-fact tone and the conversational style of the essays make them persuasive even though Searle does not work out all of his arguments with philosophical sophistication. Throughout the six essays, Searle uses analogies to persuade his readers to accept the existence of seemingly incompatible facts without attempting to reconcile them. The book is therefore thoughtful and thought-provoking, leading casual readers to accept both the premises and the views expressed and encouraging others to explore further answers to the questions raised.

Critical Context

Minds, Brains, and Science is important for two reasons. First, it explores questions that have fascinated people in the West since the time of Plato; second, it presents the material in a format apprehensible by the interested nonspecialist. It succeeds admirably at its second task and provides the nonspecialist with a cogent introduction to some important modern philosophical questions.

Minds, Brains, and Science explores questions that interest not only philosophers but also computer scientists and cognitive scientists. The six essays fit into Searle's own exploration of the questions, including his article "Minds, Brains, and Programs," which discusses the "Chinese room," and *Intentionality: An Essay in the Philosophy of Mind* (1983), which in part claims that mental properties are higher than the neurophysiological level of the brain. *Minds, Brains, and Science* explores questions of major scholarly inquiry, such as the relationship between the mind and the brain/body (see, for example, *Mind and Brain: The Many-Faceted Problem*, 1982, edited by Sir John Eccles), the relationship between philosophy and science (see, for example, Hilde Hein's *On the Nature and Origin of Life*, 1971), and artificial intelligence (as in, for example, Theodore Roszak's *The Cult of Information: The Folklore of Computers and the True Art of Thinking*, 1986). Specifically, there is a large amount of secondary critical literature that discusses both Searle's ideas and his conclusions, and *Minds, Brains, and Science* is in part an answer to essays critiquing "Minds, Brains, and Programs" and *Intentionality*.

Sources for Further Study

Anderson, David. "Is the Chinese Room the Real Thing?" in *Philosophy*. LXII (July, 1987), pp. 388-393.

Cuda, Tom. "Against Neural Chauvinism," in *Philosophical Studies*. XLVIII (July, 1985), pp. 111-185.

Donagan, Alan. *Choice: The Essential Element in Human Action*, 1987.

Landesman, Charles. "Minds, Brains, and Searle," in *Metaphilosophy*. XVII (April-July, 1986), pp. 172-182.

Rey, Georges. "What's Really Going on in Searle's 'Chinese Room,' " in *Philosophical Studies*. L (Spring, 1986), pp. 169-185.

Alexandra Hennessey Olsen

MIRROR IN MY HOUSE
The Autobiographies of Sean O'Casey

Author: Sean O'Casey (John Casey, 1880-1964)
Type of work: Autobiography
Time of work: The early to mid-twentieth century
Locale: Ireland and England
First published: 1956

Principal personages:
SEAN O'CASEY, an Irish dramatist
MICHAEL CASEY, his father
SUSAN ARCHER CASEY, his mother
ISABELLA (ELLA), his sister
EILEEN O'CASEY, his wife

Form and Content

Mirror in My House combines six books previously published: *I Knock at the Door* (1939), *Pictures in the Hallway* (1942), *Drums Under the Window* (1945), *Inishfallen, Fare Thee Well* (1949), *Rose and Crown* (1952), and *Sunset and Evening Star* (1954). The books tell the significant events in O'Casey's life from his birth in Dublin until roughly 1954, near the end of his life. The term autobiography should, however, be used with caution for a number of reasons. First, the books are less a continuous narrative than a series of "vignettes" (O'Casey's term), vivid scenes often dramatized with abundant dialogue; for many, James Joyce's term "epiphanies" is appropriate: The vignette may not represent a crucial event in O'Casey's life but may rather reveal something about him or his situation. (At one point O'Casey seems to have projected the work as a series of short stories.) Aspects of O'Casey's life may be either played down (for example, his support of the Soviet Union) or blown up (his literary quarrels) beyond what the reader might consider their real importance. A good example of his subjective approach is his treatment of the Easter Rising of 1916. It records, first, O'Casey's abortive attempt to advise the Irish Volunteers on military strategy; then comes a description of looting by the slum dwellers; then follows an account of O'Casey's own experiences as a neutral taken into temporary custody by the British; and finally O'Casey offers an imaginative account of the execution of some of the rebels (which he could not have witnessed).

As part of an autobiography, the emphasis is naturally on what O'Casey experienced, but the first three parts convey the cynicism which also appears in *The Plough and the Stars* (1926), while the last expresses a kind of grudging acceptance of the rebellion. The poverty of the area is brought up not only in the looting but also in an episode in which O'Casey is able to feed himself and his mother much better than usual because a British soldier who is guarding him compels the neighborhood shopkeeper to give him an adequate supply of food. O'Casey's technique is selective but emotionally and thematically coherent.

As a dramatist, O'Casey began his career in the tradition of naturalism, but from *The Silver Tassie* (1928) on, he made increased use of expressionistic and symbolic techniques; in the autobiographies, he frequently shifts from a relatively conventional narrative and descriptive style to passages which cannot be taken literally. For example, at the end of *Pictures in the Hallway*, the reader suddenly finds himself in the aftermath of the Battle of the Boyne in 1690 with the defeated Irish soldiers looting for food; gradually, however, the account moves to the present, where in the Church of Ireland parish where O'Casey worshiped as a youth, a low-church (Orange) faction is pitted against a faction (O'Casey's) which either is Anglo-Catholic or is so regarded by its opponents; the same disputes are going on as in the days of William III, with the happy exception that in St. Burnupus' parish the Orange faction is put to rout.

Large sections, too, would have to be classified as rhetoric, being argumentative, verbose, and heavily documented; this is true of O'Casey's quarrels with the Catholic church. Style, too, can be unconventional. Generally O'Casey writes in the third person, in an "Irish" manner which presumably echoes his own colloquial speech; nevertheless, there are numerous purple passages and others written in what George Orwell sarcastically called "Basic Joyce," somewhat in the manner of *Finnegans Wake* (1939).

O'Casey affects to look down on Latin, but the text is studded with Latin phrases. These are usually conventional phrases purposely altered, with grammatical correctness sacrificed to satiric effect. *Trio juncta in lacunae, per amica violentio lunee*, for example, combines a definition of the Trinity with the title of a book by William Butler Yeats, with various substitutions.

Analysis

In James Joyce's *A Portrait of the Artist as a Young Man* (1916), Stephen Dedalus talks of the "nets" ("nationality, language, religion," "my home, my fatherland, or my church") which the artist must "fly by" in order to fulfill himself; the novel ends when Stephen flies by the nets into exile. These same nets affect O'Casey's life, and at the end of the fourth of his autobiographies he accepts exile in England; nevertheless, this is not the end of his story, and the word "nets" does not really define his attitude toward these forces. "Themes" is perhaps a better word for them; they come in and out of the autobiographies and as much as anything give them form.

The first theme is, quite naturally, family. John Casey was born into a lower-middle-class household which enjoyed a degree of modest comfort—his father, a clerk, had a small library—but this comfort vanished with his father's illness and death. O'Casey has been suspected of exaggeration in describing the family's poverty, but even allowing for this, the picture is deeply disturbing. The problem of getting medical attention for O'Casey's diseased eyes was particularly acute. Somehow treatment was found, and his eyesight was preserved, but only with much difficulty and humiliation. Funerals, too, could be emergencies, since the family scorned a pauper's burial. Particularly depressing is the story of Ella (Isabella), O'Casey's sister, a talented woman who had trained as a teacher but who ended up bearing five children to a violent husband who had to be committed to an asylum. She died in the bed in which she slept with the five children; O'Casey became the guardian of one of his nephews and was reproved for not providing him with a sufficiently Christian education by the agent for a Protestant charity which was contributing meagerly to the child's support. What is not depressing is O'Casey's portrait of his mother, who well into her later years struggled to keep her dignity and to support her children and grandchildren as best she could. O'Casey never tried to fly by his family, though at times their needs conflicted with his desire to buy books.

What distinguished his family from most of their neighbors were religion and politics: The family members were Protestants, loyal communicants of the Church of Ireland, and they were Unionists, partisans of the British Empire. An uncle had fought in the Crimean War, and two brothers had served in the army and were proud of the fact. Ella, in the depths of her misery, decorated her room with pictures of royalty and military heroes. Eventually, O'Casey lost his faith but not his gratitude to the local vicar, who had been loyal and generous to the family in their troubles; in later life, however, the Catholic church, with its intolerant censorship, became the playwright's enemy. The Empire he abandoned for other forms of politics.

O'Casey was not ashamed of "honest poverty" and was proud of his work as a laborer on the railroad, but he made his own the grievances of his class and was for a time active in labor agitation. He was a fervent admirer of James Larkin, and the defeat of the 1913 Dublin transit strike was one of the traumatic events of his life. At the same time, he was becoming committed to the nationalist movement. He was enthusiastically involved in the Gaelic League (an ostensibly nonpolitical group); he learned Gaelic himself and taught classes and organized meetings in spite of clerical interference.

He was also involved in overtly political and even revolutionary activities. For a time, he was secretary of the Irish Citizen Army, which had been founded by James Connolly to resist police violence during the 1913 strike. By the time of the Easter Rising, however, O'Casey had become inactive. He had come to see that Irish nationalism did not combine well with labor and socialist (much less pacifist) sympathies. In the rebellion, the Citizen Army was allied with Volunteers, which O'Casey perceived as a middle-class organization that included some who had been intensely hostile to the strike. O'Casey saw the civil war in 1922 as an extension of the same class conflict between the proletariat and the middle classes; one of his most striking vignettes describes Free State partisans on bicycles pursuing and brutally killing a former comrade who would not accept the treaty with Great Britain and the resulting partition of Ireland.

As the story progresses there is more and more about O'Casey the artist and less and less about the proletarian and revolutionary. There are two crucial dates here—1923, when *The Shadow of a Gunman* was produced, and 1926, when O'Casey moved to England. Before 1923, O'Casey had done some pamphleteering and had written some plays, but from that time on his life was largely that of the professional writer. In England O'Casey enjoyed, however precariously, a degree of middle-class prosperity and a happy marriage to an Irish actress. Self-educated or badly educated himself, he could send his children to a select private school recommended by George Bernard Shaw. The rejection of *The Silver Tassie* by the Abbey Theatre was a traumatic event and led to a split with Yeats; to O'Casey's credit, the quarrel was patched up, and he always writes of Lady Augusta Gregory (who was involved) with admiration and affection. As for O'Casey's quarrels with Catholic bishops and English critics—including Orwell, who thought that refugee Irish writers should be grateful for English hospitality—one feels that O'Casey was usually in the right but that his treatment of his grievances was excessive. To be fair, O'Casey ran more risk from German bombs in the Battle of Britain than he ever did from starvation and police brutality in Dublin.

Critical Context

   Mirror in My House has analogies to a genre, the *Bildungsroman*, or educational novel, which has been popular at least since the time of Johann Wolfgang von Goethe and William Wordsworth. The protagonist's life may be recounted as straight autobiography or as fiction, but always there is development and often obstacles to the development as well. Irish examples include Joyce's *A Portrait of the Artist as a Young Man* and George Moore's *Confessions of a Young Man* (1888). Joyce's and O'Casey's books illuminate each other by comparison. O'Casey's account of the death of Charles Parnell seems to be influenced by Joyce's, and the pandy bat episode also has its parallel. Joyce's poverty is of the shabby-genteel kind which comes from improvidence; O'Casey's is the poverty of working people down on their luck. Joyce's attitude toward Irish nationalism is cool and condescending; O'Casey's, if it ends in cynicism, was at one time desperately involved. Francis Sheehy-Skeffington, whom O'Casey idolizes and who met a tragic death in the Easter Rising, is the same pacifist and feminist whom Joyce treats comically under the name of McCann.

   Mirror in My House can be used as an adjunct to O'Casey's plays, and on many points they illuminate them; yet they have generally been regarded as masterpieces in their own right. Some of the great events and social movements of the twentieth century are noted here, recorded not by an observer but by a participant. They are set down vividly and passionately; if sometimes the passion seems excessive, more often than not it seems exactly right.

Sources for Further Study

Ayling, Ronald, ed. *Sean O'Casey: Modern Judgements*, 1969.
Krause, David. *Sean O'Casey and His World*, 1976.

Lowery, Robert G. *Sean O'Casey's Autobiographies: An Annotated Index*, 1983.
_____, ed. *Essays on Sean O'Casey's Autobiographies*, 1981.
O'Connor, Garry. *Sean O'Casey: A Life*, 1988.
Scrimgeour, James R. *Sean O'Casey*, 1978.

John C. Sherwood

MORNINGS IN MEXICO

Author: D. H. Lawrence (1885-1930)
Type of work: Travel writing
Time of work: 1924-1925
Locale: Oaxaca, Mexico; Arizona; Spotorno, Italy
First published: 1927

Form and Content

The significance of travel in the writings of D. H. Lawrence often seems to reflect the author's sense of values; the troubled internal struggles of itinerant protagonists frequently seem related to the restless, wandering existence that marked much of the author's later career. In many ways, as well, the peculiar ideals espoused by some of his leading characters may have been derived from the writer's quest for exotic and primordial antecedents to modern mores in locations where traces of older cultures could still be found. Lawrence's compact volume of travel notes about Mexico is of some interest for those concerned with the writer's biography; reflections of concerns that were explored more fully in his fiction may be found in this effort as well. The work is a bright, charming, and occasionally witty series of sketches drawn from Lawrence's personal observations; in other respects, it casts some light on the author's conception of the ultimate impulses and imperatives with which human nature must reckon. In some ways, *Mornings in Mexico* illustrates the complexity of Lawrence's attitudes toward the seemingly timeless practices of ancient peoples.

Altogether, with the exception of some time he spent on a return visit to England and Europe, Lawrence's sojourn in the New World lasted from September, 1922, until September, 1925; during much of this period he remained in Taos, New Mexico. In March, 1923, he set forth, in the company of his wife and other friends, on a tour of Mexican cities, which lasted for about four months; further travels ensued in the autumn of that year, and from October, 1924, until March, 1925, another journey brought Lawrence and his companions into Mexico once again. To the south, in Oaxaca, he rented a house for the winter. The work commences with a description of sights and sounds in that city during the week before Christmas, 1924. Additional chapters deal with other times of the year. Rather than presenting a continuous narrative account, the book provides a series of impressions from episodes that struck Lawrence as particularly interesting or diverting. Some descriptive passages may have served as working exercises for Lawrence's major and controversial novel *The Plumed Serpent* (1926); other portions, it has sometimes been charged, were attached in a somewhat haphazard fashion, for the sake of variety. Although *Mornings in Mexico* did not provoke pronounced reactions among critics, some reviewers found it admirable for its sense of place; others received it with some bemusement. While in some quarters it was regarded as more palatable than Lawrence's fictional works, there were those who found the organization and choice of materials arbitrary and disjointed. One commentator, writing for *The New York Times Book Review*, pronounced it required reading for members of Congress who had to deal with Latin American developments. Most readers, however, probably found it significant for its literary qualities. Some excerpts from *Mornings in Mexico* later were used in manuals of expository writing to illustrate the means by which narrative pace had been brought into harmony with the settings and subjects Lawrence had set out to depict.

Analysis

At the outset, grand notions of national character and civilization are not foremost in the author's mind; indeed, he consciously puts aside such musings in order to set down more immediate impressions of his surroundings. Sunshine and the smell of carnations, the sound of cocks crowing, and the scent of leaves, wood resin, and coffee suggest whatever is most typical about a bright, clear morning in a small Mexican town. A pleasant day, warm enough for writing outdoors, sets in motion some gentle and unpretentious thoughts centering on Corasmin, a white, curly-haired little dog that cannot fathom the mimicry of two parrots which can "bark" in much the same way that he does. The dog's discomfiture moves the writer to speculate about the natural scheme of things.

Theories of evolution were not to Lawrence's liking, because they presume too much of an orderly sequence that reduces living creatures to causal links in an inflexible chain of events. Half seriously, he would cogitate upon Aztec cosmology, which he thought was more amenable to notions of volition and individuality. According to early Mexican beliefs, periodic outbursts of cosmic convulsions during epochs of chaos and creation have ushered in new ages in the development of life on the planet. In *Mornings in Mexico*, such reflections, which are followed by lighthearted asides, set the tone for the sketches. This effect of varying depth, in a work that never quite renounces its air of nonchalance, propels the reader quickly through encounters with people and places of the New World. One essay discusses a walk into a neighboring village, where Lawrence could not obtain fresh fruit; resignation, or peacefulness, set in toward the end of the day. Rosalino, Lawrence's native houshold attendant, supplies some opportunities for observations about the Indians of Mexico. The author is alternately attracted and repelled by individuals who seem to embody the stolid virtues and the starkly alien values of Aztec lore. Once Rosalino resisted recruitment by a revolutionary army and was beaten so badly that his back was seriously injured. In his sympathy, Lawrence expresses a horror for mass movements that he feels the Mexican servant shares with him.

The chapter "Market Day" describes the last Saturday before Christmas, 1924, as one year hastens toward its end and the next promises momentous prospects. Red and yellow flowers seem to swell in anticipation; yucca plants in bloom and majestic clumps of cactus impart a luxuriant appearance to a landscape that otherwise might appear arid and forbidding. Cloud banks and distant mountaintops, with white barred hawks wheeling in the foreground, suggest the graceful sweep of natural spirals that converge at a hidden vortex. Villagers and merchants gather in processions that draw peasants and Indians from outlying highlands; they are joined by townspeople who descend in dusty columns on roads that bustle with lines of oxen and donkeys which in turn are flanked by running men and barefoot women. Purveyors of local produce assemble near a canopy which is bedecked in colors of its own. Gregarious and mercantile impulses seem oddly intertwined among all who take part in this provincial yet distinctly variegated exchange of goods. One is expected to haggle over every centavo; sellers take such gestures as a sign of positive interest.

In this essay, Lawrence says it is rather unpleasant to bargain with leather merchants, but not because they are too grasping. He complains that shoes are treated with so much dung that they smell. The merchants, however, who are accustomed to local methods, regard it as laughable that he would raise such objections. He concludes that there is no arguing with native ways. What the Mexicans accept as a traditional means of manufacture is hardly a matter on which they might defer to the olfactory judgments of outsiders. The tide of families, coming and going with products old and new in tow, ebbs by nightfall; people return home as the vast curve of humanity expands outward in its centripetal phase.

That Indians of the New World are different from Europeans is easily established; to Lawrence's mind, however, the peculiar mystique of native peoples can be accounted for in many ways. Indians, he says, seem to have entered one branch of human consciousness which at an early stage bifurcated from the state of mind known to the white man. Neither can really understand the other, and it is vain to pretend otherwise. Even such a commonplace matter as entertainment reveals how profound the gulf actually is. Stage events that for Europeans might be riveting, that are fraught with deep cultural significance, would be regarded with uncomprehending indifference by the Indians. Abstraction and vicarious sensations seem alien to them, so much so that any effort to posit an underlying basis for literary and social values is bound to founder on the lack of any common conception of art as representation. Greek drama from past millennia can still strike evocative emotional chords among modern European readers, but no shared ground appears to exist where Indians are concerned.

Indian dances and ceremonies form the subject of several essays, and it is important to Lawrence that broad themes be treated in what he regards as their essential light. Indian processions strike him as characterized by an unswerving unanimity which subsumes any hints of individuality that under other circumstances might arise. Efforts to uncover more exalted or baser meanings, Lawrence contends, have betrayed the prejudice which affects previous accounts of Indian beliefs and practices; others have fallen into exaggeration because of the tendency to substitute sentimentality or dislike for sober judgment. The problem lies with those who think that cultural misunderstanding can be overcome where the means to do so do not exist.

In its most common form, says Lawrence, the Indians' song is a performance that can be observed without regard for any verbal content; there also is no melody recognizable to a Western listener. Representations of wild animals such as deer, wolves, bears, buffalo, or coyotes enter more directly into the mysteries of the Indians' universe. For that matter, pantomime, buffoonery, and amusements of many sorts are staged; the drama that is central to Western presentations, however, has no real counterpart in Indian productions. Although wonderment can be expressed at the world of creation, there is no God or Great Mind at the center of the Indians' conception of their natural surroundings. The mystery pageants are unmoved by any suggestion of a divine purpose. To be sure, there are certain moral imperatives which can be inferred from Indian ceremonies; lying and cowardice, for example, are to be abjured. Moreover, Indians seem to accept the Mary and Jesus Christ of Western Christianity without concern for any conflict such professions of faith might have with earlier and more deeply rooted beliefs. Each system apparently exists on separate doctrinal foundations.

Mornings in Mexico includes some fine descriptions of Indian rites that recapture some of the frenzy and the grandeur of the solemn events. Perhaps the most noteworthy is Lawrence's depiction of the dance of the sprouting corn, a procession that is held in celebration of spring planting and which takes place on the three days that follow Easter Sunday. The dark agility of the men complements the rounded, impassive features of the stolid Indian women. Rapt in an intense rhythmic absorption which produces brisk, modulating waves of movement, the dancers commemorate the change of seasons in costumes that seem at times to blend with the swaying bodies. Kilts of red, green, and black fabric are set above lovely fur and buckskin boots; necklaces of white shell cores from the Pacific coast leap and vibrate in unison with the performers. The men move in broad, graceful circles that abruptly sweep backward to form a long, straight line. For accompaniment, the solitary drummer supplies a steady rhythm of bass notes; at climactic moments, he strikes a series of high notes. An evocation of the germination of seeds in the earth, the Indian ceremonies suggest resurrection according to beliefs that antedate any received faith.

Although he had little formal expertise in this area, Lawrence's views have been thought worthy of notice among those who study Indian traditions. Intuitive but sometimes persuasive judgments are found in his essay on the Hopi snake dance, an event which he witnessed in Arizona. As a prelude, men and boys stamp about in an antelope dance. They are followed by snake-priests, men who have spent days catching reptiles and who have fasted in preparation for this ritual. Some crude, swaying movements are accompanied by deep, heavy chants, evidently directed at the snakes themselves. For a minute of two, the priests, absorbed in their calling, remain silent and transfixed in some form of primordial communion. This mystical concentration apparently is enough to appease the reptiles, for they remain quiescent throughout. Skeptics aver that the same snakes are used from one year to the next. At the first performance, Lawrence sees the spectators becoming restless and impatient after a short while; many in the audience seem disappointed that they did not actually see poisonous snakes on display. Perhaps in response to public demand, on the next afternoon, after three rounds of ritual dancing and chanting, a young priest appears bearing a long, yellowish rattlesnake with its neck between his teeth. To the crowd's astonishment, another snake bearer comes forth, and then another; in a few moments, possibly six snake-priests are on hand with their quivering animals. The older Indians seemingly can exert unseen powers over the creatures. Unblinking fascination, rather than fright or horror, spreads among the onlookers, who remain passive, as though mesmerized. Large and peculiarly attractive rattlesnakes, as well as some handsome bull-snakes and lithe, twisting whipsnakes, become docile and immobile under the eyes of the spectators. As the exhibition draws to a close, Lawrence meditates on the widely different ways by which white men and Indians have achieved mastery over nature: One vanquishes the elements by damming the Nile and laying claim to the frontiers of America, and the other conquers inner space. In this contest of mutual negation, the white man, because of his mechanical virtuosity, already has begun to win over some of the younger Indians. Nevertheless, it cannot be said that either way is innately better. Where the one holds out the hope of material progress, the other resolves his conflicts with nature in a slow, unceasing battle that has varied little since the beginning.

The last essay, which is no more than a brief afterthought, provides some reflections from Spotorno, Italy. Lawrence recalls images of America, where he had left behind the lights of Taos and his ranch in New Mexico. Even the ancient sites of the Old World are positively youthful in comparison with the ways of the Indians, which are derived from a much more distant past. Weightier concerns seem as irresolvable as ever, so Lawrence turns instead to an evaluation of American moonshine, which he has tasted, and Italian vermouth, which he has before him.

Critical Context

Mornings in Mexico has been considered one of Lawrence's more vibrant works, one in which unity of feeling and idea produces some interesting evocations of far-flung peoples and landscapes. It also reveals some elements of the author's thought that do not appear or are not stated in the same way elsewhere. Although it has not been regarded as one of Lawrence's major works in its own right, its relationship to more celebrated efforts is worthy of consideration. While Lawrence's novel *The Plumed Serpent* presents a vivid and memorable fictional depiction of Mexican lore, in that work Lawrence appears much more firmly persuaded that a void has grown in Western ideological and religious systems. *Mornings in Mexico*, on the other hand, seems to indicate that the writer was aware of limitations on the power of Aztec mythical representation. Works about Lawrence's career, such as the literary memoirs of Witter Bynner and Dorothy Brett, do not claim to resolve the problem of Lawrence's ambivalence about Mexico.

Lawrence's other writings with similar settings, such as *St. Mawr* (1925) and "The Woman Who Rode Away" (1925), while rich in thematic allusions, do not address ancient values in the same way as *Mornings in Mexico* does. In still other travel writings, Lawrence ponders the significance of timeless myths among peoples of the ancient Mediterranean world, but even there, stark contrasts between early and modern forms of thought and devotion are not so sharply drawn.

Sources for Further Study
Brett, Dorothy. *Lawrence and Brett: A Friendship*, 1933.
Bynner, Witter. *Journey with Genius: Recollections and Reflections Concerning the D. H. Lawrences*, 1951.
Cavitch, David. *D. H. Lawrence and the New World*, 1969.
Clark, L. D. "D. H. Lawrence and the American Indian," in *The D. H. Lawrence Review*. IX, no. 3 (1976), pp. 305-372.
Fay, Eliot. *Lorenzo in Search of the Sun: D. H. Lawrence in Italy, Mexico, and the American Southwest*, 1953.
Janik, Del Ivan. *The Curve of Return: D. H. Lawrence's Travel Books*, 1981.
Martin, Dexter. "D. H. Lawrence and Pueblo Religion: An Inquiry into Accuracy," in *The Arizona Quarterly*. IX, no. 3 (1953), pp. 219-234.
Nehls, Edward H., ed. *D. H. Lawrence: A Composite Biography*. Vol. 2, 1958.
Parmenter, Ross. *Lawrence in Oaxaca: A Quest for the Novelist in Mexico*, 1957-1959.
Rossman, Charles. "D. H. Lawrence and Mexico," in *D. H. Lawrence: A Centenary Consideration*, 1985. Edited by Peter Balbert and Phillip L. Marcus.
Tracy, Billy T., Jr. *D. H. Lawrence and the Literature of Travel*, 1983.
Walker, Ronald G. *Infernal Paradise: Mexico and the Modern English Novel*, 1978.

J. R. Broadus

MOSES AND MONOTHEISM

Author: Sigmund Freud (1856-1939)
Type of work: Psychology
*First published: Der Mann Moses und die monotheistische Religion: Drei
Abhandlungen,* 1937-1939 (English translation, 1939)

Form and Content

Moses and Monotheism is a psychoanalytic interpretation of the biblical story of
Moses and the Jewish exodus from Egypt and a reconsideration of the subsequent
history of the Jews and their religion in the light of this interpretation. The argument proceeds in a manner familiar from Sigmund Freud's other writings. In an
almost conversational tone, he leads the reader from one point to the next, anticipating and answering questions and objections, gently introducing psychoanalytic
concepts to illuminate the story. From time to time he admits that every doubt that
has occurred to the reader has occurred to him as well, but that the credibility of his
interpretation depends less on the proof of its parts than on the coherence and
plausibility of the whole.

The book consists of three essays of differing lengths and complexities. Essay 1,
"Moses an Egyptian," is a mere ten pages, while essay 2, "If Moses Was an
Egyptian . . . ," is thirty-seven pages long and broken into seven untitled sections
preceded by an introduction which links it to the first essay. Essay 3, "Moses, His
People, and Monotheist Religion," is longer still and far more complicated in form.
Its eighty-three pages are divided into two parts, the first of which begins with two
prefatory notes, followed by five titled sections: "The Historical Premiss," "The
Latency Period and Tradition," "The Analogy," "Application," and "Difficulties."
Part 2 of the third essay has its own preface, "Summary and Recapitulation," followed by eight sections: "The People of Israel," "The Great Man," "The Advance
in Intellectuality," "Renunciation of Instinct," "What Is True in Religion," "The Return of the Repressed," "Historical Truth," and "The Historical Development."

The structure of the work reflects the circumstances of its composition and
publication. Freud drafted the work in Vienna in 1934 but did not publish it for fear
that the strongly Catholic Austrian regime would suppress the psychoanalytic movement. In spite of himself, however, Freud could not abandon the work, which
"tormented [him] like an unlaid ghost." In 1936, he rewrote the first two essays to
make them independent, and in 1937 they were published in separate issues of the
journal *Imago.* In each essay, Freud disclaimed any idea of pursuing the subject
further, owing to insufficient historical evidence and to his own lack of strength (he
was eighty-one and had been battling cancer for fourteen years).

The following year, however, Freud returned to the work, revising the third essay
to make it cohere with the rest. He reminds his readers in the first preface to essay 3
(dated "before March, 1938") that he is living "in a Catholic country under the
protection of that Church, uncertain how long that protection will hold out" and

that he will not seek to publish the complete work until it is safe to do so. Freud wrote these words shortly before Adolf Hitler's takeover of Austria (on March 12) and the outbreak of officially sanctioned violence against Jews. With no future left in Vienna either for psychoanalysis or for the Freud family, the Freuds, after effective intervention by highly placed friends and admirers, reached London on June 6, 1938. That very month, Freud wrote a second preface to essay 3 of *Moses and Monotheism*, celebrating the change in his circumstances that opened the way to publication. At the beginning of part 2 of the third essay there appears yet another prefatory note, also written in England, explaining the organization of the work.

Moses and Monotheism is not an easy work to classify. Taken as a whole, it is an essay in the psychology of religion, for Freud seldom strayed far from the consuming passion of his life: psychoanalysis and its theoretical or practical applications. Parts of the work belong to comparative mythology, however, and parts to the history of religion. Freud himself once called it a historical novel, perhaps to underscore the element of uncertainty that clings to his reconstructions, an uncertainty acknowledged throughout the work.

Analysis

In the short first essay of *Moses and Monotheism*, Freud seeks to establish that Moses was probably not a Jew but an Egyptian. Comparing the story of the birth of Moses and his rescue from the river by the pharaoh's daughter with other stories glorifying national heroes, and drawing upon Otto Rank's psychoanalytic study, *Der Mythus von der Geburt des Helden* (1909; *The Myth of the Birth of the Hero: A Psychological Interpretation of Mythology*, 1914) as well as the more general psychoanalytic concept of the "family romance" (a common childhood fantasy of having been born to noble or royal parents and only adopted by the humbler family of reality), Freud concludes that the adoptive family in the Moses myth—that is, the Egyptian family—must have been his real family, and that the myth's birth family—the Jewish family of the tribe of Levi—was a fiction.

In essay 2, Freud discusses the source, character, and historical development of the religion an Egyptian Moses would have given to the Jewish people. Freud maintains that the God of Moses must have been an adaptation of the sun-god Aton, the god that a pharaoh of the fourteenth century B.C., Akhenaton, had tried to substitute for the many gods and sacrifices of popular Egyptian religion. After Akhenaton's death, the traditional polytheistic priesthood of Amon regained power and suppressed all mention of the worship of Aton. In Freud's conjectural reconstruction, Moses was a highly placed adherent of Akhenaton's religion who saw his ambitions thwarted, his beliefs driven underground, and himself isolated. Freud suggests that Moses—estranged from his own people—adopted the Jews as his new people, to whom he could give his cherished religion. In support of this idea, Freud identifies three points of similarity between Judaism and the religion of Aton: strict monotheism, lack of concern with the idea of life after death, and the practice of circumcision.

Following a Jewish folk tradition for which the scholar Ernst Sellin had recently found scriptural support, Freud surmises that after first accepting the leadership of Moses and his God, the Jewish people rebelled against the ethical rigor and ceremonial austerity of the new religion, murdering Moses himself. A generation or two later, the descendants of the Jews who had followed Moses out of Egypt united with related tribes between Egypt and Canaan and adopted the worship of an Arab-Midianite volcano-god, Yahweh, who demanded the very sacrifices and rituals that Moses' God had despised. The memory of the one God of Moses and His requirement of a life of justice and mercy did not completely die, however, having been kept up among a small group who remained loyal to the Moses tradition. Through their influence, the law of circumcision was retained; in time, Yahweh grew beyond the primitive localism of his origins, acquiring the greatness and power of the God of the Exodus. Eventually, with the periodic prodding and chastisement of the prophets, the God of Moses was entirely identified with the god Yahweh, and the Moses of the Exodus became identified with the Midianite priest who had introduced the Jews to Yahweh. Thus, they could unite their conflicting religious traditions in support of the rigorous monotheism which now became a source of identity and pride to the Jews, while at the same time denying the crime—the murder of Moses—which lay at the base of their history as a people. They further expiated that crime by projecting the characteristics of the man Moses onto the God he had taught them to worship, including the idea of "chosenness"; just as the Egyptian Moses had chosen the Jewish people as his people, so the God of Moses, in the revised memory of the Jews, had chosen them, bestowing upon them a special blessing and a special destiny. In Freud's account, it is this sense of being chosen, the pride and ultimate self-confidence it offers, that has enabled the Jews to survive as a people in spite of all the catastrophes that have befallen them in their history.

In the third essay, Freud ranges far beyond the history of the Jewish people and religion to the formation of religious beliefs in general and of Christianity in particular. Briefly recapitulating the argument of the first two essays, Freud reaffirms that the later Jewish religion is the ethical monotheism of the Egyptian Moses, whose God was recognized as the only God; disdaining ceremonial and sacrifice, He demands only belief in Him and a life of truth and justice. Yet the triumph of the God of Moses came only after a long period of rejection in favor of the primitive Yahweh of the Midianites.

Freud explains this delayed effect psychoanalytically by analogy to the development of a neurosis. Defense against the memory of an early trauma—the murder of their leader Moses and the rejection of his God—lies at the heart of the history of the Jews and their religion. By identifying the God of Moses with the god Yahweh, they denied that the God of Moses had ever been abandoned; by identifying the murdered Moses with the Midianite priest, they denied Moses' death. What made this crime particularly difficult either to remember openly or to forget completely was that it repeated the primal crime, the murder of the father of the primal horde by his sons, which, according to Freud's psychoanalytic anthropology, is lodged in the unconscious memory of all people.

The subsequent history of the Jews, during which the worship of Yahweh grew more and more like the religion of Moses and all remnants of the primitive religion that Yahweh represented were cast off, corresponds to the latency period of a neurosis, characterized by a psychic development apparently untroubled by the traumatic memory. After several generations of this "advance in intellectuality," however, the collective neurosis emerged in the form of guilt as the defensive repression loosened and the traumatic memory began its disturbing work. Paul of Tarsus identified the source of this guilt as "original sin." Paul's Christianity, therefore, with its repetition of the killing of the Father in the reversed and expiating form of the killing of the Son, represents the return of the repressed. Christianity, in Freud's view, was culturally regressive, in that it abandoned the high intellectuality of developed Judaism for a return to a proliferation of symbolic rites and a thinly disguised polytheism. Christianity, in other words, represented a "fresh victory for the priests of Amun over Akhenaten's god." Nevertheless, as the return of the repressed Christianity is a psychological advance over the Jewish religion, which became "to some extent a fossil."

The question of the historic relationship between the Jews and other peoples was much on Freud's mind in the Nazi era. Arguing that the essential character of the Jewish people was bestowed upon them by Moses, Freud claims that the source both of the hatred so often directed against them and of their capacity to endure this hatred and to survive until the present day is the same: their religion. Belief in a God who is universal and therefore the God of all, who nevertheless out of all peoples especially chose them, the Jews, as his own; a God moreover who is known not crudely through miracles or graven images, but intellectually through the written record, the Torah—these facts of their faith have given the Jews a self-confidence, even an arrogance, that tends to bring down the hatred and envy of others upon their heads. Yet that same self-confidence, that pride in their special destiny, is what has kept them together as a people in spite of dispersion, hostility, and persecution.

Critical Context

Freud's ideas about Moses crystallized in the ominous atmosphere of Hitler's triumph in Germany. Yet anti-Semitism was nothing new to Freud. He had lived with its Viennese manifestations all of his life, all the while taking defiant pride in his Jewishness. Notwithstanding his deep religious skepticism, it mattered intensely to him that he was a Jew. What exactly did being a Jew mean to him? Freud's perspective on Jewish identity and survival was conditioned by the critical view of religion that was an enduring theme in his work. In *Totem und Tabu: Einige Übereinstimmungen im Seelenleben der Wildren und der Neurotiker* (1913; *Totem and Taboo: Resemblances Between the Psychic Lives of Savages and Neurotics*, 1918), Freud maintained that religious beliefs and practices had originated in guilt for the primal crime of the murder of the father, and in *Die Zukunft einer Illusion*

(1928; *Future of an Illusion*, 1957), he concluded that religion is a collective neurosis which must give way to the healthy outlook of scientific rationalism. In these works, however, Freud had dealt either with primitive religions or with Christianity; in *Moses and Monotheism*, he proposed to analyze Judaism from the same critical perspective. Two factors converged in the selection of Moses as the center of this analysis. First, Freud strongly identified with Moses, seeing himself as the embattled founder of a movement whose ungrateful followers, unable to keep the faith he had revealed, murmured and rebelled against him. Second, Moses was a historically problematic figure. Contradictions and obscurities in the biblical account of his life and leadership had long attracted scholarly interest, and Freud was not the first to suggest that Moses could have been an Egyptian.

These factors help to explain why Freud could not leave the subject of Moses alone, and why, when the book was finally published, the most pained response came not from the Catholic church, as Freud had anticipated in Vienna, but from Jews, who were appalled that one of their own would seek to deprive them of their chief consolation, their faith, in their hour of greatest need. To Freud, however, the independence of mind and strength of character that permitted him to defy even his fellow Jews was itself the specific attribute of Jewishness he most valued, the cultural consequence of Moses' gift to the Jewish people so long ago, and the very grounds of Freud's identity as a Jew. Finally, he did not expect to deprive believers of their faith, for, as he put it in his excellent though sometimes idiosyncratic English, "I just produce scientific stuff for the interest of a minority which has no faith to loose."

Sources for Further Study

Bakan, David. "Moses in the Thought of Freud," in *Commentary*. XXVI (October, 1958), pp. 322-331.

Gay, Peter. *Freud: A Life for Our Time*, 1988.

Jones, Ernest. *Sigmund Freud: Life and Work*. Vol. 3, *The Last Phase*, 1957.

Robert, Marthe. *From Oedipus to Moses: Freud's Jewish Identity*, 1976.

Van Herik, Judith. *Freud on Femininity and Faith*, 1982.

Isabel F. Knight

MOTHER IRELAND

Author: Edna O'Brien (1932-   )
Type of work: Cultural criticism
Time of work: 1935-1950
Locale: Tuamgraney, County Clare, and Dublin, Ireland
First published: 1976

Form and Content

Mother Ireland is Edna O'Brien's first book-length work of nonfiction, a medium
to which she has not devoted very much attention during her prolific writing career.
In certain respects, the book is a consolidation and repetition of material which the
author had already treated fictionally in her first three novels—*The Country Girl*
(1960), *The Lonely Girl* (1962), and *Girls in Their Married Bliss* (1964)—and more
graphically and with greater art in *A Pagan Place* (1970). The autobiographical
content of *Mother Ireland*, however, is presented in the context of the author's
general observations about her native land and her native place within it, which is in
rural County Clare, in the west of Ireland. Thus, while the seven chapters of *Mother
Ireland* cover O'Brien's childhood, education, and immediate after-school life in
Dublin, culminating in her emigration to England, each chapter contains more than
a mere recitation of strictly autobiographical data. It is for this reason that the work
is ultimately one of cultural, rather than strictly personal, interest and significance.
Clearly, readers wishing to know more of the background of one of the least likely,
but best-known contemporary Irish writers of fiction will find a considerable
amount of color and detail regarding Edna O'Brien's origins, together with an
intriguing amplification of episodes from the early novels.

O'Brien's point of departure for presenting this material typically is an Irish myth
or some representative scene or experience from Irish life. Each chapter opens with
a comparatively impersonal preamble leading into the more intimate, autobiographical matter. There seems little thought, however, that the personal is necessarily
clarified by being presented in the context of a more generalized perspective. No
explicit links are made between the two modes of discourse, and the text frequently
rambles from one to the other, conveying the senses of spontaneity and improvisa-
tion which mark the author's autobiographical fiction.

The result is an idiosyncratically human document in which the possibility of
ideas about Ireland is subtly repressed in favor of a representation of the emotional
and psychological bequest of that country's culture and Catholic-derived mores. In
keeping with the work's title—a title which is a commonplace honorific designation of Ireland—the author's emphasis is on the nurturing and domestic aspects of
Irish life more than on what might be considered more eye-catching areas such as
history, politics, or art.

The text is accompanied by a number of photographs by Fergus Bourke. For the
most part, these have no direct bearing on the text (an exception is a superb portrait

of the author's father). The reader unfamiliar with the land and people of Ireland, however, will find them illuminating, and their grainy black-and-white texture and pearly light contribute effectively to the work's overall atmosphere. Readers familiar with Ireland will find their sense of familiarity stimulated.

Analysis

"I believe that memory and the welter of memory, packed into a single lonely and bereft moment, is the strongest ally a person can have." Apart from giving a sense of the author's style—note, for example, the tonality of that sentence's subordinate clause—this quotation from *Mother Ireland* speaks to one of the text's most obvious strengths, its power of recollection. Set in the impoverished and repressive atmosphere of Ireland in the 1930's, the years of World War II, and their unenlightened aftermath, *Mother Ireland* is at its most persuasive when presenting revealing moments of the provincial life of those provincial times.

At the heart of the text is an irregularly coordinated series of epiphanies illuminating experiences of, and typifying attitudes toward, class, religion, education, and entertainment. These epiphanies are almost invariably given expressive life in the context of daily, material life; *Mother Ireland* is replete with the common nouns of dress fabrics, tableware, high tea, and related staples of domesticity, whether the domicile is the author's home or the convent boarding school in which she spent most of her adolescence. Such a context clearly emphasizes the mothering theme of the work as a whole.

One limitation of this approach is that it seems to preclude the world of men and work outside the home, with the possible exception of priests, who are treated as rarefied, unworldly creatures, worthy of the greatest respect and whatever culinary honors the family can confer. The lack of a social sense that conveys a sense of manners in the broad meaning of the term deprives the reader of insights regarding life on the land during a relatively undocumented period of economic difficulty and sociopolitical uncertainty. On the other hand, such an omission creates space for this work's deft, impressionistic sketches of character and faintly gossipy overview of local life. Thus, although there is a certain unsystematic air about *Mother Ireland*, one gathers—by virtue of its persistence, if by nothing else—that this air is being deliberately cultivated in order to create an impression of the randomness and inevitable selectivity of recall.

In addition, this book's disregard of the systematic prevents O'Brien from developing a specifically feminist perspective governing her portrait of the artist as a young girl. Nevertheless, the question of what manner of woman emerges from such a context is implicit throughout, particularly in the closing chapter, where young Edna is now an economically and emotionally independent young lady. Here, however, as events suggest, the life for which she had been equipped, its vocabulary of brand names providing a characterization of material adequacy, is not particularly attractive to her. On the contrary, it is to the emotional and sexual side of her nature—the areas of existence for which no guiding provenance have been offered—that she finds herself wanting to devote most of her individual energies. In these areas it is clearly impossible to sustain for long the designation of self in the second person; in the family home, the local school, and the convent school, however, the author frequently describes herself as a "you," an anonymously typical product of the times.

Thus, Edna O'Brien finds that it is the normality of life in Ireland from which she finds herself in exile. This normality—its pretensions, its tastelessness, its crass tone and dull manner—induces the author to describe its practitioners as inhabitants of "Godot-land," an allusion to the works of Samuel Beckett which follows through on *Mother Ireland*'s curselike epigraph from Beckett's work. (Scholars of O'Brien's work may, indeed, date her increasing familiarity with, allusions to, and writing on Beckett's works from the publication of *Mother Ireland*.) In the opening chapter, and rather in contrast with the work's overall tone, there are references to a return trip to contemporary Ireland and various scathing remarks about the quality of life there, including artistic and cultural life:

> No great philosophers, no great psychiatrists, no achievement where logic is paramount; a great literary endowment, true, but lean offerings over the past thirty or forty years. Romantic Ireland, quite dead, you say, when you are sitting down to high tea, . . . imploded with drop scones, apple pie and soda bread.

The connection between logic and romantic Irleand is tenuous at best, and the rather adventitious sense of form conveyed by *Mother Ireland* suggests that the author is not perhaps the most qualified to make the connection more substantial. It is not surprising, therefore, that romantic Ireland is what has earned O'Brien's allegiance. Her frequent quotations from the rich, and not infrequently kitsch, repertoire of Irish story and legend (not all of which comes from the school anthologies of her generation) reveal part of the substance of that allegiance, as do some of the book's concluding statements: Ireland "is a state of mind as well as an actual country. . . . Ireland insubstantial like the goddesses poets dream of. . . . The impassioned, and often-violent, imaginative backdrop to the land of Ireland is invoked to colorful effect by the simple and telling means of giving the origins of the Irish place-names as they occur naturally in the course of exposition. This material, the basis for which is to be found in redactions of old Irish sagas, speaks of exalted feeling and deeds characterized by destructive finality—the antithesis, clearly, of quotidian life. In addition, there are numerous references to matters of documented Irish history and an unanalytical sense of the manner in which such matters become transformed because of their endurance in the popular mind. There is the implication that the preservation of certain grandiose, stylized versions of events in the Irish imagination has an inevitable compensatory function.

Yet, because of her country's imaginative appeal, O'Brien retains her attachment to it. This, perhaps, is the ultimate denouement of the title's parenting metaphor. For all its flaws, Mother Ireland's indestructible umbilicus still provides psychic sustenance. O'Brien's position with regard to this primal parent is typical of offspring. She remains indebted to the influences of her formative environment, while desiring to articulate, with an independent mind, her resistance to those influences. The most revealing evidence in *Mother Ireland* of that divided yet reconciled condition is the interplay between memory and imagination.

Critical Context

Mother Ireland should be seen in the context of O'Brien's career and in the context of modern Irish literature. In the first case, the work effectively marks a period in her development as a writer of fiction. Since its publication, the author has tended to produce fiction which is less interested in background than in foreground. Background was used in her early work to supply a framework of understanding through which a reader might appreciate a given character's rebarbative mannerisms or ignorant behavior. Subsequently—beginning, arguably, with the novel *Night* (1972)—the emphasis has been on passion and isolation, on protagonists suspended in the unique and not particularly communicable life of their own feelings, with an accompanying eschewal of cultural nuance. *Mother Ireland* is central to that change of emphasis. As though to underline the change in artistic orientation further, the choice of the passionate self (rehearsed in the closing pages of *Mother Ireland*) is upheld by the author's anthology, *Some Irish Loving* (1979).

Paradoxically, then, as the author establishes the peculiar remove at which her social life has placed her from Ireland and at the same time reaffirms her intimate connection with her native country, she becomes the first writer of her generation to imitate a strategy employed to good effect by Irish fiction writers of the 1930's and 1940's. Three of the main figures of this period—Seán O'Faoláin, Frank O'Connor, and Liam O'Flaherty—all wrote works of cultural criticism in a similar vein to *Mother Ireland*, voyages of rediscovery of various kinds and in a tone that varied merely in the degree of their acerbity. In a work which goes in for the salutary disabusement of tradition, Edna O'Brien aligns herself with a tradition. Since the tradition in question is a literary one, however, it is likely that she feels reasonably at ease in aligning herself with it; as *Mother Ireland* demonstrates, she has earned her place in the Irish literary tradition.

Sources for Further Study

Adams, P. L. Review in *The Atlantic Monthly*. CCXXXVIII (October, 1976), p. 115.

Eckley, Grace. *Edna O'Brien*, 1974.

Elder, Richard. Review in *The New York Times Book Review*. LXXXI (September 19, 1976), p. 6.

The New Yorker. Review. LII (October 11, 1976), p. 171.

Swan, Annalyn. Review in *Time*. CVIII (September 20, 1976), p. 90.

George O'Brien

THE NAMES
A Memoir

Author: N. Scott Momaday (1934-
Type of work: Memoir
Time of work: 1934-1976
Locale: The Southwest
First published: 1976

Principal personages:
N. SCOTT MOMADAY, a Native American writer and poet
ALFRED MORRIS MOMADAY, his father, a schoolteacher and
painter
NATACHEE SCOTT MOMADAY, his mother, also a teacher
JAMES, his uncle
MAMMEDATY, his grandfather
POHD-LOHK, a tribal storyteller, his step-grandfather

Form and Content

In 1968, thirty-four-year-old N. Scott Momaday wrote to his old friend and academic mentor, Yvor Winters, that he was planning a book of nonfiction, "an evocation of the American landscape informed by autobiographical elements and the history of the Kiowas." His goal was to write "an indigenous book." At this point in his life, Momaday, whose father was a full-blooded Kiowa and whose mother was of English, French, and Cherokee extraction, had begun to wonder about his Indian heritage and to explore his tribal and familial history. He had visited many of the places along the Kiowas' migration route from Yellowstone to the Staked Plain of Texas, worshiped in front of the sacred Tai-me medicine bundle in Oklahoma, and collected ancient stories from tribal elders, all in an effort to define his place in the traditions of his forebears. Artistically, this exploration yielded Momaday's *The Way to Rainy Mountain*, published in 1969, a year after his Pulitzer Prize-winning novel, *House Made of Dawn*. Encouraged by his editor, Frances McCullough, to write an autobiography about growing up Indian, Momaday began work on *The Names.*

The Names is divided into four parts, framed by a prologue and an epilogue. The prologue recalls the Kiowa creation story about the tribe's emergence from an underground world through a hollow log. In the epilogue, Momaday relates the last stage of his journey along the Kiowas' migration route. Entering the Staked Plain, Momaday imagines the presence of the buffalo, of his ancestors engaged in story-telling, and of the Kiowas' deserted camps. He celebrates the beauty of the land along his way, which finally leads him to a hollow log, like the one that gave birth to his tribe. The prologue and the epilogue, then, form a circle, outlining the larger racial story surrounding Momaday's personal account.

The four parts of *The Names* follow Momaday's life chronologically and geographically, from his early infancy in Oklahoma to his childhood on the Navajo reservation at Shiprock, New Mexico, and Tuba City and Chinle, Arizona, and his boyhood among the people of Jemez Pueblo in New Mexico. Within this rough structure, however, Momaday constantly moves back and forth between the present and the past, creating a sense of cotemporality, a dimension of personal time in which the boundaries between past and present are fluid.

The Names cannot easily be attributed to a single genre; rather, it is a collage of vignettes of people and places, family photographs, landscape pictures, poems, imaginary dialogues between ancestors or between Momaday and his forebears, family stories, renderings of sense impressions from early childhood, and tales of adventures and conflicts about growing up as a modern Indian in a multicultural environment. A genealogical chart and a glossary of Kiowa terms and names help the reader follow Momaday's explorations, in the course of which the author-subject negotiates myth and autobiography, tribal and individual experience, racial and personal identity.

Part 1 brings to life Momaday's European ancestors who settled in Kentucky; it relates how Momaday's mother, in tracing her Cherokee heritage, provided a model for what he himself would later pursue in exploring his father's Kiowa background. Through stories and photographs, Momaday introduces not only Kau-au-ointy, Keahdinekeah, Aho, Guipagho, and Mammedaty but also the Galyens, Scotts, Ellises, and McMillans. Of particular significance is the portrayal of Pohd-lohk, the man who gave Momaday his Indian name, because by calling him Tsoai-talee, he integrated the boy into tribal myth and landscape, affirming "the whole life of the child in a name."

Part 2 deals with Momaday's childhood years in Navajo country, but his memories of Oklahoma remain a constant presence. The two landscapes are fused into a single whole in Momaday's imagination. The long and moving story of Uncle James, which concludes this part, is a sad reminder of what can occur when an Indian fails to accommodate himself to the modern world. Momaday's tribute to his relative, who sought refuge in alcohol, underscores the need for creating a personal myth which gives order and meaning to a life between two cultural worlds.

In part 3 Momaday relives his early boyhood in New Mexico during World War II and illustrates that modern America—the films, popular songs, and football—became as much a part of his imagination as Kiowa warriors and chiefs. It also reveals some of the conflicts Momaday encountered in reconciling his modern self with his tribal antecedents, for example, when he confesses, "I don't know how to be a Kiowa," or when his shortsightedness causes this anguished response: "The Indians didn't wear glasses not the Kiowas how can you hunt buffalo with glasses on I broke my glasses." The extended stream-of-consciousness section, which makes up more than half of part 3, allows the reader to participate directly in the process Momaday called the creation of an idea of himself.

Part 4, finally, explores Momaday's formative years at Jemez Pueblo, where he grew up among the Jemez and Navajo peoples. This part of the memoir contains loving renditions of neighbors, feasts, ceremonials, and adventures in a spectacular and spiritually meaningful landscape. Like Tolo, the protagonist of the Christmas story, Momaday enters into the landscape of his adopted home, the Canyon de San Diego, appropriating it to his physical and spiritual experience. *The Names* ends with Momaday's symbolic fall from innocence into experience. The reader leaves him facing the world beyond childhood, equipped with a strong sense of self and the certainty of being rooted in an ancient tradition and a spiritually sustaining landscape. The book's form and content reflect the author's purpose in piecing together stories, images, and names from the past to create a personal myth, whole and intricately interwoven with the larger story of his ancestors.

Analysis

The Names rests on the assumption that one comes to understand who one is through an act of the imagination, and that this imaginative act relies on the power of language. Momaday's names are building blocks from which he assembles the stories in which and by which he lives. He explains that "life . . . is simply the construction of an idea of having existence, place in the scheme of things." This important tenet is introduced at the work's opening, when Momaday states: "My name is Tsoai-talee. I am, therefore, Tsoai-talee; therefore I am." Language, Momaday contends, precedes individual existence and determines it. Reflecting back to the words he heard as an infant, Momaday muses, "Had I known it, even then language bore all the names of my being." To the degree to which one explores and understands language, then, one is capable of determining one's place in a given cultural tradition.

Momaday illustrates the controlling and creative function of language in two passages which instruct the reader in the appropriate way of reading the work. In the first of these episodes, Momaday recalls a nightmare he had as a child in the course of which he finds himself trapped in a room with a mysterious presence that gradually grows into a huge and threatening mass. He tries to raise his voice against the menace but remains dumb. Without the power of language, Momaday suggests here, an individual is incapable of ordering and controlling experience. Referring to his terrifying sense of impotence, Momaday explains how the situation might have been resolved:

> I sometimes think that it is surely a name, the name of someone or something, that if only I could utter it, the terrific mass would snap away into focus, and I should see and recognize what it is at once; I should have it then, once and for all, in my possession.

In a second passage, Momaday describes his discovery of the creative power of language. As a child, he draws a boy's head on a sheet of paper. He wonders about his creation's identity and attaches a name to it; he calls it Mammedaty, the name of his grandfather. This act of naming gives rise to a great sense of wonder, for suddenly Momaday knows himself in the presence of his ancestor. His name, all of a sudden, has opened a window to the past and forged a vital link between the boy and his ancestry.

Thus the act of naming is profoundly creative in the process of formulating a personal identity. According to Momaday, "The storyteller Pohd-lohk gave me the name Tsoai-talee. He believed that a man's life proceeds from his name, in the way that a river proceeds from its source." Working with these premises, typical of an oral culture, Momaday creates an imaginative reconstruction of his childhood and youth in which history and autobiography, myth and reality, dreams and visions merge and give rise to a modern Indian's sense of belonging to an ancient and evolving tribal tradition.

Technically, Momaday uses a variety of devices which place his memoir into the middle ground between fiction and history. He frequently employs novelistic techniques to re-create events and experiences of which he could not have been a part. He freely enters other people's minds, an option closed to the traditional autobiographer, dramatizes encounters between ancestors who died long before Momaday was born or could possibly remember them, or presents an episode in his life through the eyes of an omniscient third-person narrator, as in the story of Uncle James. In using these devices, Momaday is concerned not with factual truth but rather with a subjective, emotional, personal truth.

Momaday's reality, then, is not restricted to what he has experienced directly in his lifetime but subsumes his ancestral past and tribal mythology, a reality accessible to him by way of stories and names and brought to life through the power of his imagination. The following passage is crucial to an understanding of Momaday's memoir:

> The past and future were simply the large contingencies of a given moment; they bore upon the present and gave it shape. One does not pass through time, but time enters upon him, in his place. . . . Notions of the past and future are essentially notions of the present. In the same way an idea of one's ancestry and posterity is really an idea of the self.

Momaday's descriptions of places and landscapes contain not only the palpable elements of which they consist but also the shadows of those who peopled them long before the beholder's lifetime.

The portrayal of Pohd-lohk suggests that Momaday believes in a racial component capable of shaping his life. Momaday's relation to Pohd-lohk is not a matter of blood but of a shared racial imagination. Momaday perceives himself, at least in part, as following the pattern of Pohd-lohk's experience. Pohd-lohk had searched for his past in the Kiowa calendar history, a chronicle Momaday describes as "an instrument with which he could reckon his place in the world." Momaday emulates him in this effort. Furthermore, Momaday claims that both his and Pohd-lohk's lives have been propelled by a spiritual power particular to the tribe, "a force that had been set in motion at the Beginning." Whereas Pohd-lohk examines the "yellow, brittle leaves" of his ledger for "the long swath of his coming to old age" ("swath" carrying the meaning of "footstep" or "trace"), Momaday searches for his tribal precursors in the land: "I invented history. In April's thin white light, in the landscape of the Staked Plains, I looked for tracks among the tufts of coarse, brittle grass." This parallel suggests not only the continuity of experience from one generation to the next, but also of the presence of the past in landscapes and language, in leaves of grass and the leaves of Pohd-lohk's ledger and Momaday's writings.

Momaday's symbolic and imaginative alignment with Pohd-lohk is one of many examples of his mythmaking in *The Names*. Once Momaday's readers understand and accept that they live in a world made of stories, they will have transcended the immediate personal and cultural context of Momaday's work and discovered that names are of equal significance in the shaping of their own lives.

Critical Context

In *The Names*, Momaday pursues the theme of identity which dominates his two earlier works. For him, as for many other contemporary Native Americans, tribal identity is no longer a given but rather a consciously constructed concept, which allows them to participate in the mainstream of American society without sacrificing their attachment to a cultural heritage. Storytelling is central to this process, as it has always been in tribal societies; it is not an art for art's sake but a matter of individual and communal survival.

The Names continues Momaday's exploration of tribal identity which began in his Pulitzer Prize-winning novel, *House Made of Dawn*. This novel reflects, both in form and content, the threat of personal and cultural fragmentation and disintegration which modern Native Americans often face. Momaday argues that only through trust in language, in the oral tradition, and in the continuing validity of ancient stories can a sense of wholeness be preserved. In *House Made of Dawn*, the protagonist's loss of voice accounts in large measure for his nightmarish existence between two worlds. The restoration of his voice at the end of the novel becomes one of the prerequisites for healing and reunifying him with his tribe.

In *The Way to Rainy Mountain*, Momaday charts the process of placing himself into his Kiowa background. It is the account of a physical, spiritual, and intellectual journey through stories and places, a blend of myth, history, and autobiography which crystallizes into Momaday's personal reality. While he emphasizes the relationship between racial experience and tribal consciousness in *The Way to Rainy Mountain*, he examines his sense of self in a more direct and detailed fashion in *The Names*, examining family influences and the impact of other cultures. In doing so, he offers the reader a deeper insight into the components and the process which have made Momaday the unique individual that he is.

Sources for Further Study

Abbey, Edward. "Memories of an Indian Childhood," in *Harper's Magazine*. CCLIV (February, 1977), p. 94.

Schubnell, Matthias. "Myths to Live By: *The Names: A Memoir*," in *N. Scott Momaday: The Cultural and Literary Background*, 1985.

Stegner, Wallace. Review in *The New York Times Book Review*. LXXXII (March 6, 1977), pp. 6-7.

Velie, Alan R. "The Search for Identity: N. Scott Momaday's Autobiographical Works," in *Four American Indian Literary Masters*, 1982.

Matthias Schubnell

NATIVE REALM
A Search for Self-Definition

Author: Czesław Miłosz (1911-   )
Type of work: Autobiography
First published: Rodzinnia Europa, 1959 (English translation, 1968)

> *Principal personages:*
> CZESŁAW MIŁOSZ, a Polish poet
> OSCAR VLADISLAS DE LUBICZ MILOSZ, his cousin, some thirty
>   years his senior, a poet and mystic who lived in France and
>   wrote primarily in French
> "TIGER," his friend, a professor of philosophy whose real name
>   was Juliusz Tadeusz Kroński

Form and Content

In 1951, Czesław Miłosz, the Lithuanian-Polish poet, scholar, and diplomat, defected to the West. *Zniewolony umysł* (1953; *The Captive Mind*, 1953) describes the conflict of the artist in a totalitarian society. Utilizing the plight of all intellectuals as a backdrop, Miłosz attempted to explain the motives for his defection not only to others but to himself as well. Although the book was a critical success, Miłosz, after reading its widely differing reviews and commentaries, realized that many if not most of his readers had misunderstood the book's central premises because of their inability to penetrate the cultural and historical perspective underlying the essays. Given the typical Westerner's knowledge of its histories and cultures, Eastern Europe might as well be on another planet. Any cultural awareness in the West of countries such as Poland or Lithuania is, to put it charitably, vague at best. Yet at the core of Miłosz's writings is the insistence that an individual can only be evaluated in terms of his or her cultural heritage and environment. In the introduction to *Native Realm: A Search for Self-Definition*, he asserts:

> Instead of thrusting the individual into the foreground, one can focus attention on the
> background, looking upon oneself as a sociological phenomenon. Inner experience, as
> it is preserved in the memory, will then be evaluated in the perspective of the changes
> one's milieu has undergone.

The times and places of his homeland from his birth in 1911 until the moment when he felt compelled to leave are re-created by Miłosz in *Native Realm*. It is a selective autobiography. Miłosz describes only these episodes or personal encounters which he deems of primary importance to his artistic, philosophical, and, not least, political development. Although the narrative consists of chronological chapters, Miłosz's sense of time is also selective. Events and conversations melt into a fluid panorama of past, present, and future. This journey is not simply that of one individual in his own private time and space. It is the journey of a region of the earth which has suffered tremendous crises and change in the twentieth century. *Native Realm* may be, as its subtitle indicates, an exercise in self-analysis, but, while explaining himself and his generation, Miłosz sought to give a history lesson to his Western readers. The book was written not for his compatriots from Eastern Europe but for those who cannot understand the names of the stopping places, let alone the time schedule.

Miłosz, like a good teacher, tries to start from the simple in order to work gradually toward the complex. The title of the first chapter, "Place of Birth," should indicate an easy history lesson, but in Eastern Europe, nothing is easy. Even the geography is unstable and deceptive. Miłosz, who was born in Lithuania but was educated in Poland and writes in Polish, must interpret the shifting allegiances of a long and troubled history. Vilna (Lithuanian "Vilnius" and for Miłosz "Wilno"), a city which is described in minute detail in several essays, can be taken as a prime example. In this hodgepodge of ethnic groups, religions, and national and political affiliations, even the name of the city itself was in dispute.

The contradictions inherent in Eastern European society control the structure of the work. Each essay stresses one piece of the puzzle and endeavors to fit it along-side its neighbors. For example, one of the early chapters, "Nationalities," deals with the social and ethnic strata of Vilna, especially the situation of the Jews. In a typical progression, Miłosz introduces the topic with the description of two Jewish playmates. He then fills in the historical background, explaining why they spoke a different language and went to different schools. The scope of the discussion broadens into an examination of political partisanship, that of the Jews and that of those groups that used prejudice against them for their own political motives. The chapter which had begun in the Vilna/Wilno of the 1920's ends in the death camps of the 1940's.

The tone of the work is one of melancholy. It cannot be otherwise for one who has "witnessed much of what Europe prefers to forget, because it fears the vengeance of specters" and who admits that "my first awareness came with war." From czarist Russia to Nazi-occupied Poland, the first seventeen essays are permeated with the atmosphere of war.

After World War II, Miłosz served in the diplomatic corps of the People's Republic of Poland. After several years in the United States, he deliberately decided to return home. His stay was brief. Realizing that he could not tolerate the intellectual subjugation forced upon him by the Polish-Stalinist government, in 1951 he asked for political asylum in France.

The last two chapters, "Tiger I" and "Tiger II," revolve around this painful decision, but, characteristically, they are not in any way confessional. Miłosz dispenses with his return and departure from Poland in only one paragraph. Instead, he tries to focus on his dilemma by comparing it to that of a friend and mentor who chose a different path.

The Tiger of the final essays, given that nickname because of his ability to pounce on and destroy the arguments of others, was Juliusz Tadeusz Kroński, a professor of philosophy. (In the text, Miłosz refers to him only by his nickname. As a result, when Irving Howe reviewed the 1981 reissue of *Native Realm* in *The New York Times Book Review*, he misidentified Tiger as Bolesław Miciński, a philosopher who died in 1943 while still in his early thirties. Howe's error has subsequently been perpetuated in several other sources.) Although Miłosz admired Tiger greatly and considered him a catalyst for his thought and writing, he does not always treat his mentor sympathetically. Tiger was a man who, enamored of mind games, outwardly conformed to the dictates of the Polish government and accepted a university post. Hoping for a "humanistic revolution," he believed that one must bend to the currents of history. Tiger was the one who stayed, Miłosz the one who left. The parallels and contradictions of the two men form a fitting climax to Miłosz's meditations on the paradox of Eastern Europe.

Analysis

In one of the final pages of *Native Realm*, Miłosz remembers words spoken to him in Poland before his defection: "One has the right to escape only if he finds a way to fight." Fight what? Not any specific ideology or government. Miłosz's essays are not a diatribe against Marxism, a defense of capitalism, or a nationalistic plea for Polish independence. If there is outcry, it is directed against violence, physical violence, and, above all, crimes of violence against the mind. On the other hand, men and women may willingly do emotional and psychological violence to themselves by resisting, at least inwardly. These are Miłosz's heroes.

Miłosz believes that the individual, indissolubly welded to his history, cannot be alienated from his heritage and environment. To confess alienation is also to confess a lack of humanity. This opinion is in direct contrast to much Western literature of the twentieth century, in which the alienation of the individual is a dominant motif. Therefore, underlying Miłosz's attempt to explain an Eastern European perspective is the implicit realization that, in the final analysis, it may never be fully understood by a Westerner, but one must at least make the effort.

This inability to comprehend is not merely philosophical or literary. It reveals the very essence of people's character and perception, which are, in turn, molded by personal and national history. One of Miłosz's principal criticisms of the West, especially of the United States, is that it lacks a sense of history and, consequently, a sense of the tragic. Miłosz affirms the Aristotelian belief that the individual can be purified by suffering. Nations can undergo catharsis through historical pain, and no one can deny that Eastern Europe has not passed through the fire. Miłosz cannot help but feel resentment toward those who seem to have slipped unscathed through the horrors of the twentieth century. In a telling passage, he describes the outrage he felt upon seeing for the first time the skyline of New York City, standing straight and tall, oblivious to the destruction of others. The inhabitants of New York constituted a personal affront to Miłosz because they had no empathy for his own private, inner wars. Behind him lay Warsaw in ruins while Americans, and Miłosz among them, enjoyed their trivial pleasures.

This sense of unreality finally drove Miłosz back to Poland. It is an ironic turnabout, because if Miłosz criticizes the West for its lack of historical perspective, he severely chastises Eastern Europe for its atmosphere of unreality and its lack of a definite form.

> In a certain sense I can consider myself a typical Eastern European. It seems to me that his *differentia specifica* can be boiled down to a lack of form—both inner and outer. . . . He always remains an adolescent, governed by a sudden ebb or flow of inner chaos. Form is achieved in stable societies.

Miłosz's life with its inner and outer chaos mirrors the lives of his fellow intellectuals. The most intimate revelations of these autobiographical essays are of his inner turmoil and search for some degree of metaphysical stability. This book, claims Miłosz, "is not one of feelings." Perhaps it is of choices made and not made. The choices Miłosz and his contemporaries made were never abstract. They were not the purely intellectual commitments made by a Westerner who knows that certain rights and traditions support him even if he disdains that legacy. "By choosing," Miłosz laments, "we had to give up some values for the sake of others, which is the essence of tragedy."

The final two chapters of *Native Realm* offer the life of Miłosz' friend Tiger as a significant example of the brutal consequences of choice. Miłosz attempts to describe Tiger's inner struggle, knowing that others have vehemently accused the philosophy professor of cowardice, hypocrisy, and a chameleonlike change of attitude. Tiger had two personas, that of lecturer at the Party Institute at Warsaw and that of the leader of a small group of loyal friends to whom he could vent his frustrations and express his true opinions—camouflaged, however, in the form of allegories or parables. Unable to liberate his inner demons by writing them out as his friend Miłosz did, Tiger had to be content with his mental games. Believing that man must align himself with historical necessity, Tiger outwardly swam with the current, but he endeavored to keep his inner self free from contamination. He believed that outward deception could still serve the truth, if one did not retreat into total submission. Such a balancing act required a deliberate, self-directed violence that Tiger could not long sustain. After recounting his unexpected death from a heart attack, Miłosz states that "Tiger was killed by the game. The heart, too quickly consumed by the game, is unable to keep up with the mind, straining to discern the will of God in the current of history."

Miłosz credits Tiger with keeping him honest by his mockery and sarcastic challenges. Preoccupied with his subterfuges, however, Tiger could never answer the crucial question that Miłosz repeatedly asked: What is the responsibility of the writer when the concessions cost too much and the true voice cannot be heard?

It seems that the reader, without even opening the book, must know Miłosz's answer to that question. After all, *Native Realm* is the work of a noted émigré reflecting upon the causes and situations that led to his defection from Communist Eastern Europe. After completing this memoir, however, the reader is struck by the realization that no final answer to the question has been given. Life in the West did not permit instant inner peace or guarantee artistic integrity. Miłosz compares himself to the time traveler in one of Tiger's parables who finds that he has landed in the past. The same traps (and more) lie in wait for him. Miłosz is especially troubled that even in the West his words can be twisted out of context and used as political fodder.

Nevertheless, the final tone of Miłosz's meditations, although resigned and tinged with melancholy, is not lacking in optimism. He is buoyed by a Unamunian faith in the *intrahistoria* of the land and consoles himself with the thought that those who have suffered much gain understanding and value commitment.

Critical Context

Czesław Miłosz, who received the Nobel Prize in Literature in 1980, is considered by many to be Poland's greatest living poet and one of the major poets of the twentieth century. Miłosz's first work to gain recognition in the West, however, was his study of intellectual capitulation to Stalinism, *The Captive Mind*. Miłosz, who often and scathingly criticized prevailing political ideologies and impartially flayed both East and West, was dismayed to discover that his work was being used as political propaganda by the Right. Having suffered through many of the hells of his time, Miłosz distrusted writers who advocated a justified violence for whatever reasons.

Still, protest as he might, Miłosz cannot help but be a symbol. His poetry, which deals with recent episodes in Polish history as well as past traditions and memories, has always been tremendously popular in Poland despite the prohibitions of the Polish government. A line from one of Miłosz's poems appears on the monument in Gdansk erected by Polish workers as a memorial to their slain comrades. In 1981, he was allowed to return to Poland and met with Lech Walesa, who acknowledged his debt to the poet.

Although since 1980 more attention has been paid in the West to the literary merits of his work, much of that commentary still centers on Miłosz's political ideas and status as an exile. Critical evaluation of Miłosz must pass through a filter of recent events in Poland or the situation of other Eastern European dissidents. In *Native Realm*, this seems to be precisely Miłosz's goal. He deliberately sets events in his personal life within the greater context of historical events. The essays depict the formation of an intellectual whose voice was that of a dissident. The complex interaction between man and his environment lies at the heart of Miłosz's poetry and prose. In fact, all of his work can be viewed as a protest against a literature not grounded in a sense of history and cultural legacy. His emphasis on a new direction in literary values, away from the hermetic and confessional, is a primary reason why he has been misunderstood by many Western intellectuals.

Sources for Further Study

Contoski, Victor. "Czesław Miłosz and the Quest for Critical Perspective," in *Books*

Abroad. XLVII (Winter, 1973), pp. 35-41.

Czarnecka, Ewa, and Aleksander Fiut. *Conversations with Czesław Miłosz*, 1987.

Gillon, Adam, and Ludwick Krzyzanowski, eds. *Introduction to Modern Polish Literature*, 1964.

Haas, Robert. *Twentieth Century Pleasures: Prose on Poetry*, 1984.

Howe, Irving. "The Moral History of Czesław Miłosz," in *The New York Times Book Review.* LXXXVI (February 1, 1981), pp. 3-24.

Miłosz, Czesław. *The History of Polish Literature*, 1969.

Charlene Suscavage

NATURAL SYMBOLS
Explorations in Cosmology

Author: Mary Douglas (1921-   )
Type of work: Cultural anthropology
First published: 1970

Form and Content

Natural Symbols: Explorations in Cosmology, like Margaret Mead's *Coming of Age in Samoa* (1928) and Claude Lévi-Strauss' *Anthropologie structurale* (1958; *Structural Anthropology*, 1963), addresses contemporary cultural conditions in the Western world using the insights of anthropological studies. Mary Douglas' study begins with an apparent anomaly in contemporary Western societies: While the better-educated, elite clergy of mainstream denominations (Douglas cites especially the Roman Catholic church in Great Britain) tend to devalue the inherent efficacy of traditional observances such as abstaining from meat on Fridays, many ordinary church members cling to such rituals. This split is one manifestation of a pattern of changes taking place in Western culture, a pattern generally characterized by an increasing emphasis, among elite groups, on the ethical dimensions of religious experience at the expense of the symbolic dimensions, concurrent with an increasing valuation of elaborated, rationalistic speech codes at the expense of condensed speech codes. Douglas' thesis is that these changes are part of a pattern observable in many cultures, not merely a result of inevitable secularization in industrial societies. Various relations between a society's "grid," or system of roles and hierarchies, and its "group," or level of control exerted by others over the individual person, correlate with four major varieties of religion and cosmology. Furthermore, the symbolism of the physical human body—a symbolism used in virtually every culture—responds to the social system, so that types of bodily symbolism correlate with types of grid-group relationships.

The first five chapters of *Natural Symbols* set out the terms of the grid-group system and the kinds of interpretations to which it can lead. The concluding five chapters apply those terms to a variety of religiocultural situations, providing a multifaceted demonstration of the ways in which social systems, religions, languages and linguistic systems, and symbolic codes interact.

Douglas' argument begins with the observation that family structures and linguistic modes can both be seen as ranging along two continuums. Family structure ranges from the "positional" (that is, hierarchical and rigid regarding roles and duties) to the "personal" (that is, concerned with developing sensitivity to others' emotions and ability to manipulate abstractions). Speech modes range from the "restricted" (that is, used for the purpose of reinforcing positional values) to the "elaborated" (that is, used for self-expression and critical reflection). In societies characterized by highly positional families who use highly restricted speech codes, ritual is a potent form of communication. In societies with personal families and elaborated speech codes, such as upper-middle-class England and America, ritual gives way to ethics; ironically, the highly educated religious leaders drawn from this class cannot respond to the "condensed symbols" which lie at the heart of all rituals.

Family structure and the style of control it implies do not, however, arise independently of a larger social and cosmological order. Power, Douglas argues, is made legitimate in terms of elements of a society that are not explained or even discussed by its members, but instead are so implicit as to seem self-evident. These sources of power or control can be traced along two dimensions of human interaction. The first is the amount of pressure the individual can or does exert on others and the amount they can or do exert on him. Douglas calls this dimension "group." Second, the coherence of the system by which experience is categorized she calls the "grid." The experience of any individual person within the group or the grid is not an absolute value, but relative to the experiences of others in his or her culture. Thus, for example, in an industrialized society strong grid may correlate with the presence of both strong leaders who exert great pressure on the group and a mass of people subjected to the impersonal rules of the grid; these people attach themselves comfortably to a leader as long as he is in ascendancy but break out into millenarianism when his fortunes collapse.

Human societies present an enormous variety of religious and cosmological forms, but, Douglas argues, there are four main social types, corresponding to four cosmological types. First, societies characterized by strong grid and group see the universe as just, with pain and suffering serving as appropriate punishments for misdeeds, either individual or collective. Second, societies characterized by intense identification with small groups but lacking strong grid see a war between the forces of good and evil in the universe, with evil as an alien danger introduced by outside contamination. These societies are especially prone to such religious manifestations as the exorcism of witches. Third, in societies with strong grid but weak group identification, the leaders see the cosmos as an arena in which they compete, using any means, natural or supernatural, that will assure their success. Fourth, the mass of people in strong grid, weak group societies see the universe as a place of impersonal rules followed to placate distant gods. Such people are prone to millenarian movements when the rewards for obeying the rules seem not to be forthcoming.

Within this worldwide context of societies and cosmologies, modern Westerners live with highly developed grids but relatively low group identification. The search for group solidarity manifests itself in clinging to identifying rituals (such as Friday abstinence), while the desire to transcend the impersonality of the grid leads to antiritualism in its various modern forms, including religious revivalism and secular revolts against bureaucratic and academic structures.

Analysis

If anthropology has an interest for the general reader, that interest to a great extent lies in the insights the science provides into contemporary society, even as it ranges far afield in time, space, and level of development. *Natural Symbols* addresses directly the paradox that its readers, unlike many of the subjects of anthropological study, are "people who live by using elaborated speech to review and revise existing categories of thought" and who measure their success by the extent to which they force their disciplines into new channels and maintain "a professional detachment towards any given pattern of experience." To bring such readers to understand how deeply ritualism and condensed symbolism affect many people and how impoverished is the person unable to grasp the multilevel importance of "efficacious signs" is Douglas' formidable self-imposed task. At the same time, she insists that "anthropologists must be [the book's] most important critics"; if the general reader at times finds the detailed discussions of previous studies and of fieldwork among various tribes exhausting, the professional anthropologist will find them exhaustive.

The extensive comparative descriptions of other cultures serve another of Douglas' purposes: She demonstrates, again and again, that efforts to reform Christianity by deemphasizing ritual and stressing ethics and a personal relationship with God rest upon unfounded or false assumptions. This carefully documented presentation of numerous cultures (at least thirty are discussed in some detail) shows that antiritualism is not necessarily a sign of cultural superiority or of socio-technological evolution. Contrary to what might seem logical, not all primitive religions are magical and ritualistic, and not all primitive societies lack elaborated grid and group structures. Yet, as Douglas puts it, to modern clerics "a rational, verbally explicit, personal commitment to God is self-evidently more evolved and better than its alleged contrary, formal, ritualistic conformity." To privilege the elaborated speech code and its concomitant habits of mind in this way is as limited and limiting, Douglas argues, as any other exclusive definition of true religious experience.

In addition to comparing various forms of religious experiences across cultural boundaries, Douglas compares secular and religious movements within contemporary culture. Her most sustained example is her observation that secular and religious antiritualism demonstrate a similar pattern of bodily symbolism. In each case, as the exterior forms of society are devalued, each individual person asserts a sharper split between body and spirit, with a concomitant dishonoring of the exterior—the body—demonstrated through neglect of clothing or hygiene or the adoption of bodily forms perceived as bizarre. As the concept of God becomes more personal and interior, the body is seen as increasingly irrelevant or even positively evil, the source of corruption and contamination. Hence, Douglas argues, arise the distinctive garb of monks and hippies.

Besides offering insights into religious movements, attitudes, and conflicts, *Natural Symbols* analyzes the nature of symbols and language in important ways. Douglas develops the concept of the condensed symbol, something in a culture that is "so economical and highly articulated . . . that it is enough to strike one chord to recognize that the orchestration is on a cosmic scale." Rituals such as the Christian

Eucharist may in fact be symbols of this sort. Beyond their religious significance, condensed symbols have powerful aesthetic and political dimensions. Because "symbols are the only means of communication . . . the only means of expressing value; the main instruments of thought," the absence of common symbols as norms in modern Western culture stands as a serious problem. Yet the highly educated, who decide upon the official place of condensed symbols in cultural institutions, "are only too likely to have been made, by the manner of their education, insensitive to non-verbal signals and dull to their meaning." Furthermore, Douglas asserts—in one of her most controversial passages—that "there is no person whose life does not need to unfold in a coherent symbolic system." When the condensed symbols of people are denigrated and "when ritualism is openly despised the philanthropic impulse [often proposed as an appropriate alternative to rituals] is in danger of defeating itself." To be unable to grasp the basic importance of symbols is to "cherish . . . in the name of reason a very irrational concept of communication." Throughout her book, Douglas urges a respect for the value of symbol and a skepticism toward those who would diminish the "faculty for receiving immediate, condensed messages given obliquely along non-verbal channels."

In the widest sense, *Natural Symbols* asserts the importance of structures of all kinds to human beings, whether considered as individuals or as social groups. Douglas seeks to demonstrate that nothing human can be understood as an isolated phenomenon. She shows human thought patterns to be correlative with social patterns, and individual psychological orientations to be embedded in cultural ways of seeing and responding to the cosmos.

Some readers have found Douglas' comparisons between Christianity and so-called primitive religions disturbing, considering it inappropriate to appear to equate the two kinds of experience or to suggest that Christianity, like other religious systems, correlates in important ways with the kind of society in which it is dominant. Others, however, have seen in this work a seminal analysis of the relationships between sociocultural patterns and religious beliefs and a skillful application of the analytical techniques of the social sciences to the contemporary world. In evaluating the value of such studies, Douglas asserts that one's "cosmological scheme connects up the bits of experience and invests the whole with meaning. . . . Unless we can make the process visible, we are the victims."

Critical Context

That patterns of social relation are both expressed through and created by collective rituals and belief systems is one of the central theses of Émile Durkheim's pioneering work in cultural anthropology, and Mary Douglas works squarely within the Durkheimian tradition. Douglas extends the range of such study, however, by employing techniques of linguistic analysis, especially those of Basil Bernstein (whom Douglas acknowledges throughout *Natural Symbols*). Showing correlations between belief systems, linguistic codes, and social structures, Douglas reaches across several subdisciplines within the field of anthropology. She is also the first to use the grid/group model to account for religious patterns in widely divergent cultures.

Although in her meticulous citations of sources and descriptions of fieldwork Douglas is as detached and objective as any professional social scientist, her sympathies lie always with religious belief and its expression through condensed symbols. Unlike many other anthropological studies, *Natural Symbols* draws explicit conclusions about the strengths and weaknesses not only of remote and primitive cultures but also of contemporary Western culture. Douglas' own cosmology is not value-free: To her, the failure of the clergy and the academic communities to understand the needs of ordinary people is deplorable, but capable of being remedied. It is this insistence on seeing and judging clearly that makes *Natural Symbols* an important work for readers other than anthropologists, and that makes some anthropologists uneasy when they confront it.

Among Douglas' many other works, one that is particularly relevant to *Natural Symbols* is *Implicit Meanings: Essays in Anthropology* (1975). *Implicit Meanings*, which gathers essays and lectures from 1955 to 1972, shows how different cultures organize the raw material of experience in different ways. In her preface, Douglas makes explicit the thrust of these essays, arguing for a radical relativism. While acknowledging Durkheim's pioneering efforts in demonstrating the "social factors controlling thought," she notes that he failed to extend his critique to his own attachment to modern science and the notion of "non-context-dependent" truth. In short, Douglas provocatively contends that most arguments for cultural relativism have not gone far enough: "It is no more easy to defend non-context-dependent, non-culture-dependent beliefs in things or objective scientific truth than beliefs in gods and demons."

Sources for Further Study

"Grids and Groups," in *The Times Literary Supplement*. May 14, 1970, p. 535.

Hacking, Ian. "Knowledge," in *London Review of Books*. VIII (December 18, 1986), pp. 17-18.

Rabon, Jonathan. "Conservative Cosmologies," in *New Statesman*. LXXIX (June 5, 1970), pp. 812-813.

Steinfels, Peter. "The Sartorial Shagginess of St. John the Baptist, Hippies, and Nuer Prophets," in *Commonweal*. XCIII (October 9, 1970), pp. 49-51.

Wuthnow, Robert, et al. *Cultural Analysis: The Work of Peter L. Berger, Mary Douglas, Michel Foucault, and Jürgen Habermas*, 1984.

Julia Whitsitt

NIGHT

Author: Elie Wiesel (1928-   )
Type of work: Memoir
Time of work: Spring, 1944, to spring, 1945
Locale: Hungary, Poland, and Germany
First published: Un di Velt hot geshvign, 1956 (*La Nuit,* 1958; English translation, 1960)

> *Principal personages:*
> ELIE WIESEL, an author and a survivor of Auschwitz
> HIS FATHER, who perished in Auschwitz

Form and Content

On March 19, 1944, German Schützstaffeln (SS) troops under Adolf Eichmann entered Hungary for the express purpose of rounding up the Jews of that country for extermination. Even as German armies elsewhere were retreating under pounding Russian advances, Adolf Hitler's so-called final solution was extended to Hungarian Jews—who had mistakenly thought themselves safe from German danger. A few days after the invasion, SS troops appeared in the Transylvanian town of Sighet and began the brutal process that would send almost all Sighet's fifteen thousand Jews to their deaths at Auschwitz in Poland. Among those Jews who lives were totally uprooted was a devout fourteen-year-old student of the Talmud, Eliezer Wiesel.

Wiesel's experiences from that point to eventual liberation at Buchenwald on April 11, 1945, made up an eight-hundred-page Yiddish manuscript, written after the completion of a self-imposed ten-year period of silence, study, and reflection concerning the Holocaust. *Night,* outlined within weeks after his liberation (and only one-seventh of the Yiddish original), is Wiesel's only book devoted completely to the Holocaust, although his experiences of life in Auschwitz and the loss of the six million dictate almost all Wiesel's thought and writing.

The book's nine chapters demarcate key events for Wiesel, detailing the gradual loss of the illusion of hope as the grim realities become paramount. Two interrelated concerns are woven throughout the narrative: Wiesel's agonizing loss of faith in the God of his childhood and his excruciating relationship with his weakening father. The latter is marked by filial love and concern, but also by his own devastating guilt as his father slips inexorably toward death and Wiesel anticipates freedom from his burden of devotion.

Night reveals the destruction of all aspects of the accepted universe—the shtetl (the Jewish enclave) of Sighet, family life, the training of a deeply religious child, and the illusion of a caring humanity. Yet above all, it sets forth a sequence of experiences that results in Wiesel's becoming "the accuser, God the accused." A universe is revealed in *Night* in which "anything is allowed." After seeing a truck dump babies into a burning pit, Wiesel cries,

Never shall I forget that night, the first night in camp, which has turned my life into one long night, seven times cursed and seven times sealed. Never shall I forget that smoke. Never shall I forget the little faces of the children. . . . Never shall I forget those flames which consumed my faith forever. . . . Never shall I forget those moments which murdered my God and my soul and turned my dreams to dust. Never shall I forget these things, even if I am condemned to live as long as God Himself. Never.

Following the execution of a child possessing "the face of a sad angel," a voice asserts that God "is hanging here on this gallows." Wiesel is deliberately ambiguous about the source of this assertion.

The nine chapters in *Night* are devoted to specific aspects of Wiesel's Holocaust experience: the warnings and illusion-filled prelude before deportation, the terrifying train ride to Auschwitz, the arrival at the gates of the SS hell, the loss of family members, and the early signs of a shattering faith. Wiesel recalls the slave labor at the Buna works adjacent to the central Auschwitz complex, the promise of the approaching Russian army's liberation destroyed by the SS evacuation of camp inmates, the march away from Auschwitz toward Germany, the train ride to Buchenwald, the death of his father, and his own liberation. The book's tone varies from irony to bitterness to terrible despair, with the latter perhaps being dominant. As its Yiddish title suggests (literally, "and the world remained silent"), Wiesel's book is addressed to the world that did nothing, but it also challenges a God who did nothing.

Wiesel is acutely conscious of the duty of the survivor and writer following the Holocaust to educate that apathetic world and to provide a voice for the six million murdered Jewish victims. In an interview published in the *Journal of Education* (1980), he noted, "I do not write to please the reader. . . . I write for the dead." Wiesel himself calls *Night* the literature of testimony.

Analysis

In a symposium published in *Judaism* (March 26, 1967), Wiesel declared, "In the beginning there was the Holocaust. We must therefore start over again." Most commentators would agree with Graham Walker's description, in his book *Elie Wiesel: A Challenge to Theology* (1987), of the Holocaust as an event of "ontological status which has disrupted both human history and the life story of God." *Night* is one of only a few books whose authors attempt to understand the Holocaust. Wiesel's international status as the winner of the 1986 Nobel Peace Prize, as a formidable literary figure, and as one of the leading voices speaking for the Holocaust survivors as well as the victims makes this work all the more compelling. His decision to focus on the Holocaust's significance for altering the human understanding of man's relationship to God indicates that Wiesel's views, as expressed in *Night* and in virtually every work of his since, reflect the central difficulties involved in the painful theological revisions that have occurred in both Jewish and Christian realms since 1945.

It is important to realize, however, that *Night* is not an example of the "death of God theology." At the Brandeis-Bardin Institute (January 22, 1978), Wiesel claimed that "the Covenant was broken. I had to tell God of my anger. I still do so." God is not dead for Wiesel; in fact, it is the recognition of a God that permits the monologue recorded in *Night*. Wiesel can protest vehemently to God about the state of the creation precisely because God the Creator exists.

Paradoxically, Wiesel also employs silence within this monologue. While Wiesel believes that to remain silent about the Holocaust is to betray its victims, he also knows that presuming to talk about the experience of the Holocaust is a betrayal of another kind. His words are thus chosen with extreme care, but also with a great regard for the silence between the words. In an interview with Harry James Cargas in *U.S. Catholic* (September, 1971), Wiesel observed that "there are certain silences between word and word. . . . This is the silence that I have tried to put in my work."

Although Wiesel's words and silences are intended for all readers, Jewish and non-Jewish, Hasidic Judaism and culture shaped and still influence the man. Writing in *Jewish Heritage* (1972), Wiesel attests:

> I myself love Hasidism because I grew up in a Hasidic milieu. Whenever I want to write something good, I go back to my childhood. The soul of every writer is his childhood, and mine was a Hasidic one. I love Hasidism because of its tales, because of the intrinsic fervor that makes them Hasidic tales. I love Hasidism for something else too: it contains all the themes that haunt my work.

Although Wiesel's Judaism is deeply ingrained, *Night* does not offer an uncritical view of the behavior of Jews in the face of murderous Nazi intentions. Illusion reigns for Jews in Hungary and Sighet, even with SS soldiers in their midst. No one can think the unthinkable; even the eyewitness account of a Jew who escaped from a death camp is discounted as the ravings of a madman. A woman driven to insanity while on the train heading to Auschwitz (and death) is silenced; her visions of flames and terror are ridiculed—until the sights of the death camp's huge chimneys loom near. A pie waits to be baked in the ghetto, sudden deportation having removed the family that hoped to enjoy it. Wiesel's father advises his loved ones not to fear wearing the Star of David as ordered by the SS; it cannot kill you, he argues. Wiesel asks rhetorically, retrospectively, "Poor Father! Of what then did you die?"

Nevertheless, Wiesel believes that a defining mark of Judasim has been its willingness to question. Robert McAfee Brown notes that at the center of Wiesel's work has been the urgent question of how mankind should "respond to monstrous moral evil." In *Night*, Wiesel asks why he should honor the name of the God who has done nothing about the existence of the death camp Auschwitz and relates this question of theodicy to the suffering experienced by the Jews. Concerned primarily with the "defiance of suffering," Wiesel points out in the Cargas interview that "suffering as a virtue is alien to Judaism" because "suffering is impure." Ultimately, suffering is not to be experienced as an end or as a means to some transcendent value.

The absence of transcendent affirmation in *Night* involves the creation of a new kind of protagonist—not the tragic hero of past literatures but the survivor, the sufferer. As Terrence Des Pres argues in *The Survivor: An Anatomy of Life in the Death Camps* (1976), the survivor chooses life, even on the unbearable terms of the persecutor, rather than death, which might redeem or ennoble him in the eyes of his audience. For Wiesel, survival, even with its terrible burden of guilt, denies the perpetrators a victory and allows the survivor's testimony to be handed on to posterity.

Critical Context

In *Against Silence: The Voice and Vision of Elie Wiesel* (1984), Irving Abrahamson asserts that *Night* is not merely the first work by Wiesel. Indeed, it is the center of all that follows: *Night* contains all the haunting issues permeating Wiesel's later works. Wiesel has spoken of *Night* as surrounded concentrically by his later books. Although *Night* is his only effort exclusively concerned with the Holocaust, the universe of the concentration camp is central to all of his work.

Lawrence Langer, in *Versions of Survival: The Holocaust and the Human Spirit* (1982), has argued that language to describe annihilation has yet to be devised. Literary categories that sufficed as intellectual frameworks prior to Auschwitz no longer apply. Most historians, theologians, and critics believe that Auschwitz has generated a unique class of writers. If so, the attendant literature of atrocity is operating in uncharted intellectual and moral terrain. Nevertheless, *Night*'s extraordinary power cannot be denied. All the forces that operated within the Holocaust— perpetrators, victims, bystanders—are represented in this slim volume under the scrutiny of a keenly perceptive narrator who sees these forces within the framework of a kind of receding universe. He gives no assurances about what will replace this world.

Wiesel's *Night* records this destruction of the old order—the inherited past, faith in humanity, belief in the God of the covenant with Abraham and the God of Sinai—and questions the implied nature of the emerging new order based on totalitarian misrule, the industrialized debasement of humanity, and the worthlessness of women, the elderly, and innocent children. A few critics found parts of *Night* steeped in bathos or mawkishness, but such negative views were extremely rare. Wiesel was not writing from the narrative perspective of a Henry James or a James Joyce: Having stood within feet of a burning pit filled with infants and small children, Wiesel did not find it useful to write with Olympian detachment. The influence of Franz Kafka and Albert Camus (whom Wiesel knew during his days in Paris as a journalist) is reflected in Wiesel's portrayal of the madness and absurdity of Auschwitz and in his commitment to producing literature that might help improve the human condition through appealing to conscience.

In the final analysis, *Night* is significant as a clear record of mankind's confrontation with the darkness of an overwhelming evil that operated on a vast scale in the twentieth century and which cut viciously to the core of known historical, social, humanitarian, and religious dynamics. The absolute darkness of the night that descended for all time on the six million Jewish victims will not, Wiesel argues, leave untouched anyone born after the Holocaust.

Sources for Further Study

Abrahamson, Irving. *Against Silence: The Voice and Vision of Elie Wiesel*, 1984.

Berenbaum, Michael. *The Vision of the Void: Theological Reflections on the Works of Elie Wiesel*, 1979.

Brown, Robert McAfee. *Elie Wiesel: Messenger to All Humanity*, 1983.

Cargas, Harry James. *Harry James Cargas in Conversation with Elie Wiesel*, 1976.

Ezrahi, Sidra DeKoven. *By Words Alone: The Holocaust in Literature*, 1980.

Fine, Ellen. "Witness of the Night," in *Legacy of Night: The Literary Universe of Elie Wiesel*, 1982.

Halperin, Irving. *Messengers from the Dead: Literature of the Dead*, 1970.

Langer, Lawrence. *The Holocaust and the Literary Imagination*, 1975.

——————— . *Versions of Survival: The Holocaust and the Human Spirit*, 1982.

Rosenfeld, Alvin, and Irving Greenberg, eds. *Confronting the Holocaust: The Impact of Elie Wiesel*, 1978.

Sherwin, Byron. "Elie Wiesel and Jewish Theology," in *Judaism*. XVIII (1969), pp. 39-52.

——————— . "Jewish Messianism and Elie Wiesel," in *Notre Dame English Journal*. XI (1977), pp. 33-46.

Walker, Graham B., Jr. *Elie Wiesel: A Challenge to Theology*, 1987.

Michael R. Steele

THE NOISE OF TIME

Author: Osip Mandelstam (1891-1938)
Type of work: Autobiography
Time of work: The 1890's to the first decade of the twentieth century
Locale: Riga, St. Petersburg, and nearby Pavlosk, Russia, and Finland
First published: Shum vremeni, 1925 (English translation, 1965)

> *Principal personages:*
> OSIP MANDELSTAM, a Russian poet
> VLADIMIR GIPPIUS, his teacher, also a poet
> BORIS SINANI, his school friend
> YULI MATVEICH, a friend of the Mandelstam family
> VERA KOMISSARZHEVSKAYA, a theater actress and director
> SERGEI IVANYCH, a revolutionary

Form and Content

The Noise of Time is a poet's autobiography. Osip Mandelstam, working in the Russian genre of childhood reminiscence, attempts a completely new transformation of the form. Jane Gary Harris describes it in her introduction to Mandelstam's *The Complete Critical Prose and Letters* (1979): "*The Noise of Time* is structured around fragments or vignettes involving recurrent poetic images and a density of references and associations unified by the autobiographical impulse and ordered 'according to their spatial extension.'" The genre provides an unconfining frame for the fragments, images, and associations arranged like stanzas in a poem, their juxtaposition more important to the effect than chronology or causation. The internal connection of the fragments achieves Mandelstam's interpretation of his age, his ideas about the role of the poet, the nature of the word, and his view of art. Prince Mirsky speaks of the "daring, depth, and truth" of the work's "historical intuition."

The work is divided into fourteen such fragments, each seemingly complete in itself. "Music in Pavlovsk," the first, presents in sensuous detail memories of a summer concert in the mid-1890's at the railroad station restaurant in Pavlovsk, a popular retreat from St. Petersburg, but the year-round home for the Mandelstam family in those years. Detail about Pavlovsk at that time of every kind—architectural, literary, musical, human, social, economic—saturates the three and a half pages. The description catches the moment with a fullness that combines the fresh responses of a child with the attention and understanding of the adult, letting the reader experience the way it was then for a small boy but with the irony born of hindsight.

Part 2, "Childish Imperialism," reproduces the emotional effect on the child of the militaristic images of St. Petersburg—the equestrian statues, the horse and marine guards, the navy ships, the great barracks, the Field of Mars, the "funeral pomps of some general," the military bands, the stately progress of the czar and his family through the streets. Mandelstam says that the "very architecture of the city inspired me with a kind of childish imperialism" and in a last paragraph distinguishes all that glitter from the middle-class Jewish family life of which he is a part.

"Riots and French Governesses," part 3, describes first the student riots, well controlled but nevertheless an early sign of the coming revolution. This image of disorder is supported by a memory of the three-year-old boy's responses at the funeral of Alexander III. These signs of the breakup contrast with the anglicized and frenchified fops promenading on the avenues, their inadequacy emphasized with a description of the superficial French tutors with which the boy was provided in his family's attempt to join the dominant culture.

Part 4, "The Bookcase," characterizes the Jewish "chaos" of his own home by describing the contents and arrangement of books in their bookcase. From his father's and mother's books he moves to their character, each showing a different response to the culture of which they were not truly a part. A section on the nineteenth century popular poet Semyon Nadson catches the sentimentality of the age which loved him.

Petersburgers vacationed in Finland, and the next section describes visits to a Vyborg family, Jewish but secure, "stable" and "oaken," unlike his own family life. Part 6 describes his family in greater detail, with a long section on the different speech of his mother and his father. The word is already important to the poet to come.

Part 7 returns to the theme of music, this time the Lenten concerts of a violinpiano duo who induce a "Dionysian" delight in the St. Petersburg crowds. The scene is at the classical Nobility Hall, and the virtuosi are "rational and pure," contrasting with the hysteria of the audience. The boy is growing, and part 8, at the turn of the century, finds him at the Tenishev School, an anglicized and exclusive preparatory school where Mandelstam is introduced to literature and politics. He describes his classes, classmates, and the old-fashioned head of the school.

Mandelstam characterizes the year 1905, with its abortive revolution, in the person of Sergei Ivanych, an intense, disorderly, and ineffective rehearsal coach for the revolution. Like the clash itself, the man was a "chimera," unable to face the reality of the change he advocated. Part 10 describes Yuli Matveich, a friend and arbiter in his family, an image of a wise epicurean touched with despair at death, ever a presence in the book.

Part 11 introduces the reader to Vladimir Gippius, a Symbolist poet but here a teacher of literature of the Tenishev School, where Mandelstam encounters the Erfurt Program and idealistic Marxist economic views. From that reading, it is only a step to part 12 and the young man's introduction to the intellectual Sinani family and especially to Boris, the son, half-Jewish and a spiritual Russian Populist and Socialist Revolutionary. The narrator also begins to find his way into classical and contemporary Russian poetry, but the approach of revolution and the fierce debates about its direction leave him troubled and anxious, like the time itself.

Part 13 states the purpose of the work: "to track down the age, the noise and the germination of time." His labor, he says, is to distance the past. He writes of the actress and woman director, Vera Komissarzhevskaya: spare, "Protestant," in her acting style. He lets the reader hear her voice and says, "The theater has lived and will live by the human voice." Her theater tried to be contemporary and European just before the revolution carried everything away.

In part 14, "In a Fur Coat Above One's Station," the young man recognizes himself as a *raznochinets* (an intellectual) and a writer. He sees the autobiography as making his way alone "back up the dried riverbed." The prose becomes denser with literary reference and metaphor as the nineteenth century passes to the twentieth and the brink of revolution and civil war. The narrator visits his teacher, the poet Gippius, full of joy and malice, in his disorderly apartment; through him, the young man connects with the literary tradition and sees the newcomers to poetry watch the century freeze. He feels the raw power of literature in the wintry scene.

Analysis

The Noise of Time, a collection of intensely realized scenes and vivid characterizations, resonating with all the signs of doomed nineteenth century Russian culture, is at once the story of a boy's coming of age, of his commitment to the power of the word, and of the life and death of a century. Both man and century open to a new and terrifying life.

Autobiography here becomes a highly compressed and meaningful interpretation of the "germination of time" for the poet, for the age, and for the reader. Guy Davenport calls the whole work a "spiritual inventory of the mode of life swept away by the Revolution," but it is also a search for the roots of the poet's commitment to his work. What seems a somewhat tenuously connected group of intensely realized moments in a young man's life becomes an analysis of why the Bolshevik Revolution became possible and what elements formed the poetic psyche of the narrator. Jane Gary Harris sees this personal and historical perception as revealing a "startling parallelism" of history and the aesthetic consciousness of the country and the poet. The country and the age fall apart as the poet emerges into his profession.

The poet sees the superficiality and sentimentality of 1890's Russia in the relaxed summer concert at Pavlovsk; he sees the childish and merely spectacular military regime of imperial Russia; he notes the beginning of trouble in the still easily suppressed student riots and the beginning of hysteria in the concerts at the Nobility Hall. The rumble of revolution is heard in the passionate political idealists of various camps the boy encounters at school and in Sergei Ivanych, the "chimera," both a person and the truth of the 1905 revolution. Mandelstam's image of Komissarzhevskaya is one of the rich culture still linked to the West but doomed in the turbulence to come. In *The Noise of Time*, as in Anna Akhmatova's *Poema bez geroa* (1960; *A Poem Without a Hero*, 1973), the hectic end of an era emerges, full of both the triviality which condemned the culture and superb images of the culture to be lost.

These images of superficial glamour and passionate dissent have counterpoints in the "Judaic chaos" of the narrator's family life. The characterization of his uninte-grated father and mother (despite her efforts to integrate), the alien stability of Jewish friends who make no attempt to integrate outside of business relations, the exotic quality of his encounters with the Jewish religion—all of those trouble the writer, provide another image of unresolved problems in the empire, and ultimately counter with a strong sense of reality the unreal culture about to die.

Simultaneously, the images from both the Russian and the Jewish cultures feed the boy's emerging interest in the work, his gradual commitment, not to politics, but to poetry. His teacher, Vladimir Gippius, shows him the way to himself. His father's strange speech and his mother's care to speak pure Russian make him acutely aware of language. His experience of poetry—the popular, of which he is contemptuous, the Symbolist, which he sees as over, and the great classics of the Russian tradition, which he values—is knit into every episode, both explicitly and implicitly. The theme of poetry and the poet emerges at the end, as the young adult emerges, to speak ferociously as the wintry chill of change takes hold. He is defined as the time is defined; literature has its role to play: the representation of the time, the distancing of the time, and the understanding of the time and the self. Literature is intuitive, naturally beastlike, but it is linked inexorably to personal and national history, as the work has made clear. The "noise" of time, conjoining the sounds of all the life here represented, turns at last into the sound of the poet's voice.

One underlying theme runs through the work: death. The work aims to recapture the life and the quality of the past, now dead and gone. It presents a three-year-old child at the beginning and moves through his life until late adolescence—one knows this life too must end; funerals and episodes repeatedly, as it is borne in upon the reader that all this life has passed. Art, meanwhile, is re-creating this life; art conquers time and death, just as it reflects them.

The structure of the work is clearly not as casual as it first seems. Every element recalled contributes to the effect of the whole. Episode is bound to episode by psychological, metaphorical, and associational links. Literary allusion builds a con-text of literary history as it communicates the new word of the author. The selection of episodes works to the rich development of interdependent themes, each of which sheds light on the other yet remains a representation of a unique life.

The texture of the work is also not simple. Childlike responsiveness guides the scenes, but the quality represented comes to the reader in a network of references implying the sophisticated Russian and Western culture of the adult narrator. Like a collage, the work fits bits and pieces of past literature and knowledge into a new design that nevertheless richly reveals the old. The narrator assumes the culture he uses, making claims on the reader that presume mutual values and literary experi-ences with those of the writer.

Nadezhda Mandelstam in *Vtoraya kniga* (1972; *Hope Abandoned*, 1974) writes that her husband dictated *The Noise of Time* to her, and the sound of his voice is in the prose. Sounds generate and reflect meaning. For all of their resonances, the sentences, while long, are clear and the word choice precise. Characterization is loving caricature, single features of the people drawn giving vivid impressions of the essence of their personalities, which are defined by what they do. These images nevertheless reflect also the interest and feeling of the narrator, who is otherwise little in evidence. Everything is seen through his eyes. Clarence Brown points out in the introduction to his translation of the work that Mandelstam's startling imagery, juxtapositions, and accumulation of detail "make strange" the scenes and people he depicts, using the formalist device of *ostranenie* to give a fresh and living sense of the reality.

Critical Context

The Noise of Time was commissioned by Isay Lezhnev, the editor of *Rossiya*, in the early 1920's, but he rejected the work as "not what the age demands." So far from wanting a work that brilliantly caught the world that had passed forever, Lezhnev wanted a reminiscence suitable for the new Soviet politicized literature. He himself supplied it with a story of a poor Jewish boy who grew up to become a Marxist-Leninist. *The Noise of Time* was published only in 1925, well after other Soviet publishers also had rejected it.

This disjunction between what was wanted and what interested Mandelstam culminated in Joseph Stalin's time with the poet's isolation, arrest, and death in a transit camp for political prisoners. The fissure between the poet and the new regime became apparent with *The Noise of Time*, though the poet at the end of the book accepts the responsibility of the poet to speak to and for the new age.

In his own artistic development, *The Noise of Time* represents a culmination of Mandelstam's first phase as an artist and the definition of his role. In prose, he asserts the power of the poet and poetry to be a part of the age and to transcend time. He comes to terms with his Jewish heritage and with his calling, blending autobiography and new fictional techniques to achieve a new genre. The historical milieu is not only represented but also poeticized.

Intellectual influences on Mandelstam's work are multiple. The emphases of the Acmeists in poetry, with their shift away from Symbolist transcendence to the immediate and the present; the Bergsonian view of time as space rather than succession; his friend Lev Vygotsky's link of language and history; Maxim Gorky's autobiographical trilogy; Aleksandr Blok's unfinished autobiographical poem "Vozmezdie" (retribution); Innokenty Annensky's renewal of Hellenism; Velemir Khlebnikov's interest in the origins of Russian language and culture—all of those and others contributed to the form and content of *The Noise of Time*. Jane Gary Harris sees the work also in the context of twentieth century autobiographical modes, arising from the individual search for truth, when, in Geoffrey Hartman's phrase, "personal experience becomes the sole authority and source of conviction, and the poet a new intermediary."

Sources for Further Study

Brown, Clarence. Introduction to *The Prose of Osip Mandelstam*, 1965.

_____ . *Mandelstam*, 1973.

Cohen, Arthur A. *Osip Emilievich Mandelstam: An Essay in Antiphon*, 1974.

Harris, Jane Gary. "An Inquiry into the Function of the Autobiographical Mode: Joyce, Mandelstam, Schulz," in *American Contributions to the Ninth International Congress of Slavists*. Vol. 3, 1983. Edited by Paul Debreczeny.

_____ . Introduction to *The Complete Critical Prose and Letters*, 1979.

Mandelstam, Nadezhda. *Hope Abandoned*, 1974.

_____ . *Hope Against Hope: A Memoir*, 1970.

Monas, Sidney. *Osip Mandelstam: Selected Essays*, 1977.

Martha Manheim

NOTEBOOKS, 1960-1977

Author: Athol Fugard (1932-   )
Type of work: Notebooks
First published: 1984

Form and Content

Athol Fugard, whose best-known works emerged in the late 1960's and early 1970's, is one of the world's most prominent playwrights. His messages, often couched in the existential, despairing voice of a Samuel Beckett or a Jean-Paul Sartre, concern more than anything else the singular predicament of twentieth century Afrikaners and the black and "Coloured" peoples they fear, exploit, and hope to contain. An experimenter with theater having uncommon poise and courage and one who dares write politically explosive plays in a country known for its suppression of intellectuals and artists, Fugard has given the world a number of award-winning plays which have earned for him a reputation for candor and brilliance.

In his collection of notes written over a seventeen-year period beginning in 1960 with notes for his play *The Blood Knot* (1961), Fugard recorded both miraculous moments and everyday occurrences, as well as the inspirations that events gave him. One can see how some simple observations of life in his hometown of Port Elizabeth and environs became the raw materials essential in creating great plays such as *Sizwe Bansi Is Dead* (1972), *The Blood Knot*, *People Are Living There* (1968), and *The Island* (1973).

These jottings are not random or disconnected; they show not only how Fugard gradually developed his most important themes and motifs but also how his Christian conscience gave him no rest. South Africa's racial situation made him a man without a country, for his skin color allowed him to lead a life of privilege denied to those with black or mulatto complexions. He could have easily written "safe" plays for the parochial and smug state-approved theater of Johannesburg and Cape Town and lived well. Instead, conscience, as the notebooks prove, nagged at him and helped him create the Serpent Players, a group of mainly black South Africans meeting in the area known as Korsten. In *Notebooks, 1960-1977*, one discovers how this singular group of disciplined actors came together and created a vibrant theater that would be applauded in London and New York.

Fugard's view of his world is always a subjective one, colored by his observations of drunks in black settlements, an arguing Afrikaner family, his own parents, two Coloured vagrants stumbling along looking for cast-off bottles to be redeemed for cash. Such simple observations are transformed by art; the familiar sight of moths futilely flying against an overhead lightbulb, for example, generates a startling and memorable image for *The Blood Knot*, where the moths became emblematic of the risk-taking behavior of the darkly complected brother Zach. The two ragged bottle-collectors, on the other hand, end up as his unforgettable and tragically linked couple Boesman and Lena, from the play of the same name, who search futilely for the meaning of life in a country that denies them meaning.

Direct observations alone, however, do not generate Fugard's characters; he turns frequently to the writings of Albert Camus, Beckett, and Bertolt Brecht for ideas. In their works he discovers the kind of oppressed, anguished people he needs for characters in his plays.

As he seeks to understand the thoughts and inner motivations of others, both fictional and real, Fugard also seeks the meaning of his own existence, asking such elementary questions as "Am I a pessimist or an optimist?" and "Am I too much the white man to talk knowledgeably about the difficulties of black South Africa?" The reader of these notebooks discovers the thoughts of a man obsessed by the need to understand himself and his place in society—a man who writes his plays by drawing upon the inner tensions he discovers, giving his characters some of his own shattered dreams and living hopes.

The apartheid system does not allow Fugard the luxury of living in an imagined world. Rather, its cruelties force him—as they do any South African artist of integrity—to register the damage segregation inflicts and to react against it. Morality demands that people of conscience who have the ability to influence others take a stand on apartheid, and Fugard, much to his credit, has done so, at great cost to himself and to his family. His notes record not only the destructive effects of apartheid but also the battle he waged against his own complacency and moral drift. Renouncing the safe approach to theater, Fugard finds that he must put principle before safety.

Analysis

Notebooks records Fugard's pilgrimage from the choking despair about his life in fear-ridden South Africa that he displayed early in his career toward the cautious hope that is exemplified in the later notebook entries. As his inner frustrations and rage find their proper mode of expression, his pessimism eases and he matures in outlook. He also finds a voice which is all his own. Though in his later plays he continues to take cues from other dramatists, he does so only because he chooses to, not because of artistic immaturity and lack of control. Fugard's progression from student of existentialist masters to master in his own right is superbly chronicled by these notebooks.

Involved in Fugard's quest for honest theater of a political nature is his pursuit of religious certainty. On one hand, the Calvinism present in the Dutch Reformed Church, under whose considerable influence he grew up, helped shape his outlook upon life: God seems to stalk him, testing him, revealing his laws. On the other hand, the atheistic existentialism of Beckett, Camus, and Sartre excites his imagination and helps shape his art. While at times Fugard finds it necessary to disavow Christianity, his notes are filled with the simple phrasing of the New Testament and his battle with apartheid is based on Christian love of one's neighbor. Christianity's call for soul-searching and humility and its disdain for worldly goods have also heavily influenced Fugard.

Nevertheless, Fugard's plays are most often compared with those of the existentialists, whose emphasis upon man finding his own way in an indifferent universe is mirrored by the struggles of Fugard's characters.

The greatest plays from his early period—*Boesman and Lena* (1969), *The Blood Knot, Hello and Goodbye* (1965), and *People Are Living There*—are all concerned with people who pass their lives on a kind of tightrope stretched across the void. They need to receive warmth from others around them, yet too often they do not know how to elicit that warmth. Sometimes they gather courage and take the chance to communicate with others, only to find themselves repulsed and isolated.

Fugard himself has labeled the viewpoint that informs his kind of theater "courageous pessimism." This attitude is reflected in a notebook entry in which Fugard grasps an essential truth of Camus: that in order to live authentically, one must periodically leave the human habitations which so define and restrict the individual and live in the open, in nature's realm, where words such as "success" and "failure" do not have meaning.

The notebooks are not solely self-directed. Fugard tells the reader about people who are important to him: his wife, Sheila, who serves as lover, critic, and confidante; his parents; fellow artists such as film director John Schlesinger, writer Uys Krige, and the beloved Norman Ntshinga, persecuted actor, rebel, and director. In fact, some of Fugard's most impassioned entries concern the fate of Ntshinga, one of the Serpent Players of Port Elizabeth, accused by the government of having aided and abetted the banned African National Congress. The injustice of Ntshinga's rigged trial helps fuel Fugard's hatred of the apartheid system, making even more resolute his determination to take his message about South African injustice to the world.

These notebooks are thus the work not only of a gifted playwright but also of a remarkably brave and determined human being who has placed truth in theater above all other considerations. As Fugard's international reputation has grown over the years, so has his power; he can teach people outside South Africa about its evils. Yet Fugard is no propagandist, but rather an artist whose recording of speech, whose attention to the elements that make up human personality, and whose vigorous voice crying for change have produced some of the best theater created in the last half of the twentieth century.

Critical Context

Athol Fugard's work has been influenced by some of the greatest innovators of his century, including Eugene O'Neill, Samuel Beckett, and Jerzy Grotowski. Out of the cultural ferment of South Africa have come other promising playwrights who may have inspired his writing, among them Richard Rive, B. L. Leshoai, David Lytton, Cosmo Pieterse, and Harold Kimmell.

Grotowski's contribution to Fugard's art is particularly significant. Grotowski's *Towards a Poor Theatre* (1968), to which Fugard alludes many times in the *Notebooks*, calls for the dramatist to rely upon myth rather than individual characters to forward the story. What Grotowski asks for—that the actors become reborn as men who discover their freedom—is what Fugard delivers in many of his plays.

O'Neill also had a considerable impact upon Fugard. In his later plays, O'Neill created a theater stripped bare of trappings, a theater in which characters bared their innermost selves to the audience in a way not seen since William Shakespeare. O'Neill's approach is clearly in evidence throughout Fugard's work.

Nevertheless, it is Samuel Beckett who is most often mentioned in the *Notebooks*, and he remains the single greatest influence upon Fugard. Like Fugard, Beckett relies upon two or three character plays; he uses terse dialogue and dingy settings, and his characters wander about in the midst of stark wastelands. Beckett's language impresses Fugard with its spare dignity. Fugard's people are also like Beckett's in that they have a fierce hunger for the love and affection which life denies them. Compassionate and sensitive, they find themselves out of place in a universe that betrays them.

Despite these influences and those of major figures, Fugard remains a creator of theater unmatched in Africa and rivaled by few playwrights elsewhere in the world. A flexible and innovative writer, he tries to revise his conception of the theater each time he writes a new play. His voice is the most eloquent one speaking of South Africa's tragic situation, and for those who wish to understand the genesis of his art, there is no better place to start than the *Notebooks*.

Sources for Further Study

Caute, David. Review in *The New York Times Book Review*. LXXXIX (June 3, 1984), p. 42.

Coetzee, J. M. Review in *The New Republic*. CXC (April 9, 1984), p. 25.

Coghill, Sheila. Review in *Library Journal*. CIX (June 1, 1984), p. 1124.

Fugard, Athol. "Challenging the Silence: Athol Fugard Talks to Michael Coveney," in *Plays and Players*. November, 1973, pp. 34-37.

Iyer, Pico. Review in *Time*. CXXIII (April 30, 1984), p. 76.

John D. Raymer

NOTES FROM THE CENTURY BEFORE
A Journal from British Columbia

Author: Edward Hoagland (1932-   )
Type of work: Travel writing/diary
Time of work: June 2 to August 3, 1966
Locale: British Columbia
First published: 1969

> *Principal personage:*
> EDWARD HOAGLAND, a writer who searches out aged explorers in
> the British Columbian wilderness

Form and Content

In the summer of 1960, Edward Hoagland and his wife lived in Hazelton, British Columbia, a remote village on the Skeena River, where Hoagland heard stories of an even more isolated town named Telegraph Creek. Telegraph Creek originated one hundred years earlier, when a plan to string telegraph wire from New York to London the long way required outposts along the route. The line was hung as far as Telegraph Creek when the transatlantic cable connected New York and London the short way; thus, spools of unused wire were left to rust, and the population of Telegraph Creek shrunk to native Indians and the various gold hunters and white explorers who fancied living on game and produce. The century-old Telegraph Creek Hoagland pondered in Hazelton promised a wealth of lore and glimpses of mountain men ("stories which hadn't worn threadbare with handling") were it only possible to arrive there. No one in Hazelton could accommodate the journalist, however, as the passage overland was more demanding than even the local blusterers could manage, and Hoagland returned to New York unsatisfied.

Despite correspondence from guides familiar with Telegraph Creek which discouraged the avid writer from visiting, Hoagland returned to British Columbia in 1966, divorced and lonely but eager to confirm his intuition that going into the area around Telegraph Creek would be tantamount to stepping into the previous century. *Notes from the Century Before*, a travel journal of more than three hundred pages, is the book he wrested from the inhabitants, human and animal, and the magnificent landscape. Although Hoagland labels himself a rhapsodist, and although he devotes sections of the journal to the visual wonders, the book concentrates on describing the men who live in the wilderness and the stories they had to tell: "I would be talking to the doers themselves, the men whom no one pays any attention to until they are dead, who give the mountains their names and who pick the passes that become the freeways."

The journal begins with an entry for June 2, 1966, the day Hoagland left New York, and concludes with an entry for August 3. After two weeks in Telegraph Creek, he traveled to other remote corners of British Columbia. Entries characteristically feature physical impressions of the men and women Hoagland meets. Dan McPhee, who settled in the West in 1904, "looks like a canny grandpa from Tobacco Road—long nose, floppy hat, black shirt . . . and when he tells a joke, he seems to swallow it, like a shot of whiskey." Another Telegraph Creek citizen, Mr. Wriglesworth, "looks like the prophet who walks in front of a migrating people carrying a staff, and as though his face were younger underneath the skin than outside." Entries also focus on the means these pioneers have found to thrive in this land without supermarkets. Wriglesworth's staples include grouse, salmon (slimed "with brine strong enough to blacken a potato"), black bear, mountain goat, moose, snowshoe rabbits, beaver, and a wealth of vegetables from cabbage to squash. Methods of trapping animals are discussed at length, and story after story is recorded of self-sufficient inventiveness by the mountain men. Typical of dozens is a method used by Jim Morgan, an aging explorer, who as a young man enticed wolves to approach him by flopping around on a frozen lake as if wounded.

Since the book is a journal, meditation on the place he is visiting occurs at random. Hoagland often remarks on the Indians' condition, and how their way of living contrasts with the whites. Hoagland finds the Indians of Eddontenajon, a village to the east of Telegraph Creek, susceptible to the white man's gift of liquor and their community a mess as a result. In a town such as Caribou Hide, however, the Indian's traditional life-style survives. Left to themselves, without the welfare checks distributed to the alcoholic Indians of Eddontenajon, the Indians remain Indians. Yet they also suffer periodically from starvation, a condition the white explorers find inexcusable given the wealth of game available to any hunter.

Hoagland also records descriptions of the animals. Game, he contends, is more essential than stunning scenery. Watching a caribou swim across a lake, he writes, "She was a pretty bleached tan with two-pronged antlers in velvet, and she splashed in the shallows like a filly, muzzling the bugs off her rear." A sighting of a wolf takes up two pages of diary space, as if his view might be the last:

> And their heads are large to contain their mouths, which are both hands and mouths. Their eyes are fixed in a Mongol slant to avoid being bitten. Nobody born nowadays will see a wild wolf. They are an epitome; one keeps count because they are so exceptional a glimpse.

Along with the eighty-year-old pioneers, their anecdotes, the Indians, the vast landscape, and the game, Hoagland writes of introspective moments. He feels guilty about the scavenging methods of professional journalism, and though most interlocuters speak freely and surrender their lore, some ask to be paid. His inability to stay married to a woman he loved exasperates him. He frankly admits the differences between himself and the pioneers. While admiring their stamina and indifference to the harshness of isolation, he is not tempted by their life-style. Though he has found sustained intimacy with women in civilization hard to manage, he is not inclined to withdraw. When he is concussed and bedridden after an automobile wreck in the woods, and flown to a hospital in Hazelton, he surrenders gratefully to the blandishments of the nurses: "Back to the world of women! Suddenly it was all women. It's not that there aren't any women in the bush; it's that they're so muffled up."

After recovering, Hoagland explores the region north of Telegraph Creek, including another town he wanted to visit for its possible historic significance—a "gold town" called Atlin. During the Gold Rush, Atlin had thrived. When Hoagland arrives he finds 160 old souls living just below the Yukon on a mixture of memories and alcohol: "Needless to say, I love this town. Atlin has the blue lake, the Swiss view and the swish-swash historical hurrah of the Rush, but it isn't niched into a worn river bluff like Telegraph Creek."

Hoagland's journal concludes with his departure from Atlin. The book's final chapter describes his few days in Victoria, before leaving for New York, where he hunts down and interviews one last aged adventurer, E. C. Lamarque, who led mapping expeditions during the 1930's in northern British Columbia. To Hoagland's astonishment, Lamarque gives him a ten-foot sheet of paper containing his original sketches for a map of a passage Lamarque loved the most of any place he had explored. Hoagland flies east the next day mumbling again and again to the wilderness, "I love thee. Love to thee. I love thee."

Analysis

In the journal's next to last entry, dated August 2, Hoagland describes a scene on the Tahltan River near Telegraph Creek. A landslide has filled the river, and salmon are blocked from their spawning grounds upriver. Though the river has blasted a passage through the slide, it is narrow and the water moves through like a fire hose, killing the trapped fish. Attempts by fisheries workers to carry the fish in barrels past the slide are ineffective as the salmon die in transport. Watching from the shore, Hoagland feels like crying as thirty thousand fish, many without noses because of the battering on rocks, slowly die.

The picture of large fish carried by instincts to unfulfilled obliteration is an apt concluding note to the journal. It serves to depict the condition Hoagland senses human beings face as the twentieth century draws to a close. His journal has held in focus a very small, rare generation of explorers who forsook the America of cities and highways to spend entire lifetimes in the wilderness. With all the wonder Hoagland feels for their lives, his journal, he realizes, is an elegy to a gone world, not an encouragement to future explorers. What is lost, Hoagland senses, is not a breed of men capable of living this life, but the open geography, wild and empty of settlements. Like the blocked salmon driven upriver, the rare man capable of living the all-consuming life of exploration is denied fulfillment simply because all the wilderness has been chartered.

The best man, Hoagland intimates again and again, the man most worthy of drawing breath, is the man who lives the Cro-Magnon dream. Leaving civilization is not enough. The ideal man leaves civilization to inhabit the wilderness permanently. An example of such a man, for Hoagland, is John Creyke, citizen of Telegraph

Creek whose trapping territory alone is twice as large as the state of Delaware. His life of moving on foot or behind a dogsled across a huge area has established his identity, a presence so admirable to Hoagland that he records it as heroic: "He's been south to the Nass . . . and north to the headwaters of the Yukon, and west to the International Boundary, and east into the Liard River system—one of the iron men, one of the princes." Men such as Creyke are the object of Hoagland's search. His self-appointed function as a journalist is to preserve their memory. Creyke, as it happens, can neither read nor write. Such "doers" stand above the common herd. Hoagland notes that most others have shot their dog teams, and the Indians are rarely practitioners of Creyke's passions either. After lauding Creyke in two pages of his journal, Hoagland abruptly switches to inhabitants of Telegraph Creek who are not living the dream. The Hudson's Bay clerk is a frail functionary. A preacher and a nurse exhibit inferior obsessions.

In his introduction to the journal, Hoagland writes, "The problem nowadays turns on how we shall decide to live." The person who sees as much as there is to see is to be honored. Hoagland's valuation of such people is unashamedly romantic. Jim Morgan's eyes are "extraordinary," and when they see something "they light on it. It's not that they're big; it's that they're wide." The wideness Hoagland attributes to Morgan's lifetime of seeing, not to innocence, just as the wolf's eyes have developed a slant for self-preservation. Hoagland takes pride in his own eyes, in the searching they have done to rescue these anonymous heroes. A happy moment for him is when he is assumed to be the grandson of Frank Swanell, another explorer, who is for Hoagland in the "whittled down" modern era "the equivalent of De Soto."

Hoagland also values the quality of the relationship such men have with the wildness they call home. A reader of the journal will sense that the qualities Hoagland finds to admire in the old men are projected in faith from his own sensibility, since, for the most part, the explorers and trappers are inarticulate about their feelings. The finely honed writer's awareness is everywhere transmuting the wilderness phenomena, as well as seeking it out. After seeing a cow butchered, Hoagland meditates and describes for three pages in an agony of empathy for the cow: "The pawing was redolent with woe and sharp frustration—all was dissolved." The author's capacity to be taken in by what he sees, to sustain interest, is no small part of what the journal preserves.

Notes from the Century Before is full of many expressions belonging distinctly to Hoagland. His ability to nail down what he experiences with sharp images is a phenomenon as wild and unpredictable as the wilderness itself. Seeing a group of wild horses, he writes, "They have the corrupt, gangster faces of mercenaries and that tight herding instinct." Impressionistic energy is released in describing each new face. Wriglesworth's wife's "hair is a frumpy dab, her mouth bends like a bobby pin." An Indian has "a chin like a goiter, a distorted cone of a forehead. He looked like a movie monster; he was stupendous." Leading off a paragraph with the assertion that a certain man is difficult to convey on paper, Hoagland proceeds to do what is so difficult, in two pages describing how the man chops wood, drinks from his hat, and appears blithe despite lips so chapped that he cannot smile. What strikes a reader is not so much the uncommonness of the man described, but the uncommonness of the powers exerted in the seeing.

Living on the edge of boundlessness as the settlers do, Hoagland asserts, is very healthy for the mind, both the practical, inventive side, which is daily challenged, and the imaginative side. "You're always looking for what's ahead," a Telegraph Creek trapper tells Hoagland, explaining the pleasure each day offers. Hoagland's work of searching out the people who live such lives is similarly pleasurable, as the journal logs character after character, view afer view. Hoagland's hometown, New York, cannot shape a person the way the fastnesses of British Columbia do; a writer is lucky to find people so alive, even if, as Hoagland repeatedly reminds himself, the possibility for such daily rapture died the century before. Hoagland also shows, without apology, that such pleasures are the domain of men alone. The typical wife looks like a nurse, stout and servantlike, but a man, such as Amel Phillipon of Eddontenajon, achieves serenity: "He's marked with the exuberance of the search."

Critical Context

Notes from the Century Before is written in a distinctly American literary context deriving from the nature writing of Henry David Thoreau. The writer in this context is typically an isolated figure developing in great detail the sense of an actual place. As Thoreau became synonymous with Walden Pond, Hoagland's two months of observation on the Stikine River by Telegraph Creek established a similar identity: "This is my Mississippi. I love it as I have never loved any piece of land or any other scene." The literary tradition from which this work springs includes the travel books of Herman Melville, Mark Twain's *Life on the Mississippi* (1883), Ernest Hemingway's *Green Hills of Africa* (1935), and the work of writers contemporaneous with Hoagland, such as John McPhee (*Coming into the Country*, 1977), Edward Abbey (*Desert Solitaire: A Season in the Wilderness*, 1968), and Peter Matthiessen (*Men's Lives: The Surfmen and Baymen of the South Fork*, 1986). While Thoreau could imagine a vastness of unexplored country to the west, recent nature writers are concerned with the end of the American frontier.

Placing Hoagland firmly in such a milieu is a generalization which familiarity with his work will both confirm and blur. He is an oddball, an original, a unique voice, and his searching out of other one-of-a-kinds shows that his subject is life itself, in whatever vital manifestations he finds it. Restlessness is the condition from which he writes, a restlessness which, after the book on British Columbia, carried him to the Sudan "because of its almost unequaled variety, and because it has seldom been written about." The book which resulted from that trip, *African Calliope* (1979), is filled with the same sort of voracious seeing found in *Notes from the Century Before*.

Though Hoagland writes frequently of unknown people and places, he has also written at length about New York, which he loves as much as the natural wilderness. His essay "Home Is Two Places" elucidates his contrary affections. Hoagland frequently mentions his stuttering as a painful handicap clearly relevant to his need to live in isolated places. As a teenager, he sought the company of animals, both in the woods and working as an animal tamer for a circus. His ability to describe animals is evident in *The Edward Hoagland Reader* (1979), which contains essays on turtles (several species roam the floor of his New York apartment), mountain lions, dogs, and bears.

The originality of Edward Hoagland is felt even more in his style than in his choice of offbeat subjects. Surprise is a regular experience for Hoagland readers. Horses can be described in human terms in one sentence, and as butterflies in the next. Occasionally his honesty seems excessive. A reader can be shocked by the frankness of his appraisals, such as some in *Notes from the Century Before*, which he puts down without seeming to realize that the person so described may read the description and be devastated. Yet Hoagland's honesty is what makes his writing so appealing, since his aesthetic seems to be based on the belief that something new will be found with each new person or place he sees. Vital signs—whether ferocity, mindlessness, or mediocrity—are what claim his attention and what his writing brings to readers curious enough to be attracted by the same things.

Sources for Further Study

Gardner, Harvey. Review in *The New York Times Book Review*. LXXIV (January 8, 1969), p. 16.

Grant, Annette. Review in *Newsweek*. LXXIII (January 2, 1969), p. 94.

Hoagland, Edward. "Slouching Toward Wadi Dhar: Edward Hoagland Motors Through the Mountains of Yemen and Lives to Tell About It," in *Interview Magazine*. XVIII (May, 1988), p. 96.

Updike, John. "Journeyers," in *Hugging the Shore: Essays and Criticism*, 1983.

Wolff, Geoffrey. Introduction to *The Edward Hoagland Reader*, 1979.

Bruce Wiebe

NOTES OF A NATIVE SON

Author: James Baldwin (1924-1987)
Type of work: Essays/cultural criticism
First published: 1955

Form and Content

Notes of a Native Son established James Baldwin as one of the most important black essayists in the United States. Yet, as he explained in the introduction added to the 1984 edition, Baldwin had not originally intended to produce a book of essays. His need to understand himself and his place in American culture led him to write a series of magazine articles grappling with the special problems facing black Americans. The success of his first novel, *Go Tell It on the Mountain* (1953), and of his first play, *The Amen Corner* (1954), had aroused interest in his work, but Baldwin found publishers reluctant to accept his second novel, *Giovanni's Room* (1956), because of its frank treatment of homosexuality. In order to earn enough money to go on writing fiction, Baldwin agreed to gather together nine of his previously published articles and write the title essay as well as a brief preface.

Although it originated as a series of separate magazine pieces, *Notes of a Native Son* is unified by recurring themes and by the arrangement of the essays. The book is divided into three parts and a preface, "Autobiographical Notes," which introduces Baldwin's determination to be "an honest man and a good writer." The preface's brief account of his childhood and emerging literary aspirations not only provides background for the essays that follow but also establishes the book's dominant underlying theme: a black artist's search for his identity. Baldwin explicitly recognizes that "the most difficult (and most rewarding) thing in my life has been the fact that I was born a Negro and was forced, therefore, to effect some kind of truce with this reality." He goes on to argue that the black writer must find a way to overcome hatred and fear in order to provide an honest assessment of both his own personal experience and his complex, often painful relationship to American society and Western culture.

The three essays in part 1 attack the inadequate or dishonest treatment of the black experience in Harriet Beecher Stowe's *Uncle Tom's Cabin: Or, Life Among the Lowly* (1852), Richard Wright's *Native Son* (1940), and the film *Carmen Jones* (1955). Baldwin's central point is that the traditions in which the black artist is expected to work provide false, sentimental, and dehumanizing portraits of black life. "Everybody's Protest Novel" begins with an analysis of Stowe's famous anti-slavery novel, comdemning the bad writing and sentimental self-righteousness, which, according to Baldwin, masks the author's underlying racism, the author's "secret and violent inhumanity." The essay goes on to assail the oversimplification of life inherent in novels of social protest, even those by black writers, such as Wright's *Native Son*.

Wright's novel receives more detailed and more critical attention in the second essay, "Many Thousands Gone." Baldwin insists that the United States has been afraid to face racial issues honestly and has therefore sought escape in the reductive nature of sociological analysis. This attempt to treat the black man as a social cipher instead of a complex human being is illustrated by Wright's portrayal of Bigger Thomas as a subhuman brute in *Native Son*. The novel's sensationalism and stereotyping express the nation's guilt and fear but prevent a deeper confrontation with the real problems. The desire to evade the realities of black life is also the dominant theme of "*Carmen Jones*: The Dark Is Light Enough," a brief critique of a film remake of the opera *Carmen* that used an all-black cast.

The second part of *Notes of a Native Son* consists of three essays exploring the grim realities of the black experience. In "The Harlem Ghetto," Baldwin touches on a wide range of subjects—including black leaders, the press, religion, and the relationship between Jews and blacks—but his underlying concern is with the sense of bitter desperation that he finds in almost every phase of black life. "Journey to Atlanta" explains how black Americans have been trained to distrust politicians and to despair of political change. "Notes of a Native Son," the longest essay in the book and the only one written specifically for it, marks a shift from detached analysis to the moving presentation of personal experience. By describing his reaction to his father's death and funeral, Baldwin comes to terms with his own heritage and provides his most powerful account of the corrosive effects of racism.

The third section contains four essays based on Baldwin's experiences in Paris and Switzerland. Although the ostensible subject is the black American in Europe, Baldwin's central concern in this section is with American culture, especially the complex racial heritage that distinguishes Americans from Europeans. In these essays, Europe forces the sensitive black traveler to confront his alientation from his past, his people, and himself.

The two final essays in this section rely more vividly on Baldwin's personal experience. "Equal in Paris" describes the eight days he spent in a French jail as the result of a misunderstanding involving a bed sheet a friend had taken from a hotel. Ironically, for the first time in his life, Baldwin found that he was free of racial prejudice, that he was being judged solely as an American and not as a black man. "Stranger in the Village" offers the clearest exposition of the lessons Baldwin learned from his travels in Europe. Staying in an isolated Swiss village whose inhabitants had never before seen a black man, Baldwin realized that he was irretrievably cut off from European culture and that he needed to accept and affirm his identity as a black American.

Analysis

Notes of a Native Son is best understood as the work of a young writer searching for an identity and struggling to reconcile the contradictory impulses that define his experiences as a black man, as an American, and as a writer. The essays are uneven, largely because Baldwin had not yet found his voice, and, as he himself admitted in his 1984 introduction, there was much that he was "trying to avoid." The three pieces describing his personal experiences—"Notes of a Native Son," "Equal in Paris," and "Stranger in the Village"—have justifiably received the most praise. They have a stylistic clarity, intellectual force, and emotional honesty that some of the earlier essays lack. To some extent, Baldwin resented the way he was expected to explain the black experience to a white audience, and his writing sometimes reflects an incompletely resolved struggle to free himself from the limits of conventional social analysis. For example, the essays in part 1 seem artificially detached and overly intellectualized, as though they were the products of repressed anger and confused emotion. Nevertheless, the essays in *Notes of a Native Son* constitute one of the most thoughtful explorations of the black experience in American literature.

Throughout his career, Baldwin insisted that writers needed literary traditions that enabled them to probe beneath the surface of life and take the full measure of any individual's joy or grief. Unfortunately, he found that the only traditions available to black writers falsified reality by reducing blacks to abstractions. Preferring psychological complexity to political propaganda, Baldwin clearly rejected the social protest novel as an inadequate literary form.

That in turn led to his harsh rejection of the work of Richard Wright in "Many Thousands Gone," which has provoked more controversy than any other essay in the book. It is important to realize that Wright was not only the most celebrated black American novelist but also a kind of literary father figure for Baldwin. Wright had encouraged Baldwin, had helped him to win fellowships, and was the inspiration behind Baldwin's move to Paris. Baldwin's attack on Wright put a permanent end to their friendship. As he later admitted in several interviews, Baldwin was engaged in a symbolic act of rebellion akin to the psychological process in which the growing child frees himself from his father's control in order to establish his own identity.

Many critics have complained that Baldwin's attack on Wright was unfair, and a few have even defended Stowe from the charges leveled in "Everybody's Protest Novel." The essays in part 1 are vulnerable as analyses of specific works, but they achieve more validity when regarded as the literary manifestos of a young writer attempting to pinpoint the pitfalls and obstacles blocking the roads of all aspiring black authors. Baldwin warns that a political agenda can undermine the artistic integrity of a literary work and deprive it of psychological complexity. In this respect, Baldwin's most important insight is that American culture insidiously finds means to avoid or distort the reality of race and racism. Even a work that appears to protest social injustice can be tainted by an underlying "theology" in which "black is the color of damnation."

Although he engages in social analysis, Baldwin expresses a clear distrust of all political and sociological solutions. Instead, his primary concern is with the black man's need to achieve some kind of personal moral triumph that enables him to accept a brutal reality without being brutalized or dehumanized by that act of acceptance. The essays in part 2 provide a compelling portrait of the frustrations of black life, but they are less specific and perhaps less helpful in defining the means by which blacks are to purge themselves of despair and hatred. Although he repeatedly asserts that the black man must never acquiesce to the forces that would debase and dehumanize him, Baldwin's apparent emphasis on symbolic vision rather than political change has irritated some readers. Furthermore, a few critics have also been annoyed by Baldwin's authoritative tone, which sometimes leads him into sweeping generalizations about American society and black life. Moreover, he sometimes uses an editorial "we" that appears to link him with white American society and separate him from the typical black man (the "he" of the essays).

Perhaps the greatest strength of the essays stems from Baldwin's awareness that the black experience usually provides an ironic mirror of the larger American experience. In his "Autobiographical Notes," Baldwin declares, "I love America more than any other country in the world, and, exactly for this reason, I insist on the right to criticize her perpetually." Many of his remarks are critical. He acutely delineates the failure of his country to live up to its own ideals of justice, freedom, and equality. Baldwin not only denounces all forms of overt racism but also shows a perceptive awareness of the more subtle means by which Americans deny the humanity of black people. In particular, he emphasizes a dangerous type of naïveté that leads Americans to evade reality, especially the reality of racism. If the essays about life abroad reveal that the black man must accept his American heritage, they also declare that his country's only hope lies in recognizing the humanity of black people.

In the essays about Europe in part 3, Baldwin repeatedly turns to the qualities that the black American traveler shares with his white countryman. Foremost in Baldwin's analysis of qualities uniting white and black Americans is blacks' deeply rooted sense of alienation from the past, which cuts them off from the monuments of European culture and makes them equally reluctant to explore the turmoil of American history. The distinguishing fact of American social history thus becomes the overwhelming burden of slavery and racism. The distinguishing fact of American cultural history thus becomes the overwhelming burden left by slavery and racism, but it is a burden that Baldwin requires blacks and whites to share.

Baldwin's essays are usually most effective when they rely heavily on his personal experience. It is in these essays that black life becomes a painful reality, not a mere abstraction. The reader shares Baldwin's anger when he is denied service in a New Jersey restaurant in "Notes of a Native Son" and his agonizing uncertainties as he faces the apparent cruelties of the French legal system in "Equal in Paris." "Stranger in the Village," probably the most widely praised of the essays in the book, offers a cogent analysis of the black man's intricate and difficult relationship to Western culture, but its effectiveness stems largely from Baldwin's skill at making the reader understand the wide range of uncomfortable feelings that emerge when Swiss children point at him and shout "*Neger!*"

At their best, Baldwin's essays reveal his courageous determination to face the world honestly, to acknowledge the bitter reality of black life without losing sight of hope or giving in to hatred, and to affirm his own identity as a black American artist who is true to his experience and his craft.

Critical Context

Notes of a Native Son was probably the single most impressive work of cultural criticism to emerge from the civil rights movement in the United States in the 1950's. It gained widespread attention and may have influenced the increasing sympathy for the plight of blacks among liberal Americans in the 1950's and 1960's. The black writers that followed Baldwin have had to acknowledge his presence and his ideas even when they disagreed with him. The controversy generated by Baldwin's attack on Wright and protest fiction set the course for much of the literary debate about black writing. More radical writers, such as Eldridge Cleaver, have often disapproved of Baldwin's treatment of political issues, insisting that black American writing had to be based on fervent political protest. Others, most notably Ralph Ellison, have shared Baldwin's belief in the primary need for an essentially symbolic affirmation of black humanity within American culture.

Baldwin went on to write many other essays and to produce several nonfiction books, the most important of which are *Nobody Knows My Name: More Notes of a Native Son* (1961), *The Fire Next Time* (1963), and *No Name in the Street* (1971). These works show an increasing dissatisfaction with the failure of Americans to recognize and correct the reality of racial injustice. By the time he wrote his new introduction for *Notes of a Native Son* in 1984, he complained of the years of unkept promises and saw little reason for optimism.

Baldwin also wrote novels, plays, and short stories, and during his life he was generally regarded as one of the two or three most important American black writers. The general critical assessment is that he was a writer of great talent who never quite fulfilled the promise shown in his early work. When he reviewed *Notes of a Native Son* for *The New York Times*, Langston Hughes praised it highly, stating that he preferred Baldwin's essays to his fiction. It seems possible that Baldwin's importance in American literary history may rest more on his skillful handling of the essay form in works such as *Notes of a Native Son* than on his novels.

Sources for Further Study

Eckman, Fern. *The Furious Passage of James Baldwin*, 1966.
Kinnamon, Keneth, ed. *James Baldwin: A Collection of Critical Essays*, 1974.
Moller, Karin. *The Theme of Identity in the Essays of James Baldwin: An Interpretation*, 1975.
O'Daniel, Therman B., ed. *James Baldwin: A Critical Evaluation*, 1977.
Stanley, Fred, and Nancy Stanley, eds. *Critical Essays on James Baldwin*, 1981.

Alfred Bendixen

NOTES TOWARDS THE DEFINITION OF CULTURE

Author: T. S. Eliot (1888-1965)
Type of work: Cultural criticism
First published: 1948

Form and Content

Thomas Stearns Eliot's Harvard University education, his alienation from his birthplace (St. Louis, Missouri), his repudiation of his family's Unitarianism, his reputation as a man of letters, his installation as a member of the Church of England, and his renunciation of American citizenship all contribute to the fabric of *Notes Towards the Definition of Culture.* Eliot, a consummate master and jealous guardian of the English language, preferred British English to American English; he preferred the older British elitist education to American egalitarian education; and he preferred England's colorful and orthodox Anglo-Catholic ritual to the bland patina of American religious observances. He preferred the hierarchy and brilliant pageantry of British monarchy to the leveling processes of American republicanism and a class system based upon birth and landed wealth to one based upon wealth acquired through purely capitalistic means. All these preferences, which England satsified for him at least adequately, find expression in his essay defining culture, published twenty-one years after he chose official expatriation, three years after the close of World War II and the ratification of the United Nations Charter, and the year of his receipt of the Nobel Prize in Literature.

Eliot began work on this essay in 1945, ostensibly in response to the establishment of the United Nations Educational, Scientific, and Cultural Organization (UNESCO), which called for the development and maintenance of international understanding and appreciation of the culture of the world's peoples. His determination to elucidate the meaning of "culture" gave impetus to an ambitious sociological project which resulted in not a lengthy dissertation but a tentative set of notes in the form of six essay-chapters, to which he added three radio lectures on "The Unity of European Culture" that he had presented to German listeners in 1946.

"Notes Towards," the first two words of the title, amount to an admission of the sketchy nature of the work. The six essays, however, preceded by an introduction and followed by the appended radio lectures, constitute a set of bold, if insufficiently supported, sociological assertions which, taken with the first lecture in Eliot's *After Strange Gods: A Primer of Modern Heresy* (1934) and the whole of his *The Idea of a Christian Society* (1939), reflect a credo that is both the basis of his literary criticism and the essential theme of his poetry and drama. Briefly, this credo is as follows: Religion is the matrix of culture; the Christian religion is the formative factor of European, or Western, culture; and the modern West, in its retreat from strict adherence to the Christian faith, is undergoing a cultural deterioration that appears to be without promise or possibility of arrest.

In his cultural criticism, Eliot disarmingly identifies himself as a poet and a critic of poetry who is directing his aesthetic sensibility to subjects external to his firm competence so as to lend to those subjects the perspective of a man of letters and to accommodate with his observations those readers who think enough of his poetry and criticism of poetry to want the benefit of his critical views in other areas. The introduction established Eliot's notion of the inseparability of religion and culture, the dependence of culture upon the persistence of social classes, and the impossibility of any calculated invention of culture. In chapter 1, he differentiates the cultural development of an individual, of a group or class, and of a whole society; he shows that the three types of culture must be cohesive; and he posits that culture and religion are not two separate things bound by a relationship or identifiable one as the other but different aspects of the same thing and that the culture of a people is an incarnation of its religion. Describing culture as that which makes life worth living, he concludes that "any religion, while it lasts, and on its own level, gives an apparent meaning to life, provides the framework for a culture, and protects the mass of humanity from boredom and despair." The subsequent chapters elaborate upon the class and the elite, unity and diversity with respect first to region and then to sect and cult, culture and politics, and culture and education.

Eliot's sense of class is that "higher types exhibit more marked differentiation of function amongst their members than lower types," and he identifies the elites as the differentiated groups of higher types concerned respectively with art, science, philosophy, and action. The similarity to the class system in Plato's *Politeia* (388-368 B.C.; *Republic*) becomes more noticeable as Eliot states the aim of his doctrine of elites: "All positions in society should be occupied by those who are best fitted to exercise the functions of the positions." In this context he conceives of culture as "the creation of the society as a whole: being . . . that which makes it a society." Eliot's moderation lies in his calling for class barriers that are not rigid, so as occasionally to permit those without the advantages of birth to rise in status.

In his outline, culture should be fluid and constant; each area of a region should participate in the regional culture and should both harmonize with and enrich the cultures of neighboring areas. As with areas subsumed to regions, so should it be with sects and cults subsumed to the regional religion. Eliot emphasizes that "the formation of a religion is also the formation of a culture," and the culture of the West, as a region, is accordingly derived from the formation of the Christian religion.

Eliot's concluding chapters caution against culture-consciousness, which tends to subordinate culture to politics and is conducive to political totalitarianism, and against equal opportunity in education, which contributes to the elimination of the intellectual elite and to the disintegration of class.

Eliot's theory of the dangers of equal educational opportunity may have had some validation. In the late 1960's and early 1970's, lowered standards and curricula fashioned in accordance with students' demands, in both England and the United States, resulted in a lesser quality of education to which there was ultimately a "back to the basics" reaction. The countercultural movement responsible for this lessening proved to be less the countering of a youth culture against that of an establishment than a veritable contraculture, or anticulture; comcomitant with it was another anticultural effect of which Eliot proved to be prophetic, the breakdown of the family: "The most important channel of transmission of culture remains the family: and when the family fails to play its part, we must expect our culture to deteriorate."

The appendix on the unity of European culture may be taken as an extension of the chapter "Unity and Diversity: The Region," the region being Europe with its constituent nations. Eliot's perspective remains that of the poet and critic of poetry. His focus is the interdependent literary traditions of the European nations. His definition of culture in this section is anthropological: "the way of life of a particular people living together in one place." The place is Europe, and the "dominant force in creating a common culture between peoples each of which has its distinct culture, is religion," the religion again being Christianity. Eliot mentions here and there the formative contributions to Western culture made by the Jewish, Greek, and Roman civilizations but subordinates these contributions to their amalgamation by the Christian tradition.

Analysis

In his preface to *For Lancelot Andrewes* (1928) Eliot styled himself a classicist, royalist, and Anglo-Catholic. His conservative penchant for literary tradition, monarchist politics, and ritualistic religion gives tone and direction to *Notes Towards the Definition of Culture*. It may seem odd that Eliot, whose impetus toward modernism in poetry was great, should identify himself as a classicist; he did not, however, oppose classicism to Romanticism or modernism but upheld the literature of the past as the tradition from which no poet can exclude his work. His royalism entailed the favoring of a class system determined by birth and wealth and limited to upper and lower, unbothered by middle. His religious preference culminated in his exaltation of Christianity as the true cultural determinant of Western civilization.

Consistent in his beliefs and preferences, although not always strictly logical in his presentation of them, he emerges in his attitude as part of a civilizational rearguard. This attitude underscores the pessimism of his poetry, which, although aggressively vanguardist in structure, idiom, and rhythm, is defensively expository of what he takes to be a true culture that has been rendered effete and moribund by the decline of Christianity.

In "The Love Song of J. Alfred Prufrock," Eliot personifies waning Western culture as an anxiety-ridden, stultifyingly middle-class, and middle-aged man who is no longer subjectively conversant with great art and literature and who cannot face the reality toward which his introspection is leading him. The title of Eliot's most famous poem, *The Waste Land* (1922), refers to the modern Western world as bereft of religion and consequently of culture: Fragments of the education that formerly reflected the culture are gathered together like the fragments of a broken vase whose reassemblage requires an adhesive that only religion can provide; the need for religion is likened to thirst, and the water to quench the thirst is to be found only in India, where a religion still satisfactorily sustains a culture.

In several poems Eliot also personifies the grossly sensual residue of an irreligious society as a coarse, apelike lecher named Sweeney. In *The Waste Land*, illicit sex, between a typist and a "young man carbuncular," is shown as boring and, in the absence of Christian standards of morality, an act of animal instinct and bleak impunity. Sweeney is the embodiment of the drive to perform this act.

Eliot claims in *The Idea of a Christian Society* that education in a Christian society must be religious "in the sense that its aims will be directed by a Christian philosophy of life"; he envisages his ideal Christian society as limited to England. In *Notes Towards the Definition of Culture*, he expands his horizons to include the whole of Western civilization, which, as a product of the Christian philosophy of life, must refurbish itself as a Christian society if it is to retain its culture. The tone of the latter essay, while less mockingly ironic than that of his earlier poetry, carries the same resignation and world-weariness. The didacticism is positive and not without intimations of hope, but the essay says overall that this is the way it could be and should be but will not be because the departures from the Christian way of life are too pronounced.

Eliot's argument can win little approval from non-Christian members of Western society or from those of democratically liberal persuasion. His conservatism is such that he actually condemns any variations from the pre-Renaissance Christian society of Europe. He scorns Humanism and all projected increments to the secular way of life. The anti-Semitic bias in his earlier poetry is not explicit in the essay on culture but can be inferred in it from the exclusivity with which he invests his discussion of the Christian society. His predilection for Fascism, with its organization and ordered economy, is hardly concealed, although he does not condone political totalitarianism. In effect, however, religious totalitarianism is what he advocates.

The religious totalitarianism called for in *Notes Towards the Definition of Culture* is adumbrated in *After Strange Gods*, Eliot's Page-Barbour lectures delivered at the University of Virginia in 1933. In the first of the three lectures his denunciation of the Civil War as "the greatest disaster in the whole of American history" and as destructive of a "native culture" is fully implicit with the support of the slave system that was part of the native culture. His Fascist leaning and his anti-Jewish bias are explicit in this passage from the same lecture:

> Population should be homogeneous; where two or more cultures exist in the same place they are likely either to be fiercely self-conscious or both to become adulterate. What is still more important is unity of religious background; and reasons of race and religion combine to make any large number of free-thinking Jews undesirable. . . . And a spirit of excessive tolerance is to be deprecated.

The passage is much quoted but chiefly by Eliot's opponents, of whom there were not many in his lifetime. That Eliot was not broadly attacked for his views owes largely to the almost universal respect and prestige accorded him by the academic world in the United States, England, and Germany. There was a trickle of dissent from his views in England. Robert Graves, in *The Common Asphodel* (1949), found unpalatable the anti-Jewish prejudice in Eliot's poem "Burbank with a Baedeker: Bleistein with a Cigar." L. A. Cormican, in "Mr. Eliot and Social Biology," remarks that Eliot's "orderly description of culture on p. 120 [of *Notes Towards the Definition of Culture*] is phrased throughout in such a way as to fit either Nazism or Stalinism." Nevertheless, these and other articulations of disapproval are significantly sparse. Eliot's reputation as a poet and literary critic apparently precluded concerted, discriminating challenge to his social and political prejudices, even though such prejudices were manifest in his poetry and drama.

The most serious American challenge to Eliot's views and to the questionable logic with which he presents those views was Russell Hope Robbins' *The T. S. Eliot Myth* (1951), a cool and cogent appraisal of Eliot's anti-humanism that is not deterred by the Chinese wall of Eliot's reputation. Robbins' book found its way into very few selected bibliographies of studies of Eliot; a noteworthy exception is Leonard Unger's *T. S. Eliot: Moments and Patterns* (1966). It is ignored by Allen Austin in *T. S. Eliot: The Literary and Social Criticism* (1971), although Austin, like Robbins, finds the authoritarian and stratified society envisaged by Eliot to be repressive. Robbins, however, writes as an adversary of Eliot's views, while Austin writes merely as an expositor of them. Nevertheless, Austin's summary of *Notes Towards the Definition of Culture* is chilling:

> Culture cannot exist without religion and inequality (in wealth and education). Culture is most likely to flourish in a class society based on tradition. The elite, although admitting those of exceptional talent to its ranks, should be determined by birth.

Eliot insists in his essay on culture that "Christendom should be one." He maintains that there should be a "corrective force in the direction of uniformity of belief and practice" if culture is not to suffer in its constituent elements. In *The Idea of a Christian Society*, Eliot assumes that "totalitarianism can retain the terms 'freedom' and 'democracy' and give them its own meanings: and its right to them is not so easily disproved as minds inflamed by passion suppose." For Eliot, then, monolithic unity upheld by authoritarian control is the only stabilizing force of culture; in this, as in other of his dicta, he speaks dogmatically and without argumentative logic. Also in that essay, he writes that "the only possibility of control and balance is a religious control and balance; that the only hopeful course for a society which would thrive and continue its creative activity in the arts of civilization is to become Christian." *The Idea of a Christian Society* was completed at the beginning of World War II; *Notes Towards the Definition of Culture*, its thematic companion piece, was published after the end of World War II. In both essays Eliot finds the Western democracies to be as prone to cultural defect as the Fascist and Stalinist regimes, if not more so.

In keeping with his negative prediction, Eliot does not look ahead to his ideal of the Christian totalitarian state; he looks back to it—for it did exist, in Europe, from the twelfth through the fifteenth centuries, from the time of Saint Thomas à Becket, martyred in 1170, through the time of the Grand Inquisitor Tomás de Torquemada, who died in 1498. Eliot's predilection is clearly for this age of faith, which fostered the Gothic cathedral, the mendicant orders, Scholasticism, Saint Thomas Aquinas, Dante, and those Christian corrective forces known as the Crusades and the Inquisition. As he writes in "The Dry Salvages," the third of his *Four Quartets* (1943), "the way forward is the way back."

Critical Context

Eliot's career as a poet extends from the publication of "The Love Song of J. Alfred Prufrock" in 1915 through the publication of his theological poems, *Four Quartets*. His career as a literary critic continued from 1917 until his death, but all of his most influential essays had been published before 1937. His five plays appeared during the years 1932 to 1958. In the life of this poet, literary and social critic, and dramatist, the 1930's, the decade of Eliot's forties, embrace a shift in creative activity away from poetry and literary essays toward drama. They also embrace the beginning of a preoccupation with social and cultural criticism, namely, the publication in 1934 of *After Strange Gods*, which is a combination of literary criticism and cultural commentary.

The sociological preoccupation was resumed at the beginning of the next decade with *The Idea of a Christian Society* and tapered off in 1948 with *Notes Towards the Definition of Culture*. The triad amounts to an interjection of social and cultural criticism into the late midcareer of the poet, literary critic, and playwright. That it was a less than felicitous interjection was generally recognized. Eliot's staunchest admirers conceded that these works were, to put it kindly, not Eliot's best. In them the precision and insight, the perfection of phrase, and the pointed support of general observation by impeccably selected specific examples—the constant characteristics of his essays in literary criticism—give way to editorial rhetoric, unsupported generalities, and disclaimers which do more to try the patience of than effectively to disarm the reader. They are praised only by those who believed that Eliot was infallible or by those who considered that whatever Eliot wrote was worth reading. The latter may have gone astray in their praise, but they were not aberrant in their consideration. The chief value of a work such as *Notes Towards the Definition of Culture*, at least for students of literature and literary history, lies in the explicitness with which Eliot gives voice to his most cherished convictions.

Sources for Further Study

Ackroyd, Peter. *T. S. Eliot: A Life*, 1984.
Austin, Allen. *T. S. Eliot: The Literary and Social Criticism*, 1971.
Bantock, G. H. *T. S. Eliot and Education*, 1970.
Headings, Philip R. *T. S. Eliot*, 1964.
Kojecky, Roger. *T. S. Eliot's Social Criticism*, 1971.

Ricks, Beatrice. *T. S. Eliot: A Bibliography of Secondary Works*, 1980.
Robbins, Russell Hope. *The T. S. Eliot Myth*, 1951.
Spender, Stephen. *T. S. Eliot*, 1975.

Roy Arthur Swanson

NOW AND THEN

Author: Frederick Buechner (1926-   )
Type of work: Memoir
Time of work: The 1950's to the 1980's
Locale: New York, New Hampshire, and Vermont
First published: 1983

> *Principal personages:*
> FREDERICK BUECHNER, a novelist and a writer of popular theology
> PAUL TILLICH,
> REINHOLD NIEBUHR,
> MARTIN BUBER, and
> JAMES MUILENBURG, theologians who helped shape his worldview

Form and Content

By age twenty-six, Frederick Buechner had become widely known as the precociously successful writer of two critically acclaimed novels, *A Long's Day's Dying* (1950) and *The Season's Difference* (1952). Bursting on the literary scene as "a new Henry James," Buechner, with his mandarin, contemplative narrative style, seemed to capture the essence of angst-ridden and God-forsaken America of the 1950's. Arguably, Buechner seemed destined to take his place among those despairing voices within American fiction—William Styron, Norman Mailer, Truman Capote—who looked bleakly heavenward but discovered only an empty sky bereft of divine comfort or direction. Buechner's conversion to Christianity and his subsequent seminary education altered his course irrevocably, however, and *Now and Then*, Buechner's second memoir, depicts a novelist reborn not only in spirit but also in prose style and thematic concern. The characters and predicaments of Buechner's postseminary fiction clearly reflect a new humanness and humor uncharacteristic of the somber, tortured protagonists of his earliest novels, and this second memoir chronicles the force behind this dramatic change.

Now and Then thus completes the autobiographical reflections Buechner began in *The Sacred Journey* (1982). *The Sacred Journey* details key events of Buechner's childhood and adolescence—primarily the traumatic experience of his father's suicide—and recalls the formative influences he encountered during his undergraduate years at Princeton University. This first memoir concludes with Buechner's recounting of the composition and unexpected critical acclaim of his first two novels and his eventual conversion to Christianity. *Now and Then* begins with his days as a student at Union Theological Seminary in New York City and moves on to an account of Buechner's unlikely development of three different vocations after his graduation and ordination: a chaplain and teacher in a private academy for boys, a religious novelist, and a popular theologian. Along the way, Buechner's subtext concerns the profound changes that took place in his thinking after his conversion to Christianity and how he adjusted to these shifting currents of his life within his calling as a writer.

Rhetorically, *Now and Then*, like *The Sacred Journey*, is quite terse; its scant 109 pages are divided into three chapters, each titled for one of the Buechner family's residences: New York, Exeter (New Hampshire), and Vermont. At each stop Buechner gives the reader tantalizingly brief glimpses into people, places, and events that hold meaning for him—as if one were looking out of a passenger train accompanied by the shy, modest Buechner as a tour guide. To be sure, these glimpses are poignant, well chosen, and ably reconstructed by the mature Buechner. Yet he uses the absolute minimum of verbiage to capture these scenes, occasionally leaving even the most sympathetic reader wanting more expansive treatment. Perhaps Buechner follows too well his own advice for writing that he shares with readers toward the end of the book: "If you have to choose between words that mean more than what you have experienced and words that mean less, choose the ones that mean less because that way you leave room for your hearers to move around in and for yourself to move around in too." As in any Buechner text, more important than the ostensibly important personages and conversations is the hidden meaning—the "alphabet of grace" operating within the moments recalled—that bespeaks the presence of the Divine in every human life.

Both the serendipity and the inevitability of Buechner's Christian conversion lurk behind every anecdote or character sketch in *Now and Then*. Nevertheless, in form *Now and Then* represents spiritual autobiography in almost its purest form in that it concentrates almost entirely on the believer's gradual, agonizing, and ambiguous groping toward God—the mundane pieces of daily life that when woven together form a tapestry of faith and hope. Taken as autobiography, this brief volume and its predecessor comprise a scant 210 pages, compelling the reader to place more interpretive weight on each line than would be expected or appropriate for a more expansive work. The details with which Buechner chooses to deal are those that contribute directly to an explanation of his spiritual journey and its implications for his life, work, and family life. The resulting focus does not yield the typical fare of much twentieth century biography—that characterized by obsessive concern for gossip, shockingly private revelation, or the lampooning of prominent or famous individuals.

Analysis

Despite the fact that Buechner has met, studied with, and received accolades from some of the more celebrated literati and theologians of the twentieth century, he would prefer to talk about an elderly lady in Vermont with whom he played the board game Aggravation or how empty he felt the day his daughters left for boarding school. These less public and less apparently important events and relationships speak more eloquently to Buechner of what a relationship with God demands than the supposedly significant encounters he has had with celebrities and scholars. That fact is the reigning theme of his memoir and, indeed, of each of his postseminary volumes, both fiction and nonfiction.

The renowned (and controversial) theologian Paul Tillich, one of Buechner's professors at Union, does emerge as one of the few more celebrated personalities given extensive coverage in *Now and Then*. It is Tillich's volume *The New Being* (1955) that provides Buechner with his epigraph and title for the memoir: "We want only to show you something we have seen and to tell you something we have heard. . . . that here and there in the world and now and then in ourselves is a New Creation." The opening part of Tillich's statement echoes the words of Saint John in the New Testament, explaining the impulse of the early Christians to chronicle the life of Christ: Those whose lives were touched by Christ, John explains, simply must report what they have seen with their own eyes. Yet the quotation also reflects the basic motivation behind all biographical writing: To reveal the truth of a human life one must uncover the basic narrative that underpins it. The second half of the statement is thematically an apt capsuling of Buechner's own view of narrative, which is reflected in his fiction to be sure but also in his theological texts and, certainly, his autobiographical writing. For Buechner, all life is the unfolding of a story, a narrative written, in essence, by God in history. It is "now and then," "here and there," in the ordinary footage and slippage of life, that one's purpose and calling are discovered. The role of those narrators perceptive enough to fathom this truth is to listen carefully to their own lives, recovering the inner agenda or pattern of events that unlocks the meaning of their days.

When he or she is successful, Buechner suggests, the novelist or theologian lays bare not only the meaning of specific events but also the divine presence behind them. *Now and Then* admirably exemplifies that viewpoint. The most compelling novelist or memoirist is thus not one whose own characters or personal life can be called exemplary in some unique way but rather one who is able to evoke in readers a sense of wonder at the way their own lives have unfolded. The search for self is as rewarding as its discovery.

Tillich—along with his colleagues Reinhold Niebuhr, Martin Buber, and James Muilenburg, famous theologians one and all—indeed do appear in *Now and Then* but no more and no less as literary characters might in a Buechner novel. Rather than fully developed persons, they tend to "stand for" a truth, motive, or experience that helps shape Buechner's own response to life. Their presence in this work is not to satisfy the reader looking for gossip about famous people but to underscore the importance of the overlooked detail, the seemingly trivial fact that can reveal what is truly significant in any person's life.

Oddly enough, the film actors, literary characters, and newsmakers whose images filled the mind of the young adult Buechner count for as much as the real celebrities he encountered; Buechner wonders out loud why the impact of such images in the ordinary person's life is generally ignored. According to Buechner's interpretation, God usually works "behind the scenes" in history and almost never explicitly; the exception is Christ's crucifixion and resurrection. Buechner considers fictional narrative and autobiography the most appropriate media for conveying this theological truth. It is not the logician's syllogism but the narrative of the graceful storyteller that sheds light on God's hidden workings.

The reader finds in *Now and Then* some characteristic Buechnerian styles and themes. One finds, for example, that Buechner frequently quotes his previous fiction and theological works to underscore a point about his own life. In less skillful hands, this technique might seem to betray both rank egotism and the worst sort of pedantry. Since Buechner regards the characters peopling his works as independent voices who speak both to and against him at times, however, his citations seem more like conversations with friendly adversaries than pretentious self-promotion.

Buechner revives the theme that God writes history with an "alphabet of grace," thus redeeming and imbuing language itself with a special power to transform lives:

> Words are put together out of letters, all twenty-six of them. So the alphabet is your instrument. . . . By means of vowels and consonants, you must put together the best words you can—words that, if possible, not only mean something but evoke something, call something forth from the person you address with your words. Christ himself both spoke such a word and was such a word.

With these words Buechner well describes his own narrative power. Like his most fully realized characters—Leo Bebb, the rogue preacher of *The Book of Bebb* (1979), and Godric (in *Godric*, 1980), the wizened twelfth century holy man whom Buechner found tucked away in a dictionary of saints—he refuses to explain away the tensions of faith or paint a simplistic picture of the spiritual dimensions of life that lie just beyond the horizon of man's consciousness. All the while, though, he is convinced that when a human life is examined sensitively and honestly it emerges as a series of small but real triumphs over great odds and that even the most crushing defeats can be overcome by the irresistible grace of God that operates with or without man's assistance. *Now and Then* concludes with a quotation from *Godric* that epitomizes this essential Buechnerian optimism: "'What's lost is nothing to what's found,' as Godric says, 'and all the death that ever was, set next to life, would scarcely fill a cup.'"

Critical Context

The primary audience for Buechner's work comprises two groups of readers: those for whom his Christian experience is both instructive and illuminating of their own faith and those who—with little regard for his religious conviction—admire his effortless prose and skillful depiction of the tensions and anxieties of modern life. Buechner has often said that his books are too religious for secular readers and too secular for religious readers. The truth is that throughout the winding path of his literary career, Buechner has had a consistently enthusiastic, though admittedly modest, readership among both kinds of readers.

Now and Then, though, clearly does represent a full circle in the canon of works he has created. Buechner once told a reviewer that his writing was a kind of ministry—a substitute pulpit for one ordained as a Presbyterian minister but without a congregation to shepherd. As noted already, he has argued in various works that storytelling reveals the form of human life, a pattern of events that upon investigation would divulge a divine presence and care. In his fiction, he has created credible living characters whose stories and themes exemplify this narrative vision. In *The Sacred Journey* and *Now and Then*, Buechner has exploited these narrative gifts in illuminating how his own life has unfolded. Buechner emerges in *Now and Then* as a compelling character himself; the bemused writer stands beside his own life as if producing a third-person narrative, chronicling the personalities, events, and circumstances that have given him meaning.

A rather retiring, tantalizingly modest, and unprepossessing personality emerges from this memoir. He who has had famous teachers and won prestigious literary awards shrinks from the public spotlight to allow his life—or, rather, the sometimes mundane details of his life—to speak for itself. Buechner's conviction that life is a story to be both celebrated and endured, but always a story to be told, is never more evident than in *Now and Then*. No one who has read even a small portion of Buechner's work can come away from it knowing less of himself. *Now and Then* calls attention not to Buechner as a celebrity or novelty but, paradoxically, as a notably ordinary man whose story is really no more remarkable than the reader's might be. The difference is that Buechner has taken the time to listen to the alphabet of his days. His reader may be blessed in learning how to do the same.

Sources for Further Study
Davies, Hélène. *Laughter in a Genevan Gown: The Words of Frederick Buechner*, 1985.
Gibble, Kenneth. "Listening to My Life: An Interview with Frederick Buechner," in *The Christian Century*. C (November 16, 1983), pp. 1042-1044.
McCoy, Marjorie Casebier. *Frederick Buechner*, 1988.
_____. Review in *The Christian Century*. C (March 23-30, 1983), p. 280.
Nelson, Rudolph. " 'The Doors of Perception': Mystical Experience in Buechner's Fiction," in *Southwest Review*. LXVIII (Summer, 1983), pp. 266-275.

Bruce L. Edwards

THE OAK AND THE CALF
Sketches of Literary Life in the Soviet Union

Author: Aleksandr Solzhenitsyn (1918-   )
Type of work: Memoir
Time of work: 1967-1974
Locale: The Soviet Union
First published: Bodalsia telenok s dubom: Ocherki literaturnoi zhizni, 1975
  (English translation, 1980)

Principal personage:
ALEKSANDR SOLZHENITSYN, a writer

Form and Content

For a brief period in the 1960's, Aleksandr Solzhenitsyn was favorably viewed by the Soviet regime, because *Odin den Ivana Denisovicha* (1962; *One Day in the Life of Ivan Denisovich,* 1963) was one of Nikita Khrushchev's weapons in the de-Stalinization campaign. Described by *Izvestia* as a "true helper of the Party," Solzhenitsyn came close to winning the Lenin Prize in literature in 1964.

With Khrushchev's fall in 1964, however, the de-Stalinization process was cut short. Conflict between the Soviet regime and Solzhenitsyn was inevitable, given the great disparity between their values. One of Solzhenitsyn's central beliefs is that Marxism is an "un-Russian wind from the West"; hence, the Communist regime is in every way inimical to the Russian people. Moreover, Solzhenitsyn is a fervent Christian, which places him in head-on conflict with the country's leaders. Given Solzhenitsyn's determination to speak his piece, to stand up for what he considered morally right, regardless of consequences, there was bound to be open war between author and state. In Joseph Stalin's time, the state would have silenced the author at once. By the 1960's, however, the regime, while certainly not respecting the rule of law as Westerners know it, no longer behaved like the totalitarian state of Stalin's era. The author's fame at home and abroad would have made the reincarceration of Solzhenitsyn a political embarrassment for the Soviet government. In short, the redoubtable Solzhenitsyn was able for several years to stand up defiantly to the dreaded Komitet Gosudarstvennoi Bezopasnosti (KGB), before his involuntary exile in 1974.

The Oak and the Calf is Solzhenitsyn's account of his long battle with the Soviet regime. (The title comes from the Russian proverb about the calf butting the oak—similar to the English-language "knocking your head against a stone wall"—with the calf of the book, Solzhenitsyn, having rather more success than the original calf of the proverb.) Written with a powerful eloquence, the book recounts the travails of an artist struggling to create his works in the face of difficulties quite unimaginable to a citizen of a free country. Minions of the Communist Party, memorably portrayed as ignorant dullards, try to halt Solzhenitsyn's work. Yet the words flow out to the world, both in the author's native country through the medium of *samizdat* (an acronym meaning "Self-Publishing Company," a takeoff on *Gosizdat*, or State Publishing Company, the official publishing house of the regime) and abroad, through the smuggling of Solzhenitsyn's works over the borders. Most of the book is devoted to the war between the author and his would-be masters, but there are some personal asides and some memorable portraits of important literary figures, especially of Aleksandr T. Tvardovsky, the editor of *Novy mir*.

The book is divided into five parts. The first recounts the story of the acceptance and publication of *One Day in the Life of Ivan Denisovich*, of the efforts to publish other works, and of the gradual estrangement of Solzhenitsyn and the Soviet regime. The next four parts are called "supplements" by Solzhenitsyn; they are divided chronologically (from 1967 to 1974) and cover the awarding of the Nobel Prize to Solzhenitsyn and the Soviet state's steadily growing harassment of the author, culminating in the revocation of his citizenship and his expulsion from the Soviet Union in 1974. The last part of the book is an appendix of interesting and valuable primary source material, illustrating the themes of the book.

Analysis

Since the book is a memoir, it provides many insights into Solzhenitsyn's mind, personality, and character. Nevertheless, he does not discuss in any systematic way his own creations; he does not tell his readers about the authors who have influenced him, nor does he discuss his style, his methods of work, or artistic problems that he has had to solve. Literary scholars seeking aid for their research into Solzhenitsyn's oeuvre will perhaps find this book disappointing. Moreover, except for a few comments deprecating the West as a place with nothing to teach Russia (it is quite the other way round—sooner or later it is Russia that will do the teaching, a sentiment that shows Solzhenitsyn to be firmly in the mainstream of nineteenth century Slavophilism), there is no systematic exposition of Solzhenitsyn's political views. One would have to go to his other writings to study what have been termed his "authoritarian-nationalistic" ideas.

A reader will quickly learn, however, that there is no doubt in Solzhenitsyn's mind as to his role in the world: He was sent by God to battle the forces of evil. For example, he describes his struggle with cancer and how the doctors told him that he had only three weeks to live—this after having only recently emerged from his long imprisonment in Stalin's labor camps. While in the camps he had composed and committed to memory many thousands of lines. So that future generations of Russians would know what had happened to their country under the Communists, he wanted to get these lines onto paper. Yet how could he do it in three weeks? Clearly he did not die—which he describes as a "divine miracle." As a leading authority comments, it is difficult in the mid-twentieth century, in this age of unbelief, to portray oneself convincingly to one's fellowman as God's sword. Nevertheless, no one can doubt that Solzhenitsyn is utterly sincere in his belief in his own mission. Given the enormity of the obstacles he has overcome—the years as a slave laborer, serious disease, and endless harassment from the Soviet system—one can understand his dedication to his divine mission.

In addition to being criticized for his perhaps exaggerated sense of the importance of his role in human affairs, Solzhenitsyn has been taken to task for his portrayal of many of his fellow Russians. Large parts of the book are devoted to descriptions of Tvardovsky, long the editor of *Novy mir*, a "liberal" journal in the Soviet literary scene. It was Tvardovsky who made possible Solzhenitsyn's literary career by persuading Khrushchev to allow *Novy mir* to publish *One Day in the Life of Ivan Denisovich*. Solzhenitsyn has much that is laudatory to say about Tvardovsky, but he also portrays his erstwhile mentor as an alcoholic, a tyrant over his staff, and a bureaucrat who enjoyed and insisted upon the privileges of Soviet officialdom. His treatment of Tvardovsky has evoked replies from Tvardovsky's daughter and other figures in a position to know that Solzhenitsyn's account was perhaps less than fair. Similarly, Solzhenitsyn gives a condescending portrait of Andrey Sakharov, a central figure for a quarter of a century in the Russian dissident movement. He also portrays his first wife in a most unchivalrous fashion. Other former friends who came to disagree with Solzhenitsyn are described as mendacious figures.

Indeed, the book has stimulated a spate of counterblasts from people, both in the Soviet Union and abroad, who believe themselves badly used by the great writer. There can be little doubt that Solzhenitsyn belongs to the type of self-righteous prophet who can brook no disagreement, who sees an honest difference of opinion as an immoral act. One must submit, or face the withering fire of Solzhenitsyn's great satirical powers. Consequently, those parts of the memoir dealing with people who have parted company with Solzhenitsyn—or have been cast aside by him—must be read with caution.

The memoir is without question of great value in its portrayal of the chicaneries of Soviet officialdom and of its ultimately unsuccessful battle to halt Solzhenitsyn's exposure of its criminality. Solzhenitsyn has indeed attained his life's aim: In his books published openly in the West and circulated secretly but widely in his own country, he has revealed for future generations the utter failure of the Communist regime to create a healthy society, one that would, as Karl Marx and Vladimir Ilich Lenin expected, bring general happiness to mankind. Instead, what has been created is a society replete with hypocrisy because of the vast gap between goals and reality. Instead of enjoying an economy of abundance, the Soviet people live in poverty. Instead of a society of equals, a "New Class" has come into being, composed of Party members, bureaucrats, industrial leaders, and other privileged groups, who have access to special stores, medical care, and other amenities of life unknown to ordinary Soviet citizens. Instead of the unleashing of human powers in the socialist era that was predicted by Marx, creative people in Soviet society live under the rule of philistines—except for those few like Solzhenitsyn, who by a combination of his own genius and some good luck managed to hold his own against officialdom for two decades, until his expulsion from the country.

All these shortcomings are part of the gigantic structure of immorality erected by Soviet leaders since 1917, in Solzhenitsyn's worldview. To Solzhenitsyn, it is no accident that the regime is immoral, because its central premise is the denial of the existence of God. In Solzhenitsyn's mind, it is part of the genius of the Russian people to have had Christianity at its core through the centuries. Thus, any regime that turns its back on Christianity has turned its back on its own people. Small wonder that a titanic struggle erupted between regime and author.

Solzhenitsyn describes the struggle in matchless prose, both in Russian and in English, for the book was put into English by an excellent translator, Harry Willetts. Future generations, upon reading *The Oak and the Calf*, will find risible the Soviet regime's claims to be "mankind's hope" and "the beacon of the toilers of the world." The timeserving officials are excoriated in unforgettable terms. One hapless nonentity, whose name and writings are totally forgettable, is quoted by Solzhenitsyn as complaining in a supercilious way that Solzhenitsyn sees "only the dark side" while he (the complainer) in his writing has always written "only about joyful things." Such is the "Socialist Realism" which the Party requires and which has put Russian literature in fetters. The picture of Soviet officialdom that emerges from Solzhenitsyn's pages is that of men with banal minds who prefer their creature comforts to truth and who will be scorned by Russians of a future age.

The reader marvels at the depths to which Solzhenitsyn's tormentors descended. For a long period, they mounted a systematic campaign of slander, with statements that Solzhenitsyn "deserved" his labor-camp sentence by having become a "traitor." It was even stated that he had worked for the Gestapo. (Solzhenitsyn in fact was sentenced to a labor camp for having mildly criticized Stalin's military leadership in a personal letter.) At one point the KGB started rumors that Solzhenitsyn's real name was "Solzhenitser," that is, that he was Jewish. Given the fact that the press is wholly in government hands, Solzhenitsyn had no effective way to rebut the government's campaign. He issued counterstatements through *samizdat*, but it reached only relatively small numbers.

As is natural, most of the memoir is devoted to Solzhenitsyn's own affairs, but he finds time too for remembering the other writers who struggled against the system. He tells of many writers who "have been subjected during their lifetime to abuse and slander in the press and from the platform without being afforded the physical possibility of replying." Many were subjected to violence and personal persecution. Moreover, no one will ever know the names of those who perished in the camps before their talents could blossom. It is a heartbreaking picture.

After the many pages recounting his persecution at the hands of the Soviet regime, it is refreshing to read Solzhenitsyn's credo, which would sound like a set of clichés if uttered by a writer in a free country but which must inspire the true artists of Solzhenitsyn's homeland:

> I believe that it is the task of literature to tell people truthfully how things are and what awaits them. . . . In general, the task of the writer cannot be reduced to defense or

criticism of this or that mode of distributing the social product, or to defense or criticism of one or another form of government. The tasks of the writer are connected with more general and durable questions, such as the secrets of the human heart and conscience, the confrontation between life and death, the triumph over spiritual sorrow, the laws of humanity over the ages, laws that were born in the depths of time immemorial and will cease to exist only when the sun ceases to shine.

Critical Context

To lovers of literature, writers' memoirs are almost always interesting to read for the insights they give into the authors' minds and characters. Because of the intensely personal nature of *The Oak and the Calf*, and because of the extraordinary experiences which fate has packed into Solzhenitsyn's life, his memoirs are of unusual interest. As a work of art, *The Oak and the Calf* is far superior to Konstantin Paustovsky's *Povest o zhizni* (1946-1964; *The Story of a Life*, 1964-1974), another Soviet literary memoir generally available in the West, one that seems bland and of limited interest in comparison to Solzhenitsyn's. Solzhenitsyn's work is more readily comparable to Ilya Ehrenburg's various volumes of reminiscences, for both give vivid portrayals of the Soviet Union's cultural life. Nevertheless, Solzhenitsyn's work is more focused, both in time and subject, and ultimately more revealing of Soviet realities.

The importance of *The Oak and the Calf* may be judged from the great critical attention accorded it when it came out. Leading newspapers and journals in the Western world devoted lengthy reviews to the work. While reviewers were sometimes disconcerted by Solzhenitsyn's notion of himself as a "second government," with the right to critique not only his own but all the rest of the governments in the world, they praised the brilliance of his memoir. *The Oak and the Calf* certainly takes a central place in the great Russian author's re-creation of Russia in the years before the Revolution and in the Soviet period, which he has done in his novels and in his literary-historical work, *Arkhipelag GULag, 1918-1956; Opyt khudozhestvennogo issledovanniia* (1973-1975; *The Gulag Archipelago, 1918-1956: An Experiment in Literary Investigation*, 1974-1978).

Some Westerners may become weary of reading the hundreds of pages of details of Solzhenitsyn's literary life. Most will also on occasion be affronted by some of Solzhenitsyn's more bizarre judgments, such as that Soviet atrocities have been "immeasurably greater" than those of Adolf Hitler. Yet Solzhenitsyn did not write the book primarily for Westerners. He wrote it so that Russians of the future would know what happened to their motherland in the twentieth century. Certainly one of the most lasting contributions of the book, ensuring that it will be read for generations to come, is its proof that one person can stand up to a totalitarian system and win a victory for decent values. As a chronicle of Soviet life, the book is one of the great works of the late twentieth century.

Sources for Further Study

Bayley, John. Review in *The New York Review of Books*. XXVII (June 26, 1980), p. 3.

Blake, Patricia. Review in *Time*. CXV (June 9, 1980), p. 80.

Cohen, S. F. Review in *The New York Times Book Review*. LXXXV (May 4, 1980), p. 1.

Scammell, Michael. *Solzhenitsyn: A Biography*, 1984.

Steiner, George. "Excommunication" in *The New Yorker*. LVI (August 25, 1980), pp. 94-100.

Roland V. Layton, Jr.

OF A FIRE ON THE MOON

Author: Norman Mailer (1923-   )
Type of work: History
Time of work: 1969
Locale: Cape Kennedy, Florida, and Houston, Texas
First published: 1970

> *Principal personages:*
> NORMAN MAILER (AQUARIUS), a journalist assigned to cover the
>   first manned mission to the moon
> MIKE COLLINS,
> BUZZ ALDRIN,
> NEIL ARMSTRONG, and
> PETE CONRAD, astronauts
> GENE KRANZ, the mission's flight director

Form and Content

In 1969, Norman Mailer was assigned by *Life* magazine to report on the first manned landing on the moon. Mailer worked as journalist, visiting the space centers at Houston, Texas, and Cape Kennedy, Florida. He interviewed the astronauts and other important figures in the National Aeronautics and Space Administration (NASA); studied the technical reports, publicity releases, and transcripts of the voyage; and attended various briefings and press conferences held for the media. As in *The Armies of the Night: History as a Novel, the Novel as History* (1968), however, he also covered the moon shot as a novelist, attempting to divine the psychology not only of the astronauts but also of the machines they handled and of the administration that guided them into space and into the public's awareness. In the end, Mailer produced a comprehensive portrait of his personal reaction to this historic event while also giving full value to the experience of the event itself.

Of a Fire on the Moon is divided into three parts: "Aquarius," "Apollo," and "The Age of Aquarius." As the titles of the sections suggest, the book begins by introducing its narrator, Norman Mailer, who dubs himself "Aquarius" because he was born under that astrological sign and because in this period of his life he sees himself as surrendering his personality to a time in history that may well redefine human nature and the nature of the world. Known for explicitly projecting himself onto the events he reports, Mailer suggests that in this book he suffers a loss of ego before the enormity of the moon shot. This is a historic voyage that may mark either a new beginning for the human race or possibly an ending, depending on how it responds to the new technology. Part 2 concentrates on the astronauts, on their moon voyage, and on their technological environment at NASA. Here Mailer commits himself to detailed descriptions of the science and engineering of the flight while speculating on how the human psyche has been affected by the rigid demands of a technological environment. Part 3 (much shorter than its predecessors) puts the primary focus on the narrator and suggests his need to encompass the moon shot with his own personality, to make it—as he so often says of the astronauts—an "instrument" of his will.

Each part of the work is presented in a mixture of styles. There are long passages of philosophical speculation, in which Mailer indulges his penchant for the long sentence, mining every bit of evidence for its significance and ending with shrewd insights and a host of unanswerable questions. There are also long, riveting sections of narrative in which he captures the drama and the risk involved in getting to the moon. Sometimes he is bored by the official information put out by NASA, or by the astronauts' efforts to avoid all emotion, and presents extracts from transcripts of their talk. He does not neglect the incredible volume of technical detail. Trained as an engineer at Harvard University, Mailer reveals considerable fascination with the way engineers and scientists worked together in reaching President John F. Kennedy's goal of sending men to the moon by the end of the 1960's. Mailer has numerous observations on the way he and the rest of the press cover the moon shot, and he tries to record the space launch from every conceivable point of view.

Analysis

One of the first things that strikes Mailer about the people in the space program is their use of jargon: Their words are usually devoid of personal expressions, and the astronauts feel uncomfortable when asked about their personal reactions. Being part of a team, part of NASA, means to suppress individuality. As Mailer puts it, "Yes, real Americans always spoke in code. They encapsulated themselves into technological clans." The result, however, is to make the moon shot seem unreal. Surely Mike Collins, the astronaut who would stay in the spacecraft while his colleagues descended in a specially designed vehicle to the moon, must have felt some envy or regret over not going himself. Yet Collins will not allow himself to suggest he might be disappointed. Part of the problem is that the astronauts have to play several roles at once. The complexity of their situation is unprecedented, Mailer supposes, and this accounts for their unwillingness to risk anything like an original or a daring thought. Their press conferences are boring to most of the press, yet Mailer probes for a rather intriguing speculation on the astronauts' dilemma:

> Now it was as if they did not know if they were athletes, test pilots, engineers, corporation executives, some new kind of priest, or sheepish American boys caught in a position of outlandish prominence—my God, how did they ever get into this?

Several of the astronauts have been test pilots. They are superb physical specimens ready for the rigors of space travel. Some of them have engineering degrees; some are already administrators. They are treated as heroes, and they are also somewhat embarrassed by their publicity. Mailer puts all these facts into a single sentence and a style that both sums up and expresses their awkward circumstances. Even on the subject of their own deaths they are silent, or they attempt to downplay the dangers of their mission: Rather than speaking of their "personal disasters," they employ euphemisms such as "contingency." This use of language to mask reality is profoundly disturbing to Mailer, who points out that Nazis and Communists have made a similar use of words, resorting to terms such as "liquidation" to refer to "mass murder." As a writer, he fears the damage to the human psyche when "words, like pills, were there to suppress emotional symptoms."

Mailer's forte is to find the contradictions of the moon voyage. On the one hand, the astronauts have been picked for their prowess and virility. On the other hand, for most of their time in space they are "passive bodies." In their preparations for space travel, they have submitted to every kind of hazardous experiment: He suggests, "They were done to, they were done to like no healthy man alive." They eat out of plastic tubes filled with mushed edibles resembling baby food. They are as awkwardly confined in their bulky spacesuits as a trussed-up baby still in diapers. They are protected by every kind of technology, yet their voyage could well lead to their deaths. In this respect, they are simply intensified examples of the technological twentieth century, which contains "huge contradictions [and] . . . profound and accelerating opposites." Technology has made it possible for people to live in the utmost comfort and safety, yet that same technology is capable of destroying their environment. This is why, in Mailer's view, the moon shot can be interpreted as forecasting an "exceptional future" and the "real possibility of global destruction."

The journey to the moon is an apocalyptic event, yet Mailer notices that the astronauts refuse to romanticize their roles—as if "technology and the absence of emotion . . . were the only fit mates for the brave." These spacemen are entirely too rational for Mailer's taste, which matches that of the press, who keep goading the astronauts to say something heroic or daring. Instead, they speak like cautious scientists and loyal corporate citizens.

There is no doubt in Mailer's mind that the space program is a triumph of engineering and science, but it troubles him that the public will take NASA's accomplishments as proof of the superiority of science. Referring to his own education as an engineer, he points out the fallacy of thinking of science as "an exact study with certain knowledge." On the contrary, scientists know relatively little about the structure of the world or about the nature of things. Even something as solid as the law of gravity has not really been explained. Scientists know how gravity operates, but they cannot account for why bodies are attracted to one another. Science can measure nature, but it rarely reveals nature's secrets.

Mailer presses his point by showing how nearly every spaceflight has suffered unaccounted failures and near fatalities. While NASA has employed extraordinary precautions to protect the astronauts, he suggests that "some very large chances [have] been taken" in the space program's quest to make good on President Kennedy's challenge to land men on the moon by the end of the 1960's. Astronauts have died in a fire on a launchpad; various manned capsules have spilled fuel, failed to fire their rockets properly, and suffered various malfunctions in guidance and communications systems.

Although he sees the flaws in space exploration, Mailer maintains an open mind, realizing that the results of the trip to the moon may be spectacular. He also wants to honor the efforts of men who in spite of their bureaucratic talk are plumbing the mysteries of the universe. Indeed, one of Mailer's aims is to revive the sense of wonder out of which the moon quest has sprung. It is characteristic of him to put the sense of wonder into a question: "Who was to say it was not the first step back to the stars, [the] first step back to joining that mysterious interior material of the stars, that iron of communion with cosmic origins?" When he verges on the mystical, Mailer checks himself by refusing to make sweeping statements. His prose, like the moon shot, is an exploratory voyage.

Ever alert for signs of stress in the highly controlled technicians who guide the mission, Mailer notes that their hands are "clammy to the touch." Even in the professionally cool NASA environment, he sensed the "aisles of quiet fear," the tension in the men who work on the computers' functions that were "always in as much danger of going awry as society is in danger of some final collapse into crime." Like spy masters, these men had to check for "sneak circuits" capable of interreacting "in ways no one had foreseen."

Rather than merely covering the space program as a historic event, a technological feat, or a heroic quest, Mailer tries to view the meaning of landing on the moon from every vantage point—not forgetting his role as a journalist craving news and quotable statements or his profession as a novelist searching out the deepest meanings of his perceptions. For Mailer, the moon shot is a test of his own intelligence. He frankly admits that he and most journalists did not have the technical background to understand the NASA briefings. At the same time, he makes a virtue of his ignorance, observing himself in the third person and suggesting that "it was his profession to live alone with thoughts at the very edge of his mental reach." What distinguishes Mailer's method in *Of a Fire on the Moon* is his willingness to make judgments and indulge in speculations while exposing the provisional nature of his argument.

Critical Context

Of a Fire on the Moon appeared at the very end of the 1960's, at a time when technology was coming under attack, when serious questions were raised about the advisability of spending billions of dollars on space exploration when the needs of millions of Americans were not being served by the government or the big corporations involved in NASA programs. At the same time, as Mailer points out, technology promised an easier life. There would be "spin-offs"—all kinds of new products developed out of space exploration that would benefit the domestic economy. A large segment of the public also looked upon the astronauts as heroes—although a new kind of conservative, carefully spoken figure who had almost nothing in common with the characters of science-fiction moon voyages.

Mailer took it upon himself to describe and to embody the contradictions of his culture, giving the space program a sympathetic hearing while also criticizing it and asking hard questions. At least since his ground-breaking book *Advertisements for Myself* (1959), Mailer had taken on the role not only of the political pundit but also of the novelist open to every trend in the national psyche. Covering political conventions, prizefights, demonstrations, and other public events, Mailer turned himself into a character, often describing his reactions in the third person as Henry Adams did in his autobiography, *The Education of Henry Adams* (1907).

Of a Fire on the Moon is a transitional book in the development of Mailer's literary persona. It marks a gradual shift away from his emphasis on himself to an immersion in the lives of others. Beginning with his biography *Marilyn* (1973) and culminating in *The Executioner's Song* (1979), he has moved from journalism to "novel-biography" and "true-life novel." Each of these books—starting with *Of a Fire on the Moon*—takes Mailer toward the realization that his ego, which is very much present in *Miami and the Siege of Chicago: An Informal History of the Republican and Democratic Conventions of 1968* (1969), must be jettisoned. *Of a Fire on the Moon* is an important achievement, balancing an ingenious imagination against the space program's impressive technological and organizational accomplishments. Reading Mailer's book results in a deep appreciation not only of space exploration but of the adventurousness of the author's prose as well.

Sources for Further Study
Adams, Laura. *Existential Battles: The Growth of Norman Mailer*, 1976.
Bailey, Jennifer. *Norman Mailer: Quick-Change Artist*, 1979.
Begiebing, Robert J. *Acts of Regeneration: Allegory and Archetype in the Works of Norman Mailer*, 1980.
Hollowell, John. *Fact and Fiction: The New Journalism and the Nonfiction Novel*, 1977.
Manso, Peter. *Mailer: His Life and Times*, 1985.
Mills, Hilary. *Mailer: A Biography*, 1982.
Solotaroff, Robert. *Down Mailer's Way*, 1974.

Carl Rollyson

OF GRAMMATOLOGY

Author: Jacques Derrida (1930-   )
Type of work: Literary criticism
First published: De la grammatologie, 1967 (English translation, 1976)

Form and Content

Jacques Derrida's *Of Grammatology* is the seminal work of what has come to be called deconstructionist criticism. Essentially, deconstructionist critics reduce texts to their most fundamental elements in order to reach irreducible signs. The text as narrative in effect ceases to exist in order to privilege the signs it conveys; deconstructionists see this process as necessary violence which yields positive results. Consequently, there is no definitive text of any sort at any time, only a series of signs which can be reconstituted in an infinite number of ways. For example, this discussion of Derrida's *Of Grammatology* is not his book; yet it reconstitutes its signs, the *grammai* (Greek for "the strokes of writing"), and thereby becomes a proximate model of it. Still, this discussion is far from what came from Derrida's mind, which was itself different from what came from his pen; indeed, this discussion of *Of Grammatology* is the product of this writer's deconstruction of Derrida's text as it was translated by Gayatri Chakravorty Spivak (the translation is an earlier deconstruction). In essence, the only constant in this process is the *grammé*, the single stroke.

Because it relies upon the *grammé*, not even the *lettre*, Derrida's book cannot strictly be called literary criticism; nor does it present a theory of linguistics, a discipline Derrida believes "grammatology" supersedes. Nevertheless, despite its unconventional nature, Derrida would be the last to deny the eclectic influences which one can trace in his work. Indeed "trace" is a recurring word in Derrida's vocabulary. He argues that one can discern the trace in every text; this trace remains an indelible indication of the signifier within what is signified. All writing is, therefore, a process carried out, as it were, *sous rature* (under erasure). Derrida uses this analogy because it best describes what happens in the correction process. No matter how carefully the change is made, a trace of what was before always remains. What was before itself embraces the trace of what was before that. That leaves the *grammé* as the only essential sign, the stroke of writing having no referent except itself.

Though clearly a revolutionary idea, Derrida's theory of grammatology follows quite logically from several sources and reflects the atmosphere of challenge and upheaval characteristic of scholarship in the 1960's. Four theorists were especially important in shaping Derrida's thought (though Derrida's ideas are significantly different from the ideas of these men): Friedrich Nietzsche (1844-1900), Sigmund Freud (1856-1939), Edmund Husserl (1859-1938), and Martin Heidegger (1889-1976). From Nietzsche, Derrida developed a general distrust of metaphysics as a systematic study and a suspicion of fixed values of meaning. Nietzsche had sought to liberate the signifier from its absolute identification with *logos* (word). Derrida, like Nietzsche, questions the meaning of truth and the primary signified (but Derrida criticizes Nietzsche's indefinite expansion of sign chains, which ultimately lead to undeniable truth). For Derrida, even the most apparently incontestable ideas as embodied in *logoi* contain the trace of their own contradiction; he indicates this by crossing out expressions on the page, so that the original is somewhat obscured but still legible.

From Freud, Derrida derived the notion that every concept is sustained by its opposite, that a unit of meaning necessarily admits at least the possibility of its own contradiction. For example, the pleasure principle contrasts with, yet actually serves, the death instinct. Similarly, the death instinct inspires an economy of life and manifests itself in life as inertia. Derrida refers to the permanent trace of conceptual opposites as *La différance*. The capitalized article and the spelling of "difference" with an *a* are used to convey the three notions of "differing," "deferring," and "detour"—*sous rature* in all rational processes.

Husserl distinguishes between a transcendental apprehension of consciousness (for example, each human being's understanding of an individual relationship to the world) and a pure psychology of consciousness (for example, the idea of "world"). Freud's contribution, so Derrida would argue, is in obliterating the distinction between "being in the world" and "world," even as he underscores it through the process of psychoanalysis. In more simple language, the analysand discovers that what causes individuation (the psychosis) is simply an eccentric manifestation (a *différance*).

Derrida uses Heidegger against Nietzsche. Though Nietzsche questions being as an ultimate signified, he never questions the questionings. For Heidegger then, the idea of "Being?" is surpassed by Nietzsche. Heidegger holds that the question unquestioned leaves only another element, posited as though it were irreducible. Derrida thus views Heidegger as, in a sense, anticipating his own concept of *sous rature*.

Analysis

Derrida's book begins with an "exergue," which, strictly speaking, is the empty space around the edges of a coin or a medallion. He thus avoids the semantic implication of the word "preface," that the ideas about to be presented have not already been constituted. An exergue allows him to see his subject (the relationship of writing, speaking, reading, and knowing) as a topic which can be approached in any number of ways, not merely through history. Though writing begins as something ethnocentric (in that it traces the history of the people who produce it), it is simultaneously logocentric: It is equally conscious of itself and develops its own history through what it is called upon to convey.

Despite what might be viewed as writing's evolving complexity, its having to produce methods of conveying the concepts an evolving culture produces, Derrida argues that writing immediately assumes a life of its own which simultaneously overtakes (even as writing is written) the culture which produces it. This idea can be illustrated in several ways. The pictogram (which conveys knowledge through pictures) is immediately (and increasingly) an abstraction of the ethnocentric known. The ideogram (syllabic script) encroaches immediately upon the *langue* (the spoken word). It does not, however, reproduce the *langue*; even when haltingly deciphered (as, for example, Mycenaean Linear B), it reveals nothing of the *modis loquendae* (method, manner of speaking) and nothing of the intellectual process which produces the content the ideogram conveys, so close to knowing.

One might imagine that a universal alphabetic script would break the tyranny of the letter, but even if one could posit a single script representing a single *langue*, its proximations to knowing would be no closer. If the hypothetical universal culture were technological, the jargon of the *logoi* would still overwhelm the concepts it describes; it would, futhermore, survive those concepts, outliving them to the point at which the concepts had ceased to be known or had ceased to be known as originally known.

In an attempt to discover seminal knowledge, humanity posits the sign, the unit which has no meaning beyond itself. Because of the "logocentricity" of humanity, *logos* became understood as sign. Nevertheless, it is clear that not every *logos* can be a sign; indeed, very few even remotely qualify. Antiquity and the Middle Ages attempted to resolve this problem by positing a "logological" hierarchy in which *logoi* have *logos* as their ultimate referent. One can discern elements of this principle in Plato, through his theory of forms in the *Phaedo* and Socrates' logological chains in the *Phaedrus* (c. 388-366 B.C.); Saint Augustine's *Confessions* (397-400), in which the infant's cry becomes the adult's word, becomes the convert's prayer; in Dante's *La divina commedia* (c. 1320; *The Divine Comedy*, 1802), where allegory races toward a true understanding of itself in the beatific vision.

The great break with this tradition came during the eighteenth century with the Age of Reason. This period was neoclassical in name only, for it saw the rise of modern metaphysics. Not content with an Aristotelian understanding of the transcendent, metaphysicians of the eighteenth century, such as Gottfried Wilhelm Leibniz (1646-1716), posited causal chains whose absurdities were lampooned by Voltaire (1694-1778) in his popular fable *Candide* (1759; English translation, 1759). Nietzsche called the entire study of metaphysics into question a century later with his "Genealogy of Morals," but it was Freud who argued that nearly every concept (whether "true" or "false") holds in its being stated precisely by its opposite. Derrida understands this idea as the *différance* (differing, deferring, detouring principle). "Being" implies nonbeing; "is" implies "is not"; "inside" implies outside; and "presence" implies absence. Thus, Derrida concludes that writing begins when book ends; the *grammé* and not the *logos* is the sign, that which defines itself and is its own subject and object. Positively stated, history, philosophy, and science have bowed to the *episteme* (closed, profound, comprehensive knowledge) of the *grammé*, and one can legitimately pursue its study as "grammatology."

The second part of Derrida's study focuses on the Enlightenment, specifically on the writings of Jean-Jacques Rousseau (1712-1778). For Derrida, Rousseau best illustrates the simultaneous presence of subject-signifier and material signified. Rousseau's autobiography, *Les Confessions de J.-J. Rousseau* (1782, 1798; *The Confessions of J.-J. Rousseau*, 1783-1790) insists from its beginning upon the authenticity of its author's experience, upon the author's intention to convey that experience in a wholly accurate way, and upon the individuality of that experience as never lived by any other. It is striking that Rousseau is aware of the life of his text and that he desires that his book be its writer and not simply a representation of its author's life. Rousseau's autobiography thus posits a phonological presence, the author's voice, externally and unceasingly constituting itself independently of the reader, or external referent. Derrida would say that the metonymy of using Rousseau's name alone for "Rousseau's writings" holds especially true because of this autoactuated phonological presence.

Nevertheless, the truth of any text is questioned by structuralist critics, who are generally at odds with the methods of the deconstructionists. Derrida cites the contention of one of the foremost structuralists, Claude Lévi-Strauss, that writing by its very nature implies falsehood, an idea striking when juxtaposed to Rousseau's insistence upon the veracity of his own text. Lévi-Strauss (and the structuralists generally) would argue that no text can be understood in a linear or historical sense, that it is like a plant which sends its roots in all directions—tapping what came before it, disguising that in the aspect of its own substance, and even anticipating what other texts will make of what it has done. As one example, William Shakespeare, seen in this context, is a "diachronological" (passing through and by time) embodiment of his predecessors, a "radical" (in the sense of *radix*, or root) expression of them, and one link in a chain which never achieves closure. Structuralists use this hypothesis to deduce larger, sociological, transcendent meanings from recurring structural elements in a wide variety of texts. Like the deconstructionists, structuralists believe that narrative is irrelevant, but Derrida argues that structuralists continue to privilege *logos*, that they do violence to the text merely to establish another text. In effect, Derrida accuses Lévi-Strauss of slackness of method, of a sentimental ethnocentrism which understands writing only in a narrow sense—which remains logocentric. Lévi-Strauss, seen this way (and, one must note, against his own strong objections to the contrary), becomes a deconstructionist unwilling to move against logocentrism.

Derrida repeatedly demonstrates what he holds are recurring characteristics of knowing-language-writing (all the same for Derrida). One of these is the proper name, a form of narcissism which seeks immortality and privilege for a name even as it desires to make the name common, a part of the idiom, of the *parole* (the language as spoken). This is manifested at times in wordplay (no matter whether intentional). "Hegel" (proper name) is evoked, so Derrida believes, as "eagle" (the French *aigle*, corresponding to the pronunciation of the German philosopher Georg Wilhelm Friedrich Hegel's surname), implying imperial and magisterial power. The philosopher's name is at once immortalized and effaced within the text (which is the author).

Though Derrida notes that Rousseau ultimately interrupts the unity of signifier and signified through a "supplement," the disturbance itself represents the author's desire to continue the text as a continuation of self, a wish for immortality. Perhaps that is why Derrida continues his own text through five supplements which rely heavily on fable for illustration. At this point Derrida, in effect, sets exposition to one side and becomes a fabler. Plato, who supposedly eschewed mythology as falsehood, is situated in Derrida's pharmacy, appropriately named White Mythology, for the product it sells. Rousseau, who candidly admits to frequent masturbation in *The Confessions of J.-J. Rousseau*, has an erotic dream in which his "supplement" rapes metaphysics (enters her by force).

Critical Context

The eclectic nature of Derrida's work, borrowing from recognized academic disciplines and using these borrowings in (to say the least) untraditional ways, places him in the grandly vague tradition of postmodernism. Though Derrida rejects all classifications of his work, including "deconstructionism," he is clearly an important member of the group of avant-garde intellectuals, mostly but not exclusively French (Derrida is himself a Sephardic Jew, born in Algiers), who challenged the tedium of traditional French criticism, known as *explication de texte*, in the politically, socially, and intellectually violent 1960's. Others in this tradition, each very distinctive in his methods and conclusions, include Jacques Lacan, Paul de Man, J. Hillis Miller, Geoffrey H. Hartman, and, more popularly, Harold Bloom and Umberto Eco. Eco's *Il nome della rosa* (1980; *The Name of the Rose*, 1983) presents sign theory in the form of a detective novel set in the Middle Ages. Another Italian, Italo Calvino, uses deconstructionist ideas in his novels *Il castello dei destini incrociati* (1969, 1973; *The Castle of Crossed Destinies*, 1979), *Le città invisibili* (1972; *Invisible Cities*, 1974), and *Se una notte d'inverno un viaggiatore* (1979; *If on a Winter's Night a Traveler*, 1981). These popular works are an indication of the degree to which what had been a radical and esoteric movement has found expression in popular culture.

It is easy to overlook the essential playfulness of Derrida. Caught up in the welter of metaphysical, philosophical, and psychoanalytic studies it presumes, an uninitiated reader might easily conclude that Derrida is a species of campus radical who prefers to destroy books rather than buildings. Nothing could be further from the truth. As he mischievously disentangles the verbal tapestries of philosophers as different as Plato and Rousseau, he simultaneously binds them together by using the phenomenological tool he identifies as "grammatology." The universal element of all texts is the *grammé*, the sign which seeks identification of the signifier and the signified.

It is also difficult to know what time will make of Derrida's ideas. From its publication, *Of Grammatology* was heatedly criticized, Derrida loving every harsh word as proof that writing is violently and passionately destructive. That whole departments of literature (most notably at Yale University, where Derrida has regularly been a visiting professor) have employed Derrida's ideas as important constituents in their curricula indicates their immediate importance in academic circles. If grammatological deconstruction ultimately travels the same road as French existentialism, Derrida can still argue that this oblivion merely proves the immutability of the *grammé*.

Sources for Further Study

Bloom, Harold. *The Anxiety of Influence: A Theory of Poetry*, 1973.

Brown, Norman O. *Closing Time*, 1973.

de Man, Paul. *Blindness and Insight: Essays in the Rhetoric of Contemporary Criticism*, 1971.

Hartman, Geoffrey H. *Saving the Text: Literature/Derrida/Philosophy*, 1981.

Johnson, Barbara. *The Critical Difference: Essays in the Contemporary Rhetoric of Reading*, 1980.

Robert J. Forman

ON GROWTH AND FORM

Author: D'Arcy Wentworth Thompson (1860-1948)
Type of work: Science
First published: 1917

Form and Content

On Growth and Form appeared in the summer of 1917, the second of four books D'Arcy Wentworth Thompson produced in a long career as scientist, author, translator, and editor. His only volume on a strictly scientific subject, *On Growth and Form* was conceived by the author around 1912 and had been promised to Cambridge University Press as a little book to cost no more than two or three shillings. In the course of distilling nearly three decades of observations on the forms of plants and animals, Thompson saw his book grow to more than eight hundred pages of text and illustrations; many delays in its preparation were caused by Thompson's severe criticism of his own writing as well as by wartime conditions.

At the time of the book's publication, Thompson's career had already encompassed diverse scientific studies as well as digressions into mathematics, classical literature, poetry, and philosophy. *On Growth and Form* was by intention both a scientific work and an evocation of the seemingly boundless universe of organic and inorganic form which had been revealed by modern science. Thompson's appreciation of poetry and classical literature played a significant part in its writing, and the enormous impression made by the book on its first appearance was based on its style perhaps as much as on its author's scientific achievements.

By 1922 the first edition of *On Growth and Form* was sold out, but Thompson would not then agree to its reprinting. In the 1930's and early 1940's, he completed a revision of the book which appeared in 1942 and has been reprinted frequently. In 1961, an abridged edition was prepared in the light of a widespread recognition that the 1917 version was, in some ways, a better book than the 1942 edition, in which Thompson had expanded the original text by more than three hundred pages without giving attention to necessary revisions.

Thompson has been called one of the last of the "scientist-naturalists," and a nature lover's passion for observation is the mainspring of much of his work as an author. *On Growth and Form* has two related objectives: to describe the visible forms of plants and animals—including microscopic structures—and to reveal the mathematics that underlies the vast variety of organic form. Though it is for the most part comprehensible to the layman, the text of *On Growth and Form* is augmented with lengthy and detailed footnotes and contains many quoted passages in French, German, Latin, and Greek. Formulas requiring a significant background in mathematics for their full comprehension are included in the text, but they rarely impede its flow. Thompson is said to have been an outstanding lecturer, and the skills of an able and considerate public speaker are evident throughout the book, both in its structure and in its language. Particularly effective is the author's provision of hundreds of drawings and diagrams to illustrate the issues raised in the text; in some cases, these become an almost autonomous source of interest.

Analysis

Thompson wrote *On Growth and Form* in the maturity of a career that lay somewhat outside the mainstream of the biological sciences of his day. The book is in large part a contribution to morphology, the study of organic form. This branch of the biological sciences had a flowering in the early and mid-nineteenth century but subsequently receded from the forefront of influential research. As an aspect of natural philosophy, morphology can be traced back at least to the Greek philosopher Aristotle, although the term itself is credited to the German poet-philosopher Johann Wolfgang von Goethe. In broad terms, the study was concerned with relationships of structure between diverse plant and animal species and proposed various theories to explain the observed continuity of organic forms. For example, Goethe, whose scientific and poetic work D'Arcy Thompson knew well, had asserted that all plants were modifications of an archetypal plant and that all plant organs were variations of a single fundamental organ, the leaf. The most arresting issues in morphology, however, lay in zoology and paleontology; with the appearance of Charles Darwin's *On the Origin of Species* in 1859 the fundamental problems of morphology seemed to have been resolved by reference to paths of evolutionary descent within the animal kingdom.

Thompson's early education took place during the widespread debate over the merits of the Darwinian evolutionary theories, and his scientific career, though not running altogether counter to concepts of evolution and natural selection, had a pronounced bias toward alternative perspectives on many issues. *On Growth and Form* is essentially an attempt to establish a theory of organic form based upon the physical and mathematical laws governing the development and function of organisms instead of upon the operation of the mechanisms of heredity and natural selection. In its progression of topics, *On Growth and Form* demonstrates organic form as principally determined by material forces operating upon biological structures. In the first two chapters, titled "Introductory" and "On Magnitude," the foundation of the book is set solidly upon the laws of Newtonian physics, yet Thompson carefully avoids giving the reader the impression that his personal philosophy is mechanistic:

> The waves of the sea, the little ripples on the shore, the sweeping curve of the sandy bay between the headlands, the outline of the hills, the shape of the clouds, all these are so many riddles of form, so many problems of morphology, and all of them the physicist can more or less easily read and adequately solve: solving them by reference to their antecedent phenomena, in the material systems of mechanical forces to which they belong, and to which we interpret them as being due. They have also, doubtless, their *immanent* teleological significance; but it is on another plane of thought from the physicist's that we contemplate their intrinsic harmony and perfection, and "see that they are good."

Thompson's appreciation of natural beauty is clearly attuned to his love for mathematics, an affinity which appeared early in his career and set him apart from the majority of his colleagues in the biological sciences.

Despite his reputation as a zealous geometer, Thompson avoids mere mathematical abstraction in his approach by emphasizing process in living form. Biological entities, he writes, "can never *act* as matter alone, but only as seats of energy and as centres of force." The author's conception of the vitality of biological form is implicit in his use of the word "growth" in the title of the book; he understands that the idea of "form" by itself can be too easily detached from the "dynamical" aspect of objects and phenomena. Thompson's prose often exhibits a dynamism uniquely attuned to his subject, as in the following discussion of scale:

> A certain range, and a narrow one, contains mouse and elephant, and all whose business it is to walk and run; this is our own world, with whose dimensions our lives, our limbs, our senses are in tune. The great whales grow out of this range by throwing the burden of their bulk upon the waters; the dinosaurs wallowed in the swamp, and the hippopotamus, the sea-elephant and Steller's great sea-cow pass or passed their lives in the rivers or the sea. The things which fly are smaller than the things which walk and run; the flying birds are never as large as the larger mammals, the lesser birds and mammals are much of a muchness, but insects come down a step in the scale and more.

Thompson here evokes not only the energy and movement of organisms but also the dynamism of time on complementary scales of individual and historical development.

The third chapter of *On Growth and Form*, "The Rate of Growth," introduces the notion that "the *form* of an organism is determined by its rate of growth in various directions." After a promising but brief exposition of this concept, Thompson is diverted into a somewhat superfluous argument regarding a passage from Darwin and then launches informative but pedestrian accounts of human growth and population statistics, the growth rates of insects and animal organs, and environmental factors affecting growth. This long chapter, alone among the seventeen which make up the 1942 edition, concludes with a one-page summary of its contents; its next-to-last sentence, a resigned "But enough of this discussion," lends credibility to John Tyler Bonner's editing of this chapter for the revised edition of 1961.

The fourth and fifth chapters of *On Growth and Form* concern the cell. Chapter 4, "On the Internal Form and Structure of the Cell," begins with a brief historical review of the morphological approach to cell structure, beginning with the first decades of the nineteenth century. After observing that the visible structure of the cell has been studied more exhaustively than the "purely dynamic problems" associated with cells, Thompson goes on to state, with somewhat uncharacteristic dogmatism, that the "mere study" of cell structure is essentially exhausted—a judgment that was extremely premature. In the absence of sufficiently intricate observations by which he might account for the complexity of cellular activity, he reassures the reader that "very great and wonderful things are done by means of a mechanism (whether natural or artificial) of extreme simplicity." His aim in this chapter is to emphasize the operations of "physical forces" in cells and thereby to avoid a static, mechanical model of the cell, but Thompson is here writing from a position of weakness. Historically, the study of cell structure and physiology was on the verge of far-reaching developments which might well have inspired a fresh treatment of the topic by Thompson only a few years later; on the professional side, however, his background as a naturalist with virtually no experience in experimental biology left him particularly vulnerable to the obsolescence inherent in this more specialized and more quickly advancing field of study. Thompson seems to be aware of this possibility when he states, "But our sole object meanwhile, as I have said more than once, is to demonstrate, by such illustrations as these, that, whatever be the actual and as yet unknown *modus operandi*, there are physical conditions and distributions of force which *could* produce just such phenomena of movement as we see taking place within the living cell."

There is a logical step from the chapter on the internal structure of cells to that concerning their external forms, but it should be noted that the abridged edition of 1961 eliminates "The Internal Form and Structure of the Cell" as "completely out of date" without sacrificing the continuity of Thompson's text. The conceptual progression from the molecular scale to the mammalian is such a strong element of *On Growth and Form* that the reader of the revised edition will miss much detail but no clarity of argument. Thompson's underlying hypothesis that organic form rises in great part from the action of purely physical forces upon developing biological structures is paralleled by his gradual expansion of the field of view; to the degree that he supports his arguments at each level of physical scale the structure of his argument as a whole is bolstered.

Thompson's sense of delight in the forms of organic and inorganic nature reaches a high point in chapter 5, where the general reader will appreciate the text's extensive illustrations. The mathematics which is central to the author's scientific perspective finally is given concrete significance and appeal as well. Most of the pictorial material consists of line drawings, but in this chapter there are several high-speed photographs of liquid splashes which are significant footnotes to the history of scientific illustration. Three of these photographs, reproduced within the text as "figures," first appeared in 1908 in a paper by A. M. Worthington; the others are provided as "plates" of much higher quality and were made in the 1930's by Harold Edgerton of the Massachusetts Institute of Technology (and thus are additions to the original edition). These celebrated images show phases of a splash in which a crownlike rim of liquid is in the process of dividing into droplets. Thompson uses these photographs to demonstrate analogies between various biological forms and the forms caused by the surface tension of liquids.

The last, and briefest, chapter of the first volume, "On Adsorption," is essentially an extension of aspects of the material in chapter 5, and can be thought of as an extended, digressive footnote to it. This section was justly cut from the revised edition, though it should be noted that in explaining its deletion Bonner refers to it as "a note on absorption" and somewhat misconstrues its content. The second volume begins with "The Forms of Tissues: Or, Cell-Aggregates," actually two chapters, the second of which is referred to in the table of contents as "The Same (continued)." This arbitrary division of a continuous topic can only have been intended to keep the chapters as close to a uniform size as possible, and with the exception of parenthetical sections the remainder of the book follows this pattern.

It is probably only in the second volume of *Growth and Form* that the contemporary reader will begin to feel fully acclimated to the author's style and to appreciate the degree to which the work transcends the need to impart facts and theories. Thompson seemingly tries to create a vision of the unity of the world of forms, tying together organic and inorganic structure by reference both to sense experience and to mathematical analysis. The effect of the measured progression from small to large forms, and from elements of form to the living structures they support, creates a sense of synthesis balancing the process of analysis necessary to the scientific enterprise. Chapter 6, "The Forms of Tissues: Or, Cell-Aggregates," shows Thompson at his best, integrating mathematics and natural history by the use of commonplace as well as esoteric observations. The central issue of these connected chapters is the explanation of the grouping of cells on the basis of fundamental geometric relationships, many of which are commonly seen in the arrangement of the thin films of soap bubbles. Plane and polyhedral structures found in physical systems are related to similar organic forms, and the concept of the "close packing" of volumes is given a clear and diverse treatment. Where the mathematics of the discussion might be unclear to general readers, illustrations bridge the gaps.

Chapter 9, "On Concretions, Spicules, and Spicular Skeletons," concerns forms arising from the deposition within living bodies—principally invertebrates—of inorganic materials such as calcium carbonate. Thompson proceeds from brief theoretical comments to specific considerations, such as how the forms of spicules can be artificially imitated or theoretically explained. A series of chemical experiments producing forms analogous to organic structures is described and illustrated, then the discussion is directed toward the mechanical causation of organic forms. Thompson's objection to Darwinian hypotheses comes to the fore in the midst of this chapter, where he draws attention to "the fundamental difference between the Darwinian conception of the causation and determination of Form, and that which is based on, and characteristic of, the physical sciences." He writes that "a graduated or consecutive series of forms may be based on physical causes" and that "forms mathematically akin may belong to organisms biologically remote, and . . . in general, mere formal likeness may be a fallacious guide to evolution." This is Thompson's position on evolutionary matters: Hereditary hypotheses often leave much to be desired. His glancing blows against Darwinian theory occur at such sporadic intervals, however, that their significance in Thompson's overall scheme might easily be underestimated.

For aesthetic appeal, "The Equiangular Spiral" surpasses all the others. The mathematical elements of this section are among the least formidable in the book, and the visual material—principally drawings, diagrams, and photographs of shells— is inherently fascinating. Thompson's discussion originates with a distinction between the "spiral of Archimedes," which resembles a coiled rope and the equiangular spiral, a form seen with greater or lesser clarity in shells. Thompson presents a remarkable variety of explanations of the significance of the spiral in mathematical, physical, and biological terms; each of his examples seems complementary rather than redundant. Thompson's essential point is that the growth of horns, shells, and other organic forms in which an equiangular spiral can be recognized demonstrates an increase in size coupled with an identity, or near identity, of shape or volume. The shell "does not alter as it grows; each increment is similar to its predecessor, and the whole, after every spurt of growth, is just like what it was before."

Having established a theoretical framework for the study of equiangular organic forms, Thompson proceeds to increasingly complex examples of mollusks, foraminifera, and worms for which the basic mathematics must be elaborated. In concluding this chapter, he once again brings his discussion to bear on his reasons for discounting the hypothesis of natural selection: "It is hard indeed (to my mind) to see . . . where Natural Selection necessarily enters in, or to admit that it has had any share whatsoever in the production of these varied conformations." In his opinion, the sense of natural selection can be nothing more than a vague "nexus of causes" with which "to differentiate between the likely and the unlikely, the scarce and the frequent, the easy and the hard."

The next four short sections are of varying significance. Chapter 12, "The Spiral Shells of the Foraminifera," is largely a continuation of the previous chapter on spirals. "The Shapes of Horns, and of Teeth or Tusks: With a Note on Torsion" takes the discussion into the realm of large mammalian structure in anticipation of the concluding chapters. Interjected before these important sections are a fine but unessential chapter on leaf arrangement and "On the Shapes of Eggs, and of Certain Other Hollow Structures," which is flawed by an erroneous deduction Thompson might have been expected to correct in the second edition.

"On Form and Mechanical Efficiency" is a treatment of the topic of structural form in birds, fishes, and mammals, with an emphasis on the resemblance of skeletal forms to engineered structures. Dealing with matters which are far less esoteric than most of Thompson's topics, it has the feeling of a fine, self-contained piece of virtuoso public speaking transposed to the printed page; one can easily imagine the illustrations as lantern slides for a lecture. A photograph of a bison, for example, is described parenthetically as "an unusually well-mounted skeleton, of American workmanship, now in the Anatomical Museum of Edinburgh"—a genteel flourish which would seem out of place elsewhere in the book.

The final substantive chapter of *On Growth and Form*, preceding a short poetic epilogue, is the source of most of the influential excerpts from the book found dispersed among texts on various scientific and cultural topics. The essence of "On the Theory of Transformations: Or, The Comparison of Related Forms" is simple, direct, and elegantly visual. It is a conceptualization of the transformation of a shape, or family of shapes (and volumes, as the issue becomes more refined), into related forms by means of the stretching of a system of coordinates. For example, if the outlines of the human skull are placed on a rectangular grid, a series of regular alterations of the grid can be carried out which transpose the coordinate points of the original drawing so that the drawing resembles that of a chimpanzee's skull; further warping of the grid changes the drawing to approximate the skull of a baboon. Examples of similar transformations of the shapes of leaves, crustaceans, and fishes elaborate the methodology in a convincing fashion.

Thompson uses the model of the "deformation" of biological form in two senses: to demonstrate how one form can be seen to be related to another and to show how differential rates of growth produce forms of greater or lesser levels of perceived relationship. Ultimately, however, he gravitates to the issue of discontinuity of form across the spectrum of creation, concluding that, since there is an absolute discontinuity between types of geometric forms, there are inevitable gaps in categories of organic forms. "Our geometric analogies weigh heavily against Darwin's conception of endless small continuous variations," the author states, though he admits that "this is no argument against the theory of evolutionary descent." "Physicomathematical possibility" is for Thompson an essential and perhaps the paramount component of an adequate account of the origin as well as the limits of biological diversity.

Critical Context

The position of *On Growth and Form* in the history of the biological sciences is somewhat unusual. It is one of the very few books written by a twentieth century scientist to be celebrated as a classic, yet neither the book nor its author rates mention in many comprehensive and reliable guides to modern biology. Despite the status of *On Growth and Form* in England and the United States, its influence has been intangible and indirect; few scientists, artists, and writers have directly acknowledged Thompson's legacy. P. B. Medawar has observed that there is little that can be traced in "pedigrees of teaching or research" to the book or to the scientific career on which it was based.

Thompson's analysis of form, which appeals almost equally to scientific and aesthetic modes of experience, stands apart from the conventional cultural relationships of the arts and the sciences, which continue to maintain a high degree of professional specialization and ideological exclusivity. Thompson's life's work, diversified by successful endeavors in classics and mathematics, embodies an alternative to this situation, but his example has had less currency than might have been hoped. In an essay titled "Literature and Science," Aldous Huxley recalls T. H. Huxley's advocacy of "a primarily scientific education, tempered . . . with plenty of history, sociology, English literature and foreign languages" and contrasted it with Matthew Arnold's plea for "a primarily humanistic and specifically classical education, tempered by enough science to make its recipients understand the singularly un-Hellenic world in which they find themselves living." Thompson, the son of a poet and teacher of literature, and himself the recipient of a fine classical education, transcends the dichotomy of science and art that Huxley and others have found so problematic.

Sources for Further Study

Bonner, John Tyler. Introduction to *On Growth and Form*, by D'Arcy Wentworth Thompson, 1961 (revised edition).

Hutchinson, G. E. "In Memoriam: D'Arcy Wentworth Thompson," in *American Scientist*. XXXVI (October, 1948), pp. 577-606.

Le Gros Clark, W. E. Medawar, and P. B. Medawar, eds. *Essays on Growth and Form Presented to D'Arcy Wentworth Thompson*, 1945.

Thompson, Ruth D'Arcy. *D'Arcy Wentworth Thompson: The Scholar-Naturalist, 1860-1948*, 1958.

Whyte, Lancelot Law, ed. *Aspects of Form: A Symposium on Form in Nature and Art*, 1951.

C. S. McConnell

ON HUMAN CONDUCT

Author: Michael Oakeshott (1901-   )
Type of work: Philosophy
First published: 1975

Form and Content

Michael Oakeshott, a distinguished British philosopher who is usually referred to as a conservative, wrote *On Human Conduct* in order to summarize a half century of theorizing about government and political activity. Interested in "an engagement in understanding," Oakeshott attempts to construct a general theory of political life, and he insists that he is not attempting to advance a particular ideology or political agenda. Oakeshott's values, however, have a great impact upon the conclusions of the book. With his strong commitment to individual freedom, he expresses a distrust of all forms of political power, and to the extent possible he wants the individual to be able to choose his or her own substantive purposes without government intrusion. Readers who are committed to socialism, modern liberalism, and the welfare state will disagree with many of Oakeshott's assumptions and generalizations.

On Human Conduct is composed of three related essays. The first essay is devoted to "the theoretical understanding of human conduct," with an emphasis on the perennial question of human freedom versus determinism. The second essay attempts to clarify the nature of "the civil condition" by examining the differences between "civil associations," which mandate laws for public order, and "enterprise associations," which are joined by voluntary consent. The third essay, "Character of a Modern European State," summarizes the historical evolution of how national states have developed out of heterogenous traditions, with an analysis of what major political philosophers have written about this development. In the third essay, Oakeshott argues that in the earlier stages European states could be generally classified as civil associations, but that gradually they have increasingly acquired characteristics of enterprise associations—a development that he deplores.

In order to understand Oakeshott's rather difficult book, the reader should give special attention to this dichotomy between the civil association (which he also calls *societas*) and the enterprise association (*universitas*). The former is a public institution which citizens are required to join on the basis of living within a political order, with the individual having no real choice in the matter. According to Oakeshott, the relationship within a *societas* is moral in nature, requiring strict rules and mandatory enforcement. In contrast, the *universitas* is voluntary, with members having the option of withdrawing from the association, and the relationship is founded upon a shared goal of attempting to satisfy some kind of substantive desire. Oakeshott admits that these two kinds of associations are of an "ideal character" and that they are "abstracted from the contingencies and ambiguities of actual goings-on in the world." Although based on historical experience to some extent, the dichotomy actually appears to represent Oakeshott's own conception of how the public and the private spheres are and should be divided from each other.

Oakeshott takes the position that his work in philosophy does not have any practical purpose as its goal and that he is attempting an understanding of the totality of experience for its own sake. He is not at all consistent, however, in his claims to be a detached observer. In avoiding the controversies about justice and equality, for example, he is implicitly suggesting that these are not appropriate values to promote in civil assocations. In spite of his claims that he is not trying to defend a particular ideology or practical program, his description of the civil association is manifestly related to a laissez-faire view of politics. Far from a detached observer, he makes it clear that a state should follow the model of the civil association rather than the enterprise association, writing that "no European alive to his inheritance of moral understanding has ever found it possible to deny the superior desirability of civil association without a profound feeling of guilt."

Analysis

Oakeshott rejects the determinist view that individual behavior is simply a response to a stimulus, and he insists that "human conduct" is based on choice and intentionality, with rational human beings responding to situations and anticipating the choices of other humans. In making choices, individuals are influenced by their personal histories, for they are conditioned by educational processes which result in acquired beliefs, skills, knowledge, and understanding. Although there are many constraints which place significant limits upon a person's freedom of choice, the concept of human freedom is based on the premise that a person is endowed with "reflective consciousness." In other words, a person has freedom in interpreting and understanding a situation, and "what is called 'the will' is nothing but intelligence in doing." Oakeshott explains: "Wherever there is action or utterance there is an intelligent agent responding to an understood (or misunderstood) situation meaning to achieve an imagined and wished-for outcome."

In arguing that humans have a margin of indeterminate choice, at least in their ability to use reflective consciousness, Oakeshott takes a position which is both reasonable and respectable. Critics have charged that he sometimes tends to assert his theories rather than to formulate cogent arguments and that he also tends to present either/or alternatives without considering the possibility for other perspectives. This second criticism appears to have some validity—for example, when Oakeshott criticizes the determinism found in certain schools of modern psychology, as in his conclusion that "psychological mechanisms cannot be the motives of actions or reasons for beliefs." Many psychologists would maintain that humans do indeed possess a margin of freedom but that, at the same time, unconscious mechanisms— sometimes irrational in nature—can also operate as motivations for behavior. Such a view, in fact, does not necessarily contradict Oakeshott's position about conscious motives providing a basis for the use of reasoned judgments in making decisions. It does appear, moreover, that the most intelligent of humans sometimes react to environmental stimuli without much use of conscious understanding. Even if somewhat extreme, however, Oakeshott's description of human conduct constitutes a strong case against utopian schemes such as that of B. F. Skinner's *Walden Two* (1948).

This distrust of utopian thinking is especially evident in Oakeshott's delightful interpretation of Plato's allegory of the cave dwellers. The philosopher-king, according to this interpretation, does not use the same language as the cave dwellers, and they are suspicious of his claims because he does not have any respect for their dignity. In truth the cave dwellers are correct to suspect such a pretentious theoretician: "They resent him [the philosopher-king], not because they are corrupt or ignorant but because they know just enough to recognize an impostor when they meet one." When a philosopher-king or another utopian theoretician claims to seek the substantive goals of equality and justice, Oakeshott fears that the actual consequences will be to establish a relationship of master and servant. Similarly, he believes that the goal of communal solidarity "is easily recognized as a relic of servility of which it is proper for European peoples to be profoundly ashamed." As one might expect, he is most critical of the utopianism of Karl Marx, Francis Bacon, and anyone who promises a "New Jerusalem" or "Grace Abounding."

Going beyond this anti-utopianism, *On Human Conduct* is generally consistent in its antistatism, reflecting a strong distrust of, if not dislike for, all forms of political power; although Oakeshott definitely supports the civil association as the ideal model of how a state should be organized, his description of the civil association is not very attractive. He basically endorses the authoritarian views of government which are defended by Thomas Hobbes, Jean Bodin, and G. W. F. Hegel, and he consistently describes a political relationship in terms of a sovereign ruler, obeying subjects, and the enforcement of rules. He insists that the essence of the civil association is the obligation for citizens to obey noninstrumental, sometimes arbitrary rules (or laws). Because of the diversity within all large political units, moreover, there can be no substantive objectives shared by all citizens, and to impose the character of the enterprise association upon a state where membership is compulsory constitutes "a moral enormity." To have substantive objectives in a state, in order to be morally acceptable, requires the express consent of each citizen. In contrast to liberals, Oakeshott argues that the majority does not have the right to require the minority to accept such objectives. He writes, "It matters not one jot whether this undertaking is that of one powerful ruler (or *coup d'étatiste*), a few, or a majority."

Oakeshott does occasionally concede that in modern politics the distinction between a civil association and an enterprise association has not been widely recognized, especially in regard to the existence of substantive objectives. For example, he makes favorable references to John Locke's works and the United States Constitution, both of which accept the validity of some substantive objectives. John Locke argued that the state had the substantive objectives of protecting life, liberty, and property (objectives that can be interpreted broadly or narrowly), and the preamble to the U.S. Constitution speaks of "we the people" having the shared goals to "establish justice" and "promote the general welfare." Although fearing the slippery slope, Oakeshott appears willing to tolerate such objectives as long as there are definite limits on the power of government combined with a recognition of the value of individual rights. In the final pages of *On Human Conduct*, he even concedes that the two kinds of association are not totally hostile to each other and that they can coexist as "sweet enemies." Even with that, however, it is clear that Oakeshott does not want the state to go beyond the laissez-faire approach in economic policy, and he has little patience for citizens with a "slavish concern for benefits" from the state.

A serious work of political philosophy, *On Human Conduct* is remarkable for the many topics that are generally avoided. The reader will find little about representative democracy, human rights, positive liberties, or social justice. Oakeshott does not develop much of a theoretical explanation about why different forms of conduct should be morally praised or condemned, except that he expresses a high value for individual freedom. Rather than developing criteria to separate right from wrong, he usually uses the word "morality" to refer to a system of authoritarian rules which have no justification other than that they have been decreed by a civil association. Although he often speaks about reason and intentionality in human conduct, he does not actually consider the possibility that average citizens might use critical reason in the democratic formulation of public policy. It does not appear as if Oakeshott is able to conceive of a state except from a Hobbesian point of view, and he assumes that true human fulfillment, a sense of solidarity, and shared objectives are found only in private, voluntary associations.

In making this ideal distinction between two kinds of associations, Oakeshott takes a philosophical approach that is often referred to as essentialism; that is, he considers that words have essences which can be captured in definitions, and the definitions become the foundations of key arguments. For example, when he declares that the state cannot seek distributive justice, his argument is based on his definition of a civil association, the essence of which precludes substantive purposes. In contrast to most conservative philosophers, he does not argue against such a goal in terms of how it relates to values such as liberty or prosperity. In fact, Oakeshott's definition of a civil association is not well-grounded in history, for even conservative capitalistic regimes have commonly pursued limited efforts at distributive justice, as in graduated income taxes, public education, welfare, and other social programs. In the modern world the real controversy centers not on whether states should seek distributive justice but on the degree to which they should do so.

Both admirers and critics agree that *On Human Conduct* is a difficult and challenging book. An admirer of Hegel, Oakeshott writes in an obscure style not unlike that German philosopher. Oakeshott looks upon philosophy as a form of literary discourse, and he clearly enjoys using metaphors and striking phrases. (He describes human conduct as a "conversation.") In general, critics commend Oakeshott for his literary skill, but they usually fault him for his lack of clarity. There are places, in fact, where his writing is ambiguous to the extent that one suspects that he is almost deliberately hiding his meaning. Many critics have been especially harsh about his excessive use of Latin terms (*lex, respublica*, and so on) when standard English words would suffice. Oakeshott appears to recognize that his book might be more concise, writing in the preface, "When I look back upon the path my footprints make in the snow, I wish that it might have been less rambling."

Critical Context

In most ways *On Human Conduct* represents a continuation of the arguments which Oakeshott makes in his previous works. He maintains that philosophy does not have any obvious lessons, and, as in his first book, *Experience and Its Modes* (1933), he argues that human life is primarily a matter of ideas and consciousness. He continues, moreover, to express animosity toward political power and to support laissez-faire policies. In *On Human Conduct*, however, Oakeshott makes two major modifications to the positions taken in his *Rationalism in Politics* (1962). First, he has ceased to emphasize the value of tradition; more than in the earlier works he recognizes that there has been a plurality of influential traditions with an impact on the modern world, meaning that one must choose among traditions. Second, Oakeshott no longer advances a strong argument against "rationalism," a term he had used to refer to deductions from abstract principles without concern for practical experience and tradition. Rather than attacking this kind of rationalism, in fact, he makes use of such an approach, more than he makes use of the consequences of experience, in developing his dichotomy between civil and enterprise associations.

For a work that is not supposed to have any practical application, *On Human Conduct* has generated significant controversy. In a symposium about the book, for example, Joseph Aupitz makes a positive evaluation, calling the book "a remarkably careful, compelling, and coherent body of work." In the same symposium, in contrast, Hana Pitkin concludes that the book is "rigidly dogmatic, assertive, and idiosyncratic almost to the point of being crotchety." Both of these views are rather extreme, and, as is true of most controversies of this kind, the truth lies somewhere in the middle. *On Human Conduct* is a stimulating book which is devoted to important problems of political philosophy, but at the same time there are significant weaknesses in its arguments and conclusions.

Oakeshott's arguments are especially compelling in regard to the problem of human freedom. In this area he makes a strong case for the view that human conduct is based on "reflective consciousness" and understanding. Most critics have found that he is less successful when he develops the dichotomy between civil and enterprise associations, especially when he argues that the failure to recognize this dichotomy is the major reason for confusion in modern politics. Although such a distinction is most helpful in understanding the works of Jean Bodin and Thomas Hobbes, it is not very helpful as a frame of reference in trying to make sense of the political dialogue of the last two centuries. In practice, almost all conservatives have wanted governments to seek some "substantive objectives," and it appears strange to suggest that laws should be formulated without any concern for their consequences in promoting human welfare. In almost ignoring the issues of social justice, human rights, and democracy, *On Human Conduct* appears somewhat irrelevant to the major concerns of political philosophy, especially compared with a work such as John Rawls's *A Theory of Justice* (1971).

Even if one concludes that the state should seek substantive objectives, however, there remains the important problem of deciding the limitations that should be placed upon these objectives. In fact, one could argue that that is the main problem that *On Human Conduct* poses. It is certainly true that the functions of the state have dramatically increased in all modern societies, and Oakeshott has a point in concluding that this growth has not always been consistently positive in its results. Oakeshott does formulate some strong arguments in favor of putting limits on the role of the state. Also, he is correct in arguing that most people do not have free choice in deciding whether they wish to be under the political arrangement in which they find themselves; mandatory, heterogenous associations, by their nature, are unable to provide the solidarity and shared objectives that one commonly encounters in associations which are voluntarily formed. Interpreted from this perspective, *On Human Conduct* may hold the interest of many liberals and socialists, who will find some important messages in the book. Even if they disagree with many of Oakeshott's conclusions, most readers will find that *On Human Conduct* will stimulate them into theorizing about the proper role of political associations.

Sources for Further Study

Aupitz, Joseph, et al. "A Symposium on Michael Oakeshott," in *Political Theory*. IV (August, 1976), pp. 259-367.

Barber, Benjamin. "Conserving Politics: Michael Oakeshott and Political Theory," in *Government and Opposition*. XI (Autumn, 1976), pp. 446-463.

Berki, R. N. "Oakeshott's Concept of Civil Association," in *Political Studies*. XXIX (December, 1981), pp. 570-581.

Greenleaf, W. H. *Oakeshott's Philosophical Politics*, 1966.

Parekh, Bhikhu. "The Political Philosophy of Michael Oakeshott," in *British Journal of Political Science*. IX (December, 1979), pp. 481-506.

Thomas T. Lewis

ON MORAL FICTION

Author: John Gardner (1933-1982)
Type of work: Literary criticism
First published: 1978

Form and Content

On Moral Fiction constitutes novelist John Gardner's "analysis of what has gone wrong in recent years with the various arts . . . and . . . with criticism" and his accompanying "set of instructions" on how to get artists and critics back on track. His text comprises two complementary parts: "Premises on Art and Morality" and "Principles of Art and Criticism." Of the two parts, the first is by far the more interesting and provocative. The second, probably originally intended as a practical guide for the would-be writer of moral fiction, offers material that Gardner handles more completely and satisfactorily in two posthumously published works, *On Becoming a Novelist* (1983) and *The Art of Fiction* (1984).

Necessary to an understanding of this book and, some would claim, all Gardner's works, both critical and imaginative, is his definition of and belief in "true art," which Gardner contends is essentially moral (that is, by its very nature) as well as "essentially serious and beneficial." It is a "game" but one "played against chaos and death," serving as "a tragi-comic holding action against entropy" and, more positively, as "a conduit between body and soul." Such an essentialist and therefore conservative definition of art implies the kind of stasis that would necessarily call all distinctly contemporary art into question (as redundant at best and diminished at worst). Such, however, is not Gardner's position, for part of the function of art is to preserve what is essentially human by rediscovering this antiexistential essence in each succeeding generation.

In addition to its function of preserving the essentially human against all the existential and entropic odds, art serves two other important purposes: to instruct and to discover. Art, Gardner contends, must have "a clear moral effect, presenting valid models for imitation, eternal verities worth keeping in mind, and a benevolent vision of the possible which can inspire and incite human beings toward virtue, toward life affirmation as opposed to destruction or indifference." The instruction must, however, be neither authoritarian nor didactic. Like Leo Tolstoy, Gardner believes that "the highest purpose of art is to make people good by choice." Thus the discovery function of true art (that is, moral fiction) Gardner defines as nothing less than "a way of thinking, a philosophical method," one which enables the writer and the reader to test ideas, values, and assumptions, not merely to represent (or re-present) them mimetically.

True art therefore involves a process of discovery for writer and reader that Gardner carefully distinguishes from the rational: "Fiction . . . deals in understanding, not knowledge." The writer comes to understand what is true intuitively rather than to know it rationally, and he comes to this understanding in the very process of composing his novel (a process that is for Gardner largely one of rewriting). The reader comes to the same understanding by a similar but by no means identical path—not by reading the writer's successive drafts but instead by entering that "vivid and continuous dream" that the novel has become, a dream which builds toward a Joycean epiphany that clarifies without ever quite explaining the moral truth that is its reason for being. It is this very nearly mystical belief in the power of true art to clarify and redeem human existence that Gardner rather quixotically uses to overcome, or at least hold momentarily at bay, those forces that have engendered the flowering of postmodernism in the latter half of the twentieth century: Freudian determinism, Sartrian nihilism, and the positivism practiced by Ludwig Wittgenstein's followers.

Analysis

Gardner writes,

> In a world in which nearly everything that passes for art is tinny or commercial and often, in addition, hollow and academic, I argue—by reason and by banging on the table—for an old-fashioned view of what art is and does and what the fundamental business of critics ought therefore to be.

The chief issues as well as the chief strengths and weaknesses of *On Moral Fiction* are summed up in this passage: Gardner's dissatisfaction with the present state of the arts, his vision of what the arts (the novel in particular) and criticism should be, and the table-pounding way in which he chooses to make his case. Both in tone and in effect, *On Moral Fiction* is a bold and ambitious indictment of the contemporary arts. Yet while it provokes, it does not persuade. Gardner's fervor as critic frequently degenerates into mere stridency, his self-assurance into arrogance. Just as damaging, his high-minded views often seem either substanceless or carelessly supported; argument gives way to epigram, intellectual rigor to simple assertiveness.

For example, much of the practical advice offered in the "Principles of Art and Criticism" section amounts to nothing more than windy and sophomoric lectures on truth, beauty, goodness, knowledge, and understanding; on the difference between the sublime and the beautiful; and on tradition and the individual talent. Gardner's own apparently deeply held convictions about these matters fail to convince, in part because the book is so inconsistent in its tone. At times Gardner appears to direct his argument toward novelists and critics and at other times he directs it toward the general audience that has, like Gardner, grown impatient with what those novelists and writers have been doing. The Gardner of *On Moral Fiction*, like the narrator of his fiction, appears in various guises and speaks in many voices: that of angry young novelist, concerned teacher-scholar, populist making a cross-of-postmodernism speech, romantic individualist, and lay preacher.

Without doubt, Gardner's cleverness often gets the best of him. It is, however, equally true that Gardner is sincere in his convictions and that for all the seeming didacticism that his table-pounding rhetoric implies, he believes in an artistic process that in fact cannot be dogmatically defined—an artistic process that "values chance," and "does *not* start out with clear knowledge of what it means to say" but instead discovers itself in the very act of its own composition. In his seminal essay "Technique as Discovery," Mark Schorer made much the same claim in a more rigorous and less assertive manner. What *On Moral Fiction* lacks in intellectual rigor it attempts to make up for in stridency, and nowhere is this more obvious than in Gardner's discussion of the true artist and in his remarks on the ways in which so many of his fellow contemporary writers (especially American writers) have failed to measure up to his high-minded standard.

Gardner's true artist is "a man of maximum sensitivity," so dedicated to the truth of his art that he must lash out against all that is trivial and, therefore, false. As for his own work, only the artist himself can determine whether it is true; in Plato's *Republic*, according to Gardner, the artist occupies a high station indeed. In fact, he serves in a triple capacity: as his society's "conscious guardian," and, in his role as poet-priest, as "lawgiver and comforter." The authority of the true artist derives from the part he plays in the moral order: He records the deeds of heroes who enact the standards established by the gods. The appropriateness of this line of descent to the premodern world—that is to say, the world from Homer through the Romantics—seems clear. Whether it applies to the aesthetic and social world of the realists and the modernists is, however, quite another matter. Gardner, with his firm belief in essences and universals believes it should, but others are more skeptical.

While skeptics may well agree with Gardner's claim that today's artists are "short on significant belief," there remains one question Gardner fails to ask: How is belief possible in the contemporary world? Similarly, although Gardner holds up Homer, Dante, and Tolstoy as avatars of the true artist, how appropriate are they to modern artists in modern social and aesthetic conditions? Much of Gardner's argument reflects his acceptance of the views Tolstoy propounded in *Chto takoye iskusstvo?* (1898; *What Is Art?*, 1898), written with all the zeal of a Christian missionary and social reformer. For Gardner, as for Tolstoy, art entails the reformation of the world in a double sense: to remake and to improve. Yet when he looks around Gardner sees, or believes he sees, that artists have turned against their art (against the truth of their art) and therefore against their world. He indicts the contemporary artist for failing to live according to the truth of his art and for turning to escapism, moral evasiveness, and fashionably cynical attacks on traditional values. Instead of demanding an art that is both true and moral, the popular audience as well as the community of academic critics have lavished their praise on the counter-figure of the lost, or anti-, artist.

Whereas the true artist transcends his age and its fashions, the false, or minor, artist can only reflect them, as Gardner believes Donald Barthelme does. Barthelme languishes in the moral shallows, offering his readers nothing more ennobling than the advice that it is "better to be disillusioned than deluded." That, however, is only one of Gardner's many criticisms of contemporary fiction. John Barth, he claims, is "tangled helplessly in his own wiring"; Saul Bellow writes essays rather than novels; E. L. Doctorow, Norman Mailer, and John Updike are preachy; Joseph Heller and Kurt Vonnegut are coldhearted. There is surely some truth in these assessments, but in the final analysis they are far too sweeping and largely misguided.

Overly committed to his "valid models for imitation" approach to fiction, Gardner fails to comprehend how a novel such as Joseph Heller's *Something Happened* (1974) can be a work of moral fiction because it is a work of moral irony. Obliquity of approach or method does not necessarily add up to moral evasiveness. The limitation, indeed the failure, may well be Gardner's rather than Heller's. He cannot discern the moral quality of Heller's fiction for much the same reason that he "literally cannot hear" atonal music: because he has chosen not to, and, worse, because he has decided that this preference is not a personal matter but a universal fact. If a person cannot hear atonal music the reason is not that atonality is not "musical" but that that person has been trained to define what is musical solely in terms of tonality.

In discussing the novel, Gardner makes a similar mistake: He exalts another preference to the realm of the absolute when he puts character at the very center of his conception of the novel as a genre. For Gardner, characters are all; plot exists merely so they will have something to do, and setting so they will have somewhere to do it. Consequently, novelists who fail to follow this imperative earn Gardner's godlike wrath: for turning characters into mouthpieces (Doctorow and Bellow), into cartoons (Vonnegut), into caricatures (Stanley Elkin), and, worst of all, into linguistic sculptures (William Gass).

In considering Gardner's writing, particularly his comments on fellow writers, it is crucial to understand that he writes in his capacity as self-appointed and self-defined moral critic. He seeks to place himself at the opposite extreme from the vast majority of contemporary critics who are too much concerned with matters of definition and structure, with describing how a text works, and too little concerned with what Gardner clearly conceives as higher and more demanding tasks, matters of explanation and evaluation, especially with praising what is true and condemning what is false.

Gardner may well be right, particularly in a literary age which has witnessed the separation of the critic from the general literary scene and his disappearance into the narrow world of academic specialization. In the rarefied realms of hermeneutics, textual criticism, semiotics, structuralism, and deconstruction, Gardner's "moral fiction" concept has little part to play other than that of anachronistic oddity. Unfortunately, as unintelligible as much contemporary criticism may be to the general reader, Gardner's own forays into moral criticism do little to encourage faith in his method. Simply put, it is too mean-spirited to be a valid model for imitation.

Critical Context

In 1978, the critical response to *On Moral Fiction* was deeply divided. Having just suffered through a decade or so of widely praised literary innovations, beleaguered devotees of the "traditional novel" embraced Gardner as the champion of their own conservative tastes (an odd fact, given Gardner's own reputation as one of the innovators, especially as the author of the widely popular novel *Grendel*, 1971). Others reacted in just the opposite fashion, judging *On Moral Fiction* nothing more than (in John Barth's words) "a shrill pitch to the literary right." Surely, the title Gardner chose played right into his opponents' hands; during the late 1970's Jerry Falwell's religiously Fundamentalist and politically archconservative Moral Majority was making headlines in the United States. Conceived in 1965, *On Moral Fiction* deserves to be read in the context of both the rise of innovative postmodern fiction in the 1960's and 1970's and the reaction that began to manifest itself in the late 1970's not only in religion and politics but also in academic circles. Numerous other works reflected the reactionary trend: for example, *The Culture of Narcissism* (1978), Christopher Lasch's exhaustive critique of "American life in an age of diminishing expectations," and *Literature Against Itself: Literary Ideas in Modern Society* (1979), Gerald Graff's conservative but cogently argued study of the ways in which contemporary American writers have failed to establish their own moral authority and aesthetic integrity.

Perhaps the clearest indication of the importance of *On Moral Fiction* is that the literary world felt compelled to respond to it. *On Moral Fiction* could be denigrated but not dismissed, and certainly not overlooked. Indeed, for a time it was difficult to escape it. *The New York Times Book Review* ran a front-page collection of reactions to it, *The New Republic* featured a Gardner-Gass debate, *Fiction International* devoted an entire issue to the topic, and a collection of interviews with prominent American and British novelists focused on the questions it raised. It would not be an exaggeration to say that *On Moral Fiction* and the debate it spawned changed the face of American fiction in the 1980's, a decade of little innovation and much neorealism. (Whether that was the kind of change Gardner had in mind is another matter.) It was also responsible for a strong and almost entirely undeserved reaction against Gardner's own fiction—the reviewing of his subsequent work and the reassessment of his earlier work in terms of his theory of moral fiction.

Sources for Further Study

Butts, Leonard. *The Novels of John Gardner*, 1988.

Cowart, David. *Arches and Light: The Fiction of John Gardner*, 1983.

Henderson, Jeff, ed. *Thor's Hammer: Essays on John Gardner*, 1985.

Howell, John. *John Gardner: A Bibliographical Profile*, 1980.

Morace, Robert A. *John Gardner: An Annotated Secondary Bibliography*, 1984.

Morace, Robert A., and Kathryn VanSpanckeren, eds. *John Gardner: Critical Perspectives*, 1982.

Morris, Gregory L. *A World of Order and Light: The Fiction of John Gardner*, 1983.

Robert A. Morace

ON OVERGROWN PATHS

Author: Knut Hamsun (Knut Pedersen, 1859-1952)
Type of work: Autobiography
Time of work: 1945-1948
Locale: Norway
First published: På gjengrodde stier, 1949 (English translation, 1967)

Principal personage:
KNUT HAMSUN, the 1920 Nobel literature laureate

Form and Content

At the end of World War II, Knut Hamsun, then eighty-six years old, presented a sensitive problem for the Norwegian government. During the war, Hamsun had supported the Nazis. He had believed that Adolf Hitler and the Germans, as neighbors and members of Germanic peoples, would best protect Norway's integrity and neutrality. A determined isolationist, Hamsun did not trust—indeed, had never liked—the British, and he had regarded an English incursion in support of the Norwegian underground as an example of British imperialism. Nevertheless, he had thought that Norway would have to rely on some other power, and he chose to support Germany as a kind of champion against England. If Germany defeated England, Hamsun had believed, then a great threat against his homeland would be removed. Hamsun therefore had chastised the king and his cabinet for leaving Norway and for mobilizing Norway's armed forces against Germany. He went on to appeal to Norwegians fighting for the Allies, even as late as 1944, to desert the anti-Nazi cause and return to Norway.

The Germans and the Norwegian Nazi Party took full advantage of the prestige that Hamsun's name lent to their cause in Scandinavia. Hamsun was at that time the grand old man of Scandinavian letters, a 1920 Nobel laureate whose literary career had begun in 1877. Before the war, this reclusive writer, who regarded himself as a farmer, a worker of the soil, had been a kind of national treasure; in the postwar furor against Nazi collaborators, however, his actions in support of Hitler could not be overlooked. Too many people had read his articles or listened to his radio addresses and too many people resented his acceptance of an award from Hitler's own hand. Thus, Hamsun was caught up in a wave of reaction against Nazi collaborators such as Vidkun Quisling, the notorious founder of the Norwegian Nazi Party, and against Nazi atrocities in Norway and elsewhere.

Yet even Hamsun's support of Hitler and Quisling could not erase his literary reputation. Though his publisher dared not publish his books, Hamsun himself was still regarded as a somewhat tarnished treasure and officials did not wish to treat this venerable man as harshly as they had other sympathizers. Instead, they arrested him, confined him first in a home for the elderly and then in a mental hospital, pronounced him to have "permanently impaired faculties," and finally fined him heavily and released him, a virtual pauper. *On Overgrown Paths* chronicles these three years of confinement. The book restored Hamsun's popularity among Europeans, and Gyldendal, his publisher, was able shortly thereafter to rerelease his other works. Before his death in 1952, Hamsun saw his standing as an author largely restored.

For all of its importance to Hamsun's reputation, *On Overgrown Paths* is a difficult book to classify. Insofar as it contains an account of three important years in its author's life, it is an autobiography, though it is limited to those three years. Insofar as it gives some account of Hamsun's position with regard to his collaboration, it is an apologia, though it contains no apology for and little in the way of an explanation or justification of his pro-Nazi actions. Insofar as it follows the musings of an old man's mind on a variety of subjects, it is a meditation. Yet the book is somehow all these things at once and none of them. Its primary attraction is hardly the biographical information it gives about its author, nor does Hamsun give any kind of satisfactory account of his wartime activities. In his seemingly random musings on a variety of subjects, however, Hamsun manages to convey the essential qualities that pervade his fiction, the qualities that are also his own primary character traits. The book therefore acts implicitly as an apologia, for in understanding Hamsun's character, readers were apparently able to accept, if not forgive, his actions.

The formlessness of the book allowed Hamsun to foster these multiple intentions. The book's narrative comprises 176 pages not divided into chapters. Shifts in thought are signaled by white space and an asterisk, which may occur as often as once per page or not for pages at a time. Hamsun's thought follows his gaze; he may remark on the condition of his galoshes or muse repeatedly about who might have left a copy of a book for him to read or who might own a clasp knife he has found in his quarters. Sometimes his musings reach back decades to his youthful adventures in the United States; sometimes he relates the day-to-day events of his confinement. Many of the encounters Hamsun describes are unpleasant, for people know who he is and of what he is accused, and he is, after all, confined, even though his imprisonment is little more than a house arrest. Yet many other encounters are pleasant, for even though he is in trouble, many people he meets remain grateful for his books, despite the trouble surrounding their author. Thus, while the book belongs to the genre of autobiography, its organization is meditative. Thus, Hamsun involves the reader in his thought processes, a strategy which forces a close identification between writer and reader.

Analysis

Some writers write because they decided at some point in their lives that they wanted to be writers; that is, there was a conscious decision to write. Others write because they cannot help themselves; writing is simply part of who they are. Hamsun, apparently, was of the latter party. He thought of himself as a farmer, a tiller of the soil, and his writings, in one way or another, center on characters who are much like himself. They are lonely or simply alone, isolated figures who have their own sometimes tortured vision of what life is and who live consistently within that vision, regardless of whether they suffer from the conditions they create. In this way the characters are like their creator; indeed, many of the characters are explicitly autobiographical.

Hamsun knew deep within himself that life was hard and that people were basically alone in the world, solely responsible for their own well-being. Thus, he worked the soil because it was the basic element of life on earth and because success or failure depended primarily on his own work, his own dedication. Nevertheless, a part of him simply sang, regardless of how hard life became. His first widely known novel, *Sult* (1890; *Hunger*, 1899), grew out of his experiences as a starving writer roaming the streets of Oslo. Hamsun condensed and heightened his own experiences, but the hunger the main character feels is remembered, not invented. Similarly, *On Overgrown Paths* grew out of Hamsun's difficulty; this autobiographical memoir is as fully an expression of its author's trouble as the earlier novels were. Hamsun himself seems to be at the mercy of his urge to write, as he clearly indicates:

> I know that I must not bother anyone with my speculations and recollections and perceptions; I cannot stand it in others. But my head sings with them, or perhaps it is my body or my soul singing thus. It is not the beginning of a cold or something I can cure by putting on more clothes or taking them off; hush, it is something angelic, with many violins. That is it exactly!

One should be extremely cautious about taking any writer's words completely at face value, but in this case Hamsun has apparently written for exactly the reason he claims: He cannot help himself. In fact, in another sense, Hamsun could not realistically have hoped to help himself by writing *On Overgrown Paths*. Public outrage over Hamsun's wartime activities had forced his publisher, Gyldendal, to remove all of his works from print; according to Harald Grieg, the firm's director, booksellers were simply not ordering Hamsun's books. Hamsun therefore knew that as a writer he was dead. He had no audience, no source of income from writing, and no time. Approaching ninety, deaf, and in declining health, Hamsun states over and over that he is a walking dead man, that he has no hope of reaching anyone with this, his last book.

This conclusion shows itself most clearly in the way Hamsun deals with his trials, or rather in the way he does not deal with them. This memoir of his imprisonment deals only glancingly with what must have been its central events, the several court proceedings that took place during the three years included in the book. This fact is understandable, since Hamsun's deafness must have precluded him from making much of the events in the courtroom itself, but he relates far less than he must surely have known. He includes several letters he wrote to prosecutors and a very sketchy account of his own testimony; that is all. He spends a considerable amount of space reminiscing about events from his past: his life in the United States during the

1880's, life in Helsinki in the late 1890's. He also devotes much attention to several encounters with one Martin, from Hamarøy, who wanders the countryside, scratching out his living by praying at religious meetings. As a whole, then, this memoir contains no real justification of Hamsun's actions; instead, he simply admits that he did what he did and presents himself as he is, implicitly demanding that people judge the man, not his actions.

The man presented in the writing is characteristic of Hamsun's fictional characters. In one way or another, Hamsun's protagonists are cut off from the world around them. They may be isolated by poverty, like the protagonist in *Hunger*, or they may isolate themselves as the fictional Knut Pedersen does when he chooses to wander the countryside rather than settle in one place. As he wanders, he transforms himself from carefree vagabond to prophet, converting his adventure from a lark into an isolation Pedersen imposes on himself because of his special vision. In *On Overgrown Paths* Hamsun appears in much the same light. Certain circumstances—age, poverty, deafness, infamy—have almost accidentally set him apart from the rest of humanity. Yet Hamsun's own vision of life is the real separating factor. He is alone because he has always been alone; he is not terribly upset that the world has come to agree with his own self-imposed isolation.

At the same time, Hamsun grieves over the loss of his literary standing, for he sees his writings as separate from their writer; thus, punishing the books seems to him an injustice. The writing has a life of its own, and the writer fears that he will not live long enough to rescue the writing's reputation from the damage done to it by the writer's other and, Hamsun would argue, irrelevant activities. Thus, *On Overgrown Paths* is suffused with a melancholy tone as it traces the physical decline of its author. By the end of the book, Saint John's day, 1948, Hamsun is deaf and almost blind; he is afflicted with gout and hardened arteries. Still an active walker, he describes a life that he lives increasingly by himself. He is a pitiable figure and a harmless one, one who is easy to forgive. That may ultimately be the main point of the book.

Critical Context

In at least two major ways *On Overgrown Paths* makes a fitting conclusion to Hamsun's life and his writing career. It represents a peculiar merger of biography and art, rescuing its author from an enforced obscurity and providing a fitting closure to a long literary career. From a personal standpoint, the years between Hamsun's last novel, *Ringen sluttet* (1936; *The Ring Is Closed*, 1937), and *On Overgrown Paths* gave the very public man of letters a time for rest, and the reaction against him took away the pressure of living up not only to his own reputation but also to the fact that he was regarded as the replacement for the earlier literary lions: Henrik Ibsen, Bjørnstjerne Bjørnson, and Alexander Kielland. From early in his career, and increasingly after he won the Nobel Prize for *Markens Grøde* (1917; *Growth of the Soil*, 1920), Hamsun had felt forced in his writing, forced to produce and constrained by his own literary fame. In *On Overgrown Paths*, however, he could write freely, and he managed to get back to a kind of writing he had not done for a long time, perhaps not since the early 1900's.

From a literary standpoint, then, Hamsun's last book was a breakthrough and a kind of homecoming for its author. Aside from his clear desire to be forgiven without actually apologizing for his actions, he wrote honestly and without pretension, and he made contact with his public. Released in Norway shortly after Hamsun's ninetieth birthday, the book ran through its first printing of five thousand copies and its second printing of seven thousand. A simultaneous Swedish edition and several later German editions experienced similar popular success. Two years later, just before Hamsun died, Gyldendal issued his collected works. Hamsun had accomplished the seemingly impossible task of separating the literary Hamsun from the political one. Even his publisher and longtime friend Harald Grieg could not forgive Hamsun's wartime advocacy of the Nazis, but *On Overgrown Paths* restored the literary position Hamsun had enjoyed before the war.

Sources for Further Study
Ferguson, Robert. *Enigma: The Life of Knut Hamsun*, 1987.
Jacobs, Barry. Review in *The New York Times Book Review*. LXXII (July 16, 1967), p. 5.
Lowenthal, Leo. "Knut Hamsun," in *Literature and the Image of Man*, 1957.
Naess, Harald. *Knut Hamsun*, 1984.
Updike, John. "My Mind Was Without a Shadow," in *The New Yorker*. XLIII (December 2, 1967), pp. 223-232.

William Condon

ONE WRITER'S BEGINNINGS

Author: Eudora Welty (1909-   )
Type of work: Autobiography
Time of work: The late nineteenth to the early twentieth century
Locale: Mississippi, Ohio, West Virginia, and Wisconsin

> *Principal personages:*
> EUDORA WELTY, a distinguished American author
> CHRISTIAN WELTY, her father
> CHESTINA ANDREWS WELTY, her mother

Form and Content

Against all odds and expectations, Eudora Welty's modest memoir about her childhood in Jackson, Mississippi, stayed on *The New York Times* best-seller list for almost a year after it was published. It is difficult to explain the appeal of this lyrical evocation of a sheltered and uneventful life in the small-town backwater of Mississippi. Although the title suggests that the book will offer some secrets of the wellsprings of the writer's art, one does not find much of that here. With the exception of a few paragraphs near the end of this slight, one-hundred-page meditation, Welty actually says little about the sources or secrets of her magical short stories or her richly poetic novels.

Nor is the book an autobiography, for although Welty was in her seventies when she wrote it, and therefore had had a long life about which to write, it is hardly comprehensive, primarily focusing on her early childhood, with only a few pages devoted to the early days of her writing career. Instead, it may be more properly termed a memoir or a meditation, a lyrical recollection of how one writer learned to see the world in such a way that she could re-create it in narrative.

If the book is not an analytical account of the sources of Welty's work or a detailed account of her life, what indeed is it? Welty herself was asked the same question by interviewers, and she admitted that the book is unlike anything else she had ever done, for she had never before written directly about herself. In spite of the intensely personal and lyrical nature of the book, it actually began as a series of lectures at Harvard University for the William E. Massey lecture series in the history of American civilization. As Welty tells it, when she was invited to give the lectures, she protested, saying she was not an academic and thus could not possibly say anything of value to graduate students at Harvard. Yet, when told that she could talk about whatever it was in her life that made her become a writer, she probed her keen memory to evoke the particular feel of her childhood.

The three lectures (given in April, 1983) which make up the book are titled "Listening," "Learning to See," and "Finding a Voice." "Listening," the longest of the three, deals primarily with Welty's early childhood and her relationship with her parents. It is not so much chronological as it is made up of what Welty calls the "pulse" of childhood, for childhood's learning, she says, is not steady, but consists of moments. Welty's focus, as befitting a book titled *One Writer's Beginnings*, is on her discovery of the magic of letters, sounds, words, talk, and stories. Thus, much of the first lecture deals with teachers, books, music, and films, all of which fed her hunger for the sound of story.

The lecture on "Learning to See" takes Welty out of Jackson on her summer trips to Ohio and West Virginia to visit the families of her parents. Thus more of this section focuses on her parents than on Welty herself; the primary influence is the West Virginia background of her mother's life. In vignettes that indeed could be short stories, Welty tells of her mother's running back into a burning house to get her precious set of Charles Dickens novels, which her father (Welty's grandfather) had given her for allowing her hair to be cut. Welty also recounts the remarkable story of her mother, at age fifteen, taking her father to Baltimore, Maryland, because of a ruptured appendix, and then bringing his body home alone on the train. Because, as Welty says, her mother had brought some of West Virginia to Mississippi with her, Welty brought some of it with her also.

The final section, in many ways the least memorable of the book, focuses on Welty's "finding a voice": that is, her move from Jackson to college in Wisconsin, her first job with the Works Progress Administration as a publicity agent, and the writing of her first stories—stories such as "Death of a Traveling Salesman," "Livie," "A Still Moment," and "A Memory"—which brought Welty to the attention of the influential editors, writers, and critics who constituted the New Critics at *The Southern Review*. Thus, Welty's writing was introduced to a relatively small group of discriminating readers of quality journals, where she established her early reputation. Of her writing career after her earliest works, the book says nothing.

Analysis

Much of the magic and popularity of *One Writer's Beginnings* can be attributed to the personality of Welty herself—a grand lady who with quiet dignity and grace has, without involving herself actively in the New York literary world, practiced her art with honesty and conscientiousness. She is the model of the genteel Southerner—gracious, kind, hospitable, and, therefore, difficult to resist.

Also responsible for the memorable nature of the book is Welty's ability to recreate the feel of small-town American life before the 1920's began to roar. The memoir surely appeals to a widespread nostalgia for a simpler time—before television, before nuclear weapons, before computers, and before jet airplanes. It was a time when the family library contained Dickens, Sir Walter Scott, *The Book of Knowledge*, and the *Lincoln Library of Information*; when school began with the ringing of a brass bell; and when seeing a film meant Buster Keaton, Charlie Chaplin, and the Keystone Kops. Welty's ear for the dialogue of the small-town South, her eye for the telling detail, and her uncanny memory for the precise look and feel of an era make this book fascinating.

Yet on a more basic level, the book addresses what is at the heart of all works that offer portraits of artists in their youth: What is it about the artist that sets him or her apart from others? What was it about Eudora Welty's upbringing that made her into an artist? There are two ways in which Welty answers these questions. She provides the details of the important events of her life, and she offers her own meditative consideration of the story-making process.

Perhaps the key to Welty's artistic nature, or at least as close as Welty comes in the book to identifying such a key, is her understanding of the difference between events as they happen in one's life and events as they take on personal significance. Whereas the first is chronological, the second need not be at all, for events as they take on meaning follow what Welty calls a "thread of revelation." Indeed, that is perhaps the best description of the structure of *One Writer's Beginnings*—a continuous thread of individual moments of revelation.

Those moments that make up the thread of revelation for Welty include hearing her mother read stories to her and thus learning to "hear" every line read—not in her mother's voice or even her own, but in what she calls the voice of the story itself, a voice that asks you to believe; consequently, when writing her own stories Welty hears her own words in that same voice that she hears when she reads—a voice she says she has always trusted. Hearing was also important when she listened to her mother and her friends talk. When she was a small child and a neighbor was invited to go on a Sunday drive in the car with the family, Welty would sit in the back seat between her mother and her friend and say, "Now *talk*." In this way, Welty accounts for the source of the marvelous dialogue the reader hears in such stories as "The Petrified Man" and the almost perfect monologue of "Why I Live at the P.O."

It was, however, learning to perceive the world as the stuff of story that most influenced Welty in her childhood. A typical example is Welty's account of hounding her reticent mother with the question of where babies come from. At about the same time she found two polished buffalo nickels in a box in her mother's drawer, only to learn that they were nickels taken from the eyes of her mother's first child, who died as a baby. Welty writes that the future story writer in her must have stored that episode away—not as an event but rather as an emblem. For although she had been pestering her mother to tell her where babies come from, she had received another secret, not how babies are born but how they die. This experience taught her that one secret is likely to be revealed in the place of one difficult to tell and that the revealed one is often even more appalling than the one sought.

Although her parents loom largest as influences on her life, Welty also remembers teachers and books. She says that as a child she would do anything to read, and she was frustrated by the librarian's rule that you could only check out two books at a time and that you could not take a book back to the library on the same day you borrowed it. Welty took books home and read them immediately; her only fear, she says, was of books coming to an end.

"Learning to See" is perhaps the most unified section, for it deals primarily with Welty's annual summer visits to the relatives of her parents in West Virginia and

Ohio. Although she never lived in those areas herself, it is clear that she has strong roots there, particularly in the mountains of West Virginia, where her mother was born and reared. Much of this section is filled with stories of her mother's relatives, particularly her father, a country lawyer. Welty takes obvious delight in telling stories about her mother's family, for such "family stories" are usually a child's first introduction to the "thread of revelation." In looking back on those annual trips, Welty says, she realizes they were whole in themselves, stories which changed something in her life. If life is a series of revelations, then each trip for Welty was a particular revelation for her. Thus it was inevitable, she says, that she was drawn to the short story, a form which creates its own moments of revelation.

"Finding a Voice" is the most fragmented section of the book, not having the unifying tone of nostalgia and memory of the first two sections. Welty briefly describes her first years at college, where she became a kind of humorist for her college newspaper. She also describes her first job as a publicity agent for the Works Progress Administration; she traveled all over Mississippi taking photographs and writing stories for county newspapers—an apprenticeship that gave her firsthand knowledge of the people about whom she was later to write.

It is only in this last section that Welty talks much about specific stories and the sources of them. Yet the sources of her stories are never obvious, never the central theme or character, but rather some specific, seemingly peripheral, image from which the rest of the story grows. For example, the story "Livie," a mythical piece about youth and old age, springs from the many "bottle trees" people made throughout Mississippi. Making a bottle tree was a way of beautifying the yard by putting brightly colored bottles on the ends of limbs of a tree.

She also talks briefly about her first published story, and still one of her most famous, "Death of a Traveling Salesman," a story which began with a remark she heard from a traveling man, "He's gone to borry some fire." This phrase had such dramatic overtones that it became the germ of her story. With "Death of a Traveling Salesman," she says, she discovered her true subject: human relationships.

Writing, says Welty, is a way of discovering connections, for experiences that are too indefinite to be recognized by themselves come together in story and become identifiable when they take on larger shapes. Writing develops a respect for the unknown in human life and a sense of where to look for connections, how to follow the threads, for nothing is ever lost to memory; the strands are all there and what one must do is seek for the clear line. The memory is a living thing, Welty concludes, and all that is remembered joins and thus unites the old and the young, the past and the present, the living and the dead.

Critical Context

Eudora Welty's *One Writer's Beginnings* is a firsthand account of a life lived in pursuit of story. As such, it is an almost irresistible personal testimony, a narrative which, as slight as it seems on the surface, is actually a profound document about the birth and development of an artist's consciousness. When Welty first gave the lectures that make up this memoir, students stood in line and sat in the aisles to hear her speak. The book itself was just as enthusiastically received.

The remarkable reception of the lectures and the book suggests a belated appreciation of a lifetime of careful and caring artistic creation. It seems that the older Welty gets the more precious she becomes to those who know her work. During the 1980's, she was interviewed, written about, lauded, and heaped with more academic accolades than she had ever received during the time she was doing her most celebrated work. Each Welty birthday becomes the occasion for pilgrimages to Jackson by her admirers and the excuse to publish new collections of appreciations and explications.

One Writer's Beginnings is required reading for anyone who knows Welty's fiction, for although it does not give specific sources for the material of her stories, it does provide the basis for all of her work—a keen eye for detail, a sensitive ear for the nuances of speech, and most important, a kind and noble heart. This memoir will remain a classic in American literature, for it is a deeply felt personal document about a most sensitive lady of letters.

Sources for Further Study

Brookhart, Mary Hughes. "Reviews of *One Writer's Beginnings*: A Preliminary Checklist," in *Eudora Welty Newsletter*. VIII (Summer, 1984), pp. 1-4.

Dexlin, Albert J., ed. *Welty: A Life in Literature*, 1987.

Prenshaw, Peggy W., ed. *Conversations with Eudora Welty*, 1985.

Randisi, Jennifer L. *A Tissue of Lies: Eudora Welty and the Southern Romance*, 1982.

Vande Kieft, Ruth. *Eudora Welty*, 1987 (revised edition).

Charles E. May

THE ORDEAL OF CIVILITY
Freud, Marx, Lévi-Strauss,
and the Jewish Struggle with Modernity

Author: John Murray Cuddihy (1922-   )
Type of work: Cultural criticism/sociology
Time of work: The nineteenth and twentieth centuries
Locale: Europe and the United States
First published: 1974

> *Principal personages:*
> SIGMUND FREUD, the father of psychoanalysis
> KARL MARX, the inventor of scientific socialism
> CLAUDE LÉVI-STRAUSS, the founder of structural anthropology

Form and Content

In a fourteen-page introduction, John Cuddihy sets forth his thesis: the existence of a cultural collision between the standards of civility required by "the Protestant Etiquette" (that is, the norms governing public behavior in bourgeois Western society) and *Yiddishkeit* (that is, the values, feelings, and beliefs of the premodern Jewish shtetl subculture of Eastern Europe). "The secularizing Jewish intellectual, as the avant-garde of his decolonized people," Cuddihy explains, "suffered in his own person the trauma of this culture shock, . . . caught between 'his own' whom he left behind and the Gentile 'host culture' where he felt ill at ease and alienated." Cuddihy finds this plight the motivating force behind the ideologies spawned by Diaspora Jewish intellectuals—not simply Freudianism, Marxism, and structural anthropology, but Reform Judaism, Hebraism, and Zionism. Notwithstanding their surface differences, those ideologies shared a dual thrust.

> On one hand, they have "designs" on their Jewish audience, which they wish to change, enlighten, or reform; on the other, however, they constitute an elaborate effort at apologetics, addressed to the "Gentile of good will" and designed to reinterpret, excuse, or explain to him the otherwise questionable public "look" of emancipating Jewry.

Cuddihy applies this thesis to Sigmund Freud, Karl Marx, and Claude Lévi-Strauss. He does so most fully in regard to Freud's discovery (or invention, depending upon one's perception) of psychoanalysis. The twelve chapters on Freud in part 1 of the book constitute one-third of the text. The final chapter in this section ("Reich and Later Variations") discusses how Wilhelm Reich went beyond Freud in openly attacking the hypocritical and artificial politeness of Gentile society. Cuddihy also notes how Reichian ideas about the stultifying effects of bourgeois Christian civilization entered American culture through the writing of such members of the second-generation of Eastern European Jewish immigrants as Norman Mailer, Karl Shapiro, and Saul Bellow.

Cuddihy's treatment of Marx and Lévi-Strauss is much thinner. In the three chapters in part 2 dealing with Marx, he does at least make an attempt to present evidence in support of his argument that Marx transmuted the distaste he felt for the money grubbing of his fellow Jews into an attack upon bourgeois capitalism generally. The single chapter of ten pages on Lévi-Strauss, however, does no more than state as a self-evident proposition that Lévi-Strauss' repudiation of the Durkheimian model of social solidarity deriving from tribal solidarity reflected his resentment at the "demeaning" place which that model "assigned to Judaism and, by implication, to Jews."

Part 3 ("The Demeaned Jewish Intellectuals: Ideologists of Delayed Modernization") argues that the Jewish difficulty with modernity—while having its unique features—had parallels with the experience of other groups who suffered the "self-disesteem" of being recent arrivals to modern ways. "Jewish and Irish: Latecomers to Modernity" explores the parallels between the Jewish response and that of Irish Catholics in the United States attracted to Coughlinism and later McCarthyism. The other, "Secular Jewish Intellectuals As a Modernizing Elite: Jewish Emancipation and the New Nations Compared," does the same for the postcolonial societies of the Third World.

The material in part 4 ("Children of the Founding Fathers of Diaspora Intellectuality: The Contemporary Scene") is tangential to Cuddihy's major themes and appears almost to have been tacked on to pad out what otherwise would have been too short a work for publication as a book. One of the two chapters examines the trial of the Chicago Seven growing out of the demonstrations at the 1968 Democratic national convention to suggest that contemporary American society had made adherence to bourgeois standards of decorum the prerequisite for the enjoyment of full civil and legal rights. The other is a critical appraisal of post-World War II American-Jewish writing, his principal targets being Bernard Malamud and Saul Bellow. This section is not without flashes of insight—for example, Cuddihy's complaint that "the pages of contemporary American Jewish fiction swarm with incognito Christs passing as suppositious Jews" and his description of the struggle between Jewish and black intellectuals for the culturally prestigious status of victim—but it is too brief and disjointed to be fully effective.

Analysis

A sociologist teaching at Hunter College, Cuddihy takes as his starting point the concept of modernization formulated by Talcott Parsons of Harvard University—what Cuddihy terms the "differentiation model" of modernization. "Differentiation," he elaborates, "is the cutting edge of the modernization process": the differentiation of home from job, fact from value, theory from practice, ends from means, ethnicity from religion, church from state, and the like. The crux of Cuddihy's thesis is that because of the tribal nature of traditional Jewish culture, emancipation brought Jews into collision with the differentiations of Western society. Those most alien to the shtetl subculture of *Yiddishkeit* were those of public versus private behavior and of manners versus morals. "Jews were being asked, in effect," Cuddihy sums up, "to become bourgeois, and to become bourgeois quickly. The problem of behavior, then, became strategic to the whole [problem] of 'assimilation.'" The key to that problem was what Cuddihy terms "the ordeal of civility." Civility required, at the minimum, the separation of private "affect" (feelings, emotions, desires) from public behavior, required, in short, the suppression of too much of anything that would threaten to ruffle the surface calm of civil society. Cuddihy traces how this problem of Jewish assimilation into the Western bourgeois-Christian norms of civility shaped the ideas of Diaspora Jewry's intellectual giants: Freud, Marx, and Lévi-Strauss.

His related accompanying theme is that there was a "secret" adversarial relationship between the secular Jewish intellectual and the Jewish bourgeoisie (the ordinary Jewish businessmen). The intellectual saw himself as refined and sensitive and the bourgeoisie as crude and vulgar. Yet the fear of giving ammunition to the hostile Gentile world inhibited most Jewish intellectuals from openly attacking their fellow Jews. Thus, their criticism had to be disguised in such a way as to put the most favorable gloss upon offending Jewish behavior. The favored strategy for achieving that goal was "projection onto the general, Gentile culture of a forbidden ethnic self-criticism. Shame for 'one's own kind' is universalized into anger at the ancestral enemy."

Cuddihy applies this thesis most fully and systematically to Freud. He argues that the "Yid" (Jew) pushing for social acceptance is the model for Freud's "id" pushing for admission from the unconscious to the conscious. His internal censor— or "superego"—represented the bourgeois-Christian nineteenth century culture "insisting that to 'pass' properly into Western awareness or Western society the coarse id-'Yid' should first disguise itself (assimilate) or refine itself (sublimate)— in a word, civilize itself, at whatever price in discontent." Freud thus psychologized the sociological problem of the emancipated Jew. Most important, he translated the problem of Jewish social intercourse with the Gentiles into the problem of sexual intercourse. By postulating the presence of the uncivilized id beneath the highest refinement of bourgeois-Christian gentility, Freud aimed to unmask the respectability of the European society that had deemed the Jew too lacking in respectability for social acceptance. In other words, Freud made the id into "a moral equalizer legitimating 'scientifically' social equality between Jew and Gentile."

Cuddihy similarly traces the roots of the concept of the Oedipus complex to the shame that Freud had felt as a child over the failure of his father to stand up to an insult from a Gentile. A similar sense of filial shame was widely felt by the Jews of Freud's time and place who had passed beyond their parents socially and culturally. Moreover, shame at the parents' shortcomings was accompanied by a feeling of guilt for being ashamed. Freud's solution was to reinterpret this shame (a sort of moral parricide) and the resulting guilt into the repressed desire of every man to kill his father because he desires his mother. In so doing, Cuddihy contends, Freud reconceptualized "the deepest taboo of Judaism, the taboo against intermarriage, . . . as the desire for the mother, which desire is held taboo by everyone."

Cuddihy sees psychoanalysis as Freud's way of assisting his mostly Jewish patients to adjust to the strains of living publicly in accord with the norms of bourgeois-Christian society by allowing them the opportunity to be themselves within the privacy of the analytic situation. The other great ideologist of Jewish alienation—Karl Marx—opted for a more radical solution: to eliminate the problem of Jewish acceptance by eliminating bourgeois society. His affinity with Freud lay in how he similarly universalized what polite Christian society found distasteful about the Jew. For Marx, Jewish "pariah capitalism" revealed in a more open form "the very greed that the more 'spiritual' Christian businessmen concealed beneath the proprieties and civilities of their economic and social exchanges." The major difference between the money-grubbing Shylock and the Christian gentlemen was the hypocrisy of the latter. Marx thus dismissed the whole edifice of bourgeois-Christian democracy, civility, and social ethics as "but a superstructure . . . designed to conceal the rank materialism of bourgeois capitalism underneath." Cuddihy goes on to apply the same reductionist approach to Claude Lévi-Strauss. The anthropologist metamorphosed the social antagonism between Jew and Christian into a universal system of polar oppositions: between raw and cooked, nature and culture, the rules of "how to live" of savage peoples and the rules of "how to behave" of so-called civilized peoples.

Cuddihy acknowledges that socialization into modernity is difficult for nearly everyone. The major exception is "the members of the WASP core culture descended from Calvinist Christianity." Nevertheless, coming to terms with modernity was particularly difficult for the Jews. In part, the reason was because the norms and values of modern bourgeois culture were a secularized version of Christianity; thus, their acceptance raised in acute form the issue of ethnic-religious loyalty. Yet Cuddihy goes on to suggest a point that became the source of much of the controversy that the book generated:

> A kind of predifferentiated crudeness on the culture system level, and a kind of undifferentiated rudeness on the social system level of behavior, is . . . not only an integral part of what it means to be a Jew, but integral to the *religious* essence of Judaism, and not an accidental result of Exile or of socioeconomic disadvantage.

Thus, "the modernization process is 'objectively anti-Semitic.' "

Despite this unique aspect of the Jewish encounter with modernity, Cuddihy finds the Jewish experience paradigmatic of the difficulties faced by other modernizing peoples. Therein lies the larger theme of the work: the burdens imposed by modernization upon a traditional subculture. "Ostensibly about Jewry and what Jews call 'assimilation,' " he acknowledges, "the study is, in the end, only methodologically Judeocentric." Indeed, he finds striking parallels to the response of the secular Jewish intellectuals among the elites of such other latecomers to modernization as Irish Catholics, American blacks, and Third World peoples: repressed feelings of shame about the masses of their own people, the tendency to blame the oppressions of others for the degraded condition of those masses, and claims to moral superiority as a salve for wounded self-esteem. The most important of those parallels, however, was the shared ambivalence toward modernity itself. As Cuddihy concludes,

> It is hard for the "assaulted" intellectual in the countries of delayed industrialization—or for his counterparts in the advanced world—to take up a stable attitude vis-à-vis the West. Partly Westernized himself he is deeply ambivalent, wavering between *odi* [hatred] and *amo* [love], xenophobia and xenophilia.

Critical Context

Retrospectively, the popular interest attracted by *The Ordeal of Civility* is difficult to fathom. Part of the reason for the stir occasioned by its publication was that Cuddihy was raising—even if in an oblique way—one of the central dilemmas of post-World War II American policy: how to promote economic progress and Western-style political systems, in short, modernization, in the Third World. Nevertheless, the major reason is that Cuddihy—in an extraordinarily uncivil fashion—challenged the polite intellectual's evasion of discussion of the disproportionately important role played by Jews in fashioning the radically new ideological and conceptual systems associated with modern culture.

The motivation underlying this evasion was the anxiety, in the aftermath of the Holocaust, that open discussion of the Jewish dimension of Marxism or even Freudianism might rekindle anti-Semitism. Cuddihy himself became the target of the charge that he was anti-Semitic. Those harboring that suspicion misread his argument. As an Irish Catholic (even if a lapsed believer), Cuddihy had no love for the secularized Calvinism that he identifies as at the core of modern bourgeois civility. His work is intended as an act of homage to "the great unassimilated, implacable Jews of the West . . . who exhibit a principled and stubborn resistance to the whole Western 'thing.' "

Some of the difficulties with Cuddihy's thesis are apparent even to a nonspecialist. Given Vienna's history as imperial capital and Roman Catholic bastion, one can hardly say that the city's sociocultural ambience was a secularized Calvinism. One should note in this connection how importantly Rome figured in Freud's dreams. Moreover, the supposed parallelism betwen Yid and id with which Cuddihy is so taken is misleading: The German term Freud used was *das Es*.

Cuddihy's work appears to have had almost no direct impact upon later scholarship dealing with his two major protagonists. Neither Frank J. Sulloway's *Freud, Biologist of the Mind: Beyond the Psychoanalytic Legend* (1979) nor William J. McGrath's *Freud's Discovery of Psycholanalysis: The Politics of Hysteria* (1986), for example, even lists *The Ordeal of Civility* in its bibliography. There is similarly no reference to Cuddihy's book in such examinations of Marx's intellectual development as John McMurtry's *The Structure of Marx's World-View* (1978) or Jerrold Seigel's *Marx's Fate: The Shape of a Life* (1978). In a larger, indirect way, however, Cuddihy's work has had an immense influence. Since its publication, the student of Marx or Freud can no longer ignore the relationship between their Jewishness and their ideas, even if his explanation differs from Cuddihy's.

Sources for Further Study

Alter, Robert. "Manners and the Jewish Intellectual," in *Commentary.* LX (August, 1975), pp. 58-64.

Bernstein, Richard. Review in *Time.* CV (April 7, 1975), p. 78.

Burnham, James. "The Artifice of Modernity," in *National Review.* XXVII (January 17, 1975), pp. 49-50.

Ritter, H. R. Review in *Library Journal.* C (June 1, 1975), p. 1142.

Williamson, Chilton. Review in *The New Republic.* CLXXVII (October 18, 1975), p. 27.

John Braeman

THE ORDER OF THINGS
An Archaeology of the Human Sciences

Author: Michel Foucault (1926-1984)
Type of work: History/philosophy
First published: Les Mots et les choses: Une Archéologie des sciences humaines,
1966 (English translation, 1970)

Form and Content

 The Order of Things is linked in form and content to the intellectual climate in postwar France, which was dominated by existentialism, phenomenology, and Marxism. The philosophies of the subject (existentialism and phenomenology) emphasized the concepts of individual consciousness and freedom of choice and eventually undermined the foundations of Marxist thought. By the end of the 1960's, a deep disillusionment with both Marxism and phenomenology was evident among French intellectuals. At the same time, new forms of analysis utilizing models derived from structural linguistics were gaining currency. Claude Lévi-Strauss' anthropological analyses of kinship systems and myths and Roland Barthes's semiological studies of literature and everyday life were particularly influential in promoting such linguistic models. Transcendental phenomenology was largely replaced by hermeneutics, a discipline influenced by the work of the philosopher Martin Heidegger. Phenomenology conceptualized man as a meaning-giving subject, and accordingly, phenomenologists considered the origin of meaning to be subjectivity. In contrast, hermeneutics located meaning in sociohistorical and cultural practices and texts.

 Foucault's works, while influenced by all of these currents of thought, differ substantially from them as well. Unlike phenomenologists, Foucault does not take the meaning-giving activity of an autonomous subject into consideration. Unlike hermeneuticists, he does not believe in an ultimate truth which merely needs to be discovered. He also rejects the label "structuralist," because he avoids constructing a fixed model of human behavior. His distrust in formulating rules to govern a methodology also differentiates his approach from pure structuralism. Foucault does not construct a formal theory of social relations or of the relations between forms of knowledge and social practices. Although the forms of knowledge are at the core of his investigations, he does not postulate a general concept of knowledge.

 The objects of Foucault's analysis are the systems of knowledge themselves. His investigations result neither in a definitive critique nor in a delineation of alternative modes of knowledge. Instead, he begins each analysis with the formulation of a problem which he investigates with the aid of case studies. His lack of attention to national differences, for example (for which he has often been criticized), is related to this programmatic avoidance of any pretension to scientific exhaustiveness. Instead, he attempts to determine the possibilities and limitations of formalization. *The Order of Things* is thus an exploration of the conceptual organization of the human sciences themselves. Foucault seeks to discover the laws, regularities, and rules of formation of systems of thought in the human sciences.

Foucault concentrates on three areas of knowledge: "the knowledge of living beings, the knowledge of the laws of language, and the knowledge of economic facts," relating these bodies of knowledge "to the philosophical discourse that was contemporary with them during a period extending from the seventeenth to the nineteenth century." Although Foucault largely confines his attention to that time span, the last two chapters, "Man and His Doubles" and "The Human Sciences," move into the modern era, concluding with the prospects for the human sciences in the late twentieth century.

The Order of Things is a densely written, difficult book. For the English translation (387 pages in length), Foucault added a foreword to supplement his original preface. This foreword is useful not only for its outline of the scope and aim of the work—an outline which takes into account critical responses to the French edition—but also for its indication of Foucault's idiosyncratic tone: Although in some respects *The Order of Things* resembles a traditional work of historical scholarship, it is ultimately closer in spirit to the works of Friedrich Nietzsche.

Analysis

At the core of Foucault's analysis of the human sciences in his concept of the *episteme*. The *episteme* comprises the fundamental assumptions of a culture, both explicit and unspoken, that determine the "epistemological field" in which all knowledge must find its place. Foucault's concept of the *episteme* is related to the anthropological study of classification systems, the means by which various cultures order their experience of the world. Foucault himself terms his project an "archaeology" of the human sciences rather than a history; it might also be said that he applies to Western thought the kind of analysis traditionally reserved for anthropological study of "primitive" cultures.

Foucault suggests that there have been "two great discontinuities in the *episteme* of Western culture." The first, which he locates in the mid-seventeenth century, marked the shift from the Renaissance to what he calls "the Classical age"; the second, around the beginning of the nineteenth century, ushered in "the modern age." In contrast to traditional historical thinking, Foucault does not view these shifts as necessarily progressive. His analysis does not center on the progress of reason but on the distinct ordering systems by means of which experience has been presented to the understanding.

As noted above, Foucault's focus in *The Order of Things* is on the Classical age. Measurement, comparison, and an exhaustive ordering of the world lay at the heart of this *episteme*. In contrast, the Renaissance *episteme* was concerned with uncovering the hidden secrets of nature. In the Renaissance *episteme*, Foucault contends, "real language is not a totality of independent signs. . . . It is rather an opaque, mysterious thing, closed in upon itself, a fragmented mass. . . ."

Foucault centers his arguments on the Classical *episteme*'s conception of language around the Port-Royal grammar (1660). This general grammar focused on the three operations of the mind: conceiving, judging, and reasoning. Conceiving is the most basic turning of the mind to the object; it can be purely intellectual or connected to an image. Judging is the affirmation that a thing of which one conceives is such or such, and reasoning is the correct use of two judgments to make a third.

For the Classical age, language is, however, not merely a concrete version of thought, an audible or visible translation. Language is considered a linear sequence, one which represents the totality of a mental image or thought in segmented form. *The General Grammar* can be read as the study of verbal order in its relation to the simultaneity that it sets out to represent.

In the Classical *episteme*, the modes of being of language, nature, and wealth were defined in terms of representation—language as the representation of words, nature as the representation of beings, and wealth as the representation of needs. Yet, the person for whom representation existed, the thinker who assembled the strands of representation into an ordered table, had no place in this table charted by him. All these matters were crucial to man, but within the Classical *episteme* there was no locus for man as an object of knowledge. Man was merely the clarifier of the order of the world. His was the important task of clarification but not creation; he was by no means a transcendental source of signification. He was considered a rational animal high in God's hierarchy, but he was not the representer per se.

To illustrate the problem of representation and the subject, Foucault uses Diego Velázquez's painting *Las Meninas*, showing how all the themes of the Classical view of representation are embodied in it: The painter is depicted pausing and thus appears from behind the canvas. The spectator occupies the same position as the painter's subject. The model and the spectator coincide here. The light, which can be interpreted as the light of the Enlightenment, illuminates only a mirror which seems to reveal what it represents, that is, the figures who are the models whom the painter is depicting. They can and do occupy that place for the painter, but the viewers of the painting occupy that place as well. Consequently the mirror should also reveal their image—but this it cannot do. Instead, an illuminated figure in the back serves as a representation of the spectator. The spectating function, which is not represented in the mirror, is placed next to it. These three observing functions come together in a point exterior to the picture. This point can only be an ideal one, for otherwise it would be impossibly overcrowded, but it is also a real one because it is the place occupied by the viewer.

Foucault interprets the subject matter of *Las Meninas* as representation. It lays out the idea of representation in an orderly fashion on a table, on the canvas. What is represented are the functions of representation. The painting, however, cannot represent a unified and unifying subject who posits these representations and who makes them objects for himself. The central paradox of the painting consists in the impossibility of representing the act of representing itself.

What was impossible to fathom in the Classical *episteme*—man as that being who grasps the totality of the picture and at the same time is part of the picture—

became conceptualized in the modern *episteme*. With his usual reluctance to posit causal relationships, Foucault does not explain why these changes took place but merely describes them.

Man, Foucault concludes, who was once a being among others now is a subject among others. In this sense, man is now the figure which is both the object and the condition of his own knowledge. Man is a space of knowledge, a set of relations between knowledges. This is precisely the realm in which the determinations of biology, economics, and philology operate and intersect.

Critical Context

With Jacques Derrida, Michel Foucault was one of the two leading figures in the loosely defined intellectual movement known as poststructuralism. His impact on literary studies, philosophy, and other disciplines has been enormous. Foucault in his works tried various strategies to study human beings. He attempted to avoid a merely structuralist analysis, which disposes of meaning altogether and substitutes a formal model of human behavior. He also dismissed the phenomenological tracing all meaning back to the meaning-giving autonomous, transcendental subject.

His first major work, *Folie et déraison: Histoire de la folie à l'âge classique* (1961; *Madness and Civilization: A History of Insanity in the Age of Reason*, 1965), discusses the structures of cultural exclusion and integration of madness. In his next book, *Naissance de la clinique: Une Archéologie du regard médical* (1963; *The Birth of the Clinic: An Archaeology of Medical Perceptions*, 1973), he turns his attention to the analysis of the body as corpse laid out before the doctor's scrutiny. In *The Order of Things* and *L'Archéologie du savoir* (1969; *The Archaeology of Knowledge*, 1972), he explored the structures of discourse. At the time of his death, he was at work on a multivolume history of sexuality, several volumes of which had been completed.

Sources for Further Study

Caws, Peter. "Language as the Human Reality," in *The New Republic*. CLXIV (March 27, 1971), pp. 28-34.

Cousins, Mark, and Athar Hussain. *Michel Foucault*, 1984.

Dreyfus, Hubert L., and Peter Rabinow. *Michel Foucault: Beyond Structuralism and Hermeneutics*, 1983 (second edition).

Major-Poetzl, Pamela. *Michel Foucault's Archaeology of Western Culture: Toward a New Science of History*, 1983.

Pratt, Vernon. "Foucault and the History of Classification Theory," in *Studies in History and Philosophy of Science*. VII (1977), pp. 163-171.

Smart, Barry. *Foucault*, 1985.

Karin A. Wurst

ORIENTALISM

Author: Edward W. Said (1935-   )
Type of work: Cultural criticism
First published: 1978

Form and Content

The best-known and most controversial study of its sort, Edward Said's *Orientalism* is a scholarly and polemic examination of how scholars and other writers in the West have long viewed the East. By "Orientalism," Said means three things. First, he uses the term as an academic designation for the activities of anyone who teaches, writes about, or conducts research on the Orient or the East in whatever discipline. A second meaning Said finds in the term is the related but more general notion of Orientalism "as a way of thinking based upon a binary distinction between 'the (allegedly inferior) Orient' and 'the (allegedly superior) Occident,'" which has served writers of all sorts as a starting point for theories, social descriptions, political accounts, and fictions about the Orient, its people, customs, "mind," and destiny. Said views Orientalism, third, as a corporate institution since the eighteenth century for dealing with and dominating the Orient. Despite the broad range of his definitions, however, Said's own focus in *Orientalism* is specifically and almost exclusively on the Arab Muslim Middle East, which he presumably (and gratuitously) considers a representative case study illustrative of the situation throughout Asia.

Said develops his argument and analysis in three chapters, which examine chronological stages in the phenomenon of Orientalism, defined chiefly through the works and views of representative Orientalist scholars. Chapter 1, "The Scope of Orientalism," reviews writing on the Muslim Near East before the eighteenth century and the significance of Napoleon Bonaparte's invasion of Egypt in 1798. Said argues that in this period the East was a textual universe for the West, with Orientalists interested in classical periods and not at all in contemporary, living Orientals. Chapter 2, "Oriental Structures and Restructures," treats the French and English traditions of the study of the Muslim Near East during the nineteenth century and up to World War I. Said examines the career of the leading French Orientalist Sylvestre de Sacy and such works as Edward Lane's *Account of the Manners and Customs of the Modern Egyptians* (1836) in endeavoring to demonstrate, among other things, how Orientalism has influenced and affected Western perceptions of the Arab Middle East and eventually Arab Middle Eastern perceptions of themselves. Chapter 3, "Orientalism Now," characterizes Orientalism in the 1920's and 1930's, through a review of the careers of the leading Islamicists of the day, the French scholar Louis Massignon and the English scholar Hamilton Gibb. Said notes that the latter, who served as director of the Center for Middle Eastern Studies at Harvard University, lectured on "the Arab mind" and the "aversion of the Muslim from the thought processes of rationalism" and referred to Islam as "Mohammedanism."

The concluding section of the final chapter of *Orientalism* is titled "The Latest Phase," by which Said means the period after World War II, when the center of activity for the phenomenon became the United States and the American "area specialist," trained in the social sciences, assumed the lead role from the earlier philologists. Said examines how such Middle East area specialists participate in and perpetuate the dynamics of Orientalism in their representation of Islam and Arabs in four categories. The first is "popular images and social science representations"; here Said argues that treatments of Arabs and Islam are predictably and routinely negative and derive from the transference of the popular anti-Semite animus from Jews to Arabs. Said asserts the existence of academic support for popular negative caricatures of Arab and Islamic culture. For example, the first president of the Middle East Studies Association of North America observed in 1967: "The modern Middle East and North Africa is not a center of great cultural achievement . . . [and] . . . has only in small degree the kinds of traits that seem to be important in attracting scholarly attention." Said's second category is "public relations policy," by which, in Said's view, contemporary scholars perpetuate such aspects of European traditions of Orientalist scholarship as the racist discourse and dogmas of Ernest Renan in the 1840's. His example is the work of Gustave von Grunebaum, a prominent German Orientalist for whom the Center for Middle Eastern Studies at the University of California at Los Angeles is named and whom Said characterizes as exhibiting an "almost virulent dislike of Islam." Four dogmas implicit in the work of such scholars are the absolute difference between the (rational and superior) Occident and the (aberrant and inferior) Orient, the preferability of abstractions about the Orient to direct evidence from the contemporary Orient itself, the incapacity of the Orient to define itself, and the recognition that the Orient is to be feared and controlled. A third category of contemporary Orientalist representation Said calls "Merely Islam." Here his focus is on the alleged inherent inability of the Muslim Near Orient to be as richly human as the West. As evidence, Said cites the view of a prominent political scientist, whose argument that all human thought processes can be reduced to eight includes the ancillary assertion that the Islamic mind is capable of only four. Another piece of evidence is the presumption on the part of the already cited president of the Middle East Studies Association that "since the Arabic language is much given to rhetoric Arabs are consequently incapable of true thought." The fourth characteristic of Orientalist representation of the Muslim Near East is the attempt "to see the Orient as an imitation West" and encouragement to Easterners both to judge themselves by Western criteria and to strive to achieve Western goals. Said laments the consequent fact that "the modern Orient . . . participates in its own Orientalizing."

Said's concluding remarks briefly address the positive side to the problematic of reliable scholarship in the field. He argues that the best work on the Arabs and the Near Orient is (likely to be) done by scholars "whose allegiance is to a discipline defined intellectually and not to a 'field' like Orientalism defined either canonically, imperially, or geographically." Said cites the work of the anthropologist Clifford

Geertz as an example. As for scholars with Orientalist training, he sees Maxime Rodinson, Jacques Berque, Anouar Abdel Malek, and Roger Owen as freed from "the old ideological straitjacket." Ultimately, however, Said views Orientalism past and present as an almost unmitigated intellectual failure, as an enterprise which has "failed to identify with human experience" and has "failed also to see it as human experience."

Analysis

As a Palestinian educated at Princeton and Harvard universities, Edward Said was bound to confront representations by Western scholars of his culture of birth. He read numerous patronizing characterizations of "the Arab mind" and of Islam as a monolithic phenomenon. He read a leading European scholar's reference to Arabs as people who could not think straight. Von Grunebaum saw in Islamic civilization "anti-humanism" and in Arab nationalism a lack of "a formative ethic." Said read a report by an American State Department expert, in a 1972 issue of the *American Journal of Psychiatry*, asserting that "objectivity is not a value in the Arab system" and that "the art of subterfuge is highly developed in Arab life, as well as in Islam itself." What troubled Said was not that stereotypes were part of contemporary American popular culture but that there seemed to be a tradition and institution-alization of them in scholarship. The special history of the Palestinian people vis-à-vis the Zionist movement, the establishment of the state of Israel, and the aftermaths of the Arab-Israeli wars of 1967 and 1973 made Said's concerns both in-tellectual and political issues. That Said's profession became university teaching at Columbia University and literary criticism impelled him to respond to the issues through an investigation of scholarly writing on the subject and combine the fruits of his own research with polemic purpose.

Said's agenda in *Orientalism* is essentially political: He is asking that academics, policymakers, and other American intellectuals recognize and redress long-standing and arguably systematic bias against the Arabs. *Orientalism* derives largely from Said's sense of injustices perpetrated on the Palestinian people, an awareness so intense that the author has little time to find or discern positive dimensions or sides to Orientalism or even individual Orientalists who do not fit his definition of the biased scholar. Consequently, *Orientalism* has left few readers unmoved. Reactions have been predictable and varied according to the predispositions of reviewers. For example, the Anglo-Arab Middle East historian Albert Hourani has found in *Orien-talism* a basically sound historical treatment, with its major flaw forgivable exag-geration for the sake of argument. At the other extreme is a Jewish-American view expressed by Leon Wieseltier, who is outraged at Said's pro-Palestinian perspective and takes the latter to task for advocating a cause whose adherents use oil and murder as weapons. The comparative literature specialist Victor Brombert has a more detached view and consequently assesses the book's strengths, weaknesses, and relevance beyond issues of Middle Eastern studies and politics. He finds Said occasionally guilty of setting up discredited models to make and prove points and of other polemical excesses. Brombert's most serious concern with *Orientalism* is his sense that Said exhibits in it a loss of faith in humanism—in other words, that Said seems not to believe that scholars and other intellectuals can prize disinterested scholarship and love their disciplines more than their own success, power, material comforts, and the society and institutions that support their work.

Nevertheless, it is difficult to imagine even the most negative assessment of *Orientalism* gainsaying two arguments that constitute almost the warp and weft of Said's book. First is the groundlessness and perniciousness of the idea of European identity as superior to non-European peoples and cultures. Second is the constant need to question dominative modes of contemplating, discussing, and evaluating cultures other than one's own.

Critical Context

Although far and away Edward Said's best-known book, *Orientalism* is only one in a lengthy list of literary critical studies, studies of culture, historical analyses, and meditations and proposals on the subject of the Arabs and of Western views of Arabs and Islam.

In Said's stylistic analyses in *Orientalism* and his allusions throughout to a broad spectrum of literary works, he displays the literary perspectives and erudition of such literary critical writings of his as *Joseph Conrad and the Fiction of Autobiography* (1966), *Beginnings: Intention and Method* (1975), an edited volume titled *Literature and Society* (1980), and *The World, the Text, and the Critic* (1983).

As for Said's equally long-standing intellectual concerns with the political place and image of the Arabs of the Near Orient in the late twentieth century, before *Orientalism* came a series of pamphlets with such titles as *The Arabs Today: Alternatives for Tomorrow* (1973), *Arabs and Jews: A Possibility of Concord* (1974), *Lebanon: Two Perspectives* (1975), and *The Palestinians and American Policy* (1976). Substantial studies published after *Orientalism* include *The Question of Palestine* (1979), *Covering Islam: How the Media and the Experts Determine How We See the Rest of the World* (1981), and *Blaming the Victims: Spurious Scholarship and the Palestinian Question* (1988; edited with Christopher Hitchens).

In the context of scholarly and intellectual currents in general, *Orientalism* is a prominent example of revisionist stances in various academic fields in which ethnocentric approaches, national character studies, the definition of other through self, the presumption of the possibility of scholarly objectivity, and other traditional assumptions and approaches to the investigation of foreign subject matter have been questioned and forcefully challenged. Said's historical survey is as strong as it could be in arguing that a near conspiracy can be part of scholarship. His argument encouraging scholars to avoid accepting results of such research unquestioningly is salutory. In addition, his concluding examination of post-World War II American study of the Middle East constitutes both a provocative call for better teaching, research, and scholarship methods in the academic establishment and a warning to scholars concerning the inappropriateness and moral impropriety of their working in a field which does not engage their sympathies or evoke their admiration. Little serious scholarship in the field has taken place since *Orientalism* without a consideration of Said's theses, criticisms, and proposals. In short, *Orientalism* was a watershed event in academic circles. It was remarkable that a scholarly study treating such an esoteric subject from such an unpopular perspective would become one of the most widely reviewed books of its day.

For the general American reader, Said provided a dramatic and provocative plea for fairmindedness in dealing with Arab culture. More generally, he clarified the need to transcend ethnocentric predispositions and biases in judging non-Americans and their cultures in an ever-shrinking and increasingly interdependent world and to give primary and serious attention to the self-views of others, however troubling and challenging to one's own cultural values.

Sources for Further Study

Beard, Michael. "Between West and World," in *Diacritics*. IX (Winter, 1979), pp. 2-12.

Brombert, Victor. "Orientalism and the Scandals of Scholarship: *Orientalism*," in *The American Scholar*. XLVIII (Autumn, 1979), pp. 532-542.

Hourani, Albert. "The Road to Morocco: *Orientalism*," in *The New York Review of Books*. XXVI (March 8, 1979), pp. 27-30.

Said, Edward. "Islam, Orientalism, and the West," in *Time*. CXIII (April 16, 1979), p. 54.

Said, Edward, and Leon Wieseltier. "An Exchange on *Orientalism*," in *The New Republic*. CLXXX (May 19, 1979), pp. 39-40.

Wieseltier, Leon. Review in *The New Republic*. CLXXX (April 7, 1979), pp. 27-33.

Michael Craig Hillmann

THE ORIGINS OF TOTALITARIANISM

Author: Hannah Arendt (1906-1975)
Type of work: History
Time of work: The late eighteenth and the nineteenth and twentieth centuries
Locale: Europe
First published: 1951; revised, 1958, 1966

Form and Content

The fact that Hannah Arendt was a Jewish refugee from Nazi oppression cannot be divorced from *The Origins of Totalitarianism*. Written with eminent scholarship (hardly a page lacks footnotes and in some cases the footnotes are of greater length than the text), the book nevertheless is a passionate condemnation of totalitarianism. Arendt, in short, was searching for the intellectual roots of the movement which had displaced her from her native Germany and had made her a refugee in a world decidedly unfriendly toward Jews. Clearly the book is the product not only of thought but also of suffering. In fact, it was only with the publication of *The Origins of Totalitarianism* that Arendt was able to secure an academic position. Eventually she would become a full professor at Princeton University, the first woman to receive that honor.

The work is divided into three sections: "Antisemitism," "Imperialism," and "Totalitarianism," with the latter two parts having been revised in the 1958 and 1966 editions. (As the book was revised, it grew in length, running to 526 pages in the 1966 edition.) It is Arendt's thesis that the two most important contributions to totalitarian movements have been anti-Semitism and imperialism. In the first three chapters, Arendt discusses the origins of anti-Semitism and the position of the Jews in Western European society, particularly in the late eighteenth and the nineteenth centuries. She differs from many scholars in taking issue with the Jew-as-scapegoat analysis of anti-Semitism; instead, she attempts to demonstrate that anti-Semitism arose from several causes. It was a consequence of the declining importance of Jews, particularly Jewish bankers in the nineteenth century, the rise of the nation-state, and the emergence of a new type of nationalism in which the Jews were perceived as an alien element in the nation. Moreover, Jews had historically aligned themselves with the nobility, a class which had been in a position of power and so was able to protect them. Now, the nobility was seen as the major impediment to the formation of unified nation-states, and the Jews were perceived as the nobility's lackeys.

Chapter 4 deals with the Dreyfus affair, in which Captain Alfred Dreyfus, a French officer and a Jew, was railroaded into imprisonment on Devil's Island, falsely accused of spying. Although Dreyfus was known to be innocent, his trial and imprisonment, and the attempted suppression of evidence which would have freed him, revealed the anti-Semitic climate of both the army and large segments of the population in turn-of-the-century France.

Part 2, "Imperialism," consists of five chapters. Each discusses an aspect of imperialism, but the thrust is the development of racism as a consequence of imperialism and the consequences of racism. Imperialism and racism went hand in glove, according to Arendt, and it was imperialism which brought Europeans into contact with nonwhite peoples, peoples the Europeans believed to be culturally inferior and who were increasingly seen to be racially inferior as well.

Given the presence of such colonial populations, Europeans were more easily able to abandon whatever moral scruples they possessed. Thus, the natives were never given the rights which the inhabitants of the home country were afforded and, particularly in Africa, brutality—even mass murder—was not unusual.

The expansionist climate would result in the panmovements in Europe. The philosophy of the panmovements was that all people who spoke a particular language as their mother tongue were of that nationality. For example, and regardless of political frontiers, all who spoke German were Germans and belonged within one unified German state. In short, imperialism aided the formation of supernationalist sentiments, and, by the same token, supernationalist emotions helped to create the collective mass consciousness necessary for the development of totalitarianism.

The third and final section, which consists of four chapters, deals directly with totalitarianism, concentrating upon Nazi Germany and Communist Russia, although more space is given to the former than to the latter.

Given a climate of anti-Semitism and supernationalism, Arendt adds another element: "mass man," the refugee within his own society, a man led by declassed intellectuals. Arendt grants that political ideology could and would vary from society to society, but in her view political ideology was not the basic issue. What was necessary for the rise of totalitarianism were the factors mentioned above.

A new factor was added in the twentieth century: the presence in great numbers of mass men. These atomized individuals had no attachment to job, family, friends, or class. They were available to follow a leadership which allowed them to gain identity in a mass movement. No matter how brutal or irrational such a movement might be, it nevertheless offered a sense of identity to those who had never sufficiently gained one or who had lost the one they had possessed.

Analysis

The Origins of Totalitarianism is a wide-ranging book, capacious to a fault. Indeed, some of the chapter subsections could stand alone and perhaps should not have been included; instead, they should have been published as separate historical pieces, as they are tangential to the subject of the book. Moreover, it is surprising that Arendt never precisely defines totalitarianism, although she deals with Stalinist Russia and Nazi Germany as prime examples. What emerges is a portrait of an entity which seeks to establish total control within the state, absolute control not only of the government but also of every aspect of the lives of those who reside within it. Whatever the political philosophy—and political philosophies differed greatly between Nazism and Communism—no deviance in thought or action was permitted. In fact, to a totalitarian regime, ideology is secondary. What is of prime importance is the state itself. The state is above the individual, and both the individual and the party exist for the state. The state itself is the cause, the cause to which all belong and in which all submerge their individual identities and become one.

Every agency of the totalitarian state has but one function: to enforce uniformity, to stamp out deviance. The forms of enforcement or enculturation may differ from regime to regime, as they in fact did in Adolf Hitler's Germany or Joseph Stalin's Russia, but the ultimate purpose remains the same. Thus, regimes such as Spain under Francisco Franco, Italy under Benito Mussolini, or Argentina under Juan Perón do not qualify as totalitarian, for their Fascist masters sought only absolute political control. Other areas of life, such as art, music, and literature, were left untouched. The dictators of these regimes did have their personal preferences, but they did not impose them upon the nations they governed. Totalitarianism, on the other hand, is all-pervasive and all-encompassing. Hitler himself differentiated between Fascism and Nazism in this regard.

Arendt provides an excellent analysis of the seemingly unlikely alliance of the mob and the intellectual. The underclass, whether *Lumpenproletariat* or fallen bourgeoisie, stripped of jobs, family, friends, a sense of community, and, perhaps, religious attachments, becomes atomized. Being human, however, such individuals seek a sense of identity, an identity which can be found in a mass movement, such as Communism or Nazism. In joining a mass movement, the individual identity, weak though it was, is lost, submerged in a mass—and much more powerful— identity.

The role of the intellectual was to mobilize and direct the masses, the very mass of atomized men who yearn to be mobilized and directed and to lose themselves in the collective whole. The intellectual, as Arendt defines him, need not be a formally educated person. Neither Hitler nor Stalin had much formal education; Hitler was in fact anti-intellectual, but he was a man of ideas, a man with a message.

While Arendt's discussions of Nazi Germany and Stalinist Russia are excellent, what is surprising is that China under Mao Tse-tung is omitted. That is understandable in the first (1951) edition, but the 1958 and 1966 revisions should have contained a treatment of China, which was then the world's largest totalitarian society. One suspects that Arendt did not wish to deal with China because Mao, whatever his faults, was no Hitler or Stalin, and the Chinese peasant, who had brought Mao to power, was not the European atomized man. Similarly, one can take issue with Arendt's view that while dictatorship can occur in nations of any size, totalitarian regimes can develop only in states with quite large populations. This view has been disproved by the genocidal Pol Pot regime in Cambodia, a fairly small nation. It is true that the murder of three million people by the Khmer Rouge under Pol Pot and the totalitarian nature of his regime came to light only after the last revision of *The Origins of Totalitarianism* in 1966. Indeed, the facts were not well-known until after Arendt's death in 1975, but the evidence of Cambodia does disprove her contention regarding state size and totalitarianism.

Given her background, it is not surprising that Arendt would focus upon anti-Semitism as a root cause of totalitarianism. Again, the evidence of China and Cambodia, nations without an anti-Semitic tradition, seems to contradict her on this point. Totalitarianism can exist, and has existed, entirely separate from anti-Semitism. Furthermore, as penetrating as her analysis of anti-Semitism is, it does not account for medieval and early modern anti-Semitism. Reading the book, one would gain the impression that anti-Semitism was almost a nineteenth and twentieth century phenomenon. Yet the roots of anti-Semitism lie deep within the Christian tradition as churchmen sought to distance their new religion from its parent, Judaism. It was not the Nazis who first built the ghetto walls, and it was not the persecutors of Alfred Dreyfus who perpetrated the Crusader massacres.

In a similar vein, imperialism may or may not be a cause of totalitarianism. Under Kaiser Wilhelm II, Germany acquired a colonial empire, and it seems reasonable that the experience of overlordship of nonwhite people who were considered racially inferior did in fact further an atmosphere of racism within Germany. That such racism added to the climate which brought the Nazi regime to power also seems reasonable. Yet China under Mao was clearly a totalitarian regime and it was neither imperialist nor racist. Precisely the same statement can be made for Cambodia under Pol Pot. On the other hand, Great Britain and France, the two greatest imperial powers of the modern world, never experienced totalitarianism; they evolved into parliamentary democracies.

What Arendt has done, then, is primarily to examine the roots of Hitlerian totalitarianism, and she has done so with solid scholarship, providing a number of penetrating insights. She has gone on to extrapolate from the German example to Stalinist Russia and to the nature and origins of totalitarianism as a whole. Yet the Nazi experience was only one among a number of totalitarian regimes; thus, while anti-Semitism, imperialism, racism, and the desire of an atomized population led by declassed intellectuals to gain a new sense of identity clearly contributed to the rise of Nazi totalitarianism, the same would not necessarily be true elsewhere. For example, the Stalinist regime in the Soviet Union was not openly anti-Semitic until its last days, although Russia was historically anti-Semitic. Moreover, Communist doctrine, far from being racist, openly and avowedly opposes racism. Thus the book would have been far truer to its content and scope if it had been titled "The Origins of Nazi Totalitarianism," for it is apparent that that is the subject about which Arendt knew most and is really the topic she most wished to discuss.

Critical Context

A work of eminent scholarship, although some of its basic premises can be faulted, *The Origins of Totalitarianism* vaulted Hannah Arendt into the ranks of intellectual preeminence. She would go on to author a number of books but became best known to the general public as a result of the 1963 publication of the controversial *Eichmann in Jerusalem: A Report on the Banality of Evil*. Karl Eichmann was the German officer directly in charge of the genocide practiced against the Jews in

World War II. He had been kidnapped in Argentina by the Israelis and brought to Jerusalem to stand trial.

Arendt claimed that it was wrong simply to concentrate upon one man, Eichmann, because others were also responsible: other countries which stood passively by, other Germans, and even Jews who had not acted with determination in the face of the Nazi evil. It was her view that, first in Germany and then in other parts of Nazi-occupied Europe, evil became commonplace, hence banal, and so did not garner the moral opprobrium which it normally would have aroused. From 1963 onward, the phrase "banality of evil" would be associated with her and would remain controversial.

Written between 1945 and 1949 and published in 1951, *The Origins of Totalitarianism* serves as an example of the right book at the right time. The true horror of the Nazi regime and its death factories had struck the world with awful force, and the West, then in the grip of the Cold War, was also reacting to the perceived menace of Communism, Communism not only in the Soviet Union but also throughout Soviet-occupied Eastern Europe. Thus, the time was ripe for an examination of totalitarianism. Arendt's book filled the need. It was not only erudite—it would have been recognized as a major treatise in any period—but also timely.

The Origins of Totalitarianism and *Eichmann in Jerusalem* are Arendt's best-known works. In them one sees her focus upon Nazism, the force that had displaced her from a comfortable life in her native Germany, had made her a refugee, and had murdered millions of her fellow Jews. It is no wonder, then, that the thrust of her intellectual interests thereafter would be an attempt to understand Nazism and that her clarity of vision was perhaps clouded by the anti-Semitism of Hitlerian Germany and its horrific consequences. Yet whatever its faults of conceptualization, *The Origins of Totalitarianism* will remain a major work in its field, for it provides much useful historical information and a number of profound insights into totalitarianism, a topic of crucial importance in the history of the twentieth century.

Sources for Further Study

Brown, J. F. Review in *Annals of the American Academy of Political and Social Science*. CCLXXVII (September, 1951), pp. 272-273.

Buchheim, Hans. *Totalitarian Rule: Its Nature and Characteristics*, 1968. Translated by Ruth Hein.

Cook, Thomas I. Review in *Political Science Quarterly*. LXVI (June, 1951), pp. 290-293.

Friedrich, Carl Joachim, and Zbigniew K. Brzezinski. *Totalitarian Dictatorship and Autocracy*, 1966 (second edition).

Hughes, H. Stuart. Review in *The Nation*. CLXXII (March 24, 1951), pp. 280-281.

Kohn, Hans. Review in *Saturday Review of Literature*. XXXIV (March 24, 1951), pp. 10-11.

Schapiro, Leonard Bertram. *Totalitarianism*, 1972.

Unger, Aryeh L. *The Totalitarian Party: Party and People in Nazi Germany and Soviet Russia*, 1974.

Joel M. Roitman

OVERDRIVE
A Personal Documentary

Author: William F. Buckley, Jr. (1925-   )
Type of work: Memoir
Time of work: Late autumn, 1981, with flashbacks
Locale: Primarily Connecticut and New York
First published: 1983

> *Principal personages:*
> WILLIAM F. BUCKLEY, JR., a journalist, the author
> CHRISTOPHER BUCKLEY, the author's son
> WILLIAM F. BUCKLEY, SR., the author's father
> EDWARD PULLING, the headmaster of the Millbrook School in
>   Connecticut
> ROSALYN TURECK, a musician
> FERNANDO VALENTI, a musician
> DAVID NIVEN, an actor
> RONALD REAGAN, a personal friend of Buckley

Form and Content

William F. Buckley, Jr., paused to examine his life at a peak moment, choosing a single week in the late autumn of 1981. It was a week not dominated by major world events, so that the everyday life of this politically conscious figure, and his more purely human consciousness, comes to the fore. The form of a seven-day slice of life is more novelistic than memoiristic; the refusal to rearrange life dramatically, instead cherishing its mundane texture and spontaneous moments of reflection, suggests the film documentary more than a novel—hence the subtitle. (Earlier, Buckley employed the same form in *Cruising Speed: A Documentary*, 1971.) Like a documentary, *Overdrive* leaves in all Buckley's weaknesses and warts. It becomes an apologia only when reviewing verbal duels that have vexed the author in the past and continue to haunt him; thus, he gives his side of the acrimonious disputes with Gore Vidal and Franklin Littell. Another important aspect of the memoir as document is the self-explanatory role of the many letters he incorporates verbatim.

Buckley freely admits that he eschews introspection and that his life could be called unexamined. He explains the "commotion" of his life (the experiences of just one week require him to draw vignettes of some two hundred people) as arising from a counterpoint between the search for intellectual virtue and the fear of boredom:

> The unexamined life may not be worth living, in which case I will concede that mine is not worth living. But excepting my own life, I do seek to examine, and certainly I dilate upon, public questions I deem insufficiently examined.

The narrator appears to be much like the public Buckley. He delights in the deadpan, outrageous statement. Thus, he begins his vignette of Howard Hunt with the words, "Howard was my boss during the nine months I spent in Mexico working for the CIA." Nevertheless, the personality that emerges is more relaxed than that of the public Buckley.

There are hasty nods to almost every living soul Buckley encounters in eight days; such sketches do not rise above mere name-dropping, often of obscure people. When Buckley takes the time to describe in anecdotal detail, he can produce memorable portraits. Of the two politicians, Ronald Reagan and Daniel Patrick Moynihan, who are extensively portrayed, Reagan is flat and wooden, but Moynihan is vibrant and believable. More inspired are sketches of people in the arts: for example, master harpsichordists Rosalyn Tureck and Fernando Valenti and actor David Niven.

The most vivid descriptions center on Buckley's boyhood days at the Millbrook School, with portraits of his father, the headmaster, Edward Pulling, the other masters, his brothers, and schoolmates. The foibles of the masters are drawn with a true novelist's eye; a fine contribution to the schooldays genre is Buckley's mad naturalist (and sometime baby-sitter) who had a special fondness for snakes. The section on the Millbrook School was originally published as a separate piece titled "God and Boys at Millbrook." It enters Buckley's documentary in connection with a trip on the Orient Express that caused him to miss the school's fiftieth anniversary. The Orient Express excursion (entering the memoir as he dashes off an article on it) in turn irresistibly reminds him of a hair-raising, week-long trip on a World War II troop train: "So to speak, the Upstairs and Downstairs of train travel. . . . It is terribly vexing that it isn't obvious that the one was ultimately more pleasurable in memory than the other."

Unlike the blasé, pedantic, ideological, public Buckley, the inner Buckley views much with unblushing delight and appreciation: his family and familiars, his car, peanut butter, harpsichords, boats, the sea, a good play, and every solid, mundane thing that warms a life. The "hard-working snob" (a jibe he has gleefully taken over from one of his opponents) is surprisingly unspoiled. Neither ideology nor specific ideas are dear to Buckley the author of *Overdrive*; rather, the flow of ideas as part of living is important. In Buckley's personal documentary, there is no idea without a life-form, or at least something concrete, attached.

Analysis

Buckley, generally viewed as an ideologist for his long-standing and occasionally quixotic defense of conservatism on principle, in *Overdrive* defines ideology itself as "a hierarchy of values." Such a definition explains the apparent absence of any ideology in *Overdrive*, where the concerns are chiefly about ethical and ontological questions. The author's well-known public persona, put forward rambunctiously over the years, however, impelled critics to view *Overdrive* as no more than a vehicle for the author's image. Initial disclaimers of harboring the least resentment toward Buckley routinely dissolved into parodies of both the man and his style. In reverse counterpart to the boy who cried "Wolf!" too often, Buckley had in the past cried "Sunshine!" so often that even when he was submerged in a gathering darkness, his most eloquent defender, Norman Podhoretz, chided him for showing "all light and no shadow."

Grounded more deeply than the glitter of Buckley's life are the two recurring themes in *Overdrive:* "right reason" and ghosts. Right reason is Buckley's translation of the medieval Latin *recta ratio*, whose meaning combines intellectual integrity and simple ethics. Perhaps the unique paradox of Buckley is that his version of intellectual integrity—to which he holds fiercely—is primarily an ethical matter, only secondarily an intellectual matter, and scarcely an academic matter, since it must be manifested through a real application. In fact, Buckley's wry report on how he preserved his dignity in the face of a hostile audience at Vassar College is perhaps his best example of right reason at work and triumphant. The genesis of right reason goes back to his close-knit family and the Millbrook School, an experience forming the heart of the book.

As for ghosts, Buckley's most important is Whittaker Chambers. Chambers is no doubt a troubled ghost, but Buckley does not allow himself to entertain the possibility that Chambers perjured himself. His Chambers is a soft-spoken, infinitely weary, benign shade who visits only Buckley's writing desk. By contrast, Harry Elmlark, the late newspaperman, has so robust a personality that Buckley speaks over his ashes as if Elmlark were alive.

It was no coincidence that the week chosen for the framework of the autobiography, in addition to being a relatively quiet one, was the week in which Buckley was deciding whether to contribute a commentary for the British Broadcasting Corporation's television production of Evelyn Waugh's *Brideshead Revisited* (1945, 1959). Indeed, the "haunting" novel is primarily about decay and death, particularly in the thirteen-hour videotaped version that Buckley watched in a marathon session that week. Buckley, who knew Waugh (another ghost returning), explains his commentary as an intended counterbalance to what he perceived as the production's anti-Catholicism, in accordance with Waugh's dictum that the novel was "about God," not the "fools" who misinterpret Him.

Brushed repeatedly by death, Buckley keeps refocusing on life, which abounds in small pleasures "whose resonances have been insufficiently sung." This ordinary-extraordinary week brings the news that a friend, the harpsichordist Fernando Valenti, is terminally ill of cancer. Buckley draws a poignant contrast between Valenti's enfeeblement and the vibrancy of the music he created. Then Buckley comes home to find his newly arrived houseguest, David Niven, still vivacious and irrepressible (as captured in a Buckley vignette) but already having "a most fearful time controlling his voice." (The fact that Niven was then suffering from Alzheimer's disease, known at the time of publication, is left out.)

Other guests arrive, one of whom has a bad back. For the first time, Buckley—still vital, active, taking hare-brained moonlight sails in midwinter—casually remarks, "I have chronic sinusitis, Dupuyter's contracture, and skin cancer, so I suggest that we [the back-sufferer and Buckley] devote three minutes to our several physical complaints, and then shift to sublime subjects, like David's and my books." The ambassador to France soon drops in, which leads to the recollection of a practical joke of gargantuan proportions. It is characteristic that an elaborate practical joke directly follows the book's darkest moment. Buckley's summing-up, however, makes it clear that he is not denying death, particularly in this work.

As the week ends, he muses over his closest peer, Bill Rickenbacker, and the theme of right reason returns. Rickenbacker has an inventory of accomplishments similar to Buckley's: "linguist, writer, economic analyst, humorist, pianist, and pilot." Unlike Buckley, however, this friend never "merchandised" his talents, preferring to live on a farm, issue pastoral letters, and never make any money. Buckley thinks about this road not taken, which might easily have been his:

> Self-pleasure is heady stuff, but isn't it . . . antisocial, in the grave sense of deciding not to share? . . . Some pleasures cannot be shared, but must one [not] seek to share those that can, which includes insight into right reason?

Emerging from this week, Buckley locates the source of a quotation that has been nagging at him and quotes it in full. The passage begins concretely, but concludes, "A great nothingness was before him, a great nothingness that was Something, a great nothingness that was All; and in the warm freedom from the tangible he knew his Savior and was absorbed by Him." Responding to it, Buckley exclaims, "But the radiance of the whole thing cries out, and the great mysterious dilemma is made plain." The same evening, he visits a lifelong friend who has just had a stroke. Home from the depressing visit (and it is typical of Buckley that sadness must be surmised indirectly, from the vigor of his reaction against it), he drinks in the unexpected arrival of his son Christopher, who "brings into the room freshness, affection, and informality." In the unedited welter of material that this typical yet watershed week has thrown at him, life predominated over death. For all that has gone well (and the emphasis is Buckley's), "we are *obliged* to be grateful. To be otherwise is wrong reason."

Critical Context

Overdrive and the critical reaction to it helped to bring about a quasi canonization of Buckley as the "Patron Saint of the Conservatives" (as John B. Judis aptly, if sarcastically, subtitled his 1988 biography of him). Buckley's first book, *God and Man at Yale: The Superstitions of "Academic Freedom"* (1951), indicated both his political and religious concerns. Nevertheless, the political side predominated in Buckley's subsequent writing, particularly his newspaper column *On the Right*, and culminated in his unsuccessful run for the mayoralty of New York City in 1965. A closer association between religion and politics reemerged from the 1970's onward.

An inadvertent support for Buckley's "canonization" was provided in a review of *Overdrive* by John Gregory Dunne, who saw the chief flaw of the work as its failure to address life's *stigmata*—that is, the "alcoholism, drug addiction, pederasty, pedophilia"—that infected Buckley's cast of characters, yet "not a hint of which darkens Mr. Buckley's journal." The result, for Dunne, is "a truly alarming vision of a life without shadows." The critic introduced a parodic bit of religious imagery, calling Buckley's world "a city of God from which Mr. Buckley dispenses his patronage as if it were sanctifying grace."

By contrast, Buckley's partisan apologist, Forrest McDonald, raising a lone voice against the anti-Buckley journalistic uproar, pleaded the case for Buckley the writer based in part upon Buckley's good deeds and personal virtues. Norman Podhoretz, finding the biting hostility that greeted *Overdrive* in the press to be an interesting phenomenon in itself, defended Buckley, only half jokingly, in terms of the Talmud. Podhoretz, however, can understand the resentment that many must feel toward "this 'blasphemously happy' man who is in love with the life he leads." Like Dunne, Podhoretz faults Buckley for showing "all light and no shadow."

Once launched, the new perception of Buckley, who heretofore was a primarily ideological figure, in moral and ethical terms became predominant and contributed in a subtle way to the climate of opinion about political figures generally. Buckley's followers virtually abandoned ideology and began to press their challenge to non-conservative leaders in simple terms: Is he or she virtuous? With all that makes the anticrowd position of Buckley so precarious in a democracy, is he, nevertheless, "right" in a personal moral sense? This focus contradicts Buckley's own reverence for eighteenth century American constitutional theory, which sought to make government work well and responsibly regardless of the rascals, or paragons, in charge.

Buckley's patrician probity unexpectedly dovetailed with a popular movement back to reliance on the leader's moral purity as the sole guarantee of good government (thereby ignoring the lessons of history). The frustration felt by those representing the broad spectrum of opinion to the left of Buckley's position might, however, find a remedy in the same source, turning to the nonideological ideal of right reason that Buckley shows himself attempting to live by in *Overdrive*.

Sources for Further Study

Burner, David. *Column Right*, 1988.

Dunne, John Gregory. "Happy Days Are Here Again," in *The New York Review of Books*. XXX (October 13, 1983), p. 20.

Ephron, Nora. Review in *The New York Times Book Review*. LXXXVIII (August 7, 1983), p. 7.

Judis, John B. *William F. Buckley, Jr.: Patron Saint of the Conservatives*, 1988.

Koenig, Rhoda. "Dictated but Not Read," in *Harper's Magazine*. CCLXVII (October, 1983), p. 72.

Podhoretz, Norman. Review in *Commentary*. LXXVI (November, 1983), p. 66.

Winchell, Mark Royden. *William F. Buckley, Jr.*, 1984.

D. Gosselin Nakeeb

PACK MY BAG
A Self-Portrait

Author: Henry Green (Henry Vincent Yorke, 1905-1973)
Type of work: Autobiography
Time of work: 1905-1927
Locale: Great Britain
First published: 1940

> *Principal personage:*
> HENRY VINCENT YORKE (HENRY GREEN), a novelist

Form and Content

In 1938, at age thirty-three, fearing that the incipient world war would bring about his death, Henry Green felt the necessity to create a written record of his life. He could not see that he had the time left to use his material in the less personal and, to him, better form of the novel. So he wrote this autobiography, which takes him from his earliest memories at home through his education, culminating in two years at the University of Oxford. The autobiography concludes with a brief description of his work in 1927 as a laborer in his family's foundry in Birmingham. As Henry Yorke, rather than the pseudonymous Henry Green, the author subsequently became managing director of the company. This book provides no account of the period between 1927 and 1938, during which the author was rising in the family business and publishing his second novel, *Living* (1929). He does write about the earlier composition and publication of his first novel. *Blindness* was published in 1926, while Green was still an undergraduate at Oxford.

Divided into seventeen unnumbered chapters, the autobiography is most heavily devoted to Green's years in an unnamed boarding school in Kent and to his period in preparatory school at Eton College, which he also does not name as such. A chapter detailing his life before school opens the book, and the concluding three chapters concern his two years at Oxford and his work in Birmingham. The book begins with Green admitting that he was born into money. He is living on the family estate, called Forthampton, located in Tewkesbury, Gloucestershire. His earliest memories seem to be primarily about servants: Poole, the gardener, who spoke against the author's mother but could not alter his love for her; a young maid with bad breath who played vigorous physical games with him; and Lydia, the last maid who could remember his great grandmother and whose retirement cottage he often visited. In contrast, he can remember only two contacts with his grandfather.

Green's prose in this autobiography is as impressionistic as it is in his nine novels; thus, discerning the precise facts of his life is not easy. He rarely provides dates, identifying only five actual years precisely in the whole book. So, although he says that he started boarding school at age six, he does not reveal how long he was there or at what age he entered Eton. He declines to use the names of his friends because he expects his readers (clearly he was thinking primarily of British readers coming to the book soon after its publication) to draw their emotions from the book itself and not from "associations common to place names or to persons with whom the reader is unexpectedly familiar." In short, Green aims to provide an impression of his life and not an account of it. Nor does he draw many conclusions about its meaning or significance, especially of the kind that readers of his novels might hope to discover as clues to interpretations of the fiction.

Green's account of his youthful and adolescent years alternates between the rigors and loneliness of school terms and the much shorter, happier holidays between them. Green rarely makes the schools sound attractive. Writing of going to boarding school for the first time, he says that "nothing can ever so estrange a nursery boy from himself." He calls the seventy-five-student school a fascist state and writes that the boys were all "taught to see things as our headmaster did and he saw them upside down." Although he found greater personal liberty at Eton and had a room of his own, Green still characterizes the college as "an authoritarian state." In fact, he proclaims his belief that Germany's system of government at that time was founded on the system of the British public schools. Not surprisingly, then, young Green looked forward to each end of term, recalling that the boys marked off the days on calendars "as prisoners notch the walls." In contrast, the day for returning to school went unmarked and always loomed so far ahead that a boy on holiday could almost forget it was coming.

Besides his schooling and holidays, Green deals in detail with three major events in his life. One is the death of an older brother Philip, from which he says he learned that the living cry in self-pity at the menace of death. About this same time, when Green was eleven or twelve, his home had been turned into a convalescent hospital for officers. His experiences there with men from lower social classes were important as his first real journeys outside his own class. Although Green writes little about his parents, a third major learning experience presented itself when he received an erroneous report that both parents had been killed in an accident in Mexico. He writes that when the housemaster read him the telegram, he "felt absolutely nothing at all. In my life I have had no similar experience."

Analysis

Even though this book is only about Green's first twenty-two years, it gives the impression of being exceedingly pessimistic about the success of humans of all ages in managing their words, finding happiness in any activities, and, in fact, even surviving the approaching war that Green feared would take his own life and perhaps even mark the end of the world as he knew it. Green (probably by nature a pessimist) knows that he conveys an impression of almost overwhelming pessimism. So he stops his narrative from time to time to advise his reader that he does not really mean to sound as hopeless as he naturally is. Green almost seems to tell the reader not to take the pessimism as seriously as Green himself must take it. For example, coming to the end of his account of life at the boarding school, Green

urges the reader not to think "that there was persecution or even prolonged unhappiness at our school," even though the author has provided several accounts of both.
Green's questionable explanation for the dominance of unhappy events in his book
is that humans generally remember happiness only when it is attached to some
particular action or person. Because the lives of the boys in the school were so busy,
so communal, so totally arranged by the headmaster, Green could not actually
experience individualistic events that, alone, might have brought sufficient happiness to be remembered.

Later in the book, now writing about his period at Eton, Green stops himself
again to write, "But I should give an altogether false idea of my time at school by
describing it as one long moaning and groaning." He continues, observing that
there were "things anyone could do," and he recounts a few. Still, the more consistent impression is of the unhappy times.

At another point, writing about his own compositional method of bringing events
back from the past, Green writes that it is an error "to try to recreate days that are
done." What he does rather than to re-create the past is to search out a time and to
write it down as nearly as possible to capture what it seems to him to be like at the
time of writing, not at the time of occurrence. Here is a primary clue both to
Green's impressionistic style and to his pessimistic outlook. He has a present impression of the way things once were, and it is that current impression that he wants
to convey, rather than to try to discover through memory what his impression might
have been earlier. Even if Green was not inherently pessimistic, the reader can
certainly see that in the 1938-1939 period just prior to World War II, he was filled
with despair. Surely that hopelessness colored, as Green almost admits, not only the
actual nature of his past but also the feelings that he may or may not have had
during the occurrences in the past.

Like almost everyone who writes about British social and educational life, Green
must deal with the class system. Particularly interesting is his reaction to the officers who were convalescing in his family home during World War I. Writing of the
differences in expectations and manners between his family and the wounded officers, Green remarks that the effect "on a child of my class" was to expose him to
social gulfs that were both narrow and deep. They were narrow because these men
were, after all, officers, but the chasms were simultaneously deep because the men
had "to come over that rope bridge over that gorge across which intercourse is had
on the one side by saying 'sir' and on the other 'my good man.'" Of the effect on
him of his exposure to these men, Green maintains that he probably did not
immediately learn about the fine distinctions in class, because he was too young to
absorb such a lesson, but that he saw enough to recognize the echoes when he heard
them in later situations. According to Green, manners were what he and his family
had and these wounded men did not have; he contends that the differences between
the classes are accidental, primarily the result of money. The presence of money
means that leisure time is available for the learning of manners, so anyone can have
manners who has the time to learn them. Green does not even seem convinced of

the advantages of being in the privileged class, saying that many of the privileges are illusory. Writing of the laborers in the family's manufacturing plant, with whom he worked, Green observes that "theirs is one of the best ways to live provided that one has never been spoiled by moneyed leisure." Green's quiet acceptance of both the existence of the class system and the role he had to play in it is well demonstrated in the opening sentence, where he says he was born "with a silver spoon." Although Green's phrasing and the preceding discussion may imply that British society is divided simply into those who have money and manners and those who do not, the truth for Green is much more complex, as he states that there are hundreds of well-defined social classes throughout the country.

Regarding his own personality and character, Green is equally accepting, matter-of-fact, rational, and impressionistic. Considerably overweight and possessed of few athletic talents, Green was not very good at the sports and games that were such a large part of the boarding school system. A chapter begins "Gym was harrowing," but Green hardly tells a harrowing tale. Rather, he says that the boys did not really have to take gym class seriously because the instructor was of no importance in the scheme of things; only the headmaster really counted. About leaping onto a leather horse, Green says it was the pointless torture that boys had to go through in Fascist states and in an England preparing to fight such states. As he writes, the impending war was never far from Green's thoughts. He admits to developing a short-lived appetite for games when he first arrived at Eton, but in retrospect he is not at all certain why he temporarily found enjoyment in playing. At Oxford, Green became part of a group of young men more interested in aesthetics than in athletics, and they were looked upon as lepers by the majority of game-playing students. Green asserts that he and the others did not disdain athletics then only because of their own physical clumsiness. They saw positive damage to education being done by the emphasis upon athletics. Green writes that many of the school's masters were terrible teachers who held their positions only because they had been famous athletes.

If young Green was ineffective in athletics, he was not much better at first in that other primary game of the young: romance. The picture he draws of young Henry at Eton is of a boy holding girls in total awe. They were such beautifully superior beings that Green could not imagine doing anything with them but holding conversation, and even that was nearly impossible because of "the animal mystery they held of bearing life within them." In love with love and unable to bring his exalted emotions down to the level of individual girls, Green says that he could not possibly believe that poets such as Robert Herrick were correct in saying that women "enjoyed making love." He concludes that he and his friends were lucky in being protected from "a glut of girls," which would have served only to remove the wonderful mystery of sex.

Important things began happening to Green just at the end of his penultimate year at Eton and the summer holiday that followed. He began writing his first novel, and he began to "meet girls." Well, perhaps they were not really girls. They were two beautiful sisters in their thirties, one widowed and one married. They began to take interest in the sixteen-year-old Green. Although Green characterizes his view of them as being "in a light altogether remote from any that shines on this world," he recalls that he was simultaneously "entirely uncertain of my position" with them. Writing about the experience, he supposes that they never thought of him except when they were planning another party.

The instructive climax in the relationship came at a party at Green's family's home, at which Green went to bed because he disdained dancing. The "girls" came up to his room to tease him and try to taunt him down to the party. Green writes that he had thought in vain "over and over again" why they left the dance to come to him with their "bare shoulders," but as a result of their visit he felt grown-up and "did not presume on the incident because I had the sense to realize they were not for me." Green apparently muddled through all of his romantic explorations well enough, since he closes this book with the information that as of 1939 he had been happily married for ten years.

This portrait of Green as a young man is rarely that of an incipient artist in any Joycean sense, but rather of an intelligent youth who would one day write novels. Rarely discussing art and aesthetics, Green does twice quote from and discuss early efforts at writing. He cites three expressions of moods not so much for what they describe as for "how they are written." He refers to two as "yells about self" and expresses the hope that in this book the raw wounds have been scabbed over with an objective attitude. He remains afraid, however, that his death in World War II will "come too soon, before this attitude is established" for use in novels. Green need not have harbored such fears. This book has the attitude he seemed to desire. He survived the war. Seven more novels were written.

Critical Context

Autobiographies of fiction writers regularly seem to inherit a secondary role of supplying background material helpful in appreciation of the fiction; yet Green's book can stand on its own merits. It does so not so much because it is a fascinating look at English school life early in the twentieth century, but more because it is such an objective and impressionistic look at that life. Green indulges in self-defense so rarely and stands back from himself so often that the book has many of the narrative appeals of a good first-person novel, in which the author and the narrator must be seen as two separate persons.

At the same time, it does provide insights into the nature and sources of Green's pessimism and his resigned, wry sense of humor, which also dominate his novels. This book reveals some of the sources of two closely related subjects that occur frequently in the novels: the class system and feelings of being an outsider. Green's experiences in his own home with many officers of different social classes came at an impressionable age and helped give him his dubious attitude toward strict social separations. Certainly his own experiences as a leper, what he also called an "albino," in his not being acceptable within school circles, particularly the domi-nant athletic one, had a bearing on his many fictional depictions of persons unable to make meaningful contact with others.

Green's autobiography should be read alongside other literary memoirs by his contemporaries. In particular, the reader will gain added insight into *Pack My Bag* from Anthony Powell's four-volume memoir *To Keep the Ball Rolling* (1976-1982). Powell and Green were schoolmates at Eton, and the first volume of *To Keep the Ball Rolling*, *Infants of the Spring*, includes Powell's recollections of Green both as a youth and as a fellow writer, with an assessment of Green's achievements as a novelist.

Sources for Further Study
North, Michael. *Henry Green and the Writing of His Generation*, 1984.
Odom, Keith C. *Henry Green*, 1978.
Russell, John. *Henry Green: Nine Novels and an Unpacked Bag*, 1960.
Ryf, Robert. *Henry Green*, 1967.
Stokes, Edward. *The Novels of Henry Green*, 1960.
Weatherhead, Andrew Kingsley. *A Reading of Henry Green*, 1961.

J. F. Kobler

THE PARIS AND NEW YORK DIARIES OF NED ROREM
1951-1961

Author: Ned Rorem (1923-   )
Type of work: Diary
Time of work: 1951-1961
Locale: France, Morocco, Italy, England, Germany, and the United States
First published: The Paris Diary of Ned Rorem, 1966; *The New York Diary of Ned Rorem*, 1967

> *Principal personages:*
> NED ROREM, a composer and music writer
> MARIE-LAURE, VICOMTESS DE NOAILLES, his patron

Form and Content

The Paris Diary was the first in a long series of selections from his diaries published by the American composer Ned Rorem (some other installments are included in *Music From Inside Out*, 1967; *The Final Diary*, 1974; and *Essays and a Diary*, 1983). It was followed a year later by *The New York Diary*, which takes up the chronological sequence exactly where the previous volume leaves off: in mid-Atlantic, aboard the SS *United States*, as the author returns home to America after years of expatriation in France. Though necessarily episodic, given their "intimate journal" form, together the diaries do tell a story: of the composer's continuing attempts at self-understanding, abroad and at home. Young, talented, beautiful, and successful, Rorem traces his own progress in "those three things (and there are only three) we all desire: success in love, success in society, success in our work."

For his work, Rorem charts the mysterious ebb and flow of his desire to create. He also records the professional circumstances under which various pieces were commissioned, performed, and received, but more space is devoted to aphoristic reflections on music and the arts in general, and particularly to the state of modern music in Europe and America at the historical moment in which he writes: The conflict between serialism and his own more melodic, tonal compositions, for example, remains an important concern throughout.

For society (or friendship), Rorem records, especially in the more gossipy *Paris Diary*, his meetings and developing friendships with many prominent members of the international cultural élite, including artists, writers, performers, and conductors as well as his fellow composers. Most important is Marie-Laure, Vicomtesse de Noailles, who becomes his patron and closest friend; many sections of the diaries were written at her home in Hyères. He also traces, with a candor that surprised early readers, the progress of a serious drinking problem: Whereas *The Paris Diary* presents the picture of a young charmer whose drunken antics contribute to his social success (Marie Laure de Noailles becomes his friend only after he knocks her down at a party), *The New York Diary*'s portrait is more somber, its subject now an admitted alcoholic acutely aware of getting older, trying vainly to stay sober through attendance at meetings of Alcoholics Anonymous.

Rorem's honesty about his love affairs also shocked some readers when the books first appeared, for he was among the first American writers to admit his homosexuality without making an issue of it. Almost uniquely in gay literature of the 1950's, the diaries include no hint either of apology or of defensive boasting, or even of justification or explanation. Casual sexual encounters are duly recorded, while several long-term relationships receive all the care and attention that major emotional events deserve. This is especially true of *The New York Diary*, which includes a thirty-four-page letter to a former lover, detailing with painful precision all the nuances of a rejected lover's emotional response. The honesty of these passages on drink and sex attracted the most attention among both diaries' first reviewers. Rorem's true subject, however—the one that subsumes all his categories of work, society, and love—is the search for the self, for the ability to see oneself clearly; the passages on drink and sex are only an aspect of this larger project.

The quest for this elusive self continues over the entire period covered by the two diaries, and the sense that this quest is conditioned by the passage of time is emphasized by the diary form, with its inevitable indications of gradual change. The diaries are subdivided according to the various geographical locations in which they were composed, and each of these subheadings also indicates the dates covered. Rorem is acutely aware of time as it passes: Each birthday is recorded, with growing concern as he moves from his twenties into his thirties. Although the entries are often discontinuous, even random, it is just this attempt to grasp the self even as it changes that unifies them, from *The Paris Diary*'s quizzical opening—"A stranger asks, 'Are you Ned Rorem?' I answer, 'No,' adding, however, that I've heard of and would like to meet him"—to *The New York Diary*'s concluding suggestion about the identity of the artist: "People keep wondering: where does the man leave off and the artist begin? This is where."

Although *The Paris Diary* and *The New York Diary* are often discussed as a single entity, and have been reprinted in one volume, Rorem's original decision to publish them separately is nevertheless a valid one, despite their continuity and their many formal similarities; it recognizes the equally important distinctions to be drawn between the two installments. The narrative impulse is much stronger in *The Paris Diary*, which, with its many anecdotes and its more consistent concern with professional success and with the self in society, is the more extroverted of the two books. In *The New York Diary*, the self turns inward rather than looking outward, and the diary becomes more reflective than narrative, Rorem's aphoristic style taking precedence over the anecdotal; even the sections concerned with his love affairs are more concerned with his own emotional state than with the other men. Both views of the self, external and internal, are necessary; and the movement from narration to reflection is identical, in these books, with growing up. In addition, the division of the diaries in two emphasizes the importance of time's passage for the audience as well as the author: The books' first readers had to wait a year to hear the outcome of Rorem's trip home.

Analysis

The difference between the two diaries is made explicit at the beginning of *The New York Diary*, as Rorem announces his intentions for it: "Hopefully it will be at once less frivolous and more outspoken than those Paris diaries." It is, indeed, less chatty and less concerned with social advancement than the previous installment, and more introspective. Less overtly, however, *The New York Diary* also shows the author trying—sometimes successfully, sometimes not—to resolve some of the contradictions in his views on art, love, friendship, and especially the self, that make *The Paris Diary* seem such an immediate portrait of the artist, inconsistencies and all. What *The New York Diary* may lose in the flavor of day-to-day life as it is being lived, however, it gains in artistic unity.

The Paris Diary suggests a number of different, or even mutually exclusive, views of the self. The diary format allows Rorem to hold them all: Because it is by nature discontinuous, each entry reflecting the thoughts of a different day, the diarist, unlike the essayist, can juggle contradictions within the confines of a single book.

Most important of these attempts at self-definition is the young Rorem's desire to believe in the self as unchanging, like a work of art, a desire to which, in different forms, the author continually returns throughout the volume: "Each of our *clichés* becomes new insofar as we expose it to a new person. But *we* stay the same." At the same time, he is painfully aware of the passage of time, which is periodically marked by birthdays, lists of the year's professional accomplishments, and the like, as well as by the implacably changing dates that open each section of the diary.

It thus becomes essential for the author, pursuing the ideal of a changeless self in a constantly changing universe, to identify himself with immortal art, especially with his music. The lists of compositions, even as they suggest the passage of time, thus also represent an unchanging artistic order shored up against it: "The writing of music is not of the present, it is of a domain that has nothing to do with time." It is also essential that the work of art should refer only to its creator, rather than the performer or the audience; if others find in a work something other than what the creator intended, then even art is subject to change, and that cannot be admitted:

> If Michelangelo did create for a mass (debatable) his subject matter was the same as that of lesser artists. He was great not because of his material or mass appeal, but because he was Michelangelo. The masses don't know the difference.

Such an attitude inevitably tends to isolate both art and the self from the rest of humanity, from the masses. Indeed, Rorem finds it annoying that audiences may come to know his music without knowing him: art, in *The Paris Diary*, is a way of preserving the self, unchanged, through time. Similarly, the act of creation isolates the self. The artist must withdraw from ephemeral, changing human relationships in order to pursue the eternal. Thus Rorem presents himself throughout *The Paris Diary* as a detached, ironic observer, even in love, despite its constant society gossip: He often recounts such gossip only to express his disgust with it. Paradoxically, if the self is defined in terms of artistic success, success can be measured only in terms of recognition or fame: The artist must define himself according to others' perceptions of his art. Despite his ironic detachment from society, Rorem thus also needs society's approval, if the self is to be validated. Artistic immortality can only be conferred by an audience.

Since the young diarist's identification of himself with art extends even to his physical appearance (in a charming passage, Marie-Laure takes his measurements and finds them "to be according to the classic golden law"), another paradox results. The beauty of human beings, unlike the beauty of art, must pass, as Rorem knows: Toward the end of *The Paris Diary*, he recognizes that people no longer turn to look at him in the street. This recognition of the reality of change, enforced by advancing age, is strengthened by his return home, in *The New York Diary*, to scenes of his past life. This volume turns inward, as Rorem searches for a basis for the self which is not dependent on others' perceptions, either of his talent or of his beauty. He also finds himself rejected in love for the first time, increasing the need for such a basis.

He finds it precisely in the past, which is evoked ever more powerfully on his home ground; memory plays an increasingly important role in *The New York Diary*. Moving beyond the acute sense of time passing that characterized the previous volume, the diarist moves toward a recognition that time has already passed, and thus toward a more mature, and poignant, view of the self in time: "I . . . no longer believe in my own immortality." Rather than seeing his work only in terms of himself, he now sees it as a result of his Protestant heritage: Time past, rather than the eternal, now defines the self. An important result of this new concern with the past is that the diary becomes self-reflexive. Earlier passages are now quoted and analyzed, with a recognition of just how much has changed in spite of his youthful desire for eternity: "Did I write that!"

The self, then, has come to be defined as something that changes in time; rather than an eternal, formal work of art, it has become the sum of its still-accumulating past experiences and impressions—more like the diary itself, with all of its random inconsistencies, than it is like an art-song or one of Michelangelo's statues. Such changes are recorded, and understood, internally, rather than being imposed by others; thus the author can begin to recognize that others, too, have their own independent existence, rather than existing only to validate the self as a work of art, or the work of art as an expression of the self:

> Why do I keep on, making every gesture in the fear and hope that it will be seen, remembered? Or for what reason can I say that this or that of me I have made indelible, when with a final gulp I, too, have admitted death? . . . If ever I am spoken of in whatever generations may have the funny miracle of being born, it will not be Ned Rorem *himself* who is remembered.

Though Ned Rorem himself may be forgotten, it seems likely that his diaries, like his music, will be remembered.

Critical Context

It may be useful to think of *The Paris Diary* as a late development of a subgenre of modern American literature, the expatriate memoir. Such books as Ernest Hemingway's *A Moveable Feast* (1964), Gertrude Stein's *The Autobiography of Alice B. Toklas* (1933), and Robert McAlmon and Kay Boyle's *Being Geniuses Together, 1920-1930* (1968), as well as many others, chronicle the bohemian life in Paris during the heroic age of modernism, the 1920's, especially as it was experienced by young American artists living there. *The Paris Diary* has in common with these works its setting, the presence of important cultural figures, and a peculiarly American sense of naïve excitement at being a part of it all. Rorem's book is among the last examples of this genre, however, taking place as it does in the 1950's and among comparatively minor figures: not Igor Stravinsky, but Georges Auric; not Stein, but Alice B. Toklas; not Hemingway, but Julien Green. It is also a diary rather than a memoir, and this formal difference is significant: The authors of those books looked back at a time gone by rather than chronicling it as it happened, because the expatriate life was coming to an end as New York, rather than Paris, began to dominate the international cultural scene.

It is therefore entirely appropriate that Rorem should continue his diary at home, in New York, and that *The New York Diary* should be such a different kind of book. The reflective, introspective character of this volume is an important departure from other books of its kind. No longer concerned with recording external events in the world of celebrities, its inward quest for the self was an early warning that something new was happening in American culture. *The New York Diary*, indeed—in its pacifism, in its insistence on honesty even at the risk of offending, in its acceptance of homosexuality, in its perception (in a long passage on the effects of mescaline) of drugs as tools that might be used to explore the self, and even in its youthful narcissism—can easily be seen as a forerunner of the cultural upheavals of the 1960's.

Sources for Further Study

Gruen, John. *The Party's Over Now*, 1972.

Lambert, Gavin. "Confessions of a Charmer," in *The New York Times Book Review*. LXXI (July 10, 1966), p. 46.

Mazzocco, Robert. "To Tell You the Truth," in *The New York Review of Books*. VII (September, 1966), pp. 6-8.

Miller, C. K. Review in *Library Journal*. XCI (May 1, 1966), p. 2326.

Phelps, Robert. "A Portrait of the Diarist," in *The Paris Diary of Ned Rorem*, 1966.

Slavitt, David R. "Pose and Compose: With Ned Rorem, It's Hard to Tell the Difference," in *Philadelphia Magazine*. LXXIX (May, 1988), p. 89.

Robert S. Sturges

PATAGONI

Author: Paul Metcalf (1917-   )
Type of work: History/diary/letters
Locale: North America and South America
First published: 1971

Form and Content

 Patagoni is a difficult book to classify by genre. Linking folklore to history to personal diary and letters to conflations of history texts, Paul Metcalf has made genre subservient to artistic whim. While the book resembles a long modernist poem, it concludes with a lengthy bibliography of sources Metcalf quoted or paraphrased, indicating to the reader that the text he is reading is also a research paper. However flashy and original a glance through the book suggests it to be, it is, above all, a work of meditation upon texts. Original authorship takes less space in *Patagoni* than the sections on South America and Henry Ford which Metcalf borrows from his sources.

 If the subjects Metcalf examines are not new, their arrangement, enjambment, compression, and structuring relative to one another are wholly original. Part anthropological speculation, part history, the book is a work of art and is experienced by the reader as a "poem about civilization," such as those written by Metcalf's modern ancestors Ezra Pound (the *Cantos*) and Charles Olson (*The Maximus Poems*). The visual "look" of the pages is modernist as well. Eschewing capital letters and conventional paragraphs, Metcalf builds his text like a collage. Like Pound's *Cantos*, *Patagoni* even includes bars of musical text. Thus, though the book is classified as "nonfiction" it is a challenging book to read for anyone unequipped with the decoding skills developed through contemplating the disjunctions of modern art.

 Patagoni's subject is the New World, South America and North America, rather than the southern tip of South America the title suggests. The term "Patagoni" refers to the giant natives Ferdinand Magellan reported seeing while exploring the coast: "fo bygge, that the heade of one of owr men of a meane ftature, came but to his wafte." The New World Metcalf contemplates is not the discovery Columbus made in 1492 but the primordial America of the great Indian civilizations and their obscure ancestors. Of the two continents, Metcalf favors the southern as the center of origins, especially what is today known as Peru and the Lake Titicaca region of Bolivia. The book's second section, "Tihuanacu," describes this western side of South America as it was before Europe found it, with special attention to the holistic unity in the vitality of geography, plant life, animals, and aboriginal Indians. Metcalf shows how this richly alive kingdom, untouched by the European influence, gave issue to the artifacts, religion, and brilliantly designed cities which exist today only as memories. The place Metcalf describes in "Tihuanacu" is an American Eden, far surpassing in resources the northern continent. "Tihuanacu" is a book of genesis for this place, a world so rich in life that even the clay could sustain a hungry Indian.

Metcalf's third section, "Sialia," presents the other side of his American coin: Henry Ford's doings in North America. Condensing gists from biographies and instruction manuals, Metcalf profiles the mind and energies of the inventor of the assembly line. Juxtaposing the Ford section to the South American section advances Metcalf's subject—the contrast between the New World's original or aboriginal geography and mentality and the white orientation in the less fructive northern continent.

The juxtaposition of the ancient south and the modern north is in focus throughout the book's five remaining sections. The contrast is made complex by the contrasts Metcalf finds existing within each side. Early Peru, described in the second section, is compared with contemporary Peru as described in *Patagoni*'s final section. The early Detroit described in "Sialia" is compared to the Detroit Metcalf visited in the 1950's and describes in the fifth section, "d'Étroit." The mystically fructive Eden of the second section becomes a modern wasteland in the last section, and the early successes of Henry Ford's automobile manufacture, which included a thriving and well-paid work force, become the nightmare of contemporary labor strikes and layoffs. The degenerative energy of historical process is a theme Metcalf introduces on the book's first page, where the image of stock cars racing in the Darlington 500, "chomping butyl, gorging gas, puffing smoke," foresees in reverse the edenic energies of birds and animals in the second section: "snowwhite islands black with birds, the air thick with mutterings, the hum of wings, grunts and screepy calls."

Like a symphony, the narration of *Patagoni* progresses in radically contrasting tones. The personal poet's voice of the first section is followed by the second and third sections' less personal historical narration. A page from a McGuffey's Reader is quoted at length, and a how-to process from a manual on the construction of a motor. Later, in "Diario y Cartas" (diary and letters), the author's informal personal presence is central. By quoting himself at length in words written before the composition of his book, Metcalf underlines the method of authorship he has chosen, that of the historian who cannot know his subject at first hand but is limited to the words which other men (in this case, even, himself), living in the past, chose to write down. Thus, the issue of "the perceiver" is a secondary but essential theme of *Patagoni*. The tangibility of a former world is reduced to texts, and the book's central historical individual, Henry Ford, is the person famous for saying "History is more or less bunk."

Analysis

If *Patagoni* defies convenient genre categorization, it does impose a familiar literary pattern upon its subject: tragedy. The American hemispheres Metcalf surveys in the twentieth century have nearly lost their grandeur, and *Patagoni*, juxtaposing the old glory and the new wastage like an archaeological dig, reveals that past masteries of Indian civilization and the shadow masteries of North American mechanized civilization. The contemporary Peru of Inca Cola and starving Indians, and the Detroit of the 1950's, with its historical tours and vast, empty airports, are full of echoes for the historian, and Metcalf ponders what went wrong and what has been lost.

The problem with America, for Metcalf, is the white man's presence. Through centuries the Indian developed his consciousness of dependence on his native earth. His religious rites bound his life to nature and daily reminded him in folklore and superstition of his subservience to the "great creature" on which he lived:

> the earth is a great creature, the rivers the bloodvessels, the earth turns one way and another, to warm itself at the sun . . . the first man mated with a gentle doe, and deerlike, generation by generation, the race of indians evolved . . . out of the phallus of the chief came the first maize, from his head gourds.

The Indian's intelligence evolved in harmony with his location. His architecture was a continued projection of the energies of the living earth, as trees supported verandas and building stones slid seamlessly into union. A Castillian entering this homeland was dubbed a vagabond, his wandering an indication to the Indian that the earth had not borne him: "such as were bred of ye scum of the Sea, without any other Origen or Linage, . . . that you are ydle persons, and have not wherein to imploy your selves, because you abide in no place, to labour and till the ground."

The white man ruined what the Indian so delicately constructed. Metcalf's collage elements depict an alien white intelligence converting everything it found into raw materials for its own products, the foremost of which was movement in space. Carved Tihuanacuan stone and building blocks were crushed and used as fill for railroads. Timber for railroad ties was shipped from Oregon. *Patagoni's* central theme is the incompatibility of the rooted agricultural red man and the rootless technological white man; yet, since Detroit workers today make abstract art from old tailpipes and crank-boxes, Metcalf also propounds the permanence of iconography. The explorer was moving too fast to see, but his spirit was not as alien to the Indian's as his speed made it seem. This blind movement spelled tragedy for the white as well as the Indian.

Metcalf settles on Henry Ford as a luminous example of the white man enmeshed in the tragedy he created by his foraging. Metcalf's section on Ford begins with a quotation from *McGuffey's Eclectic Fourth Reader*, which in its instructions on how speakers ought to control the pronunciation of words bespeaks reliance on mechanistic control in a world where no regional past sustained the settler. Ford is such a rich symbol for Metcalf because he was the supreme mechanist while remaining nostalgic about nature. He simply lacked native viability, and could not really inhabit his Michigan birthland the way the Indian, thanks to the patrimony of shared vision with ancestors, could inhabit his. Asked by a lawyer during a libel trial what the United States had been originally, Ford responded, "land, I guess." So much, Metcalf implies, for the "great creature" described in the "Tihuanacu" section, where the earth is shown in its redoubtable presence, the Amazon of South America, a place of titanic struggle: "waves beating from riveredge to riveredge, hour after hour, land and trees crashing, terra cahida, the roar of artillery."

Ford, unawed by geography, knew how to harness it. He placed factories alongside rivers for power and transportation. Chemurgy promised a method for transposing New World abundance into whatever a designer might have in mind. Ford built a workshop and experimented with grains and vegetables. Rumors arose that he would "perhaps grow a complete car of wheat." Cabbage, carrots, onions, melons, cornstalks, and sunflowers disappeared into his hoppers. Flora, emblem of mythic dependence for a Mayan, held possibilities for all-new being under Ford's willful genius. What had sprung from the archetypal mechanic's head was not gourds but something wholly original:

> for the nation, a car—a carnation!
> not an inca, but re-inca—in car!

> *reincarnation!*

Metcalf's vision of Ford establishes him in an America void, rather than the Indian's Eden. His cars moved across ice, mud, and mountains. When they broke down, the mechanic exulted—welcoming challenges to ingenuity—and blacksmithed repairs. Ford envisioned a life for his fellow mechanics, *his* tribe. His factory workers lived well on five dollars a day. Like the McGuffey speech rules, his mind stamped pattern on malleable substance. Metcalf quotes four pages of Ford's manual of assembly processes for a crank-box ("Tap globe-seat cap holes for cap retention. Tap drain screw seat. Tap the two overflow screw seats") and intersperses American pioneer songs ("Oats, peas, beans and barley grows . . .") to exemplify how native a music Ford's processes composed. Andean man, Metcalf shows, set flutes in the clefts of mountains for the winds to play a mountain music. Ford's American music was the pockety-pockety of his internal combustion engine.

Metcalf recurrently directs the reader to the contrast of patterns the Indian and white were geniuses at fashioning. An Indian might wear "a garment composed of thousands of the tiny goldgreen feather from the hummingbird's breast." The structure of self-sufficient propulsion Ford perfected was contrary to nature, scary to innocent roadside chickens and inspiring folklore such as the tale of the Pensacola, North Carolina, hillbilly lady who shoots the first "moll t" she sees: "ah made it let loos-a that man."

Ford's empire proved inherently brutal and antisocial. Jobless workers assembled for a hunger march at the Rouge plant on March 7, 1932, and were gunned down by thugs hired by Ford's director of personnel, Harry Bennett. Ford's genius was eccentric and his vision the same. He believed milk to be poisonous and salt good for the hair. The inventor mentality—Metcalf shows by contrasting it with the Indian's intuition of what was good for the tribe—proved selfish, shortsighted, and unnatural. Ford's assemblage of his personal nature garden mixed domestic plants, animals, and birds with foreign species. Heated bird baths did not stop the birds' migrating, and the rabbit population destroyed Ford's orchards, so he killed them. The English birds vanished in the surrounding countryside. In addition, Ford's restlessness, the very thrust which drove him to make what he made, judged his creations ultimately unsatisfying: "The Rouge is so big that it is no fun any more." Unconnected to the past ("History is more or less bunk") and bored by the present, Ford was the archetypal white forager-explorer and became the American Alexander with no worlds left to conquer.

Ford did endow America with a legacy, Metcalf demonstrates. It is the motor culture, and one of its festivals, the Southern 500 stock car race, is the book's opening denunciation of that culture. What is ugly about this culture is its use of nature— steel, rubber, gasoline—to estrange people from nature. When the race ends the spectators leave their "raffish scaffolds" and "go out like sheep, like huancayo llamas." The motors are silent "against the unmuffled thunder above. . . ." However dissatisfying the book finds contemporary mechanical America, it remains persuasive about the old options. The section "Diarios y Cartas" shows Metcalf wandering in the ancient places and advocating that his North American correspondents should pull up stakes and join him at Lake Titicaca or La Paz: "This is, beyond all doubt, THE CITY—incredible."

Critical Context

Paul Metcalf is the great grandson of Herman Melville. Like his grandparent, Metcalf's scope as a writer is broad in geographical and cultural subjects. Melville's placing a tattoo-covered savage, Queequeg, in bed with Ishmael, the white American narrator of *Moby Dick* (1851), is comparable to Metcalf's union of South American Indians and Henry Ford. The connection of pagan and civilized poses the problem many contemporary writers have addressed: Western civilized man is adrift and alienated because he lacks meaningful symbols to order his spirit and behavior.

English writers in the twentieth century have offered various opinions on this problem. T. S. Eliot was pessimistic, sensing in *The Waste Land* (1922) that cultural cohesion was impossible. Ezra Pound was more optimistic, arguing that America could be saved if Confucian principles were adopted by its rulers. D. H. Lawrence searched past civilizations and advocated abandoning civilized mores and replacing them with the sensibilities of Etruscans or Mexican Indians. Other writers have offered Eastern religion as a means of rescue. The message of *Patagoni* seems closest to Lawrence's point of view. The white American needs to return to the symbology of Incans and Mayans and recognize that a place supersedes its inhabitants and must be listened to and, ultimately, worshiped. The Indian's art had significant dialogue with his place. He was not alienated from but embraced by his environment, and his works bore testimony to his happy situation.

Metcalf's architectonic style, the joining of apparently different subjects without transitional explanation, is also typical of twentieth century writing. Unexpectedness, strangeness, freshness are aesthetic ideals this style attempts to embody. The virtue of *Patagoni* is its accessibility. Though a reader may have initial difficulty adjusting to the lack of plot, the suspension of a directing narrative voice, the book is much easier to understand than books in a similar style, such as Pound's *Cantos* and Olson's *The Maximus Poems*, which require cribs or even libraries for elucidation. Metcalf's book is not written only to a coterie of scholars but to general readers as well. Despite its readability, *Patagoni* goes unread just as Metcalf's earlier book *Genoa* (1965), written in the same collage style, goes unread. This seems mainly attributable to the publisher, The Jargon Society, which specializes in producing avant-garde books in small numbers. Yet *Patagoni* revivifies the content of history books and social studies texts that most Americans encountered in the elementary grades. Its avant-garde style is not really all that new. The critic Guy Davenport has pointed out that Metcalf's eclectic style, where almost anything pertinent will be inserted, is much like the style of his grandparent's *Moby Dick:* "Of what other novel than *Moby Dick* can you say that a chapter on any subject under the sun might fit into it?"

Patagoni's madeness stands for more than its author's attempt to be different for the sake of being different. He attempted to make a hieroglyphic, a lasting American symbol, upon which the twentieth century reader can meditate. Its obscurity seems only to heighten the quality of its vision, just as a stone covered with glyphs discovered among Mayan ruins mesmerizes its happy finder.

Sources for Further Study

Callahan, Bob. Review in *Credences*. III (March, 1980), pp. 36-37.
Campbell, Andrew. "Paul Metcalf, Geology, and the Dynamics of Place," in *Sagetrieb*. V (Winter, 1986), pp. 87-110.
Davenport, Guy. "Narrative Tone and Form," in *The Geography of the Imagination*, 1981.
The New York Times. Review. CXXI (September 15, 1972), p. 34.

Bruce Wiebe

PENTIMENTO
A Book of Portraits

Author: Lillian Hellman (1905-1984)
Type of work: Memoir
Time of work: 1905 to the early 1970's
Locale: The United States and Europe
First published: 1973

> *Principal personages:*
> LILLIAN HELLMAN, the author, a playwright
> BETHE,
> WILLY, and
> JULIA, friends or relatives who are remembered in this memoir
> DASHIELL HAMMETT, Hellman's longtime companion

Form and Content

The title of playwright Lillian Hellman's second book of memoirs is a painterly one, which Hellman defines in a brief prologue:

> Old paint on canvas, as it ages, sometimes becomes transparent. When that happens it is possible, in some pictures, to see the original lines: a tree will show through a woman's dress, a child makes way for a dog, a large boat is no longer on an open sea. That is called pentimento because the painter "repented," changed his mind. Perhaps it would be as well to say that the old conception, replaced by a later choice, is a way of seeing and then seeing again.

This elegant definition, along with the book's subtitle—*A Book of Portraits*—goes far toward explaining Hellman's method, style, and focus in *Pentimento*. The book is indeed a series of portraits, most of them devoted to people and places important only to the narrator. One might extend the painterly metaphor to describe the seven essays in the book as finely wrought miniatures, each of them more reliant on detail than on scope. In *Pentimento*, the United States' most important twentieth century woman dramatist casts herself as the repenting painter defined above, and it is her voice, her special vision, that unifies the many disparate parts of the book. In its emphases on memory, on time, and on taking responsibility for one's own actions, *Pentimento* is as much as anything else a self-portrait.

Far from being the sort of name-dropping celebrity memoir that one might expect of someone who had, by the time of the book's publication, lived in the public eye for some forty years, *Pentimento* is intensely private; only one of its chapters deals to any extent with the rich and famous. Rather, *Pentimento* is a group of seemingly unconnected reminiscences of a famous woman's off-duty hours, of the times when a public life goes underground, and of the often eccentric characters who people any life. Certainly Hellman makes no attempt whatsoever at straightforward, chronological autobiography in *Pentimento*; her earlier memoir *An Unfinished Woman*, which won the National Book Award in 1969, was as close as Hellman would ever come to conventional autobiography. A scholar trying to piece together the details of Hellman's life would be frustrated by the evasions, the chronological lapses, the omissions that characterize *Pentimento*. Though the book includes everything from Hellman's childhood in New Orleans to her years of preeminence as a playwright to her later life as a memoirist, and while the essays are arranged in a loose chronological order corresponding to the time periods during which Hellman knew the people she describes, many of the conventions of autobiography are deliberately flouted. Dates, for example, are hazy and vague, filtered through the consciousness of a narrator who is herself trying to order a series of disconnected memories.

Pentimento is divided into seven portrait-essays, each of which describes impressionistically a person or an event or both that had a strong effect on the psychic or emotional development of the narrator. The first, "Bethe," is the story of a stalwart German emigrant, a distant relative of Hellman, who becomes involved in a series of romantic liaisons with shady New Orleans characters and who is eventually implicated in a gangland murder. "Willy" describes Hellman's cavalier great-uncle by marriage, a romantic figure for whom Hellman experienced early sexual yearnings. "Julia," the third and most famous of the book's portraits—in 1977, Fred Zinnemann released a highly successful film version starring Jane Fonda, Vanessa Redgrave, and Jason Robards—is a tribute to a childhood friend of Hellman who became a heroic figure in the underground resistance to the European Fascist movement of the 1930's. Next comes "Theatre," a celebrity-filled account of Hellman's career as a playwright, followed by "Arthur W. A. Cowan," another purely personal portrait of an eccentric friend from Hellman's middle years. "Turtle" is a semimetaphysical story concerned with nothing less than life and death, while "Pentimento" serves as a sort of coda for the book and a final justification of its existence.

Analysis

Like Hellman's later *Scoundrel Time* (1976) and *Maybe* (1980), *Pentimento* is perhaps not so much an autobiography as a commentary on autobiography. Highly and deliberately subjective, foggy in regard to details, the seven essays in the book constantly call attention to their own fragmentation. Hellman catches herself confusing one meeting with another that came much later, and she shares this confusion with the reader. Throughout the book, she reminds the reader that objective documentation of the past is hard to come by: Diary notes are sketchy and vague, letters are misplaced or, when found, frequently unreliable. People themselves, blinded by their own experiences and prejudices, are notoriously unreliable witnesses, capable of presenting only distorted evidence. Like her fellow playwright Tennessee Williams' *Memoirs* (1975), Hellman's book thus reminds the reader not only of the narrator's own unreliability but also of the limits of autobiography itself, and, by extension, of the unreliability of human memory.

Indeed, most of the characters in the book seem to be people who, having once moved quickly through Hellman's life, now seem to deserve greater consideration than they have previously received. Now, in old age, the author seems to be "replacing," as the preface says, "the old conception" with "a later choice." Each character's importance to Hellman's life seems unquestionable, though Hellman's realization of his or her importance has come about only belatedly. Bethe, for example, appears to the older Hellman as the woman who gave the younger Hellman the courage to live with a man to whom she was not married; the adolescent Hellman depicted in the story, however, knows only that she is obsessed with the unremarkable Bethe, visits her frequently against her family's will, but is able to express her fascination only haltingly and cryptically. Willy symbolizes much the same kind of sexual freedom—the story contains strong hints that he and the young Hellman had a sexual relationship—but is also seen by the younger Hellman as a strong corrective to the unimaginative avarice of her mother's family (the same clan on whom the villainous Hubbards are based in Hellman's 1939 play *The Little Foxes*). No character in the book, however, receives the kind of unreserved praise that Julia does. Born to extreme wealth and privilege, gifted with great beauty and a superior intellect, Julia nevertheless sacrifices her birthright and risks her life to smuggle political refugees out of Adolf Hitler's Europe. The story centers on Julia's enlistment of Hellman's help in running a dangerous errand for the Resistance, but this intrigue plot—interesting enough in itself—is sublimated to the main theme of having the courage of one's political and ideological convictions. Julia thus serves not only as a heroine in her own right, but as a sort of wish-fulfillment projection of the aging narrator's own frequently haphazard political self.

Politics serves elsewhere in *Pentimento* as a strong secondary theme. Long known for her leftist politics and for the overtly political messages of such plays as *Days to Come* (1936) and *Watch on the Rhine* (1941), Hellman seems weary of political endeavor in *Pentimento*, where politics becomes merely another facet of human personality and ultimately doomed to failure. Hellman makes no attempt to disguise her love for Willy, nor does she camouflage the fact that he was in many ways a blatant imperialist whose business success was dependent on the exploitation of South American natives. "Arthur W. A. Cowan," the title character of which is another overt capitalist, serves to demonstrate that politically objectionable people can nevertheless do the right thing for the wrong reason. The notorious battle between Hellman and the flamboyant actress Tallulah Bankhead, star of *The Little Foxes*, over whether the cast would stage a performance of the play for the benefit of Finnish war refugees—a battle that made headlines in 1939—becomes in "Theatre" little more than a personal clash between strong personalities. Even the heroic Julia serves, by means of contrast, to illustrate the narrator's own halfhearted attempts at direct political action: Julia dies a hero's death, while Hellman, safely back in the United States by the end of the story, is left frustrated and agonized by her inability to discover the truth of what has happened to her friend. Politics, once so important a part of Hellman's life, thus undergoes the effect of pentimento as well: what once seemed life-altering now seems less so, having undergone the ravages of time and distance.

It should not be thought, however, that this sophisticated indirection detracts in any way from the book's dramatic or narrative impact. On the contrary, Hellman's deliberate sketchiness emphasizes scene over commentary, the sharply focused encounter over lengthy analysis. One critic has correctly noted that Hellman's dramatic instincts are continually at work in *Pentimento*. The crisp dialogue and sharply drawn confrontations that characterize her best plays are what make memorable such scenes as a drunken restaurant battle between Hellman and one of Julia's detractors; the many semicomic conversations between Hellman and her companion of thirty years, the mystery writer Dashiell Hammett; the darkly humorous, money-dominated dinner conversations among members of her mother's family; and the suspense-filled train scenes in "Julia." It is such climactic moments, Hellman seems to be saying, that remain in the memory long after the troublesome details of time and place have faded.

Hellman herself frequently acknowledged that Hammett served as critic, editor, and mentor throughout much of her literary career, and certainly his posthumous influence is detectable in *Pentimento*. Along with James M. Cain and Raymond Chandler, Hammett is considered responsible for creating the "hard-boiled" school of detective fiction in such novels as *The Maltese Falcon* (1929) and *The Thin Man* (1933); in fact, the sophisticated banter between Nick Charles, the hero of the latter novel, and his wife, Nora, is often thought to have been based on the unconventional relationship between Hammett and Hellman. The gutsy, urban, no-nonsense dialogue, the lack of florid embellishment, the ability to get directly to the heart of the matter in a few simple sentences—these Hammett-like attributes characterize Hellman's prose in *Pentimento* and in her three other memoirs. The spareness and simplicity made famous by her friend Ernest Hemingway, as well as the atmosphere of combativeness and heavy drinking created by both Hammett and Hemingway, are rightfully appropriated by Hellman in this memoir of a turbulent and eventful life.

Critical Context

Hellman died in 1984 amid allegations that *An Unfinished Woman*, *Pentimento*, and *Scoundrel Time* contained serious distortions of the truth, even outright lies. Though Hellman's veracity had been questioned before, the debacle reached its high point in 1980, when novelist Mary McCarthy claimed on national television that Hellman was an overrated writer and a systematic purveyor of untruths in her memoirs. Always combative, particularly when her reputation was at stake, Hellman responded by suing McCarthy for $2,225,000. While the suit never reached trial—it was on its way to court at the time of Hellman's death—it triggered a wave of similar, more specific complaints against Hellman's truthfulness. Such writers as Leo McCracken, assistant to the president of Boston University, and Martha Gellhorn, Hemingway's third wife, wrote and published detailed articles that cited specific examples of what they saw as blatant lies on Hellman's part.

Earlier, the distinguished writer and critic Diana Trilling had infuriated Hellman by attacking in print *Scoundrel Time*, Hellman's memoir of the McCarthy era, calling it one sided and dangerously misleading. Nor was Trilling the only writer to question Hellman's interpretation of the "Communist witch-hunt" of the 1950's: Both conservatives and anti-Communist liberals accused Hellman of casting herself in a much more heroic role than she had actually played in her appearance in 1952 before the House Committee on Un-American Activities, an event that forms the central episode in *Scoundrel Time*.

Perhaps the most crushing blow to Hellman's veracity came in 1983, with the publication of *Code Name "Mary": Memoirs of an American Woman in the Austrian Underground*, the autobiography of Muriel Gardiner, a woman whose life so closely matched that of Hellman's Julia that it seems almost certain that they were one and the same. When asked about Hellman's book and about the film made from it, Gardiner repeatedly stated that she could not be Julia since she had never met Lillian Hellman. Gardiner's denials went far toward establishing among Hellman's critics that "Julia" was indeed a total fabrication: what Hellman wished had happened rather than what had actually happened. (Gardiner was also said to have served as the inspiration for the character Sara Muller in Hellman's 1941 play, *Watch on the Rhine*.)

Still, for all of its intensity, this controversy was confined for the most part to the intellectual community; the general public, since the release of the film version of "Julia," had come to revere Hellman as never before. In the post-Watergate climate of the later 1970's and the early 1980's, Hellman seemed to many a doughty warrior in the fight against corrupt authority, a woman who had stood by and suffered for her convictions. Not even her detractors could deny that Hellman had indeed recognized early the Fascist threat at a time when the American government had seemed complacent about it, or that her stand before the McCarthyite inquisitors had been a courageous one. In the light of her legend, the literal truth of her memoirs seemed of little importance to those who admired her life and her writing.

On balance, however, it is the books and not the image that must be judged. While Hellman's use of artistic license in *Pentimento* and in the other memoirs seems beyond question, they are interesting and readable accounts of a fascinating life and irresistible self-portraits of a narrator to whom the reader is strongly drawn. If not the literal truth, they strongly suggest truthfulness and honesty. Further, Hellman's constant disclaimers, her frequent asides concerning the impossibility of achieving truth, her relentless questioning of her own memory, would seem to lift the memoirs outside the range of autobiography into a realm where truth and fiction merge. As her biographer William Wright has noted, her attitude toward the role of the memoirist and toward the factual basis of the stories she tells would seem to be summarized by the title of her last book, *Maybe*.

Sources for Further Study
Dick, Bernard F. *Hellman in Hollywood*, 1982.

Johnson, Diane. *Dashiell Hammett: A Life*, 1983.
Lederer, Katherine. *Lillian Hellman*, 1979.
Rollyson, Carl E. *Lillian Hellman: Her Legend and Legacy*, 1988.
Wright, William. *Lillian Hellman: The Image, the Woman*, 1986.

James D. Daubs

THE PERIODIC TABLE

Author: Primo Levi (1919-1987)
Type of work: Memoir
Time of work: The early to the mid-twentieth century
Locale: Turin, Italy
First published: Il sistema periodico, 1975 (English translation, 1984)

> *Principal personage:*
> PRIMO LEVI, a young Jewish-Italian chemist

Form and Content

Primo Levi, a Jewish-Italian novelist, short-story writer, poet, and memoirist, was also a chemist for most of his professional life. As *The Periodic Table* demonstrates, his careers as chemist and writer were inseparable. Each chapter of the memoir is named for a chemical element, explores Levi's work in the laboratory, and relates that work to his personal, social, and political experience. It is a cliché to speak of human chemistry when discussing human nature. The virtue of Levi's book is that he refreshes the cliché and shows the profound connections between chemical elements and the elements of human behavior.

Each chapter can be read as a discrete piece of work, concentrating on some episode or period in Levi's life. Nevertheless, the chapters are also unified by the author's growth in perception. As he learns more about specific chemical elements and about the procedures required to study those elements, so he also discovers life in more depth, encountering unusual characters who teach him about the meaning of their lives and about existence as a whole. The form of *The Periodic Table* is unified by chronology. After the first chapter, "Argon," which describes Levi's ancestry, subsequent chapters chart his life and career from the years just before World War II and his incarceration in a concentration camp to the decade or so following the Holocaust.

By titling his memoir *The Periodic Table*, Levi suggests that there is a structure to his writing about experience that is analogous to the way elements are analyzed in chemistry. Like the various substances the chemist tests in his laboratory, the author's experiences have different degrees of purity, different weights, and different reactions, depending upon what he uses to stimulate them. Human character in the memoir, in other words, has certain properties from the beginning, but it can be transformed in a number of ways given the changing nature of environments.

Altogether, there are twenty-one chapters or elements in *The Periodic Table*, each of which presents a peculiar problem or story Levi tells about his life and his chemistry. Some of the chapters read like mystery stories and have clear resolutions; others remain open-ended: puzzling and tantalizing. Two chapters, in italics, are fables of life suggested to the author by his career in chemistry. Each chapter has its own style, for Levi strives to achieve an absolute perfection of form and content, so that the words he uses seem to grow out of the experience they render.

Although Levi is an autobiographical writer, he does not write autobiography as such. He prefers the more flexible form of the memoir, which allows him to concentrate on certain episodes or periods without the need to cover his life in its entirety. Each chapter reads like a short story. He is careful to point out, however, how actual events often do not have the clean shape of fiction. As a result, several chapters of *The Periodic Table* do not have neat conclusions. For example, after providing a sensitive narrative of his correspondence with a German chemist who had supervised his work in the concentration camp, and just before their fateful reunion after the war, Levi receives a message announcing the man's death in his "sixtieth year of life." In one sense, the death is accidental. It could have happened before or after their correspondence. In another sense, it seems determined by the correspondence, for while the German has rationalized the death camps, it is also clear that the extermination of millions has haunted him to the "sixtieth year of [his] life" and that he wants some sort of absolution from a reluctant Levi. Levi does not say the man dies of a bad conscience, but it is difficult not to draw that conclusion. Much of *The Periodic Table* has this understated yet insistent significance.

Analysis

The Periodic Table begins with a discussion of inert gases:

> They are indeed so inert, so satisfied with their condition, that they do not interfere in any chemical reaction, do not combine with any other element, and for precisely this reason have gone undetected for centuries.

The phrase "so satisfied with their condition" is clearly an affectation. Chemists do not believe that gases are sentient. A gas does not reflect upon its own condition. Yet human beings do, and human beings are chemists. This is Levi's point: His work in chemistry has stimulated him to reflect upon the human condition and to realize that "the little I know of my ancestors presents many similarities to these gases."

In other chapters of *The Periodic Table*, the author is not so explicit. The connections between chemistry and human lives are not always specified, although the connections are there in the way Levi writes, in the way he lives. His ancestors, for example, have been inert in the sense that they have been "relegated to the margins of the great river of life." Again, the sense of something elemental suffuses Levi's style. By the second page of his memoir, it is clear that chemistry has become a part of his writer's vocabulary and that his way of life—and by extension all lives—is chemistry.

This constant parallel between chemistry and life might prove tiresome if it were not for Levi's elegant, concrete style. His ancestors may be like inert gases, but he can make them as colorful and all absorbing as gases are to a chemist. There is his vivid memory of Barbaricô, a fine doctor who disliked everything that went along with having a career. Barbaricô hated hard work, schedules, appointments, commitments, politicking—in short all the things a professional normally does to advance in the world. He loved men and women and nature. He let various women take care of him. While he was an excellent diagnostician, he preferred spending the day reading books and newspapers. If a patient sent for him, he would readily go, never asked for his fee, and accepted whatever goods his poor clients handed him. His needs were simple. He was more than ninety when he died "with discretion and dignity," Levi concludes.

In his evocation of Barbaricô, Levi conveys his deep affection for a relative, but he also views the man with considerable objectivity, measuring him like a scientist, a chemist curious about how this individual combines with other elements of life. Using another cliché, Levi suggests "the comparison to inert gases with which these pages start fits Barbaricô like a glove." "Like a glove"—the very terms of comparison make Levi's point that whether one is comparing gases or human beings, the principle of comparison is the same. If the elements fit, it is like the fit of glove to hand.

The Periodic Table, like the table of elements for which it is named, is constructed on the principle of making comparisons, of weighing and analyzing substances and experiences. Although Levi never says so explicitly, his memoir begins with a discussion of his inert relatives because he himself has been inert. In "Potassium," for example, he explains why he and his family did not leave Italy when each day brought fresh evidence that the Fascists were bent on destroying the Jews: "We pushed all dangers into the limbo of things not perceived or immediately forgotten." Their life was Italy. In the "abstract" they could have escaped, but they would have "needed a lot of money and a fabulous capacity for initiative." Having neither, and wanting to live, they imposed upon themselves a blindness, trying not to witness how circumscribed their lives had become.

Like an impure element, the Jews were driven out of Italy and into the extermination camps—a hideous irony for Levi, who spends his career examining the impurities of elements and who is constrained, as well, to contemplate the imperfections of human beings. In "Nickel" he presents what amounts to a fable of human history, a story about a mine he worked, where many years earlier (so the story was told to him) the workers had given way to every kind of chaotic behavior and sexual promiscuity, forcing the "governors in Milan to carry out a drastic, purifying intervention."

Levi's own mind, as presented in *The Periodic Table*, is like an impressionable metal that retains its own structure while becoming amazingly adaptable to the pressures exerted upon it. During the war, he worked for a Swiss scientist who put him onto fruitless projects such as discovering an "oral anti-diabetic." Although Levi put forth a few objections to his superior's wacky scheme, he immediately complied when he found the scientist's attitude "hardened like a sheet of copper under a hammer." Levi's friend, Giulia, became angry at him for humoring the superior's weird ideas, but that is Levi's strength: his pliable yet resistant nature. He goes along with nonsense without ever becoming nonsensical himself.

Levi's memoir is both a historical and a philosophical work. It is also remarkable for the way it can blend history and philosophy in a single passage, thereby showing once again the unity of all things. For example, Levi describes his feelings as a chemistry student, learning about the periodic table, treating it as a kind of densely packed poetry he has to unravel. It provided "the bridge, the missing link, between the world of words and the world of things." Working in a laboratory was also an "antidote" to the dogmas of Fascism, those unproved but deeply held prejudices. Chemistry and physics "were clear and distinct and verifiable at every step, and not a tissue of lies and emptiness, like the radio and newspapers."

Chemistry, for Levi, is at once a study of nature and of human nature. As he suggests in his conclusion, chemistry has taught him that he is a collection of cells which is "the *me* who is writing." No one has yet been able to explain how it is that a human personality has evolved in this way, or exactly how out of the multitude of choices available to him, the writer selects the signs that are put on the page. *The Periodic Table* ends with this chemical mystery which is also an assertion of human will. The memoir ends by focusing on the process of writing itself, on "this dot, here, this one," and suggests that Levi has accounted for as much of his life—and of life itself—as is possible.

Critical Context

The Periodic Table is the third volume of Primo Levi's autobiographical trilogy. *Se questo è un uomo* (1947), translated as *If This Is a Man* in England in 1959 and as *Survival in Auschwitz: The Nazi Assault on Humanity* in the United States in 1961, may still be his best-known work. The American title is somewhat misleading, for it emphasizes only the documentary quality of the memoir and not Levi's philosophical and literary concerns, which he continues in *La tregua* (1958), translated as *The Truce: A Survivor's Journey Home from Auschwitz* (1965) in England and as *The Reawakening* (1965) in the United States. Translations of his work—as these titles indicate—have varied enormously in quality and have done him a disservice. *The Periodic Table*, however, is regarded as a faithful rendering of his Italian. In cases where the translator has not been able to duplicate Levi's vocabulary—especially where the author plays on words—they are identified in notes at the bottom of the page. Even a reader unfamiliar with Levi's reputation in Italy will receive a glimmer of his exquisite literary sensibility. He is a master of the Italian language who makes frequent and subtle allusions to Italian literature from Dante to the late twentieth century.

The Holocaust is the central event in Levi's life and in his work. As many discussions of his memoirs note, his writing is remarkable for its compassion, detachment, objectivity, and lack of personal bitterness. Nevertheless, there is plenty of passion in Levi. He does not readily forgive the German chemist who seeks a meeting with him. Yet he is aware of his own complicity, his own inertness, in the face of profound evil. He does not scapegoat the Germans, making them into the source of all evil, but he also does not simply make their crimes the burden of humanity. He is specifically historical in his description of how the Jews were exterminated while realizing that the deaths of millions do raise important questions about human nature.

The Periodic Table has attracted a large foreign audience because of its perfection of form. Many of Levi's previous volumes have been just as well written, but the imaginative conception of *The Periodic Table* is at once the most ambitious, most profound, and most perfectly executed of his works to appear in English. In this memoir, Levi has found the perfect link between his personal experience and the history of mankind. In the periodic table, he has elaborated a metaphor that does justice to the complexity of reality while simultaneously making it concrete and analyzable, like the elements in his chemistry laboratory.

Sources for Further Study

Blake, Patricia. Review in *Time*. CXXV (January 28, 1985), p. 81.

Clemons, Walter. Review in *Newsweek*. CV (May 6, 1985), p. 79.

Denby, David. "The Humorist and the Holocaust: The Poised Art of Primo Levi," in *The New Republic*. CXCIII (July 28, 1986), pp. 27-33.

Eberstadt, Fernanda. "Reading Primo Levi," in *Commentary*. LXXX (October, 1985), pp. 41-46.

Howe, Irving. "How to Write About the Holocaust," in *The New York Review of Books*. XXXII (March 28, 1985), pp. 14-17.

Roth, Philip. "A Man Saved by His Skills," in *The New York Times Book Review*. XCI (October 12, 1986), p. 1.

Stille, Alexander. "Primo Levi," in *Saturday Review*. XI (August, 1985), p. 70.

Carl Rollyson

PERSONAL KNOWLEDGE
Towards a Post-Critical Philosophy

Author: Michael Polanyi (1891-1976)
Type of work: Philosophy
First published: 1958

Form and Content

  Personal Knowledge: Towards a Post-Critical Philosophy, Michael Polanyi's magnum opus, recapitulated in many ways his own intellectual odyssey. Throughout his early years in Hungary, he demonstrated the versatility that would characterize his later work. For example, while majoring in medicine at Budapest University, he was already publishing papers in chemistry and physics. By 1920, when he joined the Kaiser Wilhelm Institute in Berlin, he was one of Europe's most distinguished physical chemists. Although his main interest was in the rates of chemical reactions, he also did research in X-ray crystallography, physical adsorption, and thermodynamics. In 1933 he resigned from the Kaiser Wilhelm Institute in protest against the Nazi treatment of Jewish scientists. He then went to England, where he became professor of physical chemistry at the University of Manchester. Yet he could not ignore his experience of the political forces that were tearing Europe apart, and he tried to integrate these experiences into the objective approach to the world that had characterized his science. He began to spend so much time on humanistic issues that he became, for the last ten years at Manchester, a professor of social studies. Upon his retirement in 1958, *Personal Knowledge* was published.

  The book's appearance at the end of Polanyi's formal academic life was no accident, and its provenance owed much to his experiences as a doctor, chemist, and professor of social studies. While a scientist, Polanyi had become critical of the positivistic view of science, the doctrine that only sense perceptions can lead to genuine knowledge and that events can be understood only in terms of physical laws. He thought that this view made a mockery of such things as human responsibility and moral ideals. His experiences in Germany during the 1920's and early 1930's convinced him of the intellectual connection between positivism and the ruthless political movements of the Left and Right. He witnessed how the Nazis used a distorted Darwinism in their racist theories, and on a 1935 visit to Moscow he saw how T. D. Lysenko, a Communist ideologue, persecuted N. I. Vavilov, Russia's most distinguished geneticist. To counter these tyrannies, Polanyi saw the importance of believing passionately in certain ideals essential to a free society. He held that a complete rethinking of scientific knowledge was necessary to dispel these threats to freedom and to science itself. If moral ideals were simply matters of emotional preference, then they lacked the intellectual muscle to oppose powerful Fascist and Communist ideologies.

  To resolve what he saw as a great crisis, Polanyi did not try to make moral principles provable; instead, he tried to show how both morality and science depended upon unprovable principles. The unprovability of these beliefs did not render them worthless; rather, it showed that science was essentially a human enterprise within a community of inquirers bound together by a common faith. This conviction, burned into Polanyi's consciousness by his experiences in Nazi Germany and Communist Russia, contributed to the emergence of the philosopher from the scientist. This transformation found its greatest concretization in *Personal Knowledge*.

The book's form grew out of the circumstances of its composition. In 1951 and 1952 Polanyi delivered the Gifford Lectures at the University of Aberdeen. The Scottish jurist Adam Gifford had established the series in the nineteenth century to promote the study of natural theology. Like many lecturers before him, Polanyi interpreted the mandate quite broadly as an investigation into the intellectual foundations of theology and ethics. In particular, he saw the series as an opportunity to develop a new theory of knowledge that would have important implications for theology. He used the lectures to inquire into the nature of knowledge, its origins, and the need for a new epistemology, the rudimentary elements of which he described. In the six years after the lectures, he continued to develop his ideas, increasing the range of supporting evidence and deepening his analysis into a truly alternative ideal of knowledge. His principal theme was that the personal did not hinder but focused the activity of knowing.

The motivation behind Polanyi's book was to provide a firm foundation for humans' core beliefs. For him, scientific truth and moral goodness are not two separate categories; rather, truth is the rightness of an action, and the verification of a statement is the rationale, not wholly specifiable, for its acceptance. In the positivist view of science there is no room for personal participation. Polanyi, on the other hand, realized that the self-involvement of scientists in discovery is invariably impassioned. The joy of grasping a new scientific insight causes the mind to expand into a deeper understanding of the world and to live thereafter in a more active preoccupation with its problems. What the positivist view of science lacks, according to Polanyi, is the involving reality of individual experience.

The book's title implies that it comprises two sharply contrasting types of material. Indeed, critics who saw genuine knowledge as impersonal and objective viewed the title as a contradiction, since personal participation makes knowledge arbitrary and subjective. To counter this criticism, Polanyi marshaled evidence to show that scientific detachment exercises a destructive influence in biology, psychology, and sociology. Furthermore, he established an alternative ideal of knowledge, applicable to both the sciences and the humanities, and he used the findings of Gestalt psychology to bolster this ideal. Gestalt psychologists emphasized the doctrine that psychological phenomena are irreducible wholes, with properties that cannot be derived from their parts. Scientific knowing, for Polanyi, consists in discerning such wholes. Early in his writings he called this intuition; in *Personal Knowledge* he describes it as the tacit, or hidden, coefficient of knowing. Every interpretation of nature, whether scientific or humanistic, is based on some intuitive conception of the general nature of things. To interpret nature insightfully requires both tacit skills and passionate personal participation. Around this central idea of intellectual commitment Polanyi structured his book.

Personal Knowledge has four parts, moving from specific inquiries into the exact sciences through an investigation into the philosophical foundations of these inquiries to a justification for his general theory of knowledge. Part 1, "The Art of Knowing," examines scientific knowledge by analyzing discoveries in physics and chemistry to reveal the personal elements that are often hidden. Part 2, "The Tacit Component," shows that all knowledge is guided by personal and social factors that are rarely articulated. In part 3, "The Justification of Personal Knowledge," Polanyi considers modern philosophical and religious beliefs in elaborating his program of epistemological reform. The book's final part, "Knowing and Being," shows how the structure of human knowing mirrors the structure of being.

Analysis

Much of *Personal Knowledge* constitutes an attack on the positivist claim for total objectivity in scientific knowledge. Polanyi argues that modern scientism enslaves thought and action more tyrannically than religious thought ever did. Indeed, the ideal of scientific detachment offers human beings no scope for their most vital beliefs and even forces them to disguise these beliefs in debilitatingly inadequate ways. Yet these beliefs will not remain hidden, and through numerous examples from the history of science, Polanyi shows that scientific discoveries cannot be explained in terms of wholly explicit knowledge. In doing so, he uncovers an interesting paradox: Many scientists of the positivist persuasion insist that science rests on wholly explicit truth, but in their actions they show that science lives by discovery, and these discoveries depend on imprecise hunches and a faith in the orderliness of nature.

For Polanyi, knowledge has two faces: explicit knowledge, usually displayed in written words or mathematical formulas, and tacit knowledge, generally exemplified in skilled actions. Through his analysis of tacit knowing, Polanyi shows that scientific discovery demands intuitive and patiently acquired skills that are in principle irreducible to explicit rules. He finds that there is always something ineffable about such skills, and that they can be learned only by close association with a master and a community of practitioners. Between the subject and object, then, stands the community, which is creative like the subject and refractory like the object. Consequently, science is a vast system of beliefs, deeply rooted in history and cultivated by a specially organized section of society.

Besides his negative thesis of scientific objectivity's weaknesses as an ideal, Polanyi has a positive thesis of personal knowledge as a realistic ideal. This positive ideal centers on the notion of commitment. Without conscious commitment to value judgments the human being cannot arrive at the truth, which Polanyi sees as the least coercive relationship between man and society. To say that something is true is to express a belief and therefore to commit oneself to a course of action consonant with this belief. This commitment is both subjective and objective. In making it, the person is inevitably motivated by subjective factors rooted in his individuality, but there is something universal and therefore objective in personal commitment, since the person becomes responsible, together with sharers of his belief, for following that course of action. Polanyi insists that all knowledge takes place within a framework of personal commitment. For him, personal knowledge means the knowledge possessed by a responsible person who is part of an intellectually healthy community.

Polanyi saw the modern mind as sick, and he thought that he could cure it. The modern dilemma arises from the relation between the scientistic claim of detached knowledge and the moral dynamism of contemporary social and political movements. To bridge the gap, one needs belief. The scientist must believe that the methods of science are fundamentally sound if he or she is to acquire the skills of scientific inquiry. In the eleventh century Saint Anselm wrote that he did not seek to understand so that he might believe, but he believed in order to understand. Polanyi, too, argues that one must believe to know, for the meaning of all of one's judgments ultimately depends on realities grasped only tacitly by a mind in action. Polanyi believed that human minds are capable of making contact with reality and that the intellectual passion impelling them toward this contact will so faithfully guide their actions that they will achieve the full measure of truth.

For Polanyi, the vocation of the scientist is to uncover the truth about the natural world. What he fought against is severing scientific activity from the scientist's belief in his own power to construct a meaningful picture of reality. Detachment dehumanizes people and alienates them from society. Science does not require that one study the world and society in a detached manner; instead, science is essentially a human activity. Polanyi saw man primarily as a meaning-seeking creature whose brain has been programmed to discover systems of meaning both within and without himself. Five million centuries of evolution, groping upward along numberless paths, have led to the human being, who is, so far as is known, the only bearer of responsible thought in the universe.

From this analysis it is clear that personal knowledge has implications for religion. Polanyi rejects the traditional division between science and religion because it assumes that science proceeds by deductive logic and inductive generalization whereas religion proceeds by acts of faith that often defy logic. In his distinction Polanyi sees science as seeking to uncover realities which exist independently of people's knowledge of them, whereas religious realities are brought into being by people's creative efforts to achieve meaning in their lives. Religious realities are valid in the sense that they reveal more of what they mean as time goes on, but Polanyi thinks that it would be illusory to view them as existing before humans discovered them. Religion is related to experience as are mathematics and art. To someone prepared to live in their world, they convey their own meaning, which is related to human experience but not corroborated by external experience in the way the natural sciences are.

Polanyi recognizes that religious conversion changes a person in a way that growth in natural knowledge never does, but the difference between scientific and religious knowledge is one of degree, not of kind, since both science and religion require commitment and dynamic contexts to have understanding and meaning. In *Personal Knowledge* Polanyi states that religion builds up its own universe, using secular experience as its raw material. Every great religious system is constructed by elaborating some external experience in terms of an internal experience. The convert surrenders to this personal experience and through his life accredits its validity. God exists, then, not as a scientific fact. Like truth, goodness, beauty, and justice, God can be appreciated only in serving Him.

The conclusion of *Personal Knowledge* is a meditation on man in the universe. Polanyi sees the appearance of the human mind as the ultimate stage in the awakening of the world. Everything before man, from the big bang through the evolution of the galaxies to the appearance of the planets and the strivings of many forms of life, is part of the same endeavor toward liberation. In his final words, Polanyi sums up the contribution that these various centers of activity have made to human existence:

> We may envisage then a cosmic field which called forth all these centres by offering them a short-lived, limited, hazardous opportunity for making some progress of their own towards an unthinkable consummation. And that is also, I believe, how a Christian is placed when worshipping God.

Critical Context

In *Personal Knowledge* Michael Polanyi criticized important modern ideas and attitudes, and these criticisms called for responses from many philosophers, who, unfortunately, never made them. From the time of the book's appearance until Polanyi's death in 1976, he worked in the University of Oxford, but even there his philosophical writings were either neglected or received with suspicion. Polanyi had spent a significant portion of his life as a physical chemist, and it was natural for philosophers to look upon him as an outsider. Indeed, his relative ignorance of the field is a good example of his own thesis that any discipline contains much that is acquired tacitly, through acculturation. Despite this realization, Polanyi thought, toward the end of his life, that his work had been a failure. His purpose had been to convince intellectuals that the modern mind was in trouble and that he had a solution in his new epistemology. To be sure, he won some converts, but most Western intellectuals either ignored or failed to be persuaded by his work.

Polanyi should not have been surprised by this. England, during his time there, was dominated by analytic philosophy, and these philosophers, both logical positivists and language analysts, were unable to take him seriously. Logical positivists, who wanted to maintain the distinction between science and nonscience, saw his action of putting them on the same continuum as muddying the waters of science. Furthermore, Polanyi's treatment of personal knowledge put him, according to analytic philosophers, among the philosophes, isolated from the true philosophers.

Personal Knowledge presents many new positions on a host of thorny philosophical problems and so it is to be expected that even his followers found things to criticize. For example, Marjorie Grene, who was his assistant while he was writing the book, has criticized his notion of hierarchies—that is, his doctrine of the levels of reality. Polanyi argued that living things, within which one finds a hierarchy of organizing principles, transcend the laws of physics and chemistry. Similarly, he proposed that the brain and the mind are separate realities. For Grene, Polanyi's position constitutes a defense of dualism. Polanyi's views on life and mind are instances of his general position that beings are organized into a stratified universe in which higher types of being emerge from the lower types. Grene's studies of evolutionary theory have made her skeptical about cosmologies of emergence. Yet Polanyi has his defenders. Harry Prosch, for example, thinks that Grene is wrong in assuming that Polanyi introduced Cartesian dualism into his system. The mind and brain are certainly different for Polanyi, but he also holds that there are no unincarnate minds. Grene is correct in her view that he believed in a stratified universe, but such a belief would be unsound only if higher beings had powers that were simply the summation of the powers of their subsidiary parts.

Despite these criticisms of Polanyi's supposed subjectivism, dualism, and hierarchism, he continued to maintain that his philosophy would provide a fruitful intellectual basis for supporting a free society. At the center of his thought is the intellectual passion that impels human beings to make ever more meaningful contact with reality. He maintained that a free society could not exist unless there were basic ideals held in common by all members of the community. He himself had a profound experience of the scientific community, but he also experienced the demoralizing gap between theory and practice in the scientific life of Nazi Germany and Communist Russia. He saw the need for science to become more human and for the sciences and humanities to come closer together. In this way loyalty to mankind would increase among scientists, and scientific truths would turn from something static and detached into dynamic and creative human truth.

Sources for Further Study

Dulles, Avery. "Faith, Church, and God: Insights from Michael Polanyi," in *Theological Studies*. XLV (September, 1984), pp. 537-550.

Gelwick, Richard. *The Way of Discovery: An Introduction to the Thought of Michael Polanyi*, 1977.

Hall, Mary Harrington. "A Conversation with Michael Polanyi," in *Psychology Today*. I (May, 1968), pp. 20-25, 65-67.

Kane, Jeffrey. *Beyond Empiricism: Michael Polanyi Reconsidered*, 1984.

Polanyi, Michael. *The Anatomy of Knowledge*, 1969.

_____. *Knowing and Being*, 1969.

_____. *The Study of Man*, 1959.

_____. *The Tacit Dimension*, 1966.

Poteat, William H. *Polanyian Meditations: In Search of a Post-Critical Logic*, 1985.

Prosch, Harry. *Michael Polanyi: A Critical Exposition*, 1986.
Stines, James W. "I Am the Way: Michael Polanyi's Taoism," in *Zygon*. XX (March, 1985), pp. 59-77.

Robert J. Paradowski

PHILOSOPHICAL EXPLANATIONS

Author: Robert Nozick (1938-   )
Type of work: Philosophy
First published: 1981

Form and Content

A notable book on political theory appeared in 1971: *A Theory of Justice* by John Rawls argued brilliantly for a theory of government that would distribute the goods of its people with a Social Democratic bias toward the poor. Almost immediately afterward another brilliant book appeared which attacked Rawls's book respectfully but powerfully—*Anarchy, State, and Utopia* (1974), by Robert Nozick, a professor in the philosophy department at Harvard University. Even more interesting than Nozick's treatment of Rawls's assertions—coming down on the side of individual liberty and property—was the tone of Nozick's text. It was written in a casual chatty style, one in which powerful and dangerous assertions, rebuttals, and refutations appear and disappear in the friendly text, like sharks in custard.

In 1981 another book by Nozick appeared, *Philosophical Explanations*. Having made his bow to the public in political theory, Nozick took on the age-old, classical questions of philosophy. Individual chapters deal with the identity of the Self, self-knowledge, the possibility of knowledge, skepticism, value, free will, ethics, the meaning of life, and Martin Heidegger's ultimate query, "Why is there something rather than nothing at all?" Yet the very traditionalism of the queries is deliberate. Nozick is trying to view the fundamental questions of philosophy from a new angle, that of philosophical "explanation."

From the very first page Nozick repudiates any attempt to provide a definitive treatment of any of these questions, simply because a successful act of definition ends discussion. This definitive procedure, of attempting to answer philosophical questions once and for all, is what Nozick calls "coercive":

> The terminology of philosophical art is coercive: arguments are *powerful* and best when they are *knockdown*, arguments *force* you to a conclusion, if you believe the premises you *have to* or *must* believe the conclusion, some arguments do not carry much *punch*, and so forth.

These metaphors of combat show that philosophy has traditionally been regarded as a coercive activity. If a philosopher refuses to engage and retreats, he is not considered sporting:

> If the other person is willing to bear the label of "irrational" or "having the worst arguments," he can skip away happily maintaining his previous belief. He will be trailed, of course, by the philosopher furiously hurling philosophical imprecations. . . . Perhaps philosophers need arguments so powerful they set up reverberations in the brain:

if the person refuses to accept the conclusion, he *dies*. How's that for a powerful argument?

Nozick asks what useful purpose philosophical argument serves: "Why are philosophers intent on forcing others to believe things? . . . The valuable person cannot be fashioned by committing philosophy upon him." What does Nozick recommend? He recommends explanations rather than proofs. The reader reading an explanation engages in a gentle dialogue with the text, in which his own ideas are evoked in response to the text's gentle nudges. In this way, a cooperative process is initiated. Here philosophy becomes "a nice way to behave," a benign collective activity rather than a bullfight where the text's author is the matador and the reader is the bull.

Philosophical Explanations contains 778 pages and is divided into three large sections bearing traditional names—"Metaphysics," "Epistemology," and "Value"— each of which is divided into several chapters. The first section, "Metaphysics," includes "The Identity of the Self" and "Why Is There Something Rather than Nothing?" "Epistemology" is composed of "Knowledge," "Skepticism," and "Evidence." The third section, "Value," by far the longest section in the book, is composed of three chapters, "Free Will," "Foundations of Ethics," and "Philosophy and the Meaning of Life." Some of these titles seem ironic, as if Nozick were going back to traditional philosophical topics and, despite his attempt to avoid coercing the reader, settling them once and for all.

Analysis

In "Metaphysics," the first topic chosen is an old and traditional one—the nature of the self, the status of the individual. Nozick calls up an old and fascinating example: the ship of Theseus. If a plank wears out on the ship, it is thrown away and a new plank is fitted to the deck. Suppose all the planks and all the other equipment of the ship are similarly replaced: Does one still have the old ship, or is it a new one? As if that were not puzzling enough, suppose someone sneaks away with the discarded equipment and forms it into a ship again: Which ship is the old ship and which is the new one?

The problem is not concerned with ships but with people. The components of the body change constantly. Is one still the same person? This problem has to do with the body as material object; if this were the whole problem, it would be easy to solve, simply by denying that molecular interchange constitutes a material change. When mental "objects" are considered, however, the problem is not so easy to dismiss. For example, has a college class on philosophy changed if one of the students is absent? Or (Nozick's example) if the famous Vienna Circle of philosophers had scattered before World War II (as it did), what would have happened to the Vienna Circle if three members had emigrated to Istanbul and carried on as the Vienna Circle, only to find out at the end of the war that other members had emigrated to the United States and also carried on as the Vienna Circle? Where would the "real" Vienna Circle have been located?

In his solution to this problem, Nozick seems to be analyzing not what the "individual" really is, but what is meant when the word "individual" is used, an approach credited to Ludwig Wittgenstein. Nozick employs the notion of the "closest continuer"; whichever of the entities to be traced bears the closest "continuing" relationship with the original object would be called "the original object." Thus, in the case of Theseus' ship, most people would say that the closest continuer would be the ship from which the planks were originally taken and replaced.

The second portion of "Metaphysics," "Why Is There Something Rather than Nothing," deals with a famous metaphysical question with which philosophers from Gottfried Wilhelm Leibniz to Martin Heidegger have wrestled. The basic problem in dealing with this question, as Nozick notes, is that the answer to the question explains everything. Yet the question itself is something, part of everything, so how can a question provide an answer for its own existence? Here the problem is identified with the notion of "self-subsumption" and with the further problem, "how is explanation possible?" Here the reader sees Nozick's motive for dealing with this problem—it provides a philosophical basis for "philosophical explanations."

Is self-subsuming explanation thwarted by the fact that explanations must be deeper than what they (purport to) explain? . . . Explanatory self-subsumption, I admit, appears quite weird—a feat of legerdemain. When we reach the ultimate and most fundamental explanatory laws, however, there are few possibilities.

Either all explanations go round in an infinite circle, each explanation explaining the next, forever, or explanations have a stop; if they stop, where do they stop—at unexplainable "brute facts" or at self-subsuming laws? There are problems with both suggestions, and Nozick wrestles with them. He approaches the matter (with help from his twelve-year-old daughter) and moves toward a statistical notion: There are many ways for something to be something, but only one way for there to be nothing. Thus, if states are assigned randomly, there is a much greater chance for there to be something than there is for nothing. The philosopher can work out a principle that all possibilities will eventually occur: "All possible worlds obtain." The principle itself is part of a possible world, if it is true, however, so it is self-subsuming, and here one begins to get out of the possibility trap.

In the second large section, "Epistemology," knowledge and skepticism are covered. How can one convince a skeptic that he is eating an omelet, that he is not, in reality, merely a brain suspended in a vat which is under the impression that "he" is eating an omelet? Again, a classic problem in philosophy. Here Nozick separates the problem into two distinct parts: Can one convince the skeptic that he is wrong? (Answer: no.) Does one have to convince the skeptic that he is wrong if as a philosopher one wishes to deal with the problem? (Answer: again, no.) Here is the basis for Nozick's preference for explanations over proofs; the skeptic cannot be coerced into belief, but explanation may soften skepticism in others.

In the third large section, "Value," Nozick wrestles with the foundation of ethics.

Ethics has become fashionable again after a long interval of neglect. (Nozick's colleague at Harvard, Morton Gabriel White, has also written on ethics.) One of the main concerns of ethics is the determination of value. Value governs choice, and Nozick handles the problem by saying, essentially, that people who behave in an ethically and morally responsible manner are nicer than people who do not. Niceness for Nozick is a powerful criterion, possibly what decency is for George Orwell: a noncoercive standard that may ultimately be the only true guide to action. Saints, martyrs, and heroes end up being used by fanatics to justify their tyranny. Decency and niceness are harder to employ for these purposes. That, presumably, is why Nozick is opposed to any coercive systems, even philosophical ones.

Critical Context

Philosophical Explanations, above and beyond the treatments of the topics chosen, shows that Nozick's real interests lie in methods of philosophical description. The range of the subjects shows that it is the process of philosophizing itself that Nozick is questioning. He seems to be following in the footsteps of Friedrich Nietzsche and Ludwig Wittgenstein, in that Nozick is attacking philosophical activity itself, the possibility of describing anything. Nietzsche described philosophers as thinking that they are doctors when they are actually the disease.

Nozick's first articles dealt with decision making, which includes deciding what can be described clearly—Wittgenstein's emphasis. In this context Nozick's first book, *Anarchy, State, and Utopia*, which made a political stir upon its publication in 1974, is not really about political theory at all; it is essentially an exercise in philosophical explanation used in the realm of political theory, a "five-finger exercise" in preparation for the virtuoso performances to come.

Critics have noted that Nozick ends, despite his modest declarations, by providing proofs rather than explanations; that is, Nozick's demonstrations are sometimes so subtle and brilliant that readers can be convinced by them, even if Nozick wants only to stimulate thought. In Aesop's fable about the Sun and the Wind, the Wind fails to make a traveler remove his cloak. No matter how hard the Wind blows, the traveler merely grasps the cloak more tightly around himself. The Sun, however, causes him to remove his cloak merely by beaming upon him. Nozick would here be the Sun, gently coercing belief. His support of explanation over proof may change the present vogue for axiomatic demonstration—coercive proof in its most coercive form—in many fields of philosophy. If he succeeds, *Philosophical Explanations* may become an important book in the history of philosophy.

Sources for Further Study

Asahina, R. "Inquisitive Robert Nozick," in *The New York Times Book Review*. LXXXVI (September 20, 1981), p. 74.

Blanshard, Brand. Review in *The Yale Review*. LXXI (Spring, 1982), p. 404.

Brueckner, Anthony L. "Why Nozick Is a Sceptic," in *Mind*. XCIII (April, 1984), pp. 259-264.

Burnyeat, M. F. Review in *The Times Literary Supplement*. October 15, 1982, p. 1136.

Levin, Michael E. "Thinking About the Self," in *Commentary*. LXXIV (September 7, 1982), p. 55.

Williams, Bernard. Review in *The New York Times Review of Books*. XXIX (February 18, 1982), pp. 32-34.

Edmund L. Epstein

PHILOSOPHY AND THE MIRROR OF NATURE

Author: Richard Rorty (1931-   )
Type of work: Philosophy
First published: 1979

Form and Content

Richard Rorty began the process of plotting out the ideas and approach of *Philosophy and the Mirror of Nature* while holding an American Council of Learned Societies Fellowship in 1969-1970. The major portion of the manuscript was drafted during 1973-1974, while he held a Guggenheim Fellowship. Thus, by the time it reached final form, the book had been about ten years in the making—the rest of the work and revisions being fitted around his regular teaching load at Princeton University.

The philosophical method within which Rorty had been trained played a large role in the way that he approached, organized, and developed this book. He had been taught that a philosophical problem was

> a product of the unconscious adoption of assumptions built into the vocabulary in which the problem was stated—assumptions which were to be questioned before the problem itself was taken seriously.

By using some of the seed-work done by Wilfred Sellars and W. V. O. Quine, Rorty began to turn the tools of the discipline of philosophy upon its own underlying assumptions. By so doing, he hoped to do what he calls "therapeutic" or "edifying" philosophy as opposed to taking a systematic approach. This would be accomplished by unmasking the unstated assumptions and revealing them for what they are—"optional" tools in "a way" of doing philosophy.

Rorty divides his 401 pages into three primary parts. Within the first two parts, although sporadic attention is paid to other edifying philosophers (the prime examples of the therapeutic approach being Ludwig Wittgenstein, Martin Heidegger, and John Dewey), Rorty's main focus is upon showing and dismantling the assumptions of the analytic tradition in philosophy. He writes in the style and vocabulary of the analytic; his goal, however, is nothing less than the deconstruction of the tradition. Part 1 centers on a philosophy of mind. In it, Rorty looks closely at what he calls "the invention of the mind," going back to René Descartes' indubitable substance of man as a "thinking thing." He says that Descartes moved the focus away from the notion that the mind is reason, replacing it with the idea of the mind-as-inner-arena. A correlative shift, then, accompanied the aforementioned move in that a quest for certainty replaced the quest for wisdom.

Part 2 is concerned with epistemology. This section places the beginnings of epistemology in the seventeenth century by connecting it with the Cartesian notion of mind mentioned in part 1. Within this section, especially chapter 4, Rorty appropriates Sellars' attack on "givenness" and Quine's attack on "necessity." By amplifying these arguments, he seeks to dismantle the possibility of an epistemological enterprise grounded in certainty. His approach, instead, leads to a pragmatist conception of knowledge, seeing truth as "what is better for us to believe rather than an accurate representation of reality," to quote William James.

Part 3 finally gets to that which Rorty considers to be edifying. He borrows a term from Thomas Kuhn's *The Structure of Scientific Revolutions* (1962), "normal science," and generalizes it, saying that the idea of "normal discourse" can apply to any sort of discourse (scientific, political, theological, and the like). What makes it "normal" is the fact that it conducts its pursuits in accordance with the "givens" of the prevailing paradigm. In other words, this sort of discourse works within the bounds of a prescriptive model which aims at finding commonality and agreement from those operating according to that paradigm. On the other hand, "abnormal discourse" does not operate in accordance with the assumptions of the prescriptive model or paradigm. Whereas Descartes, Immanual Kant, and John Locke serve as primary examples of Rorty's ascription of "normal discourse" in philosophy, Wittgenstein, Heidegger, and Dewey lead the way in doing "abnormal" philosophy.

In chapter 8, Rorty uses the hermeneutical method of Hans-Georg Gadamer to develop some useful insights regarding the approach he espouses. By looking at Gadamer's hermeneutical circle, he concludes his analysis with the admonition to "continue the conversation."

Analysis

In *Philosophy and the Mirror of Nature*, Richard Rorty has attempted to find an underlying metaphor upon which the history of Western philosophy has been founded. He has turned the critic's attention away from propositions, submitting that pictures form the core of philosophical positions. Beginning with Plato, Rorty purports, Western philosophers have constructed a doctrine of the mind as a mirror of nature. Thus, the ultimate forerunner of the Western mode of thinking would have to be Plato, or at least the Platonic ontology: that there exists an external reality which is independent of the perceiving mind; it is, however, accessible—whether through intuition, sense perception, or propositions—to the mind, which is pictured to be an "inner eye."

If Plato serves as the genesis of this view of reality, René Descartes is just as important in that he provided the major connection between the Platonic ontology and modern philosophy. Descartes' epistemological turn established the commonly held version of mind-body dualism. Hence, the mind is an independent entity, a thinking thing, which knows itself better than it knows anything else, given its privileged access. Nevertheless, it achieves knowledge of "outer realities" by accurately mirroring or representing those realities. This view fit nicely with John Locke's view of the human mind as a *tabula rasa*. On this blank slate, the outer world somehow imprints itself, creating an inner impression which exactly replicates the world outside. Finally, Immanuel Kant, in his *Kritik der reinen Vernunft* (1781; *The Critique of Pure Reason*, 1873), systematizes the ideas developed by the previously mentioned philosophers. He combines a Cartesian sort of intuition with a Lockean representation allowing predication in his synthetic a priori approach to knowledge. Through all this development of philosophical thought, the metaphor of the mind as a mirror of nature held firm.

Rorty's book, decried by many because of its so-called polemics, has sought to displace the mirror metaphor. He believes that this image serves as the rallying point upon which analytic philosophers of otherwise widely diverging views have agreed. He is also convinced that it is the precursor of perennial philosophical problems, such as those of mind/body, Spirit/Nature, and consciousness. In the light, then, of these devastating problems presented to philosophy by this "optional" notion, he sets sail to deconstruct the history of philosophy by examining it without the help of the Cartesian picture. This concomitantly requires the laying aside of the common field of inquiry usually associated with that picture: the nature of privileged representations, incorrigible sensations, and understanding "raw feels." Thus, the need is expunged to ground a statement such as "my head hurts." Instead of spending needless effort on epistemological questions of how I know, or what it means to know what I think I know through privileged representation or raw feels, I can far more profitably turn my attention to the pragmatic question of finding the aspirin bottle.

This pragmatic turn, which Rorty so readily embraces with the help of the "edifying" trinity of Wittgenstein, Heidegger, and Dewey, is meant to create new kinds of conversation contra the systematizers of traditional philosophy. Interestingly, even those who are not thoroughly enamored of his approach acknowledge the important role played by this study. In his October 7, 1981, review of *Philosophy and the Mirror of Nature* in *The New Republic*, Ian Hacking said:

> Unlike Will Durant, who encapsulated the history of philosophy into an uplifting theme of better and better, Rorty, with an equally attractive historical style, tells us that the whole project is spiraling down into nothingness. Yet this very book is causing numerous young people to read philosophical classics as never before. This is the closest thing to a cult book commencing popular philosophy that we have seen for many a year. So there is an internal paradox: a death-of-philosophy book doubles interest in all kinds of philosophy.

Rorty proposes (chapter 7) that the issue at stake is the way in which the problem of knowledge is framed—epistemologically or hermeneutically. Indeed, he had been moving toward this claim throughout the book. To view knowledge epistemologically, so Rorty asserts, is to take up the project proposed by Descartes: to doubt what can be doubted until one reaches that which is indubitable. In other words, Descartes' quest aimed at finding certainty. Wittgenstein and Rorty propose a very different project. Instead of certainty, they aimed at a perpetually self-correcting understanding via a never ending methodology of revision. This is not "clear and distinct" certainty. Whereas the "epistemological project" is after truth, Rorty's "hermeneutical project" focuses on method. The former seeks propositional statements which stand beyond the need of correction; the latter sees its conclusions as always and necessarily corrigible.

Several reviewers of the book have queried what the practical effect would be of approaching philosophy as hermeneutics. Would this move, by its very nature, displace the need for a discipline called philosophy? Undoubtedly, if this model were adopted, the notion of philosophy as a foundational subject, and the philosopher as a guardian/judge of rationality, would suffer serious damage. That is, in fact, Rorty's point. The self-deception of thinking that a perspective or a system can be eternalized would eventually fall into disrepute. To answer the above question, one need look no further than Rorty's own conclusion on the matter, "Professions can survive the paradigms which gave them birth. In any case, the need for teachers who have read the great dead philosophers is quite enough to ensure that there will be philosophy departments as long as there are universities."

An inevitable question comes up when a project such as Rorty's is proposed. It centers on whether such an approach is the necessary means toward the achievement of the goal. In other words, why should "abnormal discourse" be embraced rather than "normal discourse"? No doubt, Rorty would answer this question in a thoroughly Kuhnian sense: Assumptions, like paradigms, are not necessarily permanent. Instead, they afford one way of seeing among others. Challenging our assumptions opens us to new constructs, to which we were previously blinded because of a priori commitments.

Critical Context

The traditional way of thinking of philosophy in the history of Western thought has been to see it as a foundational discipline—one that establishes the rules upon which other disciplines may operate and catalogs the ways by which they may verify their truth claims. Undoubtedly, there have been many in the analytic tradition who, like Rorty, are skeptical about traditional epistemological concerns. Their skepticism is not, however, with the epistemological enterprise as a whole; instead, they claim that genuine philosophical issues have been clouded by the epistemological formulations that have been offered. What is needed, therefore, is a reformulation of the relevant issues. This is the approach taken by many who find themselves somewhat sympathetic to Rorty's concerns. Nevertheless, Rorty points out that while such men as Hilary Putnam, Gottlob Frege, and Michael Dummett make attempts at dealing with the issues, they are still caught in the web of a veiled foundationalism. Rorty categorically rejects this.

On the other hand, given Rorty's attempted escape from a foundational approach, he has been labeled with such terms as historicism, skepticism, and relativism. If, indeed, Rorty is seeking to do away with the approach that privileges a perspective, then he would be no more amenable to historical foundationalism than he is to philosophical foundationalism. If he is suspicious of attempts to eternalize a "neutral framework" by which all claims to knowledge can be evaluated, that does not necessitate his espousal of a view which says that one cannot know what is beyond the "veil of ideas." In fact, he attacks this metaphor throughout. In like manner, Rorty is not touting a relativism that denies that there is truth. Rather, he wishes to emphasize that what is understood as "true" has been, and will continue to be, forged in the furnace of historical and sociological practice.

Though much of Rorty's approach is thought to be tendentious by those whom he describes as partaking in "normal" philosophical discourse, he suffers the same sort of fate in his peers' critique of him as do other disciplinary deconstructors who have plowed new ground. Those who undertake an "abnormal," "therapeutic," or "conversational" approach, such as Jacques Derrida (literary theory), Thomas Kuhn (science), Gene Wise or Michel Foucault (history), and Clifford Geertz (anthropology), have not initially been widely embraced by the discourse communities which they have addressed. Perhaps this is part of the personal price one has to pay for paving the way to new insights.

Sources for Further Study

Bernstein, Richard J. "Philosophy in the Conversation of Mankind," in *The Review of Metaphysics*. XXXIII (June, 1980), pp. 745-775.

Cornman, James W. *Materialism and Sensations*, 1971.

Greene, Robert. "Richard Rorty, *Philosophy and the Mirror of Nature*," in *Modern Language Notes*. XCV (December, 1980), pp. 1387-1391.

Hacking, Ian. "A Rebirth of Philosophy?" in *The New Republic*. CLXXXV (October 7, 1981), pp. 32-35.

Hoy, David Couzens, ed. "Foucault and Epistemology," in *Foucault: A Critical Reader*, 1986.

Rosenthal, David, ed. *Materialism and the Mind-Body Problem*, 1971.

Stephen M. Ashby

PILGRIM AT TINKER CREEK

Author: Annie Dillard (1945-   )
Type of work: Nature
Time of work: The mid-twentieth century
Locale: Virginia
First published: 1974

Principal personage:
ANNIE DILLARD, an American writer

Form and Content

Tinker Creek is a valley in Virginia's Blue Ridge Mountains. Annie Dillard, although born and reared in Pittsburgh, decided to make it her home for several years, and *Pilgrim at Tinker Creek* is the result. The book records her explorations and observations of the life of nature around the creek, interspersed with her meditations on the intricacies, paradoxes, mysteries, cruelties, and sublimities of the created world, and the unanswered and unanswerable questions about the intentions of the Creator. She is not a disinterested naturalist or scientist, but sees herself as a pilgrim, with her awakened senses ready for any momentary epiphany which may come her way.

The chief actors in this book are animals, insects, birds, and plants, as seen through the eyes of Dillard. Only rarely does another human being intrude into her story, and then only obliquely. The natural world provides drama enough, in numerous small ways. Dillard chances upon a small frog, for example, and as she gazes at it from a distance of a few feet it suddenly sags and crumples like a deflated football; its insides have been sucked out by a giant water bug, and all that remains is a bag of skin. Dillard is appalled; the ruthlessness and cruelty of nature is one of her recurring themes.

Sometimes she creates her own little dramas. She catches sight of a coot in the creek and improvises a game of hide-and-seek, instantly standing stock-still whenever there is a chance of the coot seeing her and taking flight. Shy coot and cunning coot-watcher, disguised as a tree whenever necessity demands, continue this unusual game for forty minutes.

She has learned the virtues of stealth and patience. She stalks a muskrat and gets within arm's reach of it; oblivious of her presence, it munches clumps of grass. She has also learned to be bold. Encountering a poisonous copperhead snake one night at a quarry, she watches it silently from a distance of four feet, knowing that it is aware of her presence. As she watches, a mosquito alights on the snake and feeds on it for several minutes, an event which astonishes Dillard and prompts her to reflect, in a manner that is typical of the whole book, on an imperfect, torn world in which everything is "nibbled and nibbling."

The book covers a year of such physical and mental meanderings, organized loosely around the passage of the seasons. Dillard will often break off her thoughts or her narrative and recall a significant event from another time and season; sometimes she flashes back to an incident in her childhood which sheds light on her present thoughts. A number of chapters are organized around a particular theme. In "Fixity," for example, she puzzles over the inability of many insects to alter their instinctive rituals even when those rituals have clearly ceased to be in their own interests. (Caterpillars will trail endlessly, playing follow-the-leader, around the rim of a vase, even when they are close to starvation and food supplies are nearby.)

Such bits of information are culled from Dillard's wide reading in the works of naturalists and explorers, mystics and quantum physicists, works which she shares enthusiastically with her reader. These sources complement her direct observations and supply another dimension to her thoughts. They feed her love of statistics and her passion for intricate detail. She enjoys divulging, for example, that there are 228 separate muscles in the head of the caterpillar of the ordinary goat moth; that in the top inch of forest soil there are an average of 1,356 living creatures present in each square foot; that water moving up a tree trunk can climb 150 feet in an hour; that a large elm makes as many as six million leaves in one season; and that the growing power of an expanding squash exerts a lifting force of five thousand pounds per square inch.

Stylistically, *Pilgrim at Tinker Creek* has two aspects. On the one hand, Dillard is informal, conversational, and sometimes colloquial. She has a keen sense of humor and enjoys telling a joke or a story. Frequently she addresses the reader directly, and her persona is that of the honest inquirer and earnest seeker who is thinking out loud, with all the intellectual vigor she possesses, about the implications of what she sees. She can also be iconoclastic and irreverent, not afraid of offering the Creator some blunt suggestions about how He might have improved His handiwork.

On the other hand, Dillard's prose is often richly poetic, dense with images, and allusive. She thinks effortlessly in similes, many of them highly arresting: a praying mantis about to disgorge its eggs looks like "a hideous, harried mother slicking up a fat daughter for a beauty pageant," and when the eggs emerge they are like "tapioca pudding glued to a thorn." Termite workers look like "tiny longshoremen unloading the *Queen Mary*"; the forests which end up as a coal bed with 120 seams must have "heaped like corpses in drawers" as they fell; and a menacing swollen creek thrashes around "like a blacksnake caught in a kitchen drawer." Whether poetic or conversational, figurative or natural, Dillard's language is always alert, fresh, and as fecund as the nature she studies so intently.

Analysis

Dillard is keenly aware of the opposites in creation—beauty and ugliness, bliss and terror. The beauty, grace, and perfect, careless spontaneity of a mockingbird as it plunges in a straight vertical descent from a four-story building impresses her deeply, but it is the grotesque phenomena in creation, such as the frog being sucked by the water bug, which prompt her more persistent and darker speculations. The questions "What's it all about?" and "What is going on here?" run like a leitmotif throughout the book. They are asked particularly in regard to the insect world, which boasts such a wide variety of puzzling behaviors, from the habit of the female praying mantis of devouring the male as they copulate to the female lacewing's eating of her own eggs. Dillard muses over the world as a parasitic place in which everything is battered, torn, preyed upon, and devoured. The world does not fit together in a way that makes rational sense; it offers testimony only to the Creator's exuberance, not to His goodness, or even to His intelligence.

Yet at other times Dillard's vision extends beyond the problematic aspects of Creation. During moments of heightened perception, she sees the world in a wholly different way, pulsing with divine fire and light. Moments such as these are also a recurring motif, and they act as a counterpoint to the insistent questioning. Indeed, the entire book can be understood as a prolonged meditation on how to see.

Normally, people see only what they have been conditioned to expect; the human brain acts as an editor without the conscious permission of the mind. Dillard draws on her reading of a book about how people who had been blind from birth reacted when their sight was restored. One girl, speechless with wonder before a tree, eventually described it as "the tree with the lights in it." Ths image gives Dillard one of her central, informing ideas. She describes how she had searched for the tree with the lights in it for many years, through all seasons. One day, out walking and thinking of nothing in particular, she saw a cedar "charged and transfigured, each cell buzzing with flame." The grass below her feet was seemingly on fire also, and charged with light. It was an epiphany, a manifestation, such as Moses had received through the burning bush, of a spirit and a power, burning in fire and light, which makes all things new. Dillard felt not only that she was seeing for the first time but that she too was being seen. The moment passed, but she lives for its recurrence; it is the moment which renders all other moments in life, and all other enterprises, inconsequential.

In this connection, Dillard makes ingenious use of the story of Xerxes, who apparently halted his army for three days so that he might contemplate the beauty of a single sycamore tree. He too, says Dillard, had seen the tree with the lights in it, and it put a halt to all of his worldly endeavors. Blaise Pascal, she notes, also had an experience of divine fire, and recorded it in a note which he sewed into the lining of his jacket, so that he would carry it with him at all times.

The moment of mystic perception comes unasked for and cannot be summoned at will. Closely related to it is Dillard's prerequisite for clear seeing: innocence, the capacity to lose self-consciousness and become completely absorbed in the object of contemplation. This involves the ability to live in the present, and Dillard devotes an entire chapter to it. She recalls one apparently insignificant incident in which she was patting a puppy at a deserted gasoline station, feeling the western wind on her face and the taste of recent coffee on her tongue, and watching a nearby mountain. For some unknown reason, self-consciousness was momentarily held in abeyance, and she felt fully alive, in the present, with the same elation she had felt when she had contemplated the cedar tree. It was a moment of innocence—but naturally it vanished the very moment she became aware of it. Dillard insists that it is self-consciousness that traps mankind in separateness, whether from God, from nature, or from one another.

On numerous occasions she seems able to overcome this built-in barrier, to make herself, so to speak, transparent before the phenomena she is observing. She watches a muskrat, for example, and later comments, "I never knew I was there"; she suggests that had an electroencephalogram been taken of her brain activity at the time it would have registered flat. She was a passive receiver, taking in but not giving out. The experience is close, as she realizes, to the loss of self the mystic knows (Dillard refers frequently to Thomas Merton, Martin Buber, and the Cabala), and it is usually accompanied by a feeling of balance, repose, and calm.

Such experiences create a strong sense of unity between the observer and the observed; they bridge the gap between subject and object. Although Dillard seems always to have possessed an acute sense of the affinity between all manifestations of life (she quotes Dylan Thomas approvingly: "The force that through the green fuse drives the flower/ Drives my green age"), in her epiphanies she seems to leap beyond simple affinity into identification, to become what she is contemplating, and the result is a sense of expansion and freedom. The loss of self is also the passage into a larger self, infinite in its variety: "Something broke and something opened. I filled up like a new wineskin. I breathed an air like light; I saw a light like water. I was the lip of a fountain the creek filled forever; I was ether, the leaf in the zephyr; I was flesh-flake, feather, bone."

Ultimately these experiences, and others like them, quiet the what's-it-all-about refrain that runs like the Devil's counter-tune to the song of praise prompted by the sight of the tree with the lights in it. In the dialectic between the analytic intellect and the visionary self—a variation on the age-old conflict between doubt and faith—it is the latter which proves to be stronger. *Pilgrim at Tinker Creek* ends on a note of exultation and acceptance of the totality of creation. No answers are provided to the questions that have troubled Dillard's rational intellect, but she is happy to go on treading the path of the Mystic Way, with her right foot saying "Glory" and her left foot saying "Amen."

Critical Context

Pilgrim at Tinker Creek was Dillard's first full-length work. It was enthusiastically received by reviewers and won the Pulitzer Prize for nonfiction, although a few dissenting voices complained about Dillard's self-centeredness. Many compared her to Henry David Thoreau and Herman Melville, and her search for the illuminated moment, what German Romantic writers called the *Augenblick*, aligns her with English Romantics such as William Wordsworth and William Blake. A comparison with Blake is particularly instructive, since Dillard, like Blake, writes about the state of innocence; she too is horrified at the parasitic aspects of nature, which parallels Blake's disgust with the state of being he labeled "Generation."

Dillard's visionary breakthroughs resemble Blake's higher world of Eden. Concern with the *Augenblick* also aligns Dillard with twentieth century writers such as James Joyce and Marcel Proust.

Dillard's next book was *Tickets for a Prayer Wheel* (1974), a collection of religious poems which record mystical experiences similar to those in her first book. She writes of seeing trees on fire, for example, and of God picking her up and swinging her like a bell (the bell metaphor is used twice in *Pilgrim at Tinker Creek*). *Holy the Firm* (1977), a visionary prose narrative, illustrates by way of parable Creation, Fall, and Redemption. It too makes extensive use of the image of fire, and reveals what is perhaps sometimes obscured in *Pilgrim at Tinker Creek*— that Dillard's concern is not with the natural world per se but with how nature reveals the infinite God. Her interests are theological rather than naturalistic.

Dillard wrote several more books during the 1980's. These included *Teaching a Stone to Talk: Expeditions and Encounters* (1982), which consists of fourteen essays, dealing mainly with the natural world and once more emphasizing transcendental experiences. Here for the first time in Dillard's work, other human beings become important to the narrative.

The autobiographical *An American Childhood* (1987) sheds interesting background on *Pilgrim at Tinker Creek*, revealing how Dillard first developed her acute powers of observation of the natural world and how this skill was accompanied by a search for transcendence.

Sources for Further Study

Carruth, Hayden. "Attractions and Dangers of Nostalgia," in *Virginia Quarterly Review*. L (Autumn, 1974), pp. 637-640.

Dunn, Robert Paul. "The Artist as Nun: Theme, Tone, and Vision in the Writings of Annie Dillard," in *Studia Mystica*. I, no. 4 (1978), pp. 17-31.

Lavey, David. "Noticer: The Visionary Art of Annie Dillard," in *Massachusetts Review*. XXI (1980), pp. 255-270.

McConahay, Mary Davidson. "'Into the Bladelike Arms of God': The Quest for Meaning Through Symbolic Language in Thoreau and Annie Dillard," in *Denver Quarterly*. XX (Fall, 1985) pp. 103-116.

McFadden-Gerber, Margaret. "The I in Nature," in *American Notes and Queries*. XVI (1977), pp. 3-5.

McIlroy, Gary. "Transcendental Prey: Stalking the Loon and the Coot," in *Thoreau Society Bulletin*. CXXVI (Summer, 1986), pp. 5-6.

Reimer, Margaret Loewen. "The Dialectical Vision of Annie Dillard's *Pilgrim at Tinker Creek*," in *Critique: Studies in Modern Fiction*. XXIV (Spring, 1983), pp. 182-191.

Bryan Aubrey

THE PINE BARRENS

Author: John McPhee (1931-   )
Type of work: Nature
First published: 1968

Form and Content

John McPhee is one of the most accomplished and respected prose artists writing in English. *The Pine Barrens* is perhaps his most well-known work, and in many respects it exhibits to best advantage the salient characteristics of all of his writing. First, the subject is a modest one for an essay: McPhee does not choose for his subjects the famous, the newsworthy, the popular, or the attractive. Instead, he writes about the places, people, and events that lie just below the level of popular consciousness, and he writes about them in a way that affords the reader a look beneath the superficial.

McPhee's canon includes works about a headmaster at a small New England private school, a basketball player, a chef, the state of Alaska, a tennis player, and oranges. In each case, the reader is first amazed that whole books are dedicated to these seemingly unassuming subjects and then astonished that upon completion of the work a significant amount of knowledge about the subject has been painlessly learned because of McPhee's impressive and lucid prose.

In *The Pine Barrens*, the subject is a geographic and ecological area of the state of New Jersey. As a place, the Pine Barrens are practically invisible, but under McPhee's close scrutiny and tender handling, they become a complete world, a fragile, balanced, human ecological system. The subject is large, but McPhee encompasses it with his prose, making it understandable and fascinating. Categories can be deceiving. *The Pine Barrens* is literally a book about some woods and the people who live in them. This is an alluring place, but few readers have the wherewithal to realize this fascination, even if the opportunity to visit and explore the place were available. McPhee does the work for his readers.

The book is a single long essay divided into nine chapters, each one of which could serve as a finished work. In effect, the nine essays offer a survey of the natural world of the Pine Barrens, the history of the area, an examination of its people and their customs, the wildlife of the barrens, and a glimpse of several possible futures for the area. This book is not, however, an ecological tract or (at least not overtly) a plea for a particular method of management or preservation. Nor is it a technical or scientific description of a landscape. To the contrary, McPhee's singular talent is the ability to condense scientific data and concepts—as well as his own observations—into prose that not only is accessible but also gives the reader an appreciation of the scope and size of the subject. All the subjects McPhee writes about are "bigger" than they first appear. His task, admirably performed, is to convince one of that fact. McPhee can make anything interesting. One need only trust him.

Analysis

McPhee's work may not at first seem a proper subject of "literary" analysis. *The Pine Barrens* is nonfiction prose. In addition, it is not, at least at the level at which most people read it, rhetorical. There is no blatant effort to convince the reader to take a particular political position, no attempt at persuasion. McPhee is not literary, in the sense that he makes no effort to force the facts of his story to engage larger systems of thought or structure. On the other hand, the book is not mere journalism. The success or failure of *The Pine Barrens* does not depend on the objectivity of the narrator or on his reportorial skill. The reader does not judge this book as he would a work about current affairs, sociology, or history. There is no "theory" to be proved, applied, or demonstrated.

The closest approximation of what McPhee and his book are and do may be found in the world of travel writing. Here, the reader expects personal insight, demanding accuracy but tolerating interpretation of accurate description. The presence of a narrator is constantly felt, no matter how objective he may make himself. Historical background is accepted if it illuminates some aspect of the entire subject. Glimpses of people the writer offers are enjoyed, both as a community viewed from a distance and as individuals viewed in some detail. The reader practically demands the unusual, the fascinating, the exotic, and the new.

The Pine Barrens provides these components in abundance, but there is also the writer's method to consider; thus, any analysis is not a matter of interpretation but is primarily an appreciation of McPhee's skill as a writer and an organizer. The book begins with a literal overview. Almost cinematically, McPhee positions the Pine Barrens geographically and socially. The most impressive aspect of his discussion in the first chapter, "The Woods from Hog Wallow," is the very presence of this wilderness in a state that has become an archetype of industrial development and residential density. McPhee is careful to expand the view to include the additional irony of finding this area in the center of the Eastern megalopolis that stretches from Richmond to Boston. It is a most unlikely place for the Pine Barrens, but the Pine Barrens is a most unlikely place.

After this sweeping overview, McPhee zeros in first on the town of Hog Wallow and then on an individual who will remain as a "guide" to what the Pine Barrens is and what it means. Fred Brown, offered by the writer as the prototypical denizen of the pines, is allowed to speak and act, without the narrator interrupting the action. Indeed, the narrator's presence is noted only when he wishes it.

The first example of McPhee's shifts from close observation back to expansive comment is worthy of close examination. Upon leaving Fred Brown's house to get water from the pump outside, McPhee leaves Fred as a subject as well. When McPhee operates the pump, it is as if he were pulling knowledge from the ground. Just as surely as the water rises from the earth, he describes its quality, the natural reservoir from which it comes, and the condition of that source as compared to others in the country. The reader is moved far away from Fred's house in the Pine Barrens and yet paradoxically remains there, because McPhee is still there. With the comment on the quality of the water, the focus returns to Fred. Both transitions have been so smoothly done that they are hardly noticeable.

Fred's knowledge of the pines becomes McPhee's, as the narrator describes the journeys the two men make around the area. The simplicity of Brown's observations, and McPhee's selection of them, makes the reader immediately familiar with the pines and the history they contain. The past that Fred carries with him is the final focus of the chapter, and the reader is left with the realization that the pines, despite their unique position and their isolation, may not be now what they once were and may not be in the future what they are now.

After this introductory chapter, McPhee offers a condensed history of the Pine Barrens. The people who have lived here share Fred's desire to "get well in away from everybody." Fred refers primarily to the location of houses and the distance that separates denizens of the barrens, but McPhee turns this phrase into a marker of the attitudes of the "pineys." McPhee concentrates on the incongruity of the history of the barrens: Settled by expatriates, fugitives, smugglers, and exiles, the region was eventually industrialized by a mining effort that was crude and doomed from the start. The lost industrial attempt produced the "vanished towns" that make the area seem not only empty but also abandoned. Ironically, the inhabitants prefer the conditions that exist now in the barrens, even though those conditions suggest a life of deprivation. McPhee suggests that there is more courage in continuing to live in an abandoned area, one that has "defeated" attempts to civilize it, than there is in living in an area that is merely primitive.

What the pineys have instead of industry is the gifts and advantages that the barrens give them. McPhee summarizes these in "The Separate World." Again, McPhee works the reader's perception of the pineys against their own. The reader is treated to a world that is "separate" because it is based on the employment of the seasons, the cycles of the pines. People make the best of what nature offers them, gathering, harvesting, and collecting the gifts of the forest in 'a way that is almost idyllic. Just when the description of this life reaches its most attractive, McPhee discusses the most appalling and distressing aspects of life in the pines. Separation has its price: illiteracy, inbreeding, the stigma of misperception by outsiders. The synthesis of the internal and external views is, finally, identity. "Piney" becomes a word acceptable when used by another piney but is insulting when used by an outsider. This sense of identity is central to the discussions which follow. In detail, McPhee examines those aspects of the barrens which exist in any society: religion, myths, legends, crime, popular history, the fear of catastrophe, and, most important, the prospect of the future. An overused word, microcosm, fits this description. The barrens are a world unto themselves, the pineys a people apart, despite every effort to "civilize" them and give them a future.

That future is the topic on which McPhee resolutely refuses to comment. In most books that concern themselves with ecology, the environment, or natural history, politics play an important role. Aspects of land and water management, the maintenance of wilderness areas, the overuse of recreational facilities, and the ruin of soils and water by human waste are unavoidable topics. In most cases, the political methods a writer prefers are clearly stated and supported.

Yet McPhee avoids dogmatism. Not, presumably, because he has no opinion but perhaps because he has a larger point to make. He clearly outlines the possibilities for the future of the Pine Barrens. He even updates their status in the 1981 edition of the book. Nowhere, however, does McPhee use the forum he has created as a soapbox. He notes simply that the barrens have always survived the encroachment of civilization, casting out every attempt at industrialization, every plan for subdivision, every intention to construct the world's largest jetport, and every design to make a utopia in the forest. Such a history might create the perception that the barrens will live forever, resolutely repelling the best efforts of man to tame and civilize them. True, the area as a whole resists organized invasion, but slowly, almost like a glacier, the perimeter of the area shrinks. This process, McPhee suggests, is perhaps even more insidious because it is completely without control. The complete transformation of the area would at least be direct and would be made because of a decision. The slow destruction of an area that the destroyers probably do not even realize exists is a sad event indeed.

Critical Context

McPhee's work is rarely treated in a critical fashion, although he is almost universally respected as a skillful prose artist. This neglect may be the result of most of his books having been compilations of articles written for *The New Yorker*, the magazine for which McPhee is a staff writer. It is convenient to place McPhee in the upper echelon of popular writers who write well about mostly unfamiliar subjects.

The question remains: Why has not McPhee made the jump from writer to New Journalist and near artist, as have other nonfiction stylists, such as Tom Wolfe, Hunter S. Thompson, and Norman Mailer? The reason is probably that McPhee takes up far less space in his own work than these other writers. *The Pine Barrens* is an excellent example of this phenomenon. The reader is never aware of an authorial presence in McPhee's books; the emphasis is on subject not on writer as subject or on writer as stylist. McPhee has no interest in making his audience see the familiar in a different way; instead, he insists that the unfamiliar be seen as it is.

Such work is not readily convertible to art, even though it may have a profound effect on the reader. It is not evasive to suggest that McPhee escapes theories and interpretation for this reason: He is dedicated first to the reader, to whom he offers lucidity, experience, and immense descriptive skill; that is enough to satisfy the desires of most of his audience and is an enviable ability on any scale.

Sources for Further Study

Clark, Joanne K. "The Writings of John Angus McPhee: A Selected Bibliography," in *Bulletin of Bibliography*. XXXVIII (January-March, 1981), pp. 45-51.

Gillespie, Angus K. "A Wilderness in the Megalopolis: Foodways in the Pine

Barrens of New Jersey," in *Ethnic and Regional Foodways in the United States: The Performance of Group Identity*, 1984. Edited by Linda K. Brown.

Lawrence, Sally. "Structure and Definition: Keys to John McPhee's Style," in *Technical Communication*. XXXIV (November, 1987), p. 296.

Miers, E. S. Review in *The New York Times Book Review*. LXXIII (May 12, 1968), p. 18.

Natural History. Review. LXXVII (August, 1968), p. 80.

David P. Smith

POINTS FOR A COMPASS ROSE

Author: Evan S. Connell, Jr. (1924-   )
Type of work: Prose poetry
First published: 1973

Form and Content

"Compass rose" is a cartographic term, referring to a visual device which is an aid to navigation and a help to travelers. Found on maps, the rose is a circle divided into thirty-two points, the longest of which aims toward true, or magnetic, north, while the others determine the points of the compass. In many maps, especially those from earlier times, the compass rose is often elaborately ornamented with fantastic designs, making it both pleasing and useful. Yet above all else, it determines direction.

Evan Connell's choice of title was apt, for *Points for a Compass Rose* is built upon the structure of a voyage of discovery and exploration. In Connell's case, however, while the voyage is both external and internal, it is primarily within the hearts and minds of human beings, and the discoveries are the heights of nobility and the depths of baseness to which human ability can reach.

Points for a Compass Rose is classified as poetry only for want of a more precise term. In fact, it is a book which does not fit in any established genre, and to call it poetry is misleading. In form, the text has the look of free verse, but Connell's lines lack the rhythmic signature and the economy of expression that distinguish poetry (even the freest free verse) from prose. In its organization, however, the book resembles many a modern poem, shifting rapidly from subject to subject. It is given unity by certain recurring themes and concerns which obsess the first-person narrator. These key themes are few, but they are capable of almost endless elaboration and explication: the nature and corrupting effects of power upon individuals and nations; the mysteries of nature; the relationship between science and magic; and, above all, human history and its impact on cultures and the individual. Connell does not arrange these themes in any consistent pattern, but allows them to flow together by association, one topic suggesting the next, then a third arising to comment upon the earlier subjects, and so on.

Points for a Compass Rose is essentially a personal meditation in quasi-poetic form, and in addition to the motifs which recur, certain structural devices help tie the work together. These are the repeated use of nautical imagery, particularly navigational coordinates; interspersed notations from chess games; historical references, most often to the Holocaust and the United States' involvement in Vietnam; and the first-person narrator. Together, these elements help provide some coherence and unity.

The first three elements relate to Connell's themes; the fourth provides a more personal aspect. The narrator is a person who has not one name, but many, and whose character continually changes. He provides much information about himself, but it is misleading and contradictory. He adopts the persona of such figures as the astronomer Johannes Kepler, the scientist Sir Isaac Newton, and the alchemist Paracelsus. In this fashion, Connell manages to connect his work with a single voice yet underscore the point that this work is a view not of one man but of entire cultures and civilizations.

Analysis

Points for a Compass Rose is held together by a system of associations and images, rather than by logical or narrative development. Although this method involves the reader in sudden shifts in subject, time, and character, it is essential to Connell's central concern, which is the confused human response to uncertain times. He asks toward the end of the work, "Do human events exceed human understanding?" In a sense, this book is his attempt at an answer to that question.

The first cluster of themes found throughout the work concern travel and exploration; it is a topic announced even in the book's title, with its reference to maps and navigation. Connell announces his intention early: "Listen. I've decided to take a trip," and he urges his readers to accompany him:

> I don't plan to return
> altogether ignorant, and you're welcome to join me.
> So what do you say? Come along. Let's travel together.
> God our suzerain has a duty to protect His vassals;
> but with Him or without we'll go back and forth
> along the dusty ways choosing all knowledge
> as our provenance. Interspersing fact with lore,
> interpreting experience in terms of moral purpose. . . .

Throughout the book, references are made to travel, journeys, and explorations. On one level, the image of the journey becomes a symbol for the acquisition of knowledge, an undertaking which Connell clearly regards as a moral, even a religious, duty. Just as explorers clear away the blank spaces of the map with detailed features of the landscape, so attentive men and women can clear away the dark spaces of human character—and perhaps prevent or mitigate the crimes and atrocities which are so often noted in *Points for a Compass Rose*.

On a second level, the theme of exploration and discovery addresses this topic of human violence. Connell hints broadly at this theme in six passages, where he gives precise geographical locations, noted in degrees of latitude and longitude. Each location is a site where European culture interacted, mostly destructively, with indigenous cultures: for example, at the mouth of the Congo, where the slave trade began; off the coast of South America, where the conquistadors destroyed the ancient civilizations of Inca and Maya; and in the seas off Southeast Asia, where collisions between the East and the West, including the Vietnam War, occurred repeatedly.

In this sense, the theme of exploration blends into the theme of cultural interaction, which for Connell can take two forms: mystery and mastery. His book is filled with oddities, strange facts from foreign lands which cannot be explained by conventional wisdom. There are many things which could be learned from those people dismissed as savages: "Let me warn you: Don't lapse into the vulgar practice/ of decrying what you don't comprehend." Yet decrying, even destroying, is the most likely result of interaction between cultures, as Connell sees it. This concept leads to his third, and perhaps dominant motif, that of power and how it is exercised.

In a way, *Points for a Compass Rose* is a meditation on power and violence, a consideration of how nations and empires, from Egypt to Rome to the United States, become great but are then undone by their reliance on sheer power, adrift from its moral compass. Connell is more than abstract in this concern, for his work is often a philosophical and poetic polemic that directly confronts the American involvement in Vietnam, a conflict that was still raging when *Points for a Compass Rose* was written. Clearly, Connell fears that his country has gone astray, and he seeks to restore its natural sanity and health:

> Look, I'm writing a gnomic book about America
> because not long ago when the entrails of an eagle
> were studied for fatidic signs a vile odor spread
> and the heart was found misplaced.

In images such as this Connell links the ancient Roman Empire with the modern American state, connecting the Roman practice of examining the prophetic signs found in the organs of sacrificed animals with the symbol of the American eagle. Further, Connell uses specific, concrete references to locate his poem in contemporary history: The names of American presidents, Lyndon B. Johnson and Richard M. Nixon, and verbatim quotations concerning alleged American atrocities in Vietnam tie the action to modern times.

A problem is thus posed for the reader: Does this technique make the book merely a polemic? Is the work weakened by its close ties to one specific period in American history? *Points for a Compass Rose* is successful because its theme of power is approached in a universal, rather than a specific, fashion. The United States is not the only nation called to account for its misuse of power; throughout the book, Connell produces numerous examples of states and monarchs, rulers and empires crushing others, or trying to do so. Other references include scenes of torture and cruelty from Europe's wars of religion and its conquests in the New World. Perhaps the most powerful presentation of this theme is the simple, chilling citation of the names of Nazi death camps, followed by the numbers of their victims. In the end, Connell is no more limited by his references to Vietnam than Thucydides is by the Peloponnesian War, or Vergil by the destruction of Troy.

Connell makes this clear by using the metaphor of a chess game, raising the question of power and force to its most abstract level. Throughout the book he sprinkles the gnomic notations of chess moves: P-K5, R-K1, Q-K2, and so on, giving the movements of the pieces as the two opponents struggle for mastery of the board. In the end, the only tangible action that results is PxP, or pawn captures pawn. Despite all the maneuvers of the powerful kings, queens, bishops, knights, and rooks, the ultimate result is that one lowly pawn, the weakest piece on the board, has eliminated another pawn, equally helpless. Such is Connell's final comment upon the powerful of the world, and their glorious victories.

There remains, however, one thread which runs through the entire work, and that is the individual—in this case, the person who has fashioned this poem called *Points for a Compass Rose*. Throughout, Connell plays a guessing game with the reader, revealing a variety of purported authors, only to shift to a new persona without apology or explanation. He claims to be a bewildering cast of historical figures, from Paracelsus to Isaac Newton. In this, as in so much else in *Points for a Compass Rose*, the reader is presented with definite, solid facts, only to have those very facts refuted or withdrawn within a few lines or pages.

Connell's point here brings him back to his original theme of travel and exploration: No human being is complete and final. We change, adapt, mutate. Like Alfred, Lord Tennyson's Ulysses, we become part of all that we have met. What the reader must do is recognize that and attempt to hold fast to that which is valid and enduring: "Appearances pass; the truth abides."

Points for a Compass Rose thus charts travels and changes for an entire culture, a mighty nation, and an individual narrator. Its method is part of its meaning, and the fact that its narrator has no name—or so many names—is central to the message it carries:

> If you find yourself either troubled or exasperated
> by my pseudonyms, postures and elaborate disguises
> remember that this has been a private testament
> made of odd details with a touch of the commonplace.

One of the most attractive aspects of *Points for a Compass Rose* is its language and style. The tone is conversational as Connell (or Raymond Lully, Pythagoras— whoever the narrator claims to be at any particular moment) moves from subject to subject, offering fascinating individual facts and novelties which are gradually and almost imperceptibly woven into the larger meaning of the work. At the same time, *Points for a Compass Rose* imparts much knowledge. The range of Connell's references is great, and he frequently slips into brief phrases from other languages, especially Latin. Because of the lightness of his touch, however, the learning is never obtrusive. Connell's purpose is, ultimately, education in its broadest and best sense:

> I've set down these things for your instruction
> because I know that the earth with its many facts,
> wonders and immensities, as well as the adventures
> which befall pilgrims passing through it,
> are astonishing and greatly worth narrating.

Critical Context

Points for a Compass Rose is an important statement about the troubled times in which it appeared and represents a reaction of a significant portion of the American people to their country's involvement in the Vietnamese conflict. The work was published in 1973, a time when there was considerable and often anguished debate about the role which the United States had taken in Southeast Asia. Connell's position on the matter is quite clear, but he moves beyond polemic and momentary relevance by connecting the American experience with those of other great powers— Rome, Spain, Great Britain.

In a sense, Connell is asking questions about the nature of national power and its use, about the role of the individual in a nation. Such concerns are hardly new for Connell, but his approach—a long, discursive "poem"—was certainly unique for the period in which it was written. In this light, *Points for a Compass Rose* both comments upon its own time and manages to move beyond it, because of the many links and connections it makes with history.

Points for a Compass Rose also reveals its author's artistic interests and abilities at an exceptionally high level. All Connell's writings demonstrate an awareness of other cultures and an interest in the quirks and wonders of human nature, but this intelligence is never showcased. In *The Connoisseur* (1974), for example, his knowledge and mastery of pre-Columbian art is held in check by the narrative of the novel; the essays in *The White Lantern* (1980) never wander far from their central subjects. Still, in these and in Connell's other writings, there is the sense that a great body of knowledge and lore lies hidden, waiting only for the right vehicle in order to be revealed.

In *Points for a Compass Rose* and its predecessor, *Notes from a Bottle Found on the Beach at Carmel* (1963), Connell found that vehicle. The loose, almost rambling system of these idiosyncratic works allowed him to introduce both fascinating fact and intriguing legend without concern for narrative consistency or the limitations of space; at the same time, the flexible framework he constructed enabled him to make the various bits and pieces cohere.

While Connell undoubtedly will continue to be best known for his novels, particularly the black comedy *Mrs. Bridge* (1959), his two book-length "poems" are his most innovative works. Connell adapted the method developed in these books for his greatest popular success, *Son of the Morning Star: Custer and the Little Bighorn* (1984), a historical meditation centering on the life of General George Armstrong Custer.

Sources for Further Study

Bach, Bert C. Review in *Library Journal*. XCVIII (March 15, 1973), p. 874.

Dillard, Annie. "Winter Melons," in *Harper's Magazine*. CCXLVIII (January, 1974), p. 87.

Edwards, T. R. "Surprise, Surprise," in *The New York Review of Books*. XX (May 17, 1973), pp. 35-37.

Fahey, James. Review in *Best Sellers*. XXXIII (June 15, 1973), p. 136.
West, Paul. Review in *The New York Times Book Review*. LXXVII (April 29, 1973),
     p. 7.

Michael Witkoski

THE PRESENCE OF THE WORD
Some Prolegomena for Cultural and Religious History

Author: Walter J. Ong (1912-   )
Type of work: Cultural criticism
First published: 1967

Form and Content

One of the dominant themes in modern studies of human culture has been the impact that communication and communications media have on persons and societies. The most famous exponent of this school is Marshall McLuhan, whose often-repeated phrase "the medium is the message" has become a slogan of cultural criticism. An equally important though perhaps less well-known figure is Walter J. Ong, who studied under McLuhan and later developed his own thoughtful and carefully researched studies on the relationship between communications media and culture.

The Presence of the Word presents the foundations of Ong's explorations in this area. The subtitle of the volume is *Some Prolegomena for Cultural and Religious History*, and the work is precisely that: a preliminary discussion, or prolegomena, that outlines the material to be studied. In other works, Ong goes into more detail, but in *The Presence of the Word* he offers a general view of the subject.

The genesis of the book was a series of Terry Lectures which Ong delivered at Yale University in April, 1964. These lectures seek to bring into focus the relationship between religion and advances in science and the humanities, a goal perfectly suited for Ong, a Roman Catholic priest and a cultural historian who gives particular emphasis to the role of the spiritual in human development. *The Presence of the Word* combines human concerns with theological implications.

Ong structures his work in a series of steps which move from the specific and concrete to the more universal and abstract. He first lays the groundwork for determining the roles of the senses and the "word" in human culture. By "word," Ong means both the spoken language and the spiritual presence associated with that language. He next traces the development of human culture through what he terms the "transformations of the word." This development has a three-part movement. First, there is the oral-aural culture, in which human beings communicate solely through speech. This stage gives way to the second, the print or script culture, which comes about with the invention of writing systems, especially the phonetic alphabet. Writing has a great impact on culture, primarily because it shifts the relationships of the senses; hearing, which dominated in the oral-aural culture, now becomes less important than vision. The invention of printing makes the script culture more dominant than ever. Finally, a third stage arrives with the development of electronic media such as telegraph, telephone, radio, and television. There is a combined oral-aural and print culture at this third stage, and once again the impact is felt throughout human society.

Having established this tripartite movement, Ong examines its implications in more abstract realms, such as its impact on the causes and nature of human conflict or on humans' spiritual development and their relationship with God, or the word in its most spiritual sense. The six parts of the book thus lead upward from a study of human culture to link that culture with the divine.

Analysis

Human societies are shaped by a number of forces, but during the second half of the twentieth century increasing emphasis has been given to the study of how forms of communicatión and the media affect the development and nature of societies. The three scholars most important in these studies have been Harold Innis, Marshall McLuhan, and Walter Ong.

Innis, in two slim books, laid the foundation for future studies in this field. In *Empire and Communications* (1950) and *The Bias of Communication* (1951), Innis pointed out how changes in communication techniques caused changes in the society that used them. The introduction of a new medium, such as the printing press, meant society had to adapt to the new device; often, this adaptation occurred in totally unforeseen ways. The introduction of the printing press in England, for example, seems to have caused renewed interest in the spoken, or oral, literature of plays, thus creating the appropriate culture for a figure such as Shakespeare.

Marshall McLuhan developed Innis' theories, most notably in two influential books, *The Gutenberg Galaxy* (1961) and *Understanding Media* (1964). McLuhan came to a startling but logical conclusion regarding the introduction of new media into a culture: It is not the content of these media, but the media themselves that cause changes. In other words, the mere fact that a book can be printed in endless, uniform copies has more impact on a society than the content of that book, however important or controversial. In the same way, McLuhan argued, the forms of modern electronic media—such as radio and television—were paramount, and those who thought otherwise had missed the point. In McLuhan's terms "the medium is the message."

According to McLuhan, that is so because the introduction of new media causes shifts in the ratios of the human senses; one sense will be favored by the new media and thus achieve dominance. The spoken word emphasizes the ear; the printed word favors the eye. It is McLuhan's contention that such shifts in emphasis and sense ratios are a primary cause of changes in human cultures. His reasoning is based on the assumption that information received through sound is perceived differently from information received through sight. Human beings organize the world according to their perceptions; therefore, when the source of information changes, the perceiver's world changes.

In *The Presence of the Word*, Ong builds on the work of these two earlier writers, and many of his concepts are remarkably similar to McLuhan's. In the first half of the book, Ong discusses what he terms "the sensorium," which is the totality of human senses, and how different media favor different senses. Like McLuhan, Ong sees a distinct difference between oral-aural cultures and print or script cultures, and he points to three essential stages which have characterized Western society and its progress.

The first was the oral-aural stage, when humans were adept at using spoken language but knew nothing of writing it down and preserving it. Such a culture's worldview is strikingly different from that of a literate society. There is a greater sense of community, a togetherness that stems from knowledge as much as from anything else, because to know something in an oral culture is to have been told something. Learning depends on human interaction. Poetry assumes the function of a teaching tool and reference source; thus, Homer's *Illiad* and *Odyssey* are in part manuals for practical activities, such as forging swords or building ships. In an oral-aural culture, people exist in the present, in a close-knit community, and in a world that seems invested with magical powers.

The first movement away from the oral-aural world came with the invention of writing, especially with the development of the phonetic alphabet. Such a movement, according to Ong, marked the dawn of the modern world. The rise of writing caused the spoken word to be deemphasized; in McLuhan's terms, the alphabet gave mankind "an eye for an ear." The development and spread of printing in the late Middle Ages further exaggerated the visual shift and caused the last remnants of the old oral-aural culture to be submerged under the new print culture, which was marked by individualism, specialization, and sequence. Practical results were the assembly line, industrialization, and the rise of the consumer society. The sense of community was greatly weakened, and knowledge became a private pursuit involving silent reading in a library or study.

Before the new print culture firmly took hold, however, there was a final flowering of the older forms, marked in England by the Renaissance drama of such masters as Christopher Marlowe, William Shakespeare, and Ben Jonson. Such a development is not really surprising; Innis pointed out that the introduction of writing into ancient Greece seems to have spurred the development of that dramatic tradition, and McLuhan found that one of the results of presenting a new technology is a sudden interest in the older forms which it is supplanting. Perhaps, as Ong suggests, one cannot really recognize or appreciate a medium until it is on its way out; until then, its presence is so pervasive that it is invisible.

The third and current stage of human culture is the era of the electronic media. These include a wide range of devices: the telegraph, the telephone and television, the radio, the motion-picture camera, and the computer. They have increased the rate of production and the spread of printed information, but they have also encouraged a return to the oral-aural forms of communication that existed before writing and printing. Ong maintains that there is no paradox in this, because new media do not erase old forms but rather build upon them. The electronic media embrace both the print culture and the oral-aural culture.

What we are faced with today is a sensorium not merely extended by the various media but also so reflected and refracted inside and outside itself in so many directions as to be thus far utterly bewildering. Our situation is one of more and more complicated interactions.

These complicated interactions are the theme for the final half of Ong's volume, and his central concern is humans' relationships with their fellows and with God. For Ong, the development of the word is both a social and a religious phenomenon. As he views it, the word—sound, language, and spirit—is a means to unite human beings, to form them into groups and then link these groups into communities, societies, and ultimately an entire human world. He definitely sees an upward progression in human beings' use of the word. Here Ong differs most markedly from McLuhan, for Ong has a theological orientation, whereas McLuhan is much more secular in most of his discussions.

Ong concludes *The Presence of the Word* with "Man's Word and God's Presence," a section discussing the relationship of human beings to the divine. In this section, he brings together on the highest level the concerns and topics that run throughout the book. He unites a study of culture, communication, media, and language with enduring questions which transcend culture and history.

Critical Context

Two themes are central in Ong's investigations: the theological, or spiritual, and the cultural. Throughout his writings, Ong consistently seeks to discover the points where the spiritual and the material interact and where human beings express, through language, their fullest potential as creatures who possess a spirit or soul. In this sense, Ong combines both secular and religious concerns.

Because of this, the term "word" has particular importance for Ong. He approaches it both in its literal sense, that is, the combination of sounds used in human languages, and as the divine *logos*, or the spirit of God (specifically, of Christ) as conceived by Christian theology. "Word" appears frequently in Ong's titles; in addition to *The Presence of the Word*, his titles include *Interfaces of the Word* (1977) and *Orality and Literacy: The Technologizing of the Word* (1982). Clearly, this concept is central to Ong's theories and their development.

The Presence of the Word is probably Ong's most concise and direct presentation of his overall view, and it therefore holds a central place in his canon. In this work, he outlines clearly his theory of a three-part evolution of human culture based on communication systems: a transition from an oral-aural culture to a script culture and the subsequent emergence of an electronic culture which combines the best of the two previous stages, bringing human beings yet closer to the word in all its various senses.

These same themes are developed in others of Ong's works, sometimes with greater attention to particular details or historical events, as in *Ramus, Method, and the Decay of Dialogue: From the Art of Discourse to the Art of Reason* (1958) or *Rhetoric, Romance and Technology: Studies in the Interaction of Expression and Culture* (1971). Yet, it is in *The Presence of the Word* that Ong presents his views most clearly and convincingly, and this volume is therefore essential for the serious observer of modern culture and religion.

Sources for Further Study

Cargas, H. J. "Walter Ong, S. J.," in *Catholic Library World*. XLVII (November, 1975), p. 185.

Cox, Harvey. "The Medium Is the Word," in *The Christian Century*. LXXXV (April 10, 1968), p. 456.

Farrell, Thomas J. "Developing Literacy: Walter J. Ong and Basic Writing," in *Journal of Basic Writing*. II (Fall/Winter, 1978), pp. 30-51.

Kermode, Frank. "Free Fall," in *The New York Review of Books*. X (March 14, 1968), pp. 22-26.

Rycenga, J. A. Review in *Library Journal*. XCII (December 1, 1967), p. 4420.

Wimsatt, William K., and Cleanth Brooks. *Literary Criticism: A Short History*, 1957.

Michael Witkoski

THE PRIME OF LIFE

Author: Simone de Beauvoir (1908-1986)
Type of work: Autobiography
Time of work: 1929-1944
Locale: France, Spain, Italy, Germany, and Greece
First published: La Force de l'âge, 1960 (English translation, 1962)

> *Principal personages:*
> SIMONE DE BEAUVOIR, a novelist, philosopher, and political
> activist
> JEAN-PAUL SARTRE, her lifelong companion, the founder of
> modern existentialism

Form and Content

The first volume of Simone de Beauvoir's autobiography, *Mémoires d'une jeune fille rangée* (1958; *Memoirs of a Dutiful Daughter,* 1959), traces her successful revolt against French Catholicism and bourgeois idealism. Significantly, this second installment begins with this observation: "The most intoxicating aspect of my return to Paris in September, 1929, was the freedom I now possessed." *The Prime of Life* describes how de Beauvoir guarded and used that freedom for the succeeding fifteen years.

Her life during this period, like the historical events that impinge upon her despite her best efforts to escape their effects, divides into two parts, and so does the book. The first, and longer, section treats her experiences during the 1930's, as she establishes her relationship with Jean-Paul Sartre and gropes her way toward becoming a writer. For her this is a decade of splendid isolation and introspection, brought to a jarring end by the invasion of Poland and the outbreak of World War II.

Quoting diary entries to help portray the years between 1939 and the liberation of Paris in 1944, de Beauvoir in the second part traces her growing realization that the personal freedom she treasures must not be pursued, indeed cannot be maintained, without concern for others. During the war years she matures into the engaged intellectual that she remained until her death. As she becomes more conscious of the relevance of world affairs to her own life, they assume a larger role in her book, so that *The Prime of Life* presents a sensitive, firsthand account of life in occupied France.

Because Sartre was in many ways her second self, *The Prime of Life* offers a dual autobiography. It describes the development of Sartre's existential philosophy, as well as his hobbies (such as playing with a yo-yo), his aversions (to tomatoes, for example), and his pleasures. One sees de Beauvoir and Sartre traveling, eating, arguing, reading, enjoying films and plays, walking across mountainous landscapes and through museum corridors. De Beauvoir treats their lives, individually and together, with careful attention to detail; yet, as she warns her readers in the preface, she has "no intention of telling them everything. . . . There are many things which I firmly intend to leave in obscurity." As is so often true of authors, a full picture of her life and thoughts emerges only in her fiction.

For a dozen years, from 1931 to 1943, de Beauvoir taught philosophy, first in Marseille and later in Rouen and Paris. Her intention was to train her students to think as she did, and her didacticism is evident in *The Prime of Life*. At the end of each part she presents a brief summary of the lessons she has learned, the ways in which her life was changed, and the distance she has yet to travel between the young woman who is the subject of the book and the middle-aged woman writing it. She adheres to her determination "to set out the facts in as frank a way as possible, neither simplifying their ambiguities nor swaddling them in false syntheses," and she acknowledges that "self-knowledge is impossible." Yet the older de Beauvoir cannot escape becoming a character in the account and serves as a chorus to guide the reader's interpretation.

Analysis

De Beauvoir's importance and interest derive from several sources. Because she was a feminist, her life serves as a model of how to avoid the pitfalls described so well in *Le Deuxième Sexe* (1949; *The Second Sex*, 1953). As a prizewinning novelist, she reveals the evolution of a writer and the way life is transformed into art. Even though Sartre published a brief autobiography, *Les Mots* (1963; *The Words*, 1964), and some of his diaries have appeared posthumously, de Beauvoir's account of her relationship with a leading proponent of existentialism must concern anyone seeking to understand contemporary French philosophy. Finally, even in her attempt to remove herself from the historical currents of her age, she represents the French intellectuals of the Left during the 1930's; thus her life becomes a microcosm of the world in which she moved. Though these different strands are interwoven to create the pattern of her narrative, one may examine them individually to gain a clearer understanding of the woman and her book.

At the end of the first section of *The Prime of Life*, de Beauvoir concedes that "when certain critics read this autobiography they will point out, triumphantly, that it flatly contradicts my thesis in *The Second Sex*." More precisely, *The Prime of Life* shows how a woman may escape the curse of dependence that de Beauvoir believes blights the lives of the vast majority of women. Early in the book she makes two important decisions. Sartre has been offered a post in Le Havre, she a job in Marseille, hundreds of miles from her beloved Paris. She thus faces separation from the person and place that mean the most to her. Sartre proposes that they marry so that they can remain together at a school close to the capital. Acknowledging her opposition to matrimony, Sartre nevertheless argues that it is "stupid to martyr oneself for a principle."

She instantly rejects his solution, both for herself and for Sartre. Marriage would increase her responsibilities, and Sartre would have to surrender even more freedom than she. They have agreed to a relationship that binds neither; marriage would destroy that existence. She observes that had she wanted children, she would have decided differently, but children, like marriage, would interfere "with the way of life upon which I was embarking." In *Memoirs of a Dutiful Daughter* she is shocked when a friend declares that being a mother is just as important as being a writer. Having found her vocation, which she likens to a religious calling, she refuses to surrender to society's expectations. In refusing to marry she is not martyring herself to principle but rather avoiding martyrdom.

Yet rejecting marriage does not in itself guarantee her independence. Her victory is not complete until she decides to accept the post in Marseille. Standing on the stairs of the railway station of that city, cut off from all familiar faces and surroundings, she feels exhilarated rather than depressed, for now she is truly on her own. Alone in a new region, she uses her freedom to explore the countryside, refusing to allow her gender to restrict her movement. She demonstrates great physical strength as she climbs mountains (in Greece, Sartre was unable to keep up with her pace), rejecting warnings that such solitary ramblings were unsafe. As she writes, "I had no intention of making my life a bore with precautions of this sort."

Her autobiography is thus not a contradiction of *The Second Sex* but an alternative to it. *The Prime of Life* shows that the price of personal freedom is eternal vigilance, that only through the assertion of will and intelligence can a woman escape dependence—but she can do it.

The rigorous hikes across the French countryside are important to de Beauvoir as a writer as well as a woman. When she was a child she wanted to visit every place in the world, and that desire for travel never left her. She is constantly going places or planning a trip somewhere, for she wants to miss nothing. That same impulse takes her to films, plays, and nightclubs. André Gide once commented that the essence of Spain can be found in its hot chocolate, so she forces herself to drink cups "of a black, saucelike liquid, heavily flavored with cinnamon." Travel books say that slums reveal a town's true quality, so she visits them nightly even though she finds them uninteresting. She wants to take a grueling fourteen-hour train trip to see the Meteora monasteries in Greece; when Sartre, who has heretofore acceded to her proposed expeditions, balks, she cries in "pure rage" and tells herself that she is missing "all manner of marvels."

In listing the writers that influenced her, de Beauvoir observes that Dashiell Hammett and Fyodor Dostoevski provide models for dialogue, and William Faulkner and Franz Kafka fascinate her because of their psychological probing. She also admires Ernest Hemingway's use of the vernacular and his description of setting through the eyes of his characters. Her list of readings includes Henry James, too, and her autobiography seems to be a *mise-en-scène* of his injunction to the would-be author to be one on whom nothing is lost. Seeing her literary—and hence her life's—mission to save the world from oblivion, she constantly strives to acquaint herself more fully with that world.

Convinced as she is that she is destined to convert experience into literature, for many years she is unable to grasp what she calls "the crux of the art of letters." Her first two attempts at writing a novel end in failure because she remains detached from her work. At length, Sartre exclaims, "Why don't you put *yourself* into your writing? You're more interesting than all those Renées and Lisas," characters she had used in her work to express her views but for whom she had little or no sympathy. The notion of drawing on her own personality frightens her, but she realizes that Sartre is correct. *L'Invitée* (1943; *She Came to Stay*, 1949) thinly veils her relationship with Sartre and Olga D., a philosophy student who fascinated Sartre for a time. *Le Sang des autres* (1945; *The Blood of Others*, 1948) is based on her wartime experiences, and *Les Mandarins* (1954; *The Mandarins*, 1956), which won the Prix Goncourt in 1954, draws from her postwar life.

In this matter, as in others, Sartre showed himself to be the ideal companion. He not only helped de Beauvoir find her true subject matter for fiction, he also recognized and fostered her desire for independence. He was mentor and inspiration. His play *Les Mouches* (1943; *The Flies*, 1946) prompted her to write the two-act *Les Bouches inutiles* (1945; useless mouths). She read Sartre's *L'Être et le néant* (1943; *Being and Nothingness*, 1956) several times before it was published; her own *Pyrrhus et Cinéas* (1944; Pyrrhus and Cineas) builds on the views he expressed there.

As with every other aspect of their relationship, their intellectual debt was mutual. Her knowledge of art was more sophisticated than his; at the Prado in Madrid she taught him to regard style and technique, while he reminded her not to disregard the content. Having taken her degree in philosophy at the Sorbonne, she could discuss and exchange the latest theories in the field and so help Sartre sort out his own views.

Through de Beauvoir's record of these conversations, one sees the development of Sartre's metaphysics, his belief in "the autonomy of the irrational mind" and his discovery of Edmund Husserl's phenomenological philosophy. She shows how Sartre's fiction also developed. Thus, she introduces Jacques Bost, one of Sartre's students and the model for Boris in *L'Âge de raison* (1945; *The Age of Reason*, 1947). Chez Alexandre, a café which Sartre and de Beauvoir frequented in Rouen, became Chez Camille in *La Nausée* (1938; *Nausea*, 1949). Lobsters and crabs appear in that novel and in *Les Séquestrés d'Altona* (1959; *The Condemned of Altona*, 1960). *The Prime of Life* explains their origin: Sartre once took mescaline, and for months afterward he imagined that giant crustacea were pursuing him. Yet another revelation concerns the effect on Sartre of being a prisoner of war. After his repatriation, he became much more doctrinaire and committed to a life of action.

De Beauvoir admits that she was unprepared for this change in Sartre; for a decade both had believed that the individual must stand alone to preserve his or her freedom. Hence they had refused to join any party or act to aid causes they supported. When the Spanish Civil War began, they favored the Republicans and assumed that that side would win. They could admire the commitment of André Malraux and others who went off to fight, but they could not imitate such action. Like Léon Blum, the French leftist premier, and the radical Socialists, they chose a course of nonintervention. The conclusion of the Munich Pact filled them with relief; de Beauvoir was convinced that the democracies had acted properly to secure peace.

The German invasion of Poland forced de Beauvoir, as it did many others on the Left, to rethink her political views. In 1939, many shared the sentiment expressed by the wife of an author at Gallimard: "What difference does the war make? It does not change my attitude to a blade of grass." De Beauvoir's own naïveté is exemplified by her response in the mid-1930's to the question, "What is a Jew?" She had replied that only individuals exist, that one need not concern oneself with any identity that linked one to a group. As she describes her attitude before the war, "I had followed my own bent, learning about the world and constructing a private pattern of happiness. Morality became identified in my mind with pursuits such as these."

The Nazi occupation taught her how wrong she had been. No longer could she cling to innocent optimism; yet she refused to surrender to despair. Where she had previously hoped to find happiness and freedom through isolation, she now chose a different path: "To act in concert with all men, to struggle, to accept death if need be; that life might keep its meaning—by holding fast to these precepts, I felt, I would master that darkness whence the cry of human lamentation arose."

Critical Context

In his *Essais* (1580-1595; *Essayes*, 1603), Michel Eyquem de Montaigne wrote, "I am eager to make myself known." The self that de Beauvoir reveals is one with a great capacity and desire for happiness, one who pursues that goal and attains it. The movement of *The Prime of Life* is comic, tracing de Beauvoir's odyssey from isolation to commitment. It is also a work suffused with hope. Sartre's existentialism concentrates on the problem of confronting evil in a world that does not allow for redemption from the divine. De Beauvoir shares Sartre's philosophy but emphasizes another aspect, the working out of one's salvation in a godless universe. Though she would probably not find the comparison flattering, her autobiography retells John Bunyan's *The Pilgrim's Progress* (1678-1684) in a modern idiom, with intelligence as grace, freedom as the New Jerusalem, and herself as the secular pilgrim seeking that shining but elusive end.

What she might observe of all of her other works she may say with Montaigne here: "I am myself the matter of my book." Yet her discretion (or reserve) makes the autobiography less revealing than her novels. Anyone wishing to trace the development of her fiction must read the memoirs, but anyone seeking to understand the author must turn to the fiction. *She Came to Stay*, for example, describes a *ménage à trois* that parallels the experience of de Beauvoir, Sartre, and one of their students. In *The Prime of Life*, de Beauvoir confesses to some irritation with Sartre's infatuation. In *She Came to Stay*, de Beauvoir's surrogate, Françoise, reacts more strongly: She murders the character based on Olga. Clearly, the feelings that de Beauvoir conceals in her autobiography surface in the novels.

Nevertheless, the memoirs capture what Henry James urged all writers to record, "the look of things, the look that conveys their meaning, . . . the colour, the relief, the expression, the surface, the substance of the human spectacle." The fiction is psychological, the autobiography realistic, but both exhibit the same qualities of mind that make de Beauvoir an important figure in twentieth century life and letters.

Sources for Further Study

Ascher, Carol. *Simone de Beauvoir: A Life of Freedom*, 1981.
Evans, Mary. *Simone de Beauvoir: A Feminist Mandarin*, 1985.
Keefe, Terry. *Simone de Beauvoir: A Study of Her Writings*, 1983.
Madsen, Axel. *Hearts and Minds: The Common Journey of Simone de Beauvoir and Jean-Paul Sartre*, 1977.
Marks, Elaine, ed. *Critical Essays on Simone de Beauvoir*, 1987.
Whitmarsh, Anne. *Simone de Beauvoir and the Limits of Commitment*, 1981.

Joseph Rosenblum

PRIMITIVE CLASSIFICATION

Authors: Émile Durkheim (1858-1917) and Marcel Mauss (1872-1950)
Type of work: Sociology/anthropology
First published: De quelques formes primitives de classification: Contribution à l' étude des représentations collectives, 1903 (English translation, 1963)

Form and Content

Émile Durkheim, along with Max Weber and Karl Marx, is commonly considered one of the founding fathers of modern sociology, as well as a profound shaper of the discipline of anthropology, especially in England. The British anthropologist Robin Horton claims that now more than ever it may be appropriate to "accord Durkheim the accolade of 'The Master,' " owing to the longevity of his influence in those disciplines.

His writings cover such diverse topics as the evolution of social structure in *De la division du travail social* (1893; *The Division of Labor in Society*, 1933), sociological method in *Les Règles de la méthode sociologique* (1895; *The Rules of Sociological Method*, 1938), and the sociology of suicide in *Le Suicide: Étude de sociologie* (1897; *Suicide: A Study in Sociology*, 1951). In 1898, he founded the periodical *L'Année sociologique* (sociological yearbook), the forum in which he published, along with his nephew and pupil Marcel Mauss, his first substantial work on the sociology of knowledge: *Primitive Classification*.

The work, now seen as a precursor of Durkheim's magnum opus on the sociology of religion and knowledge, *Les Formes élémentaires de la vie religieuse: Le Système totémique en Australie* (1912; *The Elementary Forms of the Religious Life: A Study in Religious Sociology*, 1915), was essentially an extended journal article addressed to his peers in the scientific community. Taking the form of a long essay outlining a specific problem in the human sciences and indicating a new approach to its solution, *Primitive Classification* appears more as a provocative suggestion than as a definitive, self-contained work. Indeed, one gets the sense of having followed Durkheim and Mauss through the very process of thinking out their solution. The conclusion leaves the reader far from where he started; it points forward rather than summarizes.

The actual structure of the work parallels the authors' conception of the nature of the problem. An introductory chapter outlines the question to be addressed—the nature and source of the "mechanism by virtue of which we construct, project, and localize in space our representations of the tangible world." The introduction argues for a sociological approach to that question. Durkheim and Mauss follow the presumed evolution of the classificatory function in four chapters representing three stages in the evolution of human cognition: two on the Australians as the most "primitive," followed by a chapter on the Zuni and Sioux Indians, and finally a chapter on the Chinese. Although they can prove no historical connections among these instances, it is argued that they represent three "stages" in the evolutionary process which culminates in nineteenth century Europe. The concluding chapter then purports to explain the essential nature of this evolution in terms of the role of sentiment, or emotion, in the ordering of ideas about the world.

Durkheim and Mauss hold that the human mind lacks an innate capacity for such ordering; thus, classification must be inspired by some extra-individual source. It is their contention that such a source is society itself, that the groupings into which people delineate in the course of social interaction provide the model for the articulation of the world, and that the relations among such social groups are the inspiration for the presumed relations between the categories. Their method for substantiating this view, as always, is to trace the development of the phenomenon from its most primitive, or simplest, manifestation through its subsequent development in order to find the golden thread of human cognition.

Analysis

Durkheim and Mauss array themselves at the outset of the work against "Logicians" and "Psychologists," both of which, they argue, treat the process of classifying things, events, and facts about the world as at worst innate and at best individually constituted; that is, they assume that there is one essentially uniform way of ordering the world that is common to all people. In contrast, Durkheim and Mauss mobilize the anthropologist's ubiquitous argumentative weapon: the historical and crosscultural variability of nearly any human phenomenon. Indeed, they contend, that which is commonly understood as classification is of rather recent origin, having its true birth in the thought of Aristotle. This historical origin of logical classification presupposes an extended prehistory, during which humanity (or at least one part of it) gradually removed itself from its original "state of indistinction."

Durkheim and Mauss document this indistinction, or "mental confusion," which, they argue, is in places and at times so extreme that "the individual himself loses his personality." Human consciousness, in its primitive state, is a continuous and unregulated flow of representations bleeding into one another. The phenomenon of totemism—the belief in a relation of consubstantiality between members of a social group and a category of things (for example, bears, eagles, and lightning)—is a vestigial product of this sort of thought. The primitive inability to distinguish aspects of the world is taken as evidence that in the beginning, at least, humanity lacked the capacity to classify and that, consequently, such a capacity must be acquired from somewhere.

If it is not the human mind which provides this model, as a priori philosophers such as Immanuel Kant would have it, then perhaps the groupings and relations of things are inherent in the things themselves; perhaps, as David Hume and the empiricists claimed, it is nature itself which indicates how things should be perceived. Durkheim and Mauss reject this option as well, arguing that the inherent resemblances of things are not sufficient to determine the complex schemata by which they are apprehended. Having rejected both of these solutions, Durkheim and

Mauss resolve the situation by, as Steven Lukes, Durkheim's biographer, has put it, "restating the old epistemological questions in sociological terms."

The sociological thesis is boldly stated at the outset of the first chapter on Australian (aboriginal) classification. The Australian tribes are generally divided into two major, complementary sections called moieties, and each moiety is composed of two marriage classes (within which marriage is proscribed) composed of a number of clans, or groups of people of common descent. "The classification of things," Durkheim and Mauss argue, "reproduces this classification of men." Among the tribes of the Bellinger River, for example, all nature is divided into two classes corresponding to male and female. Such schemes are often overlaid by another corresponding to the four marriage classes; thus, one group will be associated with a certain set of natural species and things (for example, opossum, kangaroo, dog), another group with a different set (for example, emu, bandicoot, black duck). On the basis of such examples, Durkheim and Mauss draw the analogy between moiety and genus on the one hand, and marriage class and species on the other.

Yet it soon becomes clear that not all Australian systems are so clear-cut. Thus Durkheim and Mauss proceed to explain the variations from this central theme in a second chapter on "other" Australian systems. First they argue that many such systems which do not on the surface appear to correspond to the more "regular," or typical, ones can actually be shown to derive from or presuppose the existence of the typical scheme; some process of change has simply altered their apparent form. This discussion of the possibility of decay, or alteration, hints at a radical redefinition of the authors' position, a redefinition which is never really pursued, namely that the changes in social morphology which have produced the deviant classificatory forms are actually "due in part to the classifications themselves." Durkheim and Mauss here suggest that the epiphenomenon of mental representations may actually exist in a mutually determining relationship with their "cause" (social groupings and relations).

This form of argumentation—explaining away variation by recourse to hypothetical historical changes—can produce befuddlement as well as theoretical insight. In the chapter on the Zuni and Sioux, for example, Durkheim and Mauss discover discrepancies among accounts of Zuni distribution of game in different categories but claim in a footnote that these can be "easily explained" by changes in the "orientation of the clans," although no such explanation is given. Where explanations are attempted, the degree of apparent manipulation is alarming, and it is never clear to what extent the authors' claims are statements of fact or historical reconstructions based upon sociological principles. In documenting the supposed transition among the Zuni from the classification by clans (a vestige of the more primitive Australian type) to a classification by "quarters" (that is, the four spatial quadrants of north, south, east, and west), the authors argue that the new schema was too clearly opposed to the "facts"; thus, the Zuni were forced to alter their classifications in order to correspond in a satisfactory manner with the objective world. This process is claimed as fact but remains merely an ingenious hypothesis.

If this hypothesis seems once again to lead Durkheim and Mauss away from the initial thesis of the exact correspondence between social organization and classification, the final ethnographic chapter on the Chinese "system" doubtlessly does so in an even more extreme fashion. Indeed, they claim at the very outset that this system has been independent of any particular social formation for as long as it has been known. The Chinese system is said to comprise a multiplicity of layered schemata—such as a classification by the four cardinal points, which are subdivided into eight sections corresponding to eight powers, over which is superimposed a classification by a set of five elements (which, by the way, is said to be reducible to the former, if only some elements are eliminated and others merged).

Far from being determined by Chinese social organization, this system in fact exists in the reverse relationship with society; the classificatory system is said to regulate the social conduct of members of Chinese society (through a divinatory calendrical cycle). It is possible for the system to become liberated from the determining influence of social morphology because its complexity allows it to "grasp reality closely enough to provide a fairly useful guide to action." The process of adapting to the "facts" of the objective world which was at work among the Zuni has here to a certain extent freed Chinese thought, through reflection on its "clearly primitive" base, from the simplicity and powerlessness of primitive thought.

It is here that a distinction finally emerges which has underpinned the argument all along: the distinction between the religious nature of primitive classifications and the scientific, or technical, classifications characteristic of rational, logical thought. The movement from the former to the latter corresponds (at least implicitly in Durkheim and Mauss's thought) with an increasing freedom from social determination and an increasing capacity to explain the world adequately (which implies a capacity to direct action rather than merely reflect it).

The two types of classification are, however, connected; both are speculative attempts to understand the world, and the latter has evolved from the former. It is in their conclusion that Durkheim and Mauss offer an explanation for exactly how it is that primitive classifications are modeled on social relations and, at the same time, an explanation of the nature of the evolution from primitive to scientific. These explanations lie in the role of sentiment in both social organization and thought. Social relationships are said to be based upon sentiments of affinity between groups or individuals, and it is these same sentiments which humans employ in their attempts to understand the world. It is a condition, however, which primarily affects "primitives"; for them, a species is not only a species but also an object of "a certain sentimental attitude." The movement from primitive to scientific thus consists in the gradual removal of this emotional element from cognition and a resulting clarity, or delineation, in man's thought about the world. Ultimately, emotion arises in Durkheim and Mauss's work as the enemy of scientific—that is, individual and reflective rather than social and automatic—thought. Vestiges of such prescientific thought patterns may remain, but it is their gradual disappearance which has characterized the evolution of human classification.

Critical Context

Because *Primitive Classification* was initially published in a French academic journal and was not translated into English until 1963, its impact outside Continental sociology has been relatively mild in comparison to that of Durkheim's *The Elementary Forms of the Religious Life*, of which it is commonly considered a precursor. The latter work, a much longer and more completely thought-out treatment of many of the same topics addressed in *Primitive Classification*, is easily one of the most important works of all time in the social sciences.

Yet *Primitive Classification* did have an impact on French sociology. It represented an important step in the development of the Durkheimian school, signifying as it did a shift in emphasis toward the study of both religion and thought in sociology. As such, it inspired writers such as Lucien Lévy-Bruhl, author of *Les Fonctions mentales dans les sociétés inférieures* (1910; *How Natives Think*, 1926), to treat such topics in depth. Durkheim's *The Elementary Forms of the Religious Life*, published two years later, was in part a response to and criticism of Lévy-Bruhl. A reading of all three works provides an interesting study of the development of (and change in) Durkheim's thought, for Durkheim and Mauss's work is much closer to Lévy-Bruhl than a reading of only *The Elementary Forms of the Religious Life* would suggest.

The influence of Durkheim and Mauss's work has perhaps been greatest on the field of anthropology, especially in France and Great Britain, although once again it is overshadowed by Durkheim's later work. Much of the work of the great British anthropologist Edward Evans-Pritchard arose from the dispute between Durkheim and Lévy-Bruhl. Other anthropologists such as Mary Douglas and Claude Lévi-Strauss can also be said to owe a great intellectual debt to the collective work of both Durkheim and Mauss in general, and their collaboration on *Primitive Classification* in particular. The book has clearly shaped the work of at least two disciplines and continues to be read for both the light it sheds on the intellectual development of two of history's greatest sociologists and the insights it offers into the perennial mystery of human thought.

Sources for Further Study

Bloor, David. "Durkheim and Mauss Revisited: Classification and the Sociology of Knowledge," in *Studies in History and Philosophy of Science*. XIII (1982), pp. 267-297.

Fenton, Steve. *Durkheim and Modern Sociology*, 1984.

Giddens, Anthony. *Capitalism and Modern Social Theory: An Analysis of the Writings of Marx, Durkheim, and Max Weber*, 1971.

Gieryn, Thomas. "Durkheim's Sociology of Scientific Knowledge," in *Journal of the History of the Behavioral Sciences*. XVIII (1982), pp. 107-129.

Horton, Robin. "Lévy-Bruhl, Durkheim, and the Scientific Revolution," in *Modes of Thought*, 1973. Edited by Robin Horton and Ruth Finnegan.
Lukes, Steven. *Émile Durkheim, His Life and Work: A Historical and Critical Study*, 1972.

Mark Rogers
Elizabeth Marberry

THE PRINCIPLE OF HOPE

Author: Ernst Bloch (1885-1977)
Type of work: Philosophy
First published: Das Prinzip Hoffnung, 1954-1959 (English translation, 1986)

Form and Content

The multidimensional nature of *The Principle of Hope*, Ernst Bloch's most important work, cannot be comprehended without a closer look at his personal development and background. Born into the drab community of Ludwigshafen, the son of assimilated Jews, he experienced a youth lacking the more varied cultural opportunities of the neighboring city of Mannheim. The difference between these two cities of his youth would sharpen his perception of class distinctions in German society and would help him understand the appeal Fascist ideology held for the lower classes.

In 1905, Bloch began his university studies. He first went to Munich to study philosophy and German literature; he then attended the University of Würzburg, where he studied music, physics, and experimental psychology. He also became interested in the cabala and Jewish mysticism. In Berlin, he took up studies in sociology and later became interested in Christian mysticism. His intense interest in all areas of culture and his thirst for knowledge in many disciplines informed his philosophy and shaped the form and content of *The Principle of Hope*.

As a pacifist he went into exile to Switzerland at the outbreak of World War I. When the Nazi Party took power in 1933, Bloch, who was immediately blacklisted, left Germany to seek exile in Switzerland, France, and finally in the United States, where *The Principle of Hope* was written. His experiences in the United States thus also found entry into this extensive, multifaceted account of hope on all levels of political, cultural, and psychological experience.

In more than thirteen hundred pages divided into five major parts—"Little Day-dreams," "Anticipatory Consciousness," "Wishful Images in the Mirror," "Outlines of a Better World," and "Wishful Images of the Fulfilled Moment"—Bloch explored the emancipatory powers of hope. He mapped out the genesis of what he calls the Not-Yet-Conscious in social, political, artistic, scientific, and individual psychological expressions. As an unorthodox Marxist thinker, he believed that anticipatory illumination within culture provides the possibility to transform the material base through the superstructure. Art illuminates the missing qualities of contemporary life as they are experienced by the individual artist. As such, they encourage the recipient to determine the specific aesthetic formulation of lack, or want, and thus enable him to become involved in cultural development. In detecting the anticipatory illumination of a work of art, the reader or spectator is instilled with hope. This hope provides an impetus for change. Bloch's belief in this potential for art, which illuminates the path toward a more humane future, is the central focus of the three volumes of *The Principle of Hope*.

As in his other works, Bloch was concerned with developing a philosophy that would go beyond the rationalism of the Enlightenment, providing at the same time a more subjective method for understanding one's own experiences and historical situation and offering methods of dealing with such pressing problems of late capitalism as alienation.

Analysis

German Idealism influenced the philosophical categories Bloch used to establish his ethical and political ideal. The subjective factor in German Idealism first suggested by Immanuel Kant and developed by G. W. F. Hegel served as the basis of Bloch's Utopian notions, which he combined with the objective quality of the materialist philosophy of Karl Marx and Friedrich Engels. His concept of continuous progress was taken from his interpretation of Hegel's concept of progress. By continuous or open process succeeding ages have the opportunity to "re-utilize" or "re-function" materials from the past to accommodate their ideological needs. These ideological requirements can be either progressive or reactionary.

The Principle of Hope compiles a list of occurrences of the so-called surplus of Utopian thought throughout the ages. Bloch understands Utopia not as an impossible ideal but as a concrete state which can be achieved politically. He sees the development of Socialism as the modern expression of the Utopian function which effects this change, the goal toward which the process of history is impelled.

History, however, is not mechanically determined in Bloch's philosophy. It advances through possibility. Possibility is itself an open process which is not determined solely by the subject. Bloch postulates that the object itself contains layers of possibility resulting in the real Possible, which for him is an objective quality. It is the true synthesis of the subjective and objective realizations of the world.

Because of this attempt at synthesis Bloch has often been placed in the Romantic tradition, where imagination and the material world are ideally fused. One of the major differences between Bloch and the philosophies of German Romanticism, however, is that Bloch insists on the inclusion of the possible development of the object, on the material objective process, while the Romantic philosophers were primarily concerned with the subjective perceptions of man. Bloch emphasizes the dialectical interaction of the subjective and objective aspects. Through this, he derives the political task of humanizing material conditions. Only by working theoretically and practically to realize the possibilities of the world can man create a more humane, less alienated environment. Thus, the question of the dialectics of freedom and order, which Bloch sets out to illuminate in his work, remains an important one.

Art has the power to reveal not yet realized meaning through the presence of the Not-Yet-Conscious. The enlightening ability of the Not-Yet-Conscious can be revealed in what Bloch calls *Vorschein* ("preappearance" or "anticipatory illumination"). Works of art contain a border over which the Not-Yet-Conscious is allowed to flow when regressive interpretations or static thinking are abandoned. As such, art provides a wealth of guiding images that are able to point beyond the stagnant representation of the world.

Bloch's analysis of the Not-Yet-Conscious contains not only political and social implications but also individual psychological ones. Because of his emphasis of the emancipatory qualities of psychological reality directed toward the future, Bloch criticized contemporary psychoanalysis. He considered a preoccupation with past events too limiting. Above all, he condemned the interpretation of repression. Examining past events to understand the origin of neurosis was to ignore present and future conditions. At the same time, he faulted Sigmund Freud for disregarding the social causes of repression. Thus, psychoanalysis provided no concepts and solutions for future developments. In Bloch's opinion, only changes in society could improve the psychological situation of the individual. To ignore social causes was to deal exclusively with superficial symptoms without addressing the underlying cause.

The inner substance of hope is "real humanism." Because this goal can never be wholly achieved, however, it cannot be defined completely. One is able only to point in the direction of real humanism. Utopian hope—what Bloch terms the "oldest conscious dream of humankind"—anticipates the overthrow of those social conditions which enslave the individual. Daydreams can therefore be extremely useful, since they take place in semiconsciousness and point to objective possibilities. Daydreams, by themselves unproductive, can, in portraying the possibility of achieving certain wished-for goals, serve as the means through which humans form themselves. Such dreams provide the stimulus to move out of the current ideology's hold. It is at this point that art and literature perform their Utopian function.

Bloch, however, was no mere visionary; he intended his philosophy to be concretely Utopian. His philosophy requires active involvement with the world rather than contemplation alone. As such, *The Principle of Hope* compiles historical accounts of hope against the danger of total annihilation. At the same time, it provides practical guidelines for everyday life in an age of cultural demise, when the achievement of a more humane society seems unlikely. Bloch points toward a Socialist theory based on hope. *The Principle of Hope* envisions a society in which the individual can live and work meaningfully and with satisfaction.

Bloch refrains from providing answers or definitions; instead, he provokes readers to explore his images and their connotations. Thus, *The Principle of Hope* is rich with aphorisms, fables, and anecdotes. Bloch's expressionistic style has been said to "shock" his readers into an awareness of their own needs so that they would abandon those conditions preventing communication and collective action.

Indeed, with his often-cryptic language Bloch wanted to remove both himself and his readers from customary thought patterns. Only through a revitalization, reordering, and refunctioning of language could conventionality be overcome. To avoid the staleness of language, with its underlying complacency, Bloch uses montage techniques. His bourgeois heritage had to be reutilized to allow his novel Utopian undercurrent to be displayed. Bloch contended that bourgeois capitalism itself had created an empty space, *Hohlraum*, that needed to be filled with new content in new forms. He thus incessantly experimented with new images, seeking to refine them and endow them with anticipatory illumination, or hope. Thus, anticipatory illumination is intrinsic in Bloch's style: An image will be integrated into the argument before it emerges as a full metaphor. These images function as hidden metaphors, seemingly aimless, then surface again with new significance, thus mirroring Bloch's theory of the continuing legacy of Utopian content. His use of metaphor is based on his conviction that in metaphor the secret signatures of the world's meaning are contained. Literature therefore does not primarily imitate life but reveals its secrets.

Critical Context

Bloch's wide-ranging interests and expertise in several disciplines were decisive in his personal and political development. He remained unconventional and provocative, willing to revise his thoughts in the light of new developments. He attempted to blend his cultural heritage, dominated by German Idealism, with his individual brand of revolutionary Utopianism, informed by his study of Karl Marx. In his first major work, *Geist der Utopie* (1918; spirit of utopia), he delineated the Utopian qualities of art and literature. *Thomas Münzer als Theologe der Revolution* (1922; Thomas Münzer as theologian of revolution) combined Communist thought with religious mysticism. In *Erbschaft dieser Zeit* (1935; heritage of this time), Bloch explored the fascination Fascism had for the lower classes by formulating the categories of synchronism and nonsynchronism. Contrary to most analysts of Fascist character, Bloch emphasized that the response of the lower classes was not merely reactionary. Modern technology had created a disorienting emptiness in people's lives which produced a longing for the stable values only past traditions could provide. Fascism appealed precisely to these needs. *The Principle of Hope* combined and altered many of the ideas and categories formulated in these earlier works. It is the culmination of Bloch's philosophy and cultural critique.

Sources for Further Study

Buhr, Manfred. "Critique of Ernst Bloch's Philosophy of Hope," in *Philosophy Today*. XIV (Winter, 1970), pp. 259-271.

Furter, Pierre. "Utopia and Marxism According to Bloch," in *Philosophy Today*. XIV (Winter, 1970), pp. 236-249.

Habermas, Jürgen. "Ernst Bloch: A Marxist Romantic," in *Salmagundi*. X/XI (Fall, 1969/Winter, 1970), pp. 311-325.

Hudson, Wayne. *The Marxist Philosophy of Ernst Bloch*, 1982.

Oliver, Harold H. "Hope and Knowledge," in *Cultural Hermeneutics*. II (May, 1974), pp. 75-87.

Wren, Thomas E. "The Principle of Hope," in *Philosophy Today*. XIV (Winter, 1970), pp. 250-258.

Karin A. Wurst

PRISON NOTEBOOKS
Selections

Author: Antonio Gramsci (1891-1937)
Type of work: Notebooks
First published: Quaderni del carcere, 1948-1951, 6 volumes (English translation, 1971)

Form and Content

On November 8, 1926, Antonio Gramsci, the Italian Marxist and fierce anti-bourgeois, anti-Fascist journalist and deputy, was arrested by Benito Mussolini's police and deported to the tiny island of Ustica. His sentence was twenty years. Until his release from incarceration on April 21, 1937, six days before his death, he was variously confined at Turi near Bari, at Formia, and at Milan, until his return to his native Sardinia. A small man physically, with a deformity that gave him the appearance of a humpbacked dwarf, he suffered from tuberculosis and arteriosclerosis. Despite these infirmities and under the eyes of his Fascist jailers, he wrote 219 letters (published in 1947) to his wife and a handful of other family members. Most important, he managed to produce roughly twenty-eight hundred pages of social analysis, philosophy, and political prophecy that constitute his *Prison Notebooks*, containing his singular commentaries and reflections. Gramsci's covert writings were essential to his psychic survival: He had a fierce determination to be heard.

The substance of the notebooks was not developed sequentially. Gramsci was a thinker working under immense pressure and stress. Consequently, portions of an essay would be written at one time; months or years later it would be amended and appended.

The notebooks consist of a sequence of essays—a series of reflections. They are Marxist, but Sardinian rather than German or Russian. Gramsci's personal background was that of a high meridional, middle-class culture. Yet his was a bourgeois family that was thrown into desperate poverty. The suffering of the poor was not something he had to imagine; it had been an intimate part of his daily experience.

Substantively, *Prison Notebooks* falls into several related sections. One section deals with problems of historical materialism. It includes Gramsci's introduction to the study of philosophy and historical materialism, some problems for the study of the philosophy of praxis, critical notes on a tentative popular manual of sociology, and an essay on Benedetto Croce, who had a profound influence on Gramsci, and historical materialism.

A second intellectually coherent section of the notebooks deals with the philosophy of Praxis (action as opposed to theory). In this essay, Gramsci discusses Antonio Labriola's philosophical writings on the subject of praxis (which involved the influences of a number of Soviet and German Marxists) and discusses the intellectual roots of the concept of praxis. In Gramsci's verbal shorthand, praxis could well be represented by the thought of G. W. F. Hegel, the great German philoso-

pher, joined with the principal ideas of David Ricardo, the English classical econo-
mist. Gramsci's point was that since Karl Marx had been a student of Hegel and,
indirectly, of Ricardo, Marxist thought evolved in a fairly unified manner from the
nineteenth century into his own day; that is, its intellectual roots evolved from
main-line European culture. Thus, praxis, the philosophy of action, was a product
of an ineluctable historical process. The final sections of this essay discuss Marx's
contributions.

Other sections of the notebooks deal with such subjects as historical sociology,
politics, civilization, and culture. Each essay contains brief reflections, critiques,
and conclusions—all related to examinations of various socialisms and their relationships, historical and intellectual, to Gramsci's views on Marxism.

Analysis

Since Gramsci is considered by many to be one of the seminal political thinkers
of his time, a genius of sorts, interpretations of Gramsci's *Prison Notebooks* must
begin with an understanding of the author's own singular cultural view of himself
and of the society with which he was most directly familiar.

To be sure, Gramsci was Italian, but despite the unification of 1866, Italy's
cultural divisions and distinctions had deep and ancient roots. Gramsci was a
Sardinian, about as Italian as the Irish, Scottish, or Welsh were English, as Corsi-
cans were French, or as Basques were Spanish. The inhabitants of Sardinia, which
had resisted one invader after another through its history, are traditionally tough,
laconic, and self-analytical members of a closed folk society who saw themselves as
outsiders and whose heroes were rebels and outlaws. Gramsci, who possessed these
characteristics himself, became a leading folklorist of his native Sardinia. Indeed,
his ideas on how popular culture shapes social structure and class relationships
would profoundly affect the intellectuals of his time. Even if Gramsci had never
embraced Marxism, he would have opposed the political and social structure that
had been imposed upon the Sardinians and their culture.

In the years just prior to his imprisonment, as a leader of the Italian Communist
Party Gramsci sided with the Joseph Stalin/Nikolay Bukharin majority in the Communist Party against Leon Trotsky and the so-called left. The thrust of his critical
attack was that the Russian Communist Party was tearing itself apart while being
callously unmindful of its responsibilities to the international proletariat (working
classes) whom it was obliged to help liberate. By the time of his arrest, therefore,
he was as much in danger of extermination by Stalin as he was by Mussolini's
Fascists.

The notebooks are the work of a gifted, learned, and independent thinker. Gramsci sharply reminded the Russian leadership that Party unity and discipline could
not be coerced; unity and discipline, he thought, must emanate from genuine
loyalty and conviction. He held, too, that even the enemies of Joseph Stalin had
played important, positive, and instructive roles in the party's development.

In his limited, at times despairing physical and psychological circumstances,

Gramsci managed to develop fresh historical explanations for the evolution of socialism. He also raised a number of seminal questions that were to revivify and revitalize discussions about socialism. His ideas would continue to be a source for Marxist writings and political polemics in years to come.

What Gramsci had to say about social structure, for example, was subtler and more complex than the traditional Stalinist party line. This party line essentially posited the existence of an exploitative capitalist imperialist class abetted by its bourgeois allies, whose actions were producing an increasingly inpoverished and oppressed working class. The ultimate consequences of this unjust situation would produce international revolution under direction of a temporary dictatorship of the proletariat, directed from Moscow. Gramsci's views, however, were what Marxists would then have called "revisionist."

Gramsci doubted that international revolution was imminent, indeed even foreseeable in the near future. However desirable the advent of communism appeared, many of its realities failed to square with the hopes of its proponents. Gramsci found orthodox Marxist class explanations inadequate and unconvincing. According to Gramsci, societies were not composed of abstractly distinct functional strata. Multiple levels of culture linked and transcended "subaltern" (lower and ostensibly oppressed classes) with "hegemonic" (or dominant capitalist) classes. What he defined in his sociological observations as "good sense" and "common sense" pervaded all elements of cultures and societies and were not the singular distinctions of any specific groups alone.

Perhaps because of the extraordinary range of his subject matter, Gramsci's *Prison Notebooks* contains certain contradictions and ambiguities. He argues that folklore should be elevated to a worldview; yet he claims elsewhere that folk culture is a collection of anachronisms that the new Marxist order should simply abolish. His terminology is often difficult: Terms such as "passive revolution," "organic intellect," "integral state," "war of position," "national-popular," and "hegemonic" are not always easily grasped. Indeed, the contextual illusiveness of such concepts has been the source of provocative and productive studies by European Marxists and non-Marxists.

Yet a certain amount of obscurity does not detract from the remarkable breadth of knowledge amassed by Gramsci. His allusions and references in the notebooks to the prominent philosophical, political, and intellectual figures of his day as well as to seminal thinkers of earlier centuries constitute a tour de force. Hegel, Immanuel Kant, Giambattista Vico, and Machiavelli are only a few of those who became grist for his mill.

As founder of the Italian Communist Party, Gramsci was confronted with the fact that Italians preferred to consider their personal well-being over participation in civic life or in formal political organizations. They seemed to prefer more clandestine and covert organizations: gangs, mafias, or closely knit family networks. An important theme of Gramsci's *Prison Notebooks* is that these Italian characteristics were a result of the insidious effects of capitalism. The triumph of Communism, according to Gramsci, would restore and revitalize Italian political life and civic-mindedness. Yet, as he was probably aware, the cultural characteristics and popular mores that he sought to reform long predated Italian capitalism. Indeed, after Gramsci's death, they "infiltrated" and marked the Italian Communist Party itself.

None of these points detracts from Gramsci's immense achievements both of intellect and the spirit, or from the gift of controversy passed on by him to his intellectual successors.

Critical Context

Gramsci's *Prison Notebooks*, like his *Lettere dal carcere* (1947; *Letters from Prison*, 1973), reflect Italy's confused and unhappy situation, the result of the difficulties during and after World War I. Originally allied with the Germans and Austro-Hungarians, the Italian government, with promises of extensive Austrian, Adriatic, and Dalmatian territorial concessions by Great Britain, France, and Russia, switched sides. Poorly equipped and wretchedly led, the Italians experienced a sequence of disasters during the war. At the war's end, the promised territorial concessions were disputed contemptuously by the victorious powers.

Political chaos was rife within a largely impoverished Italy. Individuals, factions, and nationalist political parties arose to claim by force what they believed was denied them through negotiation. Mussolini, a former socialist, organized the violence that effectively stabilized internal affairs, but at the cost of quelling all serious opposition. As the bound bundle of sticks composing the Fascist symbol indicated, Italy was to be one by force. Gramsci was a stick that did not fit into the Fascist corporatist bundle. Gramsci's *Prison Notebooks* displays a sense of Italy's philosophical and historical distinctiveness and achievements—replete with a humanism that is not entirely or abstractly Marxist. It displays, too, Gramsci's vision of an Italy that would maintain its cultural variety and complexity under a Communist government that reflected this variety and complexity.

Sources for Further Study

Barzini, Luigi. *The Italians*, 1968.
Buci-Gluckmann, Christine. *Gramsci and the State*, 1980.
Femia, Joseph. *Gramsci's Political Thought: Hegemony, Consciousness, and the Revolutionary Process*, 1981.
Gramsci, Antonio. *Selections from the Prison Notebooks*, 1971. Edited by Quintin Hoare and Geoffrey Nowell-Smith.
Joll, James. *Antonio Gramsci*, 1980.
Sassoon, Anne Showstack, ed. *Approaches to Gramsci*, 1982.
_____. *Gramsci's Politics*, 1980.
Simon, Roger. *Gramsci's Political Thought*, 1982.

Clifton K. Yearley

PROLOGUE TO AN AUTOBIOGRAPHY

Author: V. S. Naipaul (1932-   )
Type of work: Memoir
Time of work: 1932 to the 1980's
Locale: The Caribbean, India, and Great Britain
First published: 1983

Principal personages:
V. S. NAIPAUL, a writer
SEEPERSAD NAIPAUL, his father

Form and Content

V. S. Naipaul's "Prologue to an Autobiography" is a hybrid of memoir and autobiography. In his illuminating foreword to *Finding the Center: Two Narratives* (1984), Naipaul explains that the book's first extended essay, "Prologue to an Autobiography" (which had first appeared in *Vanity Fair* in April, 1983), is "not an autobiography, a story of a life or deeds done"; rather, it is "an account of something less easily seized: my literary beginnings and the imaginative promptings of my many-sided background." Besides its overall aim, the essay has an autobiographical emphasis in the first of its six numbered sections, which details the thoughts, feelings, sensations, and events attending the composition of Naipaul's *Miguel Street* (1959), his first publishable, though not his first published, book. Yet the essay's preponderant focus on Naipaul's milieu—geographical, social, and especially familial—bespeaks memoir more than autobiography. Ultimately, the essay's main subject emerges as Naipaul's father, Seepersad, from whom the son derived the model of a writer as well as the urges toward pursuit of the literary profession.

Because the work attempts in its seventy-odd pages (22,000 words) to deal with "something less easily seized" than straightforward biography, as well as with a "many-sided background," its form is not simply chronological or linear, as first might be supposed from the use in the book's subtitle of the term "narrative." Possessing a novelistic quality because of vividly and pungently described people and events, the work begins *in medias res*. After an opening account of Naipaul's composing in the early 1950's of the first two chapters of *Miguel Street* (though the book is never referred to by title in the text), the work flashes forward to the successful writing and publication of three more books and then others in the late 1950's and following decades. Subsequently it flashes back to a report of salient facts of his father's life in the first three decades of the twentieth century.

Subtle and complex, the work's structure is a combination of pendulum and spiral. The essay continually oscillates between past and future, causes and effects, Trinidad and India, the Caribbean and England, father (or family) and son. Concurrently, the essay repeatedly cycles back to facts and events, giving them a new perspective or revealing underlying determinants by the disclosure of new information, much of which Naipaul himself discovered only later in life. The concluding paragraph of the work, for example, cycles back to its opening paragraphs, which deal with Naipaul's use of a British Broadcasting Corporation office, typewriter, and script paper to begin composing *Miguel Street*; in the essay's final paragraph, however, that event is given an emotionally resonant depth, for Naipaul reveals the startling facts that his father had died the previous year and that his family back in Trinidad was in distress.

The transition between the beginning of each numbered section and the end of the preceding one is careful, whether implicit or explicit, and contributes to the sense of order and sequence in the essay's overall structure. For example, the third section's beginning reference to Naipaul's seeing the real person, Bogart, who served as the basis for the fictional portrait in the first chapter of *Miguel Street*, stresses temporal terminology: "after twenty-seven years . . . again." This reference to time implicitly connects with the statement in the second section's last paragraph that "to write, it was necessary to go back" in time and place. The fourth section's opening paragraphs, about Naipaul's knowledge of family, regional, and world history, are implicitly linked with the third section's concluding reminiscences of Bogart's and a Mayan peasant's religious rituals being made meaningless because they were devoid of historical knowledge and foundation. Explicitly, the end of the first section and beginning of the second are linked by repetition of the key word "ambition" (important throughout the essay), suggesting the genesis of Naipaul's career from Seepersad's life, work, and encouragement. Similarly, the end of the fourth section and beginning of the fifth are linked by repetition of the word "pundit," in its East Indian sense, suggesting that Seepersad's religious vocation, appointed in childhood, was in a sense realized by the special and sanctified career of writing, enabled by the journalistic guru (Naipaul's word) Gault MacGowan.

Many of the essay's topics and themes occur elsewhere in Naipaul's fiction and nonfiction. Such themes include the sources, motives, and techniques of writing; the degree of correspondence between art and life; the tension between colonial and colonizer; the dynamics of kinship relationships (including that of father and son); Trinidad society; the interest of individuals' defining traits and eccentricities; the psychological and intellectual effects of the physical environment on the individual; individuals' diversity in their attempts to mold their lives, and the results of these attempts; and the impact of East Indian culture on East Indian emigrants to Trinidad. Overarching and implicit throughout the essay is the topic of knowledge: how well an individual understands his environment (for example, geography) or his past (its people, events, or documents).

Analysis

Imparting an apparent casualness, a ruminative tone, and the irony of delayed disclosures and discoveries, the essay's cyclical, spiral form is repeatedly used to convey many of the work's themes. For example, Naipaul mentions anxiety (another key iterative word in the essay) in the first section's first paragraph, in reference to beginning *Miguel Street*. After seven pages describing the real Bogart's life story as known up to that juncture, Naipaul returns to his starting point, now revealing that he had already had two failed attempts at novels, which deepens the reader's understanding of the intensity of that anxiety. Moreover, after references in intervening sections to Seepersad's troubled mind and life, in the essay's final two paragraphs Naipaul discloses his belief that his father had transmitted not only the ambition to write but also a profound anxiety that necessitated and was associated with writing. Further, Naipaul's revelation in these paragraphs of then-current family distress completes his unfolding of the anxiety mentioned in the essay's first paragraph.

Other spiral revelations (listed here in their order of first occurrence in section 2 of the work), are numerous. Seepersad's newspaper beat in Chaguanas, Trinidad, is revealed forty-two pages later in section 6 as a cause of Seepersad's passionate love-hate relationship with his in-laws, the Tiwaris, since his stories required him to become in effect the family's publicist, both laudatory and condemnatory. Having made passing mention of a "gift one year of a very small book of English poetry," his only token of contact with his absent father, Naipaul reveals fifty pages later that this book is one of his few surviving mementos of his father. The newly revealed details of author, title, price, and inscription suggest Seepersad's poverty, bequeathed love of literature and writing, and admirable moral values. The letters that six-year-old Naipaul found in his father's desk and cherished as uncomprehended magical documents, with their impressive raised letterhead, are revealed forty-eight pages later as "brusque" correspondence rebuffing Seepersad's appeals for reinstatement in his old job on the Trinidad *Guardian* newspaper. First mentioned only casually, Seepersad's unused British passport that the young Naipaul found in his father's desk is shown forty-five pages later to have been representative of the timidity that prevented Naipaul's father from escaping a circumscribed, saddening, and at times mentally unbalancing life in Trinidad. The ledger containing Seepersad's newspaper articles, which the young Naipaul found and venerated as one of his central childhood books, is revealed thirty-six pages later, at the end of section 5, as significantly incomplete as an icon of his father's elevation, writing career, and family history.

One thematic function of the essay's structure is its mimetic representation of both Naipaul's disjointed past life and his discovery and recovery of his personal history. In section 2, explaining that order existed only in his school life, Naipaul says, "But my family life . . . was jumbled, without sequence. The sequence I have given it here has come to me only with the writing of this piece." Intertwined with the topic of self-knowledge, and also suggested by the essay's structure, is the theme of the relationship between the literary vocation and the author's roots. After explaining the parallel between his own life and the *Miguel Street* narrator's escape (though a college scholarship to England) from the confinement of Trinidad, in a typical, forceful, and ironic antithesis Naipaul says: "To become a writer . . . I had thought it necessary to leave. Actually to write, it was necessary to go back. It was the beginning of knowledge." The pivotal word "back," important for Naipaul's self-discovery, the realization of his writing career, and the essay's structure, is repeated in the essay's last staccato sentences (again helping to create its cyclical, spiral form): "In my eleventh month in London I wrote about Bogart. I wrote my book; I wrote another. I began to go back."

In much of the essay, as in his other nonfiction and fiction, Naipaul is an ironist. Besides the irony in Naipaul's discovery that return rather than flight or escape is required for his writing career, explicit and implicit ironies cluster around Bogart and Seepersad. For example, because Naipaul does not know what has become of Bogart when he composes the first chapter of *Miguel Street*, he feels free to invent a surprising, "cruel," and satiric conclusion to this story. When he meets Bogart twenty-seven years later, however, Naipaul learns that life has imitated art, for Bogart indeed fled Trinidad for sensual reasons and virtually became the bigamist of the fictional story's end.

A devastatingly ironic episode in Seepersad's life, one which contributed to his mental breakdown, concerned the newspaper coverage of vampire bats in Trinidad. Cyclically, Naipaul mentions in section 5 that this coverage got editor MacGowan and reporter Seepersad in trouble, and later in sections 5 and 6 explains the difficulties of MacGowan and Seepersad, respectively. MacGowan came into even sharper conflict with his publishers, who were irritated by what they considered MacGowan's discouragement of the tourist trade and were shortly to discharge the editor because of such contention. Because of pressure and threats from anonymous Kali worshipers (who may have included his own kin), Seepersad suffered the humiliation of having to abandon, temporarily but publicly, his enlightened, reform-minded Hinduism and perform an old-fashioned animal sacrifice to Kali, whom devotees were superstitiously (in Seepersad's published view) attempting to appease in order to end the bats' attacks on cattle. Explicitly, Naipaul notes the irony that Seepersad, trained to be a pundit, for the first time performed a religious ritual— unwillingly. A further implicit irony is that Seepersad's early newspaper columns, as mentioned twelve pages earlier in the essay, had been signed with the pen name "The Pundit."

Naipaul's prose style, elegant though not ornate (as is customary in both his nonfiction and fiction), is artfully used to express irony, reserve, control, intensity, and reflectiveness. One of the essay's most prominent stylistic features, antithesis, recurs within sentences or between them, expressing the ironic contrast between expectation and outcome, the conflict between one value system and another, or the tension between one of a number of oppositions in Naipaul's life and world.

Naipaul's sentences have a notable balance, marked by a semicolon between main parts, which suggests both the essay's artful symmetry and a continual thoughtful weighing or balancing. Naipaul's distinctive use of anaphora contributes similar effects. The frequent parenthetical material in sentences, often punctuated with dashes, is used for reflective qualification as well as irony.

Related to the sentence structure's suggestion of reserve and control in the essay's tone is Naipaul's striking suppression of the colorful Trinidad vernacular that so enlivens his first four novels but is merely alluded to when Naipaul explains that an aunt, in providing oral family history, used English and referred to a "galvanize roof." This reserve is also suggested by Naipaul's never directly naming his father in the essay; only in a quoted newspaper article is the name Seepersad used.

Yet the essay is by no means without vividness and intensity. Naipaul's preference for short sentences (often five or six words) at climactic points within his paragraphs creates stylistic vigor and impact, while a number of devices (additions punctuated by semicolons, series sentences, various kinds of parenthesis) are used to provide vivid, novelistic details. In his emphasis on particularity, Naipaul shows an affinity with Charles Dickens' work, some of which (as he mentions in the essay) Seepersad had read to him in childhood.

Critical Context

Besides its polished prose, astute ideas about and observations of humanity, and artistry as memoir, "Prologue to an Autobiography" has important connections with Naipaul's other works. With regard to Naipaul's fiction, the essay sheds light on the autobiographical material in *The Mystic Masseur* (1957), *Miguel Street*, *A House for Mr. Biswas* (1961), *The Mimic Men* (1967), and *The Enigma of Arrival* (1987)—particularly on the second and third of these books. Further, it contains exceptionally keen analysis of the technique and construction of *Miguel Street*, and by extension general comments on these matters. The essay's crucial theme of self-realization and the corresponding fear of extinction is strongly manifested in individuals' struggles in *The Suffrage of Elvira* (1958) and *Mr. Stone and the Knights Companion* (1963), as well as all the other aforementioned novels.

Glancingly, the essay touches on specific travel and historical material in Naipaul's nonfiction books *The Loss of El Dorado: A History* (1969), *The Middle Passage: Impressions of Five Societies—British, French and Dutch—in the West Indies and South America* (1962), and *An Area of Darkness: An Experience of India* (1964). More broadly, in these and other nonfiction books by Naipaul about his travels, experiences, and observations in Third World cultures, he adopts, as he does in "Prologue to an Autobiography," an unobtrusive, almost self-effacing posture. Nevertheless, the reader is continually aware (partly from the use of first person) that the various phenomena of experience are being registered on and by a particular human being, who is often addressed by people met in his travels. With sensitivity, philosophical musing, irony, and a sharp eye for characterizing or symbolic detail, Naipaul's experiences are transmuted by lucid prose into art that is abiding because of the unforgettable human beings it records.

Sources for Further Study

Cudjoe, Selwyn R. "V. S. Naipaul and the Question of Identity," in *Voices from*

Under: Black Narrative in Latin America and the Caribbean, 1984. Edited by William Luis.

Healy, J. J. "Fiction, Voice, and the Rough Ground of Feeling: V. S. Naipaul After Twenty-five Years," in *University of Toronto Quarterly.* LV (Fall, 1985), pp. 45-63.

Huston, Larry Alan. "From Autobiography to Politics: The Development of V. S. Naipaul's Fiction," in *Dissertation Abstracts International.* XLIV (January, 1984), p. 2154A.

Padhi, Bibhu. "Naipaul on Naipaul and the Novel," in *Modern Fiction Studies.* XXX (Autumn, 1984), pp. 455-465.

Norman Prinsky

PROSPERO'S CELL
A Guide to the Landscape and Manners of the Island of Corcyra

Author: Lawrence Durrell (1912-   )
Type of work: Travel writing
Time of work: 1937-1941
Locale: Corfu, Greece
First published: 1945; revised, 1975

Principal personages:
LAWRENCE DURRELL, a novelist
NANCY DURRELL, his first wife
THEODORE STEPHANIDES,
ZARIAN,
COUNT D., and
MAX NIMIEC, his friends

Form and Content

Prospero's Cell is an account of Lawrence Durrell's life on the island of Corfu from 1937 to 1941. In 1937, Lawrence Durrell, his wife, his mother, and her other three children moved from England to Corfu. In *Prospero's Cell*, only one brother is mentioned as being on Corfu; the book is largely structured around the life of Durrell and his wife. This book, as is true for three other books Durrell wrote about living on the Greek Isles, is most properly described as literature of residence since it concerns the life of someone who has gone to a place to live, not simply to visit as a tourist. *Reflections on a Marine Venus* (1953) concerns Durrell's residence on the island of Rhodes. In *Bitter Lemons* (1957), Durrell tells of going to live on Cyprus from 1953 to 1956. These two and *Prospero's Cell*, however, have for audience mainly those concerned with modern literature and culture. They do give information valuable for the inquisitive tourist, but of greater importance is that they tell of the culture of the islands during times of political and social change: the coming of World War II in *Prospero's Cell*, the governance of Rhodes by the British after the war in *Reflection on a Marine Venus*, and the rebellion in Cyprus against British annexation in *Bitter Lemons*. A fourth book, *The Greek Islands* (1978), is a well-written and well-illustrated travel book, a guide to the Greek Islands.

Prospero's Cell was written in Alexandria, Egypt, and incorporated notes that Durrell had made about the years when he and his first wife, Nancy, lived on Corfu. In the published form, the format of a journal was retained, and each section is dated, the first being 10.4.37 and the last being 1.1.41. The epilogue to the book was written in Alexandria as Durrell recalls the couple's escape to Crete when World War II was declared. At the time the book was written, he was working in Alexandria for the British embassy. There is an appendix for travelers who desire information about the history of Corfu and the twentieth century way of life. There is also a brief bibliography of books in English about the island. The revised edition (1975) has a preface by Durrell and one more chapter.

Most of the information about Corfu in the book is given through conversations between Durrell and four friends of his who lived on Corfu at the time. The book is dedicated to them: Theodore Stephanides, Zarian, the Count D., and Max Nimiec. During conversations held at the count's country estate, the white house where Durrell and his wife lived, and The Sign of the Partridge (a tavern), the friends argue about the history, legends, and customs of Corfu. Through these dramatic scenes, the reader learns of the different people who have controlled the island, what they contributed, and why they were defeated. One learns much about the food, drink, and customs of Corfu, since most of the conversations occur during meals or celebrations.

Knowing that he must provide objective as well as personal information, Durrell, includes chapters outside the format of the journal which tell, for example, of Saint Spiridion, the island saint. He also writes of the history of the island and reviews those who have written about it. Always, Durrell is concerned to show how the past relates to the present: customs that have ceased or continued and qualities of the inhabitants that are constant.

Analysis

Although Durrell's main concern is to give the reader an understanding of the landscape and manners of Corfu, he also gives a portrayal of life as it was on the island before World War II. Being barely twenty-five at the time of the first journal entry, he gives an impression of youth, optimism, and naïveté—though the young Durrell is very much a man of the world in conversations with his friends. The book communicates the ease and delight of life spent in the sun by a young man and woman who have no financial worries but who do have interesting friends. There is, though, a note of nostalgia in the journal entries for a way of life whose passage Durrell regrets as he lives it, knowing that this time of youth will not come again.

Clearly reflected in *Prospero's Cell* is Durrell's ability as a writer of fiction. Even though his emphasis is on the land and its people, the reader knows what shade of blue the sea has, how the sand feels, the taste of bread dipped in olive oil. Legends—such as the story that descendants of Judas Iscariot, the disciple who betrayed Jesus Christ, took up residence in Corfu—are mentioned and their sources given. (After relating that legend, Durrell tells of his visit to a shoemaker named Iscariotes, but gains no new information despite the similarity of names.) Speculation about history is as important in *Prospero's Cell* as recorded fact because Durrell places much importance on human inquiry.

Ancient religious beliefs and artistic achievements are presented in a contemporary context. Count D. owns a sixth century statue of a woman; as he and his friends look at it, the count discusses the period in which the statue was carved and recounts his understanding of women. The existence of Pan, a god of the ancient Greeks, is recalled by the count as he tells of local belief in a mischievous house sprite who resembles Pan, having cloven hooves and pointed ears. When marriage customs and religion are discussed, it is to explain the behavior of a young couple in love, or of a man and woman who have been married for years, or of a priest of the Greek Orthodox church, now the state church of Greece.

Through the quality of the prose, one understands that Durrell is as much concerned with his own writing as with the life on Corfu. Mention is made of writers admired, or read, by Durrell and his friends. William Shakespeare is mentioned—not only because the title of the book refers to one of his last plays, *The Tempest* (1611), but also because Durrell greatly admired Elizabethan writers. The main character in *The Tempest* is Prospero, a great magician put ashore with his daughter on an island; Count D. argues that Corfu was that island. Durrell presents the view that the ancient Greek poet Homer also wrote about Corfu in his epic poem the *Odyssey* (c. 800 B.C.). According to Durrell, when Odysseus' men were lost in a storm at sea, he was washed up on Corfu, where he met the princess whom Homer names Nausicaa. Little mention is made of contemporary authors, although Durrell does refer to his friend Henry Miller, an American novelist who lived in Paris at the time and visited Durrell on Corfu in 1939. Durrell had published *Pied Piper of Lovers* (1935) under his own name and under the pseudonym Charles Norden published *Panic Spring* (1937). It was on Corfu that he first read Henry Miller's *Tropic of Cancer* (1934), which was banned in the United States. Under the influence of this book, Durrell wrote *The Black Book* (1938), in which, he said, he first heard the sound of his own voice.

In *Prospero's Cell* Durrell once again hears the sound of his own voice: complex diction, strong dialogue, and dramatic situations, all of which are intended to illustrate what he has called "the spirit of place." Place for Durrell, in this case Corfu, is not simply a geographical and historical terrain. It is as well his own particular experience with the native culture. As a young man, his experience of Corfu was different from that of the more mature one who would move to Cyprus in 1953 and then write *Bitter Lemons* about his residence.

The reader learns much about the traditional way of life on Corfu. The gathering and pressing of olives and grapes to make olive oil and wine are seen through Durrell's eyes. The economy of his part of the island depends on the success of these crops. Of equal importance, these practices are ties to the traditional life in Corfu; so Durrell tells of the beliefs and ceremonies as they have been practiced for centuries and of the changes that have been introduced. The book ends with Durrell's return after an absence of almost five years to see how the old ways have fared, so the nostalgic tone that was present in the beginning continues to the end.

Critical Context

Prospero's Cell is part of the tradition of recollections by British writers who have been attracted to the Mediterranean. Norman Douglas wrote reminiscences titled *Old Calabria* (1915) and the novel *South Wind* (1917), among other books, about his own experiences. His characters speak self-consciously of art and the emotions; in

Durrell's book, the count remarks on one occasion that he himself is beginning to sound like a Norman Douglas character. E. M. Forster, also a British novelist, who lived in Greece, Italy, and Egypt, wrote a travel narrative about a different part of the Mediterranean world, *Alexandria: A History and a Guide* (1922). Closer to Durrell in thought and style is D. H. Lawrence's *Twilight in Italy* (1916).

Though Durrell certainly was aware of these writers and their works, the matter of influence is not relevant. Yet Durrell does write about Egypt in *The Alexandria Quartet*, the four-volume novel that led to his international fame. The first novel, *Justine*, was published in 1957, the same year he published *Bitter Lemons*, and was followed by *Balthazar* in 1958, *Mountolive* in 1958, and *Clea* in 1960. His later novels all have something to do with the Mediterranean world. *Tunc* (1968) and *Nunquam* (1970) are set in England and Switzerland but the key events have their origins in Greece and Turkey. Five subsequent Durrell novels are largely concerned with the area of France known as Provence. The series takes its title from one of the major cities of Provence, Avignon. *The Avignon Quintet* consists of *Monsieur: Or, The Prince of Darkness* (1974), *Livia: Or, Buried Alive* (1978), *Constance: Or, Solitary Practices* (1982), *Sebastian: Or, Ruling Passions* (1983), and *Quinx: Or, The Ripper's Tale* (1985).

In his fiction, Durrell reverses the emphases of his three books about living on Corfu, Rhodes, and Cyprus. History and local custom are used to provide detail and believability to the characters and events of the novels. In the books discussing his residences, however, the creation of characters and dramatic situations serves as an interesting way for readers to learn.

Sources for Further Study

Dickson, Gregory. "Lawrence Durrell and the Tradition of Travel Literature," in *Deus Loci: The Lawrence Durrell Quarterly.* VII, no. 5 (1984), pp. 43-50.
Durrell, Gerald. *My Family and Other Animals,* 1957.
Fraser, G. S. *Lawrence Durrell: A Critical Study,* 1973 (revised edition).
Friedman, Alan Warren. "Place and Durrell's Island Books," in *Critical Essays on Lawrence Durrell,* 1987.
Markert, Lawrence W. "Symbolic Geography: D. H. Lawrence and Lawrence Durrell," in *Deus Loci: The Lawrence Durrell Quarterly.* V (Fall, 1981), pp. 90-101.
Pinchin, Jane Lagoudis. *Alexandria Still: Forster, Durrell, and Cavafy,* 1977.

Frank Kersnowski

THE PROTESTANT ETHIC AND
THE SPIRIT OF CAPITALISM

Author: Max Weber (1864-1920)
Type of work: Sociology
First published: Die protestantische Ethik und der Geist des Kapitalismus, 1904-
1905 (English translation, 1930)

Form and Content

    The Protestant Ethic and the Spirit of Capitalism, without a doubt the most widely recognized work by the preeminent German sociologist Max Weber, takes the form of a book-length scholarly essay published in two parts—of roughly one hundred pages each—titled "Das Problem" (the problem) and "Die Berufsethik des asketischen Protestantismus" (the ethic of the calling in Protestant asceticism). Each part is further divided into a number of subparts (or sections) and is accompanied by an extensive body of notes—84 for part 1 and 309 for part 2—in which Weber not only cites his sources but also elaborates on many of his arguments by providing a plethora of detailed and often-lengthy examples and explanations. Taken together, these notes serve to elevate the essay from a mere collection of sociological assertions to a well-argued and painstakingly documented example of modern research in the social sciences—an example embracing Weber's oft-stated and, in terms of present-day sociology, highly visionary belief that all studies of man and society should be firmly rooted in the scientific method (valid experimentation, statistical documentation, and the like).

    When Weber republished *The Protestant Ethic and the Spirit of Capitalism* as part of his *Gesammelte Aufsätze zur Religionssoziologie* (collected essays on the sociology of religion) in 1920 and 1921, he expanded the already monumental aggregate of notes to incorporate the various criticisms of his fellow sociologists and, additionally, supplied the essay with a short preface outlining several of the most important responses to the work since its first appearance in 1905. These responses included Felix Rachfahl's *Kalvinismus und Kapitalismus* (1909; Calvinism and capitalism) and Lujo Brentano's *Die Anfänge des modernen Kapitalismus* (1916; the beginnings of modern capitalism), which implied among other things that Weber was the first to hypothesize a direct relationship between Protestantism and capitalism. Contrary to the assertions of Weber's critics, however, this relationship had—as Weber himself acknowledges—already been variously postulated since the inception of Protestantism in the early sixteenth century. Indeed, Weber wrote his famous essay with the express intent of explaining, not simply stating, the fact that capitalistic economic systems tend to exist in areas of the world where the rise of Protestantism with its attendant religious, economic, and social ideologies has been most pronounced. Not surprisingly, he chose the highly industrialized nations Germany, England, and the United States, which pair free-market economies with large Protestant populations, as the major focus of his study.

In addition to explaining the complex relationship between Protestantism and capitalism, Weber's work is aimed at describing the sociological basis of the Protestant faith while at the same time demonstrating the importance of the rising (Protestant) middle classes in Germany, England, and the United States for the economic, social, and political development of the Western world. In addition, Weber stresses the significance of the Reformation as the actual catalyst behind the emergence of capitalism as a modern economic system. Not to be overlooked here are the work's comments on Protestant religious life in the United States, which Weber no doubt hoped would provide his European readers with valuable insights into early American history.

In the first part of his essay, Weber outlines the ideologies underlying the Protestant work ethic, which include a utilitarian frame of mind, an ascetic life-style, and a strict career orientation. He ends this part with the important observation that many of these ideologies were products of the Reformation, which by extension is responsible for the emergence of capitalism as a living embodiment of the Protestant ethic. In part 2, written after his tour of the United States in 1904, Weber elaborates on some of the specific religious beliefs common to the numerous Protestant sects of Europe and especially of the United States and, beyond that, provides an informative introduction to the ascetic life-style traditionally associated with the Protestant ethic and thus also with capitalism itself.

The Protestant Ethic and the Spirit of Capitalism is written in a clear and concise manner, utilizing straightforward, nontechnical language. The tone is decidedly neutral (that is, never polemical), and all arguments are constructed in a highly logical and thus easily comprehended fashion. Weber doubtlessly intended this work not only for experts in religion or sociology but also for all individuals who desire a background in the complex interrelationship between the Protestant work ethic and the practical and theoretical bases of modern capitalism and between religious ideology and the social, political, and economic structure of society.

Analysis

As mentioned previously, Weber wrote his ground-breaking essay for the primary purpose of finding a fitting answer for what he, in the heading accompanying part 1, aptly termed "the problem": Why have the predominantly Protestant nations of the world traditionally provided a much more fertile breeding ground for capitalism than their Catholic counterparts? He answers this question by underscoring a fundamental difference in the worldviews of Catholicism and Protestantism: The former religion places its greatest emphasis on the afterlife, while the latter stresses wordly life, the here and now. As Weber notes, Catholics are taught that God, who generally casts a benevolent eye upon His earthly children, will reward human goodness and adherence to Christian virtues (piety, humility, the forsaking of material wealth) with eternal salvation. Protestants, on the other hand—especially Puritans and Calvinists—learn that God views man in a rather unfavorable light, granting salvation on a strictly random basis and then only to a chosen few. They also learn that humans cannot endear themselves to the grace of God through the performance of so-called good works—a fact which ultimately renders all traditional attempts at being a good samaritan utterly superfluous.

At this point, Weber poses another important question: How do Protestants—in the apparent absence of God's love—find happiness and fulfillment in life? The answer, he maintains, lies within the Protestant individual, who holds his destiny in his own hands. Instead of hoping for a better afterlife, he does everything in his power to make the most of his existence on earth, thereby becoming the rugged individualist anticipated in Benjamin Franklin's well-known Puritan adage, "God helps them that help themselves." Weber notes that a good and productive life is defined by Protestantism as one which is totally dedicated to the attainment of worldly riches (money, property, influence, and power) through education, hard work, a disdain for anything deemed impractical and wasteful (such as art and entertainment), and—most important—a willingness to accept significant financial risk. Here it becomes evident that many Protestants believe in a direct, causal relationship between commitment to one's work and material wealth and, as a logical consequence, between wealth and personal "goodness"—a belief characterized by Weber as the "Protestant ethic" and, beyond that, as the "spirit" of this ethic's large-scale organized form, capitalism.

Weber asserts that the Protestant *Weltanschauung*, as it is outlined above, gave rise to a new breed of entrepreneurial individuals who ultimately became the founders of the present-day capitalistic economies in Western Europe and the United States. These individuals are marked by intense industriousness, competitiveness, and frugality. Unlike Catholics, they do not work to live (or merely to subsist) but instead live only to work, to produce, and to maximize profits. Weber terms the sober and utterly utilitarian life-style of these individuals "ascetic," while defining that of Catholics, who apparently perceive no sin in pairing work with pleasure and diversion, as "aesthetic."

Toward the end of the first part of his essay, Weber asks a final important question: What brought about the Protestant work ethic, the basis of all capitalistic systems worldwide, in the first place? The Reformation, he argues, liberated the individual from the shackles of Catholic dogma, giving him the power of economic, religious, and, in a rather limited sense, even political self-determination. Above all, however, the Reformation—with all of its rational and practical implications— gave the individual the freedom to pursue his own best interest, thus effectively motivating him to begin his relentless quest for wealth and profit. According to Weber, the Protestant ethic is also closely tied to Martin Luther's personal assertion that the *Beruf* (or career calling) is the ultimate, God-inspired focus of human existence. By following this calling, the individual can, as Luther implies, not only achieve his own greatest potential but also demonstrate his Christian worth. Not to be forgotten here is that the career-minded, self-actualizing person valued in Lutheran ideology (and indeed in Protestantism in general) is also the undisputed hero of modern capitalism.

In the process of explaining the close relationship between the Protestant ethic and capitalism, Weber cites specific examples of how this ethic actually manifests itself in such capitalistic nations as Great Britain, Germany, and the United States. He begins by indicating that the Protestant emphasis on productivity and efficiency in the workplace (with no squandering of time, effort, or material) translates directly into the development of modern factory-based production facilities in the wake of the Industrial Revolution. These facilities, he maintains, are exemplified by the notorious sweatshops of the nineteenth century, where an underpaid work force toiled for up to sixteen hours per day, and by assembly lines in the twentieth century, where the capitalistic dream of monumental profits through mass production was realized for the first time.

The myth of the self-made man—so prevalent in capitalism—is, as Weber points out, a further outgrowth of the Protestant work ethic, which idealizes the compulsively driven, hardworking overachiever, who has only profitability on his mind. Weber also describes the Protestant emphasis on rationality and practicality as being responsible for capitalism's general abandonment of the arts and humanities in favor of science, industry, and technology—the traditional tools of the capitalistic corporate establishment. Finally, Weber states that the unequal distribution of wealth, influence, and power between the upper and lower classes (that is, between proletarians and corporate owners) in capitalistic societies is linked directly to the Protestant—or rather Calvinistic—belief that workers should be kept chronically poor so that they may be motivated to work longer and harder hours.

Not surprisingly, *The Protestant Ethic and the Spirit of Capitalism* has always met with a high degree of controversy. Some critics find Weber's explanation for the close relationship between Protestantism and capitalism to be somewhat tenuous. Others view his contention that Catholics lack the work ethic necessary for successful participation in capitalistic economies as a personal affront. Nevertheless, the critics do seem to agree on one important point: Weber's essay, controversial as it may be, provides an overwhelming body of evidence in support of the fact that religious ideologies (regardless of their origin) exert a considerable amount of influence on—and even serve to shape—the economic, social, and political structure of nations.

Critical Context

The Protestant Ethic and the Spirit of Capitalism is, by virtue of its broad appeal among Western European and American readers, Weber's most widely recognized work internationally. Indeed, to many laymen Weber's name has become almost synonymous with the concept of the Protestant work ethic. This fact shows that most people are unaware not only of Weber's important contributions to the disciplines of history, economics, law, and psychology but also of his writings on such distinctly non-Protestant religions as ancient Judaism and the religions of the Far East, including Confucianism, Taoism, Hinduism, and Buddhism.

Yet despite its obvious importance for Weber's career, *The Protestant Ethic and the Spirit of Capitalism* attains its greatest significance only when viewed in the context of sociology on the whole. It represents nothing less than a ground-breaking attempt at fusing the subjective evaluation of man and society with the objective and eminently positivistic methodology of the so-called hard sciences. This attempt has yielded what has generally been hailed as one of the first truly modern sociological studies to be systematically constructed on a solid body of statistical and factual evidence. The significance of Weber's essay is further underscored by the fact that it spawned countless investigations in sociology—and indeed in all the social sciences—employing the now standard practices of valid experimentation, logical argumentation, and careful, highly detailed documentation. Seen in this light, it greatly helped to raise sociology, considered by many to be an utterly subjective and thus unprofitable course of study, to its proper level of scientific respectablity.

Sources for Further Study
Bendix, Reinhard. *Max Weber: An Intellectual Portrait*, 1960.
Eisenstadt, S. N., ed. *The Protestant Ethic and Modernization: A Comparative View*, 1968.
Eldridge, J. E. T., ed. *Max Weber: The Interpretation of Social Reality*, 1970.
Freund, Julien. *The Sociology of Max Weber*, 1968.
Giddens, Anthony. *Politics and Sociology in the Thought of Max Weber*, 1972.
Mommsen, Wolfgang J. *The Age of Bureaucracy: Perspectives on the Political Sociology of Max Weber*, 1974.
Robertson, Hector M. *Aspects of the Rise of Economic Individualism: A Criticism of Max Weber and His School*, 1933.
Samuelsson, Kurt. *Religion and Economic Action*, 1957.

Dwight A. Klett

PROUST

Author: Samuel Beckett (1906-　　)
Type of work: Literary criticism
First published: 1931

Form and Content

Samuel Beckett's first book, *Whoroscope* (1930), a ninety-eight-line poem which deals with the life of the French philosopher René Descartes and the subject of time, won for the impoverished twenty-four-year-old writer ten pounds and publication by Nancy Cunard's modest Hours Press. Two of Beckett's writer friends, Richard Aldington and Thomas McGreevy, immediately urged Charles Prentice, an editor at Chatto and Windus, to commission Beckett to write a monograph on Marcel Proust, the major modernist French novelist of the first half of the twentieth century, for its Dolphin series. Prentice, impressed by *Whoroscope*, agreed.

At first delighted by the assignment, Beckett promptly set to work. He wrote *Proust* in Paris, where he had just finished a two-year teaching term at the École Normale Supérieure. Every day he sat in the Café de l'Arrivé across from the Luxembourg Gardens, struggling with what eventually became a seventy-two-page essay. When he grew tired, he would walk through the nearby park to reenergize himself. Before long, however, delight turned into frustration. Beckett increasingly came to find his labor tedious, and finally even hateful. Nevertheless, he completed it late in the summer of 1930 and soon thereafter returned to Dublin, near which he had been born and spent his youth, to begin teaching at his alma mater, Trinity College. *Proust* appeared on March 5, 1931. Several positive reviews of it appeared, and it sold well enough for Beckett to be able to pay back to Aldington some money he had borrowed so that he could remain in Paris while working on his monograph.

The form of *Proust* may suggest some of the difficulty Beckett experienced while working on it. Clearly it suggests a Proustian emphasis on creative associative reasoning rather than careful critical argument. It contains no chapters in the conventional sense. Rather, it is composed of ten short, concentrated, slightly disjunctive sections, separated from one another by white space or asterisks. Some sections are no more than one paragraph in length, some are up to ten pages long. Often the logic of the section order is tenuous at best, and toward the end of the book clear and smooth transitions from paragraph to paragraph evaporate. Throughout, Beckett avoids the biographical and the anecdotal, concentrating instead on the philosophical and the aesthetic. Although Beckett would begin composing his fiction and drama primarily in French from the 1940's on, he wrote *Proust* in English; he has said that he does not want it translated into French because such an action seems pretentious to him.

For Beckett, Marcel Proust and James Joyce were the two greatest novelists of the twentieth century. Consequently, the tone of Beckett's critical essay is generally sympathetic, respectful, and admiring. Its style, which is often fairly lucid and pared down, marks a departure from the linguistic gymnastics and highly elliptical prose of his earlier critical pieces such as "Dante . . . Bruno. Vico . . Joyce" (1929). It also marks the obstipated antithesis of Proust's ornate and convoluted style. Beckett, however, is ultimately dissatisfied with his essay, having scrawled in one copy of it: "I have written my book in a cheap flashy philosophical jargon."

While contemporary critics often read *Proust* as a gloss on Beckett's own work, Beckett actually intended it as an introduction to Proust's seven-novel masterwork, *À la recherche du temps perdu* (1913-1927; *Remembrance of Things Past*, 1922-1931), whose experimental symphonic design explores the consciousness of an author, isolated in his study, remembering the *belle époque* high society of aristocrats, men of fashion, and *demimondaines* who frequented France at the turn of the century, while ultimately attempting to transcend the prison house of time itself through the production of art. Beckett's book is aimed at a scholarly audience and is concerned with examining Proust's "double-headed monster of damnation and salvation—Time." Such a concern looks back directly to the theme of Beckett's first book, *Whoroscope*, which was still fresh in his mind as he sat down to write *Proust*, and looks forward to the theme of many of Beckett's most famous novels and plays, including *L'Innommable* (1953; *The Unnamable*, 1958), *En attendant Godot* (1952; *Waiting for Godot*, 1954), *Krapp's Last Tape* (1958), and *Comment c'est* (1961; *How It Is*, 1964).

Analysis

Central to *Proust* are Beckett's notions of habit and memory. People are, he argues, victims of their past. It is easy to fall into comfortable and familiar habits, believing that they lend the world a sense of safety and coherence. This boring succession of habits, however, generates a kind of haze of preconceptions and conventions that eventually clouds over reality and hides the essence of objects. Hence, human beings usually exist in a kind of narcosis. One must create the world every moment of every day, and one tends to create it in ways that have become habitual. Only during periods of massive change in one's life—during, that is, breaks in habitual behavior—does one fully live. Habit dulls perception. During change, however, one's perception sharpens and one enters "the perilous zones . . . dangerous, precarious, painful, mysterious and fertile, when for a moment the boredom of living is replaced by the suffering of being." Although these periods produce an increase of anxiety, they also cause an intensification of the cruelties and enchantments of reality. One learns to see and feel more clearly. One becomes, in other words, an artist, creating one's world anew. Proust's work exhibits this death of habit, both in its experimental form, which shocks its readers into seeing the universe in a revitalized way, and in the lives of many of its characters, who are forced by dramatic events to perceive reality in new ways.

Beckett goes on to make a distinction between two types of memory. The first he calls "voluntary." Voluntary memory is the memory of habit. It recalls what happened with a kind of scientific precision that gets all the facts right and all the events in the correct order. The second type of memory Beckett calls "involuntary." Involuntary memory is the sort that breaks the bonds of habit. It is "explosive," associative rather than logical. It forges creative connections that others have never seen before, thus revealing reality beneath convention. "But involuntary memory is an unruly magician and will not be importuned," Beckett writes. "It chooses its own time and place for the performance of its miracle." In Proust's work, Beckett argues, it appears twelve or thirteen times. The most well-known example is when the narrator in the first book of *Remembrance of Things Past* dips his madeleine in his cup of tea and suddenly is confronted by a chain of associations which leads him into the reality of his past. At such moments, the imagination triumphs over time. Beckett argues that Proust's work may be seen as a monument to involuntary memory.

Several other key ideas guide Beckett's Proustian meditation on Proust. Beckett stresses that for Proust art is solitude. Art is created and exists apart from others. Since such notions as society and friendship are governed by conventions—by habit—it follows that the purest art is produced outside the social realm. Beckett carries this line of reasoning to its logical conclusion by asserting that in art there is no communication: "Either we speak and act for ourselves—in which case speech and action are distorted and emptied of their meaning by an intelligence that is not ours, or else we speak and act for others—in which case we speak and act a lie." That is, either the artist creates for himself, in which case he is bound to be misinterpreted by those who live by habit, or he creates for others, in which case he becomes a prisoner of habit and begins to live a lie. Since morality depends upon a system of socially accepted habits, true art is amoral. Beckett's conclusion, which he asserts with characteristic pessimism, is clear: "We are alone. We cannot know and we cannot be known."

Nevertheless, at least two positive results paradoxically follow from this bleak diagnosis. First, Proust—and those like Proust who shatter habit—transcends time and even death itself through the very creation of his experimental art. Second, Proust's experimental art momentarily awakes the reader accustomed to conventional narrative from his or her habitual narcosis. Through his nonlogical form, dense style, and exploration of reality rather than convention, Proust engages the reader and makes him or her see things "as they are—inexplicable."

Philosophically, Beckett's monograph rhymes with many of the major tenets of existentialism, which surfaced in the middle of the century in the writing of such thinkers as Jean-Paul Sartre, Martin Heidegger, and Albert Camus. Both the existentialists and Beckett argue that man has become estranged from his own being. Both assert that man is alone in an inexplicable universe. Both believe that man has become caught in habitual systems of thought that separate him from reality; both hold that only when those habitual systems of thought are broken, casting man into a state of anxiety, does man come to experience true being. Both hold, finally, that real thought begins only when Cartesian logic is overthrown and irrationalism—Beckett's involuntary memory—is embraced.

Beckett's ideas in *Proust* also have much to do, as a number of critics have indicated, with those of the German philosopher Arthur Schopenhauer. As young men, both Proust and Beckett admired Schopenhauer, and, although Beckett mentions the philosopher's name only four times in his essay, Schopenhauer's influence upon him is clear. In addition to their generally anti-intellectual view of art, Schopenhauer, Proust, and Beckett share many common beliefs: that objects are distinct and unique, not members of categories; that the artist should deal with the concrete rather than the conceptual; that in good art intuition must replace reason; that the real artist is a will-less subject; and that music is the embodiment of the Ideal.

Proust is also a subtextual argument against Descartes, whom Beckett had first studied in 1928 and 1929, shortly before he began work on his critical essay. In Beckett's mind, Descartes came to stand for reason in Western culture and for the Enlightenment belief that all sciences might one day be unified through a rational method. Beckett, however, subverted Descartes' ideas by focusing on the gap between the mind and the body that is inherent in Descartes' assertion that "I think, therefore I am." In order to do this, Beckett turned to Arnold Geulincx, a Flemish follower of Descartes whose writing Beckett encountered in 1930. Geulincx radicalized Descartes' notions. For him, there existed a mental world that was divorced from the physical one. Each person, according to Geulincx, is alone and locked in the prison of his or her mental life. In a very real way, then, Beckett is in agreement with Proust: Man cannot know and cannot be known. He is truly adrift in an inexplicable universe. Within this context, Beckett's famous assertion in "Three Dialogues" (1949) concerning the role of the artist makes sense: "The expression is that there is nothing to express, nothing with which to express, nothing from which to express, no power to express, no desire to express, together with the obligation to express."

Aesthetically, Beckett's monograph rhymes with the Russian Formalism espoused by such critics as Viktor Shklovsky, Osip Brik, and Boris Arvatov, who argued that the primary goal of art is to defamiliarize everyday perception. In conventional literature, the Formalists believed, the reader has come to expect certain perspectives and techniques; artistic devices have been backgrounded. In the best literature, however, artistic devices should be foregrounded in such a way that habitual modes of perception are disrupted. The result will be that the reader, through his or her disorientation, will suddenly see the object or event described in a fresh way. That, according to Beckett, is just what Proust does. Such an impulse is diametrically opposed to the realist tradition in art, since the purpose of the realist work is to reinforce conventional perception, to background its techniques, and to convince the reader that he or she is not reading a fiction but is actually viewing reality. From Beckett's point of view, realism is an art which speaks and acts for others, and hence is a lie. Proust's work, on the other hand, intends to foreground its own processes and makes the reader see anew. In this way it shares much with modern art and literature by such creators as Pablo Picasso, Gertrude Stein, and James Joyce. It also looks forward to the radical experimentation found in the postmodern works produced by such writers as Alain Robbe-Grillet, John Barth, and Beckett himself.

Critical Context

Beckett's *Proust* is an important critical essay for two reasons. First, it serves as a strong thematic and aesthetic introduction to Proust, focusing on many ideas that the Irishman and the Frenchman share: time and loss, habit and its relationship to time, and the failure of the intellect. Second, it serves as a strong introduction to Beckett's own canon. At the same time that Beckett explains Proust he takes on Proust, wrestling with the greatest French writer of the early twentieth century, continually redescribing the Proustian universe so that it comes increasingly to resemble his own. The result, as Vera Lee has shown, is that Beckett now and again misreads Proust. For example, Beckett often forces *Remembrance of Things Past*, which in the final analysis is a work full of affirmation and promise, into a grim, pessimistic interpretation.

In any case, *Proust* marks the apex of Beckett's interest in critical theory. It also marks the first full gesture Beckett made toward articulating his personal aesthetic. Many of the philosophical and aesthetic ideas he discusses in his pages on Proust inform his later work. *Waiting for Godot*, for example, reveals the boredom of living which Didi and Gogo experience, while its intent is to cast its audience into the suffering of being. *Krapp's Last Tape* amorally probes how people are all victims of the past. *The Unnamable* and *How It Is* explore the inability to express and assert that one cannot know and cannot be known.

Beckett, then, appropriates many of the obsessions of a modernist writer and transforms them to suit his own early postmodern enterprise. While it is true that Proust dismantled existential illusion after illusion, it is equally true that the culmination of his work is an act of transcendence through the very act of creation. Proust, a quintessential modernist, sought desperately for a metanarrative—an overarching belief system that would shape his life and give it meaning—and he believed that he had found it in art itself. Beckett, on the other hand, in a quintessentially postmodern gesture, never locates a metanarrative. In fact, from his earliest work such as *Whoroscope* and *Proust*, he takes a certain dark comic delight in the belief that there are no answers, that there is nothing to express, nothing from which to express, and nothing with which to express—but that there is a need to express the fruitlessness of expression.

Sources for Further Study

Acheson, James. "Beckett, Proust, and Schopenhauer," in *Contemporary Literature*. XIX (1978), pp. 165-179.

Bair, Deirdre. *Samuel Beckett: A Biography*, 1978.

Ben-Zvi, Linda. *Samuel Beckett*, 1986.

Jones, K. "Schopenhauer and Beckett's *Proust*," in *Études irlandaises*. XI (December, 1986), pp. 71-81.

Lee, Vera G. "Beckett on Proust," in *Romanic Review*. LXIX (1978), pp. 196-206.
Zurbrugg, Nicholas. "From 'Gleam' to 'Gloom': The Volte Face Between the
Criticism and Fiction of Samuel Beckett," in *Journal of the Australasian Univer-
sities Language and Literature Association*. LV (May, 1981), pp. 23-35.

Lance Olsen

RADICAL CHIC AND
MAU-MAUING THE FLAK CATCHERS

Author: Tom Wolfe (1931-   )
Type of work: Essays
Time of work: 1968-1970
Locale: New York and San Francisco
First published: 1970

> *Principal personages:*
> LEONARD BERNSTEIN, a conductor, composer, and contributor to
>   liberal causes
> DON COX, the field marshal of the Black Panther Party
> CHARLOTTE CURTIS, the women's news editor of *The New York
>   Times*
> JOSEPH ALIOTO, the mayor of San Francisco
> JOMO YARUMBA, the coordinator of Youth of the Future

Form and Content

In June of 1970, at the time when the first version of "Radical Chic" was published in *New York* magazine, Tom Wolfe was considered by many to be America's foremost exponent and practitioner of what had come to be called the New Journalism. Spawned by the turbulent 1960's and more opinionated than the old-fashioned, who-what-where-when-why school of objective reportage, "participatory journalism," as it was sometimes dubbed, was experimental in style, sardonic in tone, and intimate in point of view. In *The Kandy-Kolored Tangerine-Flake Streamline Baby* (1965) and *The Electric Kool-Aid Acid Test* (1968), Wolfe had employed language and grammar to fashion moods that were dazzling, rhythmic, and almost surreal. Like Truman Capote's *In Cold Blood* (1965) and Norman Mailer's *The Armies of the Night: History as a Novel, the Novel as History* (1968), Wolfe's best work seemed a blend of truth and imagination, forming a new genre: the nonfiction novel. More important, Wolfe was a consummate satirist of contemporary popular culture, or more aptly, the plethora of subcultures representing variations on the pursuit of the American Dream. Casting a jaundiced eye, he invented new methods of dissecting and capturing the myths, mores, and flawed nobility of various groups within the social landscape. Thus, his essays have sociological importance as well as relevance as primary source works for students of contemporary American history.

As the title suggests, *Radical Chic and Mau-Mauing the Flak Catchers* consists of two separate, distinct stories about black rage and white guilt, the first approximately twice the length of the second, but each easily consumed in one sitting, like a novella or a full-course meal. Both focus on bizarre, ritualistic meetings between ghetto residents and Establishment figures—in one case elite social aristocrats, in the other case government bureaucrats. A New Yorker who had documented San

Francisco's Haight-Ashbury subculture in *The Electric Kool-Aid Acid Test*, Wolfe was familiar with both East Coast and West Coast locales. In "Mau-Mauing the Flak Catchers," he satirizes the confrontations which angry militants were staging as a sidelight to President Lyndon Baines Johnson's "War on Poverty." The custom of "mau-mauing," Wolfe quips, had become by 1968 almost as American as marathon encounter sessions or zoning board hearings. In fact, the Office of Economic Opportunity encouraged the charade in order to identify and placate minority leaders in the Bay area. Since, in Wolfe's opinion, the poverty experts did not know any more about ghetto culture than about Zanzibar, they waited for self-styled militants to come to them—or, more specifically, to a designated toady or lifer whom Wolfe nicknamed a "flak catcher." The most menacing and outrageous "mau-mauers" generally received money for their ghetto programs.

On the East Coast, meetings between activists and the Establishment took a different form. "Radical Chic" describes a cause party held on January 4, 1970, hosted by maestro Leonard Bernstein and his wife, Felicia, at their thirteen-room Park Avenue residence. The avowed purpose was to raise money for the legal defense of twenty-one Black Panthers, who had been indicted on charges of conspiring to bomb five department stores, a police station, a railroad facility, and the Bronx Botanical Garden. Bernstein's reputation as a popularizer of classical music assured a glittering turn-out among New York's East Side townhouse set—including writer Lillian Hellman, actor Jason Robards, photographer Richard Avedon, director Otto Preminger, journalist Barbara Walters, Julie Belafonte (wife of Harry Belafonte), civil rights spokesman Roger Wilkins, and Charlotte Curtis, women's news editor of *The New York Times*. This party was at least the fourth such fashionable fund-raiser for the paramilitary Panthers. As Wolfe observes with tongue in cheek, radical chic had also spawned "soirees" for grape pickers, American Indians, Students for a Democratic Society, the Young Lords (a Puerto Rican group), G.I. Coffeehouses (an antiwar group), the University of the Street (a counterculture group), the Friends of the Earth (an environmental group), and the financially strapped radical-liberal editors of *Ramparts* magazine.

By and large, despite periodic breakdowns in communication, the Bernstein fund-raiser seemed to go well. Charlotte Curtis' account in *The New York Times* was uncritical. Yet it inspired a scathing editorial rebuttal, which characterized the affair as "elegant slumming" that degraded both the patrons and the patronized. Picked up by the wire services, the news account of the party played to a chorus of horse laughs and jeers. Conservative columnist William F. Buckley called it an object lesson in liberal masochism. Ridiculed as "Mr. Parlour Pink" and attacked by Jewish groups, Bernstein tried to explain that he had merely convened a meeting, not to endorse the Panthers but to ensure the protection of their civil liberties. Even so, thereafter, identification with the Panthers was no longer chic. Once the Panthers became pariahs, it was safer and more fashionable to worry about sables and leopards and other endangered animal species. Faced with a threat to their status, Bernstein's circle of New Society nabobs modified their behavior. Hardly surprising, as Wolfe writes, because "Radical Chic, after all, is only radical in style; in its heart, it is part of society and its traditions."

Analysis

Wolfe's skewering essay was not responsible for the initial wave of derision which caused "radical chic" to unravel and become passé, but his detailed observations about the foibles of the "New Society" put it in historical perspective. The roots of the debacle, in Wolfe's opinion, lay in the aristocratic tendency to romanticize things primitive and proletarian as a way of asserting superiority over the placid life-styles of the middle-class. The French had a phrase for this inverted form of snobbery—*nostalgie de la boue*, or, literally, nostalgia for the mud. It surfaced in the early 1960's in excursions to the Peppermint Lounge to dance the twist with killer Joe Piro and in the infatuation with pop art and Andy Warhol. Left-wing cause parties went back at least to the 1930's, and many of Bernstein's friends within the communications industry were "red diaper babies" who had been weaned on liberal-left political traditions. A double-track mindset was at work, with subtle contradictions, encompassing noblesse oblige but also a longing to be attuned and avant-garde. In the case of the charismatic Panthers, the envy was almost palpable. Quite aside from the political issues involved, what excited Bernstein's guests about the Panthers was their hip life-style, language, and mode of dress—in short, their raw, vital presence. As one woman put it: "These are no civil-rights *Negroes* wearing gray suits three sizes too big—these are *real men*!" They were "righteously" cocky, in contrast to black moderates who excoriated themselves for their failure to ameliorate ghetto rage. In their presence, Bernstein's assembled guests, in their Pucci dresses, Capucci scarves, and Gucci shoes, resembled "a bunch of leaping, prancing, palsied happy-slobber Saint Bernards."

Wolfe is at his most hilarious in describing the mental gyrations accompanying the planning of the cause party. For example, how to dress? Avoiding something frivolous, pompous, or artificially funky, Felicia Bernstein settled on a simple black frock and plain gold necklace. Employing black maids would be a *faux pas*, so Felicia hired white South Americans dressed in black uniforms with white aprons to serve the cheese morsels, asparagus tips, and miniature meatballs. (Felicia's Chilean background had proved so useful in finding domestics that her friends joked that she headed the Spic and Span Employment Agency.)

The cause party itself opened with some droll introductory remarks by mutton-chopped "movement" attorneys Leon Quat and Gerald Lefcourt, including jokes poking fun at Spiro Agnew and Hubert Humphrey. Then Field Marshal Don Cox from Oakland and Defense Captain Henry Miller from Harlem—accompanied by their lithe, beautiful, well-dressed women—put forth the Panthers' militant ten-point platform, as well as a pitch for the Panthers' breakfast program. Frequently quoted was Defense Minister Huey P. Newton on the necessity of class struggle, the virtues of armed self-defense, and the willingness to risk revolutionary suicide in the face of a racist, intransigent police state.

During questions and answers, some guests expressed alarm that the Panthers were becoming anti-Semitic and were threatening moderate black leaders. Gallery owner Richard Feigen wondered who to call in order to give a party. The host speculated about whether the Panthers felt infuriated just walking into such a gathering, causing Field Marshal Cox to reply, "We want the same thing as you, we want peace. We want to come home at night and be with the family . . . and turn on the TV . . . and smoke a little *weed* . . . you dig? . . . and we'd like to get into that bag, like anybody else."

Dominating the discussion was the maestro himself, whom Wolfe sometimes calls Lenny, almost as if he were behaving like an adolescent. Bernstein is portrayed as a voluble egotist: "the Great Interrupter, the Village Explainer, the champion of Mental Jotto, the Free Analyst, Mr. Let's Find Out." Anxious to find common ground with the self-styled revolutionaries, he ruminated that most of his assembled guests also had feelings of not being wanted. Wolfe describes a prophetic recurring vision of Bernstein's in which he makes a fool of himself by giving a concert audience an antiwar speech that began with the words "I love." "Radical Chic" does not so much heap ridicule on Bernstein personally as on his social circle's facile assumptions about brotherhood and class harmony. Wolfe dissects the dichotomy between their radical-liberal political sympathies and their aristocratic life-style.

During the late 1960's, "mau-mauing" evolved into an art form similar to a ghetto game called "the Dozens," where the rhetorical patter (or "rap") is theatrically violent and insulting, the object being to shatter your opponent's cool. When directed against a bureaucratic "flak catcher," the posturing was intended to instill a sense of panic. According to Wolfe, "mau-mauing" was a "shuck," a put-on employed against willing civil servants—number-two men—who, according to Wolfe's scenario, responded to the verbal assaults with guilt-ridden grins and eyes frozen into ice balls. As statistics would later confirm, the path to upward mobility was not in enrolling in a job training program but in becoming part of the bureaucratic apparatus itself. Wolfe wrote: "Everybody but the most hopeless lames knew that the only job you wanted out of the poverty program was a job *in* the program itself."

Doing a "savage number" on "the man" was considered a "beautiful trip" that brought a sense of empowerment to groups especially interested in self-respect. Face-to-face confrontations were more exhilarating and easier to organize than mass marches or demonstrations. They played on white liberal guilt and fear of the black man's masculinity. If the flak catcher's dubious manhood had to be sacrificed, that was the price of averting lawless and potentially revolutionary behavior. Poverty officials nevertheless employed flawed logic in assuming that their tormentors were natural ghetto leaders rather than just gangsters or con artists. By and large, they were, in fact, street-corner hustlers posing as freedom-fighting warriors.

Wolfe uses the phrase "Ethnic Catering Service" to define the role played by the character actors in the mau-mauing ritual. Dashikis, sunglasses, and combat boots were among the favored props. Assembling some two dozen angry-looking youths—"wild niggers," to use Wolfe's phrase—was standard operating procedure, although one enterprising soul-brother simply filled a sack with weapons, dumped the contents on a conference table, and claimed, "These are some of the things I took off my boys last night."

Chicanos, Chinese, and even Samoans got into the act. Wolfe describes how a group of Samoans once surrounded a functionary who resembled a seedy version of television announcer Ed McMahon. Bigger than professional football players, attired in blood-colored island shirts and sandals with straps the size of reins, the Polynesians banged their tiki canes in unison and demanded emoluments. "Listen, Brudda," one said. "Why don't you give up your pay check for summer jobs? You ain't doing——."

The intense competition for poverty money required the ingenuity of a Jomo Yarumba (formerly Bill Jackson), who led sixty Youth of the Future members into San Francisco's City Hall. They threatened to stay all night and despoil the hallowed lobby with candy, soda pop, and other junk food, until Mayor Joseph Alioto himself came out and promised to purchase some sewing machines for Yarumba's dashiki factory. That was small change compared to the $937,000 grant which Chicago's Blackstone Rangers had extorted the previous year.

Critical Context

For social critic Wolfe, the unhinged, helter-skelter burst of unchartered change was a troubling, though fascinating, facet of 1960's American culture. Nothing offended his sensibilities more than those who remained willfully blind to reality. In "Mau-Mauing the Flak Catchers," he ridiculed a white college professor who read aloud passages from Eldridge Cleaver's *Soul on Ice* (1968), only to receive her comeuppance from a street-smart black student, who dismissed it as jive intended for gullible white folks.

In Wolfe's opinion, the Black Panthers were a media-hyped handful of radicals with hardly a toehold in San Francisco's ghettos. Their Ten-Point Program was written in the North Oakland Poverty Center. While admired by street blacks for their courage, they were into a seemingly suicidal "trip"—fighting the Pigs (police)—on which few wished to embark. What was emulated was their swashbuckling posture, which for a time vied with the supercool "pimp" style of Sly Stone vests, black beaver fedoras, thin nylon socks, outlandish slacks, and effeminate shirts. Collegians at San Francisco State, for example, looked so "righteous," in Wolfe's words, "that Che Guevara would have had to turn in his beret and get bucked down to company chaplain if he had come up against it."

What do Wolfe's two essays have in common, aside from their acerbic tone and the author's signature style? Both poke fun at stumbling efforts to establish dialogue across class lines. Yet both the "New Society" cause parties and the mau-mauing confrontations brought together two different worlds in ways that were mutually rewarding, not merely in assuaging white guilt and venting black rage. Quite the reverse. The meetings (and that is what Bernstein insisted they were) opened windows of opportunity, at least slightly, for black participation in the system in ways which enabled both groups to assert their superiority to dreary, conservative middle-class folks—both black and white. Behind the radical posturing and sloganeering, both groups were acting in their own selfish interests. Behind the cant, Wolfe believes, lay the inherent self-interest of human nature. Meanwhile, there were more delicious contradictions to be exposed as the United States headed into the "Me Decade," a phrase Wolfe coined to described the self-absorbed 1970's.

Sources for Further Study

Coyne, J. R. Review in *National Review*. XXIII (January 26, 1971), p. 90.

Edwards, T. R. Review in *The New York Times Book Review*. LXXV (November 29, 1970), p. 4.

Epstein, Jason. Review in *The New York Review of Books*. XV (December 17, 1970), p. 3.

Foote, Timothy. Review in *Time*. XCVI (December 12, 1970), p. 72.

Howe, Irving. Review in *Harper's Magazine*. CCXLII (February, 1971), p. 104.

Mewborn, Brant. "Tom Wolfe," in *Rolling Stone*. November 5, 1987, pp. 214-219.

James B. Lane

THE REBEL
An Essay on Man in Revolt

Author: Albert Camus (1913-1960)
Type of work: Philosophy
First published: L'Homme révolté, 1951 (English translation, 1953)

Form and Content

The Rebel, first published on October 18, 1951, represented the culmination of the intellectual and spiritual development of Albert Camus, the great Algerian-born French novelist, essayist, dramatist, journalist, existentialist philosopher, and Nobel Prize winner. This massive philosophical essay on the meaning and development of Western rebellion and revolution was the product of at least nine years of intense work. His motives for writing this study were both intellectual and personal. Camus struggled to understand the origins and the character of the age of confusion and upheaval into which he had been born. He concluded that the first half of the twentieth century had been an age of fear, servitude, and mass murder perpetrated by states in the name of abstract ideologies. He sought to understand how noble Western aspirations and traditions of rebellion and freedom had come to be betrayed by two hundred years of revolutionary fanaticism, bloodshed, and dictatorship. Yet Camus also strove to find a means to improve the lot of humanity without adding to the violence of the past.

Camus' starting point is the absurd. While humans desire meaning, he says, the world is fundamentally irrational. For Camus, the true rebel is in revolt against the absurdity of oppression, cruelty, and suffering. The rebel says no to slavery and tyranny for the sake of others, and affirms his solidarity with other human beings. For the true rebel, oppression and injustice represent the violation of limits; the rebel seeks to create a freedom that respects the rights of all, rather than approving the mindless destruction of societies and individuals.

Camus then sets out to compare revolt to its sequel and its extreme form, revolution. He surveys the entire tradition of Western revolt and revolution from the Greeks to the mid-twentieth century, with an emphasis on the eighteenth through twentieth centuries. Unfortunately, says Camus, revolutions destroy the original intention of rebellion. Revolutions respond to the absurd by defining a variety of ideologies that justify murder. They sacrifice the present happiness of imperfect individuals to a hypothetically perfect future, and thus justify sacrifice of liberty to tyranny.

The Rebel was written in the immediate aftermath of Nazism and in the last terrible years of Stalinism in the Soviet Union and the Stalinization of Eastern Europe. At this time some former allies of Camus, such as the important French philosopher Jean-Paul Sartre, were still defending Communism as a hope for humanity. By writing this book, Camus himself became a rebel against the extremes of the Left and the Right.

After defining authentic rebellion, Camus discusses what he calls metaphysical rebellion. The danger of such revolt is to negate everything, inevitably establishing an absolute alternative system of belief. An example of the metaphysical rebel is the eighteenth century Marquis de Sade. Sade denied God in the name of nature, glorified sexual desire, and practiced libertinism rather than liberty. Camus also considers the dandified heroes of Romantic literature metaphysical rebels. They began as rebels but then created a make-believe world and became a law unto themselves.

Fyodor Dostoevski and Friedrich Nietzsche illustrate the appeal and dangers of nihilism. Dostoevski's character Ivan Karamazov denies the possibility of a merciful God who can tolerate the murder of innocent children, yet makes the dangerous assertion that all revolt is therefore permitted. Nietzsche openly proclaimed that God was dead and urged men to define their own values through becoming an elite of supermen. The Nazis easily perverted this idea into racial murder.

The final portion on metaphysical rebellion discusses literary revolt and focuses on the Surrealist movement. Some of the extreme Surrealists exalted random crime and murder as a way of attacking bourgeois society. Rebellion could now become an end in itself.

Camus then turns to the more concrete and serious forms of historical rebellion: revolutions. While rebellion starts with experience and creates ideas, revolution begins with absolute ideas and imposes them on a complex reality. The result is crimes justified by reason. For Camus, modern history begins on January 21, 1793, the date of the execution of King Louis XVI by French revolutionaries. They called divine-right monarchy a crime and sought to create a heaven on earth patterned after reason and created by terror. The revolutionary government executed in the name of the people.

The process begun by the French Revolution led eventually to the ideas of the German philosopher G. W. F. Hegel, who identified God's purposes with the unfolding of history and the development of the state. There are no values outside history. Salvation lies at the end of history, and the state can commit crimes in order to hasten this salvation. Hegel thus became the spiritual ancestor of both Soviet Communism and German Nazism.

Though Camus displays sympathy with some nineteenth century anarchists and fighters against tyranny, he concludes that individual terrorism paved the way for state murder, which reached its most extreme forms in the Nazi and Bolshevik movements. Nazism arose out of a philosophy of racial hatred and purported to save the world by exterminating the Jews. Soviet Communism arose from the more rational and humane ideas of Marxism, but resulted in a monstrous tyranny. A true rebel wants to live and let live, while the revolutionary is willing to kill in the attempt to produce a perfect human being.

Camus concludes that the true rebel is the artist. Art corrects reality and inspires human beings to improve society, but also creates limits and affirms life.

The final section, "Thought at the Meridian," is a passionate, lyrical exhortation to rediscover a truly humane rebellion, to reject excess and affirm moderation, and to choose the Mediterranean love of life, the sea, and the sun over the murky search for the absolute that characterizes German thought. Man must go beyond nihilism not through absolute beliefs but through freedom.

Analysis

The Rebel is a book of immense learning, reflection, and literary skill. Camus writes in the tradition of the French moralists that includes Michel Eyquem de Montaigne, Voltaire, and Émile Zola. This, his largest work, is an analysis of Western tradition and a plea for liberty, enlightenment, and moderation.

Camus tried to salvage and re-create the Western tradition of liberal humanism. As an existentialist, he held that man must discover values by his own efforts, bereft of religion and ideological dogma. Camus himself was an activist in the cause of truth and justice. His entire life, reflected in *The Rebel*, was a model of courage, decency, and integrity.

In the main, the broad arguments and illustrations of *The Rebel* are probing, stimulating, disturbing, and often brilliant. Camus' insights are frequently couched in striking aphorisms in the tradition of the great French moralists. He provides an impressive framework for explaining the excesses and horrors of the twentieth century.

Yet a work that has set for itself the very ambitious goal of charting and explaining more than two centuries of Western revolutionary development is bound to have some flaws. The book is almost too rich in its references to writers, historical characters, and fictional and mythical personages. This book of more than three hundred pages mentions an almost equal number of names. Unless the reader is unusually well-read, it will be difficult to make sense of all Camus' arguments in one reading.

Paradoxically, the illustrations that Camus uses to emphasize his points are too selective. His main examples are drawn from the French and Russian revolutions and emphasize German thinkers such as Hegel, Karl Marx, and Nietzsche. Unfortunately, Camus fails to consider the American experience. The American revolution was bloody, yet this struggle for freedom resulted in a tradition of gradualist reform, liberty, toleration, and stability—the same values and practices that Camus defines as true rebellion. Was the violence justified by the freedom that it gained? Camus does not address this question.

It is possible to take issue with Camus' methodology. His narrative can be wonderfully eloquent and insightful, but it lacks the rigor that a familiarity with the social sciences would have brought to it. The emphasis is mainly on thinkers and writers. Camus simplistically believes that men and women have been led astray from true rebellion by extremist ideas. He overlooks the fact that evil can also result from abuse of power and human corruptibility. Upheavals can be caused by more than simply a sense of the absurd or a belief in nihilism; economic, social, political, and geographic forces are often crucial. Revolutions can also spring from personal problems and dissatisfactions. In addition, the disasters of the twentieth century cannot simply be laid at the feet of certain important thinkers of the nineteenth century. The contributions of Marx, Hegel, and the Surrealists were wide-ranging and not limited to the negative effects Camus draws from them. Thus, Camus sometimes engages in oversimplification of historical forces and of moral issues.

There seems to be a marked dissonance between the body of *The Rebel* and its conclusion. The main portion of the book is concerned with the degeneration of revolt into despotism. The closing portions of the book are completely devoid of analysis; here Camus sounds a lyrical call for moderation, tolerance, and respect for individual freedom. There is nothing new about such a plea; these are the basic values of Western liberal humanism. Short of advocating trade unionism, organized protest against evil, and artistic integrity, Camus does not show how true revolt can be realized. He defines the Mediterranean ethos as a love of life and moderation, but ignores the convulsions of the ancient Greek world, Italian Fascism, and the violent oscillations of French history.

It may also be asked whether there can be such a thing as moderate revolt. The economic and social conditions of European peasant societies were far more desperate than the stabilized conditions of Europe in the 1950's. Camus does not seem to realize that revolution is a profoundly tragic phenomenon: While without revolution many societies would be doomed to widespread misery and slow, unrecorded death, with revolution there is a different price to be paid in the deaths of the innocent and in the danger of tyranny and fanaticism. In any case, by 1950 the age of revolution was over in Europe. Camus' desire that Europe abandon nihilism and excess was already on its way to being fulfilled in 1951, the year *The Rebel* was published.

Despite its shortcomings and contradictions, *The Rebel* was one of the few books of its time to address the question of where and how Europe and its intellectuals had gone astray. Camus' exposure of the traditions and dangers of dogmatic extremism of any kind is a warning that is as timely in the late twentieth century, especially for Third World countries, as it was in midcentury. Man can least of all afford to play God in a nuclear age.

Critical Context

The Rebel takes its place among Western nonfiction classics. It belongs among the important works of the immediate post-World War II period that signaled a retreat from extremism and pointed the way toward moderation and democracy. These great works include George Orwell's *Animal Farm* (1945) and Hannah Arendt's *The Origins of Totalitarianism* (1951).

The Rebel was well received in the English-speaking world as a brilliant work that dissected the dangers of ideological tyranny, affirmed the rights of the individual, and pointed the way to life and hope for Western civilization. Some critics found fault with Camus' loose generalizations, oversimplifications, and lack of a firm logical structure. Yet on the whole, *The Rebel* was hailed as the most eloquent of the affirmations of postwar reconstructive humanism.

The major controversies over the book erupted in France. Camus had addressed his book mainly to postwar French intellectuals, who were still characterized by ideological extremes and who were by no means well-disposed to Camus' brand of liberalism. Liberals and progressive Catholics welcomed Camus' individualism and democratic anti-Communism; Communists and their sympathizers, as well as the Surrealists, predictably attacked the work.

The publication of *The Rebel* resulted in the final break between the two existentialist giants of French philosophy and letters, Camus and Sartre. Sartre accused Camus of abandoning his former activist outlook and ignoring the realities of political action. Camus replied that Sartre was bowing to expediency by defending servitude (in the Soviet Union) in the guise of humanitarianism.

It is clear that as existentialists Sartre and Camus opposed preconceived ideas of human nature. Yet Sartre (though not a card-carrying Communist) remained sympathetic to Marxism, viewing it as a philosophy of hope and social liberation despite its distortion by the Soviets. Camus placed his faith in the individual as rebel and maintained that freedom of artistic expression was incompatible with Marxist ideology. Camus and Sartre never spoke or collaborated again after the publication of *The Rebel*.

Camus was killed in an automobile accident on January 4, 1960. Sartre then justly eulogized him as a noble figure of his turbulent time. He characterized Camus as one of those rare individuals who understand the malady of their time, lay it bare, and strive to affirm what is best in man. Camus questioned everything except human freedom, limits, decency, and the love of life. In the end, Sartre realized that his friend and antagonist Camus was indeed the indispensable rebel of his time.

Sources for Further Study

Chiaromante, Nicola. "Sartre Versus Camus: A Political Quarrel," in *Camus: A Collection of Critical Essays*, 1962. Edited by Germaine Bree.
Cruikshank, John. *Albert Camus and the Literature of Revolt*, 1960.
Lottman, Herbert. *Albert Camus: A Biography*, 1979.
Rhein, Phillip. *Albert Camus*, 1969.
Thody, Philip. *Albert Camus: A Study of His Work*, 1957.

Leon Stein

RELATIONS IN PUBLIC
Microstudies of the Public Order

Author: Erving Goffman (1922-1982)
Type of work: Sociology
First published: 1971

Form and Content

Erving Goffman's book deals with the connections between social relationships and public life, that is, with face-to-face interaction in activity involving mingling in the public domain. The book contains a preface, an author's note, six main chapters, an appendix (which functions as chapter 7), and an index. There is, despite the extensive use of references in the text, no bibliography. The preface, which is subdivided into three small sections, discusses the focus of the book, its methodology, and its drawbacks. Goffman's chief concern "is with the ground rules and the associated orderings of behavior that pertain to public life—to persons co-mingling and to places and social occasions where this face-to-face contact occurs." His primary methodology—unsystematic, naturalistic observation—leads to the problem of statements about groups without sufficient data, particularly since the identity and the boundaries of the groupings studied are not clearly known.

The author's note describes the relationship of the chapters to one another. The six chapters that make up the bulk of the book were written to be published together and have as a common denominator the public domain as the setting for studies of different types of face-to-face interaction. The chapters are sequential in the sense that the continuing discussion builds on terms that have been defined previously. Each chapter, however, can be read separately since, according to Goffman, "I snipe at a target from six different positions unevenly spaced." The seventh chapter, although a previously published paper, is included because it repeats, and is an application of, the major points in the book.

Chapter 1, "The Individual as a Unit," analyzes the individual from two perspectives: as a vehicular unit and as a participation unit. Goffman points out that the individual as a vehicular unit—that is, a pedestrian—operates on informal understandings of the various ground rules that provide public order on sidewalks and other public thoroughfares. Second, Goffman distinguishes the individual who appears in public as a single (alone) from the individual who appears in a "with" (in the social company of one or more persons). He analyzes the different approaches that are elicited from others when the individual is single and accompanied.

In the first two subsections of chapter 2, "The Territories of the Self," Goffman describes eight kinds of territories, each of which is situational or egocentric. He also discusses the various kinds of markers—signs that indicate a claim to a preserve—for the territories of self. In the next two subsections, he deals with the modalities of violation and offers an analysis of types of territorial offenses. The last section underscores the point made throughout the chapter that territories, markers, and violations often have a socially determined variability, which is dependent on the setting.

Chapter 3, "Supportive Interchanges," deals with positive support rituals in brief face-to-face encounters. In this chapter's six subsections, Goffman comments at length on certain terms (such as "ritual" and "contact") and then focuses on greeting and farewell behaviors. He categorizes these as access rituals which provide brackets around various kinds of joint activities. He also looks at functional equivalents to complete verbal rituals.

Chapter 4, "Remedial Interchanges," is one of the longest. After a general discussion of norms and social control, Goffman describes the function of remedial work: to transform the meaning of an apparently offensive act so that the act becomes acceptable. He analyzes the three main devices—accounts, apologies, and requests—by which that work is accomplished and describes the role of dialogue and of body gloss in that process. He divides the structure of remedial ritual into two basic moves (appreciation and minimization). He concludes the ten sections of this chapter with comments about the presence of an unwritten, assumed set of values by which society judges propriety and offense in interpersonal relationships and speculates about the source of that ideology.

"Tie-Signs," chapter 5, examines evidences about relationships which can function as rituals, markers, and change signals. After a discussion of social relationship in general, Goffman restricts the discussion of tie-signs to anchored relationships and uses as his chief focus for analysis the practice of hand-holding. The discussion, in five subsections, covers related topics such as information control and ritual idiom.

Partly because of its length, chapter 6, "Normal Appearances," is divided into three parts, with subsections within each part. In part 1, after comments about alarms, Goffman discusses *Umwelt*, the egocentric area fixed around a claimant from within which potential sources of alarm exist. He deals with the process by which an individual determines threats to himself and with the role of normal appearances in that process. Part 2 moves to an analytical discussion of the structure of *Umwelten*—the furnished frame, lurk lines, access points, and the social net. In part 3, Goffman summarizes and comments on the vulnerability of public life and on the intricacies of mutual trust presupposed in the public order.

"The Insanity of Place" is reprinted, with some editorial changes, from *Psychiatry: Journal for the Study of Interpersonal Processes* (November, 1969). The discussion centers on the relationship between mental symptoms and the organization in which they occur, with specific reference to the family. Goffman makes distinctions between medical symptoms, which are involuntary and for which remedial work can be done, and mental symptoms, which are consciously offensive and for which there is no remedial ritual except the admission of insanity. The manic, in Goffman's context, is defined as someone who refuses to contain himself in spheres and territories allotted to him and overreaches himself—that is, someone who does not "keep his place."

Analysis

Goffman, in this book as well in his previous books, follows what some consider to be unorthodox methods to gather his data and to reach his conclusions. His manner is that of careful and perceptive observation of various kinds of routines, behaviors, and interpersonal exchanges in a wide variety of settings in public life. He then generalizes about the similarities and parallels he sees in the patterns of behavior in widely different situations. There are, however, no experiments to test his hypotheses; there are no interviews with the people observed. He observes and then infers meaning from people's actions.

This method leaves him open to accusations that he ignores an enormous body of allied and experimental material in the field and that he lacks a systematic, scientific approach to his studies. His methodology can be defended, however, on the grounds that, in Goffman's view, "the realm of activity that is generated by face-to-face interaction and organized by norms of co-mingling . . . has never been sufficiently treated as a subject matter in its own right." Examinations of interaction practices in daily routines had been used as frameworks or props in other studies, but only recently had the field of what he calls "public life" begun to receive attention on its own. There was, therefore, little if any scientific material on which he could draw apart from observation. That was particularly true of some of the specific behaviors, such as hand-holding, that he chooses to analyze.

His observations and subsequent hypotheses are buttressed by supporting data from a wide variety of sources. He does draw on books and published and unpublished studies and papers by sociologists, anthropologists, and ethnologists. The lack of supporting literature specifically focused on his areas of concern, however, accounts in part for his drawing on some unlikely sources. His footnotes include references to narrative and dialogue in novels, to newspaper reports that illustrate his theories, to conversations with other sociologists, and occasionally even to the contents of a "Dear Abby" letter or to a character in an Alfred Hitchcock film.

Goffman is at his least controversial when closely concentrating his analysis on routine, ritual behaviors that are part of everyone's everyday life. As he studies a limited act of social behavior and observes when, how, and by whom it is performed, he catalogs the complexities of the signals that occur habitually but generally go unnoticed because they are so ingrained. Virtually everyone in modern American society has had either direct or indirect experience of some of what Goffman describes. His observations of the intricacies of ritual greetings and farewells, the consistency of the rules governing pedestrian traffic, and the complexities in the function and meaning of hand-holding are verifiable, to some extent, by the average person. The structures and the patterns he discerns, in fact, serve to make intelligible automatic behaviors that are rarely considered or analyzed.

Goffman's book, which is aimed at a general audience, is accessible largely because of his manner of presentation. Although he does use technical terms from several disciplines, he defines words and concepts for the layman throughout the discussion. His presentation alternates in a balanced fashion between data, theory, and supporting examples; he thus generally avoids a dry and abstract tone. The relevance of his use of apparently unlikely sources comes into play here in two ways. By drawing on spy novels, films, and the like, he not only widens the scope of demonstration for his theories (thereby strengthening his arguments) but also makes references to material that is accessible to the general public. Use of a passage from *The Autobiography of Malcom X* (1965), for example, or of a Charlie Chaplin routine to illustrate a theory moves the discussion into an arena that is comfortable for the average reader. Many of the examples Goffman uses put even the untrained reader in a position to evaluate the strength and relevance of his theories and analyses. His prose style is conversational rather than academic and pedantic, and this too makes the book accessible.

Although the discussion is serious, Goffman lightens the tone of his material not only by his conversational tone but also by his use of humor. At times the humor stems from irony. When describing the damage done by students to President Grayson Kirk's office during the 1968 demonstrations at Columbia University, Goffman notes that the appropriate sociological question is not why humans act this way, but "How come persons in authority have been so overwhelmingly successful in conning those beneath them into keeping the hell out of their offices?" At times the humor catches the reader off guard. Goffman occasionally lists a series of elements that are not ordinarily classed together in a way that gives rise to laughter, as, for example, when he makes a particular point "about criminals—and other social desperadoes such as children, comics, saboteurs, and the certified insane." His use of humor is unexpected—most often occurring in the footnotes—but it punctuates his text often enough to deflect any heaviness in tone and to keep the discussion lively.

Although Goffman's book is a definite attempt to document and establish certain theories, some of his discussion is consciously speculative. He often raises issues that have not been explored and questions that have not even been asked before. Some of these questions deal with issues that are peripheral but relevant to the discussion at hand. One footnote in chapter 4, for example, briefly touches on smiles and their role as transfix markers, as devices for bracketing a time period, an event, or an activity. Goffman proceeds to remark that "little smiles are made by everyone all day long, but we never think to study them syntactically." At other times, the questions he raises are directly pertinent to the discussion. In his chapter on remedial interchanges, he speculates on the source of the assumed—but never discussed—set of rules governing social behavior in public life. In his view, there is indeed a common core of beliefs that undergird that unwritten system of behavior, but "this common core of beliefs which links Western societies has been slighted by students of behavior."

Although Goffman aims to be definitive on certain issues, he also leaves many issues open-ended and asks questions that point in many directions. His book, then, becomes not only a study of some aspects of behavior in the public order but also a seedbed of ideas, suggesting new avenues of research and generating concepts that are worthy of further development.

Critical Context

Erving Goffman, a Canadian-born sociologist, educator, and author, is well-known for his analyses of human interaction of various kinds and for his theories that people strive to formulate their identities by means of routine social actions. His reputation was established by such books as *The Presentation of Self in Everyday Life* (1956), *Asylums: Essays on the Social Situation of Mental Patients and Other Inmates* (1961), *Behavior in Public Places: Notes on the Social Organization of Gatherings* (1963), and *Interaction Ritual: Essays on Face-to-Face Behavior* (1967). In many ways, *Relations in Public* reflects a further development and extension of the theories and discussions in his earlier works.

In previous works, Goffman had generally explored the field of social behavior in public places. Here, he repeats some of his theories but also closely analyzes a number of specific sequences of social behavior. As he details the rules and rituals inherent in particular behaviors, these analyses serve as further demonstration and additional applications of his earlier theories.

The same is true in his study of the social behavior of the mentally ill. His interest in that arena is not new, but the discussion in this book expands earlier concepts and is an instance of an application of his social theories in general. Thus, from Goffman's perspective, a manic can be described as an individual who breaks rules of access and territoriality by committing willful improprieties in an attempt to create a certain pattern of relationships.

Goffman's earlier works hypothesize that routines of daily life function according to ritual order. This book adds documentation for that theory. In the same way that ethologists have been establishing a science for animal behavior, the corpus of Goffman's work has aimed in the direction of developing a new science of human behavior. This book is one more move on Goffman's part to develop a science which focuses solely on social interaction in public places—that is, the science of "relations in public."

Sources for Further Study

Argyle, Michael. "Rules and Rituals of Everday Life," in *Science*. CLXXVI (May 12, 1972), pp. 627-628.

Berman, Marshall. Review in *The New York Times Book Review*. LXXVII (February 27, 1972), p. 1.

Black, Kurt W. Review in *The Annals of the American Academy of Political and Social Science*. CDI (May, 1972), p. 206.

Manning, Peter K. "Goffman's Framing Order: Style as Structure," in *The View from Goffman*, 1980. Edited by Jason Ditton.

Storr, Anthony. Review in *The Washington Post Book World*. V (November 28, 1971), p. 14.

Marsha A. Daigle

THE RIGHT STUFF

Author: Tom Wolfe (1931-   )
Type of work: History/New Journalism
Time of work: 1947-1963
Locale: Edwards Air Force Base, California; Cape Canaveral, Florida; and Manned
    Spacecraft Center, Houston, Texas
First published: 1979

> *Principal personages:*
> CHUCK YEAGER, a United States Army test pilot
> JOHN GLENN,
> ALAN SHEPARD,
> WALTER SCHIRRA,
> DONALD K. "DEKE" SLAYTON,
> GORDON COOPER,
> VIRGIL "GUS" GRISSOM, and
> SCOTT CARPENTER, the original Mercury astronauts

Form and Content

Neither a conventional historical account nor a historical novel, Tom Wolfe's *The Right Stuff* is one of the finest extant examples of what is usually termed the "nonfiction novel," a genre that Wolfe helped to create. In telling the factual story of the early stages of the United States' manned spaceflight program, Wolfe uses many of the techniques of fiction. While such factual considerations as time, place, technical and scientific data, and biography are scrupulously accurate, the fictional techniques of point of view, stream of consciousness, and characterization are given free rein. Wolfe has combined the good historian's exhaustive research and attention to detail with the novelist's imaginative license, and the result is not only as reliable an account as one is likely to encounter of America's love affair with spaceflight but also a highly enjoyable comic novel.

For the most part, *The Right Stuff* is organized in chronological order, an important exception being a flashback chapter devoted to the legendary test pilot Chuck Yeager, who throughout the book epitomizes "the right stuff." While the entire book serves as an extended definition of the title, Wolfe succinctly defines it in the second chapter; speaking of military test pilots, from whose ranks were drawn the seven original Mercury astronauts, Wolfe writes:

> As to just what this ineffable quality was . . . well, it obviously involved bravery. But it was not bravery in the simple sense of being willing to risk your life. . . . No, the idea here (in the all-enclosing fraternity) seemed to be that a man should have the ability to go up in a hurtling piece of machinery and put his hide on the line and then have the moxie, the reflexes, the experience, the coolness, to pull it back in the last

yawning moment—and then to go up again *the next day*, and the next day, and every next day, even if the series should prove infinite—and ultimately, in its best expression, do so in a cause that means something to thousands, to a people, a nation, to humanity, to God. . . . A career in flying was like climbing one of those ancient Babylonian pyramids . . . and the idea was to prove at every foot of the way up that pyramid that you were one of the elected and anointed ones who had *the right stuff*.

This definition sets the tone and the style for Wolfe's treatment of the military test pilots with whose exploits the book is concerned. *The Right Stuff* is a celebration of a uniquely American sort of heroism during an age that desperately needed heroes. Set against the backdrop of the Cold War, *The Right Stuff* chronicles the United States' "battle for the stars," beginning with the experimental flights of the Army Air Forces (later the United States Air Force) at bleak Muroc Field in California in the years immediately following World War II. The most significant event of this early period, Chuck Yeager's breaking of the sound barrier on October 14, 1947, serves also as one of the central episodes of the book and as the symbolic beginning of the American space race. Though relatively little of *The Right Stuff* is directly devoted to Yeager, he remains an offstage figure of mythic proportions, his heroic feats in the Air Force's X series of aircraft opening and closing the book and providing both a parallel and a contrast to the better-publicized Mercury and Apollo space programs.

The bulk of *The Right Stuff* describes vividly and imaginatively the selection, training, and missions of the original seven Mercury astronauts. Wolfe describes with humor and insight the originally negative response of military test pilots to the burgeoning space program, the sometimes comical indoctrination and training programs undergone by the astronaut candidates, the internecine strife that accompanied the formation of the National Aeronautics and Space Administration (NASA), and, significantly, the role played by the press in transforming the seven Mercury astronauts from relatively obscure military fliers into public heroes. The book closes with the beginning of the Apollo program, which would land an American astronaut on the moon in 1969. By that time "the right stuff" and those who possessed it had had an incalculable effect on America's sense of national identity and its role in the world.

Analysis

In a foreword to the 1983 paperback reprint of *The Right Stuff*, Tom Wolfe writes that

immediately following the First World War a certain fashion set in among writers in Europe and soon spread to their obedient colonial counterparts in the United States. War was looked upon as inherently monstrous, and those who waged it—namely, military officers—were looked upon as brutes and philistines. . . . The only proper protagonist for a tale of war was an enlisted man, and he was to be presented not as a hero but as Everyman, as much a victim of war as any civilian. . . . *The Right Stuff*

became the story of why men were willing . . . to take on such [high] odds [for death]
in an era literary people had long since characterized as the age of the anti-hero.

Wolfe is speaking here of the unapologetically heroic mode in which *The Right Stuff*
is written. In a century in which literature is filled with such antiheroes as the desperately wounded Jake Barnes in Ernest Hemingway's 1926 novel *The Sun Also
Rises* or, a generation later, the tragically beleaguered Willy Loman in Arthur
Miller's landmark 1949 drama *Death of a Salesman*, the nonliterary public seems
never to have lost its taste for the kind of old-fashioned valor symbolized by the
Mercury astronauts. In an ostensible effort to bridge this gap between literary
output and public taste, Wolfe creates in *The Right Stuff* what might be termed a
latter-day heroic mode, drawing upon elements from the ancient Greek epic, the
Old Testament, and the medieval romance. In its scope and tone, *The Right Stuff* can
truly be called a modern epic—a work of literature that chronicles the deeds of
great persons engaged in a heroic quest. In *The Right Stuff*, the quest is for the
"control of the heavens," and the nemesis is the seemingly invulnerable Soviet
Union.

Biblical imagery abounds in the book, lending an appropriate tone of religious
fervor to America's space race and to the zeal with which the book's heroes seek
"the right stuff." In describing the test pilots' climb up the mythic pyramid described above, Wolfe appropriates Calvinist terminology: Those who make it to the
top are "the elect," "the anointed," while those who fall behind are, presumably,
"damned." The very term "the right stuff" is at times transmuted into "the righteous stuff," as though those who possess it have been chosen by the gods of the
sky. The force that kept each of Yeager's predecessors from breaking Mach 1 is
called a "demon," so that in breaking the sound barrier, Yeager becomes by
implication a Sir Gawain-like knight subduing a celestial Green Knight, or Saint
George slaying a dragon. (It should not be thought, however, that the book's heroes
ever consciously conceive of themselves in such grandiose terms; indeed, part of
possessing "the right stuff" is being unable or unwilling to articulate it, to give it a
name. The heroic imagery in the book is very much an interpolation by a mythmaking narrator.)

The most carefully sustained biblical image in the book is that of the single
combat warrior. In chapter 5, Wolfe writes that "in single combat the mightiest
soldier of one army would fight the mightiest soldier of the other army as a
substitute for a pitched battle between the entire forces." He goes on to explain this
"ancient superstition of warfare" as having its roots not in a concern for minimizing
human bloodshed but rather in mysticism: The will of the gods could be determined
by the outcome of the single combat. Wolfe cites as the most famous incident of
single combat the Old Testament battle between David and the giant Goliath, a story
which seemed to find a modern counterpart in the underdog United States' battle
for the heavens with the seemingly infallible Goliath of the Soviet Union. Without
even realizing it, says Wolfe, the American public was responding to some deep

primordial instinct, some long-forgotten ancestral ritual, by showering the Mercury astronauts with adulation such as the country had never seen before.

Indeed, the hoopla surrounding the space program is a vital part of *The Right Stuff*. Wolfe is careful to point out that the history-making experiments with the X series at Muroc Field and Edwards Air Force Base were conducted largely in secret; even Yeager's breaking of Mach 1 received little publicity, partly because of the government's insistence on secrecy. Thus Alan Shepard, Gus Grissom, Deke Slayton, and the rest of the astronauts, reared as they were in the austerity and secrecy inherent in military test flying, were unprepared for the massive press coverage accorded the Mercury program. Having gone overnight from the obscurity of test flying to the white-hot spotlight of astronauthood, both the astronauts and their wives found themselves uncomfortable in the roles of national heroes. The only real exception was the photogenic John Glenn, adored by the press for his all-American image, whose hunger for publicity contrasted sharply with the shyness of his wife, Annie. Throughout the book, the ambitious Glenn is treated ambiguously by Wolfe, as though "the right stuff" were tainted in Glenn's case with a certain sanctimoniousness.

Press coverage of the Mercury program is never far from Wolfe's mind in *The Right Stuff*; the book constantly asks whether the heroism of the astronauts attracted the press or whether the press created an astronaut cult. Wolfe, himself a journalist, is comic and incisive in his treatment of "the fourth estate," characterizing it variously as "the genteel beast" and "the Victorian gent," labels which emphasize the tendency of the press to observe an often inappropriate decorum in covering the space program. While Wolfe's book is concerned with the colorful truth behind the astronaut myth, contemporary press coverage consistently sanitized the astronauts' images, right down to airbrushing the blemishes off the wives' faces in publicity photographs. Wolfe covers in depth the conservative image created by the partnership between the Mercury program and *Life* magazine, which early bought the exclusive rights to the astronauts' stories and became the official medium between the seven astronauts and a public hungry for whitewashed versions of their lives.

It is no accident that this carefully structured book begins and ends with Chuck Yeager, who all along symbolizes the original meaning of "the right stuff." Wolfe seems concerned with how the original quiet bravery of the test pilot was compromised and eventually perverted by the space program, until the rough-and-ready world of Yeager and Edwards Air Force Base was lost in the maze of cameras and microphones surrounding the Mercury astronauts. The book provides a forceful argument that the X series test flights carried on at Edwards from the late 1940's through the early 1960's, though overshadowed by the attention accorded the Mercury program, were in fact of much greater technological and historical importance than the space program. Certainly at the Mercury program's inception, the "true brethren" at Edwards considered the astronauts, deprived as they were of real control over the computer-operated space capsule, something less than pilots. By the end of the book, however, the astronauts have become the epitome of "the righteous stuff," and the same test pilots who had once been critical of the fledgling space program are opting for astronaut training over military test flight. In ending *The Right Stuff* with Yeager once more looking death in the face in the skies over the California desert, Wolfe seems to be writing an epitaph for the sort of unsung bravery that existed before the news cameras and the flashbulbs changed things forever.

Critical Context

Along with such writers as Hunter S. Thompson and Jimmy Breslin, Tom Wolfe is credited with founding what is known as the New Journalism, a style of writing that seeks to combine the objectivity of journalism with the subjectivity and verbal freedom of fiction. This style began in earnest in the early 1960's and in many ways hit its stride with Truman Capote's 1966 "nonfiction novel" *In Cold Blood*, the story of a brutal multiple murder in rural Kansas. Though far removed from Wolfe's normally lighthearted tone and subject matter, *In Cold Blood* makes use of many of the same fictional techniques as *The Right Stuff*: frequent shifts in point of view, strong characterization, heavy emphasis on setting and physical description, and dialogue.

If Capote, along with Norman Mailer in such books as *The Executioner's Song* (1979), is the tragedian of the New Journalism, Tom Wolfe has often been its chief satirist. With the publication of *The Kandy-Kolored Tangerine-Flake Streamline Baby* (1965), a collection of essays devoted to the popular culture of the early 1960's, Wolfe proved himself to be one of the most comically accurate observer-critics of American culture. *The Electric Kool-Aid Acid Test* (1968), which treats the West Coast drug culture of the 1960's, further established Wolfe's reputation as both a cultural critic and a prose stylist of the first order. In the 1970 *Radical Chic and Mau-Mauing the Flak Catchers*, his subject is fashionable political radicalism among the American ruling classes, while *The Painted Word* (1975) and *From Bauhaus to Our House* (1982) take on, respectively, the worlds of art and architecture.

The Right Stuff, which won both the American Book Award and the National Book Critics Circle Award in 1980, remains Wolfe's most honored book. Its colorful diction, its astute reading of the national psyche, and its bold sense of the absurd and the simply comic all make it vintage Wolfe. In some ways, though, *The Right Stuff* is unlike Wolfe's other books, for in it the author seems willingly to relinquish some of the critical detachment that characterizes much of the rest of his work. In *The Right Stuff*, Tom Wolfe joins the rest of the American public in unabashed admiration for the men who daily put their lives on the line in their quest for the stars.

Sources for Further Study

Bryan, C. D. B. Review in *The New York Times Book Review*. LXXXIV (September 23, 1979), p. 1.
Grimwood, James M., et al. *This New Ocean: A History of Project Mercury*, 1966.
Grissom, Betty, and Henry Still. *Starfall*, 1974.

Prescott, P. S. Review in *Newsweek*. XCIV (September 17, 1979), p. 93.
Sheppard, R. Z. Review in *Time*. CXIV (September 24, 1979), p. 81.
Yeager, Chuck, and Leo Janos. *Yeager: An Autobiography*, 1985.

James D. Daubs

THE ROAD TO WIGAN PIER

Author: George Orwell (Eric Arthur Blair, 1903-1950)
Type of work: History/essays
Time of work: The 1930's
Locale: Northern England
First published: 1937

Form and Content

For most countries the Great Depression began following the New York stock market crash of 1929. In Great Britain, the Depression merely worsened an already depressed economy that had been hard hit by the consequences of World War I. Between mid-1922 and 1929, the British economy had lurched from one crisis to another, with almost one-fifth of the adult male working force being on welfare (the dole) by 1929. Following the American stock market crash, the situation worsened, especially in northern England, the heart of British heavy industrial strength, where unemployment soon reached the one-third mark. Faced with an economic catastrophe of unparalleled magnitude, British politicians were unable to adopt measures which might have dealt humanely with the misery. Many intellectuals of the period, having lost faith in the political parties of the day, turned to socialism or to Marxism for cures to their country's economic maladies.

One group, the Left Book Club, provided its forty thousand subscribers with a monthly book whose aim was "to help in the terribly urgent struggle *for* World Peace & a better social & economic order & *against* Fascism, by giving . . . such *knowledge* as will immensely increase their efficiency." Coeditors Victor Gollancz, Harold Laski, and John Strachey commissioned authors to write works suitable to this task. One of the authors selected was George Orwell, then considered to be a developing voice for socialism. What the editors envisioned was a work in the tradition of Friedrich Engels' *Die Lage der arbeitenden Klasse in England* (1845; *The Condition of the Working Classes in England in 1844*, 1887) or Charles Booth's *Life and Labour of the People in London* (1891-1903). What the editors received was not quite what they had anticipated.

Orwell was asked in January of 1936 to make a study of the unemployed in depressed areas of northern England. Over the following two months, he visited Coventry, Birmingham, Liverpool, Manchester, Wigan, Sheffield, and Leeds, among others. Living with the people about whom he was to write, Orwell kept an extensive diary of observations. Upon his return, he transformed these observations into an intimate and illuminating account of the poverty, squalor, and hunger that he had witnessed. Yet his work transcended simple reportage. J. R. Hammond described it as "a social document of enduring worth . . . which is now acknowledged as a classic of the genre and as one of the seminal works of the inter-war years."

In part 1 of *The Road to Wigan Pier*, the literary genius which served Orwell well in later works such as *Animal Farm* (1945) and *Nineteen Eighty-Four* (1949) is amply demonstrated. In seven essays, Orwell describes his reactions to working-class life in northern England. Through Orwell, the reader can live and feel the pain, the suffering, and the hopelessness that the working class was enduring. Victor Gollancz wrote in his introduction to the work, "For myself, it is a long time since I have read so *living* a book, or one so full of a burning indignation against poverty and oppression." What Gollancz and his colleagues did not enjoy was Orwell's part 2, which is of a length equal to that of part 1. The six essays of this section are a passionate appeal for a less theoretical and a more human form of socialism than that espoused by many intellectual socialists.

To the credit of the Left Book Club, the book was published, although Gollancz did include a foreword which noted that he would like to argue with "over a hundred minor passages" in part 2. Since its initial publication, the book, in full or abridged form, has rarely been out of print. Despite its unevenness, the book is recognized as one of the most significant social documents of the Depression era in Great Britain. Its call for a humane solution to human misery is one that affects every generation.

Analysis

As noted above, *The Road to Wigan Pier* is divided into two parts of equal length. Part 1 is primarily a journey through despair. Orwell intended for his readers to be transported into the workplaces and slums of northern England. He therefore provides them with an account of squalid living conditions, the hopelessness of the unemployed, and the attitudes of the working class. More important, he describes people and their feelings; he wanted his reading public to know that his subjects were real people. Part 2 is his call for action. For Orwell, socialism is neither theory nor numbers; it has a human face. To him, intellectual snobs who believed that they had no prejudices and who thought that they could solve all the world's problems were out of touch with the reality that was the Great Depression. Orwell did not want to destroy socialism; he only wanted to humanize it.

The first essay of part 1 is the most literary of the seven which make up his portrait of northern England. Orwell's first-person description of life in the dreary Brooker lodging house is easily the most memorable segment of the book. He writes, "It is a kind of duty to see and smell such places now and again . . . though perhaps it is better not to stay there too long." By putting himself on the level of those about whom he would write, Orwell sought to gain immediate credibility. He wanted to be identified as a concerned and caring observer who was describing his own feelings regarding his observations. Those feelings serve to humanize his topic. This essay constitutes the pattern for the rest of part 1.

The following six essays, while more documentary in form, are nevertheless prose pictures of the underclass of British industrialism. Chapter 2, in which Orwell describes his descent into a coal mine, is a remarkable evocation of how it felt to be in such a mine. The heat and noise, the danger and difficulty of working the coal face, and the distances and time involved come alive in his narrative. He closes the essay by reminding his readers that human beings are responsible for the comfort which they enjoy: "Miners sweat their guts out that superior persons can remain superior." Succeeding chapters describe in similar fashion worker hygiene and nutritional habits, slums, social conditions, and industrial pollution.

In every chapter of part 1, Orwell attempts not only to portray a slice of working-class life but also to arouse the anger of his readers. Rarely is he analytical and dispassionate; each essay conveys deeply felt convictions. Orwell takes great care to show that workers are not mere statistics; they are living, breathing human beings who are in need. He concludes part 1 by noting that his experiences have reminded him that "our age has not been altogether a bad one to live in." Yet his seven essays show that for many of the underclass it was a miserable time to be alive.

Following this account of his tour of northern England, Orwell sounds, in part 2, a call to action. Orwell believed socialism to be not an economic creed but a humanitarian vision. He was angered by those socialists who were aloof from the working-class world and knew little about those they desired to manipulate. These six essays are considered almost unanimously, however, to be inferior to those in part 1. The reason is simple: In part 2 Orwell's statements and conclusions are generally polemical in nature and acerbic in tone. Yet he made them so for good reason. He was angry at the attitude of many socialists, and he feared the consequences of the failure of the doctrine. To Orwell, the only alternative to a viable socialism was totalitarianism. He desired to challenge socialists to improve their commitment to the cause.

Yet part 2 cannot be dismissed as mere polemic. In this section Orwell again makes clear his genuine concern for the workers. Nowhere does he define absolutely his version of socialism, but the reader can ascertain it quite easily. It is a humanitarian vision of justice, liberty, and decency for humankind. He believed that most socialists of his era were too aloof, doctrinaire, and impractical to attract converts. In great detail he outlines and discusses the aspects of socialism which repelled potential sympathizers. For example, "Socialism . . . is unattractive largely because it appears . . . to be the plaything of cranks, doctrinaires, parlour Bolsheviks and so forth." These cranks, he believed, would gradually become less significant in the socialist movement if practical, democratic socialists would assert themselves.

Of far greater concern to Orwell was the snobbery of many of the socialist theoreticians. He considered many of the leaders of the class struggle to be outright snobs who were quite disinterested in workers as a human beings. Chapter 9 is a brief autobiographical sketch in which he states that he himself had been "an odious little snob" as a youth but that he had cured the disease. For socialism to become a reality, he insists, other socialists would also have to cure that disease. His concluding chapter is a call for socialists to become familiar with the workers and to work with them in common cause. In particular, he calls for a socialism which would be "compatible with common decency."

Critical Context

The Road to Wigan Pier is a graphic, compelling account of George Orwell's visit to Lancashire and Yorkshire during the depths of the Great Depression in England. In it he also attempts to sketch a solution to the misery that he both witnessed and felt. The book itself was a pivotal work for him as many of the ideas and ideals which he had been been developing in earlier works such as *Down and Out in Paris and London* (1933) and *Keep the Aspidistra Flying* (1936) emerged clearly and powerfully in *The Road to Wigan Pier*. Moreover, despite some flaws, its style is far superior to that of his earlier efforts, and the work adumbrates the classics which he was later to write.

Orwell's political maturation is evident in *The Road to Wigan Pier*. From his autobiographical sketch in chapter 9 and from other biographies it is evident that Orwell, from a very early age, resented the class and caste barriers of his society. He was a deeply caring and idealistic humanitarian who viewed socialism as the only cure for a malaise-ridden industrial society. He greatly feared totalitarianism and believed that only socialism provided an alternative. *The Road to Wigan Pier* was clearly a watershed work for him, for it states clearly and forcefully that which he had only hinted in earlier works. Following it, he was a writer with a mission. The themes of dozens of essays, plays, and novels during the remaining years of his writing career reflect the conclusions reached in this seminal work.

While *The Road to Wigan Pier* is an example of political maturity which eventually resulted in modern classics such as *Animal Farm* and *Nineteen Eighty-four*, it was also a crucial work in the development of Orwell's writing style. Had he been content merely to cite and document his travels, the book would hardly have been memorable. His greatest ambition was to become a successful writer, and his earlier works demonstrate his efforts to discover a writing style which best suited him. With *The Road to Wigan Pier* he found his style. It was to be honest and straightforward, yet feeling and interpretive. His word pictures do not mask the appalling, nor do his polemics fail for lack of force. Orwell vented his passion on the printed page, and he continued to do so throughout the rest of his all too brief lifetime.

Sources for Further Study

Atkins, John. *George Orwell: A Literary and Biographical Study*, 1971 (revised edition).

Crick, Bernard. *George Orwell: A Life*, 1980.

Hammond, J. R. *A George Orwell Companion: A Guide to the Novels, Documentaries, and Essays*, 1982.

Hoggart, Richard. "George Orwell and *The Road to Wigan Pier*," in *Critical Quarterly*. VII (1965), pp. 72-85.

Meyers, Jeffrey. *A Reader's Guide to George Orwell*, 1975.

Stansky, Peter, and William Abrahams. *Orwell: The Transformation*, 1979.

Woodcock, George. *The Crystal Spirit: A Study of George Orwell*, 1966.

Zwerdling, Alex. *Orwell and the Left*, 1974.

William S. Brockington, Jr.

ROOTS
The Saga of an American Family

Author: Alex Haley (1921-   )
Type of work: History
Time of work: 1750-1975
Locale: West Africa and the United States
First published: 1976

> *Principal personages:*
> KUNTA KINTE, an eighteenth century Afro-American
> ALEX HALEY, the author

Form and Content

The inspiration for *Roots* came from a series of stories which the author, Alex Haley, heard from his grandmother during his childhood in Tennessee. These stories concerned the life of Kunta Kinte, an African born in the Gambia River region of West Africa. The stories relate that Kunta Kinte, when only a young man, fell victim to a slave-raiding party. Placed aboard a ship bound for Annapolis, Maryland, he entered a life of permanent servitude. According to the genealogies included in his grandmother's stories, Haley, a Coast Guard veteran and free-lance writer, was a direct descendant of Kunta Kinte.

Among the information passed on by Haley's grandmother was a smattering of terms from an unknown African language. Upon discovering that many of the characters in his grandmother's stories in fact were listed in census records in the United States National Archives, Haley became interested in discovering the birthplace of his ancestor. Questioning every colleague and resident African in the United States he could find, Haley eventually found his way to Jan Vansina, a noted African historian at the University of Wisconsin and an authority on oral tradition. Vansina tentatively identified the language of Haley's terms as Mandinka, which is spoken in Gambia and Senegal.

Haley's quest now took on the character of an obsession. He flew to Gambia and combed its villages in search of people who might know of the Kunta Kinte story. At length he discovered a *griot*, an elderly, prestigious bearer of oral history, who could recount the history of upriver Gambia in enormous detail. In the midst of the *griot*'s narrative came the tale of Kunta Kinte, his youth and his abduction, almost exactly as Haley's grandmother had told him as a child in the 1930's. Nearly overwhelmed by this discovery, Haley rushed home to compose *Roots*, six hundred pages that created a literary and public sensation.

The biography of Kunta Kinte comprises nearly two-thirds of *Roots*. The detail is as rich as if Haley had consulted archives and memoirs rather than the keepers of oral tradition. Kunta Kinte was born around 1750 to a Muslim family living in what is now Gambia. He went through the usual rites of passage for young men.

Already in their early years, Kunta Kinte and his friends heard from their parents of the dangers of *toubob*, white slavers who prowled the countryside in search of victims, and the nefarious *slatee*, Africans who abetted the slavers in their enterprises. (*Roots* also informs readers of the widespread practice of slavery within West Africa itself, as Kunta Kinte endeavors to learn from elders about the nature of slavery and servitude.)

Shortly after his initiation into manhood, Kunta Kinte himself stumbled into a *toubob* trap and was captured. According to Haley's archival research, Kunta Kinte and about 140 other enslaved Africans departed Africa aboard the American vessel *Lord Ligonier* in the summer of 1767.

Haley's account of the horrors of the Atlantic crossing almost defies belief. Crowded in chains into deck platforms so cramped that they could not sit up, racked by pain from whippings and body sores, forced to lie for days in their own body wastes, fed with indifferent slop, allowed only a few hours of exercise a week, weakened by contagious diseases, more than one-third of the slaves died during the crossing (along with a similar proportion of the white crew).

Even more than the physical suffering, the dread of the unknown was a source of anguish for the newly enslaved. Few had ever seen the ocean or a large ship; many thought that they were being taken to cannibals. Although the urge to fight back was strong among the slaves, before the crossing ended they had given in to despair.

Kunta Kinte, who refused to adapt to slavery despite repeated whippings, was the sole exception. Once in America, he escaped several times from his original owners, but on each occasion the unknown environment and the bloodhounds defeated him. Finally, to ensure that there would be no more escapes, Kunta Kinte's owners cut off the front part of one of his feet, leaving him a crippled domestic servant for the rest of his life.

Through the rest of Kunta Kinte's life, he underwent a slow transformation into the stereotype of a Southern slave. Although he became his master's carriage driver, was married, and had children, the indignity of slavery was never far away. The final humiliation—and his disappearance from the narrative—came when the master sold Kunta Kinte's daughter, Kizzy, to another owner. His spirit crushed, Kunta Kinte committed a symbolic suicide by destroying the gourd of stones which he had used for so many years to count lunar months and keep track of his age and the festivals of Islam.

The remainder of *Roots* sketches the lives of Kunta Kinte's descendants through Kizzy's line. Based on family recollections, the reconstruction moves rapidly through seven generations, covering the nineteenth and early twentieth centuries, including characters both slave and free, until it reaches Haley himself. Throughout these generations, the few terms from Mandinka which Kunta Kinte had passed on to his daughter were carefully preserved and transmitted, so that Haley would hear them as a child from his grandmother.

The final three of the 120 short chapters in *Roots* contain Haley's personal narrative of his exposure to the Kunta Kinte story and of his life as a youngster, as a member of the Coast Guard, and later as a free-lance author. They relate his personal quest to confirm the story and the dramatic moments in which his archival research and his conference with the *griot* revealed the ancestral link to Africa.

Analysis

Roots is much more than a book, even a very successful one. (It sold 1.5 million copies in the first year alone.) The appearance of *Roots* created a major sociological and cultural phenomenon. It captured the public imagination as few other works by American authors in the twentieth century have. In January, 1977, a seven-part serialization of *Roots* appeared on national television. Even though the dramatization was one of the earlier examples of the miniseries genre, ten years later several episodes of *Roots* remained among the ten highest rated offerings in the history of television. Any assessment of the impact and nature of this work must account for this unusual fact: In its first several years of publication far more people "watched" *Roots* than read it.

The central scholarly question about *Roots* is a simple one: Is the work history or fiction? Was the genealogical reconstruction sound? Was it possible to glean such enormous detail about the life of Kunta Kinte, an eighteenth century character with nothing extraordinary in his background, from a contemporary *griot*?

Haley characterized *Roots* as a work of "faction," implicitly somewhere between "fact" and "fiction." The numerous literary citations given to the work, including the National Book Award and a Pulitzer Prize, acknowledged that *Roots* belonged in a special category. To Haley, "faction" was a genre in which documented historical facts were held together by a fictionlike narrative informed by generic works on the periods or topics in question. The genealogy in *Roots*, Haley claimed, rested on documents and sound scholarship; the kinship links were real and not imagined. Most of the details of Kunta Kinte's life came from Haley's knowledge of what the youth of an eighteenth century Muslim male in the Gambia region must have been like.

Roots has been severely criticized in terms of both of the major elements of "faction." Although Haley had done some interviewing in the course of his free-lance career, he had no formal training in genealogical research. Scholars who attempted to verify his findings turned up innumerable discrepancies in data and method. Specialists in African oral history discovered that Haley's main informant in fact was not an officially recognized *griot* but only a local—and not particularly respected—storyteller, aware well in advance of the sort of information Haley sought.

In the opinion of historians, Haley's efforts to date the Kunta Kinte story through his informant's obtuse references to the appearance of English soldiers in the area are unconvincing. Virtually every genealogist who examined Haley's African material concluded not only that Haley failed to establish a credible link between the Kunta Kinte story of the Gambia and that of his grandmother but also that the evidence, properly handled, weighed heavily against such a link. Several doubt that

Kunta Kinte ever existed, either in Gambia or in North America.

The extent of Haley's mismanagement of genealogical material is all the more apparent in that he bungled the relationships even among the owners of the slave Toby, whom Haley believed to be Kunta Kinte under a name given by his masters. Kunta Kinte mysteriously disappears from *Roots* after Kizzy is sold, according to Haley, to a new owner in another state. Yet genealogists who examined relevant title deeds more carefully than Haley later showed that the two white familes involved in this slave sale were next-door neighbors.

Roots, in short, does not begin to meet the rigorous standards of modern genealogical research. The evidence strongly suggests that the links Haley established among himself, his family, Kunta Kinte, and the Gambia region are invalid.

The historical research which informs Haley's "faction" also bears little resemblance to scholarship. As Haley informs his readers in the final chapters of *Roots*, he gathered material indiscriminately from books, conversations, personal experience, and a variety of media. *Roots* contains no bibliographical citations; several other authors subsequently filed lawsuits alleging that Haley had taken material from their works on Africa. (The courts dismissed all but one of these suits.)

The fictional portions of *Roots* reflect a popular stereotype of slavery and the transatlantic slave trade more than they do recent historical research. Many of the more lurid passages in *Roots* are derived from generalized and impressionistic sources written earlier than, or without reference to, systematic and exhaustive historical research in African history begun in the 1960's. Widely accepted stereotypes about slavery and the slave trade need to be qualified in terms of time period, geographic locality, and local conditions; some do not stand up at all to careful scrutiny.

One historian, for example, took issue with the kidnapping of Kunta Kinte, pointing out that slave traders in Gambia in the eighteenth century seldom, if ever, resorted to raiding. At that time the region was under the sway of the Mandinka state of Niumi, a well-organized and sophisticated entity quite capable of retaliating against any European who brought such chaos to the country. *Roots*, it would appear, is something other than simply bad genealogy. It is also bad history.

How, then, does one account for the phenomenal success of *Roots*? Why did this work touch the hearts of so many Americans? Why did thousands of black Americans actually create a tourist boom in Gambia as they sought to walk where Haley had walked? Part of the answer must lie in the timing of the book's appearance. It coincided with celebration of the bicentennial of American independence, a time of heightened public awareness of every aspect of the national heritage.

Many analysts have suggested an even deeper meaning to *Roots*. The United States is an entire nation of immigrants and descendants of immigrants. Long before Haley published *Roots*, popular interest in genealogy had been on the rise. *Roots* expressed a widespread yearning among Americans for the security of a knowable past as distinct from the systematic doubt of professional historical research. If it confirmed myths, it did so because myths are important.

Prior to the appearance of *Roots* few black Americans had entertained the thought that tracing their families back to specific localities in Africa was feasible or even possible. *Roots* suggested that the sense of heritage and ethnic continuity so important to other immigrant communities in the United States might also be articulated by black Americans, that they also might understand themselves, as other groups do, as part of, yet apart from, the United States.

Perhaps the most important reason for the success of *Roots* was simply that Haley believed, and his readers believed. Alex Haley brought his own passion to this work. His readers thrilled because Haley's own heart raced when he found documentary evidence of his ancestors. *Roots* will continue to be a cherished work and an important event, not because of its veracity or lack of it, but because when he heard of Kunta Kinte from the lips of the Gambian, its author broke into tears.

Critical Context

Alex Haley's only other major work is *The Autobiography of Malcolm X* (1965), for which he interviewed the subject and produced a biography at the latter's request. (Critics have charged that Haley actually did a better job of abiding by the standards of oral testimony in this work than he did in *Roots*.)

One of the difficulties of assessing *Roots* lies in the fact that the book created its own critical context. The impact of the book can never be separated entirely from the consequences of the television production. Criticism also has been arrayed in the context of much broader questions, such as that of the contrasting roles of scholarly and popular history in affecting culture, or the question of what constitutes legitimate limits for the genre of "faction." Essays and reviews about *Roots* thus have an astonishing variety of scholarly pedigrees. The breadth and depth of the criticism itself helps to ensure that *Roots* will remain an important episode in twentieth century American literature and history.

Sources for Further Study

Baldwin, James. Review in *The New York Times Book Review*. LXXXI (September 22, 1976), p. 1.

Gerber, David. "Haley's *Roots* and Our Own: An Inquiry into the Nature of a Popular Phenomenon," in *Journal of Ethnic Studies*. V (Fall, 1977), pp. 87-111.

Haley, Alex. "In Search of 'The African,' " in *American History Illustrated*. VIII (February, 1974), pp. 21-32.

——————. Interview by J. F. Baker, in *Publishers Weekly*. CCX (September 6, 1976), pp. 8-9.

Massaquoi, H. J. "Alex Haley: The Man Behind *Roots*," in *Ebony*. XXXII (April, 1977), pp. 33-36.

Mills, Gary B., and Elizabeth Shown Mills. "The Genealogist's Assessment of Alex Haley's *Roots*," in *National Genealogical Society Quarterly*. LXXII (1984), pp. 35-49.

_____. "Roots and the New 'Faction': A Legitimate Tool for Clio?" in *The Virginia Magazine of History and Biography*. LXXXIX (January, 1981), pp. 3-26.

Reuter, M. "Two Writers Question the Originality of *Roots*," in *Publishers Weekly*. CCXI (May 2, 1977), p. 20.

Sheppard, R. Z. Review in *Time*. CVIII (October 18, 1976), p. 108.

Waters, H. F., and V. E. Smith. "One Man's Family," in *Newsweek*. LXXXVII (June 21, 1976), p. 73.

Wright, Donald R. "Uprooting Kunta Kinte: On the Perils of Relying on Encyclopedic Informants," in *History in Africa*. VIII (1981), pp. 205-217.

Ronald W. Davis

RUSSIAN THINKERS

Author: Isaiah Berlin (1909-   )
Type of work: Historical essays
Time of work: The nineteenth century
Locale: Primarily Russia
First published: 1978

> *Principal personages:*
> LEO TOLSTOY, an author well-known for his novels, short fiction,
>   and other writings
> ALEKSANDR HERZEN, a Russian writer and political philosopher
> MIKHAIL BAKUNIN, a Russian thinker known for his anarchist
>   leanings
> VISSARION BELINSKY, a prominent literary critic
> IVAN TURGENEV, a well-known writer of prose fiction

Form and Content

While Isaiah Berlin's writings have dealt primarily with political philosophy and the history of ideas, at times such categories have been broadly defined. Moreover, though problems and patterns in British and European thought have been his most prominent concerns, issues affecting Russia's position in the wider context of Western intellectual life have fascinated him as well. Some of Berlin's most celebrated and provocative pronouncements have dealt specifically with matters of this sort, where the ideas of Russian thinkers took on a wider significance largely through the operation of theoretical conceptions in unusual but appropriate settings.

The essays collected in *Russian Thinkers* were delivered or published between 1948 and 1970; several of them originally were public lectures, while others appeared as articles in academic journals or in other published formats. There is much continuity among the various works in this collection, while editorial selection has limited any effects of repetition or undue prolixity.

Many of the traits commonly associated with Berlin's writing are in evidence in these essays. From outwardly modest beginnings major ideas take hold and sentences build breathlessly upon one another as new images and thoughts are constructed in what at times seems to be a tumultuous array of facts and concepts; the more informal though no less complex delivery found in his lectures has been preserved in those essays that have been taken from that format. At times Berlin appears attentive to the interests of his audience; some statements resound with dramatic effect, while others provide color and vividness to what otherwise might have been rather recondite matters. There is also a kind of boldness, and a willingness to take on vast and challenging topics; indeed, the author was hardly daunted by the large and perplexing tasks that he had set for himself. There are few reservations or modifications that he has felt constrained to make even amid sweeping judgments that go beyond the received wisdom about intellectual change in Russia. Still, Berlin displays a certain specific charm and an active sense of sympathy, where it is due, for the historical personages he treats.

Analysis

The first article reproduced in *Russian Thinkers* considers the position of Russia during the revolutionary year of 1848. While major outbreaks swept over much of continental Europe, Russia remained unmoved; the seemingly unshakable power of the autocracy left many authors and journalists in despair. For a time, it had been possible for ideas to be discussed openly in Russian cities. Some interest was expressed in French utopian socialism; other stances critical of the existing order had been addressed as well. Russian writers had, during much of the 1830's and 1840's, turned away from the stultifying versions of official ideology that were promoted under government auspices. By 1848, with the czarist regime's stern and unyielding reaction to unrest elsewhere on the Continent, a spirit of resignation descended upon the nation's writers. In the absence of any appreciable social basis for the support of liberal or radical ideas, in a society where the peasantry had little political power and industrial growth had scarcely begun, few expectations for social transformation existed in any immediate sense. Subsequently, even with the advent of relatively new and different ideological trends, pronounced and long-lasting divisions set in; many important figures embraced values that were grounded in national and religious ideals, while others turned toward increasingly radical and intransigent postures. Thus, paradoxically, the weakness or absence of any significant revolutionary or reform movement during the middle of the nineteenth century foreshadowed the mounting polarization of educated public opinion that later was characteristic of Russian politics and social thought. Moreover, even earlier literary controversies had assumed much wider implications, and problems of values and ideas arose repeatedly in connection with later concerns.

The most famous of Berlin's Russian essays is "The Hedgehog and the Fox," in which the theory of history implicit in Leo Tolstoy's major fiction is discussed in relation to problems of systematic thought in a number of leading figures. Enlarging upon a phrase taken from a verse fragment by the classical Greek poet Archilochus, Berlin posits distinctions among creative and critical thinkers which would divide those from many traditions and historical periods into two groups. This distinction has been received readily and applied in many places beyond those where Berlin originally employed it. For Berlin, some individuals conceive of ultimate facts as embraced within a single system; others regard essential reality as evading such rigid criteria. Any effort to formulate all-encompassing rules that would apply to experience is subject to modifications and exceptions. Among those who belong to the first category, of hedgehogs, are Plato, Dante, G. W. F. Hegel, and Fyodor Dostoevski; Herodotus, Aristotle, Johann Wolfgang von Goethe, Alexander Pushkin, and James Joyce are cited as outstanding examples of foxes. This schema is not merely intended to distinguish between those who, on philosophical grounds, could be regarded as monists or pluralists, though the differences may be envisaged partly in this sense.

A peculiar and fascinating feature of Tolstoy's thought, as expressed primarily in his great novels, is that by attempting to demonstrate the validity of one single truth he reached results of a rather different order. In *Voyna i mir* (1865-1869; *War and Peace*, 1886), problems of historical meaning led to wider concerns with issues of causation that were examined at many points in Tolstoy's research and writing. The tension between individual experience and human action on a grand scale was reflected in the contrasts he drew between the inner lives of his protagonists and the political careers of historical characters, such as Napoleon and Alexander I, who could be taken as exemplifying both personal and national influences upon the historical process. Whether history was subject to impersonal laws, and whether it could, or indeed should, attain the status of an exact science, were questions that would affect his handling of major historical events.

In certain respects Tolstoy was inclined to take liberties with the historical record which had formed the basis for his original research—in his novel he transformed the Russian commander Mikhail Kutuzov into a heroic figure who was depicted in somewhat more grandiose terms than was warranted for his real-life counterpart. Tolstoy's views on historical matters owed much as well to other thinkers; he read the works of Jean-Jacques Rousseau, the French social and political philosopher, and he had perused Stendhal's fiction, partly for the sake of its literary evocation of actions during the Napoleonic Wars. Berlin has uncovered as well some of the more unusual sources of the Russian writer's thought. Tolstoy also pondered the writings of Joseph de Maistre, the émigré political and religious theorist who in his opposition to the French Revolution had produced essays and dialogues during a prolonged sojourn in St. Petersburg. Although on other counts Tolstoy was hardly in accord with de Maistre's conservative and antirationalist position, the Russian writer was intrigued with the notion that military operations, and other mass movements, were essentially chaotic and unpredictable; according to this view, facile expectations that social progress was inevitable, and that patterns of historical change could be discerned, were vain and impracticable.

Among explicitly political thinkers Berlin has singled out Aleksandr Herzen and Mikhail Bakunin as the most significant and representative writers of the Russian revolutionary tradition; the differences between them illustrate the divided paths by which socialism and anarchism became part of Russian ideologies of the nineteenth century. Although the two men at times were friends, their ideas could not be reconciled. Both opposed the autocracy and both placed particular hopes in the advancement of the peasantry; both rejected middle-class values and were profoundly distrustful of religious systems. Yet Herzen, in recoiling from the ethereal systems proffered by European thinkers, retained a balanced sense of critical realism; Bakunin, on the other hand, professed an abstract devotion to humanity which did not, in the end, restrain him from advocating terrorism and destruction in their most extreme forms. On many points Herzen found fault with broadly inclusive doctrines that offered some solace for humanity's plight; he remained in many respects a skeptic who was adept at noting that many expectations for social improvement could not be sustained. Vital in his thought was the conviction that moral principles were not to be repudiated or dispensed with; Herzen was prepared to uphold the value of individual freedom against fraud, violence, or oppression. For his part, Bakunin was adept at destructive argumentation; in exposing the pretenses and equivocation of conventional moral thought, his writings evinced a powerful simplicity that, to some, was attractive largely because of its undeniable rhetorical impact. Still, in urging the overthrow of established governments and institutions he promoted ideas that had no deeper means of support. While invoking the ideals of liberty and equality, he was able to arrive at no particular means by which such values could be preserved. According to Berlin, this inability to achieve a suitable equilibrium between social purposes and moral aspirations, which in varying forms could be found in Herzen as well as in Bakunin, was a recurrent problem in Russian political thought which affected the ideas of later activists down to the Revolution of 1917.

The origins of the intelligentsia in Russia, however, could be found in an earlier period. The longest essay in this work, which originally comprised a series of articles and lectures, deals with "A Remarkable Decade," the years between 1838 and 1848, when a number of major writers became involved in literary and philosophical controversies. Western thought, both French utopian socialism and German metaphysics, was received with some alacrity by Russian thinkers; even with this quite unabashed enthusiasm for foreign systems, some typically Russian features emerged in major publications of this era. The moral dimensions of art and literature and the conviction that some higher purpose should guide intellectual pursuits were almost universally accepted among writers of consequence. During this time, Dostoevski, Turgenev, and others first came into prominence as literary men, while Herzen and Bakunin began to concern themselves with social issues. The most noteworthy and significant figure among them was the literary critic Vissarion Belinsky. Berlin maintains that social criticism originated in Russia and appeared specifically during this period; moreover, Belinsky, who was recognized as the leading proponent of moral ideas in literary theory, devoted much of his career to the searching and fearless exposition of the enduring values great literature was meant to evoke. He provided Russians with the first outlines of a literary history which could distinguish between the outmoded relics and the lasting achievements of past writers; in addition, in his relentless quest for truth he instilled in others the conviction that art was in every sense answerable to life and that great literature could not endure without commitments to social justice and equality. To be sure, there was much that could be considered superficial, or overwrought, about Belinsky's positions; he often wrote in some haste, and without regard for the relationship ideas had to one another. Yet the undeniable force of his convictions could greatly impress his contemporaries.

In connection with the initial development of social thought, there is also a discussion of Herzen's early years, when he manifested some of the traits which would make him, in Berlin's estimate, "the most arresting Russian political writer in the nineteenth century." Even at the outset, before he emigrated from Russia in 1847, he appeared to have become uneasy at the specter of victimization and human suffering that might attend any effort to implement even the most high-sounding and outwardly altruistic principles. On the other hand, and perhaps in keeping with the example of his friend Belinsky, Herzen seemed markedly uncomfortable with any position which might suggest compromise or intellectual complacency. This fundamental outlook, which in time took form as the libertarian humanism for which Herzen was noted, eventually set him at odds with both revolutionary and conservative groups. More than that, however, even from a distant vantage point he could grasp the unfolding of wider processes leading ultimately to the Russian Revolution without condoning the drift toward intolerance and the advocacy of violence that began to affect subsequent political agitation.

The remaining articles deal with Russian populism, Tolstoy's theories of enlightenment, and the political implications of Turgenev's fiction. In a short essay on Tolstoy's views about education, Berlin contends that, while he often seemed to suggest that formal learning and moral scruples were in some sense incompatible, upon closer examination the great writer's views were rather more complex; as with his historical theories, Tolstoy did not easily disclose the full contours of his thought. Turgenev had often been reproached for remaining aloof from political controversies; many of his protagonists were cast as archetypal figures who resembled the very embodiment of political attitudes, and troubled questions of his own times were raised in rather forthright ways in some of his most famous writings. Nevertheless, Turgenev seemed rarely to express his own views, or to suggest whether he had any particular positions or affiliations. Even in his well-known novel *Ottsy i deti* (1862; *Fathers and Sons*, 1867), in which he composed some vivid and provocative depictions of young nihilists, it was not certain where Turgenev's sympathies actually lay. Turgenev was acutely sensitive to charges that were leveled against him, but he remained stalwart in his conviction that literature should serve the purposes he had found for it. By recognizing the political dilemmas of his own age, Turgenev implied that moral fervor should not take the place of understanding. Indeed, Berlin concludes that his doubts may have been well founded in the light of the turmoil and destruction that more rigid forms of political commitment later caused.

Critical Context

Although most of Berlin's other writings have dealt with other intellectual traditions, some affinities of subject matter may be found in various works. In his first major study, *Karl Marx: His Life and Environment* (1939), he dealt with the philosophical ideas and assumptions that were prominent in the views of the most important single socialist thinker; problems of causation and determinism were of some significance in his evaluation of Marx and his theories. Issues that Berlin found salient in Tolstoy's view of history were discussed against a much more general background in *Historical Inevitability* (1953). In other studies of Western thought, the distinction between monists and pluralists has often been raised, sometimes in a variety of contexts. Another problem that frequently arose in Berlin's discussion of Russian intellectual life has been considered on a more extensive basis in *Two Concepts of Liberty* (1958). Elsewhere, Berlin has published several articles dealing with the Soviet intelligentsia and major issues in modern Russian culture, which concern developments during the twentieth century; in these, the author notes the contrast between Soviet thought, which had become rather constrained and muted, and the vigorous and wide-ranging activity of earlier generations. Although Berlin has preferred to present his works in the form of essays and lectures and thus has not attempted to provide a comprehensive or thoroughgoing assessment of major movements in modern ideas, his studies of important Russian thinkers form part of a wider body of writings which provide penetrating and far-reaching interpretations of significant intellectual currents of the modern centuries.

Sources for Further Study
The Christian Science Monitor. Review. June 28, 1978, p. 19.
Hausheer, Roger. "Isaiah Berlin and the Emergence of Liberal Pluralism," in *European Liberty: Four Essays on the Occasion of the Twenty-fifth Anniversary of the Erasmus Prize Foundation*, 1983.
The New Leader. Review. LXI (September 25, 1978), p. 17.
Ryan, Alan, ed. *The Idea of Freedom: Essays in Honour of Isaiah Berlin*, 1979.
The Times Educational Supplement. Review. July 7, 1978, p. 28.
The Washington Post Book World. Review. June 18, 1978, p. E6.

J. R. Broadus

S/Z

Author: Roland Barthes (1915-1980)
Type of work: Literary criticism
First published: 1970 (English translation, 1975)

Form and Content

By 1970, when *S/Z* first appeared, Roland Barthes had already established his reputation in France as the most influential formulator and advocate of the philosophical approach to literature, film, myth, and other cultural artifacts known as structuralism. Yet, in spite of the publication of several theoretical pieces by Barthes, anthropologist Claude Lévi-Strauss, and others, which explored the implications of structuralism and its usefulness for understanding myth and popular culture, the approach still lacked a full-scale practical application of its methods to a literary work. It is this deficiency that Barthes sought to remedy with *S/Z*, his tour de force study of a single fictional work.

Although structuralism seems to work best when used to approach either highly formalistic myths and folktales or twentieth century avant-garde works, Barthes chose for his exercise in practical structuralist criticism a little-known novella by the great nineteenth century French realist Honoré de Balzac titled *Sarrasine* (1831). Whereas Balzac's novella is only about twelve thousand words long, Barthes's discussion of the work is approximately seven times that length. Although *S/Z* is an exercise in detailed close reading somewhat reminiscent of the poetry explications of the American formalist critics of the 1940's and 1950's, because of structuralism's divergence from formalism's focus on poetic unity and thematic integrity, it is quite distinct from that approach.

Instead of attempting to show the organic unity of the work, the intrinsic relationship between the content and style, and ultimately the central theme, as a formalist critic might, Barthes instead wishes to show that the work is pluralistic rather than unified, inconclusive rather than thematically solid, and self-reflexive rather than mimetically referential. In keeping with this atypical and iconoclastic purpose, Barthes's method is similarly unique.

First of all, Barthes breaks up or decomposes the novella into 561 units of meaning; some of these units, which Barthes calls "lexias," are sentence-length, some are merely phrases, and some are groups of sentences. He then examines each lexia separately and consecutively throughout the book in a sort of sentence-by-sentence annotation. The commentary on each lexia is not, however, based on the formalist assumption of the relationship of technique to theme, but rather on the structuralist assumption that a literary work communicates by participating in, or drawing from, various conventional literary and cultural codes. Thus, each commentary identifies each lexia in terms of the code or codes on which it depends.

Barthes defines five codes which inform the work: the *proairetic*, which governs the way the plot of the story is organized; the *hermeneutic*, which governs the presentation of puzzles and their solutions; the *semic*, which determines the way characteristics are attributed to personalities and thus create character; the *symbolic*, which enables the reader to move from details in the text to thematic meanings; and the *referential* code, which provides a cultural matrix of values from which the story draws.

In addition to this division of the work into code-bound lexias, Barthes provides ninety-three brief digressions, most of them a page or so in length, in which he comments on the theoretical and practical implications, for literature in general or narrative in particular, of the code-determined lexia which he has just discussed. Many critics believe that it is the methodology of analyzing the work in terms of codes and the digressions, miniature essays on theoretical matters, that constitutes Barthes's major contribution in *S/Z*. It is not the interpretation of Balzac's novella that constitutes the work's importance, for it is not an interpretation of the story that Barthes is seeking, but rather an exemplum of the means by which narratives communicate—not what *Sarrasine* means, but rather how *Sarrasine*, and therefore narrative in general, means. Balzac's novella, reconstituted in its original form, although with each lexia numbered, is included at the end of the book in an appendix, along with an index of the lexias identified.

Analysis

Roland Barthes's approach to Balzac's novella is based on several important theoretical assumptions about the nature of literature derived from the study of linguistics. What the structuralist attempts to do, says Barthes, is decompose an object (a literary work, a film, or any other cultural creation) and then reconstruct the object in such a way as to make clear the rules by which the object functions— that is, the very means that make it possible for the object to be a cultural object and communicate itself as such. For Barthes, although an artwork may seem to copy something outside itself (for example, the novel *Huckleberry Finn* may seem to copy or "be about" the adventures of a young boy in mid-nineteenth century America); it is not the nature of the copied object that makes the work an artwork, although that is a prejudice of a realistic approach to literature. Instead, what makes Mark Twain's novel a novel is the technique that differentiates it from the hypothetical "real world" that it seems to imitate.

What the structuralist activity succeeds in creating, says Barthes, regardless of whether it is engaged in by an artist or by a critic, is a simulacrum or similitude of an object or an experience which differs from the original object in that the simulacrum makes clear or lays bare the means by which the original object is perceived; that is, its functions or structure. The structuralist activity thus makes the object intelligible or meaningful.

This approach is based on the basic assumption of modern linguistics and semiotics (the study of signs and sign systems) that the meaning of anything which can be communicated is determined not by its essence but by differences within a patterned structure; what makes the object meaningful is its position within the pattern, that is, its difference from, or boundaries between, other objects. There is no essential connection between the sound a person makes when he says "zipper" in English (what structuralists call the "signifier") and the mental concept he has when he utters or hears that sound (what structuralists call the "signified"); there is only an arbitrary connection which speakers of English have agreed upon. The sound "zipper" refers to a fastener, while the sound "sipper" refers to one who drinks slowly only because of the difference between the *s* and the *z*, that is, that the *s* is a voiceless dental sound and the *z* a voiced dental sound.

Moreover, structuralists such as Barthes argue that in trying to understand a story such as Balzac's *Sarrasine*, one cannot understand the narrative as it exists as a similitude of actual events. Such events which take place in time, as they seem to do in everyday life, are, after all, merely "one damn thing after another"; in order to render these events intelligible, one must decompose them, break down their sequence into units, and then recompose them according to some principle other than simply that they take place in time. One must break up the temporal flow of the events which follow the principle of combination (what structuralists call the "syntagmatic") into sets of events that follow the principle of similarity of function (what structuralists term the "paradigmatic"). This is what Barthes does in *S/Z*. By using the five codes, he decomposes the "one-damn-thing-after-another" temporal flow of the story into lexias (that is, separate bits of information) based on their derivation from the five paradigmatic codes; then he "reads" the story in terms of the relationship between the paradigmatic codes, not in terms of the syntagmatic narrative flow.

Finally, Barthes makes a distinction between two kinds of narrative works to make his purpose in *S/Z* clear. One is typified by the so-called realistic works of the nineteenth century, works such as *Sarrasine*, in which the primary emphasis is to direct attention to its so-called referent, that is, what it seems to be about. These works Barthes calls *lisible*, or "readerly." The connection between the signifier and the signified in such works is so firmly grounded in the reader's "realistic" notion of reality that he does not make a distinction between them. He assumes that when one is talking about the work (which is after all a map of some assumed real "territory"), one is indeed talking about the territory itself. On the other hand, there are works which Barthes calls *scriptible*, or "writerly." In these works, the reader is not led to forget the work as a work or map and to leap immediately into what the work seems to be about, but rather to focus on the means by which the work makes the reader think it is "about" something outside itself. In "writerly" works, the reader is made to focus on the "literariness" of the work itself, that is, its existence as a map made up of differences rather than reality made up of some hypothetical essential actuality.

In effect, what Barthes does by analyzing a "readerly" work such as *Sarrasine* is to demonstrate that even the most "realistic" work is actually not realistic at all, but rather drawn from artistic and cultural conventions and codes which in fact constitute their very being as artworks. Although the title *S/Z* refers to the initial letters of the two primary characters in the novella, the sculptor-protagonist, named Sarrasine, and the object of his desire, the beautiful opera singer Zambinella, it could just as easily refer to the basic example of "difference" he uses in his essay "The Structuralist Activity" (1963); that is, the voiced and voiceless difference between the sounds [s] and [z]. For it is indeed difference, and particularly a difference that is not easily perceived as difference, which motivates the narrative. The basic premise of the plot is that Sarrasine falls in love with Zambinella ignorant of the fact that she is not really a woman at all, but rather a *castrato*, a castrated man who Italian custom dictated had to play the soprano part in opera.

Although Barthes is indeed interested in the thematic implications of this pot-boiler plot, for in many digressions he discusses the issue of masculinity and femininity and the complexity of one parading as the other, he is interested in using the work as an excuse for practicing his sophisticated "structuralist activity," the most important aspect of which is the creation of the five master codes. In order to understand how important Barthes's notion of codes is, one must realize that for the structuralists the very stuff which makes up literature is not raw "life," for that in itself cannot be communicated, but rather the literary and cultural conventions which make the creation and communication of meaning possible. For Barthes, the text of a work is actually a meshing of many previous, already-written texts; thus, when we speak of texts, we are really speaking of intertextuality. Every lexia in *Sarrasine* owes its existence to one or more of the five codes Barthes determines; the lexias, or coded elements, are fragments, he says, of that which has already been read, seen, done, experienced, or written.

The hermeneutic code (from a Greek word which designates the art of interpretation) includes the lexias which either formulate a question or pose a response to a question. Because stories always progress as a series of questions and answers (the basis of suspense), the hermeneutic code is the primary code of storytelling itself. For example, a question such as "Is he her husband?" belongs to the hermeneutic code because it poses a question which the story moves toward answering. The proairetic code, from a Greek word referring to the ability to determine the result of an action, is simply the code of sequence; it determines the syntagmatic flow of the narrative as being one thing following another in sequence. For example, in the opening sentence of *Sarrasine*, "I was deep in one of those daydreams," the act of "being absorbed" is an example of an event determined by the proairetic, or action, code. The notion of being in a daydream, however, makes this opening lexia also part of what Barthes calls the symbolic code, because it sets up a tension between two states—"day" and "dream"—an antithesis which is so frequently repeated throughout the story that it takes on thematic significance.

The final two codes Barthes describes are culturally bound. The semic code encompasses culturally stereotyped characteristics which readers attach to particular proper names, thus making them take on the role of fictional characters. The referential code is the most clear-cut cultural code, because it embodies the knowledge, wisdom, or values of the culture from which the work derives. For example, a sentence that refers to the long and laborious time it takes to become a sculptor partakes of a referential, or cultural, code of art which suggests a difficult apprenticeship, whereas Sarrasine's distracting himself in church by whittling on a pew is part of a semic code of Sarrasine's impiety which makes him a transgressor in the eyes of the reader.

Throughout *S/Z*, as Barthes divides the story into lexias and places each within the code that makes it meaningful and gives it communicative power, he also pauses to digress on those aspects of the lexia which deserve further generalization and commentary. These ninety-three digressions constitute some of the most salient points and theoretical implications of Barthes's study. It is within these digressions that he makes clear the logic that underlies his use of codes, the text's inevitable intertextuality, the distinction between a "readerly" and a "writerly" text, the means by which narrative creates character, the means by which the text creates thematic meaning—in short, the very means by which any text becomes a text, a narrative that paradoxically can communicate in a purely temporal way that which exceeds temporality. The many mysterious means by which meaningless action is transformed into meaningful discourse are the subjects of these theoretical mini-essays. Taken altogether—the concept of dividing the work up into lexia, the attributing of each meaningful unit to a preexistent artistic or cultural code, and the many theoretical ideas which derive from this process—all this makes Barthes's *S/Z* one of the most important critical documents in twentieth century literary studies.

Critical Context

Most critics and commentators agree that *S/Z* is Roland Barthes's masterwork, a *summa*, or compendium of his views, a model of practical structuralist analysis. The work has even been called one of the most celebrated masterworks of contemporary criticism. Barthes's method has been much imitated since the publication of *S/Z*, and the ideas which Barthes generated in the many "digressions" in the work have proved fruitful for subsequent critics. Much of what is now called "narratology," that is, the theoretical study of narrative structure, derives from *S/Z*.

The book falls into a tradition of critical analyses which use individual works from which to derive theoretical knowledge about the nature of narrative. Although the tradition is as old as Aristotle's study of tragedy in the *Poetics*, the most immediate predecessor within the twentieth century formalist tradition is Vladimir Propp's *Morfologiya skazki* (1928; *Morphology of the Folktale*, 1958). Other, more recent, works within this tradition are Claude Lévi-Strauss' structural study of myth in 1955 and Tzvetan Todorov's study of Giovanni Boccaccio's *The Decameron* in 1969.

In terms of Roland Barthes's own life's work, many critics believe that *S/Z* not only constitutes a high-water mark in his career but also signals Barthes's impending shift from structuralism to poststructuralism, for in the work he moves beyond structuralism's concern with discovering "deep structures" of unity and totality toward the purposeful fragmentation and undermining of such an effort which is typical of modern "deconstruction." Regardless of whether readers see *S/Z* as the high point of structuralism or the harbinger of deconstruction, no one interested in modern literary theory can afford to ignore it. When structuralism as a methodology and deconstruction as a point of view pass away from current literary criticism to be replaced by yet another critical perspective, *S/Z* will still remain for the valuable insights it provides readers into the nature of narrative.

Sources for Further Study

Culler, Jonathan. *Roland Barthes*, 1983.

––––––––––––. *Structuralist Poetics: Structuralism, Linguistics, and the Study of Literature*, 1975.

Hawkes, Terrence. *Structuralism and Semiotics*, 1977.

Johnson, Barbara. *The Critical Difference: Essays in the Contemporary Rhetoric of Reading*, 1980.

Leitch, Vincent B. *Deconstructive Criticism: An Advanced Introduction*, 1983.

Scholes, Robert E. *Structuralism in Literature: An Introduction*, 1974.

Sturrock, John, ed. *Structuralism and Since: From Lévi-Strauss to Derrida*, 1979.

Charles E. May

THE SACRED JOURNEY

Author: Frederick Buechner (1926-　　)
Type of work: Autobiography
Time of work: 1926-1954
Locale: The United States and Bermuda
First published: 1982

　　　　Principal personages:
　　　　FREDERICK BUECHNER, a writer, teacher, and Presbyterian
　　　　　　minister
　　　　GRANDMA BUECHNER, his paternal grandmother
　　　　NAYA, his maternal grandmother

Form and Content

　　The Sacred Journey is a narrative of Frederick Buechner's first twenty-seven years of life, interspersed with the insights he gained from remembering and telling the story.

　　The book begins with an introduction and then is divided into three parts: "Once Below a Time," which describes his life until he was ten, up to the day his father killed himself; "Once upon a Time," the account of his years from ten to seventeen, when he was graduated from preparatory school; and "Beyond Time," which tells of the next ten years until he started theological seminary. The whole book is 112 pages long, with approximately thirty-five pages given to each main part.

　　The contents of the book are stories of those events that had the greatest impact on the spiritual development of the author. The story is striking because the end result was so unlikely. Buechner was born into a family that had nothing to do with Christianity, and he enjoyed very little church influence in his formative years. In addition, he had to endure the devastating losses of his father and uncle to suicide, raising the fear that he too would be touched by that plague. Those events could easily have led him to believe that life is meaningless at best, or evil at worst, but instead he came to believe that life is the gift of a good Creator. As an adult, he became a Presbyterian minister and a writer of lucid, accessible theological books.

　　Focusing as he does on his spiritual life, his sacred journey, Buechner leaves out much that he could have included. In the sequel to *The Sacred Journey*, titled *Now and Then* (1983), he notes that in the earlier book he had left out everything that had to do with sex, money, travel, health and films, all of which were of great importance to him. In addition, he pays almost no attention to the public events of the world around him. He describes formative events (such as his father's death and the family's move to Bermuda), the most important people (especially his grandmothers), and the characters in books who profoundly influenced his imagination. The most important stories for him were those in which he was touched by the mystery from beyond that he did not know how to name during most of the period this book covers.

The central theme of the book is that God continually guides and speaks to human beings, but does so through their daily experiences, both good and bad. Buechner shows how he was drawn to Christ by events that he did not recognize at the time to be manifestations of the presence and guidance of God. Thus, his purpose in writing is not only to illuminate his sacred journey but to encourage others to see their own lives as such a journey. He invites readers to remember their own past and try to discern the ways in which God has been speaking to them through it.

The reader Buechner addresses is the literate adult interested in spiritual matters. He does not assume that his readers are Christians, nor that they know much about the Christian viewpoint. Instead, he writes in language that is free from theological jargon, focusing on human experience in general, so that all sensitive readers can identify with the story and find parallels in their own lives.

The tone of the book is confessional, not self-laudatory. Buechner is one of the foremost American religious writers, so the book could have been a celebration of success, but instead it is a celebration of the gift of God's coming. Constantly the author stresses his own weaknesses and failures while pointing to the grace of God at work in hidden ways that only became apparent in hindsight.

Analysis

Buechner's central thesis in *The Sacred Journey* is that God speaks to individuals in their daily lives, through the events that strike home to them. He stresses that the meaning of those events is often mysterious, ambiguous, cryptic, when first they appear. Indeed, in his own life the steps on his sacred journey were usually unrecognized as such when they happened. Only later, upon reflection, seeing where he had finally arrived, did he understand that many small events were actually divinely guided turnings on the road that led finally to service to Christ. He wrote this book to present some of those events in his own life, hoping that the theological truth he had discovered would shine through to others. He hoped that when others saw how small events could have eternal importance, they would learn to look at their own lives in the same light. Therefore, the most appropriate way to suggest something of the substance of the book is to recount a few of the more striking incidents that the author presents.

During his first decade of life, the period called "Once Below a Time," Buechner was sick for almost a year. At that time, he became an avid reader of the Oz books, especially loving one of the characters, King Rinkitink. This king was plump and somewhat foolish, given to bursting into tears, but had remarkable strength, resilience, and courage. Though he was vulnerable and silly in many ways, he was strong and wise in others, so that he always managed to overcome his troubles, riding away on the back of his goat, Bilbil. The greatest of the services Rinkitink offered to the young invalid Buechner was through advice he received from a magic white pearl. The pearl told the king that the world is filled with wonders, and Buechner found that to be great wisdom which remained with him throughout his life. In addition, the way Rinkitink succeeded in life prepared the young Buechner for the later wisdom of Saint Paul, who said that God chose those who are foolish, weak, and low as the agents by whom to redeem the world.

When his father committed suicide, Buechner's childhood ended. With his mother and his brother, the ten-year-old boy left the United States to live in Bermuda. That beautiful island became his own Land of Oz. It was a place where the terrible past could be forgotten and a new life begun. The most memorable of the experiences the young boy had there took place just before he left, at the age of twelve. As he sat with a girl his own age on a wall beside the harbor, their bare knees happened to touch. The effect was to fill him with panic, anguish, and longing for he knew not what. Into his whole being swept a hungering love for the beauty of the universe, which he later came to realize was a hunger for Beauty itself, which lies at the heart of and behind the universe. For the first time in his life he was a giver of love, not simply a receiver, which made him reach out for Paradise, longing to find an ineffable something that he could not identify. Recognizing that he had been given a gift in this overwhelming longing, he wondered if there was a Giver behind it.

Such memorable moments became for Buechner the promptings of a crazy, holy grace. It is crazy because it is totally unexpected: Out of the longing and pain and joy of daily life, something arises that touches and moves and exalts one. It is holy because it comes from farther away than Oz and produces healing. Thus, these moments are stages on the sacred journey, one that is a search for whatever lies deeper than one can see. The human being searches for his true self, and for other selves to love, and for work, but even when those are found the journey has not been finished. Something is still missing, and the search for that unfound thing must continue.

In Buechner's search during those adolescent years, Jesus began to enter in. One of his vivid memories is of a pastel drawing of the head of Jesus by Leonardo da Vinci. The face is tired, with eyes closed, looking like the face of a man to whom everything had happened. For some reason the picture moved him; it seemed to afford him an authentic glimpse of who Jesus really was and so remained alive in his memory.

Another gracious gift was given to him at Lawrenceville School, where he went in 1940. There he had an English teacher, Mr. Martin, who led him to see that words have power, that they can evoke much more than they mean, that they can make things happen by bringing characters and events to life. One day Mr. Martin gave him a perfect grade of 100 for a character sketch, a grade that was clearly a gift, and it had the effect of turning Buechner in the direction he went thereafter: He decided that he wanted to be a writer. Among the things he wrote were many poems which made references to Jesus. For some reason that the older Buechner could not identify, Jesus was present in those poems as He is surprisingly present in many other times and places and characters. For the young man of seventeen, the strange presence of Jesus was a sign of the Something he could not name, the haunting and mysterious spark of a reality mostly known by its absence.

Another ray of that divine light shone on Buechner in the army, on a cold wet evening as he sat in the mud. Hungry, he got a turnip from another soldier, a turnip covered with mud. Slowly eating the turnip, with mud still on it, he realized that both were good, that even the drizzle and the cold and the army were good. It seemed that the whole of the world was good, that the ultimate goodness and joy of things was such that if you ever really took them to heart you would have to rise up and praise someone for it. Who exactly to praise he was not sure, but the praise bubbled up and prepared him for the time when he would know.

After two years in the army, he returned to Princeton, where he concentrated on becoming a writer. He began his first novel and through that experience deepened his understanding of life. As he created a plot for his novel, he came to see that life itself may have a plot, that events that seem random can have a direction of their own. Instead of the story being aimless, it can be seen as the result of something secretly at work within one, leading one toward significance. The first line of his novel describes a man in a barber chair looking like a priest—a whisper of the direction in which Buechner was heading. That first novel was a best-seller, the one that made him famous. He saw it as a gift, an undeserved success, something that he needed to work hard to justify.

During those years immediately after college, one more whisper of the divine voice broke into what he calls his self-centered life, when a friend and fellow teacher cried out for help over the telephone. Buechner was at dinner with his mother at the time, and she was very upset at the thought of his leaving abruptly, voicing all the excuses that he had been preparing to make. Hearing them spoken openly, however, he realized that this selfishness was appalling. His friend's voice came then to be the voice of God, calling him out of his comfortable world into the dangerous battle where Christ is found. He came to see that only by journeying for others does one really begin to come alive: a new turning on his sacred journey.

Finally, in 1953, he went to New York to become a writer and heard the preaching of George Buttrick, one of the foremost Presbyterian preachers in the country. One particular sermon lifted him to the skies, when Buttrick said that Jesus is crowned in the hearts of people in confession and tears and great laughter. The phrase "great laughter" so moved him that it brought this stage of his journey to an end. He stepped through the door that he realized had been open for him for some time. He discovered what he had been seeking most of his life: He found Christ, and heard a call to enter the ministry. The next fall, he entered Union Theological Seminary.

Critical Context

The Sacred Journey can most appropriately be seen as a chapter in the long story of Christian confessions, those in which the writer shows how God graciously pursued him until he finally heard His calling. The most famous is perhaps Saint Augustine's *Confessiones* (397-400; *Confessions*), but the one that is most comparable to *The Sacred Journey* in the twentieth century is perhaps C. S. Lewis' *Surprised by Joy: The Shape of My Early Life* (1955). Lewis, too, tells a story of being touched by the mysteries when he was young and then gradually, over many years, being drawn to realize that the One who was calling him was Christ. There are two central parallels between Buechner's and Lewis' life stories. Both were highly imaginative young readers who loved fantasy and found themselves living in the wondrous worlds that the fantasy writers created. Buechner's world was Oz, Lewis' was the world of the Greek and (especially) the Norse myths. Furthermore, both of them found these fantasy worlds arousing in them a longing for something that they could not define. Lewis calls this longing "joy"; the Germans call it *Sehnsucht*. For both men, this longing for something that glimmered in their experience drove them to seek until they finally found the Mystery that lies at the heart of reality.

The major difference between Buechner and Lewis is that the latter was a rationalist in addition to being a lover of imaginative fantasy. Lewis believed that a certain amount of God's truth could be distilled and presented in rational form that believers could rationally accept. Buechner, on the other hand, stresses the mystery of God, never seeking to prove the reality of the divine in the way that Lewis did in his apologetic works.

Finally, *The Sacred Journey* must be seen in the context of the author's two other works of autobiography. The earliest is *The Alphabet of Grace* (1970), in which he describes God's presence and speaking in a single day of his life. The last of the three is *Now and Then* (1983), in which he takes up the story from his entrance into the seminary until the time of his writing of the book.

Sources for Further Study

Buechner, Frederick. Interview with J. F. Baker, in *Publishers Weekly*. CCXXI (February 12, 1982), pp. 32-34.

_____. Interview with Shirley Nelson and Rudy Nelson, in *Christianity and Literature*. XXXII (Fall, 1982), pp. 9-14.

_____. "Listening to My Life." Interview with Kenneth L. Gibble, in *The Christian Century*. C (November 16, 1983), pp. 1042-1045.

Lischer, Richard. Review in *The Christian Century*. XCIX (October 13, 1982), p. 1025.

McCoy, Marjorie Casebier, and Charles S. McCoy. *Frederick Buechner: Novelist/ Theologian of the Lost and Found*, 1988.

Price, Reynolds. "The Road to Devotion," in *The New York Times Book Review*. LXXXVII (April 11, 1982), pp. 12, 28-29.

Woelfel, James. "Frederick Buechner: The Novelist as Theologian," in *Theology Today*. XV (October, 1983), pp. 273-291.

Peter W. Macky

A SAFE-CONDUCT

Author: Boris Pasternak (1890-1960)
Type of work: Autobiography
Time of work: 1900-1930
Locale: The Soviet Union
First published: Okhrannaya gramota, 1931 (English translation, 1945)

Principal personages:
BORIS PASTERNAK, a Soviet poet
RAINER MARIA RILKE, a German poet
ALEKSANDR SCRIABIN, a composer
HERMANN COHEN, a German philosopher
AN UNNAMED WOMAN, Pasternak's beloved
VLADIMIR MAYAKOVSKY, a Soviet poet

Form and Content

The death by suicide of Vladimir Mayakovsky in 1930, partly a result of that poet's deep disillusionment with the changes in Soviet society and literature at the rise of Joseph Stalin, precipitated a "second birth" in the artistic activity of Boris Pasternak. Begun before Maykovsky's death, *A Safe-Conduct* is the poet's first autobiography, written when he was under forty. This prose work is an assessment of formative influences on his work as he attempts a new approach to his poetry.

Pasternak said he conceived of the work as "something midway between an article and artistic prose, dealing with the way in which life was transformed into art, and why." The work appeared first serially, in two parts in different journals, before it appeared as a separate volume in 1931.

A Safe-Conduct is by no means a detailed chronology of the poet's first forty years, but accounts of a series of encounters with key people, together with meditations on these episodes. The work begins with a childhood memory and ends with the death of Mayakovsky. It is in three parts, each made up of short sections. These accounts include straight narrative, sensitive representations of landscape, conversations with the key figures in the poet's coming to define and accept his role, other random details of his life at each period, and his thoughts about the experiences represented.

A Safe-Conduct is dedicated to the contemporary German lyric poet Rainer Maria Rilke, who is shown to be essential to Pasternak's views. The extent to which Rilke influenced Pasternak is clear in Pasternak's words, "I am not presenting my reminiscences to Rilke. On the contrary, I myself received them from him as a gift." The poet first met Rilke on a train when he was ten; in a later discussion, he describes finding Rilke's poems among his father's books and drawing sustenance from them throughout his life.

The next section skips three years to a time when the Pasternak family became acquainted with the Scriabin family. The boy's first idol was Aleksandr Scriabin, the composer. With his mother being a pianist and his father a painter, Pasternak at first saw himself as a musician and composer: "More than anything in the world I loved music, and, in music, more than anyone else, Scriabin." Pasternak was, however, aware that he did not have perfect pitch, and when as a teenager he played his compositions with great success for Scriabin, the older man's failure to acknowledge the same defect in himself showed his feet of clay. When Pasternak's idol's hold on him broke, the boy's commitment to music broke as well, though in retrospect he sees that he was using Scriabin's reaction only as a pretext; he had already intuited that he would not be a composer.

Pasternak turned then to the study of philosophy, first in Moscow and then in Marburg, with the famous professor Hermann Cohen. A statue of the thirteenth century Elizabeth of Hungary, patron saint of Marburg, made a deep impression on him; he was moved by her compassion for suffering people. He met the intellectual challenge of philosophy at the university with ease, but a visit to Marburg of the young woman whom he loved brought to a definitive end his potential career as academic philosopher. Pasternak proposed to the girl, but she rejected him; the cataclysm of his emotional reaction taught him more about himself than all of his philosophical investigations. "I was surrounded by changed things. Something never before experienced had crept into the essence of reality." The encounter led to Pasternak's sustained thinking about the nature of art and to his career as a poet. A commitment to reality in art, and his definition of that reality, emerged from the new life afforded to him by the young woman's rejection.

One other important event occurred in Marburg. The night before he was to meet Cohen to announce his new commitment to poetry, he had a prescient dream of war, a forecast of the coming world war. He distinguishes the "because" mind of his professor from the intuitive artistic understanding that knows what it knows without a reason.

A short visit with his family in Italy intervened; he offers brilliant images of Venice and Venetian architecture and painting. "I, too, had the fortune of discovering that day after day one could go to meet a piece of built-up space as though it were a living personality." Venetian painting helped him to understand more about the way art mirrors reality and about the continuity of Western culture. He realized that Russia too participates in that stream.

Part 3 finds the poet back in Russia. Briefly joining a group called Centrifuga, he entered the world of the "innovatory" art emerging in the years before the Revolution. The leading light of the dominant new group, the Futurists, was Vladimir Mayakovsky, and this giant of a poet was the next hero for the young Pasternak to worship, though Mayakovsky was about his age. Pasternak provides a vivid sketch of the enormously talented Mayakovsky, whose poem *Vladimir Mayakovsky* (1913; English translation, 1968) made a tremendous impression: "Actually I carried the whole of him with me that day from the boulevard into my life." Yet he could not get accustomed to Mayakovsky's work, so novel was the poetry. When, after the

Revolution, Mayakovsky began to propagandize in his poetry, however, Pasternak's interest in him waned. Despite the close, deeply respectful relationship of these two poets, their reactions to the demand for poetry to serve politics finally drove them apart. Mayakovsky's sympathetic understanding of Pasternak's very different poetry, and the innovations in technique and content that Mayakovsky's best poetry provided, had moved Pasternak along in his definition of poetry and his understanding of his own role as a poet.

The autobiogaphy ends with an account of Mayakovsky's suicide. The importance to the poet of facing death was mentioned early in the work; the close of the work praises Mayakovsky as the only poet truly of the new epoch, representing the Revolution and all the change, the only one so far to have mastered the future. Clearly Pasternak here turns to his own future.

Analysis

A *Safe-Conduct* is an intellectual autobiography, tracing in memory Pasternak's choice of poetry as the dominant preoccupation of his life. The turning points arise from subconscious motives, but the work is the effort to bring these choices into the light of the mind, showing the poet's emerging understanding of art and of his poetic aims. A *Safe-Conduct* is rich in the theoretical formulations that, carried out in his works, constitute the real life, the biography, of this artist. Just as he sees the value of Rilke's poetry in its influence on his own work, so Pasternak's unique legacy is his ideas about art, embodied in his works. His autobiography shows the coming into being of these governing preoccupations.

A safe-conduct is a document allowing a person to proceed without interference. What Pasternak seems to have meant by this title is some benevolent protection, perhaps within himself, allowing him to find his way to his vocation. The purpose of the account is to achieve a new artistic orientation. The method is reflection on past events involving five significant human figures in his life: Rilke, Scriabin, Cohen, a beloved girl, and Mayakovsky.

In *A Safe-Conduct*, the importance of Rilke is in Pasternak's definition of what the biography of a poet must contain. It cannot follow the "vertical" line of chronological narrative. The subconscious of the poet operates in the lives of his readers, as Rilke does in his, and it is in these multiple responses that the "life" of the poet is written.

Pasternak's ten-year absorption in music and Scriabin throughout his adolescence he sees as a means to self-definition: "We have all become people in the measure in which we have loved people and had the opportunity to love." Failure to love unreservedly is to be afraid of the "sacrifices tradition demands of childhood," to choose to remain common, uncreative. Scriabin, responding favorably to the young Pasternak's musical compositions, emphasized simplicity as necessary in great art; works rich in content, he said, are simple. According to critic Henry Gifford, Pasternak's intense experience in music and his insights from Scriabin's music and personality inform his later poetic techniques. He learned intricate organization of sound effects, the power to communicate meaning through sound devices, and musical structure in verse and prose.

While still ostensibly committed to music, Pasternak began to explore more general questions about the nature of art. He describes his student existence with random details: reading in philosophy, becoming acquainted with poets such as Andrey Bely and Aleksandr Blok, the way the sun moved over the house where he lived. This randomness becomes part of his theory of poetry: What causes poetry to be born of this reality? He answers that experience comes in irregular ranks. Love and the sun (or weather) are the most important elements, but the slower ranks of experience lag behind; a backward glance at them is the source of inspiration.

Pasternak devotes almost a third of *A Safe-Conduct* to the time he spent in Marburg studying philosophy. The exploration with Cohen of primary works of philosophy and the rigorous discipline of scientific thinking left a lasting imprint on Pasternak's work. He continued to pursue his effort to see the eternal in the momentary. Nevertheless, the young man realized that philosophy was only an aspect of his interest, not the center.

The visit of the girl he had loved since age fourteen, and her rejection of his marriage proposal, precipitated the perception of reality that became the key to his approach to poetry. The city looked totally changed after the emotional torrent at his rejection, a change that showed him that poetry (and art in general) concerns such "coming into being." Art records the dislocation of actuality caused by feeling; the new world exists independently of himself.

> We cease to recognize reality. It presents itself in some new category. This category seems to us to be its, not our, condition. Except for this condition everything in the world has been named. It alone is unnamed and new. We try to name it. The result is art.

The insight accounts for the disappearance of the poetic "I" in Pasternak's work; his poetry depicts the outward. The function of the artist is to name the reality newly seen; finding out how to describe the external brings it into being, and that is the excitement of the poem. Almost any detail of the reality may be chosen, since it all participates in the eternal reality. The poet must choose, in his haste to catch what he sees, established words that must be newly understood.

Pasternak's dream before he left Marburg shows how the poet knows what he knows. The dream made clear that the intuitive life of poetry is the life he must follow. The deep encounter with Mayakovsky provided the means for distinguishing further the nature of Pasternak's own poetic gift from that of other poets. The vitality of the groups committed to new poetry sharpened his understanding of his own views; he could not long stay a part of any group, so individual was his stance. In characterizing Mayakovsky, Pasternak develops his concept of the Romantic poet. Mayakovsky's poses represent the highest self-expression, never achieved among the untalented, but this presentation of the self becomes "biography as spectacle." It is in fact a view of poetry as the life of the poet, what Pasternak calls Romantic. He sees that this view is "vivid and irrefutable in its symbols," but he himself rejects it because it "needs the veil of mediocrity in order to be seen." Romanticism requires philistinism.

Pasternak sees the discontinuity between the outward and the inward Mayakovsky, and he deeply admires Mayakovsky's representation of reality and, in his early work, the "infinity which opens out in life from any point and in any direction." Pasternak, however, chooses to deemphasize the self, finding it displaced in "the created world and the world yet to be created." The background of his own work is not mediocrity but the miracle of being.

By the time Pasternak absorbed the fact of Mayakovsky's suicide, his own direction as a poet was defined. He sees Mayakovsky's life, "now utterly past," as moving down into and becoming "some quiet tree-planted street." Mayakovsky is the one who has had the "newness of the times climatically in his blood," as strange himself as the new age is strange and half realized. The new age provides a displacement of reality paralleling the displacement Pasternak suffered upon his rejection by the woman he loved. The future, which Mayakovsky had understood but violated in his propaganda poetry, is the focus at the book's conclusion.

Angela Livingstone's translation of *A Safe-Conduct* gives an accurate sense of its richness of style. Pasternak later repudiated this shifting, metaphorical style in favor of greater simplicity, but readers find the style of the early autobiography valuable in itself. The tone is contemplative and appreciative. The book's vividly realized details seem at times casually chosen as if the writer could choose others and more, suggesting the richness of the world represented. At other times the details are selected with great discrimination and economy, to communicate the quality of important characters and episodes.

Critical Context

A Safe-Conduct gained resonance from Pasternak's second look at the same years. Toward the end of his life, he published an additional autobiographical essay: *Avtobiograficheskiy ocherk* (1958; *I Remember: Sketch for an Autobiography*, 1959). This work reevaluates the people so crucial to the author's development, this time in the light of their meaning for his central work, the novel *Doktor Zhivago* (1957; *Doctor Zhivago*, 1958). Leo Tolstoy therefore figures as the underlying inspiration as Rilke does in the earlier work, which focused on poetry. In the later work, Pasternak shows that Scriabin's emphasis on tradition nevertheless allowed the renewal of an art "from its very foundation." He deemphasizes his relation to Mayakovsky and clearly condemns suicide; his own survival when others gave up he attributes to strength drawn from memory. The importance of autobiography to Pasternak is emphatic, both in assessing the values of the poets close to him and in understanding the shape of his own artistic development.

The reputation of *A Safe-Conduct* is very different in the Soviet Union from its reputation in the West. Immediately attacked as subversive when it was published as a book in Pasternak's homeland, it was banned and withdrawn from libraries as not appropriate to the Soviet literary policy of Socialist Realism just emerging into official definition in 1931. Nevertheless, Pasternak's continuing commitment to the Revolution and some curious respect on Stalin's part for the poet kept him alive and free when many artists of the 1930's were arrested and imprisoned or exiled. The rejection of his work by the Soviet literary establishment grew; Pasternak was required to refuse the Nobel Prize in 1958, and he was officially isolated for the rest of his life.

A Safe-Conduct became known in English translation in the West, where the political context did not impinge, only after 1945. It has been considered all during the growth of Pasternak's international reputation as a major source of the poet's literary biography, valued for its slender biographical data and its insight into his aesthetic.

Sources for Further Study
Davie, Donald, and Angela Livingstone, eds. *Pasternak*, 1969.
Erlich, Victor, ed. *Pasternak: A Collection of Critical Essays*, 1978.
Gifford, Henry. *Pasternak: A Critical Study*, 1977.
Hughes, Olga Raevsky. *The Poetic World of Boris Pasternak*, 1974.
Mallac, Guy de. *Boris Pasternak: His Life and Art*, 1981.

Martha Manheim

SALVADOR

Author: Joan Didion (1934-)
Type of work: Cultural criticism/current affairs
Time of work: 1982
Locale: El Salvador
First published: 1983

Form and Content

In the summer of 1982, American novelist, essayist, and journalist Joan Didion visited the war-torn Central American nation of El Salvador; *Salvador* is the record of what she found there. Didion's stay in El Salvador came at a time when the United States' policy in this tiny republic was very much under fire, and her analysis never strays far from the essentially political question of what the United States government hopes to gain in a seemingly irreconcilable conflict. Part reporter's notebook, part ironic travelogue, *Salvador* defies categorization. It is perhaps best described as an extended meditation on the hopelessness of communication between North and South American cultures and, by extension, on the futility of the colonial drive to "Americanize" a culture with a different history and geography.

The political situation into which Didion steps is complex. After years of brutal civil war between factions of the Right and Left, an American-style election has recently brought to power José Napoleon Duarte, the United States-backed "centrist" candidate for president. According to Didion, the administration's official view of the election as a success, a demonstration of democracy in action, is simplistic and grotesquely optimistic. To the American government, El Salvador is a strategic stronghold in the fight against creeping Central and South American Communism; Didion's El Salvador, contrasted throughout the essay with the official American interpretation, is a morass of incompetence, corruption, and bloodshed. Both the Cuban- and Soviet-backed Sandinistas on the Left and the forces of the Right, backed by the nation's ruling classes and headed by Roberto D'Aubuisson, are, to Didion, equally to blame for the slaughter endemic to the area. Bodies literally line the streets of San Salvador, the capital city, and are thrown into huge dumps in outlying areas, victims of "death squads" affiliated with both ends of the political spectrum. Political allegiances, so important to the American government, lose their significance in Didion's analysis, in which the most appalling aspect of the situation is neither left- nor right-wing extremism but the nonchalance with which daily "body counts" are taken.

Salvador (ironically, the word means "savior" in Spanish) is organized roughly chronologically according to Didion's stay in El Salvador, beginning with her landing at the improbably located national airport and ending with her anxiety-ridden departure from that same airport. The middle portions of the brief book are concerned with various excursions, each of which becomes part of the pervasive sense of unease that to Didion characterizes the country and its people: lunch with the American ambassador, Deane Hinton; a day trip to the war-ravaged town of Gotera; a pointless and irritating cultural festival in the village of Nahuizalco; a symbolically significant visit to El Salvador's National Cathedral, site of the murder of Archbishop Arnulfo Romero. While any of these events might figure in a conventional travelogue, each takes on an eerie "through the looking glass" quality in Didion's treatment, interspersed as these episodes are with Didion's commentary on the surreal atmosphere of this illogical and cruel place and with ironically placed quotations from official State Department documents about the American government's role in the "democratization" of El Salvador. Two strictly "literary" quotations, taken from the works of the Polish-born British novelist Joseph Conrad and the Colombian novelist Gabriel García Márquez, lend the essay the illusory and symbolic quality of fiction.

Analysis

Since the journalist-narrator of *Salvador* is so often at a loss for words, since the time-honored practices of her trade seem so often to fail her in this alien territory, it is fitting that the word "ineffable" appears so frequently in this disturbing book. Didion seems constantly unable to "report" this story in conventional terms, for the rules keep changing and the lines are not clearly drawn. "Objectivity" seems impossible. The "gringa" writer well-known for her 1975 essay "On the Mall" writes of a visit to San Salvador's largest shopping mall:

> This was a shopping center that embodied the future for which El Salvador was presumably being saved, and I wrote it down dutifully, this being the kind of "color" I knew how to interpret, the kind of inductive irony, the detail that was supposed to illuminate the story. As I wrote it down I realized that I was no longer much interested in this kind of irony, that this was a story that would not be illuminated by such details, that this was a story that would perhaps not be illuminated at all, that this was perhaps even less a "story" than a true *noche obscura* [dark night].

Elsewhere, Didion writes of a dinner meeting with the grandson of a former El Salvadoran dictator, that for the "first time in my life . . . I had been in the presence of obvious 'material' and felt no professional exhilaration at all, only personal dread." The professional journalist is rendered helpless not only by the illogical nature of the place but also by the omnipresent sense of personal danger. Mindful that American and European journalists have been murdered and that their murderers have gone uncaptured, Didion writes more than once of being "humiliated by fear." Thus, *Salvador* is less a story than a mood piece about an unspeakably terrifying time and place.

The sense of place is ubiquitous in *Salvador*, Didion's thesis being that the country itself, the very landscape, goes far toward explaining the seemingly irrational behavior of its people and the indecipherable political situation that obtains in the last quarter of the twentieth century. Once again, Didion links the climate of

El Salvador with her own background and with earlier essays with which her readers might be familiar. Recalling perhaps her 1966 essay "Some Dreamers of the Golden Dream," which speaks of the nerve-shattering effect of the Santa Ana wind of Southern California, Didion tells of the contagious nervousness brought on by "earthquake weather" but then as quickly denies the link between El Salvador and the California of her childhood: "It is always earthquake weather in San Salvador, and the jitters are endemic." Nervous tension is terminal in El Salvador, a ghastly by-product of climate and geography.

Like a good reporter, Didion tries at one point to link the political situation in modern El Salvador with the country's history, with the usurpation of native culture by European and North American colonialism, but then realizes that such a linkage would be facile, since there was very little native culture to usurp. Writing of the cultural festival mentioned earlier, Didion recalls that El Salvador has always been a sort of no-man's-land, "even before the Spaniards arrived. The great Mesoamerican cultures [such as that of the Aztecs] penetrated this far south only shallowly. The great South American cultures [such as that of the Incas] thrust this far north only sporadically." Deprived of both native tradition and a distinguished modern history—Didion tellingly points out that El Salvador has no *libertador*, no great national hero—Salvadorans lack the sense of national identity that North Americans and even most other South and Central Americans take for granted, an absence which adds yet another aspect to the confusion.

This through-the-looking-glass atmosphere, this sense of having stepped into a dark and sinister other world, is reflected in the Salvadoran use of language; indeed, linguistic illusion is a strong secondary theme in *Salvador*. Didion, adopting the persona of a journalist accustomed to the literalness of words, writes of the chilling Salvadoran usage of the word *desaparecer*, meaning "to disappear":

> [It] is in Spanish both an intransitive and a transitive verb, and this flexibility has been adopted by those speaking English in El Salvador, as in *John Sullivan was disappeared from the Sheraton; the government disappeared the students*, there being no equivalent situation, and so no equivalent word, in English-speaking cultures.

"Disappear," with its magical connotations, is used in El Salvador to describe people who have been abducted and very probably murdered either by government forces or by left- or right-wing death squads. That murderers usually go uncaptured or unidentified, that the motive behind political murders often goes unexplained, makes the notion of "disappearance" both appropriate and criminally self-delusory. This national capacity for metaphor extends, says Didion, to the Salvadoran use of numbers and statistics, which seldom bears much correspondence to the truth. Didion notes that Salvadorans tend to use numbers subjectively: A million, for example, might be used to denote any very large number, a practice that makes the use of statistics nonsensical.

Yet this persistent use of figurative language is not limited to Salvadoran nationals; English speakers, including American journalists and representatives of the

United States government, have begun to adopt Salvadoran syntax "as if a linguistic deal had been cut." Didion observes that high-flown language is often used to camouflage the brutal truth of the political situation: The muddled election, for example, is referred to as *la solución pacífica* (the peaceful solution), while the mass murder of troublesome insurgents is termed "pacification." Didion seems here to be recalling the British essayist and novelist George Orwell, whose 1946 essay "Politics and the English Language" argues that shoddy terminology leads to shoddy political thought and, ultimately, to political travesties being hidden beneath imprecise words. Certainly Didion would agree with Orwell that the complicity of the United States in the chaos that is El Salvador begins with the decision to accept duplicitous rhetoric.

Nor is Didion herself exempt from the corrupting influences of the place, its language, its climate; she admits at several points to falling victim to the pervasive atmosphere of confusion and terror. After a few days in El Salvador, this sensitive *norteamericana* becomes as desensitized as any Salvadoran to the nightly accumulation of bodies in the streets and at "body dumps"; after a few nights, this celebrity journalist becomes as skittish and paranoid as any Salvadoran wife, mother, or sister. Further, El Salvador induces in her a new way of seeing. In one of the book's most darkly comic passages, Didion describes an American-style beauty contest, the "Señorita El Salvador" pageant, which is televised on the same evening that the earthquake occurs. In trying to get at the essence of the absurd events of this day—Didion had met earlier in the day with the former dictator's grandson— she quotes a passage from García Márquez's 1975 novel, *El otoño del patriarca* (*The Autumn of the Patriarch*, 1975). The quotation has to do with the novel's hero, a South American dictator, taking as his lover a girl from the slums. García Márquez, modern Latin America's well-known novelist, is famous as a member of the literary school of Magical Realism, a style more reliant on fancy than on fact, on memory than on documentation. In his brilliant novels and short stories, for example, children are born with tails and old men sprout wings. Didion then admits that on the day of the luncheon, the beauty pageant, and the earthquake, she began to see García Márquez "in a new light, as a social realist." Thus, El Salvador has forced Didion to see things as a Salvadoran would see them; no longer a teller of fantastic tales, García Márquez has become for her an objective observer of social and cultural reality.

Perhaps the most devastating comment on the perceptual change that El Salvador has on Didion, however, is contained in the book's epigraph, a passage from Joseph Conrad's *Heart of Darkness* (1902), the narrator of which has been sent into the African interior in search of his long-lost countryman, Kurtz, who has earlier been charged with "civilizing" the natives and colonializing the region. In the passage Didion quotes, the narrator, Marlow, has come upon an eloquent and rational report that Kurtz has written for his superiors at the International Society for the Suppression of Savage Customs. At the end of the document, however, Marlow finds a chilling postscript:

There were no practical hints to interrupt the magic current of phrases, unless a kind of note at the foot of the last page, scrawled evidently much later, in an unsteady hand, may be regarded as the exposition of a method. It was very simple, and at the end of that moving appeal to every altruistic sentiment it blazed at you, luminous and terrifying, like a flash of lightning in a serene sky: "Exterminate all the brutes!"

Never again in the course of the book does Didion refer back to this passage, nor does she need to, for the import is clear: Having been indoctrinated to El Salvador and its savagery, its seemingly incurable "vocation for terror," Didion is able at least in part to empathize with the rage that the crazed Kurtz felt at the alien culture in which he found himself. Didion makes a profound comment on the colonial impulse to Westernize, Christianize, Europeanize, Americanize members of other cultures when she admits her momentary urge instead to "exterminate" them.

Critical Context

The Reagan Administration's Central America policy was much on the minds of many Americans at the time of Didion's visit to El Salvador; to many, the administration seemed, both in El Salvador and in Nicaragua, to be repeating the mistakes that had sunk the United States in the quagmire of Vietnam some two decades earlier. To the administration's critics, the urge to halt the spread of Marxist regimes south of the United States' borders was both unnecessary and futile; the conservative Reagan Administration, however, insisted that Soviet influence lay behind the flourishing of Marxist rebellion and cited the Monroe Doctrine as justification for putting down left-wing insurgence.

Joan Didion's readers already knew, at the time of *Salvador*, that she was no left-wing intellectual. Right of center in her politics, she was but one of many thinking Americans who found American solutions to the Salvadoran problem misdirected and, to use one of Didion's favorite phrases, "beside the point." In the confusion of El Salvador, Didion found a perfect outlet for her formidable powers of observation and cultural criticism; earlier, she had written near-legendary studies of cultural chaos in the essays "Slouching Towards Bethlehem," a study of the San Francisco countercultural movement of the early 1960's, and "The White Album," which considers the frantic revolutionary years of the later 1960's. Both essays share much in common with *Salvador*: the alienated narrator desperately trying to make sense of a senseless situation, the characteristic sharp observation of minute detail, the darkly comic sense of irony. In 1987, Didion turned her attention to the Cuban community of southern Florida, and the result was a book-length study titled, simply, *Miami*.

Sources for Further Study

Forché, Carolyn. "El Salvador: An Aide-Memoire," in *The American Poetry Review*. X (July/August, 1981), pp. 3-7.

García Márquez, Gabriel. *The Autumn of the Patriarch*, 1975.

Hoge, Warren. Review in *The New York Times Book Review*. LXXXVIII (March 13, 1983), p. 3.

Lyons, Gene. Review in *Newsweek*. CI (March 28, 1983), p. 69.

Sheppard, R. Z. Review in *Time*. CXXI (April 4, 1983), p. 76.

Sontag, Susan. "Trip to Hanoi," in *Styles of Radical Will*, 1969.

Whitehead, Laurence. Review in *The Times Literary Supplement*. June 24, 1983, p. 663.

James D. Daubs

SAVING THE APPEARANCES
A Study in Idolatry

Author: Owen Barfield (1898-   )
Type of work: Philosophy
First published: 1957

Form and Content

Owen Barfield's thought in general is difficult to place within the usual categori-
cal limits of history, philosophy, psychology, or aesthetic theory. At its center is
Barfield's concept of the role of imagination in the evolution of human consciousness, and the consequences of that evolution on human understanding of physical
nature, philosophically conceived reality, time, and history. Implicit in this notion is
his understanding of how consciousness itself works, how it formulates representations (ideas or images) of the outside world, how its participation in the outside
world generates and completes that world's felt reality, while realizing its own, and
how awareness of the changing meaning of words reveals not merely semantic
growth or decay but also the evolving mind of the past and of the world it possessed
and partially created.

These linked ideas—developed from primarily literary or linguistic models in
his earlier works, such as *Poetic Diction: A Study in Meaning* (1928) and *History in
English Words* (1926)—are focused primarily in *Saving the Appearances: A Study
in Idolatry* on two issues: the failure of post-Renaissance Western scientific thought
to establish a consistent epistemology and the consequences of that failure for
Western man's understanding of the relation "between human consciousness on the
one hand and, on the other, the familiar world of which that consciousness is
aware." *Saving the Appearances* begins from the premise that two things currently
obscure that relationship, one an omission and the other an assumption. What is
omitted is an effective awareness of the participation of the human mind in the
creation and the evocation of the phenomena of consciousness—a participation
which philosophy has been emphasizing at least since the work of Immanuel Kant,
and to which science itself has been calling attention as it continues to detail the
enormous difference between the actual structure of physical reality and its appearance. What is misleadingly assumed is that whatever the truth may be about the
relation between man and nature, that relation is fixed and unchanging, "the same
now as it was when men first appeared on earth." The twenty-five tightly reasoned
chapters of *Saving the Appearances* sketch provocatively what happens when that
assumption is challenged and that omission remedied.

The first stage of the argument—occupying the first three chapters of the book—
fixes the reader's awareness on the evolutionary nature of this process of participation: That is, at various roughly definable historical periods, the dynamics of the
process are seen to change, resulting in significantly different human perceptions of
nature and man's relation to it. In the course of the development of this idea,

Barfield insists on two others: that the illusory assumption of a static relation between man and nature may be traced to historical causes; and that a dramatically
different vision of man and nature results if one keeps steadily in mind and takes
seriously the combined insight of science and philosophy regarding the gulf that
yawns between physical nature and its appearance, and regarding the mind's evolving role in bridging that gulf. The final three chapters examine the historical and
theological consequences of this altered vision.

Analysis

Barfield begins by describing how and what the human mind knows of the
physical world. The world "rainbow," he notes, signifies a consciously shared
representation, experienced as the outcome of the sun's light striking particles of
moisture and stimulating sight. The reality of a rainbow exists outside subjective
consciousness, but the individual only knows it when he either experiences the
word's meaning or participates through the sense of sight in the outside phenomenon (light striking particles). Science has clearly demonstrated that all matter,
a tree, for example, consists of "particles"—"the atoms, protons and electrons of
modern physics . . . now perhaps more generally regarded, not as particles, but as
notional models or symbols of an unknown supersensible or subsensible base." In
Barfield's language, these particles are "the unrepresented." If these particles are
there and are all that is there, then, since the particles are no more like the thing
called a tree than the raindrops are like the thing called a rainbow, it follows that
the appearance of a tree is just as much a shared collective representation as is
a rainbow. The whole non-ego, outside world—which science investigates, and
which existed in the past—is a perceived system of shared or collective representations realized imagistically in consciousness by the mind's participation in sense
experience, and managed by language.

The mind's conversion of sense contact with the unrepresented into conscious
perception requires another process which Barfield terms "figuration." One does
not hear undulating molecules of air, one hears sound; one hears, for example, a
thrush singing. To experience that perception it is necessary to hear not with the ears
alone but with "all sorts of other things like mental habits, memory, imagination,
feeling and (to the extent at least that the act of attention involves it) will." Without
figuration, the familiar world of collective representations would be closed to the
mind. Figuration makes thinking possible. Barfield distinguishes two ways of thinking: "alpha-thinking," that is, thinking about the phenomena that figuration produces as if they were wholly objective and independent of one's perception—the
sort of thinking science generally attempts—and "beta-thinking," that is, thinking
reflexively about the processes of thinking. Through "beta-thinking" one discovers,
for example, that the phenomena are not totally outside and independent of oneself.
The book's subsequent investigation into the relation between mind and matter
proceeds from this epistemological base.

Barfield's term for the interaction of the two is "participation," a rather difficult concept to grasp in his thought since he uses it to refer to a changing, indeed evolutionary, process that must be grasped analogically. Original participation, the sort experienced by the primitive mentality, is very different from that which is common in the modern West. Citing the findings of anthropology as evidence, Barfield argues that primitive alpha-thinking was substantially different because figuration at that time was different. The primitive mind does not dissociate itself from phenomena—does not, that is, perceive itself as distinct from them, as modern people habitually do. Such a mind, in its act of original participation, perceives representations as synthetic wholes from which the percipient is not distinct, wholes that include

> an awareness which we no longer have, of an extra-sensory link between the percipient and the representations. This involves, not only that we think differently, but that the phenomena (collective representations) themselves are different.

Barfield sees the evolution of collective representations that determines the evolution of thought and language as correlative to and reciprocal with the evolution of phenomena themselves. As a practical consequence of that view, he argues that one can have no accurate or expressible knowledge of the appearance of the earth before the arrival of man—since what was going on in the unrepresented at that time could not have been constructed into reality through a consciousness capable of figuration. The prehistoric evolution of the earth, as described for example in H. G. Wells's *The Outline of History* (1920), "was not merely never seen. It never occurred." If in one's efforts to understand the past one naïvely projects backward into it the modern West's collective representations, one is creating what Francis Bacon might have called "idols of the study," and it is precisely the evolution of such idols that has made up much of the development of Western thought.

The history of consciousness in the West shows a gradual diminishing of original participation and a concomitant increase in self-consciousness; the mind becomes more and more isolated within a vacuum of meaninglessness and peers out longingly at inert phenomena that are conceived of not only as objective and independent realities but indeed as the ultimate and only realities. In the nineteenth century, the enormous power of Darwinian evolutionist thought accelerated this tendency, since it proceeded from sophisticated and disciplined alpha-thinking which never questioned the integrity of its own epistemological assumptions. So captivating was this idol of the study that its radiance blinded scientists in many fields of inquiry— in anthropology, for example, requiring the postulation of a primitive man whose blank consciousness faced and was informed by the same phenomena (collective representations) that modern people experience.

The historically real evolution of consciousness had, in fact, followed a much different course. There is, Barfield argues, sufficient philological evidence enshrined in the thought and art of earlier Western periods to demonstrate convincingly that forms of original participation, experienced as modes of knowledge, lasted into the late Middle Ages and perhaps well beyond them. Though how the process worked was a matter of dispute, philosophical thought from Aristotle to Saint Thomas Aquinas assumed that conscious knowledge meant assimilating the representational appearance of reality to grasp in some way the unrepresented—which is not to deny the increasing subjectivization of thought that was then occurring. Barfield believes that the chief difference between primitive (original) participation and the kind experienced in later ages is that in original participation the connection between self and phenomena is experienced directly, not achieved by beta-thinking of any kind. Such original participation was, however, susceptible to idol making of its own, for implicit in it was the sense that "there stands behind the phenomena, *and on the other side of them from man*, a represented, which is of the same nature as man." The divine injunction given to ancient Israel held in check that tendency toward idolatry and moved the Jews away from the kind of original participation that fostered it. For Western man in general, however, the demise of original participation was a less dramatic process effected by the relentless evolution of consciousness toward a state of self-consciousness. By the seventeenth century, the Cartesian and empiricist split between subject and object had the effect of achieving the near-total isolation of the ego which seems so characteristically modern. The intellectual ground was prepared for the Darwinian idolatry of a later period.

At this point in his sketch of Western thought, Barfield cites the appearance of certain "symptoms of iconoclasm," the chief of which was the Romantic movement in both its literary and its philosophical manifestations. He theorizes that extreme self-consciousness produced in the mind images of remembered phenomena "detached or liberated from their originals" and thus at the disposal of the human imagination, which might, if it chose, impart meaning to them. Romantic artists such as William Wordsworth and Samuel Taylor Coleridge so chose. Adopting thereby what Barfield calls "a directionally creator" relationship to nature, manipulating images of phenomena to half-create what they perceived and hence knew, they did, "*pro tanto*, with the remembered phenomena what their Creator once did with the phenomena themselves." The movement, however, never achieved in Barfield's view the full maturity it might have, for while Romantics such as Coleridge understood the way the mind participated in the evoking of reality, they failed to realize imaginatively the nature of man the creator, the relation between whose conscious and unconscious mind generates phenomena, through whom the Logos, the Divine Word, is disclosed. Coleridge may have known intellectually, Barfield implies, that the immanent life in nature—the ultimate unrepresented—was also in him; he may have known that the phenomenal world is man's collective consciousness, but that knowledge was never experienced by him as it was by Wordsworth, who felt directly and realized in his poetry what Coleridge could better explain discursively.

Johann Wolfgang von Goethe's early scientific work, Barfield holds, reveals a disciplined imagination that had allowed him to create partially and give meaning to phenomena while simultaneously experiencing them directly. He was thereby enabled to make botanical and anatomic discoveries because his imagination had reached a point where it enhanced figuration itself, as a result making previously unperceived parts of the whole field of phenomena perceptible. This kind of participation Goethe applied to the task of finding pattern in nature, earning Coleridge's commendation for having transferred the uses of the imagination from literature and art to science.

It is, however, in the thought of the mystic Rudolf Steiner, the founder of anthroposophy, that Barfield claims to have discovered the keenest insight into a systematic use or training of the imagination that may make possible "final participation" and the vanquishing of intellectual idolatry. Because of the esoteric nature of Steiner's thought, though, Barfield's efforts to secure for him a wider hearing have clearly put off more traditionally minded critics and students of philosophy.

At the historical point now achieved in the evolution of human consciousness, Barfield's imagination discerns the possibility of fateful choices to be made. Western man may elect the course of increasing intellectual idolatry and continue, with greater and greater efficiency, to treat phenomena as if they had independent existence. Barfield's prophecy is that such a course would lead mankind to a world chaotically empty, to a state of idiocy "in which fewer and fewer representations will be collective, and more and more will be private, with the result that there will in the end be no means of communication between one intelligence and another." Another option, perhaps still available, is to profit from the insight of the Romantics and to model future imaginative thinking on theirs, following the lead of men such as Goethe and Steiner on the difficult journey to final, conscious participation in nature. This course assumes both that human beings are indeed capable through exercise of imagination of achieving "a directionally creator" relation to the phenomena of nature and that if such power is achieved it will be beneficently used. There are, Barfield warns, no guarantees of such an outcome. Conceivably, people might use such participation to move forward to a fantastically hideous world. In the eloquent coda which closes the book, the author leaves no doubt of the kind of choice he believes must be made, despite the dangers. The vision that beckons him is grounded in Barfield's Christian belief and hope. Encouraged by the Scriptures to believe that as men and women we have been uttered by the Word, we feel, Barfield concludes, "the seed of the Word stirring within us, as imagination." That stirring makes iconoclasm possible.

Critical Context

As Barfield is keen to acknowledge, the most fundamental intellectual theme in *Saving the Appearances* has its roots in the literary and philosophical traditions of nineteenth century Romanticism. The idea that the human mind does not merely observe the outside world but, in perceiving, partly creates it as well echoes Coleridge and the thrust of the German Idealistic school that Coleridge had appropriated. In *Poetic Diction*, Barfield noted that his own theory of knowledge had been born of his experience with English Romantic poets, an encounter that led eventually to his *What Coleridge Thought* (1971). Earlier, his discovery of the work of the turn-of-the-century mystic and philosopher Steiner allowed him to test his own inferentially developed ideas on the role of the imagination in the historical evolution of consciousness against those of a thinker who claimed direct knowledge of sustained experience with a world that transcended the ordinarily perceived one. Steiner had elaborated his reflections on that experience into voluminous teachings on spiritual science or anthroposophy, which Barfield has described elsewhere as "nothing less than Romanticism grown up."

Saving the Appearances seeks to examine within a historical context the notion of an evolving human consciousness, to show, as one commentator has put it, "that there is an interior aspect to evolution," an appreciation of which is vital to intellectual and moral well-being. The clear implication of the book is that to study the historical development of Western thought up to the present is to study the various idols that have resulted, and continue to result, when phenomena—instead of being grasped as representations—are held to have an independent and objective existence. Barfield observes that "a representation, which is collectively mistaken for an ultimate—ought not be called a representation. It is an idol." Iconoclasm, required of people individually and collectively, is the first step, he believes, on the way to final participation in nature. Breaking free of intellectual idolatry is rendered especially difficult, however, because of the currently prevailing materialist view of the world. That view is abetted by modern science, Barfield argues, through its failure to grasp its own epistemological opportunities and limits.

Saving the Appearances takes its title from a phrase invoked frequently by medieval philosophers as they sought to explain the nature of hypothetical thinking. It meant that a hypothesis was valuable insofar, and only insofar, as it explained or "saved" appearances—but was not on that basis to be regarded as true. By the seventeenth century, however, owing largely to the debate over the Copernican cosmic hypothesis, the phrase had acquired a new implication: that if a hypothesis saves all the appearances (that is, explains the phenomena), it is identical with truth. A new theory about the nature of theory had arisen; because of its historical context, it coincidentally diminished Western man's appreciation of the representational element in phenomena. Barfield's book sketches a hypothesis aimed at explaining all realities—including the representational ones—underlying phenomena. It aims at saving all the appearances.

Sources for Further Study

Grant, Patrick. "Belief in Thinking: Owen Barfield and Michael Polanyi," in *Six Modern Authors and Problems of Belief*, 1979.

_____. "The Quality of Thinking: Owen Barfield as Literary Man and Anthroposophist," in *Seven: An Anglo-American Literary Review*. III (1982), pp. 113-125.

Mood, John J. "Poetic Language and Primal Thinking: A Study of Barfield, Wittgenstein, and Heidegger," in *Encounter.* XXVI (August, 1965), pp. 417-433.

Reilly, R. J. *Romantic Religion: A Study of Barfield, Lewis, Williams, and Tolkien*, 1971.

Sugerman, Shirley, ed. *Evolution of Consciousness: Studies in Polarity*, 1976.

Tennyson, G. B. "Owen Barfield and the Rebirth of Meaning," in *The Southern Review.* V (January, 1969), pp. 42-57.

Francis J. Morris

THE SCAPEGOAT

Author: René Girard (1923-   )
Type of work: Cultural criticism
First published: Le Bouc émissaire, 1982 (English translation, 1986)

Form and Content

The concept of "persecution texts," central to the argument of *The Scapegoat*, is defined by René Girard as "accounts of real violence, often collective, told from the perspective of the persecutors, and therefore influenced by characteristic distortions." In this book, Girard undertakes the task of showing how to identify such distortions and to reveal the arbitrary nature of the violence as a prelude to correction. The paradigm Girard chooses to start his discussion of the cultural significance of scapegoats is that presented by Guillaume de Machaut, a French poet of the mid-fourteenth century whose *Jugement du roy de Navarre* (c. 1349; *Judgment of the King of Navarre*) refers to the story of the persecution of the Jews, presumably during the Black Death. To Girard, the crucial point about this account is that Machaut accepts the accusation that the Jews poisoned the well water and caused the otherwise inexplicable horror and suffering brought about by the plague. In Girard's opinion, Machaut's text paradoxically attains a measure of reliability precisely because it combines the probable elements of what was historically true and the improbable elements of what the persecutors wanted to be true. With these built-in distortions, Girard argues, Machaut's text unconsciously provides later generations with an example of a persecution text that reveals the act of scapegoating and the collective violence which engendered it.

This poetic account of a historical event demonstrates the four characteristics — Girard calls them "stereotypes" — of the scapegoating mechanism. The first stereotype is the description of a social and cultural crisis which results in a generalized loss of differences. The second is the crime that eliminates differences. The third is that those perceived to have committed these crimes possess the marks of a victim. The fourth is the violence itself.

Having defined the stereotypes of persecution texts, Girard demonstrates, in the rest of *The Scapegoat*, the universal applicability of this pattern; he analyzes myths of the Greeks, Dogrib Indians, Aztecs, Scandinavians, and Romans as well as historical events, such as the witch trials in the United States and the fate of the Jewish doctor of Queen Elizabeth I of England. That this pattern has hitherto not been recognized, Girard argues, is a result of the inability to decode, or demystify, documents because of the degree to which such violence is concealed or "mystified" in various texts.

Girard offers his analysis of the myth of Oedipus as told by Sophocles as an exemplary persecution text. The first stereotype of persecution, that of a social crisis, is evident in the plague from which Thebes suffers. The second stereotype, that of a lack of differentiation, is fulfilled in the crimes that have been committed:

The acts of parricide, when Oedipus kills his father, and of incest, when he marries his mother, obliterate the differences between the individual and the community, which is why these crimes have almost universally been abhorred. Oedipus' markings as a victim, the third stereotype, combine several factors by which victims are identified: a physical disability such as Oedipus' limp; the suggestion of abnormality in his exposure as an infant; and the two ways in which he is a marginal figure, first as a newcomer to Thebes and second by virtue of his position of authority as a king and the son of a king. His violent fate, decreed by the oracle as the condition which will end the plague, completes the fourth stereotype.

Girard then moves on to those harder cases in which the scapegoating mechanism exists but which do not seem to contain the stereotypes of persecution. Aesthetic and literary texts, in this respect, are among the most creatively camouflaged persecution texts, Girard says, because the poet has so many ways to hide this pattern. Girard, for example, identifies such Aristotelian terms as "hamartia" as the poetic way to minimize the crime of collective violence; the term suggests only a minor flaw, not the evil which seeks to expel violence from the community by committing violence on one victim or on a minority group.

Finally, Girard devotes several chapters to an analysis of the Gospels, for he regards the story of Christ's persecution as the ultimate key to demystification of the scapegoating mechanism. Because Christ accepts His death as an atonement for the sins of the human race, He clearly identifies Himself, and His role, as a victim. The process by which the communal victim is chosen, sacrificed, and then frequently deified tends to obscure the violence which originated the pattern. The victim, who was sacrificed in order to avert or atone for a catastrophe, subsequently becomes a godlike figure who may be appealed to or must be ritually appeased to prevent other catastrophes. Because the story of Christ's persecution reveals this pattern so clearly, it nullifies the characteristic distortions and, by rejecting the pattern, serves to confirm it. The crucial difference Girard sees in the Christ story is the difference between identifying the scapegoat of the text, where the scapegoating mechanism is the structural principle but hidden, or a scapegoat in the text, where the scapegoating mechanism is clearly the visible theme.

Analysis

The Scapegoat continues to elaborate and develop ideas already set in motion in René Girard's previous works. The notion of the persecution text's first stereotype—the loss of differentiation—can be traced back to, indeed, can only be clearly understood with reference to *Mensonge romantique et vérité romanesque* (1961; *Deceit, Desire, and the Novel*, 1965). Instead of the usual dichotomy of the Self and the Other in literature, Girard argues that there is instead a triangle: the Self, the Other, and the desire to be the Other. Rivalry results because the Self in the novel wishes to imitate the desire of the Other, then desires the same object, leading to violence. The congruence of desires eliminates the difference between the Self and the Other.

From this first study based on literary texts. Girard has expanded his attempts to explain culture at large. Like some of his previous studies, *The Scapegoat* draws from several disciplines—anthropology, psychology, sociology, philosophy, and religion. His hypothesis that the victimage mechanism explains all cultural phenomena is developed in several books. In *La Violence et le sacré* (1972; *Violence and the Sacred*, 1977), Girard argues that the relationship between tragedy and society must be understood in terms of the scapegoats, who, regardless of their guilt or innocence, are treated with violence so that society as a whole may escape it. His controversial assertion that the scapegoat paradigm results from real historical events and is pervasive in historical and religious texts is developed in *Des choses cachées depuis la fondation du monde* (1978; *Things Hidden Since the Foundation of the World*, 1987) as well as in *The Scapegoat*. His assertion that the Bible is a prime source of demystification is the central argument in *La Route antique des hommes pervers* (1985; *Job, the Victim of His People*, 1987).

Throughout *The Scapegoat*, Girard's clearly argumentative, sometimes defensive, tone suggests the ongoing and provocative nature of his hypothesis. René Girard offers nothing less than an explanation of the origins of religion and myth and ritual; furthermore, it is an explanation that posits the real, not the symbolic, violence at the heart of those origins. The argumentative tone is inevitable, for, as Girard realizes, his hypothesis that the scapegoat pattern in texts refers to real events runs counter to some of the prevailing theoretical principles of the last twenty years, among them the idea that the "referent," meaning the subject of a text, remains basically inaccessible. For critics who adhere to this principle, Girard notes, the only possible subjects for study are the "ambiguous and unreliable relationships of language."

Girard rejects this critical skepticism and "cognitive nihilism," not only maintaining that the referent is accessible but also describing what that referent is and how universal it is. Girard replaces what he calls the principle of "unlimited mistrust" with his golden rule of persecution texts: "The mind of a persecutor creates a certain type of illusion and the traces of his illusion confirm rather than invalidate the existence of a certain kind of event."

Another scholarly group with which Girard's discourse concerns itself is the ethnologists, for he is not an apologist for Western ethnocentrism. His hypothesis, intended to demystify all myths and religions, asserts vigorously that the Gospels provide a key to such demystification.• Anticipating the criticism and counterarguments that ethnologists might put forth, Girard, explaining the violence at the center of the Aztec religion, for example, points out that ethnologists eagerly describe the extraordinary privileges that the victims chosen for sacrifice enjoyed before their death and warn against judging an ancient culture by current standards. Girard finds condescending these scholarly attempts to justify the "bloody orgies" by accepting the self-glorifying image of the persecutors: A violent act must be recognized and revealed for what it is, for only then can human beings separate the glorification of the myth from its shameful origins.

Such an ambitious design has its intrinsic problems. On one hand, Girard's analyses of specific myths from the point of view of his hypothesis have been praised for their insights into the texts. Moreover, his theories have provided other critics with a useful and productive frame of reference for the study of specific literary texts. The very ambitiousness of his theory, however, has led to criticism about his vagueness and the excessiveness of his claim to explain all religions and myths. Is it possible, one reviewer argues, to have a "key to all mythologies," especially when Girard offers no statistical evidence to back up such a conviction?

A related problem in Girard's assertion that the scapegoat mechanism is universal lies in the inherent danger that all literary texts might then be reduced to a single pattern. Girard's own analyses in *The Scapegoat*, as well as his critical work elsewhere on such traditional classics of the canon as Shakespeare's *Hamlet* (1600-1601), however, refute such fears. Though he has said explicitly that he believes "all human thinking ultimately goes back to the mimetic mechanisms" he explores, he has also observed that literary texts are enormously diverse in the degree to which they reveal or dissimulate this scapegoating mechanism. In crudely practical terms, while Girard's enumeration of the four stereotypes may seem simplistic, they still allow for much critical thought, not to say ingenuity, in deciphering the details by which texts manifest the scapegoating mechanism. Still, Girard admits that his interest in texts is selective, limited to those which will help him to understand his hypothesis.

The most appealing facet of Girard's passionate tone in *The Scapegoat*, as in his other major studies, comes from his conviction that intensive study of such persecution texts leads not only to an exercise of the intellect but also to the discovery of a universal self-deluding pattern of human thought and behavior which, once identified, will be a step toward ending human violence.

Critical Context

The Scapegoat is an important work of intellectual inquiry in several respects. First, Girard's argument that the Gospels provide a key to decoding the scapegoat mechanism asserts the importance of biblical studies and may be seen as part of a larger trend, the renewed interest in the Bible as the "supreme supertext of Western civilization," as Gerald Gillespie has expressed it in a review. Thus, for example, along with Girard's *The Scapegoat*, Gillespie discusses Northrop Frye's *The Great Code* (1983), and Frank Kermode's *The Genesis of Secrecy: On the Interpretation of Narrative* (1979).

Second, as an elaboration of Girard's continued interest in the relationship between violence and religion, the scope of *The Scapegoat* places it in the category of those interdisciplinary studies which attempt to deal with large philosophical issues rather than narrow specialities. Though perhaps rather incidental to Girard's main purpose, the results for the study of literature have been salutary. By rejecting the obsessive concern with the intricacies and problems of language in recent literary studies, Girard reaffirms the value of literature, arguing that it too can reveal the true nature of violence. Finally, Girard's style, in sharp contrast to the dense and complex styles of many poststructuralist critics, is relatively simple and clear. As in *The Scapegoat*, Girard's belief in the power of ideas to effect cultural change gives rise to an impassioned style that invigorates intellectual inquiry.

Sources for Further Study

Dumouchel, Paul, ed. *Violence and Truth: On the Work of René Girard*, 1987.

Farenga, Vincent. Review of *Violence and the Sacred* in *Comparative Literature Studies*. XXXII (Fall, 1980), pp. 419-424.

Gillespie, Gerald. "Bible Lessons: The Gospel According to Frye, Girard, Kermode, and Voegelin," in *Comparative Literature Studies*. XXXVIII (Summer, 1986), pp. 289-297.

Hamerton-Kelly, Robert G., ed. *Violent Origins: Walter Burket, René Girard, and Jonathan Z. Smith on Ritual Killing and Cultural Formation*, 1987.

Juilland, Alphonse, ed. *To Honor René Girard*, 1986.

Palmer, N. B. Review in *Choice*. XXIV (January, 1987), p. 751.

Winch, Peter. Review in *The Times Literary Supplement*. March 20, 1987, p. 290.

Shakuntala Jayaswal

SCULPTING IN TIME
Reflections on the Cinema

Author: Andrey Tarkovsky (1932-1986)
Type of work: Film criticism
First published: Die versiegelte Zeit, 1986 (English translation, 1986)

Form and Content

This penetrating essay on filmmaking is a serious examination of cinema as art. Reflecting the author's philosophy, *Sculpting in Time* is a powerful plea for honesty, faith, and individual expression in an art form too long identified with literature, from which it is often adapted, or mass consumerism, which it often reflects. Tarkovsky discusses this subject from the perspective of his own films, which have had deep influence on filmmaking in the West but which have been little understood by bureaucrats in his native land.

His films include *Ivanoro detstvo* (1962; *Ivan's Childhood*), *Andrey Rublyov* (1969), *Solaris* (1972), *Zerkalo* (1974; *The Mirror*), *Stalker* (1979), *Nostalghia* (1983; *Nostalgia*), and *Offret* (1986; *The Sacrifice*). As a student at the State Institute of Cinematography in Moscow, Tarkovsky, with Andrey Mikhalkov-Konchalovsky, made two films in 1959; one of these won first prize in the New York Students' Film Competition. *Ivan's Childhood*, a surrealist depiction of a young boy during wartime, won the Golden Lion Prize at the Venice Film Festival in 1962 and other awards at film festivals in Acapulco and San Francisco. The film about Andrey Rublyov, the saintly medieval icon painter, received a prize at the Cannes International Film Festival, as did *Solaris*, a psychological exploration of man's reactions to scientific achievements in space.

The author reveals his own artistic growth by recognizing the dimly perceived ideas set forth in his early films, ideas which prompted Soviet cinematic bureaucrats to limit the number of his creations. They regarded his films as too subjective and puzzling for Soviet patrons. (Interestingly, that was precisely the reaction of Western audiences.) Denied the freedom to make films the way he wanted, he was persuaded finally to seek residence abroad. During the filming of *Nostalgia* in Italy in 1982, he made the decision not to return home.

With the help of Olga Surkova, the work of Tarkovsky is reconstructed from diaries, conversations, lectures, and notes over a period of a generation. Some repetition and lack of organization are evident. Consisting of nine chapters, including an introduction and a conclusion, the book deals with topics such as the relationship between film and poetry (Tarkovsky quotes freely from the works of his father, the poet Arseny Tarkovsky), the director's freedom to alter a script, the distinctions between art and science and between film and literature, the connection between art and religious faith, and the importance of human memory. The author discusses his principles for the selection and retention of actors and describes his favorite and not-so-favorite performers. Tarkovsky also addresses the role of time, rhythm, editing, and cinematic music. He is not at one with Sergei Eisenstein, who regarded editing as the creative essence of filmmaking. To Tarkovsky, each frame suggests rhythm, a movement in time. The importance of editing is that it enhances the art of what the camera has already produced. The process does not create art. Above all, Tarkovsky stresses the responsibility of the director to be true to himself, not to the demands of the mass audience or the state.

Tarkovsky decided to write this book to clarify his artistic vision both for the East and for the West. The book was published in the West in the year of Tarkovsky's death; thus, it constitutes a kind of testament to his career. In fact, the chapter on his last film, *The Sacrifice*, was dictated during the final weeks of his fatal illness.

Analysis

Compiled from different media over a long period of time, with essays on a wide range of film topics, *Sculpting in Time* has no single theme. Nevertheless, Tarkovsky is clearly preoccupied with several ideas. He insists upon abandoning commercial, consumer-type filmmaking. (One wonders, as one reviewer suggested, whether Tarkovsky could have found the money to film *Andrey Rublyov* in the West, or whether Shakespeare was less an artist because he desired in part to entertain.) Tarkovsky writes, "It's only possible to communicate with the audience if one ignores that eighty per cent of people who, for some reason, have gotten into their heads that we are supposed to entertain them." It is the duty of the director to tell people the truth, he says: "Any one who wants can look into my films as into a mirror in which he will see himself."

In this quest for truth, a director needs total freedom, including the right to alter the script, if necessary; after all, writers write screenplays. Tarkovsky relates film to poetry, not to the linear stories of prose. While the art of film lies in the ability to communicate, cinematic art must be separated from literature. Although the reader perceives words subjectively as the viewer perceives images in cinema, there is no place for literary symbolism in film. As with music and poetry, film should be free of ideology. Similarly, Tarkovsky sees film as akin to religious faith, a theme explored in *Andrey Rublyov* and, even more directly, in *The Sacrifice*.

The director must encourage the audience to ponder, to ruminate after leaving the film. In film, thought does not develop logically—the same is true for both poetry and religious faith, a position demonstrated in *The Mirror*. It is wrong to provide a final deduction for the viewer, whose participation is essential to the success of film art. Tarkovsky says that he witnessed Ingmar Bergman's *Persona* (1966) "a great many times," each time seeing something new. He regards that film as a true work of art, since it allows him to interpret it differently at each viewing. Tarkovsky dislikes the cinema of his much-heralded countryman Sergei Eisenstein, whose montage technique in a work such as *Potemkin* (1925) results in mere thought control; Eisenstein's editing deprives the viewer of his interpretive role, providing nothing elusive.

According to Tarkovsky, filmmaking is very close to life, but not in the classic realist manner of depiction. Everyday life is filled with suggestions, innuendos, nuances, poetry, and mystery—elements of filmmaking which the supporters of realism often ignore. Hence, the surreal in cinema is closer to real life than is often imagined. Life depends also on individual expression (*Andrey Rublyov*), on the reassertion of conscience (*The Sacrifice*), and on memory (*Nostalgia*). If an author, he writes, is moved by a chosen landscape, if it brings back memories and suggests associations, even subjective associations, then such a memory will also move the audience.

As for actors, Tarkovsky takes the unpopular position that only the immediate scene should be understood by the performers. He never tells the actors about subsequent developments, because the conclusions may intrude upon what should be spontaneous performances in each scene: "I am adamant that the actor should not connect any piece he plays with the whole, sometimes not even to his own immediately preceding and following scenes." Tarkovsky contends that actors are freer without this knowledge, but he readily concedes that not all actors are able to recognize that. His favorite performer, and one who worked in several of his films, was Anatoly Solonitsyn, a man who retained a kind of childlike faith in the director. Indeed, that was the rule of the game. Cerebral, analytical performers, even when knowledge of the plot is withheld from them, invariably try to guess the conclusion and unconsciously play the "end product." Among Tarkovsky's other favorite actors were Margarita Terekhova, Danish actor Max von Sydow, who never performed above the situation wherein his character was placed, and Charlie Chaplin, whose hero never notices the illogical world about him.

As with most theorists of artistic expression, Tarkovsky is concerned with preserving freedom and individuality. The director should be free from political or commercial restrictions, the actor should be free from the constraints of the plot, and cinema should be free from the critical standards of literature. Yet freedom is not absolute. The artist has no freedom to abandon truth or discipline. He is not free to cancel his love of mankind. Tarkovsky makes clear the director's varied responsibilities to his profession. Indeed, freedom—according to Tarkovsky—is misunderstood in both East and West. Denied expression in the East, it is too often equated with selfishness in the West. Freedom for all people, not simply for cinematic artists, is inseparable from self-discipline.

In *Nostalgia*, Tarkovsky reveals his Russian ties. Although filmed in Italy for distribution in the Soviet Union, it is a quintessential Russian film because of its exploration of the Russian national character. The leading figure, like Tarkovsky, develops an unsettling attachment to an alien landscape but still longs for home. Russians, Tarkovsky argues, make the worst emigrants, because they resist absorption by another culture. They are too bound by their past traditions. Although *Nostalgia* was based upon an authentic historical character, the mood of its protagonist is the mood of the director. While filming, Tarkovsky was ever conscious of Russians' ties to family, land, and culture. Even his most favorable impressions of

Italy were colored by what seemed to him like "unrequited love, like a symptom of the hopelessness of trying to grasp what is boundless, or unite what cannot be joined."

Nostalgia has little plot. In fact, Tarkovsky is wholly uninterested in plot; he is interested only in a person's inner world, his feelings of life. "Why crowd this theme with mere happenings?" he seems to ask. It is vital to show that "people are not alone, are not abandoned in an empty universe, but are linked by countless threads with the past and the future." Are these not the same words that might have been uttered by Ingmar Bergman or Federico Fellini? Characterization is unique in Tarkovsky's cinema. His figures seem weak but have an inner strength. They are people who cannot adapt to the pragmatism of the world. Rublyov looked at the world with naïve, childlike eyes, only to be confronted with savagery and brutality of the worst order. In the end he recovered his sense of man's goodness and love.

To Tarkovsky, audiences are overly concerned with symbolism. For him, rain, fire, wind, and sunshine are not symbolic but merely the stuff of life to be enjoyed for their own sake. He reminds readers of the snowflakes which fall on the eyelids of the brutally murdered girl in Bergman's *Jungfrukällan* (1960; *The Virgin Spring*). They have no symbolic meaning; their function is to heighten the audience's emotional reaction to the tragedy. Yet Tarkovsky admits to the use of a symbol when at the end of *Nostalgia*, he inserted a Russian house inside the ruins of an Italian cathedral.

The apotheosis of Tarkovsky's career is his last film, *The Sacrifice*, made in Sweden with the famed cinematographer Sven Nykvist. Somewhat reluctantly, Tarkovsky employed more plot, more poetic drama, as he says, than in many of his previous films. In part, the film concerns a man stricken with cancer who goes to bed with a witch and is miraculously cured (Solonitsyn had just died of cancer and Tarkovsky himself had recently been diagnosed as having the disease). Deliberately constructed so that the viewers could interpret it in differing ways, this film was less firmly rooted in everyday life than his other works.

In *The Sacrifice* familiar themes of depression, weariness, despair, and the emptiness of human speech appear as the products of the relentless march of modern technology. The film climaxes when the hero turns to God in prayer and vows no longer to speak. In his silent world, he violates common conventions and adopts a role which evokes the image of the holy fool in medieval Russia, a figure whose very presence disturbs people's normality—a normality which Tarkovsky sees as the prevailing philosophy of positivism. There is no better example of the latter than commercial cinema, of which this last film is a repudiation.

Above all, the principal theme of *Sculpting in Time* is the decline of the spiritual dimension of modern man, something which can only be prevented by the recovery of artistic truth. While such a view may suggest the spiritual egotism of the Renaissance *virtu*, Tarkovsky is explicit in identifying spirituality with religious faith. Armed with a passionate opposition to Marxist theory, Tarkovsky asserts that the aim of all art is to help mankind to restore its participation in the future, a goal attainable only when man can return to a belief in the immortality of the soul. Art teaches man to see the relationships between actions and conscience.

Critical Context

The theory of cinema found in these pages represents the culmination of an aesthetic movement begun by Ingmar Bergman and supported by Federico Fellini, following the production of his *Le notti di Cabiria* (1957; *The Nights of Cabiria*). Bergman's preoccupation with religious belief and Fellini's trenchant critiques of material values via his surrealist techniques in *Giulietta degli Spiriti* (1965; *Juliet of the Spirits*) and later films launched a movement that enjoyed critical favor for a generation. Tarkovsky especially liked the Spanish work of director Luis Buñuel. He liked Buñuel because films such as *Viridiana* (1961) were protest films devoid of political ideology.

Like Bergman, Fellini, and Buñuel, Tarkovsky swam upstream against the tide of popular filmmaking. Ironically, his style was more acceptable in the West during the 1960's, when his own films were limited in distribution. Having emigrated to the West in the 1980's, he made it his candid mission to help rescue filmmaking from the crass materialism of capitalism, yet by then, the aesthetic movement of the 1960's and 1970's was yielding to a new realism. His own films never received the acclaim of those of other radical directors, partly because of the limited distribution of Soviet films and partly because of the waning of that style. Hence, through *Sculpting in Time*, Tarkovsky seeks to explain his type of art to a generation unacquainted with it.

Sources for Further Study

Birkos, Alexander S. *Soviet Cinema: Directors and Films*, 1976.

Green, Peter. "Andrei Tarkovsky (1932-86)," in *Sight and Sound*. LVI (Spring, 1987), pp. 108-109.

Insdorf, Annette. "Faith in Movies," in *The New York Times Book Review*. XCII (September 20, 1987), p. 20.

Kennedy, Harlan. "Tarkovsky: A Thought in Nine Parts," in *Film Comment*. XXIII (May/June, 1987), pp. 44-47.

Montagu, Ivor. "Man and Experience: Tarkovsky's World," in *Sight and Sound*. XLII (Spring, 1973), p. 89.

John D. Windhausen

SEA AND SARDINIA

Author: D. H. Lawrence (1885-1930)
Type of work: Travel writing
Time of work: January, 1921
Locale: Sicily, Sardinia, and Civitavecchia, Italy
First published: 1921

> *Principal personages:*
> D. H. LAWRENCE, a British novelist, poet, essayist, and playwright
> FRIEDA (THE Q-B) LAWRENCE, his wife

Form and Content

Sea and Sardinia is chronologically the second of D. H. Lawrence's Italian travel books, after *Twilight in Italy* (1916) and before *Etruscan Places* (1932), which was written two years before Lawrence's death and published posthumously. In most respects, *Sea and Sardinia* is not like a travel book at all, at least not as one normally understands that genre, for there is little in the way of specific guidebook commentary or romantic reflections. Though written almost as a journal of the brief trip to and through Sardinia which he and his wife, Frieda von Richthofen Lawrence, took from their home on Sicily, *Sea and Sardinia* is actually a highly subjective collection of Lawrence's impressions. The Lawrences made their excursion in order to investigate the possibility of living on Sardinia, but the normal considerations of those seeking a new home appear only obliquely behind the motifs of inertia and mobility, freedom and bondage, masculinity and femininity which are important elements in other Lawrence works.

Lawrence, predisposed to melancholy in most of his first-person writings, is predictably irascible throughout much of the trip. His mood contrasts markedly with Frieda's determined amiability. Lawrence grumbles about everything, from the cold weather they face upon setting out to the general filth of the port of Palermo, the arrogance of peasants they meet, and the low rate of currency exchange. At times, he appears even to resent Frieda's ability to accept it all with good grace. Nevertheless, in the midst of one of these tirades, he will burst out in extravagant praise of some detail of scene which he considers worthwhile or beautiful. His Palermo steamer is crowded and unbearably small, but its maple panels and ebony fittings are wonderful, old-fashioned, and splendid. The Sardinian peasantry is either uncommunicative or rude, but their universal black-and-white costume is magnificent because it allows them to stand as individuals.

The contradictions in these observations do not concern Lawrence. He notes the individuality of the Sardinian peasantry even as he observes its unvarying clothing. He generalizes repeatedly about what he calls "the races" but objects when Italians consider him typically English. He inveighs often against local discourtesy yet enthusiastically shakes the hand of the fat peasant who sits beside him at the play he attends. He admires their generosity and spontaneity, and he is sorry to leave them.

Above all, Lawrence is candid in these sketches, often embarrassingly so; though he is inconsistent at nearly every turn, it is the honest inconsistency which troubled him throughout his life. The working title of *Sea and Sardinia*, which Lawrence abandoned before its publication, was "A Diary of a Trip to Sardinia." Though neither a diary nor a conventional travel book, it nevertheless retains a naïve intimacy which tells as much about Lawrence's personality as a revealing biography.

Analysis

Sea and Sardinia, though written quickly, contains several motifs which lend it coherence. The first of these, which appears at its very beginning and which readers of Lawrence's *Fantasia of the Unconscious* (1922) will probably recognize, is the antithesis of movement and inertia. Lawrence is determined that the time has come to go somewhere and he questions only what the destination will be. He enumerates various possibilities (Girgenti in southern Sicily, Syracuse on the southeastern coast, Tunis in North Africa) but eliminates them all. The surrounding scenery is exquisite, but Lawrence feels impelled to go—anywhere, but obviously not anywhere, since he eliminates all possibilities save for the comparatively primitive and difficult-to-reach island of Sardinia. Movement, so Lawrence contends in *Fantasia of the Unconscious*, is identifiable with the male and that which is masculine. Conversely, immutability, permanence, and inertia are feminine. Lawrence believes that since the Renaissance, man has largely entered the female mode; thus, *Sea and Sardinia*, in its first pages at least, is filled with an almost manic passion for movement.

Paradoxically, on the morning scheduled for their journey to begin, it is Frieda, referred to only as the queen-bee and subsequently as the q-b, who provides all the impetus and enthusiasm the trip requires. It is she who prepares the tea, sandwiches, and apples to pack in the satchel (called the "kitchenino") which she will carry. All the while, Lawrence laments about his stopped American watch, the darkness, the threatening weather, and almost everything else. It seems a major effort to get beyond his own garden wall, and once outside the single feature of landscape clearly visible in the morning darkness is Mount Etna. Lawrence perceives even the volcano as a symbol of inertia, and he believes that he must escape. Etna, for him, is a "mistress," a Circe-like witch who drives men mad. These details portray the trip as a masculine assertion, though only in its conception, a spontaneous Homeric adventure with Lawrence as a modern Odysseus.

It is clear by the start of the trip, however, that Lawrence is no Odysseus. Immediately upon arriving at the railroad station, he starts noting, inevitably in unflattering ways, the types of Sicilians with whom he is traveling. Either they are enormously fat or (less often) grotesquely thin; they are loud, and those men who are commuting to office jobs in Messina are vainly proud of the clothes which distinguish them from their fellow travelers who are laborers or factory workers. Repeatedly in *Etruscan Places*, Lawrence admires the Italian willingness to touch and be touched, seeing it as the naturalness which distinguishes them from northern Europeans, but here he finds it merely a distasteful and typical affectation.

Lawrence is equally repelled by the greasy, narrow sidewalks and filthy streets of Palermo. Again, he finds these, as well as the delays encountered on the relatively brief railroad trip to the steamer, intolerable and typically Italian. Lawrence's preoccupation with social classes and ethnic characteristics does not, however, allow him to see the inconsistency of his anger at being deprecatingly identified as English. In the midst of it all, he asserts his individuality, declaring that he is himself above all, that he owes nothing of his behavior to any class or group.

Lawrence particularly admires ritual wherever he sees or believes he sees it. In *Twilight in Italy* he is enamored of church architecture because he believes this preserves a living link with the past. In *Etruscan Places*, fanciful and often-inaccurate descriptions of tomb paintings at Tarquinia and Cerveteri sketch the Lawrentian positions on love, life, death, and resurrection. *Sea and Sardinia* contains similar motifs in Lawrence's enthusiastic descriptions of a religious procession in the Sardinian village of Tonara and of an old man roasting a goat on an open fire in the inn at Sorgono. He most enjoys the antique detail and beauty of the costumes worn by those participating in the procession and compares the roaster's fire to gold, but he decries the modern statue of Saint Anthony which stands by the altar, finds appalling the simpleminded sermon of the priest, and loathes the wretched inn at Sorgono. For nearly every positive impression, Lawrence discovers some negative element which reduces or cancels out the good he sees.

Ritual provides Lawrence with an element of timelessness and continuity which serves as an antidote to the movement of time, and he understands the word in the broadest possible sense as any action performed the same way over the course of many years and despite external circumstances. Ritual continuities thus become a motif in all Lawrence's later writings, not only in *Sea and Sardinia*, and Lawrence sought them out as a means of establishing what he saw as uncorrupted natural primitivism, as a way of living which was free of the taint of modern intellectual civilization. In the years after World War I, he pursued this search with manic urgency. It would drive him to Mexico and result in *Mornings in Mexico* (1927), to the American Southwest, then to Etruscan Italy. In Sardinia, he hopes literally to discover the end of the earth but is nearly always disappointed in what he finds.

Lawrence's search for uncorrupted primitivism on Sardinia inevitably leads him to seek close contact with its peasantry, but his English reserve, coupled with his marginal Italian and the peasant inclination to distrust outsiders, never allows any meaningful encounter. He observes the costume of a handsome, elderly peasant in Cagliari; the man's leather vest becomes a cuirass, his hat an ancient Phrygian warrior's cap. Though he admires the man's appearance, modern etiquette allows no personal contact. Ironically, circumstances often force conversation when Lawrence does not wish it; in such cases, Lawrence's descriptions become a parody of his own ideas. An obese couple on the train to Palermo become a fat Jupiter and Juno, and Lawrence mocks their middle-class superiority and fastidious attention to clothing.

In fact, Lawrence is all too aware of his own middle-class Edwardian background, and he vacillates between flaunting it (as, for example, when he finds himself in a restaurant which does not serve coffee because there is no sugar) and asserting his preference for traveling in third class because there is space, air, good spirits, and lively conversation. When he finds himself in a third-class railway coach, however, he is appalled by the boorishness of his traveling companions and, on one occasion, is nauseated by a young woman with motion sickness.

Such inconsistencies will perplex the reader who looks for coherent philosophy in *Sea and Sardinia*, but their candor reveals Lawrence as he was: earnest, often naïve, all too aware of his inner conflicts, and given to relentless self-deprecation and parody. At Mandas, Lawrence tries to be affable; in the manner of many travelers having a less than perfect trip but not entirely willing to admit it, he proclaims to the innkeeper how much he likes the Sardinians. When the innkeeper presses him to say why, Lawrence responds that it is because they are more open and honest than the Sicilians. At this, the innkeeper frowns suddenly and turns away. Only then does one of the diners tell Lawrence that the innkeeper himself is Sicilian.

Despite such encounters, one after the next, the Lawrences bravely follow their itinerary, moving from one village to the next northward through Sardinia. Increasingly, Frieda becomes angry with Lawrence's impatience and tendency to romanticize. At Sorgono, she rejects his search for nonexistent moral ideals, and her anger makes Lawrence all the more sullen. He curses all of his thoughts about a noble peasantry and the q-b as well for interfering with his anger. This scene marks the low point of the Lawrences' odyssey and emphasizes the masculine character of the trip Lawrence had planned against its unsatisfactory reality. When the Lawrences leave Sorgono, without having had breakfast or even dinner the night before, it is in the first-class section of the bus, though Lawrence rationalizes that this will allow them to see better.

Perhaps it is the accumulated effect of these experiences which causes Lawrence to begin his sketch on the village of Nuoro with a panegyric to the glories of the modern automobile. His seat on the bus from Sorgono has, at least for a time, altered his black mood, even if at the expense of his social theories. The food is better at Nuoro, and the end of the journey is in sight. Lawrence is extravagant in his praise of both the meal and his host at Nuoro, and by way of contrast with his reception at Sorgono he notes its moderate cost. Another peasant girl experiences motion sickness, but the good meal and decent manners of the Nuoroesi allow Lawrence to cope with the situation with considerably more grace than he had displayed on the train to Palermo.

On the road to Terranova, their final stop before boarding the steamer, the Lawrences are again weary, and Lawrence is predictably irritable. There is the usual disappointing search for food and complaints about a much less satisfactory bus than the one which took them from Nuoro. This time, in a curious analogy which could describe Lawrence himself, he christens his new driver "Hamlet"; this epithet is presumably based on the driver's searching, abstracted expression and lean appearance, but it becomes humorous when a peasant boards with two little pigs, one in each arm, and is required to pay full fare for each.

The Lawrences' journey is circular, beginning and ending on Sicily and connected by an often-difficult ride up the Sardinian coast. Since it is a hero's odyssey, at least in the Lawrentian sense, it is fitting that Lawrence introduces one final motif: death and resurrection. As they pass through Orosei, throbbing with the reflected light of the sea, and look on its gray houses and olive groves, Lawrence's thoughts suddenly turn to death. The difficulties somehow make possible the triumphant unity he feels with the Italian audience with whom he attends a play in Civitavecchia. When the play is over, he vigorously shakes the hand of the man sitting beside him, glad to have come through it all.

Critical Context

In early 1912, Lawrence, not yet twenty-seven and already a writer of great promise, went to the home of Ernest Weekly, his former languages tutor at Nottingham University. He was hoping for Weekly's advice about his career but while there met the professor's wife, Frieda, the daughter of Baron von Richthofen, the German aristocrat and soldier. In what became a *cause célèbre*, Frieda left her husband and three children for Lawrence, journeyed with him to the Continent, and was married to him after receiving her divorce in July, 1914. Edwardian sensibilities were offended by their conduct, and many who probably never would have read Lawrence's works took it as a sacred mission to forestall their publication and rigorously enforce censorship laws in order to modify them.

Critics have discerned elements of this affair in Lawrence's novels *The Rainbow* (1915) and *Women in Love* (1920), and it is certain that the restless existence of his life from 1912 to its end in 1930, not to mention the equivocal feeling he had for England, stemmed from this experience. Victorians and Edwardians perceived a freer moral climate in what they called "the South," referring generally to the Mediterranean basin but specifically to Italy; by journeying to Italy, Lawrence added his name to a long list of talented but discontented artists who sought relief there.

Still, Lawrence found no peace in Italy, as anyone who reads his Italian travel books can see. If anything, he becomes more restless and ill at ease during the years between *Twilight in Italy* and *Sea and Sardinia*; the series of small unhappy experiences which fill his trip to Sardinia are but one indication of the psychological and physical malaise he felt at the time. Readers who come to his third travel book, *Etruscan Places*, without first reading *Mornings in Mexico* might well have the impression that Lawrence had limited his search for happiness to Italy, but such was not the case. He and Frieda never moved to Sardinia, but they did spend two years after the final publication of *Sea and Sardinia* in both Mexico and New Mexico. For a time, Lawrence was seriously considering a kind of utopian community near the town of Taos, New Mexico; indeed, a modern artists' colony continues to thrive there.

Sea and Sardinia is not important as a romantic travel book, and it is certainly not a tourist's guide to the island. It does, often with disarming candor, describe the pathetic and tragic condition of Lawrence in his final years. It also sets forth his philosophical perspective, frankly and with all the inconsistencies which characterized the man himself.

Sources for Further Study

Ellis, David. "Reading Lawrence: The Case of *Sea and Sardinia*," in *D. H. Lawrence Review*. X (1977), pp. 52-63.

Gersh, Gabriel. "In Search of D. H. Lawrence's *Sea and Sardinia*," in *Queens Quarterly*. LXXX (1973), pp. 581-588.

Janik, Del Ivan. *The Curve of Return: D. H. Lawrence's Travel Books*, 1981.

Meyers, Jeffrey. *D. H. Lawrence and the Experience of Italy*, 1982.

Tracy, Billy T., Jr. *D. H. Lawrence and the Literature of Travel*, 1983.

Weiner, S. Ronald. "The Rhetoric of Travel: The Example of *Sea and Sardinia*," in *D. H. Lawrence Review*. II (1969), pp. 230-243.

Robert J. Forman

SEA OF CORTEZ
A Leisurely Journal of Travel and Research

Authors: John Steinbeck (1902-1968) and Edward F. Ricketts (1897-1948)
Type of work: Nature
Time of work: 1940
Locale: Monterey, California; the Baja Peninsula; the Gulf of California; and
  Mexico
First published: 1941

> *Principal personages:*
> JOHN STEINBECK, an American writer
> EDWARD RICKETTS, an American biologist
> ANTHONY BERRY, the owner of the *Western Flyer*
> TINY COLLETTO, a crew member of the *Western Flyer*
> SPARKY ENEA, a crew member of the *Western Flyer*
> TEX TRAVIS, an engineer on board the *Western Flyer*

Form and Content

In March, 1940, John Steinbeck and Edward F. Ricketts began serious preparation for a six-week biological expedition to the Gulf of California, which they designate by its earlier name, the Sea of Cortez. Ricketts, the owner of the small Pacific Biological Laboratories in Monterey, California, had long been interested in the invertebrate marine life of the California coast. Steinbeck's best friend for eighteen years, he exerted a profound influence on the novelist's thought and became the model for Doc in Steinbeck's *Cannery Row* (1945). Steinbeck, who financed the voyage, had long shared his friend's interest in marine life. Tired of the adulation and controversy that followed publication of *The Grapes of Wrath* (1939), he viewed the expedition as a peaceful and revitalizing interlude in the turbulent career of a writer. The expedition departed from Monterey on March 11, 1940, and returned on April 20; actual exploration in the gulf occurred from March 17 through April 12. *Sea of Cortez*, a genuine collaboration by the two explorers, consists of a narrative account of the expedition from its preparation stages until the beginning of the homeward voyage on April 13, along with an annotated scientific catalog of species taken.

Ricketts viewed the gulf expedition as an extension of his previous study of invertebrates along the California coastline, which culminated in the publication of his and Jack Calvin's *Between Pacific Tides* (1939). The expedition was designed to study the invertebrate marine life of the gulf's littoral, that portion of the coast between tide levels. Since tides inside the gulf are relatively high, the littoral, with its numerous tidal pools, offered a wide expanse for collecting. Capturing, preserving, cataloging, and describing the greatest possible number of species and individual animals formed the group's major activities. Beyond collecting and making taxonomic descriptions, the authors envisioned important discoveries about patterns and the distribution of marine life in the gulf.

Apart from illustrations and introductory matter, *Sea of Cortez* divides into two major parts: a narrative account and a phyletic catalog of the species collected. The narrative portion, republished by Steinbeck in 1951 as *The Log from the Sea of Cortez*, represents the tradition in American nature writing that originated with Henry David Thoreau and continues through writers such as John Muir and Joseph Wood Krutch. It reports and describes scientific discoveries and natural phenomena and offers philosophical reflections, human interest, and human perspective. While informing the reader about unknown or unappreciated facets of nature, it places discoveries in a human context and illuminates through reflection. The Steinbeck-Ricketts narrative portrays the gulf as teeming with marine life, a contrast to the barren and inhospitable land along its shores. Primarily an account of the expedition, the narrative bears a resemblance to travel literature; among Steinbeck's writings, the log most nearly resembles his later *Travels with Charley* (1962).

Following the introduction, the narrative is divided on the basis of date, each chapter usually opening with an account of the locale chosen for that day's collecting, followed by descriptions of the major species found and reflections on the experience. There are, however, gaps in the dates. A few daily entries describe shore visits to Mexican villages and towns along the coast.

The "Annotated Phyletic Catalogue and Bibliography," included as a long appendix, lists and describes approximately five hundred species collected and identified during the expedition. While the explorations concentrated on the littoral, a few species from deeper waters are included. Among the numerous species, one finds ninety snails, fifty-four crabs, and twenty-two fish (the only vertebrates taken). For each phylum, the work lists species arranged by class and family. Under each such heading, previous studies are listed and thoroughly annotated; then each species is separately entered with observations about its condition, abundance or scarcity, and geographical distribution. For each phylum, a summary section provides species totals and comments on the general significance of the discoveries.

Analysis

The catalog lists, in logical scientific form, the discoveries made during the expedition. It represents a taxonomic report and little more, like numerous other reports derived from observations in nature. It reflects scientific inquiry of a basic and systematic kind that advances knowledge through the steady accumulation of data. In the log, Ricketts and Steinbeck offer philosophical perspectives and scientific speculation to justify and transcend the limitations of this inductive approach.

The varied log section represents a complex account of the journey, beginning with the preparations, detailing the long voyage to the mouth of the gulf, and proceeding with a discussion of each successive stop where specimens are collected. Interspersed throughout are reflections and discourses on a wide range of topics: nations and societies, human relationships, mistakes of the expedition, humorous mishaps and adventures, and philosophical speculations.

The authors embarked at a time when the world stood on the brink of cataclysm, and they could only assume that the war engulfing Europe would widen to involve the United States. This awareness leads to pessimistic reflections on war, though the expedition avoids newspapers and radios for six weeks. The authors also reflect on poverty and unemployment, still major social problems in the United States late in the Depression, and see no remedy. They take little consolation in the assurance by a Mexican that all Americans own Fords and are therefore affluent.

During preparations for the expedition, they find only incredulity among the practical sardine fishermen of Monterey when they seek to charter a boat for science. With luck they find a receptive newcomer, Anthony Berry, with a seventy-six-foot boat, the *Western Flyer*. When they discover that its engine room is immaculate, a point of importance to Steinbeck, they hasten to secure it for the expedition. In official circles, they encounter similar skepticism. They receive little encouragement from the State Department; the Mexican government is uncertain and hesitant, yet it finally grants them permission to collect specimens in the gulf and along its shores. Because the Mexicans they meet during their stops are skeptical about the expedition's scientific purpose, the authors concoct the story that they are selling the collected specimens to wealthy Americans as souvenirs. This reassuring and more plausible explanation leads to such cooperation from the basically friendly Mexicans that they begin bringing valuable specimens to sell to the collectors.

The journey involves humor, good fun, and not a little drinking, reflecting the book's subtitle, *A Leisurely Journal of Travel and Research*. Although the crew members grow skillful in helping to collect, they never become accustomed to placing scientific interests above personal and practical ones. They are eager to collect fish for eating, not preserving, and Tiny Colletto enjoys harpooning giant rays in an attempt to capture one for a photograph. Numerous frustrations arise because they depend on an unreliable outboard motor to power a small boat to the shore for collecting while the *Western Flyer* rests at anchor. The engine, dubbed "Hansen's Sea Cow," almost invariably fails, with the result that the crew members find themselves having to row; the frustration causes the narrator to attribute a perverse personality to the engine. Other humorous accounts involve interactions with the Mexicans. On one occasion, the authors buy two live chickens, which they must catch; in the process, they discover that chickens are good athletes. Numerous villagers join the chase, which succeeds only through wearing the chickens down. Among other anecdotes that suggest the descriptive power of Miguel de Cervantes, Steinbeck and Ricketts narrate their stop for beer at an isolated cantina, where they buy drinks for a group of forlorn young men who seem to have no other occupation than loitering.

In addition to these adventures and misadventures, the authors freely acknowledge their mistakes in planning and preparation. They packed too few bottles and tubes for storing specimens and were thus unable to preserve as many as they might have. They brought cameras but no photographer and, as a result of being too busy themselves, made little use of the equipment. On the whole, however, the expedition achieved most of its objectives.

As critics have noted, the heart of the book lies in the "Easter Sermon," chapter 14, the essay on nonteleological thinking. This section is heavily indebted to Ricketts' journal, a major source for the entire log portion; Steinbeck, untypically, did not keep a journal during the expedition. The chapter develops intellectual support for ideas about biology that Ricketts began to formulate as a student at the University of Chicago under William Allee, an early advocate of ecology. During their collecting, Steinbeck and Ricketts were particularly fascinated by animals that lived in colonies or moved in groups. Repeatedly, they note commensal living and patterns of symbiosis which suggest that life is more complex than is generally thought, indeed that all life is interrelated. From this perspective, they draw frequent analogies between animal groups and human society, emphasizing man's closeness to other species. From a biological standpoint, then, proper study is not of species but of species living together in a system. Thus, Ricketts believed that study of the littoral's marine invertebrates would result in larger discoveries about cooperative living.

In keeping with these concepts and values, the authors attack teleological thinking, reasoning which assumes a chain of causes leading to an end and strives to remedy, ameliorate, or solve problems by removing or modifying their causes. To the authors, this mode of thinking, typical of Western civilization, almost invariably oversimplifies by selecting one contributing cause and seeking to remedy it, without taking other possible causes and consequences into account.

As an example of the failure of teleological analysis, they cite as an example a declining willow grouse population in Norway. The Norwegian authorities attributed their decline to predation by hawks and consequently attempted to solve it by killing as many hawks as possible. To their dismay, the rate of the grouse decline increased. They then discovered that the decline was caused not by predation but by disease. The hawks had actually slowed the decline by killing birds weakened by disease, thus removing sources of contagion. While teleological thinking would then seek to cure or prevent the disease, the authors argue that nonteleological thinking would likely view the disease as only one of numerous contributing causes.

Nonteleological thinking, which the authors advocate, views life as part of a complex system; it first tries to understand existing entities and their functions, rejecting shortsighted solutions. This dichotomy in modes of thought, eloquently championed by Steinbeck and Ricketts, has severe limitations, for the examples given by the authors clearly oversimplify the concept of teleological thinking. Yet nonteleological thinking offers a rationale for the kind of exploration that Ricketts preferred, study of animal groups living together in a defined area, and it addresses the charge that his and Steinbeck's kind of exploration represents only taxonomy.

Critical Context

As a scientific account of invertebrate marine life of the gulf, *Sea of Cortez* holds a modest but secure place among similar studies. While scientists are inclined to view it as the work of amateurs, the ample data and cumulative species totals make it useful. Its discoveries about patterns of distribution of species in the area are significant, though the methodology was not sufficiently rigorous to establish major generalizations; those generalizations offered in the narrative, including reflections on the distribution of species within the gulf, remain tentative. On the other hand, it should be noted that Ricketts and Calvin's *Between Pacific Tides* remains a pioneer work of its kind; it has seen numerous reprintings.

As nature writing in the tradition of Henry David Thoreau, John Audubon, and John Muir, the log portion seems assured of a significant place. It portrays an area then little known except to the fishermen who benefited from its abundance. The combination of vivid description, humorous narrative, and philosophical reflection make the work rewarding to read.

Drawn from eclectic sources, the book's scientific and philosophical ideas are heavily dependent upon those of Charles Darwin, yet they include ideas, like the chain of being, that predate Darwin. An early example of an ecological approach to natural science, the book emphasizes the interdependence of living things, the abundance of forms and individuals, the ordering of nature to promote species survival, and symbiosis. To illustrate these ideas at work, the authors call attention to complex life communities, which Ricketts refers to as superorganisms, and to mass patterns of behavior such as those of schools of fish, freely drawing analogies to human life. These ideas, particularly of human beings as part of a social structure, recur in Steinbeck's later fiction. Gradually, however, emphasis on collective behavior gives way to inner conflict as Steinbeck creates individuals who are responsible for their ethical choices.

Sources for Further Study
Astro, Richard. *John Steinbeck and Edward F. Ricketts: The Shaping of a Novelist*, 1973.
Benson, Jackson J. *The True Adventures of John Steinbeck, Writer*, 1984.
Ferrell, Keith. *John Steinbeck: The Voice of the Land*, 1986.
Fontenrose, Joseph. *John Steinbeck: An Introduction and Interpretation*, 1963.

Stanley Archer

THE SECOND SEX

Author: Simone de Beauvoir (1908-1986)
Type of work: Essays
First published: Le Deuxième Sexe, 1949 (English translation, 1953)

Form and Content

Originally published in France in two successive volumes, *The Second Sex* was conceived as one comprehensive study but its two parts—book 1 and book 2— differ somewhat in format. The historical approach and presentation of established data in book 1 permit the author to conclude each essay with a brief summary and an evaluation of stated facts. The more subjective and speculative nature of book 2, which contains Simone de Beauvoir's observations of women of her own generation, must remain without such summaries. Instead, book 2 offers a final chapter fully devoted to recapitulating salient points about the status of women at the time of its writing. Apart from this final chapter, simply titled "Conclusion," de Beauvoir's study consists of twenty-five essays, arranged to be read in sequence but, at the same time, independent of one another, with only occasional references to previously mentioned material. An index follows the actual text of this substantial collection.

Book 1 of the study is divided into three parts with eleven essays and bears the subtitle "Facts and Myths." It examines women's bodies, souls, and economic status in terms of biology, psychoanalysis, and historical materialism. It also presents the reader with an overview of women in history, from primitive societies through classical antiquity, the Middle Ages, the French Revolution, and modern times. A final discussion is devoted to women and myths in general, as well as to the specific myths of women in the works of D. H. Lawrence and four French authors—Henry de Montherlant, Paul Claudel, André Breton, and Stendhal.

Book 2 (divided into four parts and comprising fifteen essays) is subtitled "Woman's Life Today" and presents a study of the status of contemporary women and its basis in recent tradition. It is concerned with women known to a French, Catholic, upper-middle-class author of the late 1940's, when French women had just received the right to vote and French morality was largely determined by the teachings of the Roman Catholic church.

De Beauvoir perceives the course of a woman's life in essentially two stages: the formative years (childhood, adolescence, sexual initiation, with a separate chapter on lesbianism) and the years of confinement within the permanent situation or condition reserved by traditional society for the mature woman (marriage, motherhood, prostitution, life after menopause). The final section of the study deals with the question of justification for women's acceptance of the tyranny of established traditions (narcissism, love, religious experience), and, in a brief essay, the relatively rare case of independent women who managed to defy tradition and establish themselves as writers or artists is considered.

Educated in the French classical tradition, de Beauvoir shows her erudition by providing her readers with a seemingly endless supply of examples from and references to many sources spanning more than two thousand years of Western civilization. Her friend and lifelong companion, the philosopher and writer Jean-Paul Sartre, is one of her favorite authors, along with the philosopher Gaston Bachelard, the anthropologist Claude Lévi-Strauss, some psychoanalysts (such as Sigmund Freud and Alfred Adler), and several French and Anglo-American writers of fiction.

Analysis

It seems appropriate that the first comprehensive and widely influential feminist study of recent times should focus on the deceptively simple but absolutely essential task of defining what a woman is in modern times. Unlike earlier American feminists, the author rejects as too abstract and unreal the concept of a common humanity without clearly defined sexual distinctions. De Beauvoir provides her readers with a highly logical exercise in examining and systematically refuting some generally accepted statements by scientists and theoreticians such as Charles Darwin, Sigmund Freud, and Friedrich Engels, whose combined efforts shaped the image of women during the first half of the twentieth century. At the same time, she establishes her own concept of women as not significantly different from men biologically yet socially far removed from the superior position occupied by men. De Beauvoir's compelling arguments against existing perceptions and in favor of her own inventive feminist interpretation of known facts are well-grounded in modern philosophy and anthropology (the theories of Martin Heidegger, the father of French existentialism, and Claude Lévi-Strauss, the foremost representative of structuralism, are cited).

De Beauvoir fully agrees that the human race shares its biological differences between male and female with other species, but she also insists that membership in a species is insignificant in human terms, because human beings create societies with set human values and impose customs, restrictive as well as supportive, on their members. This social imposition on the human female is the determining factor in her existence. (De Beauvoir's dictum that one is not born but rather becomes a woman is now one of the mainstays of feminist theory.) Emphasizing the mutual need for a willed coexistence in both male and female, de Beauvoir rejects the psychoanalysts' view of women as alienated from their biological and psychological destiny and frustrated in a vain attempt to be men. She sees alienation for both men and women as an existential dilemma precipitated by the burden of self-determination and the exercise of free will. She rejects Engels' theory that the oppression of women is merely the result of men acquiring private property with a subsequent profit-oriented need for slave labor done by women. Instead, she traces women's enslavement to the invention of tools, which became the exclusive province of men.

The invention of tools brought about a profound change enabling man to settle and to liberate himself from the uncertainties of his environment. The new life-style eliminated the need for women to function as the incarnation of the secrets of nature; women, however, failed to transcend their established status and remained in bondage to life's mysterious processes, while men created productive work for themselves. This disturbance of a previous existing equilibrium led to women's devaluation and their oppression in modern societies. Women's failure to share in men's way of working and thinking excluded her from human *Mitsein*, a commonly shared existence. It is de Beauvoir's view that women's alterity, once it is recognized and clearly defined as a social rather than biological condition, is not irreversible or absolute and that there exists no real reason to continue to deny women access to human *Mitsein*.

De Beauvoir's theory rests on two important concepts: "otherness" and the related ideas of "transcendence" and "immanence." She unequivocally stands behind otherness as a fundamental category of human thought. The Other is usually set up by individuals or groups who need a foil in an inferior position to define themselves as superior. Therefore, the Other never exists as a wholly autonomous entity on its own terms. Otherness produces separation, but it also creates the bond of need between two entities wanting to define themselves, a conception de Beauvoir has taken from the work of G. W. F. Hegel. In the relationship between men and women, otherness is bound to the constant desire of man to possess what he is not and to seek a union with the Other, which he is not.

The terms "transcendence" and "immanence" represent opposing conditions. Transcendence implies activity, freedom, being in charge, while immanence means confinement within an uncreative, passive, and limited existence. Man has long been seen as *Homo faber*, the doer who invented tools and created society's fabric, while woman remained restricted to a narrow cycle of repetitious duties of childbearing and nurturing, and of what is compatible with the task of reproduction— namely, household chores. The ovule, motionless and in a state of expectation, has been thought to symbolize immanence, with the agile and vigorous sperm representing transcendence. De Beauvoir argues that human gametes play a fundamentally identical role and cannot be divided into a passive, inferior female and an active, superior male. Men, however, are favored from a biological standpoint, because their sexual life is fully integrated with their existence as a person. Women, on the other hand, are profoundly alienated because of their enslavement to reproduction, which, according to de Beauvoir, is unwillingly accepted. Women, too, feel the urge to transcend but are biologically destined to give life in a society which values posterity in its offspring. Facing the constant temptation to forgo liberty and become objects rather than affirm their subjective existence, women have failed to set up female values in opposition to male values.

It is not until menopause that women are delivered from the servitude imposed on them by their organism. Postmenopausal women, in a sense, form a "third sex," not male but also no longer female. In de Beauvoir's opinion, women of all ages will regain their urge and ability to transcend once they are permitted to affirm their status as subjects through an active and productive existence. In practice, nothing but gainful employment will guarantee their liberty. They will set new goals to play a vigorous role in economic, political, and social life; they will escape the prison of immanence "to emerge into the light of transcendence."

De Beauvoir's influence on feminist thought is tremendous. Her statement that "in a properly organized society, where children would be largely taken in charge by the community and the mother cared for and helped, maternity would not be wholly incompatible with careers for women," though actually referring to a Socialist model, heralded a revolution in Western capitalist societies. Early American feminists blindly subscribed to de Beauvoir's contention that economic independence and integration into the productive labor force could not fail to bring full equality to both sexes. Her suggestion of reorganizing a family-oriented society into one where the care of children would become the responsibility of the community as a whole has remained a viable concept reflected in many attempts to solve the lingering child care question on a state and federal level.

Critical Context

If feminist theory has evolved through several stages, then de Beauvoir's essays belong to the first stage: the refutation of existing male-dominated ideas. Since the middle of the twentieth century, several other stages have evolved and, in some cases, superseded de Beauvoir's theories. Lévi-Strauss' structuralism, a major influence on de Beauvoir, has given way to poststructuralism. The rejection of Freud's and Adler's placement of women in a position of inferiority to men has been reversed; Jacques Lacan's theories of physiologically determined psychological immanence have been accepted by a new generation of French and American feminists. De Beauvoir's own expectation that the problems of women would resolve themselves automatically in a context of Socialist development has not been fulfilled, because, as the author stated in an interview thirty years after writing *The Second Sex*, Socialist countries are not really socialist. De Beauvoir was appalled by the re-mystification of motherhood and the reintroduction of the idea of the "Eternal Feminine" in the early 1980's.

Perhaps the most controversial of the many issues touched upon in de Beauvoir's study is that of women's responsibility for and involvement in shaping centuries of an oppressive existence. Consistent with her existentialist worldview, de Beauvoir never wavers in her contention that one is not born but rather becomes a woman and that women are exploited but have also permitted themselves to be exploited in the name of love. Many feminists are not willing to accept this premise and hold that women's destiny was shaped entirely by forces outside their realm.

Sources for Further Study

Ascher, Carol. *Simone de Beauvoir: A Life of Freedom*, 1981.

Evans, Mary. *Simone de Beauvoir: A Feminist Mandarin*, 1985.

Keefe, Terry. *Simone de Beauvoir: A Study of Her Writings*, 1985.

Leighton, Jean. *Simone de Beauvoir on Woman*, 1975.

Okely, Judith. *Simone de Beauvoir*, 1986.
Schwarzer, Alice. *After the Second Sex*, 1984.

Rita Terras

THE SECRET HOUSE
Twenty-four Hours in the Strange and Unexpected World in Which We Spend Our Nights and Days

Author: David Bodanis (1947-   )
Type of work: Science
First published: 1986

Form and Content

David Bodanis' *The Secret House* (1986) is, as its subtitle indicates, the story of twenty-four hours in the strange and unexpected world in which we spend our nights and days. With a degree in pure mathematics from the University of Chicago, Bodanis has published widely in such newspapers as *The Washington Post*, *The Times Literary Supplement*, and *The International Herald Tribune*, as well as in *Reader's Digest*. He also authored *The Body Book* (1984). The idea for *The Secret House* came to him while he was living in a small French village in a four-level house dating back to the twelfth century. Each level had its own particular atmosphere, its own psychology. "What would it be like," Bodanis wondered, "to work out this psychology for the contemporary home?"

The plan he finally hit upon for his study of the contemporary home was to describe the immediate environment of such a home as its occupants go through a typical day from morning to night. After a few months of false starts in the drafting of chapters, he finally found the approach that seemed right. "It turned out to be a sort of benevolent personality," he says. "I am benevolent, though the facts stay impersonal." The approach he uses, moreover, is a scientific one, relying heavily on scientific terms appropriate to the modern world.

The book is divided into two parts, "Daytime" and "Night Time." These parts are in turn divided into three chapters each. "Daytime" includes those chapters titled "Morning," "Midday," and "Late Afternoon," while "Night Time" includes those titled "Early Evening," "Dinner Continues," and "Bath and Bed."

"Morning" begins with the ringing of an alarm clock and the onslaught of shock waves that flow throughout the bedroom as the occupants are aroused from their slumbers. A radio is turned on, a window is opened, feet patter to the bathroom, and teeth are brushed. Following these ablutions comes the preparation of breakfast. All these activities are embellished with detailed scientific facts that give them a complexity almost beyond the ken of the human imagination. The same is true for all the chapters of the book.

The second chapter, "Midday," shows the empty house after its occupants have left for their workday. While one might think that the absence of human activity and the placidity of emptiness would indicate a house in which nothing is happening, the contrary is actually the case. Bodanis talks about everything from carpeted floors to walls to windows, and the house shakes, breathes, slithers, and writhes. When the woman of the house comes home early, the scene shifts to the back garden, where she sits contentedly sipping a Coke. Here Bodanis presents a scientific treatise of what is occurring several feet under the lawn as various kinds of soil creatures carry on their own daily existence.

"Late Afternoon" brings the house's other occupant home, and the activity in the house becomes frenetic indeed, as voices reverberate and preparations for the evening meal get under way. In the process Bodanis gives the reader dissertations on such things as microwave ovens, the slaughtering of beef, salmonella, human hair, and clothes, as the house's occupants prepare to entertain dinner guests.

The preparations continue in the next chapter, "Early Evening," as dressing continues and the vacuum cleaner is run. Bodanis moves from an analysis of these activities to the arrival of the carpet destroyers—the guests who carry millions of particles of sand on their shoes. Handshaking, sneezing, talking, eating, breathing, and toilet flushing are all examined by the author with the minuteness of detail that marks the whole book.

"Dinner Continues" presents the activities of the dinner party and all the drama that goes on unseen by the human beings going through their social rituals. Beginning with a discussion of air in the dining room, Bodanis moves next to the storm that has been brewing all day, which arrives with a clap of thunder. Wind, rain, and lightning are all subjected to his microscopic treatment. The storm, however, does not stop the serving of dessert, a cake. While the guests eat the cake, the reader is taken through a process that runs from the formulating and packaging of cake mix to the baking of it and, finally, to the piling of ice cream upon the finished product.

Following dessert, some guests light cigarettes and deluge themselves and their companions with poison chemicals. The evening, however, is almost over, and the guests, like all good guests, leave.

"Bath and Bed" brings the time of purging all the effects of the day's activities. A bath is high on the relaxation list, and the bath is what Bodanis focuses on next. Starting with the history of the modern bathtub, he takes the reader through the bathing ritual and on to the female's efforts to maintain attractive facial skin. The house's occupants now retire to bed—but a faucet is dripping, and, true to form, Bodanis does not leave this phenomenon untreated. On that note that book ends.

Accompanying the lively prose of *The Secret House* are numerous photographs of superb quality. From fibers in a synthetic shirt to dust fragments to the cranking hands of a wrist watch, these photographs add a graphic dimension to the text that contributes significantly to the overall success of Bodanis' efforts.

Analysis

Although *The Secret House* is not a work of fiction, it reads with the same sense of drama as does good fiction. One could say that Bodanis uses no characters to achieve this sense of drama, or one could say that he uses billions, even trillions. There are no human characters other than the faceless and nameless occupants of the house and their dinner guests, and they are mere stage props. On the other hand, Bodanis parades before the reader endless masses of insects, germs, bacteria, and other invisible inhabitants of the secret house. In a very real sense, they are the characters of the book.

Bodanis is interested in those realities that lie behind daily existence, which most people take for granted. The secret houses that humans inhabit seem to be one thing to the naked eye, but to the microscopic eye they are something vastly different. By focusing on a typical day in the life of one house and its two occupants, Bodanis provides the reader with a microscopic eye and thus brings to light the secrets of the secret house.

Having brushed their teeth with toothpaste made up of 30 to 45 percent water, chalk, some titanium dioxide to make it white, some gummy molecules from seaweed, paraffin oil, and a large helping of detergent, the occupants of the house descend to the kitchen for breakfast. This meal, for many people, is a culinary highlight; for others, it is simply a quick cup of coffee to get the body ready to face the day. After reading Bodanis' treatment of the breakfast scene and all that goes into it, one might wish that the normal eating routine consisted of only two meals per day—or better yet, none at all. They are aware of neither the ingredients that have gone into their toothpaste nor the hordes of bacteria that await them in the kitchen. After a description of the egg in the refrigerator that has been absorbing bacteria all night through microscopic holes in its shell, Bodanis turns to the kettle in which the water is boiling for coffee. Reminiscent of long-gone cretaceous lagoons, the kettle's interior is populated by great numbers of floating creatures that merge and grow in their bubbling home, exuding an ancient form of oxygen that wafts across the kitchen. Some of these creatures make it into the coffee cup, perhaps to be joined there by bacteria from the milk used to dilute the coffee.

Next comes the margarine, which was invented during the reign of Napoleon III as a cheap scource of fat for those who could not afford butter. Today soy fat joins fat from squished herrings and fat from pigs as the base for margarine—an unpalatable mess indeed. Low-grade milk is added, however, along with extra-strong dyes and flavorings, to make it all resemble the pictures of sunkissed meadows on the package, before it is spread thickly over toast, rolls, pancakes, and the like.

Following the kitchen drama, the occupants of the house prepare to leave for work. Bodanis describes the male occupant's tugging and yanking of his trousers to get them on and the resultant unseen tearing of threads that weakens the garment. While the male struggles with his trousers, the female is punishing her lips with a concoction of shortening, soap, castor oil, petroleum wax, perfume, food preservatives, fish scales, and red dye—lipstick. Long forgotten, apparently, is the occasion in 1924 when the New York Board of Health considered banning lipstick because of the fear that men might become poisoned from kissing women who wore it.

If the woman's application of lipstick may seem an act of vanity, then consider the man's shaving. Though his trousers suffer tears and rents as he puts them on, his face is brutalized to an even greater extent during the act of shaving. Although facial hair is dead, skin cells are not, and those cells that surround whiskers are slashed and ripped by what to them (if cells could think) must seem to be a jagged and rusty giant metal rake. Bodanis gives some consolation as, by comparison, he describes earlier methods of shaving that relied on rough bronze knife blades or filed flints. The modern male then braces his face with after-shave lotion—essentially 40 to 60 percent pure ethyl alcohol, with an anesthetic and some perfume added—and he too is ready to face the world.

This irony of the often-threatening reality that encroaches upon the lives of oblivious human beings is underscored by juxtaposition: for example, Bodanis moves from a description of medieval feasting habits to an analysis of the modern dinner party, where people still gobble food with little concern as to what is in it—the "living fungus bodies, great writhing colonies of the stuff, safely nestling within the cavities of the Roquefort cheese, let alone the huge numbers of bacteria, swimming, gliding, bouncing, and plodding through everything else." As the guests sniff the food, dribble it, spill it, and wipe it, the air heated by their bodies rises from the floor and gets trapped in clothing or in bodily crevices. Carried by this air are such travelers as grit, pollen, fungus spores, asbestos particles, mite corpses, and sweat residues—none of which would seem to be compatible with an evening of dining.

As if all the above were not enough to make dining a somewhat precarious event, some dinner guests complete their repast with a cigarette. Bodanis notes that the average cigarette smoker takes about eleven puffs from each cigarette he lights up. Thus, he inhales very little of the cigarette's smoke, most of which then floats across the room. Bodanis paints a frightening picture of the poisonous chemicals turned loose by the cigarette smoker. He calculates that something on the order of two billion clotted chemical balls bounce out from a single cigarette. These balls float up into the air before they fall to cling to whatever they hit first—hair, clothes, carpet, furniture, and the like.

In discussing the bath at the end of the day, Bodanis ranges from the mysteries of the whirlpool created as the water drains out to why the National Aeronautics and Space Administration (NASA) chose to put its launch site in Florida. While her companion relaxes in the tub, the woman of the house works diligently to remove the day's germs from her face. Bodanis points out that people are indeed fortunate that they cannot see the horde of creatures that live on the human face. Cold cream may remove dried makeup, but it has no chance against these armored mites that are anywhere from 30 to 50 microns across. Not to worry, says Bodanis, these creatures are relatively harmless, and it might well be dangerous to try frantically to wash them off, because they tend to multiply after a washing.

The inhabitants of the house eventually get to sleep, but the house itself, with all its secrets, never sleeps.

Critical Context

Taken strictly as a work of popular science, *The Secret House* would merit great praise. David Bodanis' lucid exposition bears comparison to the best of John McPhee or Stephen Jay Gould. The thrust of his work, however, is much different from theirs. At its core, *The Secret House* is a satire. Bodanis' closest literary relatives are not nature writers or science writers; he has blood ties with the Russian Formalists, and certainly with Jonathan Swift, whose giant Brobdingnags resemble the occupants of Bodanis' house.

Formalists such as Viktor Shklovsky delighted in what they called "defamiliar-ization" or "making strange." Habit dulls perception; it is the function of art, Shklovsky suggested, to make the familiar strange, so that the reader or viewer might perceive reality afresh. As a device, "making strange" can serve various ends, ranging from irony to lyrical celebration. In *The Secret House*, the ends to which it is put are consistently satiric. Bodanis defamiliarizes not only the house and its appurtenances but also the experiences of its tenants. Their conversation is comically reduced to the physics of speech—explosions of sound bouncing off walls. The erotic is similarly deflated. A sequence of "heat images," showing a woman entering a bath, soaking, getting out, and drying, defamiliarizes the nude, while the couple's lovemaking is obliquely described via a virtuoso account of its effect on "bedspring molecules"; there is even a historical digression on Robert Hooke, the seventeenth century savant "who first described these laws of spring action." Comical, yes, but Bodanis' vision of humankind is generously laced with Swiftian disgust for the messy physicality of these creatures who go about their daily routines oblivious to perhaps 95 percent of reality.

Sources for Further Study

Appraisal: Science Books for Young People. Review. XX (Summer, 1987), p. 21.

Baldwin, J. Review in *Whole Earth Review*. LV (Summer, 1987), p. 110.

Best Sellers. Review. XLVI (December, 1986), p. 356.

Hoelterhoff, Manuela. "Bookshelf: Of Mites and Men," in *The Wall Street Journal*. March 11, 1987, p. 34.

Science Books and Films. Review. XXII (May, 1987), p. 302.

Stepp, Carl Sessions. "Close Up on the World Around Us," in *The Washington Post Book World*. XVI (October 12, 1986), p. 8.

Wilton Eckley

SEDUCTION AND BETRAYAL
Women and Literature

Author: Elizabeth Hardwick (1916-   )
Type of work: Literary criticism
First published: 1974

> *Principal personages:*
> ANNE BRONTË,
> CHARLOTTE BRONTË, and
> EMILY BRONTË, three sisters, nineteenth century English novelists
>   and poets
> JANE CARLYLE, a nineteenth century diarist, the wife of Thomas
>   Carlyle
> F. SCOTT FITZGERALD, a twentieth century American novelist
> ZELDA FITZGERALD, his wife, also a writer
> HENRIK IBSEN, a nineteenth century Norwegian-born dramatist
> SYLVIA PLATH, a twentieth century American poet
> VIRGINIA WOOLF, a twentieth century English novelist, essayist,
>   and short-story writer
> DOROTHY WORDSWORTH, a nineteenth century diarist, the sister of
>   William Wordsworth

Form and Content

As early as 1959, Elizabeth Hardwick declared, "The proper study of mankind may be man, but the subject for women is other women. . . . It is a subject upon which one can speak with something like authority." *Seduction and Betrayal* bears out that conviction. It collects essays on women that Hardwick, a founding editor of *The New York Review of Books*, originally published in that journal, though some have been altered and others expanded since their initial appearances. A few of the essays were read as papers: The title essay was presented at Vassar College in 1972, and the essays on Dorothy Wordsworth and Jane Carlyle formed part of lectures given for the Christian Gauss Seminar in Criticism at Princeton University. Although there is a unifying theme insofar as the book considers women and literature, *Seduction and Betrayal* has no central argument. The ten essays in the slim volume (208 pages long) address women as authors, novelists, or poets; as fictional characters; and as close associates of literary men. They do not offer close textual readings or historical data but rather sensitive interpretations of lives, personalities, and literary themes in accordance with the vision of a cultivated critic who is herself a novelist.

The essays are arranged in five sections. The long opening biographical essay on the Brontë sisters is followed by "Ibsen's Women," a section of three essays devoted to the female characterizations in *Et dukkehjem* (1879; *A Doll's House*, 1880),

Hedda Gabler (1890; English translation, 1891), and *Rosmersholm* (1886; English translation, 1889). The third section, "Victims and Victors," comprises individual essays on Zelda Fitzgerald (construed as victim) and on Sylvia Plath and Virginia Woolf (victors). Under the heading "Amateurs" follow individual essays on two talented women who, to Hardwick's regret, never fully exercised their gifts and were dwarfed by their men: Jane Carlyle, the wife of historian and essayist Thomas Carlyle, and Dorothy Wordsworth, the sister of poet William Wordsworth. Finally, balancing the opening essay, the long title essay, "Seduction and Betrayal," discusses seduced and betrayed women characters in the Western literary tradition, principally in English, American, Russian, and French novels, though opera and narrative poetry are mentioned too. Although the arrangement of the essays does not constitute a progression, the title essay, easily the most provocative piece, nevertheless serves as a culminating statement by virtue of its challenging claims.

Eminently readable and presented without documentation (except for a single note to the Woolf piece), the essays are directed to the intelligent nonspecialist, male or female, and, while informed by a strong awareness of the problems created by gendering, are not noticeably feminist in tone but reflective and urbane.

Analysis

Hardwick's essays are stylistically elegant, written in a polished, often-epigrammatic prose that sparkles with witty insights and striking claims. Her critical approach is moral and psychological rather than formal. She investigates not techniques or structures or, as a rule, aesthetic issues, but rather values and personalities in pieces that, perhaps reflecting her reviewer's training, are often musings around a center rather than tightly reasoned arguments. (Her essay on Virginia Woolf, which begins as reflections on Bloomsbury, is particularly discursive.) The tone of the essays remains objective; any anger Hardwick may feel at literary women's plight is kept so carefully controlled that her essays will interest male readers without accusing or affronting them.

Nevertheless, Hardwick has no particular feminist position to argue even if she has opinions about women. She is dissatisfied with women's subordinated lot and indignant at their victimization; she consistently admires independent-minded and ambitious females. The essays as a whole, however, do not maintain any sustained theoretical perspective on women in literature. Hardwick does not write with a special consciousness of women authors as differing from their male counterparts or embedding subtexts in their work; she does not have a particular affection for such historically characteristic forms of female writing as the letters and journals. Except when discussing the Brontës, she treats her material ahistorically; her women, unlike those of most feminist critics, are figures without a social background that may have conditioned them. Written as individual pieces, her essays remain discrete entities, valuable as individual comments on literature and life issuing from an intelligent and perceptive mind, although it is one which still views literature through a masculine critical perspective.

Nevertheless, Hardwick called to public attention in the early 1970's topics neglected until the renascent women's movement. Her essay on the Brontë sisters, for example, honors women whose achievement Hardwick considers heroic. Though restricted by their class, their situation, and even their temperaments, they created an honorable way of life for themselves by developing their talents. Hardwick sees them challenging the fate of women in the nineteenth century, when chaperones and fatuous rules of deportment and occupation drained the energy of intelligent, needy females and when even opportunities for independence crushed the spirit. Despite society's contempt for the prodigious efforts such women made to survive, despite the emotional burdens of an eccentric father and a weak-natured brother, the sisters persisted in their writing to escape the hard destiny of being governesses. The indomitable spirits of the Brontë sisters have a renewed hold upon their readers' admiration.

Similarly, in an essay inspired by Nancy Mitford's biography of Zelda Fitzgerald, Hardwick asks the reader's admiration—and "respectful pity"—for Zelda Fitzgerald, whose desperate attempts at independence were perpetually foiled. Zelda's creative urge to dance, paint, or write was neither understood nor valued by those in charge of her fate, though F. Scott Fitzgerald cavalierly appropriated the fruits of her literary talents. She had not only an extraordinary zeal to cure her schizophrenia but also the ambition to work at something that would diminish her dependence on Scott. Hardwick solicits respect for that "astonishing desire" of a beautiful, indulged woman for a work of her own.

Hardwick is clearly sensitive to talented women whose lives were subordinated to those of their men. Yet whereas she can admire Zelda, she writes critically of "amateurs" Dorothy Wordsworth and Jane Carlyle, whose efforts at self-definition through works remained sporadic and casual; she demands of them more authenticity and independence than they chose to show. She is struck by the evidence, in Dorothy's journals, of a woman who responded to the emotional deprivation of her youth by narrowing her vision to the pictorial and eschewing generalization; whereas brother William poured meaning into nature, for Dorothy it was "pure sensation that held the meaning of her life without clearly telling her what that meaning was." Nor does Dorothy analyze people; no real people inhabit her journals. She clung to her dependency so desperately, Hardwick concludes, that she dared not risk writing anything but descriptions of the scenery amid which she lived.

Because of Jane Carlyle's "subversive irony" and her ambivalent feelings for her husband, Hardwick finds her the most interesting of the mid-Victorian literary wives—but also one too easily gratified. Although her brilliant letters show that she could have been a fine novelist, she lacked ambition and the psychic need for a creation that would stand outside herself; she could be satisfied with her daily social contacts and chores and in being a collaborator in Carlyle's sacred mission. All this would not, however, save her from the bitter, debilitating unhappiness that was to come because of Carlyle's friendship with Lady Ashburton. Nor had she serious writing to sustain her. To Hardwick, who has great faith in the powers of literary endeavor—provided it comes in canonical forms such as the novel or poetry—the letters and journals of Jane Carlyle, like those of Dorothy Wordsworth, were regrettably inadequate to comfort her and support her self-esteem. "What strikes one as the greatest personal loss of these private writing careers," Hardwick comments, "is that the work could not truly build for the women a bulwark against the sufferings of neglect and the humiliations of lovelessness."

Ironically, though Hardwick does not remark it, their less private careers were unable to provide such bulwarks for the two great writers whom Hardwick dubs "victors" despite their respective suicides: Sylvia Plath and Virginia Woolf. Hardwick unreservedly admires Plath, whom she deems likely to remain one of the most interesting American poets for the precision and intensity of her verse: "Overwhelming; it is quite literally irresistible. The daring, the skill, the severity. It shocks and thrills." To Woolf, however, Hardwick has ambivalent responses: she is put off by Woolf's Bloomsbury snobbery and aestheticism. Woolf's abstractness elicits only respectful admiration from her readers rather than a sense of deep engagement with her fictional worlds. Granting Woolf her feminism—"she thought and wrote seriously not only about being a woman but about the defaults and defects of a world made by men"—Hardwick is skeptical of Woolf's androgyny, that fusion of feminine and masculine traits as a writer for which contemporary critics praise her. To Hardwick, "androgyny" is merely "a way of bringing into line the excessive, almost smothering 'femininity'" of Woolf's fiction, so lacking in the salutary masculine (earthbound) knowledge of a writer such as George Eliot. Yet Hardwick must acknowledge superior technique and a great mind working in Woolf's novels; she even affirms Woolf's *Between the Acts* (1941) as one of the century's two most powerful literary images of the cycles of life and culture (T. S. Eliot's *The Waste Land*, 1922, is the other).

Among female characters, whose psychodynamics interest Hardwick, she finds herself drawn to Henrik Ibsen's women because it seems to her that Ibsen thought hard about what it may mean to be born female. (It emerges that he had a distaste for women's power over men.) His free-spirited Nora of *A Doll's House* counters notions that an independent and brave woman cannot also be pleasure loving, domestic, and charming. Nora may leave her husband and children to find herself but, challenging the usual assumptions of Nora's growth, Hardwick insists that she does not become free in the act; she has always been free spirited. Yet Ibsen errs in Nora's casual abandonment of her children, slipping into the masculine perspective that refuses to allow children to be an impediment to self-realization—or so it seems to Hardwick, from the perspective of the 1970's. Ibsen's Hedda Gabler, "one of the meanest romantics in literature," who attracts by her powerful style and aristocratic pride yet simultaneously repels is more male than female; she has turned away from all those props by which nineteenth century bourgeois women tried to invest life with hope and warmth. Yet it is she, Hardwick believes, rather than Nora, who prefigures the future; hardly a woman in Ingmar Bergman's films would be imaginable without her. As for *Rosmersholm*'s Rebecca West, who has created a love triangle, Ibsen withholds full sympathy from her, unwilling to grant women the right to live accountable only to desire. The unspoken moral of his plays—appealing to the moralist in Hardwick—is that ultimately nothing is worth the destruction of others or oneself.

Hardwick's final essay on seduction and betrayal is a powerful analysis of the fictional motif of the betrayed woman, viewed from the perspective of Hardwick's own moral emphasis. Her conclusion is noteworthy, for having traced outstanding expressions of the theme from Wolfgang Amadeus Mozart's *Don Giovanni* (1787) and Samuel Richardson's *Clarissa: Or, the History of a Young Lady* (1747-1748) to Theodore Dreiser's *An American Tragedy* (1925), Hardwick regrets the loss to literature of seduced and betrayed heroines as subjects and as occasions for the reader's compassion or admiration, now that sex no longer has the status of a tragic, exalted subject and morality is indeterminate: "The old plot is dead, fallen into obsolescence. You cannot seduce anyone when innocence is not a value. Technology annihilates consequences." For contemporary readers, the illicit has become a psychological drama, not a moral one; the value scheme, like the sense of reality, is subjective and relative. How greatly Hardwick regrets the loss not only to literature but to life as well is indicated by her choice of a closing quotation from the work of Émile Zola: "Venus was rotting." Predictably, her enthusiasm for seduction and betrayal has not endeared her to other, more pronouncedly feminist critics.

Critical Context

Elizabeth Hardwick's place in contemporary feminist criticism lies among the more conservative critics. She has been grouped by more radical thinkers with critics such as Mary Ellmann in *Thinking About Women* (1968) as epitomizing the critic who does not write as a woman, who never says, "I, as a woman, think," but instead talks about other women writers as if they were a third sex and is careful not to be too angry or earnest in her feminist pronouncements, thus deflecting male criticism. In terms of the influential distinction made by Elaine Showalter in "Towards a Feminist Poetics" between feminist critique and gynocritics, Hardwick practices feminist critique, that version of feminist criticism in which woman as reader principally seeks out the errors of omission and commission concerning women in past criticism, the terms of her investigation coming out of male critical thought. Feminist criticism, however, has thrived through the plurality of its approaches; although Hardwick's book has become less significant than it was when first issued in 1974, hers is still a respected voice among the moderates. Notably, she was less conservative by the time of *Seduction and Betrayal* than she had been in her 1962 *A View of My Own: Essays in Literature and Society*, in which, repeating an opinion from the 1950's, she was convinced that women writers could never compete with men because of their ineradicably differing life experiences. By 1974 she did not condone limitations on women's performance. Whatever her changing views on women, an impeccable style of writing and an assured literary sensibility have been characteristic of Elizabeth Hardwick's criticism from the start.

Sources for Further Study

Aldridge, John W. "Writing About Women," in *Commentary*. LVIII (August, 1974), pp. 75-78.

Dinnage, Rosemary. "Men, Women, and Books: The Rule of Heroism," in *The Times Literary Supplement*. November 29, 1974, p. 1333.

Humm, Maggie. "Feminist Literary Criticism in America and England," in *Women's Writing: A Challenge to the Theory*, 1986. Edited by Moira Monteith.

Marcus, Jane. "Nostalgia Is Not Enough: Why Elizabeth Hardwick Misreads Ibsen, Plath, and Woolf," in *Women, Literature, and Criticism*, 1978. Edited by Harry R. Garvin.

Solomon, B. R. "Of Women Writers and Writing About Women," in *The New York Times Book Review*. LXXIX (May 5, 1974), p. 4.

Harriet Blodgett

THE SEVEN STOREY MOUNTAIN

Author: Thomas Merton (1915-1968)
Type of work: Autobiography
Time of work: 1915-1941
Locale: England, France, Bermuda, New York, and Louisville, Kentucky
First published: 1948

> *Principal personage:*
> THOMAS MERTON, an American religious thinker and writer

Form and Content

The publication in October, 1948, of his autobiographical work *The Seven Storey Mountain* marked the true beginning of Thomas Merton's extraordinary literary career. Seven years earlier, Merton had entered the Trappist abbey of Gethsemani in Kentucky. Encouraged by his abbot, Dom Frederic Dunne, Merton wrote his autobiography in order to describe his transformation from a nonpracticing Anglican into a convert to Catholicism who abandoned a promising academic career in order to enter a cloistered monastery. During the last twenty years of his life, Merton wrote extensively on such diverse topics as war and peace, the ecumenical movement, racial and social injustice, Eastern and Western monasticism, and the relationships between traditional Christian beliefs and the modern world. Although Merton never composed a formal autobiography after *The Seven Storey Mountain*, he did write several fascinating journals, including *The Sign of Jonas* (1953), *Conjectures of a Guilty Bystander* (1966), and his posthumously published *The Asian Journal* (1973). In 1968, he undertook his first extended trip away from his monastery: On December 10, 1968, he was accidentally electrocuted while attending an international conference of Eastern and Western monks in Thailand.

Before the publication of *The Seven Storey Mountain*, Merton was not entirely unknown in literary circles. In 1944, his first book, *Thirty Poems*, had appeared in print. This thin volume included his exquisite poem of consolation "Sweet Brother, If I Do Not Sleep," written in memory of his brother John Paul, a soldier killed in World War II. Encouraged by both his abbot and his publisher, Merton continued his literary career. During the twenty-seven years he lived in Gethsemani, Merton spent two hours daily on research and writing. This discipline enabled him to produce an impressive number of books, essays, and poems. People as diverse as Popes John XXIII and Paul VI, Evelyn Waugh, Graham Greene, and the Dalai Lama believed that Merton's writings revealed how a profound commitment to spiritual and moral values can give meaning to life.

Merton divided his autobiography into three sections. The first part deals with the years between his childhood and the physical breakdown he suffered in 1936. The second section describes his extended period of recuperation, his conversion to Catholicism in 1938, and his decision in late 1939 to enter a seminary. The third section describes his thoughts before and after he entered the Gethsemani Monastery in December, 1941.

The title of Merton's autobiography refers to the seven levels in Dante's *Purgatorio* (c. 1320; *Purgatory*). Divine grace enabled Merton to move from the lowest to the highest levels of spiritual understanding. *The Seven Storey Mountain* describes in a direct and unpretentious style Merton's gradual change from a haughty and apathetic young man into a fervent and mature believer who found contentment as a contemplative monk. Since its publication in 1948, *The Seven Storey Mountain* has touched the hearts of numerous readers.

Analysis

In the beginning of *The Seven Storey Mountain*, Merton portrays himself as a prisoner of a materialistic world. This comparison of the modern world to a prison has struck many readers as excessive. The eminent British writer Evelyn Waugh published a thoroughly revised version of *The Seven Storey Mountain* under the title *Elected Silence* in 1949. Waugh eliminated what he considered the exaggerations in both Merton's style and his assessment of the world outside his monastery. Although Waugh did improve certain passages in Merton's book, Merton believed that the urbane and refined style preferred by Waugh could not properly convey to readers his visceral reaction to his experiences before and after his conversion. Merton wanted the readers of *The Seven Storey Mountain* to understand that his life would have been meaningless had he not received the gift of faith from God; his conversion had radically transformed his perception of the world.

The Seven Storey Mountain has been favorably compared to such classic autobiographies as those of Michel Eyquem de Montaigne, Saint Augustine, and Jean-Jacques Rousseau. Such praise of Merton's autobiography is entirely appropriate because he also analyzed with almost brutal honesty the weaknesses and strengths of his character. Merton never attempted to mislead his readers by presenting himself in an overly positive light. His subjective analysis of his own life never seems artificial. His consistent attempt to understand the true motivation for his moral choices persuades his readers both to respect Merton's perception of the world and to appreciate the universal elements in Merton's spiritual and psychological growth: The chronological structure of this autobiography enables the reader to understand the gradual changes which caused Thomas Merton to convert to Roman Catholicism and then to enter a cloistered monastery.

Thomas Merton had a difficult childhood. He was born near the Spanish border in the French village of Prades on January 31, 1915. His parents were both artists, and they moved frequently. His mother, an American, would die in 1921 and his father, a New Zealander, would die nearly ten years later. Merton spent his childhood and adolescence in France, England, Bermuda, and the United States but never felt at home anywhere. The artificiality and selfishness of modern society depressed him. Because of his profound sense of alienation, Merton yielded to many self-destructive urges: After he entered the University of Cambridge in 1933, he began to drink heavily and then fathered a child out of wedlock. Both his former mistress and their son would die during a Nazi air raid on London. While writing his autobiography, Merton recalled that a friend from Cambridge had committed suicide. He became convinced that only the grace of God had protected him from a similar fate and that he had accomplished nothing positive during his years in England. He moved to America in 1934, never again returning to Europe. In this first section of *The Seven Storey Mountain*, the despair and alienation which many people felt after the horrors of the Holocaust and the destruction of World War II is powerfully and movingly expressed.

In the second part of *The Seven Storey Mountain*, Merton reveals that he needed both divine grace and the moral support of his friends in order to grow spiritually. After Merton arrived in the United States, he enrolled at Columbia University, where he met two professors, Mark Van Doren and Dan Walsh, who profoundly influenced his personal development. Van Doren taught Merton to think critically, to value truth for itself, and to distrust all forms of specious reasoning. Ironically, Merton had never intended to meet Van Doren. At the beginning of his junior year at Columbia, Merton went to the wrong classroom. When Van Doren came in and started talking, Merton decided to take that course instead of his intended history course. Merton viewed this fortuitous accident as part of a divine plan to help him accept the gift of faith. Van Doren, who was a Protestant, became one of Merton's closest friends, corresponding with him for years and often visiting him at Gethsemani. Although he did not share Merton's religious beliefs, Van Doren strongly supported both his conversion to Catholicism and his decision to enter the monastery. Whenver he had personal problems, Merton knew that Van Doren would be there to help and guide him.

Another close friend from Columbia was Robert Lax. He encouraged Merton to take a course on medieval Scholasticism which Dan Walsh, a visiting professor of philosophy from Sacred Heart College, was to teach at Columbia. Walsh taught Merton that no opposition need exist between the acceptance of traditional Christian beliefs and the philosophical search for truth. After he became a Catholic, Merton spoke to Walsh of his interest in the priesthood, and Walsh suggested the Trappist monastery in Gethsemani. At first, Merton rejected this suggestion, but within two years he would become a Trappist. Most of his friends at Columbia were not Catholic. Nevertheless, they attended his baptism in 1938. Eleven years later, his Columbia friends would travel to Gethsemani for his ordination. Friendship enriched Merton's life and gave him the inner peace which he needed in order to accept the gift of faith. Whatever their religious beliefs, his readers can identify with Merton's thoughtful analysis of the close link between friendship and the search for happiness.

The third part of *The Seven Storey Mountain* describes his reasons for entering the Cistercian monastery and the great joy which active contemplation brought to him there. After considering several religious orders, he at first rejected the cloistered life. Nevertheless, after many conversations with his friends from Columbia and two retreats in Cistercian monasteries, Merton concluded that only the contemplative life would enable him to grow spiritually. He wrote to Gethsemani and was accepted for what he was: a rake whom the free gift of faith had transformed into a fervent believer. At Gethsemani, Merton would experience for the first time the pleasures of true emotional and intellectual satisfaction.

When Merton reached Gethsemani on December 10, 1941, he saw the words *Pax intrantibus* (peace to those who enter) inscribed over the entrance gate. In Merton's mind, this Latin greeting defined the paradoxical nature of the monastic life. The numerous and often-petty rules in a contemplative order are in fact designed to bring monks inner peace by freeing them from the artificiality of the materialistic world. Thus, the peace he wished to acquire was the wisdom to accept everything as part of the divine plan. Yet this trust in divine providence would soon be severely tested.

Only a few months after his arrival at Gethsemani, he was called to his abbot's office. Merton's brother, John Paul, then a sergeant in the British army, had come to the abbey in order to receive religious instruction, wanting to be baptized as soon as possible. By a curious coincidence, Father James Fox, who would serve as Thomas' abbot and spiritual mentor from 1948 until early 1968, was asked to prepare John Paul for baptism. As his newly baptized brother was walking away from the monastery, Thomas suddenly realized that they "would never see each other on earth again." Within a year the recently married John Paul was killed in action. Thomas coped with his grief first by praying and then by writing "Sweet Brother, If I Do Not Sleep." His complete acceptance of divine benevolence persuaded Thomas that John Paul's "unhappy spirit" had finally been called "home" by God. Only a brief epilogue, "Meditatio Pauperis in Solitudine" (meditation of a poor man in solitude), follows this powerful analysis of the last meeting between Thomas Merton and his only sibling.

Critical Context

When they agreed to publish *The Seven Storey Mountain*, the editors of Harcourt Brace hoped to sell five thousand copies of this work, believing that Catholic readers might be interested in the reasons for Merton's conversion. The appeal of *The Seven Storey Mountain*, however, has never been limited to Catholics. Within two years of its first publication more than 600,000 hardcover copies had been sold in the United States alone, and Merton's autobiography has continued to fascinate readers and critics. In *The Seven Storey Mountain*, Merton expressed with extraordinary sincerity and insight the universal elements of his spiritual growth.

The Seven Storey Mountain was Thomas Merton's first important work. Nevertheless, it contains all the major themes which he would develop during the remaining twenty years of his life. In such profound works as *The Sign of Jonas, The Wisdom of the Desert* (1960), and *New Seeds of Contemplation* (1961), he would explore more thoroughly the meaning of the ecumenical movement, the nature of contemplative prayer, and the complex relationship between Eastern and

Western monasticism. Yet *The Seven Storey Mountain* remains his most psychologically powerful work. Merton's moving analysis of his search for meaning in his life should continue to fascinate readers for generations to come.

Sources for Further Study

Forest, James H. *Thomas Merton: A Pictorial Biography*, 1980.
Furlong, Monica. *Merton: A Biography*, 1981.
Hart, Patrick. *Thomas Merton, Monk: A Monastic Tribute*, 1974.
Mott, Michael. *The Seven Mountains of Thomas Merton*, 1984.
Rice, Edward. *The Man in the Sycamore Tree: The Good Life and Hard Times of Thomas Merton*, 1970.
Shannon, William H. *Thomas Merton's Dark Path: The Inner Experience of a Contemplative*, 1981.
Wilkes, Paul. *Merton: By Those Who Know Him Best*, 1984.

Edmund J. Campion

SEVEN TYPES OF AMBIGUITY
A Study of Its Effects on English Verse

Author: William Empson (1906-1984)
Type of work: Literary criticism
First published: 1930

Form and Content

One of the most remarkable books of literary criticism of the twentieth century, *Seven Types of Ambiguity: A Study of Its Effects on English Verse* was composed in three weeks at the end of its author's brilliant undergraduate career at Magdalene College, University of Cambridge. While there were many influences at work upon William Empson during the composition process, nothing he learned from others can be said to account, really, for this remarkable production of a truly rare mind.

The organization of the book into seven chapters, each devoted to progressively more complex poetic ideas, is somewhat deceptive. Instead of the precise gradations of a coherent system, the seven chapters serve as a frame within which the poetic samples sometimes overlap, sometimes seem inconsistent, as Empson himself readily admitted. It is the close verbal analysis, ranging over a considerable variety of English literature, that remains the heart of the work, the work that introduced modern readers to the pleasures of poetry's multiple meanings.

At the time Empson went up to Cambridge in October, 1925, the university was filled with the intellectual excitement of scientific discovery, particularly in the fields of physics and astronomy. In fact, Empson had won a scholarship in mathematics to Magdalene College and took a First in the subject in 1926. Then, in his third year, he changed to English under the lively influence of I. A. Richards, who had brought out *Science and Poetry* in 1926. For a mind as agile and innovative as Empson's, Cambridge offered unusually exhilarating prospects in the 1920's. That fertile atmosphere is re-created in Sir James Jeans's *The Universe Around Us* (1929) and in Sir Arthur Eddington's *The Nature of the Physical World* (1928). At the very time that the horizons of science were broadening dramatically, literature was being subjected to new approaches and stimulating revision. Besides Richards' influence, there were some distinguished visitors to Cambridge in 1926 who may have contributed to Empson's change to English: Gertrude Stein, who gave a lecture titled "Composition as Explanation," and T. S. Eliot, who gave the Clark Lectures at Trinity College on the Metaphysical poets. When Empson began publishing poetry in 1927, he did not abandon science; true to the interdisciplinary attitude that was so strong at Cambridge then, he incorporated it, particularly in his diction and metaphors. Having applied an analytic method to the reading of a wide range of English poetry, he was awarded the highly unusual distinction of a starred First in part 1 of the English Tripos.

As the story has been repeatedly told, Richards, who was Empson's director of studies, was startled by the exceedingly well-read younger man's deft interpretations of a Shakespearean sonnet, readings like those recorded by Robert Graves and Laura Riding in *A Survey of Modernist Poetry* (1927). When Empson suggested off-handedly that this sort of analysis could be done with any sort of poetry, Richards took the opportunity of sending him away to make good on his claim. The next week the undergraduate was still typing his manuscript, and shortly thereafter he presented Richards with thirty thousand words of the soon-to-be-completed text. This extended analysis, which Empson submitted in part as his original composition for the English Tripos, became *Seven Types of Ambiguity*.

As for the book's organization, the seven categories of ambiguous meanings, if not taken too rigidly, do stimulate and guide the imaginative reception of literature of the highest order. First, there are details of language that are effective in several ways at once. Second are alternative meanings that are completely resolved into the one meaning the author intended. The third type is the apparently unconnected meanings occurring in one word, as in puns. Fourth are the alternative meanings so combined as to convey the complicated state of mind of the author. The fifth, also called a fortunate confusion, is a simile that incompletely suggests two incompatible things so that the author is found to be "discovering his idea in the act of writing." Sixth are the statements that are so patently contradictory or irrelevant that the reader is forced to create his own interpretation. Lastly, the seventh type is a statement so fundamentally contradictory as to reveal a division in the author's mind.

As a second and then a third edition followed the first, Empson submitted his book to some revision in the interest of clearer articulation of the verbal analysis. In the first edition there was neither an index nor chapter summaries. In a preface to the second edition, Empson explained that he had "cut out a few bits," not to suppress any "analysis that would be worth disagreeing over," but to remove those that "seemed trivial and likely to distract the reader's attention from the main point." He was surprised, he said, at how little he wanted to change. Also included in this preface is a lengthy passage from a criticism of the book which Empson undertakes to answer, confirming his perceptions of sixteen years before. In 1953, another brief comment was added as a note for the third edition, on two interpretations that had attracted some dissent, the first concerning the "bare ruined choirs" of William Shakespeare's Sonnet 73 and the second George Herbert's "The Sacrifice." Thus, the third edition offers more guidance and the benefit of second thoughts, while the first reflects the original expression of Empson's mind in the process of discovering how his principle worked in practice.

It is the individual example, not the classification system, that made the book so influential. Neither the theoretical superstructure nor even the term "ambiguity" itself is fixed or final. The thrust of the study is discovery, the discovery of the richness of individual poems and of the minds of poets. As that quest proceeds, Empson readily modifies or questions his tools of discovery.

The selections themselves are drawn from English poetry and drama, largely from the sixteenth, early seventeenth, and eighteenth centuries. The influence of Eliot's work on Shakespeare and the Metaphysical poets is in strong evidence.

Fewer in number but important are the examples from the twentieth century.

These individual analyses are memorable as much for their zest as for their literary acumen. Empson conveys a sensitivity, an admiration, an argumentative edge, and a wit, each in turn as the process of teasing out the meanings advances. It is true that the book originated as a senior thesis and is a thesis book—thus the youthful high spirits as well as the abundance of abstraction. Still, the personal style—casual, offhand, breezy—contributes an excitement and engagement that lives on the page.

Analysis

First and foremost, *Seven Types of Ambiguity* is an extended examination through logical analysis. In the opening chapter Empson reminds those who might object to a scientific approach to literary criticism that "the belief that Reason can be applied to the arts is as old as criticism, and fundamental to it." In the preface to the second edition, he restates that "the method of verbal analysis is of course the main point of the book" but goes on to mention "two cross-currents" that found their way into his work. The first was Eliot's reevaluation of the Metaphysical poets, which implicitly questioned the value of the nineteenth century poets. The second cross-current was "the impact of Freud," or more generally the issue of unconscious conflict. One of the reasons the book gained such a reputation was that it did without the familiar historically based approaches.

Empson's aim in his close analysis is not to identify the one "right" meaning, but to explore the expanding possibilities of alternate, multiple, and simultaneous meanings. He begins in chapter 1 with a single line from Shakespeare's Sonnet 73, "Bare ruined choirs, where late the sweet birds sang." The simplest type of ambiguity, as Empson defines it, occurs when "a word or a grammatical structure is effective in several ways at once." This is Empson's breathtaking analysis:

> The comparison holds for many reasons; because ruined monastery choirs are places in which to sing, because they involve sitting in a row, because they are made of wood, are carved into knots and so forth, because they used to be surrounded by a sheltering building crystallised out of the likeness of a forest, and coloured with stained glass and painting like flowers and leaves, because they are now abandoned by all but the grey walls coloured like the skies of winter, because the cold and Narcissistic charm suggested by choir-boys suits well with Shakespeare's feeling for the object of the Sonnets, and for various sociological and historical reasons (the protestant destruction of monasteries; fear of puritanism), which it would be hard now to trace out in their proportions; these reasons, and many more relating the simile to its place in the Sonnet, must all combine to give the line its beauty, and there is a sort of ambiguity in not knowing which of them to hold most clearly in mind.

Thus, selecting brief passages and paraphrasing the meanings as he finds them in the New English Dictionary, Empson builds his case for the enriching power of ambiguity.

The second type of ambiguity involves two or more meanings which are resolved into one, as in Shakespeare's Sonnet 16, where "lines of life" conveys time's wrinkles, lineage or descendants, lines drawn with a pen, the lines of a poem, and destiny. To show that poetical ambiguity was already underway in Geoffrey Chaucer's time, Empson analyzes some lines from *Troilus and Criseyde* (1382), and as he proceeds he points out that a long poem accumulates imagery, thereby producing increasing reserves of associated meanings. As with this example, many of Empson's analyses are both minute and sustained; some go on engagingly for pages.

Some readers find Empson's wit tiresome upon rereading, and others find it more revealing of serious meaning than they like. He moves from "beating about the Chaucerian bushes," for example, and turns to "the very sanctuary of rationality," the eighteenth century English poets: They endeavored to be "honest, straight-forward, sensible, grammatical and plain," and Empson has made it his business "to outwit these poor wretches, and to applaud them for qualities in their writings which they would have been horrified to discover." He looks at the idea of power in Samuel Johnson's *The Vanity of Human Wishes: The Tenth Satire of Juvenal Imitated* (1749) and the vivacity of the ambiguous "charm" in Alexander Pope's "Essay on Women." It is also in chapter 2 that Empson includes one of the few selections from twentieth century poetry, *The Waste Land* (1922), where the word "poured" imbues with wavering fluidity the dressing table, its jewels, and cases in "A Game of Chess." He pauses then for one of his characteristically personal touches before moving on to emendations of Shakespeare: "Some readers of this chapter, I should like to believe, will have shared the excitement with which it was written, will have felt that it casts a new light on the very nature of language." Even if doubtful about his impudence and his breezy language, few readers are immune to Empson's personal appeal; there is emotion there, as well as thought. He is constantly aware of the risks he is taking in insisting on so many alternatives. After examining and reexamining the word "dis-eate" from a speech in *Macbeth* (1606), he makes this apology: "I am sorry to appear so fantastic, but I can form no other working notion of what this unique mind [Shakespeare's] must have been like when in action." Recreating the mind that made the poetic decisions is at the heart of Empson's purpose.

In summarizing Empson's work, it is easy to overemphasize his ingenuity, even though he makes a point of undercutting it. His readings make it clear that he possesses "an intuitive intimacy with nature" and "a conception of nature in terms of human politics," just as he said of Pope when analyzing his lines foretelling the eventual destruction of the house of the Duke of Chandos. This example appears in chapter 3, where the ambiguity arises from two ideas, both relevant, being given in one word. He goes on to warn explicitly against too much ingenuity, especially in analyzing Shakespeare, and pronounces literary conundrums "tedious." In a long examination of John Donne's "A Valediction, of Weeping" in chapter 4, he at last reaches the limits of close scrutiny: "The machinery of interpretation is becoming too cumbrous here, in that I cannot see how these meanings come to convey tenderness rather than the passion of grief which has preceded them." One more way in which Empson's criticism surprises is in its frank uncertainty when feeling its way.

Types six and seven are the most complex and, indeed, are a mark of the best poetry. The alternative meanings in the first contradict one another, or are irrelevant or repetitious, so that the meaning is brought to nought. Here Empson takes up George Herbert, who in his lines "Affliction" says both that he was "*betrayed*" into the life of contemplation and "*entangled*" in the life of action, showing him "doubtful which he would have preferred," even now. The following lines present the puzzling tautology: "Ah, my dear God, though I am clean forgot,/ Let me not love thee, if I love thee not." Let me be consistent, Empson poses as one interpretation; let me love you not only in will and deed but also in calm assurance, is another; even if you do forget me, "damn me if I don't stick to the parsonage," is a determined third.

Herbert provides one of the better known examples for the seventh type, again expressing most poetically a fundamental conflict in religious faith. This last type is defined as opposites that "show a fundamental division in the writer's mind." In "The Sacrifice," the unresolvable contraries in Christ, the "scapegoat and tragic hero; loved because hated," produce the possibility of reading these lines, "Only let others say, when I am dead,/ Never was grief like mine," to include the wish that there be retribution as well as the desire that there never again be a death like Christ's. "I am not sure how far people would be willing to accept this double meaning," Empson goes on; "I am only sure that after you have once apprehended it . . . you will never be able to read the poem without remembering that it is a possibility." One other verse is particularly striking:

> Oh all ye who pass by, behold and see;
> Man stole the fruit, but I must climb the tree,
> The tree of life, to all but only me.
>   Was ever grief like mine?

Empson uncovers suggestions of a Christ sinless, yet a criminal, and shows Herbert's poem to be a masterpiece of simplicity in complexity.

Critical Context

Empson did not initiate the method of close reading that he employs in *Seven Types of Ambiguity*, but he did establish a landmark with his controversial first book. More systematic than other analytic texts (even though its system was flawed), it was also the broadest and richest in imaginative sympathy. Even those who object to some, or many, of the readings find them difficult to refute. The book had a pronounced effect on the teaching of English, especially at Cambridge, and it modified the vocabulary of literary criticism in English.

With *Seven Types of Ambiguity* Empson initiated a line of thought about complexity and simplicity in poetry that he continued in *Some Versions of Pastoral* (1935), then further developed in *The Structure of Complex Words* (1951); these books continue to dwell on double meanings. In *Milton's God* (1961), Empson argues against the kind of close reading done by what he called the neo-Christians, critics who insisted on the autonomy of the text and its deep or irrational content in order to fend off rational objections to, for example, the illogical and sadistic. In the decades after his first book, Empson became concerned that his kind of analysis was being turned into a rationale for pious zealots who wanted the poem to be seen as an inviolable artifact, a "verbal icon." Both the man and his writings have resisted assimilation into any school or dogma; they do not tread the beaten path, nor do they oversimplify. Therein lies their integrity.

Sources for Further Study

Bradbrook, M. C. "The Ambiguity of William Empson," in *William Empson: The Man and His Work*, 1974. Edited by Roma Gill.

Gardner, Philip, and Averil Gardner. *The God Approached: A Commentary on the Poems of William Empson*, 1978.

Hardy, Barbara. "William Empson and *Seven Types of Ambiguity*," in *The Sewanee Review*. XC (Summer, 1982), pp. 430-439.

Jensen, James. "The Construction of *Seven Types of Ambiguity*," in *Modern Language Quarterly*. XXVII (September, 1966), pp. 243-259.

Norris, Christopher. "The Importance of Empson (II): The Criticism," in *Essays in Criticism*. XXXV (January, 1985), pp. 25-44.

Sale, Roger. "The Achievement of William Empson," in *The Hudson Review*. XIX (Autumn, 1966), pp. 369-390.

_____. *Modern Heroism: Essays on D. H. Lawrence, William Empson, and J. R. R. Tolkien*, 1973.

Willis, J. R. *William Empson*, 1969.

Rebecca R. Butler